DATE DUE

DEMCO 38-296

Business
Plans
Handbook

Highlights

Business Plans Handbook, Volume II (BPH II) is a collection of actual business plans compiled by entrepreneurs seeking funding for small businesses throughout North America. For those looking for examples of how to approach, structure, and compose their own business plans, *BPH II* presents 26 sample plans, including those for the following businesses:

❑ Kennel
❑ Microbrewery
❑ Talking Photo Frame Manufacturer
❑ Automobile Assembler
❑ Mobile Photo Studio
❑ Freelance Editor
❑ Delicatessen Franchise

❑ Newsletter
❑ Public Relations Firm
❑ Online Search and Retrieval Firm
❑ Virtual Shopping Kiosk
❑ Sports Collectibles Producer
❑ Restaurant
❑ Film and Video Producer

OTHER FEATURES

BPH II also provides additional resources for the business owner in need of guidance or the entrepreneur preparing to research and compose their business plan, including:

- A **Business Plan Template** providing all of the essential elements of a plan. Also in this section are two fictional business plans used by small business counselors as examples for their clients.

- An expanded directory section. **Organizations, Agencies, & Consultants** provides a listing of associations and consultants of interest to entrepreneurs, in addition to the 10 Small Business Administration Regional Offices and all of the Small Business Development Centers. These valuable resources can provide you with informative materials, offer business counseling and support, and give you a place to begin networking with other business owners and contacts.

- A **Glossary of Small Business Terms** providing insight into the often confusing lingo of entrepreneurship.

- An expanded **Bibliography** of materials for further study and sources for research.

- **Expanded coverage of financial information**. Business plans in *BPH II* contains more financial data, including Cash Flows, Balance Sheets, Income Statements, and more.

Business Plans

A COMPILATION
OF ACTUAL
BUSINESS PLANS
DEVELOPED BY
SMALL BUSINESSES
THROUGHOUT
NORTH
AMERICA

Handbook

VOLUME

2

Kristin Kahrs,
Editor

 *Gale Research*

An ITP Information/Reference Group Company

Changing the Way the World Learns

NEW YORK • LONDON • BONN • BOSTON • DETROIT
MADRID • MELBOURNE • MEXICO CITY • PARIS
SINGAPORE • TOKYO • TORONTO • WASHINGTON
ALBANY NY • BELMONT CA • CINCINNATI OH

Editor: Kristin Kahrs

E. Koek, Susan B. Martin, Jennifer Arnold Mast, Holly M. Selden
Associate Editors: Kelly Hill, Eva M. Felts

Managing Editor: Deborah M. Burek

Contributors: Jodie S. Jaworski, Amy Lynn Park, Angela Shupe, Deborah J. Untener

Production Director: Mary Beth Trimper
Assistant Production Manager: Evi Seoud
Production Associate: Deborah Milliken

Art Director: Cynthia Baldwin
Graphic Services: CJ Jonik

Data Entry Manager: Benita L. Spight
Data Entry Coordinator: Gwendolyn Tucker
Data Entry Associate: Lysandra Davis

ISBN 0-8103-9395-6
ISSN 1084-4473

Printed in the United States of America

I(T)P™   Gale Research Inc., an International Thomson Publishing Company.
ITP logo is a trademark under license.

Contents

Gale Research Inc.

Introduction

NEW TO THIS VOLUME

When we began compiling the second volume of *Business Plans Handbook*, we sought the advice of those who had used the first volume to help improve this new collection of plans.

In addition to 24 genuine business plans (including one reprinted from the first volume), *BPH II* also includes several examples of revised business plans. With the increased emphasis on strategizing and pre-planning, many business owners are finding it helpful to revise their business plans to consider different conditions than the original plan assumed. For instance, entrepreneurs may revise their plans to include new approaches to changing economic conditions, new or departing personnel and subsequent job re-definitions, expansion plans, or others factors that result in a significant strategy alteration. In short, revised plans often recognize that even the best laid plans can be foiled by the real world. To this end, three sets of business plans in this volume are examples of "before and after" business planning. They are the Newsletter, Media Production, and Restaurant (Nonprofit) plans. (The original restaurant plan is reprinted from the first volume alongside its revision for comparison purposes.) Look for changes in operations and perspective, celebrations of success, adjustments in goals, and re-dedication to the business as themes in these revised plans.

The second volume, like the first, offers genuine business plans used by real people. *BPH II* provides 24 business plans used by actual entrepreneurs to gain funding support for their new businesses. Only the business and personal names have been changed to protect the privacy of the plan authors.

In accordance with feedback from users of our first volume, we have also expanded the coverage of small business resources. For instance, you will find: an enlarged directory section, which, in addition to listing all of the Small Business Development Centers (SBDCs), now includes entries for associations of interest to entrepreneurs and hundreds of consultants, listed geographically, who specialize in small business advice and planning; enhanced coverage of print business resources in the bibliography with the inclusion of periodicals; the addition of an Appendix containing a business plan template, which provides a comprehensive overview of the essential components of a business plan, and two fictional plans used by small business counselors; and improved inclusion of the financial data usually presented in conjunction with a business plan, such as Income and other Projections, Cash Flows, Balance Sheets, and other financial statements often requested by lenders.

Finally, in *BPH II* you will find a slightly revised page layout that accommodates more text per page and gives us more room to include financial tables, while still keeping the book to one compact volume.

If you already have the first volume of *BPH*, with this second volume you will now have a collection of 56 real business plans (not including one reprinted in the second volume from the first or the two fictional plans in the second), contact information for hundreds of organizations and agencies offering business expertise, a helpful business plan template, a foreword providing new planners with advice and instruction on how to begin their research, more than 400 citations to valuable small business development material, and a comprehensive glossary of terms to help the business planner navigate the sometimes confusing language of entrepreneurship.

FEATURES AND BENEFITS

BPH II offers many features not provided by other business planning references including:

○ Twenty-four business plans, providing examples of what entrepreneurs in your situation have done. Each of these real business plans represents an owner's successful attempt at clarifying (for themselves and others) the reasons that the business should exist or expand and why a lender to should fund the enterprise.

○ Two fictional plans that are used by business counselors at a prominent small business development organization as examples for their clients. (You will find these in the Business Plan Template Appendix.)

○ An expanded directory section that includes listings for all Small Business Development Centers with full contact information, including phone, fax, and contact names. In addition, this Appendix also contains a section listing associations of interest to entrepreneurs; Small Business Administration (SBA) Regional Offices; and consultants able to provide valuable advice on the business planning process. It is strongly advised that you consult supporting organizations while planning your business as they can provide a wealth of useful information.

○ A Glossary of Small Business Terms to help you decipher the sometimes confusing terminology used by lenders and others in the financial and small business communities.

○ An expanded bibliography, citing sources for easy follow-up and further reading. It now lists periodicals as well as books.

○ A Business Plan Template providing a model to help you construct your own business plan. This generic outline lists all the essential elements of a complete business plan and their components, including The Summary, Business History and Industry Outlook, Market Examination, Competition, Marketing, Administration and Management, Financial Information, and other key sections. Use this guide as a starting point for compiling your plan. Also in this section are two fictional plans used as examples by professional business counselors.

○ More of the financial documents that accompany a good business plan. You will find more tabular data, such as Cash Flows, Balance Sheets, Income Projections, and other financial information included with the textual portions of the plan.

ACKNOWLEDGEMENTS

The Editor wishes to thank all of the members of the Small Business Resources and Technology team, especially Kelly Hill, Karin E. Koek, Susan B. Martin, Jennifer Arnold Mast, and Holly M. Selden, all of whom contributed to this project in unique and valuable ways.

Thanks are also in order for the many contributors to *BPH II*, a number of whom have very good timing and whose business plans will serve as examples to future generations of entrepreneurs; the users of the title who called with their helpful suggestions; and Tim Dixon, of the Edward Lowe Foundation, who provided valuable commentary and insight: Your help was greatly appreciated.

Gale Research Inc.

COMMENTS WELCOME

Your comments on *BPH II* are welcome. Please direct all correspondence, suggestions for future volumes of *BPH*, and other recommendations to the following:

Business Plans Handbook II
Gale Research
835 Penobscot Bldg.
Detroit MI 48226-4094
Phone: (313)961-2242
Fax: (313)961-6815
Toll-Free: 800-347-GALE
Telex: 810 221 7087
E-mail: SmallBus@gale.com@galesmtp

Kristin Kahrs

Business
Plans

Automobile Assembly

BUSINESS PLAN   DREAM CARS

2000 Seaside Blvd.
London, ON, Canada N6A 3X1

May 1993

This component vehicle assembly business provides buyers with replicas of luxury automobiles and other specialty cars. The following plan outlines specifics on successfully working with other specialty car manufacturers to provide buyers with a personalized and rare vehicle.

- MISSION STATEMENT
- OVERVIEW
- COMPETITION
- SUPPLIERS
- CUSTOMERS
- ADVERTISING
- PRICING
- OPERATIONAL COSTS

- SALES SUMMARIES 1ST AND 2ND YEAR
- PROFITABILITY
- STAFFING
- LOCATION
- SETUP REQUIREMENTS
- FINANCIAL
- RETURN ON INVESTMENT
- CONCLUSION

AUTO ASSEMBLY BUSINESS PLAN

MISSION STATEMENT

Dream Cars, a manufacturer of replica and specialty automobiles, will help people realize their dreams of owning a luxury, sport or sports luxury automobile, without the high cost of importing a similar vehicle.

OVERVIEW

North America's love affair with the automobile will never end. The automobile has not only become a necessity, but a direct statement on who the person is that drives it. The individuality of one's vehicle is very important. You see various vehicles that are the same make and model, but are seldom identical because of personal touches added by the owner. There is an abundance of makes and models available to the everyday car buyer, but it is not the everyday car buyer to whom Dream Cars will cater.

Dream Cars is a component vehicle assembly facility. We assemble vehicles that are not of the ordinary, but more personal to the buyer. To explain further, a component, or specialty, vehicle is a domestic automobile combined with the "kit" from a different manufacturer. Kits that are available range from a reproduction 1955 Chevrolet convertible to a custom-designed, exotic-looking sports car that, for looks, will give any Ferrari or Lamborghini a run for their money. Performance can be enhanced in these vehicles as well, not only giving the exotic look, but also the power associated with this type of vehicle.

Day-to-day goings-on of the business will be the purchase of selected "donor" vehicles starting with a Datsun 240Z to be re-fitted to look like a 1968 Ferrari Vella Rossa Spyder. The re-body components will be purchased from selected dealers throughout North America, with preference given to Canadian companies. Another kit to be purchased will be the 427 Cobra replica from LA Exotics. These kits will be assembled and the finished product sold. 427 Cobra replicas are the most popular component cars on the market today.

Findings from the research conducted on this type of business show that the average gross profit from the sale of a component vehicle is between $9,500 and $10,500, ranging as high as $15,000. The overall objective of Dream Cars is to build and sell eight vehicles by the end of the first fiscal year, and double that total for the second year.

COMPETITION

There is competition in this market, but not in London or the surrounding area. There is one Cobra Replica kit dealer in London, but he is not a manufacturer or assembler. The closest competition found is in Windsor, and this firm specializes in the Lamborghini replicas. There are 3 other builders in southern Quebec, two offering Pontiac Fiero re-bodies and the other specializing in the Cobra replica. Dream Cars will assemble and offer these vehicles, but also several others for a more diversified and consumer demand-oriented platform.

SUPPLIERS

Various suppliers will be used throughout North America. Preference will be given to Canadian companies, then the United States, then Europe. The supplier of the Cobra kits will be a company called Luxury Ltd., out of Carmel, California. This supplier was chosen because of the quality of service and product, as well as a guarantee of availability of parts. They have also granted Dream Cars dealership rights in Canada for their Cobra replicas. Parts availability has been a major problem for some of the larger manufacturers of these kits. For the Fiero parts, either Red Dragon Inc. out of Winnipeg or Sassy Stuff Inc. from Sarnia will be used. For specialty orders from customers, suppliers will be sourced on an as-needed basis.

Dream Cars will cater to a customer base of 35 years old and up, married, male with an income above $35,000 per year. Of course there are always exceptions to the demographics, but this will comprise the majority of our customers. This data is derived from inquiries to the magazines that support this trade, as well as the other similar businesses and a survey of 1000 people who have purchased or are going to purchase a pre-assembled component vehicle.

With the customer base expanding to all four coasts, there is a very large clientele. We are expecting, however, the majority of our customers to be from the west coast, namely the lower half of British Columbia, down into the Portland, Oregon area. This constitutes a population of approximately 10 million. Taking 30 percent of that figure to represent the adult population leaves 3 million prospective customers. Out of that 3 million, approximately 20 percent will be in a position to purchase our product. This leaves a customer base of 600,000 people. This will more than satisfy the goals of selling eight cars the first year and sixteen the second. Dream Cars will, however, arrange to have a vehicle shipped anywhere in the world.

CUSTOMERS

This audience will be reached through advertisements in such magazines as "Trader," "Peterson's Kit Car," "Specialty Car," and "Road & Track." Other publications will be used as dollars permit.

Twenty percent of gross profits will be budgeted for this expense, which will allow approximately $1,450 per vehicle sold. During the first fiscal year the total advertising budget will be $11,600 or $967 per month.

ADVERTISING

The suggested retail selling price of a component vehicle will be approximately 30 "points" above product cost. The total cost of production is divided by .7 and rounded to the next highest thousand, which will give the suggested retail price. This will, of course, leave some room for negotiation on the actual selling price.

PRICING

Labour costs for the assembly will run about $2,000 per vehicle. The average time required to assemble a Cobra kit, for example, is between 150 and 200 hours. With building operations costs and salary overhead of $71,548 per year (shown below), every vehicle will have an assembly cost of $8,943.50 in the first year with eight vehicles sold. This will drop to approximately $6,060.33 in the second year. This is with 16 vehicles sold and a five percent inflation rate taken into consideration.

OPERATIONAL COSTS

OPERATIONAL COSTS...*continued*

Cost Breakdown (1st year)

Description	Per Month	Per Year
Rent for shop	$750.00	$9,000.00
Utilities (hydro, phone)	500.00	6,000.00
Advertising	967.00	11,604.00
Insurance	240.00	2,880.00
Business Tax	22.00	264.00
Yard Maintenance	200.00	2,400.00
Salaries for office (incl. principal)	3,500.00	42,000.00
	$6,179.00	$74,148.00
Labour for eight vehicles	1,333.00	16,000.00
Total operational costs 1st year	$7,512.00	$90,144.00

Cost Breakdown (2nd year)

Description	Per Month	Per Yer
Rent for Shop	$787.50	$9,450.00
Utilities (hydro, phone)	525.50	6,306.00
Advertising	1,015.35	12,184.20
Insurance	252.00	3,024.00
Business Tax	23.10	277.20
Yard Maintenance	210.00	2,520.00
Salaries for office (incl. principal)	3,675.00	44,100.00
	$6,488.45	$77,861.40
Labour for sixteen vehicles	2,800.00	33,600.00
Total operational costs 2nd year	$9,288.45	$111,461.40

PROFITABILITY

Purchase:

427 Cobra Replica Kit	$15,595.00*
Less 5% Builder's disc.	779.75
Builder's cost	14,815.25*
Canadian Exchange 36.28%	5,374.97
Duty @ 3.2%	646.09
G.S. Tax (7%)	1,458.54
Kit total cost Canadian funds	$22,294.85
Shipping California to Manitoba	1,253.00
Total cost (FOB Selkirk)	$23,547.85

*U.S.

Extra Parts Needed to Complete Vehicle

302 V-8 Engine	$1,700.00
5 Spd Transmission	1,500.00
Drive shaft	150.00
Steering Wheel	150.00
Miscellaneous	1,000.00
Total extra parts	$4,500.00
G.S. Tax	315.00
Total	$4,815.00
Total Vehicle Cost	$28,362.85

Sell:

LA Exotics 427 Cobra Replica MSRP (cost/.7)	$40,995.00
Total revenues	$40,995.00
Less Expenses	28,362.85
Gross Profits	$12,632.15

Because of the average profits in the sale of component vehicles being between $9,500 and $10,500 and an overhead of approximately $9,000 per vehicle, this leaves between $500 and $1,500 net profit for the company. This translates to around $850 per month for debt servicing the first year and over $5,000 per month for the second.

With all optional costs taken into consideration, the break-even point in the first year for Dream Cars will be seven vehicles sold. In the second year we will break even on the 10th vehicle sold. The initial year of operations targets for eight vehicles sold and second year sales will be 16 units. This is translated into the the dollar figures seen below, taking into consideration that half of the vehicles sold will be Cobra replicas and the other half will be a mixture of others. All figures are derived from the lowest acceptable price (in parentheses) for each vehicle sold and are in Canadian finds.

First Year	Sales	Costs
Four 427 Cobra replicas ($36,500.00 Can.)	$146,000.00	$113,451.40
One 1929 Mercedes replica ($18,000.00)	18,000.00	12,659.10
One La Grande XT (Fiero) ($38,000.00)	38,000.00	27,516.50
One Ferrari Vella Rossa (24,500.00)	24,500.00	11,342.90
One Ford TG-40 Replica ($84,000.00)	84,000.00	63,872.90
Total first year sales:	$310,500.00	$228,842.80
Gross Profits 1st year		$81,657.20
Operations cost 1st year		71,548.00
Net profit 1st year		$10,109.20

SALES SUMMARIES: 1ST AND 2ND YEAR

**SALES SUMMARIES:
1ST AND 2ND YEAR**
...continued

Second Year	Sales	Costs
Eight 427 Cobra replicas ($38,325.00)	$306,600.00	$238,247.94
Two Ford GT-40 Replicas ($88,200.00)	176,400.00	134,133.09
Two 1929 Mercedes Replicas ($19,500.00)	39,000.00	26,584.11
One Rhino GT (Ferrari rep. $23,000.00)	$23,000.00	11,910.05
Two Arteros (Fiero $38,900.00)	77,800.00	54,463.40
Total Second Year Sales:	$622,800.00	$465,338.59
Gross Profits 2nd year		$157,461.41
Operations Costs 2nd Year		96,965.20
Net profit 2nd year		$60,496.21

The vehicles described are just speculations on what vehicles will be built and sold by Dream Cars, but do reflect the type of sales figures expected from similar automobiles. Market research shows the Cobra to be the most popular replica available. We expect at least half of our sales to be Cobra replicas. The Ford GT-40 replicas are very popular as well. The only hindrance is the high price tag. This is the reason for fewer sales of this particular automobile. The others are reflections of potential customer orders.

STAFFING

Accomplishing the eight sales in the first year would require two full-time employees as well as myself for efficient operations. By the middle of the second fiscal year, a second mechanic will have to be hired. A journeyman mechanic will be hired in the first year to ensure the vehicles meet all safety requirements as determined by law. An accounting/promotions expert will also be hired to look after the advertising/customer service as well as the day-to-day operations of bookkeeping and other general accounting duties.

For customer protection, Dream Cars will offer a complete bumper-to-bumper warranty for parts and labour for mechanical failure caused by "normal use" for a period of one year from the date the customer takes delivery.

LOCATION

The business will be operating on a lot in the area. This spot was chosen for the following reasons:

a) Centrally located with regard to North America.
b) Large seven-acre lot with plenty of room for expansion.
c) Good-sized shop and offices already on the premises.
d) Rent is very reasonable with option to purchase property.
e) The location is a great place to raise a family.

**SETUP
REQUIREMENTS**

The nature of this type of business requires the acquisition of various permits, licences and bonds. These include an automotive dealership bond, an automotive dealership license, and liability insurance in the amount of one million dollars. These will be obtained as soon as the premises are secured.

The shop has a compressor and lines. Other tools will be supplied by myself and the journeyman mechanic hired. The office equipment, including a computer and accounting software, has already been obtained.

Inventory:

FINANCIAL

Purchase Cobra Kit as described above.	$28,362.85
Purchase 2nd Ferrari VR replica parts	9,342.90
Shop supplies (misc. tools and equipment)	5,000.00
Office supplies (computer, software, desks etc.)	7,600.00
Setup Charges - utilities	250.00
Yard cleanup	150.00
Operating capital (6 month)	45,072.00
Total startup costs	$95,777.75

Less Equity:

Computer & Software	3,500.00
Office furniture	500.00
Office equipment	250.00
Office supplies	100.00
Tools	2,400.00
Cash	15,000.00
	21,750.00

Total Investment required	$74,027.75

For the investment of $75,000, Dream Cars is offering an interest rate of 12% amortized over the next 15 years payable bi-weekly.

(Amortization schedule, normally included, was excluded for this publication.)

RETURN ON INVESTMENT

Market research shows an upward trend in both the home-building and the professional assembly of replica automobiles. With the necessity of both husband and wife having careers nowadays, the home-building of the replica vehicles is on a down turn and professional assembly is being opted for more and more often, sheerly because of lack of time required to build them. Being an integral part of this market is not only lucrative financially, but very rewarding personally as well. It is always good to know you have helped someone achieve their dreams.

CONCLUSION

Freelance Editor

BUSINESS PLAN

THE SCRIVENER

752 Kenwood Dr.
Silver City, NV 75002

June 1995 to December 1995

The following plan features an approach to home-based freelancing that seeks to combine professionalism and state-of-the-art technology with a broad range of editorial and publishing services. The plan includes discussions of marketing strategy, services, and a variety of other issues of interest to those intending to launch a freelance editorial or similar enterprise.

- EXECUTIVE SUMMARY

- MANAGEMENT AND ORGANIZATION

- SERVICE PLAN

- MARKETING PLAN

- FINANCIAL PLAN

- OPERATING SYSTEM

- GROWTH PLAN

- APPENDICES

EXECUTIVE SUMMARY

The Scrivener was formed as a sole proprietorship in November 1993 in Silver City, Nevada. It is a Nevada certified woman-owned business. The Scrivener will be seeking Nevada Department of Transportation certification as a woman-owned business in the first quarter of 1996.

The Scrivener, located in Silver City, Nevada, increases their client's share of the market by ensuring that each piece of written material is accurate, comprehensible, creative and effective. The company provides Writing Works solutions to businesses, government, non-profit organizations, and individuals. An array of products and services varying from simple data input to developing complex marketing materials, from technical manuals to newsletters rests beneath this umbrella. The Scrivener will handle any project needing to be researched, written, edited, typeset, illustrated, and produced.

The Scrivener is the only writing and editing service in the Silver Valley region. Other companies offer graphic design, some ad copy, or fill-in-the-blank resume services. The Scrivener delivers a comprehensive product from concept to binding. The Scrivener offers research services that use the latest in electronic technology and state-of-the art computer systems. The Scrivener is the only company in the region with an active presence on the Internet. The Internet/CompuServe resources allow The Scrivener to swiftly answer the needs of its clients for accurate timely information.

Our marketing focus in order of precedence is:
    1) Businesses / Government entities
    2) Non-profit organizations
    3) Individuals

The Marketing Plan seeks to increase our position as a full-service partner to our client base. All businesses have a need for our services. Our job has two segments: educate local businesses that an effective flyer, brochure, etc., is more than a secretary with a desktop publishing program, and secondly, demonstrate that using a professional delivers measurable positive results.

The Scrivener is a home-based business. It uses state-of-the-art Macintosh platforms and peripherals. Through telecommunication technology, The Scrivener is able to service clients in Europe and Australia. The company contracts out large printing jobs and occasional work overruns. The business is seventeen months old. The services offered by The Scrivener have been altered and honed to meet the needs of its clients. We are in daily operation, and we are currently investigating future services to offer.

Jane Austen has previously worked as a technical writer, documentation and learning systems designer, and a writer of articles for a variety of regional, national, and international markets. Ms. Austen edited and published an international newsletter which appeared throughout Europe. She is the decision-maker, primary designer and writer, and marketing specialist for the company.

James Baldwin, retired from the Los Angeles Police Department, performs routine input, document and graphic scanning, graphic and photographic editing, project design, graphic design, copy editing duties, and Quality Assurance duties.

The company will eventually be expanded (estimate Spring 1996) to include an office manager/designer, and a solid stable of contracting writers. Expansion options include segmenting the company into divisions handling advertising/marketing, technical documentation, newsletters, training programs, and consumer clients.

The Scrivener will be evaluating its business status in late 1995 according to advice from the accountants. At this time The Scrivener is considering the benefits of Limited Liability Companies and Schedule S Corporations.

The Scrivener will seek certification as an Enterprise Zone business prior to hiring any personnel.

The Scrivener will be trademarking its name, and its logo in the first quarter of 1996. It plans to service mark "Writing Works."

The Scrivener delivers global quality written communication services at a regional price. The company focuses on providing complete marketing and documentation services to businesses, government entities, and non-profit organizations. The Scrivener meets general consumer needs for letters, specialty projects, and resumes.

MANAGEMENT AND ORGANIZATION

Jane Austen, sole proprietor, handles all decision-making administrative and financial recordkeeping, and most of the project development. She is the primary writer and researcher. She is a graduate of the FastTrack II program. The Scrivener plans to become either a Limited Liability Company or a Schedule S Corporation by the third quarter of 1996. The company plans to hire an administrative assistant/writer-designer by the first quarter of 1996.

The management team is volunteer or hired as advisory consultants; their fees, if any are paid as part of the expense of doing business.

Management Team

The primary management team consists of:

Decision-maker - Jane Austen
Co-Decision-maker - James Baldwin
Small Business Advisor - Jesse James, Director of the SBDC at Silver City
Banker - George Eliot, Vice President Business Account, Bank One Silver City
Lawyer - To be selected
Accountant - B. Jones at Jones & Associates, Silver City, NV.

The secondary management team consists of:

Contacts on CompuServe and the Internet
Outside experts brought in by the SBDC
Clients

Jane Austen has over thirteen years of experience in writing genres ranging from analyzing information for technical publications for a quasi-illiterate audience to motivational marketing documents. She has the drive to succeed and pays attention to details. She is passionate about her occupation. She has used computers for over fifteen years. She will concentrate on the project management and development aspects of the business. Marketing is handled by Ms. Austen.

James Baldwin, co-decision-maker concentrates on graphic development, input, and proofing of projects. He is learning how to design and develop projects. The primary management team will be briefed on The Scrivener's activities, goals, projects, and processes at approximately two-month intervals, or on an as-needed basis (lawyer).

The secondary management team is consulted on an as-needed basis. The administrative assistant/writer-designer position will require someone who is familiar with Macintoshes, the American-English language, and who possesses very good interpersonal/customer handling skills. The ideal candidate will possess organizational skills, excellent typing and proofing skills. The Scrivener is willing to consider JTPA candidates.

Compensation

When The Scrivener makes money, (after paying off debt accumulated to purchase capital equipment and to pay operating expenses) a salary will be drawn by Jane Austen and James Baldwin. The appropriate financial retirement/health benefits will be set up with the accountant's advice. A bonus of 25% of net income is payable to Jane Austen and James Baldwin at year end.

Contractors for overflow work will be paid between $5.50 and $25.00 per hour based on project requirements. The administrative assistant/writer-designer will be paid between $4.75 and $8.50 depending on the skills brought to The Scrivener.

Contract Agreement

No outside employees at this time. When employees are hired, they will sign non-compete agreements valid for one year, and a trade secrets agreement regarding client lists. Employees will sign a confidentiality agreement as a condition of hire.

Insurance

Schornack & Associates Insurance has prepared a policy through the U.S. Insurance Co. The Scrivener's personal agent is Steven Schornack. The policy has the following coverages:

General Liability	$1,000,000
Products - Comp/Op Agg [E&O]	$1,000,000
Personal & Adv Injury	$1,000,000
Each Occurrence	$1,000,000
Fire Damage (Any 1 fire)	$50,000
Med Exp (Any 1 person)	$10,000
Business Contents	$50,000
Deductible	$250

When the Business's capital debts have been repaid, a life insurance policy will be placed on Jane Austen, and possibly on James Baldwin.

Purpose of the Service

The Scrivener eliminates the "huh??" in written documents. Some people regard writing as an inherent skill, and the services of a third party as a luxury. Yet, most people peruse at least one document each day where they use precious time deciphering directions, memos and reports, and other company's service offerings.

The Scrivener provides clearly written communication. Clearly written communication is necessary for the success of any business or industry. Applications of creative effective written communication range from advertising to technical documentation. By using such a service clients reach target markets, comply with regulations, increase the ability of their workers to perform, and streamline specific functions via a coherent written document.

Unique Features

☐ Flexibility, creativity. The Scrivener provides a global quality product at regional accessible prices. Access through telecommunications enhances the material/resources available to the local area.
☐ Our system of checklists ensure the high quality of the final product.
☐ We offer a variety of project options/payment plans.
☐ Our top-of-the-line equipment allows us to work faster and provide a higher quality product than any other local service.
☐ Experience of Ms. Austen in a range of corporate, military, technical, and academic settings.
☐ Comprehensive writing/editing/desktop publishing services.
☐ Ability to function as client's marketing and/or technical documentation department.
☐ Use of telecommunication and courier services allow client service across the globe.

Stage of Development

The business is seventeen months old. The services offered by The Scrivener have been altered and honed to meet the needs of its clients. We are in daily operation, and currently investigating future services to offer.

Trademarks and Copyrights

The Scrivener plans to trademark its logo and its name within the next six months - October 1995 to March 1996. Copyrights of work are not registered but held in house as per the 1976 law. Work for hire agreements are handled by contract. To date there are no royalty or license issues. The Scrivener adheres to copyright law requirements in all projects. Clarification is sought on an as-needed basis.

Product Liability

(Excerpt from Letter of Agreement Elements - See Appendix 1 for complete text.)

Prepatory Work (sketches, copy, dummies, and all prepatory work created or furnished by The Scrivener) shall remain our exclusive property and no use of same shall be made, nor any ideas obtained therefrom be used, except upon compensation to be determined by The Scrivener.

Alterations represent work, performed in addition to the original specifications. Such work shall be charged at current rates and supported with documentation upon request.

Color Proofing - Because of differences in equipment, paper, inks, and other conditions, a reasonable variation in color between color proofs and completed job shall constitute acceptable delivery.

Proofs shall be submitted and returned marked "O.K." or "O.K. with corrections" and signed by client. We regret any errors that may occur undetected, but cannot be held responsible for errors if the work is printed per client's O.K., and shall not be responsible if client returned proofs without written indications of change or has instructed The Scrivener to proceed without submission of proofs.

We will, of course, make every reasonable effort to assure that the text, artwork, photos and color of your (brochure, mailer, annual report, etc.) are correct before printing. However, inasmuch as we can never be as familiar as you with your (operations and products, activities, etc.) and because subjective decisions are often unnecessary, we require your approval at key intervals in the production process. Typically this includes signing off on text drafts, typeset copy, page proofs, printing dummies (bluelines/salt prints), and color and press proofs. The Scrivener assumes no legal or financial responsibility for content errors or omissions.

The Scrivener carries a general and professional liability policy. Liability is possible if a client has an accident at our office. We endeavor to meet clients at their offices.

Limitations

Most writing materials need to be periodically updated. It is possible to develop a high quality product that the client uses it as a template. Clients may take material to another service provider for copying at a total reduced cost.

Related Services and Spin-offs

One-stop convenience for marketing and technical documentation.

Services offered as of 1 June 1995

Annual Reports
Newsletters
Booklets
News Releases
Brochures
Product Literature
Business Letters
Proposals and presentations
Directories
Proofreading
Desktop Publishing Research (Electronic & Library)
Document Scanning
Reports
Editing Resumes and Cover Letters

Flyers
Rewriting
Manuals & Other Forms of Documentation Special Occasion Booklets
Job Descriptions
Technical Editing
Technical Writing
Thermal Binding
Word Processing
Grant Writing
Training Program Development & Documentation
Training Sessions

Presentation materials, i.e., Computer generated slide shows, transparencies, CBT (Computer-Based Training) scripts.
Alliance with computer training providers/printing houses

Spin-offs are limited by manpower, innovation, expertise, and funding.

Current production is readily handled by Jane Austen and James Baldwin. An administrative assistant/technical writer will be added when volume reaches a steady workload of 100 hours per week. Technical writers will be used as contractors on an as-needed basis until that point. Printing is handled by print shops and service bureaus.

Currently the only "waste" produced is paper, which is used in our fireplace. If volume increases to the point where paper recycling is feasible, then the paper will be sorted, shredded, and recycled. Various products such as toner, etc. are disposed of per the packaging guidelines.

The Scrivener is a smoke-free environment.

Writing services encompass all forms of written media from specialist to generalists, from concept to delivery of bound materials. As larger industries trim their staffs, the specialists in marketing and training are dismissed. Some of these individuals become contractors to their former employer; others seek more traditional employment opportunities.

Every business, non-profit, educational, and governmental entity has an on-going demand for high quality, value-priced writing services. Some companies choose to purchase desktop publishing software to be operated by clerical staff. These products vary from loathsome to excellent.

Successful writing service operators cater to a global clientele with educated tastes. Materials are exchanged through facsimile, on-line telecommunications, and courier services. The Scrivener is at the cutting edge of its industry. The market is growing for writing services to function as an independent marketing/documentation "department." Writing and other professional services are no longer tied to a specific geographic area.

Spin-offs

Environmental Factors

MARKETING PLAN

Industry Profile

"Lone Eagles are entrepreneurs or professionals--writers, brokers, analysts, lawyers, accountants, management consultants (marketing gurus, futurists, trainers and so forth), among others--who move to America's small towns or rural areas, where they continue to practice their trade and deliver products and services to faraway markets.

Whatever their motivation, Lone Eagles are knowledge workers who live by their wits, are heavy users of computers and advanced telecommunications, and remain connected to their markets and the outside world by faxes, modems, express mail, and airplane tickets." [Phil Burgess & Colleen Bogg Murphy - Center for the New West] (Sullivan, "Workstyles: Ten Years After," *Home Office Computing*, 126, March 1995).

There do exist concentrations of writing services in metro areas, the Northeast Corridor, DC beltway, and Los Angeles. The trend is for remote servicing using telecommunication equipment and courier services, however. Investment in equipment/software is key to profitability once client base is established.

Little capital is required to open a writing service. Traditional requirements are telephone, stamps, table, chair, and a typewriter. Today most homes have personal computers, a printer, and a word processing package.

Our competitive advantage to these wannabees are experience in diverse written communication products, flexibility, reliability, and state-of-the-art equipment. We actively solicit Letters of Recommendation and include these in our presentation and marketing materials.

Some clients do offer seasonal opportunities. Some local clients are seasonal based on income from recreational visitors. The winter Holiday period for family newsletters etc. is a growing market.

Customer Profile

Primary clients are:
- Business - owners and managers
- Non-profit/educational
- Government

Secondary clients are:
- Resume clients
- Non-business consumers

Target Market Profile

The Scrivener targets businesses and organizations needing Writing Works. We tailor our products to the needs of real estate agents, non-profits, and educational groups. Our clients seek to increase their market share through the use of our services.

- Business - owners and managers
- Non-profit/educational
- Government

The Scrivener primarily relies on clients referred by satisfied customers and the local Yellow Pages listings. The company will be expanding its client base through networking, seminar presentations, and a series of direct mail campaigns.	**Market Penetration**

Prospects receive a package with a brochure, two business cards, two letters of recommendation, and a tailored solutions letter. Follow-up with telephone calls after a ten-day period.

An 8.5 x 11 newsletter will be mailed to clients and prospects on a bi-monthly basis. The newsletter will present practical tips, inform clients about The Scrivener's services and accomplishments, discuss the need for Writing Works.	**Advertising and Promotion**

The Scrivener is an active member of the Silver City Chamber of Commerce and regularly attends networking opportunities. The Scrivener is a member of the National Association of Desktop Publishers and the National Association of Female Executives. The Scrivener will be joining the Society of Technical Communication in the third quarter of 1995.

Referrals from the Small Business Development Center from an important source of clients. The SBDC also provides professional services to The Scrivener.

The Scrivener uses the following avenues to promote its services:

- 800 AT&T yellow pages. Cost: $110/mo. Discontinued as of October 1995 due to poor return.
- Silver Valley Directory. Cost: None.
- Silver City Chamber of Commerce Directory. Cost: None
- Brochure displays at: Commercial Productions, Silver City Chamber of Commerce, Office City, Graphics Unlimited.
- The Silver Valley Weekly. Cost: $44/mo. Women in Business issue - $50.00
- Dynamic Silver City column. Cost: Time to write column
- Interaction on Internet and CompuServe forums. Sign messages with our name, mission, and 800 number. In the Desktop Publishing forum, the Work from Home forum, and the Writers Forum, have file describing The Scrivener's services.
- The Scrivener is investigating the cost of advertising on CompuServe and the Internet.

- Training Seminars - Internet, client-defined topics - Technical documentation/Employee handbooks - Newsletters for clubs & organizations - Church bulletins - Presentations/proposals for executives, contractors, and engineers - Bi-monthly regional magazine	**Future Markets**

Please see the Service Fees list included in the Appendices. Prices are evaluated in March, June, October, and December of each year. The Scrivener offers the following service discounts:	**Pricing Profile**

Pricing Profile
...continued

Non-profits - 50%.
Educational organizations - 25%.
SBDC referred clients - 30%.
Long Term Agreements - 20% with 15% for independent projects

Payment Policy

☐ Projects below $50: payment is due upon job completion.

☐ Projects between $50 and $100: $50 is due upon job acceptance, the balance is due upon completion.

☐ Projects over $100 are divided into thirds, with one-third due upon job acceptance, the second third due upon delivery of the first draft, and the balance due upon job completion.

Gross Margin on Products

The Scrivener uses a variety of industry publications, (National Writers Union, Creative Business, Writer's Marketplace etc.) and conversations with peers to establish service prices. Industry standard pricing is too expensive for this region, therefore The Scrivener has evolved a reduced pricing structure as compared to the rest of the industry.

The Scrivener requires $10.00 of each hourly billing to meet overhead costs. The profit margin varies with the rate charged.

Management Benchmarks

No one client should contribute more than 25% of yearly income. A good mix of existing to new client work is about 2 to 1 (66%) for freelances and midsize firms (up to 12 employees). Jobs from existing clients frequently produce profit that is up to 30% higher. [Creative Business - March-April 1995].

FINANCIAL PLAN

Business History

Nineteen ninety-four was our first year in operation. In addition to the "standard" development of a start-up business, there were additional problems. These incidents account for the sometimes negative growth of a viable growing business. Existing computer systems also proved unable to handle the volume and quality of work necessary to succeed.

The Scrivener invested $12,000.00 drawn from personal savings in new computer equipment and software in August 1994.

Ratios for a Creative Business*

Quick: [Short term assets divided by short-term liabilities]. Ideal = 1.0 to 1.5. The Scrivener as of June 1995 has a ratio of 1.25.
Debt to Asset: [Total liabilities divided by total assets]. Ideal = 0.3 to 0.6. The Scrivener as of June 1995 has a ratio of 0.5.
****Return on Equity**: [Net profit divided by owner's equity]. Ideal = 15% to 35%. The Scrivener as of June 1995 has a ratio of 18%.
Return on Net Working Capital: [Net revenue divided by short-term assets minus short-term liabilities]. Ideal = 5 to 10. The Scrivener as of June 1995 has a ratio of 6.

*Creative Business Newsletter   **Business performance index

Sales - $2,000.00 per month based on a workload of eighty hours per month at an average cost of $25.00 per hour.	**Assumptions**
Newsletters - 2 per month at an average billing of $300.00 each	
Repay nearly $15,000 in personal loans to start business at a monthly cost of $486.70 Pay monthly overhead and expenses, excluding loans, average of $600.00 Pay business Visa charges, currently $200 per month.	Accounts Payable
Projects below $50: payment is due upon job completion. Projects between $50 and $100: $50 is due upon job acceptance, the balance is due upon completion. Projects over $100 are divided into thirds, with one-third due upon job acceptance, the second third due upon delivery of the first draft, and the balance due upon job completion.	Accounts Receivable
1.75% monthly interest (21% APR) is charged on accounts over 30 days old. Bad Checks are sent to the Silver County Attorney's office.	
The Scrivener has not had to pay income tax, nor does it collect sales taxes.	**Taxes**
The Scrivener uses M.Y.O.B. ver. 5. Client project times are kept by Time slips, a report listing client, project, and activity is printed for each invoice activity. An accountant will be auditing the books and amending any errors which occurred during the set-up phase.	**Accounting System**
	OPERATING SYSTEM
☐ Clients receive Courteous, Prompt, Reliable service. ☐ A series of checklists is used to ensure the high quality of client's project. ☐ Appendix 2 contains the checklists used to handle clients and their projects. ☐ Administrative policies and procedures are maintained in The Scrivener Ops Manual. This manual contains a master listing of how to handle the business. This Business Plan is a companion document. ☐ The Scrivener is an equal opportunity employer and does not discriminate against color, sex, creed, political affiliation, marital status or age. It is the company's practice to fill vacancies by promoting from with whenever possible. ☐ The normal work week is Monday to Friday, 9 am to 5 pm with a one hour break for lunch. ☐ Outside hires will be made in accordance with Enterprise Zone requirements whenever possible.	**Administrative Policies and Procedures**
Employees must call in by 10:00 with the reason for their absence.	Absences
Employees will be paid semi-monthly by check on the 15th and the last day of the month. All contract workers will be paid within 15 days of receipt of their invoice.	Pay periods

Evaluations	Employee evaluations will be monthly, quarterly, semi-annually, and annually. An evaluation sheet will be filled out on each employee by the manager. The manager and the employee will sign the sheet after the session. A copy of the evaluation will be retained by the employee, by the manager, and by the Human Resources department.
Time Off Policy	Full-time employees are allowed 30 calendar days off during the year. Vacation and sick time is included in this time to allow the employee maximum flexibility. A maximum of 15 days may be carried over into the next year. Any time carried over must be used within six months. January 1 and 2, Presidents Day, Good Friday or Easter Monday, Memorial Day, July 4th, Labor Day, Thanksgiving Thursday and Friday, Christmas Eve, Christmas Day and Boxing Day (December 26) are Company Holidays.

•Each month the employee will earn 2.5 days of vacation-sick time.
•First year employees receive no pay for these periods.
•Second year employees receive 25% of their daily wage.
•Third year employees receive 50% of their daily wage.
•Fourth year employees receive 100% of their daily wage.

Family Leave	An employee is able to take as much unpaid family leave as necessary. Family leave covers maternity and paternity leave, catastrophic illness of a family member, and other instances on a case-by-case evaluation by management. All cases will be evaluated in accordance with the current provisions of the Family Leave Act.
On-Site Daycare	The Scrivener provides on-site daycare for its employees.
Insurance	No insurance or company benefits are being offered at this time.

Administrative Controls

Project Initiation	The Client Handling checklist is used to set up project accounting.
Billing	☐ Projects below $50 are invoiced upon job completion. ☐ Projects between $50 and $100: $50 is due upon job acceptance, the balance is invoiced upon project completion. ☐ Projects over $100 are divided into thirds, with one-third due upon job acceptance, the second third is invoiced upon delivery of the first draft, and the balance is invoiced upon job completion. Terms are Net 10 days.
Collecting Accounts Receivable	Outstanding invoices are tracked and an overdue reminder is sent after 30 days. If a billed customer has not paid or made arrangements for payments by 60 days, the account is turned over to National Credit Systems for collection activities.

1.75% monthly interest (21% APR) is charged on accounts over 30 days old.
Bad Checks are sent to the Silver County Attorney's office.

Bad Check Policy	Checks marked "Returned for Insufficient Funds" are resubmitted once. Checks returned a second time are prepared in accordance with the Silver Attorney's office Bad Check handbook. The bad check is photocopied, a bad check letter is filled out and mailed to the client. Failure to pay the debt with cash, money order or certified check sends the client's check to the Silver County Attorney's office.

Bad Check Charges:

Checks Up to $100	$20.00
$101 to $300	$45.00
$300+	$70.00

Inventory is kept to a minimum. Office supplies are purchased in bulk whenever possible. Graphic supplies, software, and hardware are purchased on an as-needed basis.

Inventory Control

① A Letter of Agreement is generated for each project over $100.00, excluding resumes.
② The Client Handling Checklist will be followed.
③ The Accounting Checklist will be followed.
④ The customer will be required to proof and sign/initial the proof before the master documents are made.
⑤ Clients will be informed of delays in work schedule by telephone with a letter to confirm.
⑥ All work in progress will be tracked on a daily basis. A project schedule board will be made up, showing each stage of the project. Completion dates will be assigned to each stage and updated daily.
⑦ Invoices will be prepared the day the work is complete and will accompany the final artwork.
⑧ Deposits to the bank will be done on a daily basis.

Documents and Paper Flow

Sales Projections - are inflated slightly. Hours would have to fall below 400 to harm cash flow. If this happens, then the household loan repayments would cease, and planned purchases (computer hardware/software) would be eliminated for the duration of the episode.

Risk Analysis and Alternative Plans of Action

Older computer equipment and software is being sold with the monies to be reinvested in the business. If the Scrivener were to close, all equipment would remain with Jane Austen and James Baldwin. Every effort would be made to collect Accounts Receivable.

Salvaging Assets

◆Must have cash flow to pay writers at least bimonthly.
◆Must train them in the Scrivener's method of project accounting for client tracking.
◆Their computer systems and software must be compatible with ours & with clients'.

Contractors

Subcontractors, their specialties, and rates:

C. Bronte	$15.00	Technical documentation
Henry James	$15.00	Technical documentation
Beth Walden	$10.00	Library research/documentation
Sandy Smith	$10.00	Admin Ass't/Tech documentation
Jimmy Faulkner	$10.00	Admin Ass't/Tech documentation

Exit Strategies

① Sell stock
② Franchise
③ Go out of business and liquidate assets
④ Find employment with another company
⑤ Start new venture and transfer assets to the new company.

The ideal exit strategies are #1, #2, and #5.

GROWTH PLAN

Expansion options include segmenting the company into divisions handling advertising/ marketing, technical documentation, newsletters, training programs, and consumer clients. When volume reaches $30,000 in a particular market segment, then a division with a full-time writer will be created.

Eventually the Scrivener plans to have satellite offices in major metropolitan areas with contracted freelancers. Franchise opportunities are an option, as well.

The Scrivener will be evaluating its business status in late 1995 according to advice from the accountants. At this time The Scrivener is considering the benefits of Limited Liability Companies and Schedule S Corporations.

Capital Requirements

Small Business Loan - January 1996

☐ Purchase new PowerMac 8100/AV, two page monitor
☐ Purchase color inkjet printer
☐ Purchase software for new workstation
☐ Purchase office equipment for new workstation
☐ Professional services: attorney, accountant
☐ Trademark/servicemark search
☐ General operating expenses

Personnel Requirements

Administrative Assistant/Writer-Designer will provide administrative support, project oversight, clerical work, telephone support, design projects and write copy.

Service Fees (as of 1 July 1995)

(Fees subject to change without notice)

The Scrivener provides a complete range of Writing Works services. We have a policy of CPR (Courteous Prompt Reliable) Service. We believe in satisfying our customers.

Educational groups receive a 25% discount on services. Non-profit and Non-for-profit groups receive a 50% discount on services.

Service	Fee (per hour, unless otherwise specified)	**Service Fees (as of 1 July 1995)** ...*continued*
Brochure		
(Design)	$50.00	
(Copy Writing)	$45.00	
(Copy Editing)	$30.00	
(DTP-Input/Edit)	$50.00	
Arrange for printing	Enquire	
Business Letters	$50.00 and up	
Consultation	$40.00	
Consumer Letters	$15.00 and up	
Desktop Publishing		
(Design)	$50.00	
(Copy Writing)	$45.00	
(Copy Editing)	$30.00	
(DTP-Input/Edit)	$50.00	
Arrange for printing	Enquire	
Graphics		
Creation	$35.00	
Editing	$30.00	
Foreign Document Translation (Spanish, German, French)		
Translation	$25.00	
Manuscript		
Typing	$20.00	
Proofreading	$20.00	
Copy Editing	$20.00	
Rewriting	$30.00	
News Releases		
Business	$50.00 each	
Non-profit/Education	$25.00 each	
Newsletters		
(Design)	$25.00-300.00 per design	
(Copy Writing)	$45.00	
(Copy Editing)	$30.00	
(DTP-Input/Edit)	$40.00	
(Research) $30.00		
Proposals (Service includes)		
(Design)	$50.00	
(Copy Writing)	$45.00	
(Copy Editing)	$30.00	
(DTP-Input/Edit)	$40.00	
Research	$30.00	
Does not include connect fees.		
Names, Addresses or Telephone Numbers	$1.00 each	
	$10.00 for 15	
Rewriting	$30.00	

**SERVICE FEES
(AS OF 1 JULY 1995)**
...continued

Resume Services
(Service includes two usable resumes, a camera ready copy, and an emergency white copy and two envelopes)

1-page	$25.00-70.00
Visually enhance basic information/address change	$25.00/ea
Evaluate client work history, current resume and targeted employer(s)	$25.00/hr.
2-page	$35.00-100.00
Visually enhance basic information/address change	$35.00 each
Evaluate client work history, current resume and targeted employer(s)	$25.00/hr.
3-page	$45.00-125.00
Visually enhance basic information/address change	$45.00 each
Evaluate client work history, current resume and targeted employer(s)	$25.00/hr.

Job Application Letters/Cover Letter	$25.00/ea

Additional copies

Camera ready	$5.00/ea.
Resume paper	.10/sheet
3.5 inch disk copy	$5.00/disk

Scanning

Document	$20.00
Graphic	$25.00

Technical Editing	$35.00
Technical Writing	$45.00
Training	$30.00

Thermal Binding
$1.50/vol: up to .50 inch plus $15.00/hr. labor charge for client-provided materials.

Cost per volume if we arrange copying from client master:

Copybind (2-15 sheets)	$1.70-3.00
1/8 inch (16-33 sheets)	$3.10-4.80
1/4 inch (34-65 sheets)	$4.90-8.00
3/8 inch (66-98 sheets)	$8.10-11.30
1/2 inch (99-130 sheets)	$11.40-14.50

Sizes larger than 1/2 inch are available upon request.

Typing	$20.00

Letter of Agreement (a)

???? hereby retains The Scrivener for writing services as explained below, commencing ??? and continuing monthly thereafter, until ???. Either party hereto may terminate this agreement earlier by tendering a 30-day written notice of termination. This agreement covers only services, not printing, materials, photocopying, etc.

For these services, ??? agrees to pay a fee of ??? in ??? and a monthly fee of ???. The monthly fee shall be due and payable in advance and in the following manner:

◆ The first month's fee shall be due and payable by ???, and ??? shall be due on ???.

◆ If the client elects not to use the retained services within the agreed upon time span, then the client forfeits the use of that service for that time period.

◆ Expenses shall be billed by invoice and shall be due and payable within fifteen days of the invoice date. No expense shall be incurred by the Scrivener on the client's behalf without the client's prior approval.

In the event that any legal action is required to enforce this agreement or any portion thereof, the prevailing party of such legal action shall be entitled to recover from the other part the reasonable attorney's fees and legal costs thereof.

Additionally, is offered a 15% reduction on services for projects outside the terms of this retainer.

Services Retained (Monthly)

Meetings/Consultation
Copywriting
Copyediting
Desktop Publishing
Design
Research

Value of Services Retained

??? will receive ??? of service for the amount of ???. This represents a 20% savings over the project rate.

Prepatory Work (sketches, copy, dummies, and all prepatory work created or furnished by The Scrivener) shall remain our exclusive property and no use of same shall be made, nor any ideas obtained therefrom be used, except upon compensation to be determined by the Scrivener

Proofs shall be submitted and returned marked "O.K." or "O.K. with corrections" and signed by client. We regret any errors that may occur through production undetected, but cannot

Letter of Agreement
...*continued*

be held responsible for errors if the work is printed per client's O.K., and shall not be responsible if client returned proofs without written indications of change or has instructed the Scrivener proceed without submission of proofs.

We will, of course, make every reasonable effort to assure that the text, artwork, photos and color of your projects are correct before printing. However, inasmuch as we can never be as familiar as you with your (operations and products, activities, etc.) and because subjective decisions are often unnecessary, we require your approval at key intervals in the production process. Typically this includes signing off on text drafts, typeset copy, page proofs, printing dummies (bluelines/salt prints), and color and press proofs. The Scrivener assumes no legal or financial responsibility for content errors or omissions.

If the balance is not paid within 30 days, the entire balance shall become due and payable upon demand, plus the cost involved of notification, either by regular or registered mail, that this account is past due, plus any collection fees or attorney fees necessary to collect the stated amount. A monthly minimum service charge of $3.00 will be added to all accounts over 30 days. Claims for defects, damages, or shortages must be made by the client within a period of thirty (30) days after delivery. Failure to make such a claim within the stated period shall constitute irrevocable acceptance and an admission that they fully comply with terms, conditions, and specifications. The Scrivener's liability shall be limited to stated selling price of any defective goods, and shall in no event include special or consequential damages, including profits (or profits lost).

In the event that any legal action is required to enforce this agreement or any portion thereof, the prevailing party of such legal action shall be entitled to recover from the other party the reasonable attorney's fees and legal costs thereof.

Signing this Letter of Agreement constitutes permission to proceed with the work indicated under the specified terms. Please Keep a copy for your records.

Letter of Agreement (b)

??? hereby retains The Scrivener for writing services as specified below.

All services, including consultation, research, writing, editing, designing, proofing, and other tasks normal and incidental to the completion of this project will be charged at these rates:

Project:

Design	$20.00/hour*	
Technical Writing	$20.00/hour*	
Technical Editing	$12.50/hour*	
Desktop Publishing	$17.50/hour*	
Graphic Creation	$17.50/hour*	
Graphics Editing	$15.00/hour*	
Research	$12.50/hour*	
Training	$12.50/hour*	
Meetings	$20.00/hour	*Non-profit rate

Workbooks can be thermally bound (perfect bound, ex: paperback book) at a cost of $15.00 per hour plus $1.50 per cover.

Preparatory Work (sketches, copy, dummies, and all prepatory work created or furnished by The Scrivener) shall remain our exclusive property and no use of same shall be made, nor any ideas obtained therefrom be used, except upon compensation to be determined by The Scrivener.

Alternations represent work performed in addition to the original specifications. Such work shall be charged at current rates and supported with documentation upon request.

Proofs shall be submitted and returned marked "O.K." or "O.K. with corrections" and signed by client. We regret any errors that may occur through production undetected, but cannot be held responsible for errors if the work is printed per client's O.K., and shall not be responsible if client returned proofs without written indications of change or has instructed The Scrivener to proceed without submission of proofs.

We will, of course, make every reasonable effort to assure that the text, artwork, photos and color of your (brochure, mailer, annual report, etc.) are correct before printing. However, inasmuch as we can never be as familiar as you with your (operations and products, activities, etc.) and because subjective decisions are often unnecessary, we require your approval at key intervals in the production process. Typically this includes signing off on text drafts, typeset copy, page proofs, printing dummies (bluelines/salt prints), and color and press proofs. The Scrivener assumes no legal or financial responsibility for content errors or omissions.

For projects under $50.00 payment will be upon project completion. For projects over $50.00 payment shall be 1/3 net total upon job initiation, 1/3 net total upon final proof approval, remaining balance upon delivery unless otherwise provided in writing on proposal. All discounts and terms other than these will appear on the invoice. If the balance is not paid within 30 days, the entire balance shall become due and payable upon demand, plus the cost involved of notification, either by regular or registered mail, that this account is past due, plus any collection fees or attorney fees necessary to collect the stated amount. A monthly minimum service charge of $3.00 will be added to all accounts over 30 days. Claims for defects, damages, or shortages must be made by the client within a period of thirty (30) days after delivery. Failure to make such a claim within the stated period shall constitute irrevocable acceptance and an admission that they fully comply with terms, conditions, and specifications. The Scrivener's liability shall be limited to stated selling price of any defective goods, and shall in no event include special or consequential damages, including profits (or profits lost).

Expenses shall be billed by invoice and shall be due and payable within fifteen days of the invoice date. No expense shall be incurred by The Scrivener on the client's behalf without the client's prior approval.

In the event that any legal action is required to enforce this agreement or any portion thereof, the prevailing party of such legal action shall be entitled to recover from the other party the reasonable attorney's fees and legal costs thereof.

Letter of Agreement
...continued

Appendix 2:

Client Handling Procedures

Checklist

A. Client requests services/meeting
  1. Listen to need
     a. Restate for clarity
     b. Don't specify how job will be done - just if it is possible to meet client's request.
  2. What are client's expectations?
  3. What is client's budget?
     a. How to handle project changes?
     b. Increased costs/time?
B. Fill out project spec sheet.
  1. Status: individual/Business/Educational organization/Non-profit
  2. Reporting periods
C. Fill out project Letter of Agreement for work valued at over $50
  1. Is money due up front?
  2. Payment options
D. Set up Project Sheet (TT)/DTP project master
  1. Time activate steps
  2. @all board
  3. Gannt chart
E. Set up Timeslips Tracker
F. Set up job number in MYOB
G. Complete project
H. Run checklists
  1. Print out applicable checklists
  2. Use checklists
I. Invoice project - Use Accounting Checklist
J. Deliver project to client/Evaluation form
K. Within 3 working days = Telephone follow-up
L. Within 7 working days = Thank you note.
M. Add to DB, contact a minimum of every 2 months with Scrivener info/new services etc.

Project Specification Worksheet

1. Description:
   brochure   ad   catalog   press release
   annual report   newsletter   manual   other:
2. Pages: Number   Size
3. Print: One-color   Two-color   Four-color
4. Illustrations: Yes   No
a. What is the nature of the assignment?
   Size   Colors
   Number of pieces   Medium
   Technique   Complexity
   Style   Other
b. What sketches, reference material or art direction will be provided?
c. How much consulting/meeting time is estimated?

d. What is the usage?

        Medium (e.g. publication)

        Distribution

        Exposure (e.g. circulation)

        Other:

e. What is the timing?

        When can I begin?

        When is the first sketch needed?

        When must the final be delivered?

f. What rights are requested?

        One time   Limited   All Rights

g. Do I retain the original art?

        Yes   No

Estimating Considerations (hours):

    Research

    Thinking/conceptual

    Drafting

    Revision

    Finish

    Optimism factor (Add 10% to 15%)

        Total

Additional Considerations:

1) Will the illustration be published with a credit line/copyright/my signature?

2) Will tear sheets or copies be provided?

3) Does this assignment require me to work other than normal hours, and does the fee reflect it?

4) Is the price or my estimate approximately 15% of the ad price for a similar unit of space?

5) Does the job have showcase/fun value?

6) Is the client likely to pay without hassle?

7) How much money will I really make on this job (billing minus overhead & job expenses?)

8) Other:

5. Photographs: Yes   No

        Color   Number

        B&W   Number

Special Requirements

6. For use: in house as training information other
outside as advertising public education other

7. Audience: Age range   Knowledgeable in client's field?   Yes   No

Sex: Predominantly male   Predominantly female   Mixed

Education: Elementary   High School   College   College+

Occupation(s):

Geographic Locale:

Project Specification Worksheet

...continued

Project Specification Worksheet
...continued

8. Project Objectives:

9. Product Features:

10. Customer (User) Benefits:

11. Support for Benefit Claims:

12. Competition:

13. Creative Considerations:

14. Distribution Considerations:

15. Single Most Important Point:

16. Primary Contact/Phone

   Project Manager/Phone

   Other

17. Will advance or progress payments be provided?

   Yes $ No

18. What expenses are allowable?

   Models   Deliveries   Travel

   Stats   Research   Other

19. Is there a kill fee, or will I bill for time at my hourly rate if the job should not go to completion?

   Kill fee   Hourly Rate   Neither

20. Has budget been established?

   Fixed   Ball Park   Estimate Required

21. Will there be a purchase order, or will I need to prepare a letter of agreement?

Purchase order Letter of Agreement

22. Materials Supplied by Client:

23. Deadline Schedule:

   Materials to writer

   Outline

   First Draft

   Revisions Noted

   Final Draft

Notes:

Estimating Worksheet

Date: Revision#:

Client

Project

Job #   Client PO #

Proposal required by:

Projected start date:

Projected finish date:

Job Specifications

Dimensions/format/size/scope:

Number of pages/images/item:

Quantity:

Colors:

Paper/fold/presentation:

Number of photos/illustrations:

Number of words:

Number of charts/graphs/graphics:

Special considerations:

Input Time

	Hours	x	$Rate	=	Total

Initial meeting(s)
Additional meetings
(No.)   Client interviews
Background research
Travel time

Conceptual Time

	Hours	x	$Rate	=	Total

(No.)   In-house meetings
Creative research
Strategizing evaluating
Concept/development
Design/write/sketch

Execution Time

	Hours	x	$Rate	=	Total

Client meetings
Full layout/draft/sketch
Copywriting
Copyediting
Scanning
First revision
Second revision
Author's alternations
Travel Time

Sub-Contracted Services

	Hours	x	$Rate	=	Total

Interviewing Suppliers

	Estimate	x	Markup	=	Total

Copywriting
Design/layout/execution
Illustration
Original photography
Stock photography
Mfg/production/printing

Production Time

	Hours	x	$Rate	=	Total

Project management
Art direction
Typesetting
Mechanical/boardwork
Prepress
Printing supervision

Estimating Worksheet
...continued

General expenses

	Estimate	x	Markup	=	Total

New type fonts
Clip Art
Special supplies/software
Copies & stats
Delivery services
Cabs/tickets/mileage
Meals/hotels
LD telephone/fax
Service bureau charges

Miscellaneous

Additional usage rights

Administrative expense (small jobs) +5-10%
"Optimism factor" compensation + 10-20%
Job/client difficulty factor
Competitive factor

Estimated Total

Proofreading Checklist

All drafts, except Final:

Independently checked?
Material read aloud by 1 person and type-checked by another.
Proofing done without a break

If 1 person proofing:
       Read text all the way through forward for sense.
       Read text backward, word for word, for mistakes.
       Read text forward for sense.

Check:
       Photos/captions
       Headlines
       Text references
       Format consistency

Final draft:

Run Grammar Check Program

Client: Project:
Job #:   Stage:

This proof must be returned by ?? to make our production schedule, which calls for ?? to be provided to you next on: ??

☐No changes required on this proof. .
☐Make changes where indicated on pages
☐Submit a revised proof.
☐No need to submit a revised proof.

Signature: Date:

Note: Changes resulting from author's alterations (those not caused by errors or omissions) may result in additional charges or delays.

Client: Project:
Job #:   Stage:
This proof must be returned by ?? to make our production schedule, which calls for ?? to be provided to you next on: ??

☐No changes required on this proof.
☐Make changes where indicated on pages
☐Submit a revised proof.
☐No need to submit a revised proof.

Signature: Date:

Note: Changes resulting from author's alterations (those not caused by errors or omissions) may result in additional charges or delays.

1. Finish work/bill client
   a. Print Timeslips worksheet for project
   b. Card file in MYOB: Name, address, telephone, discount, account due information
   c. Jobs list General Accounts - is project listed? If not, then list.
   d. Item invoice:
      1) Invoice number key (505-0100) 5=year 05=month 01=invoice number 00=subsequent invoices for this project
      2) use Timeslip worksheet for information
      3) Include job number on invoice
      4) Record the invoice
      5) Save data
      6) Print invoice
2. Receive $
   a. Write check number on invoice stub
   b. Photocopy check
   c. Apply payment to outstanding invoices
   d. Save data
3. Deposit $
a. Stamp back of each check
b. Fill out deposit slip
c. Record on deposit slip
d. Deposit $
e. Record deposit in checkbook.

Accounting Checklist

Freelance Editor

BUSINESS PLAN   WORD FOR WORD

668 Sycamore Dr.
Pine Bluff, FL 55379

April 1995

The following plan represents another example of a home-based editorial services company started fulfill the author's goals of independence and career control. Whereas the previous plan was for a company offering a broader range of services, this author has found a niche for her unique skills.

- EXECUTIVE SUMMARY

- CONCEPT

- OBJECTIVES

- MARKET ANALYSIS

- PRODUCTION

- MARKETING

- EDUCATION

- ORGANIZATION AND PEOPLE

- FUNDS FLOW AND FINANCIAL PROJECTIONS

- OWNERSHIP

FREELANCE EDITOR BUSINESS PLAN

EXECUTIVE SUMMARY

This business plan describes the sole proprietorship run by Joan Beaufort. It answers who, what, where, when, why, and how, which are summarized in this section.

Who

Professional business writer Joan Beaufort is establishing a sole proprietorship known as Word for Word. I have 15 years of communications experience that covers both non-profit and corporate work. In the non-profit sector, I worked in marketing and public relations in the health care industry and in the arts. I have a bachelor's degree in journalism, and a master's degree in international education.

After eight years in non-profit work, I began a job as an editor and writer for IBM Denmark in Copenhagen. After three years, I was promoted to a communications management position with IBM Netherlands in Amsterdam. After two years, I took a senior project management position with RR Donnelley Europe's translation subsidiary, also located in Amsterdam. From Amsterdam, I managed projects located in 12 countries, including Japan.

What

I am primarily a business writer and editor, which means I will limit this business to this activity. Projects that do not have anything to do with writing, will be turned down. The most important thing is for me to define the skills I offer and stick to them. It is not possible to be all things to all companies.

Where

For the first two years I will work from my home office. After that time, I plan to move to an office outside of my home. I should be established enough at that point to do so.

When

This business will begin in May, 1995.

Why

I am starting this business because I want to be in control of my own work. I do not want to be limited by managers as to what projects I can work on, nor do I want anyone else to set my hours. I want to offer the best quality service possible, and to continually improve on this service. For example, if I want to take an important course that meets during the day, I do not want an employer to turn this down because of production schedules.

I believe in the service I am offering, I know how business works both nationally and internationally, I have researched the market, and I am certain there are potential buyers. I am limited only by my own creativity, imagination, drive, and vision.

How

I will set up a home-based office with computer, printer, modem, fax, extra phone and fax lines, 35mm camera, and tape recorder.

My clients will be a mix of public relations and advertising agencies, translations companies, technical companies, and newspapers and magazines.

My business concept is to offer high-quality business writing and editing services with a fast turn-around time to both domestic and non-domestic companies. The advantage of this service is that it can be utilized by companies during peak periods on a project basis. Companies do not have to pay the high cost of overhead to employ extra employees who may sit idle during slow periods. Instead, the company gets the skills needed, the desired high quality at a reasonable price, and deadlines met without (as much) in-house, last-minute panic.

CONCEPT

OBJECTIVES

Personal Objectives

◯ To continue to work as an international project writer and editor.
◯ To write and publish at least one magazine or newspaper article each month.
◯ To increase my business experience by working with many types of businesses and organizations throughout the world.
◯ To increase my skill level by trying new types of projects and working with people in many jobs/disciplines to which I have not yet been exposed.
◯ To learn and grow professionally by taking advantage of courses, seminars, and workshops in my field.
◯ To learn and grow personally by meeting my goals and objectives each year.

Business Objectives

◯ To make a minimum of $30,000 my first year in business.
◯ To increase my second year's income to $50,000.
◯ To increase my third year's income to $60,000.

MARKET ANALYSIS

In the last five years, many companies have down-sized their publications and communications departments. This is a well-documented international phenomenon. However, the need for publications, advertising, and public relations has not decreased. Indeed, in many cases it has increased.

South Florida has a special business climate because it is geographically so far from the rest of the United States. Not many major corporations have headquarters here. Instead, there are thousands of small- and medium-size companies. There is also a strong Latin American influence, which requires many companies to produce both English and Spanish publications. Often companies produce the Spanish publications in-house, but contract out the English language communications work. In addition, many Europeans are buying property in South Florida and setting up small companies.

In my conversations with potential buyers of my services, I have been told "there are not enough business freelance writers in South Florida — we just can't find the people we need;" "you would think a large company like us would have a large freelance bank, but we don't;" "not many business writers can write both technical and marketing literature — that's an unusual and valuable skill;" "with your international experience, I can already give you a list of companies that could use your services."

These types of discussions both surprised and thrilled me. It was clear that truly professional writing services offered by a person with both international and corporate experience is rare in South Florida.

Likewise, when I have corresponded with companies in other parts of the world, they tell me it is hard to find business writers with experience editing text written by non-native English speakers. They said they would rather work with a writer with this experience, combined with general international experience, because that person most likely will have a greater appreciation for everything from cultural differences to time differences.

Successful translation companies in other parts of the world often have text translated in the country where the language is spoken. If this is not possible, they will often ask an editor in that country to look over the text to make sure it sounds natural. Judging from industry reports, few editors in this country have the international experience to approach these translation companies abroad and offer editing services.

In terms of newspapers and magazines, competition is definitely stiff. But after reading no less than 10 books on freelance writing over the last year, it is clear that there is always room for good writers who approach their writing as a business. Writers who understand the editorial needs of the publications they want to write for are far more successful than those who do not.

PRODUCTION

To produce high-quality publications and documents, a good-quality printer, computer, fax, and modem are needed. In addition, Word and WordPerfect word processing programs are essential for delivering compatible files to clients. Other programs will be purchased and learned according to client requirements. A 35mm camera is also important because most writers also take their own photographs. A tape recorder is essential for taping interviews. A laptop computer is desirable.

A home office dedicated for just that purpose will increase efficiency and give a professional image to clients. A small office at another location is the ultimate goal, but that will not happen until the business's third year.

An additional telephone line for the business is desirable, as is a separate fax line.

MARKETING

Technical Companies

To start, I will accept short-term contract technical writing positions in order to bring in consistent income and build contacts. This will probably require working at the client's location, which will cut back on the marketing I can do for my other services.

This is going to be a hard one to judge. The income is important, but for the longevity of the business, marketing is also important. Eventually I will have to cut back on the contract work and concentrate full time on developing other sides of the business. The plan is to make enough contacts to get technical writing assignments that I can do from my home office.

Technical writing is a lucrative skill. It will be important to use this skill to "jump start" the business, and it also will play an important supporting role as other aspects of the business grow.

Since virtually all of these agencies keep an active freelance file, I will send a biographical statement with brief resume and cover letter to well-known agencies operating in South Florida. Several I have personal contacts with; others I know of from reading trade publications. I will then follow up with a phone call and try to make as many appointments as possible. I will then call the agency every three-four weeks to remind them I am interested in working with them.	**Public Relations and Advertising Companies**
I will send query letters to regional magazines and local newspapers for the first year. I will then begin sending queries to national publications.	**Newspapers and Magazines**
I will approach this locally in much the same manner as with public relations and advertising agencies. Internationally, I will use my contacts from former jobs to get my name placed on active freelancer lists. I know from experience that these lists are long, but that there are only a few freelancers considered good enough for project work at these agencies.	**Translation Companies**
I will use my own contacts from previous jobs to re-establish professional relationships and get referrals. These companies range from technical to publishing.	**Companies Located in Other Countries**
I plan to join and become active in Women in Communications. I also plan to do community work as a responsible businessperson. This will increase my visibility, as well as allow me to learn more about the community I am contributing to.	**General Marketing and Visibility**
The following estimates show how I plan to spend my time in the next three years. All figures are based on a 50-hour week.	**Percentage of Time**

Percentage of Paid Time — First Year

Technical	60%
Public Relation/Advertising Agencies	15%
Newspapers/Magazines	10%
Translation Companies	5%
Companies Located in Other Countries	5%
General Marketing	5%

Percentage of Time
...continued

Percentage of Marketing Time — First Year

Technical	25%
Public Relation/Advertising Agencies	25%
Newspapers/Magazines	25%
Translation Companies	10%
Companies Located in Other Countries	10%
General Marketing	5%

Percentage of Paid Time — Second Year

Technical	30%
Public Relation/Advertising Agencies	40%
Newspapers/Magazines	10%
Translation Companies	0%
Companies Located in Other Countries	20%
General Marketing	0%

Percentage of Marketing Time — Second Year

Technical	10%
Public Relation/Advertising Agencies	20%
Newspapers/Magazines	10%
Translation Companies	5%
Companies Located in Other Countries	50%
General Marketing	5%

Percentage of Paid Time — Third+ Years

Technical	15%
Public Relation/Advertising Agencies	30%
Newspapers/Magazines	5%
Translation Companies	5%
Companies Located in Other Countries	40%
General Marketing	5%

Percentage of Marketing Time — Third+ Years

Technical	15%
Public Relation/Advertising Agencies	15%
Newspapers/Magazines	10%
Translation Companies	5%
Companies Located in Other Countries	50%
General Marketing	5%

In this field it is extremely important to stay on top of new technical and creative developments. I plan to take courses regularly at Broward Community College, which has a strong communications program. I also will stay on top of new releases of computer programs, and buy these programs according to my client's formatting needs.

EDUCATION

I will operate and manage this business entirely on my own. I do not intend to hire anyone, except an occasional researcher.

ORGANIZATION AND PEOPLE

This business will be run in the simplest way possible — a cash basis. I will have a separate checking account for the business and all income and expenses will be handled through it. This is the easiest way to track all funds coming in and going out.

FUNDS FLOW AND FINANCIAL PROJECTIONS

My general cost per hour will be $40 plus expenses in the first and second years. It will rise to $55 in the third year. Income should be proportionate to the percentages given in the marketing section.

Computer with modem	$2,500
Printer	300
Fax	300
Extra phone and fax lines (per month)	30
Letterhead	60
Business cards	20
Total	$3,210.00

Start-Up Costs

As sole proprietor, I will be the owner of this business. If something happens to me, the business will not continue under the management of anyone else. In the third year, I will incorporate the business for tax purposes. If something happens to me, my husband, Jason Parker, will take over the business.

OWNERSHIP

Kennel

BUSINESS PLAN

BEST FRIEND KENNELS

PO Box 54669
Terra Verde, Arizona 85635

July 1995

The following business plan provides details on purchasing an existing business in need of improvement and additional construction. Highlights include detailed explanations of services, cost/benefit analysis, and the equipment and financing needed for a boarding and grooming business with a special niche in breeding and handling.

- STATEMENT OF PURPOSE

- THE BUSINESS

- MARKETING

- FINANCIAL DOCUMENTS

- INVENTORIES

STATEMENT OF PURPOSE

Best Friend Kennels provides expert pet grooming, boarding, training, handling, pet cemetery and pet cremation services for Terra Verde and the surrounding area. Our physical address is 47883 S. Longbranch Rd., Terra Verde, Arizona. Our mailing address is above.

Our objective is to acquire 70% of the grooming market, 75% of the boarding market, 90% of the training market and 100% of the pet interment market in the Terra Verde area within the next five years. We plan to accomplish our objectives by always meeting or exceeding the customer's expectations and going the "extra mile" with the best in customer service.

Best Friend Kennels was founded in 1986 and has a multi-year profit-making history. Best Friend Kennels has operated successfully under its current owner since February of 1993. Ms. Bradley brought over 20 years of retail merchandising experience and over 18 years of experience in grooming and showing various breeds of dogs to Best Friend Kennels. She has strong interpersonal communication skills, an incredible ability to organize, prioritize, and maximize time, personnel, assets and equipment. Ms. Bradley's years of retail experience and personnel management skills coupled with her previous experience as a department manager for a national department store have been a strong asset for the business. Ms. Bradley has experience in targeting specific markets, having worked for such renowned businesses as Durango's and Brooksman's. Both of these jobs provided in-depth training on selecting target markets and tailoring sales techniques to the target market. Ms. Bradley co-authored several successful business and marketing plans for diversified local businesses. Unbound copies of these plans are available upon request.

In November of 1994, Best Friend Kennels applied for a loan from the Small Business Administration in the amount of $495,000.00. $445,000.00 of this loan will be used to obtain clear title to Best Friend Kennels from the previous owners. The remaining $50,000 will be used to complete construction of the South Kennel ($32,000.00) and to build training and play areas on the facility ($18,000.00). Loan repayments are made from the profits of the business. This loan is secured with the inventory from the business, the equity available from payments to the previous owners and the owner's personal assets.

THE BUSINESS

Business Description

This 16-acre pet services facility consists of three environmentally controlled cinder block kennel buildings housing a total of 76 dog and 23 cat runs, ten grooming runs, grooming and bathing shop, pet cemetery, training area, owner's home and three continuously occupied rental units. Each kennel building has its own food preparation area and a stereo system for the guests' enjoyment. Runs are sized to accommodate larger guests and multiple guests whose owners want their pets boarded together. Canine guests are provided with blankets, toys and individual food and water dishes. We provide feline guests with individual litter boxes, cat furniture, toys and individual water and food dishes.

Our Main Kennel Building has 29 covered indoor-outdoor dog runs and 17 indoor cat runs. The Cattery has 10 covered indoor-outdoor runs, 6 indoor runs and its own bathing facility. Our South Kennel features 34 open air indoor-outdoor runs for guests who are used to the great outdoors. A large play area for owners visiting their pets borders the South Kennel and serves the entire kennel facility.

The grooming shop incorporates six preparation/drying stations, three grooming stations, a two-station bathing facility, a laundry and a reception area. Ten covered cinder block grooming runs house pets waiting for their owners before and after grooming and bathing.

■**Legal Structure:** Best Friend Kennels operates as a sole proprietorship. At an undetermined point in the future, Best Friend Kennels may be incorporated and may offer stock to the general public under the guidelines of the Arizona Corporation Commission.

■**Business type:** Best Friend Kennels is a service business providing pet grooming, boarding, training, handling, pet cemetery and pet cremation services to Terra Verde, Geronimo County and the surrounding areas.

■**Services and Products offered:** Best Friend Kennels offers expert pet grooming and boarding, professional obedience training, competition handling and concerned, caring cemetery and cremation services to our customers. We are one of two facilities in the local area providing pick-up and delivery service for boarding and grooming clients.

■**Business History:** Best Friend Kennels was founded in 1986 and has become the premier grooming, boarding, training, handling and cemetery facility for Terra Verde, Geronimo County and the surrounding area's pets. In February, 1993, Ms. Corinne Bradley saw the tremendous potential of Best Friend Kennels and purchased the business from the previous owners. Ms. Bradley expanded and diversified Best Friend Kennels, establishing Grosvenor Exotics, Ten Rapids Handling and the Altimont Canine College (ACC). Grosvenor Exotics raises, breeds and markets Emu—large flightless birds related to the ostrich. Ten Rapids Handling's professional staff provides competition handling for all dog breeds. Their Champion Pointer breeding program is nationally recognized. Altimont Canine College trains aspiring kennel owners/managers and obedience trainers in the day-to-day operation of diverse kennel and training facilities. Best Friend Kennels is an on-going, profit making enterprise. Under Ms. Bradley's ownership, Best Friend Kennels has steadily increased its clientele and income since February, 1993.

■**Growth Opportunities:** The pet services market will continue to expand as the population of the area continues to grow. Both city and county populations have risen steadily since 1980. The city population grew 27.4% and the county population by 17%. Camp Penneman, a large military installation, is located nearby. The Camp supplies significant percentages of our grooming and boarding clientele as well as percentages of other services. The Camp is not in danger of closure under the Base Realignment and Closure Commission's recommendations and will also continue to expand for the next several years. Our "extra mile service," positive, goal oriented philosophy and exemplary customer relations policies allow us to continuously increase our share of the boarding, grooming, training, handling and pet mortuary markets in the local area.

Business Description
...continued

Business Description
...continued

■ **Business Hours:** Our business hours are 7:00 A.M. to 5:30 P.M., Monday through Friday, and 7:00 A.M. to 3:00 P.M. Saturday. We are closed on Sundays and major holidays. We expand our operating hours based on customer demand for our services.

■ **Unique Aspects of the Business:**

√ We are one of two pet care facilities in the area offering pick-up and delivery service for our boarding and grooming clients.

√ We are the largest pet care facility in Terra Verde and are able to board and groom pets when other similar facilities have reached their maximum capacity.

√ We are the only facility in the area with a pet cemetery. We offer free pick-up service for deceased pets.

√ The Owner and several staff members live on the property and provide 24-hour care for our guests. We employ roving security patrols to further ensure the security of our customer's pets.

√ We are the only facility in the area that offers all pet services at a single location: boarding, grooming, training, handling and pet interment.

√ We are one of two facilities in the area who are members of the American Boarding Kennel Association.

√ We offer special arrangements for check-in and check-out when our customers have emergencies.

√ We are one of the few facilities in the area that offer tours of our facility without appointment. We encourage pet owners to tour our facilities to see for themselves the cleanliness of our facility, where their pet will stay and how our facility operates.

√ We offer financing through American General Financing for long term boarding, training and handling clients.

√ Our application for accepting credit card purchases is being reviewed by a local financial institution. Financing and credit card purchases are expected to increase our revenue by at least 50%.

√ We do not charge additional fees for showing winning dogs in additional categories (group bonuses, Best in Show, etc.).

√ We do not charge our handling clients board on the day of any show.

√ We do not charge our handling clients for expenses.

■**Goals and Objectives:**

❖One Year Plan (1995 Annual Goals):
  1. Inaugurate full-time all-breed handling program
  2. Membership in Professional Handlers Association
  3. Increase boarding & grooming income by 25%
  4. National advertising for breeding & handling
  5. National advertising for Altimont Canine College
  6. Establish first cemetery memorial

❖Three Year Plan (1998 Annual Goals):
  1. 10-15 handling clients per show
  2. Consistently finish Championship title dogs
  3. Establish nationwide Breeder Referral Program
  4. Graduate 5-7 students per year from ACC
  5. Equip ACC with classroom/library/computer assisted instruction
  6. Consistently train 8-10 obedience clients per week
  7. Add Assistant Training Director to keep pace with client demand for services
  8. Increase boarding/grooming income 25% per year
  9. Employ 5 groomers and 5 bathers to keep pace with customer demand
  10. Expand grooming shop
  11. Construct additional kennel building

❖Five Year Plan (2000 Annual Goals):
  1. Establish second location for grooming and boarding within Terra Verde city limits
  2. Achieve national recognition as one of the top Pointer breeders
  3. Achieve recognition as top handling organization in Southwest
  4. Establish second cemetery facility

❖Objectives: To attain our goals through customer satisfaction, diligence and positive, progressive customer relations.

Products and Services

Best Friend Kennels provides pet grooming and boarding services, dog obedience training, professional handling on show circuits and pet mortuary services for our clients. We pick-up and deliver grooming and boarding clients for a reasonable charge. We offer pick-up services for deceased pets free of charge.

Management

Best Friend Kennels has been owned and managed by Ms. Corinne Bradley since February of 1993. Ms. Bradley brought over 20 years of retail and management experience to Best Friend Kennels. She is the former intimate apparel and ready-to-wear department manager of Brooksman's, a large department store in Cheyenne, Wyoming. During one six-month period, Ms. Bradley increased the retail sales in her Brooksman's department from $900,000 to $3 million using her skills in promotional advertising and multiple selling.

As manager, she was responsible for personnel, advertising promotions, merchandising, scheduling and inventory. Ms. Bradley is proficient in short and long term planning and budgeting. She possesses exemplary interpersonal communications skills and a personality pleasing to clients and vendors alike.

Ms. Bradley also brings over 18 years of dog breeding and handling experience to Best Friend Kennels. She has competed in all-breed and specialty shows, consistently placing in the top 4 of entered classes. In 1994, one of her dogs ranked nationally in the top 5 in obedience within the breed. She has handled and pointed over 50 different breeds from all groups. Ms. Bradley has won multiple group placements with dogs from regular classes and from the "Best of Breed" classes. She won at Nationals with 3 different breeds. She's won at specialties in breed, futurity and sweepstakes. Ms. Bradley's pointer breeding program has over ten years of continuous success and one of her dames is listed in the top producing bitches of the decade (1983-1993).

A complete list of her professional accomplishments and her resume are available upon request. (Highlights omitted for privacy, but appeared here.)

Ms. Bradley has also co-authored two marketing plans as well as a training and operations manual for local businesses. She understands the necessity of clearly defining goals, employee responsibilities and standards. She has the background in personnel management to translate this knowledge into workable training manuals and employee programs.

Personnel

Best Friend Kennels employs one full-time bather, one full-time and one part-time groomer, one full-time receptionist, a full-time kennel manager, four part-time kennel assistants, training director and handler. Personnel are cross-trained to perform all non-specialized jobs within the kennel. Future plans call for 100% cross-training in those jobs that do not require specialized instruction, i.e. training, grooming and handling. The experience level of our specialized employees ranges from ten to twenty years. Our Head Groomer is currently working toward her Master Groomer Certification. Ms. Bradley is currently seeking admission to the Professional Handlers Association.

Methods of Recordkeeping

Primary financial records are maintained using Quicken Version 7.0 for DOS. Quicken is a general purpose accounting and financial program used by many small businesses for recordkeeping and analysis. Best Friend Kennels also contracts Ms. Cheryl Jerrardini, ExecuComp Tax and Accounting, 77675 Gable St., Terra Verde, AZ as our accountant. Keeping accounting data in the same software application that Ms. Jerrardini uses reduces accounting costs for Best Friend Kennels. Marketing projections, etc. are assembled using software appropriate to the analysis. Employee and administrative records are automated, as is payroll. Two sets of backup disks are kept as a minimum, in separate locations. The computer used to maintain automated records is not located within the facility and is accessible only to the owner and kennel manager through password protection. All automated systems have a paper-and-pencil backup. Kennel records will be automated as soon as funding becomes available. Kennel records are currently kept on paper. The receptionist maintains and completes kennel records with the Owner's supervision.

A "Key Man" insurance policy is in effect, sufficient to cover business liabilities. Best Friend Kennels is named as the beneficiary. Insurance premiums are paid from the proceeds of the business. Fire, theft, injury, liability, etc. coverage is in effect with Foremost Insurance. Coverage will remain with Foremost unless better coverage at lower cost can be obtained elsewhere.

Insurance

Cash is removed from the business and deposits are made daily. No cash is stored overnight in the facility. All financial and proprietary information is stored outside of the facility. Multiple copies of financial and proprietary data are kept at separate locations. There is presently no electronic security system installed within the facility. Access to the Best Friend Kennels facility is restricted by security gates and chain link fencing. Entrances are chained and locked during non-business hours. Members of the staff, including the Owner, Kennel Manager, and Head Groomer live on the property, providing 24 hour security. We also employ roving security patrols from Terra Verde's top security force—Reliable Security, Inc.

Security

The Main kennel, grooming runs, Cattery and grooming shop are completely surrounded by additional chain link barriers, ensuring that pets going to and from the grooming facility do not interfere with other activities in the kennel area. The South kennel provides similar protection for that area. Each dog and cat run features positive locking doors. Runs are double locked, preventing even the craftiest pets from getting outside of their run.

The marketing plan is broken down into the same categories as the business itself. There are different marketing considerations for each facet of the business. The primary and secondary current and target markets are addressed separately.

MARKETING PLAN

Target Markets

Our current primary clients are owners of dogs and cats requiring boarding within a 50-mile radius of the business. Current secondary clients are owners of other small animals requiring boarding. Primary target market are all small animal owners within a 50-mile radius of Best Friend Kennels. Secondary target market is Equine and Ratite owners within a 50-mile radius of Best Friend Kennels.

Boarding

Our current primary clients are owners of dogs and cats requiring grooming within a 50-mile radius of the business. Current secondary clients are owners of other small animals requiring grooming. Our primary target market are all small animal owners whose animals require bathing and grooming within a 50- mile radius of Best Friend Kennels. There is no secondary target market for grooming.

Grooming

Our current primary clients are owners of deceased dogs and cats requiring private or communal burial or cremation services within a 100-mile radius of the business. Current secondary clients are owners of other small animals requiring mortuary services. Our

Cemetery

primary target market is any pet owner within a 100-mile radius of Best Friend Kennels. Our secondary target market is owners of deceased pets who want their pets memorialized by placing nameplates on memorials at our cemetery facility.

Training

Our current primary clients are dog owners who want their dogs trained in on- and off-leash private obedience training or confirmation training within a 50-mile radius of Best Friend Kennels. Our current secondary clients are dog owners within a 50-mile radius of Best Friend Kennels who want private advanced obedience training. Our primary target market is dog owners who want group obedience and advanced obedience training within a 50-mile radius of Best Friend Kennels.

Handling

Our current primary clients are owners of American Kennel Club (AKC) recognized breed dogs within a 50-mile radius of Best Friend Kennels who want their dogs to achieve a "Champion" title in the confirmation ring, and owners of AKC recognized breed dogs within a 50-mile radius of Best Friend Kennels who want their dogs to achieve obedience titles ("Companion Dog (CD)", "Companion Dog Excellent (CDX)", "Tracking Dog (TD)", and "Utility Dog (UTD)." Our current secondary clients are purebred dog owners within a 50-mile radius of Best Friend Kennels who want their dogs to achieve field titles ["Junior Hunter (JH)", "Senior Hunter (SH)", "Master Hunter (MH)", "Field Champion (FDCH)"], and dog owners who want their dogs to achieve other AKC recognized titles ["Canine Good Citizen (CGC)", Agility, Lure Coursing, etc.]. Our primary target market is owners of American Kennel Club (AKC) recognized breed dogs within the Southwest who want their dogs to achieve a "Champion" title in the confirmation ring, and owners of AKC recognized breed dogs within the Southwest who want their dogs to achieve obedience titles ("Companion Dog (CD)", "Companion Dog Excellent (CDX)", "Tracking Dog (TD)", and "Utility Dog (UTD)." There is no secondary target market for handling.

Competition

Boarding

There are 4 pet boarding establishments listed in the local yellow pages in the Terra Verde area.

Grooming

There are 7 pet grooming establishments listed in the local yellow pages in the Terra Verde area.

Cemetery

There are no other pet mortuary facilities listed in the local yellow pages in the Terra Verde area.

Training

There is one other training establishment listed in the local yellow pages in the Terra Verde area.

Handling

There are no other handling establishments listed in the local yellow pages in the Terra Verde area. Although handling is a high profit, low expense endeavor, few handlers advertise in printed publications. Most handling referrals come through word-of-mouth advertising or by publication in national or specialty publications.

Methods of Distribution

Boarding

Customers call for reservations. Drop-ins are welcome on a space available basis. Advance reservations are requested during extremely busy periods such as Thanksgiving and Christmas.

Grooming

Customers call for an appointment. Drop-ins are welcome on a space available basis. If pets cannot be groomed on a space available basis, we attempt to reschedule the pet for grooming at a convenient time for our customers.

Cemetery

Customers may elect to purchase pre-need communal or private burial plots or wait until the need arises. Customers also have the choice of communal or private cremation services, sub-contracted through Manistee Services Inc. of Manistee, AZ. We offer free pick-up service from the customer's home, veterinary clinic or other location for burials and cremations.

Training

Customers call for an initial appointment with a member of our training staff. Contracts detailing the specifics of the training desired are negotiated. Contracts range from single-visit behavior counseling to 16 week training sessions encompassing all on- and off-leash commands. Training is tailored to the desires of the customer.

Handling

Customers call for an initial appointment with a member of our handling staff. Contracts detailing the specifics of the handling desired are drawn and signed. Contracts range from single show to full Champion titles in confirmation and obedience titles. Pre-confirmation handling is required in all handling contracts to allow the dog to become familiar with, and bond to, the handler.

Advertising

Best Friend Kennels uses a multi-media approach to advertising.

√The local yellow pages carry our advertisement under the categories of "Pet Boarding," "Pet Cemeteries and Crematories,""Pet Grooming," and "Kennels."

√We distribute flyers on a regular basis announcing special events and discounts in all facets of our operation.

√Word-of-mouth advertising from our customers results in many new clients. We offer a discount to first time boarders and multiple pet boarders.

√Best Friend Kennels occasionally uses newspaper advertising to promote training, boarding and grooming.

√Best Friend Kennels distributes brochures detailing all of our services. Brochures are placed in strategic locations throughout Terra Verde and the surrounding areas. We also distribute business cards to other businesses within Terra Verde and the surrounding areas.

√Best Friend Kennels advertises in industry specific publications such as "Pointer Points", "Dog World", and "Dog Fancy" for training, handling and breeding.

Pricing

Boarding

Our boarding prices are competitive with other boarding facilities in the area. Boarding prices are determined by the size and weight of the pet being boarded. Dogs up to 30 pounds are charged at the rate of $8.00 per day. Dogs 31-80 pounds are charged at the rate of $10.00 per day. Dogs 81 pounds and over are charged at the rate of $11.00 per day. Cat boarders are charged at the rate of $8.00 per day, regardless of size. We offer a 25% discount to first-time boarders and 10% discount to owners who board multiple pets at the same time. Guests requesting a bath and grooming before going home are not charged for boarding on the day the guest leaves, provided that the guest checks out during normal business hours. Only guests being bathed and groomed receive a free day's board when more than one guest from the same family stays at our facility. The rest of the family must pay for the last day of boarding. We charge $5.00 round trip to pick-up and return boarding guests. Financing is available for all boarding services.

Grooming

Our grooming prices are competitive with other grooming facilities in the area. Grooming prices are based on the size and breed of the pet, the type of grooming desired and the condition of the pet's coat. Nail trimming and expressing of the anal glands are included in the complete grooming prices. Prices for simple bathing and brush-out are somewhat lower, but still based on size, breed and condition of coat. We charge $5.00 round trip to pick-up and return grooming clients.

Cemetery

Best Friend Kennels is the only facility in the local area offering pet mortuary services. Our interment and cremation charges are reasonable. Cremation charges are set by our sub-contractor, Manistee Services, Inc. Cremation charges are based on the size of the pet and the type of cremation requested (communal or private). Burial charges are based on the size of the pet and type of burial requested (communal or private). Prices range from $75.00 for a small pet communal burial to $225.00 for a large pet private burial. There are additional charges for graveside services and special requests. Private burial costs include nametag, casket, burial and choice of color gravel for the top of the deceased pet's grave. Communal burial costs include burial and nametag. All burial contracts include a 25-year renewable plot maintenance contract. Financing is available for all cemetery services.

Training

Our prices are competitive with others in the city. Prices are based on the length and complexity of the training contracted. Boarding costs are included in private training prices. Prices range from $40.00 for a one-time behavioral counseling session to hundreds of dollars for advanced off-leash training. Financing is available for training services.

Handling

Our prices are competitive with other unadvertised handlers in the local area. We charge $35.00 per show per dog to show puppies (6-9 month and 9-12 month classes), $45.00 per show per dog to show open class, and $55.00 per show per dog to show in breed specialties (Champion titled dogs competing for Best of Breed). Boarding and grooming charges are not included in handling prices. Boarding and grooming charges are based on pet size and duration of pre- and post-show boarding and the amount of grooming required. Board is not charged on the day of any show. Best Friend Kennels does not charge additional fees for showing winning dogs in additional categories (group bonuses, Best in Show, etc.) or for expenses.

The pet services industry is directly related to population growth. Demand for all of our services will continue to increase as nearby Camp Penneman, Terra Verde and the surrounding areas increase their population. Between 1980 and 1993, the population of Terra Verde and Geronimo County increased 27% and 17% respectively. Training services will increase as the demand for well mannered pets is mandated by City ordinance. Demand for handling services will increase as the status of having a "titled" dog becomes more and more popular. Through outstanding customer relations and "extra mile" policies, we have overcome the negative business reputation of the previous owners and enjoy consistently increasing profits through word of mouth advertising. Demand for pet mortuary services is on the rise and is not expected to level off in the near future.

Industry Trends

Pet Care and Training Services Offered in the Local Area

	Kennel	Boarding	Grooming	Training	Cemetery	Delivery Svc
Cherokee Animal Hotel	X	X				
Duffy's Favorite	X		X			
Critter Pals		X	X			
Jessie's Poodle Palace			X			
Best Friend Kennels*	X	X	X	X	X	X
Clipper Ship Grooming			X			
Pet RoundUp			X			
Sally's Boarding & Training*	X	X		X		X
Continental Dog Grooming			X			

* Member, American Boarding Kennel Association

FINANCIAL DOCUMENTS

Summary of Financial Needs

Best Friend Kennels requires approval of a Small Business Administration Loan in the amount of $495,000.00 to procure free title to the business from the previous owners and to complete planned improvements.

Sources and Uses of Funds Statement

The Small Business Administration will disburse the loan funds as follows:

  ❖ $445,000 of the loan will be used to obtain free title to the business from the previous owners.

  ❖ The remaining $50,000 will be used to complete renovation of the South Kennel ($32,000.00) and to build training and play areas on the facility ($18,000.00).

Cash Flow Report   *1/1/95 Through 6/30/95*

INFLOWS

Altimont Canine College Gross Sales	66,547.68
Other Income	810.00
Rent Income	5,760.00
TOTAL INFLOWS	**$73,117.68**

OUTFLOWS

Accounting	206.67
Advertising	1,997.23
Electricity	1,780.19
Heat	1,231.81
Interest on Kennel Loan	20,204.29
Misc	809.12
Postage	152.41
Repairs	1,905.95
Tax Sales	147.72
Supplies	1,655.84
Telephone	3,867.50
Trade Dues	25.00
Wages	23,516.38
Dog Shows	759.01
Veterinary	906.45
Cemetery	133.51
Dog Food	3,358.45
Altimont Canine College	6,662.81
TOTAL OUTFLOWS	**$69,320.34**
OVERALL TOTAL	**$3,797.34**

Estimated Projection and Forecast of Earnings

1994-1996
GROSS PROFITS

	1994*	1995	1996
Boarding & Grooming	$182,111.37	$202,143.62	$224,379.42
Breeding	$11,400.00	$12,700.00	$14,000.00
Handling	$32,000.00	$40,000.00	$55,000.00
Training & Play Area	$42,000.00	$47,000.00	$52,000.00
Gross Profit	**$267,511.37**	**$301,843.62**	**$345,379.42**

Notes:
•*Boarding and grooming income are on track for 1994.*
•*Breeding income will not meet 1994 projections. To keep pace with customer demand, Best Friend Kennels hired additional groomers. The tradeoff for the increased grooming and administrative payroll was to do less breeding.*

•*Handling will not meet 1994 projections. Best Friend Kennels did not have sufficient financial resources to devote to national advertising. We relied on word-of-mouth advertising.*
•*Training and Play Area income will not meet 1994 projections. There were no funds available to expand the current training and play areas.*

A complete break even analysis is not included in this business plan. Pet grooming is a very labor intensive/low profit facet of our business and therefore, requires a higher number of customers to break even. Cemetery operations are low labor/high profit, requiring fewer customers to break even. Expenses associated with boarding are directly dependent on the number of pets boarding in the facility and the number of buildings used to house the boarding pets. A break even analysis for training is presented below. Training is an independent function of Best Friend Kennels and training expenses can be calculated on a cost-per-dog basis.

Break Even Analysis

Break Even Analysis
For Training

I. DRY FOOD EXPENSES
  √40# Bag @ $16.35/Bag
  √640 Ounces/Bag or 80 Cups/Bag
  √$0.0255 per Ounce ($0.03) or $0.2043 ($0.20) per Cup
    ➲ 2/Day @ 3 Cups/Feeding = $1.20/Day
    ➲ 2/Day @ 2 Cups/Feeding = $0.80/Day
    ➲ 2/Day @ 3 Cups/Feeding = $6.00/Wk
    ➲ 2/Day @ 2 Cups/Feeding = $4.00/Wk

II. CANNED FOOD EXPENSES
  √13.5 Oz Can @ $0.50/Can
  √$0.0370 per Ounce
  √2.7 Ounces/Feeding
    ➲ 2/Day @ 2.7 Oz/Feeding= $0.10/Day
    ➲ 2/Day @ 2.7 Oz/Feeding= $0.50/Wk

III. LABOR EXPENSES
    ➲25 Min/Run @ $4.25/Hr = $1.77/Day
    ➲25 Min/Run @ $4.25/Hr = $8.85/Wk

IV. UTILITIES EXPENSES (ESTIMATED)
    ➲$1.00/Day = $5.00/Wk

V. TOTAL EXPENSES PER TRAINING DOG
  √Per Day @ 2 x 3 Cups/Day = $4.07
  √Per Day @ 2 x 2 Cups/Day = $3.67
  √Per Week @ 2 x 3 Cups/Day = $20.35
  √Per Week @ 2 x 2 Cups/Day = $18.35
    ➲Difference = $ 2.00
VI. TRAINER SALARY

Break Even Analysis For
Training...*continued*

√$29,900/YR OR $2,491.66/MONTH
➲Salary/Day = $115.00
➲Salary/Week = $575.00

VII. TRAINING DOG/WEEK
√Income = # Dogs X $100.00
√Expense = Total Expenses/Dog/Wk + Trainer Salary/Wk

➲Difference

One (1) Training Dog/Week
Income: $100.00
Expense: $593.35
Diff: -$493.35

Two (2) Training Dogs/Week
Income: $200.00
Expense: $611.70
Diff: -$411.70

Three (3) Training Dogs/Week
Income: $300.00
Expense: $593.35
Diff: -$293.35

➲Ratios Remain Constant and Are Omitted for Brevity

Seven (7) Training Dogs/Week
Income: $700.00
Expense: $703.45
Diff: -$003.45

Eight (8) Training Dogs/Week
Income: $800.00
Expense: $721.80
Diff: +$ 78.20

As of 3/31/95   **Balance Sheet**

ASSETS

Cash		$4000.00
Trade Notes and Accounts Receivable	$2943.00	
Less Allowances for Bad Debts	$588.00	$2355.00
Buildings and other Depreciable Assets	$218,658.00	
Less Accumulated Depreciation	$14,432.00	$204,266.00
Land		$134,000.00
Other Assets (See Schedule)		$143,000.00
TOTAL ASSETS		**$487,581.00**

LIABILITIES AND CAPITAL

Accounts Payable	$1000.00
Motgages, Notes, Bonds Payable in One Year	$310,000.00
Capital Accounts	$176,581.00
TOTAL LIABILITIES AND CAPITAL	**$487,581.00**

Schedule of Assets

Goodwill	$90,000.00
Dogs	$34,000.00
Horse	$4000.00
Furniture, etc.	$15,000.00
Total	**$143,000.00**

Profit & Loss Statement   *1/1/93 Through 12/31/93*

INCOME/EXPENSE

Income

Grooming	$74,283.25
Boarding	$71,248.06
Cemetery	$5,455.00
Miscellaneous Income	$23,779.13
Rental	$10,400.00
Total Income	**$185,165.44**

Expenses

Merchandise	$2,294.55
Accounting	$332.57
Advertising	$7,120.04
Auto	$3,510.00
Cartons	$220.00
Electricity	$2,669.67
Entertainment	$200.00
Freight	$462.47
Heat	$894.07
Insurance	$336.42
Legal	$4,400.00
Licenses	$2,548.38
Office Expenses	$286.70
Rent (interest & principle on Kennel Loan)	$69,878.75
Repairs	$494.10
Tax-Sales	$3.75
Supplies	$7,724.61
Telephone	$2,733.39
Trade Dues	$302.00
Travel Expenses	$665.00
Wages	$50,954.67
Handling Expenses	$3,484.10
Veterinary Expenses	$1,329.70
Publications	$89.95
Cemetery	$1,543.65
Dog Food	$5,338.27
AKC	$257.00
Child Care	$607.00
Total Expenses	**$171,044.77**

TOTAL INCOME/EXPENSE	**$14,120.67**

| **Profit & Loss Statement**

INCOME/EXPENSE

Income

Grooming	$78,956.95
Boarding	$79,238.57
Cemetery	$4,440.00
Miscellaneous Income	$3,308.00
Rental	$11,520.00
Altimont Canine College	$8,476.00
Total Income	**$185,939.52**

Expenses

Accounting	$550.13
Advertising	$7,310.65
Auto	$1,205.86
Contributions	$361.00
Dog Shows	$4,143.00
Electricity	$3,338.55
Entertainment	$95.23
Heat	$1,257.04
Insurance	$2044.68
Interes	t$48,778.65
Laundry	$20.37
Legal	$7,025.75
Postage	$311.96
Repairs	$843.17
Tax-Other	$3380.30
Supplies	$4,028.59
Telephone	$5,111.96
Trade Dues	$420.00
Wages	$63,468.32
Handling Expenses	$3,484.10
Veterinary Expenses	$550.30
Publications	$55.00
Cemeter	y$1,193.51
Dog Food	$6,919.22
AKC	$52.00
Child Care	$325.00
Security	$600.00
Altimont Canine College	$7,359.55
Total Expenses	**$171,865.85**
TOTAL INCOME/EXPENSE	**$14,073.67**

Gross Income

1985-1994

	Grooming	Boarding	Cemetery	Training	Total
1985	$29,829.48	$33,145.56	$4961.00	N/A	$67,936.04
1986	$36,362.70	$41,171.10	$5727.50	N/A	$83,361.30
1987	$43,126.30	$41,137.20	$6405.00	N/A	$90,668.50
1988	$57,797.63	$49,965.06	$8247.54	N/A	$116,010.23
1989	$63,008.27	$55,881.53	$6689.95	N/A	$125,579.75
1990	$69,970.96	$69,748.78	$9285.00	N/A	$149,004.74
1991	$72,280.30	$70,869.77	$7805.00	N/A	$150,955.07
1992	Unknown*	Unknown*	Unknown*	N/A	$157,000.00
1993	$74,283.25	$71,248.06	$5455.00	N/A	$150,986.31
1994	$78,956.95	$78,238.57	$3308.00	$8476.00	$174,419.52

* *Current owner bought kennel in 1992. Some figures provided by previous owners have proven inaccurate.*

INVENTORIES

Kennel Inventory

Item	Qty	Price Ea	Total
Blanket	50	10.00	500.00
Bleach	29 Cs	6.00	174.00
Boots, Rubber		0.00	15.00
Bowl, 2 Qt	46	4.23	194.58
Bowl, 3 Qt	38	5.82	221.16
Bowl, 4 Qt	79	5.15	406.85
Bowl, 5 Qt	34	7.20	244.80
Box, Whelping, Galvanized	1	35.00	35.00
Boxes, Litter	22	5.00	110.00
Bucket, Metal, W/Clips	10	17.00	170.00
Bucket, Mop	1	50.00	50.00
Bucket, Rubberm, 12 Gal	6	10.00	60.00
Bucket, Rubberm, 14 Gal	3	15.00	45.00
Bucket, Rubberm, 30 Gal	7	20.00	140.00
Bucket, Water, 15 Gal	2	20.00	40.00
Cart, Roller	1	25.00	25.00
Cart, Roller, Show	1	50.00	50.00
Casket	20	50.00	1000.00
Clipboard	102	2.00	204.00
Clips	50	1.00	50.00

Item	Qty	Price Ea	Total
Crate, Fiberglass	1	210.00	210.00
Crate, Size 100	5	24.88	122.40
Crate, Size 200	3	31.18	93.54
Crate, Size 300	9	46.25	416.25
Crate, Size 400	11	54.68	601.48
Crate, Size 500	1	67.85	67.85
Crock, Large	7	3.38	23.66
Crock, Small	30	2.06	61.80
Dryer	5	638.00	3190.00
Fan, Osc, Free Standing	1	35.00	35.00
Fan, Oscillating, 12"	1	20.00	20.00
Fan, Oscillating, 20"	2	25.00	50.00
Furniture, Cat	13	0.00	500.00
Generator, Honda	1	300.00	300.00
Hose, 50'	9	25.00	225.00
Ladder		0.00	10.00
Lamp, Heat	3	25.00	75.00
Mats, Crate, Green	4	18.00	72.00
Oven, Microwave	1	120.00	120.00
Pen, Exer, 8 Panel, 48"	3	116.00	348.00
Pen, Exer, 8 Panel, 48"	2	78.85	157.70
Pen, Exercise, 3'x3'	5	115.00	575.00
Pooper Scooper	2	12.00	24.00
Rack, Hose	8	25.00	200.00
Refrigerator 18 Cf	1	200.00	200.00
Refrigerator, 14 Cf	1	150.00	150.00
Shade, Clothes, 20 Sq Ft	2	15.00	30.00
Shelf, 6'	2	20.00	40.00
Shelf, 6'	2	100.00	200.00
Stereo, Cd W/Speakers	3	125.00	375.00
Sunscreen, Canvas	2	75.00	150.00
Supplies, Cleaning		0.00	400.00
Toys, Assorted		0.00	200.00
Trailer, 2 Wheel	1	1000.00	1000.00
Traps, Fly	4	25.00	100.00
Vaccination	60 Sh	4.50	270.00
Van, Dodge, 1978, New Eng	1	3500.00	3500.00

TOTAL VALUE OF KENNEL INVENTORY   **$17,581.77**

Kennel Inventory

...continued

**Grooming Shop
Inventory**

Item	Qty	Price Ea	Total
Art Work	5	40.00	200.00
Boards, Bulletin, Large	2	25.00	50.00
Boards, Bulletin, Small	9	10.00	90.00
Cabinet		0.00	650.00
Cabinet, Filing 4dwr Lg	1	250.00	250.00
Cabinet, Filing, 3 Cube	1	60.00	60.00
Cabinet, Filing, 4dwr Med	3	125.00	375.00
Calculator	1	25.00	25.00
Cart, Rolling	2	25.00	50.00
Chairs	10	20.00	200.00
Closet		0.00	1000.00
Computer	1	1000.00	1000.00
Desk	1	100.00	100.00
Desk, W/Shelves	1	50.00	50.00
Dryer, Cage	1	200.00	200.00
Equip, Groom, Corinne's		0.00	1500.00
Equip, Office, Misc		0.00	1000.00
Hose	18	5.00	90.00
Leash/Collar	10	10.00	100.00
Library		0.00	2500.00
Machine, Washing	1	125.00	125.00
Pot, Coffee, W/Acc	1	50.00	50.00
Rack, Filing, Metal	1	50.00	50.00
Ribbon	30	5.70	171.00
Rinse, Creme	17	1.29	21.93
Rinse, Creme, Blow Dry	7	5.00	35.00
Shampoo, Conc, 5 Gal	1.33	75.00	150.00
Shampoo, Conc, Mr Crystal	5	35.00	175.00
Shapmoo, Mixed Bottles	130	1.00	130.00
Smocks, Grooming	7	20.00	140.00
Table, Folding	1	50.00	50.00
Table, Grooming & Arm	1	131.75	131.75
Telephone	2	110.00	220.00
Towels	75	4.00	300.00
Towels, Show	15	5.00	75.00

TOTAL GROOMING SHOP INVENTORY   **$11,314.68**

Item	Qty	Price Ea	Total	
Axe	1	7.00	7.00	**Tool Room and Maintenance Shop Inventory**
Bar, Leverage	1	19.00	19.00	
Barrow, Wheel	6	60.00	360.00	
Bits, Drill, Assort			15.00	
Blade, Sewing	1	7.00	7.00	
Blocks, Concrete	50	4.00	200.00	
Cabinets, File	7	25.00	175.00	
Can, Fuel, 5 Gal	5	8.00	48.00	
Clamp, "C"	3	6.00	18.00	
Come-Along	1	29.00	29.00	
Cutter, Bolt	1	38.00	38.00	
Cutter, Tile	1	6.00	6.00	
Digger, Post Hole	1	18.00	18.00	
Dolley	1	20.00	20.00	
Drill 1/2"	1	50.00	50.00	
Driver, Nut		0.00	9.00	
Fencing		0.00	530.00	
Files, Assort		0.00	8.00	
Fork, Garden	1	12.00	12.00	
Funnel	2	3.00	6.00	
Grinder, Bench	1	25.00	25.00	
Grinder, Dice	1	125.00	125.00	
Gun, Grease	1	7.00	7.00	
Gun, Putty	1	5.00	5.00	
Hacksaw	2	6.00	6.00	
Hammer	2	12.00	24.00	
Hammer, Masonry	1	7.00	7.00	
Hammer, Sledge	1	14.00	14.00	
Heater, Electric	1	20.00	20.00	
Heater, Kerosene	5	60.00	300.00	
Hoe	1	10.00	10.00	
Ladder, Extension	2	32.00	64.00	
Ladder, Folding, 8'	1	30.00	30.00	
Level, 24"	1	14.00	14.00	
Level, 48"	1	35.00	35.00	
Level/Square 12"	1	12.00	12.00	
Light, Work	1	7.00	7.00	
Lobber	1	26.00	26.00	
Materials, Carpentry		0.00	275.00	
Materials, Landscaping		0.00	150.00	
Measure, Tape, 100'	1	18.00	18.00	
Mixer, Cement	1	300.00	300.00	
Mower, Lawn	4	125.00	500.00	
Pick	1	16.00	16.00	
Pounder, Fence Pole	1	20.00	20.00	
Pruner	1	12.00	12.00	
Puller, Fence	1	30.00	30.00	

Tool Room and Maintenance Shop Inventory...*continued*

Item	Qty	Price Ea	Total
Puller, Nail	1	5.00	5.00
Punches, Assort	2	4.00	8.00
Rake	2	18.00	36.00
Rake, Leaf	2	9.00	18.00
Saw, Bow	1	7.00	7.00
Saw, Coping	2	10.00	20.00
Saw, Jig	1	45.00	45.00
Saw, Portable Cut off	1	130.00	130.00
Saw, Power, 7 1/4"	1	60.00	60.00
Saw, Rip	2	7.00	14.00
Saw, Table	1	120.00	120.00
Saw, Tree	1	6.00	6.00
Scrapper	2	5.00	10.00
Screwdrivers, Assort	15	6.00	90.00
Set, Plier	1	29.00	29.00
Set, Socket	2	18.00	36.00
Shovel, Flat	1	16.00	16.00
Shovel, Pointed	2	15.00	30.00
Snake, Plumbing, 25'	1	12.00	12.00
Snake, Plumbing, 50'	1	17.00	17.00
Snip, Tin	1	5.00	5.00
Spade	1	11.00	11.00
Sprayer, Chemical	1	15.00	15.00
Square, Quick	1	7.00	7.00
Supplies, Drip Irr Sys		0.00	200.00
Supplies, Electrical		0.00	175.00
Supplies, Insul/Cooling		0.00	75.00
Supplies, Paint		0.00	315.00
Supplies, Plumbing		0.00	450.00
Supplies, Roofing		0.00	430.00
System, Satelite	1	1500.00	1500.00
T-Square	1	11.00	11.00
Tank, Air	1	10.00	0.00
Thatcher, Garden	1	15.00	15.00
Tool, Screening	1	5.00	5.00
Tools, Finishing, Cement	11	5.00	55.00
Tools, Hand, Gardening	6	7.00	42.00
Trimmer, Hedge	1	24.00	24.00
Vaccuum, Blower	1	15.00	15.00
Vice, Bench	1	11.00	11.00
Weed Eater, Gas Operated	1	125.00	125.00
Welder, Electric, Arc	1	450.00	450.00
Wrench, Adj, 12"	1	16.00	16.00
Wrench, Adj, 15"	1	20.00	20.00
Wrench, Adj, 6"	1	7.00	7.00
Wrench, Pipe	1	11.00	11.00
Wrenches, Box & Open End		0.00	12.00
TOTAL VALUE OF TOOLS/SHOP INVENTORY			**$8,348.00**

Maternity Aid

BUSINESS PLAN

NEST IN COMFORT

1116 Logen St.
Santa Fe, NM 62024

March 1989

This following plan for this small enterprise outlines the qualities necessary to take a European-born product and successfully market it in the United States. The plan features a discussion of the use of direct mail and an overview of requirements, as well as a Pro Forma Income Statement and a Cash Flow Forecast.

- THE PRODUCT

- THE MARKET

- FINANCIAL TABLES

- BACKGROUND TO PROPOSAL

- PURPOSE OF BUSINESS PLAN

- OVERALL PHILOSOPHY

- MARKETING STRATEGY

- DIRECT MAILING DETAILS

- CAPITAL REQUIREMENTS

- PERSONNEL REQUIREMENTS

- FACILITIES REQUIREMENTS

- COMPUTER REQUIREMENTS

- TELEPHONE COSTS

- FREIGHT & SHIPPING

- SUMMARY OF SIGNIFICANT FORECAST ASSUMPTIONS

THE PRODUCT

Nest in Comfort is a pillow that was originally developed in Holland by a mother, pregnant with twins, for her own use based upon her experiences with previous births.

The final product proved successful and resulted in demands from family and friends. A cottage industry evolved and subsequently grew into a full-time business. Approximately three years later, the pillow is established and latest information indicated a desire to expand into other European countries, starting with West Germany.

This is the only known product devised specifically for use both during and after pregnancy. In use, the pillow adjusts to individual needs and conforms gently, but firmly, to body contours. Unlike conventional pillows, the wrap-around styling does not flatten or lose shape and "stays put" in whatever shape into which it is molded.

The distinctive features are the consequence of its curved configuration and the composition of its filling medium. Considerable research and testing were conducted to determine the type and amount of filling which would provide optimum performance. The filling medium is precisely metered into an inner casing to ensure the correct balance between firmness and flexibility.

For the expectant mother, the innovative U-shaped design provides comfort for relaxation and sleep while it helps maintain supported positions recommended by childbirth educators. Mother-to-be users report that sleeping on one side without turning is considerably easier than the sleep-interrupting routine of tossing and turning while trying to rearrange three or four ordinary pillows.

New mothers confirm that the Nest in Comfort provides firm back and arm support as well as gentle cradling for their nursing infants. Use of the pillow helps hold the nursing baby in the correct position, thereby eliminating difficulties sometimes associated with breast feeding. Breast feeding twins is made simple since each baby can be cradled on opposite sides of the pillow.

The emphasis on breast feeding and the fact that the pillow's inventor was a mother of twins influenced the design of the original brochure and the marketing thrust. This, in turn, translated in to the emphasis which we--neophytes in the maternity market--followed in our approach to the U.S. market.

As a result, we discovered the hard way that:
1. The brochure is unsuitable for the U.S. market.
2. Breast feeding, although increasing, is still less favored in the U.S. than formula feeding, and is still a controversial subject.
3. Pre-natal use is the preferred emphasis.

Aside from its intended use, there is a variety of additional potential applications and markets. These include: chiropractic, the elderly, the bedridden and chair-bound and - more frivolously -- "couch potatoes", audiophiles, bedtime bookworms, golfers, gardeners etc.

Nest in Comfort comprises a sealed inner casing containing the filling material and a removable, machine washable outer case, which features a recessed zipper for safety and convenience.

The pricing structure is $39.95 for the pillow and a choice of nursery design outer covers for $18.95, or plain covers for $12.95. UPS shipping and handling $5.00.

Of the 100 units sold, one customer ordered the pillow without a cover, one ordered the plain cover, and three requested patterns other than "bright colored nursery prints." The latter requests were met by shipping muted-striped covers from original samples.

The goal is to avoid opening and resealing boxes, plus avoid mixed inventory. Therefore, the plain cover option should be eliminated, but if sufficient demand impacts sales, a neutral option should be offered, at $18.95.

THE MARKET

Annual birthrate for the United States during 1989 and 1990 is projected at 3.8 million.

Discount .8 million for multiple births, teenage pregnancy, etc., and assume 3 million as total national market.

Assume 10% as potential achievable long-term share. 300,000 units annually x $58.90 = $17,670,000 gross sales. Assume gross profit of $35 per unit = $10,500,000 GP. A 2% market share would yield $3,500,000 in sales and a GP of $2,000,000.

History

The product has been well proven in Holland, where it was first developed. It sells there for around $80, and as far as is known, sales average 200 units per month after 2 1/2 - 3 years. Since the population of Holland is relatively low, it is sold there mostly by word of mouth.

The product is unique. There are one or two "nursing pillows" available at around $30 and one "Puff as I Grow", but none are as well-designed, and none are dual-purpose.

We first became actively involved with the pillow in April, 1988. Our first ad ran in the summer issue of "Maternity" magazine.

In retrospect, it was a poor ad, possibly offensive to some and emphasizing the breastfeeding use of the pillow. Orders were received, but not enough to justify the ad costs. An upgraded version of the ad was used for regional and local advertising with better, but still not cost-effective results.

A total of $15,000 was invested in space advertising and brochure printing for a return of $2,800 in sale. Obviously, the $15,000 included "first time" photography and production costs. The summer ad in "Maternity" entitled us to an accompanying listing in their "Parenting Directory" of booklets and samples. They failed to do this and by way of recompense offered a free listing in "the next available issue", Fall 1988. That listing, without any accompanying ad, produced 1204 inquiries. We carried out a test mailing to 500 of these during the last two weeks of November, and by December 12, had received six orders, a return of 1.29%. By the end of December, we had recorded a return of 1.8%; after 60 days, we had 2.4% with no more product to ship. 3.0% took a total of 120-180 days.

Conclusions

1. Space advertising is not the way to go in terms of yield and cost effectiveness, yet, it should still be included in the overall scenario for purposes of exposure.

2. Our initial emphasis was wrongly placed on breastfeeding, when it should have been pre-natal use.

3. The original brochure definitely works against us. A four-color brochure (tri-fold) is assembled and ready for production. I believe that a return of 5% would have probably been achieved using a brochure.

4. Cost per mailing was approximately $1.00 using brochure, envelope, and regular postage. Assembly time was approximately 1 hour per 100 pieces. These would both be considerably reduced with a tri-fold self mailer using bulk postage rates.

5. Telemarketing professionals with whom we have consulted indicate that the normal 1-2% return on direct mailing is increased to 25% - 35% nationally. This holds true for telemarketing targeted market segments. Mailing lists of pregnant women are available at $70 per 1,000; minimum 10 lists. These are available by state, by zip code and by month of pregnancy, plus phone numbers. We would use lists that provide the names of women in their 5th or 6th month of pregnancy. 80,000 new names are added weekly.

FINANCIAL TABLES

Pro-Forma Income Statement

Scenario #1 (Budget) 2% Return on Mailing, 10% on Telemarketing

Month	1	2	3	4	5	6	7	8	9	10	11	12	Totals
Gross Sales-Units													
Start-Up			200	200	1,000	1,000	1,000	1,000	1,000	1,000	1,000	1,000	8,400
Gross Sales-$													
Start-Up			11,780	11,780	58,900	58,900	58,900	58,900	58,900	58,900	58,900	58,900	494,760
Mailing	5,000	5,000	5,000	5,000	5,000	5,000	5,000	5,000	5,000	5,000	5,000		55,000
Telemarketing			5,000	10,000	10,000	10,000	10,000	10,000	10,000	10,000	10,000	10,000	85,000
Finished Goods	3,000	3,000	3,000	15,000	15,000	15,000	15,000	15,000	15,000	15,000	15,000	15,000	129,000
Bank Charges (Visa)		360	360	1,767	1,767	1,767	1,767	1,767	1,767	1,767	1,767	1,767	14,856
Total Cost of Sales (57%)													
	8,000	8,360	13,360	31,767	31,767	31,767	31,767	31,767	31,767	31,767	31,767	31,767	283,856
G.P.(43%)													
	(8,000)	3,420	(1,580)	27,133	27,133	27,133	27,133	27,133	27,133	27,133	27,133	27,133	210,904
Total G&A (22%)													
	5,845	7,095	7,995	8,795	8,795	8,795	10,460	10,625	10,625	10,625	10,625	10,625	110,875
NBT (20%)													
	(5,845)	(15,095)	(4,575)	(10,375)	18,338	18,338	16,673	16,508	16,508	16,508	16,508	16,508	99,999
Provision for Taxes					4,585	4,585	4,168	4,127	4,127	4,127	4,127	4,127	33,973
Net Earnings	(5,845)	(15,095)	(4,575)	(10,375)	13,753	13,753	12,505	12,381	12,381	12,381	12,381	12,381	66,026
Retained Earnings													
Period Begin		(5,845)	(20,940)	(25,212)	(35,890)	(22,137)	(8,384)	4,121	16,502	28,883	41,264	53,645	
Retained Earnings													
Period End	(5,845)	(20,940)	(25,515)	(35,890)	(22,137)	(8,384)	4,121	16,502	28,883	41,264	53,645	66,026	66,026

Accompanies Scenario #1 Income Statement Forecast   **Cash Flow Forecast**

	1	2	3	4	5	6	7	8	9	10	11	12	TOTALS
Cash- Beg. of Per.	100,000	66,155	51,060	46,485	36,110	54,448	63,976	80,649	97,157	101,243	117,751	134,259	100,000
Cash From A/C Receivables Start-Up	11,780	11,780	58,900	58,900	58,900	58,900	58,900	58,900	58,900	58,900	494,760		
Cash Paymts: Op Exps	(9,000)	(8,000)	(9,360)	(13,360)	(31,767)	(31,767)	(31,767)	(31,767)	(31,767)	(31,767)	(31,767)	(31,767)	(292,856)
	(5,845)	(7,095)	(7,995)	(8,795)	(8,795)	(8,795)	(10,460)	(10,625)	(10,625)	(10,625)	(10,625)	(10,625)	(110905)
Payment of Income Taxes					(9,170)			(12,422)			(12,381)		(33,973)
Total Cash: Provided by (Or Appld) Ops.	(14,845)	(15,095)	(4,575)	10,375	18,338	9,528	16,673	16,508	4,086	16,508	4,127	57,386	
Inventory Purchases	(3,000)												(3,000)
Office Fixtures	(6,000)												(6,000)
Operating Eqpmt	(10,000)												(10,000)
Total Cash (Appld)	(33,485)	(15,095)	(4,575)	(10,375)	18,338	9,528	16,673	16,508	4,086	16,508	16,508	4,127	38,386
Cash: End Per	66,155	51,060	46,485	36,110	54,448	63,976	80,649	97,157	101,243	117,751	134,259	138,386	138,386

Accompanies Pro-Forma Income Statement Scenario #1   **G&A Support Details**
Salaries:

	1	2	3	4	5	6	7	8	9	10	11	12	
Officers	2,000	2,000	2,000	2,000	2,000	2,000	3,000	3,000	3,000	3,000	3,000	3,000	30,000
Office	1,500	1,500	1,500	1,500	1,500	1,500	1,650	1,650	1,650	1,650	1,650	1,650	18,900
Warehouse		1,500	1,500	1,500	1,500	1,500	1,500	1,650	1,650	1,650	1,650	1,650	17,250
Total	3,500	5,000	5,000	5,000	5,000	5,000	6,150	6,300	6,300	6,300	6,300	6,300	66,150
Pyrll Tax	450	600	600	600	600	600	715	730	730	730	730	730	7,815
Insurance	150	150	150	150	150	150	150	150	150	150	150	150	1,800
Phone	200	200	200	1,000	1,000	1,000	1,000	1,000	1,000	1,000	1,000	1,000	9,600
Utilities	500	500	500	500	500	500	500	500	500	500	500	500	6,000
Travel	100	100	100	100	100	100	100	100	100	100	100	100	1,200
Auto	100	100	100	100	100	100	500	500	500	500	500	500	3,600
Dprciation	120	120	120	120	120	120	120	120	120	120	120	120	1,440
Accounting	125	125	125	125	125	125	125	125	125	125	125	125	1,500
Rent	1,000	1,000	1,000	1,000	1,000	1,000	1,000	1,000	1,000	1,000	1,000	1,000	12,000
Misc	100	100	100	100	100	100	100	100	100	100	100	100	1,200
Total G&A	5,845	7,095	7,995	8,795	10,460	10,625	10,625	10,625	10,625	10,625	10,625	10,625	110,875

BACKGROUND TO PROPOSAL

Nest in Comfort was first introduced to Harold Monroe by an old friend, Sonya Dennings, a Danish citizen living in Southern California.

The two decided to embark on a joint venture whereby Harold and his then partner, Marty Richmond, co-owners of Chesapeake Industries, Inc., would market the product in the U.S., with exclusive marketing rights. Sonya Dennings and her then partner, Mary Jane Landis, would manufacture the product.

This came at a time when Chesapeake Industries was plodding along at a break-even point after 2 1/2 years in business and was looking for new ventures outside the local Santa Fe market.

Six months later and some $30,000 into this joint venture, Sonya Dennings suddenly developed a serious illness resulting in her leaving the U.S. Mary Jane was unwilling to continue alone, so the manufacturing source was gone.

Marty Richmond decided that he preferred to devote Chesapeake's remaining resources to supporting some embryonic computer software projects which the partners were developing concurrent with the pillow marketing plan. Eventually, Harold and Marty decided to go their separate ways.

Chesapeake Industries still exists as a corporation, but it is not actively trading. It is solvent, carries no debt and has excellent trade references. Fiscal year end was June 30, and liquidation of assets has occurred, other than residual cash on hand reserved to cover any tax liabilities. All that remains is to dissolve the corporation unless either party wishes to re-activate as sole owner.

Harold Monroe has been assigned full rights to the pillow by Sonya Dennings, and it is his view that unless any advantage can be seen in assuming full ownership of Chesapeake, he will soon be forming a new corporation.

In order to attract working capital for start-up and operating over the first six months, sale of stock in the corporation of up to 25% is envisaged.

PURPOSE OF THE BUSINESS PLAN

This plan was created by Harold Monroe for two distinct purposes:

The first goal is to design a set of strategies to maximize opportunities for success. In the context of a unique and constantly regenerating market segment, it is essential to determine objectives and the strategies necessary to achieve them. This cannot be done in the abstract, and the objectives only become meaningful when the means to achieve them are analyzed in detail.

Please keep in mind that such a planning apparatus is associated with the type of opportunity where the challenge lies in determining what needs to be done, not simply how to do it. Honors go first to those who accurately identify, then act upon those needs.

The second goal is to attract innovation-oriented investment banking/venture capital relationships to achieve funding with which to formally commence company operations. According to forecast, working capital after six months will be provided from receivables (cash) with no need for receivables financing or inventory encumbrance.

Nest in Comfort is a small, low-profile operation, employing minimum personnel. It has high gross profit, minimum overhead, and is computerized. Marketing is implemented primarily via mail order to targeted market segments. The company is structured to go from low to high volume rapidly without the corresponding increase in space requirements and overhead.

Focused on maternity/children's market, initially with own unique product, the company follows the child from prenatal through teenage years by adding specialty products (imports from Europe) and developing a mail order catalog. The company is building its own mailing list from the initial customer list.

As new products are added, we intend to test market from the mailing list of existing customers and, for real "winners," extend exposure to commercial mailing lists.

The goal is to build a profitable, high cash flow mail order based business with unique and specialty products aimed at a specific, constantly regenerating, market.

The ultimate objective is to generate wealth by selling the company to a large firm (Johnson & Johnson, Fisher-Price etc.), or by public offering. This objective will be met by two conditions:

1. An unencumbered, enforceable patent being issued.
2. Successful results from direct mail and telemarketing strategies which will generate the profit margins and cash flow to grow the organization.

OVERALL PHILOSOPHY

Based on Scenario #1

1. Direct mailing of 10,000 per month commencing month two from start up date.
2. Telemarketing commences month four from start up date.
3. Review at end of month six to decide whether to:
    a. maintain mailing and telemarketing activity levels through year end.
    b. increase levels of either or both.
    c. discontinue either or both.

Step 3a would be logical and prudent if results were as forecast.

Step 3b would be determined by whether a clear difference in returns was obvious. If a return of better than 5% was achieved via direct mail, it would be easy to increase the volume and maintain the telemarketing at existing levels. Equally, given the cash flow available, it would be possible to increase the telemarketing, but care would be needed to assess the impact on administration capability.

Step 3c would be activated if mailings were running at 5% plus and telemarketing was at the same level. To save cost, the company would discontinue telemarketing and double up on mailing activity.

4. Set up agents (eventually 100) nationwide. A $100 investment buys them one demo pillow, 100 brochures, and a set of pictures or slides. We drop-ship to the customer, agent pre-pays us and collects from customer, $15 discount (25%).

MARKETING STRATEGY

5. We also have two requests on file from maternity stores wishing to offer the pillow. This is an area for periodic review, with considerations being reduced margins versus increased administration inherent to marketing in this way.

6. Test additional applications and markets for the pillow. Space advertising in general circulation magazines is cheaper than specialized publications--in some cases free for new products. This is a good way to test mail order type products.

7. Research new products for the targeted market, for inclusion in own mail order catalog.

DIRECT MAILING: THE CRUCIAL NUMBERS

Cost of direct mailing to 10,000 prospects

1st 10,000	Per Piece	Total
Four color brochure, tri-fold mailer, includes one-time production costs	.30	3,000
List cost @ $70 for 1,000	.07	700
Affix pressure sensitive address labels	.01	100
Bulk mailing	.01	100
Postage (third class)	.167	1,670
Mailing permit, good for one year	.006	60
Total	.563	5,630

Brochure price comes down to .20 and possibly .18 on regular volume, with prices guaranteed for one year. The labeling and bulk mailing, including free delivery to the post office, is done by the mailing list company, whether we use their list or supply our own.

2nd and subsequent 10,000		
Brochure	.20	2,000
List	.07	700
Labels	.01	100
Mailing	.01	100
Postage	.167	1,670
Total	.457	4,570

Assume:
1. Gross profit of $35 per unit
2. Sales of 200 units @ 2% return on mailing

1st 10,000 mailings @ .563	=	$5,630		
Gross profit @ $35 per unit	=	7,000		
Less cost of mailing	=	1,370	= 12%	of gross sales
3% return would give GP of		10,500		
Less cost of mailing	=	4,870	=28%	of gross sales

5% return would give GP of		17,500		
Less cost of mailing	=	11,870	=	40%

2nd and subsequent mailings				
@ $.45	=	4,570		
GP	=	7,000		
After mailing	=	2,430	=	21%

3% return GP	=	5,930	=	34%
5% return GP	=	12,930	=	44%

See how critical the numbers are at the lower percentage return, versus "cost of sales" (mailing). If you add seven cents each to the first 10,000 mailing costs, a 2% return is dragged down to a profit of $670 from $1,370. This is what kills a lot of newcomers to mail order. If you can get your production costs (printing) to equal your mailing costs, then you are ahead, and this is what the big mail order houses aim to achieve.

Things for us to look closely at are: minimizing printing costs, consistent with employing the best possible quality sales tool; seeing if the mailing list prices come down with regular quantity orders and, of course, going for a 5% return as the first target.

Actual experience on our 500 piece test mailing proved a return of 1.8% during the first 30 days, 2.4% after 60 days and 3.0% took a total of 120 - 160 days.

Although I believe that with the right brochure our return would probably have been 5%, it is prudent to use the 2% number for our own projections and planning purposes. 3% makes a whole world of difference and really accelerates things, so the layout and quality of the brochure are key in accomplishing maximum response.

Start-up

CAPITAL REQUIREMENTS

Incorporation	1,000
Patent	5,000
Brochure Design	1,000
Office/Warehouse	6,000
Computer/Phones	10,000
Filling Equipment	1,500
Printing and Supplies	500
Raw Materials and Packaging	3,000
	$28,000
Operations - first 6 months	
	$36,000
Reserve	$36,000
Total	$100,000

PERSONNEL REQUIREMENTS

1. Harold Monroe will function as General Manager
2. Office Supervisor will be responsible for order entry, data input, and coordinating telemarketers.
3. Warehouse Manager will also be trained for order entry.
4. Telemarketers (3). One full-time supervisor, plus four part-time, each working four hours per day. There will be trial and error here, covered separately under "support details". It could be that six part-timers under the direction of the office supervisor will be the most viable. $5,000 per month has been budgeted for this function under "cost of sales". This includes an incentive structure with override for the supervisor, designed to maintain performance levels.

FACILITIES REQUIREMENTS

Assume

1. Combined offices/warehouse. Cerrillos - White Rock - Santa Fe area.

      a. Offices sufficient to house

          one General Manager
          one Office Supervisor
          three Telemarketers
          one Warehouse Supervisor   1,000 square feet.

      b. Warehouse area sufficient to stock one month's inventory (approximately 1,000 units) plus filling and shipping.

Pillows, boxed are 6 x 16 x 20 inches.
An area 20 ft. x 50 ft. will hold 1,920 units, 10 per pallet, 2 pallets high.

                                    1,000 square feet.

Total requirement for year 1 =   2,000 square feet.

COMPUTER REQUIREMENTS

ITT Model 316 has sufficient capacity to handle all data associated with sales up to 2,000 units per month. Beyond that level, a "mini-mainframe" computer would be needed. Capital cost would be $50,000-$70,000. Existing software would be used on the larger system.

Software developed at Chesapeake handled:

      1. New customer entry (for own mailing list)
      2. Invoice
      3. Shipping label

Needed to complete the picture is the program to be written to generate UPS data. A provision has been made for this under "software support". This facility would automatically generate all UPS data upon order entry, with printout appearing in warehouse, eliminating manual entries in UPS books, etc.

Incoming 800 calls. (Order lines)

> $250 per line deposit.
> Free installation until October 10, 1989.
> $20 per month fee plus usage for incoming over local line.
> Day rate 22 - 25 cents per minute.
> > 5% discount after $50
> > 10% discount after $351

Outgoing Watts lines (3 for telemarketing)

> "Pro 2" Program
> 24-26 cents per minute (30 seconds on bill if client hangs up).
> Assume average call of 2 minutes = 50 cents per call = approximately 5,000 per month
> > for 10,000 calls.

Note: Outgoing Watts will be a fixed cost of sales.

Incoming 800 calls (orders) can be assumed for budget purposes at 20% of unit sales.

No freight costs are shown in the P&L projection. This is because freight is pre-paid by the customer. A charge of $5.00 per unit is made which covers UPS charges plus a small profit.

In the case of shipping to agents, we would charge the actual UPS cost and allow discretion to the agent whether to absorb or pass on charges to their customers.

As of the date of this forecast, March 1, 1989, "The Company" has not been formally or legally organized. It is the intention of Harold Monroe to utilize this forecast to obtain capital funding monies with which to formally commence company operations.

Once the necessary funding has been achieved through a funding agreement, the company will commence sub-contract manufacturing and direct-mail marketing of Nest in Comfort, simultaneously applying to complete or renew the patent application. It is recognized that this is probably not the customary sequence, however it is felt that sufficient "de facto" protection exists in view of the prior history of manufacture and sale of the product. From a marketing perspective, the best protection lies in getting the product established as a "must have," generic product as rapidly as possible. Further, the method of marketing via direct mail/mail order ensures a low profile whereby high volume sales can be generated without attracting the attention of would-be competition.

A vigorous pursuit to secure the patent is essential for ultimate protection and to enhance the value of the company. A positive outcome to the patent application is indicated by the patent attorney who was originally retained.

Financial Forecast

The financial forecast is Harold Monroe's estimate of the most probable results of operations for the forecast period. Accordingly, the forecast is his best judgement, based on present circumstances, of the most likely scenarios and their outcomes. The assumptions disclosed herein are those which he believes are significant to the forecast or are key factors upon which the financial results of the company depend. Some assumptions may not materialize and unanticipated events and circumstances may occur subsequent to March 15, 1989, the date of these forecasts. Therefore the actual results achieved during the forecast period may vary materially from the forecast.

Sales Revenue

Sales revenue will be generated initially from one source, Nest in Comfort. The retail selling price is $58.90. The test marketing program, plus input from childbirth educators, indicates this price is appropriate. Future sources of potential additional revenue include:

1) Additional markets for the pillow; same pillow, different cover; different applications, e.g., "Gardener's Pillow," "Night Reader's Pillow," etc.

2) Additional specialty products for mail order to the targeted market via our own catalog. Some excellent quality developmental toys, games, etc. are available, particularly in Europe. Several manufacturers whom we have contacted have shown a keen interest in entering the U.S. market. From time to time, small domestic entrepreneurs generate new products.

Direct Cost of Sales

Will be comprised of three factors:

1) Direct mailing costs.
2) Telemarketing costs.
3) Finished goods (sub-contract manufacture).

Based on actual experience and recent quotes, the cost of the pillow should be a maximum $12.00. For forecasting purposes, a conservative approach has again been taken by assuming a cost of $15.00. This allows for any possible increases to cover filling and packaging, whether this is to be done by the manufacturing sub-contractor or in-house at our facility.

Additional "headroom" is also available by eliminating the vinyl interior cover in favor of plain cotton. The vinyl cover was introduced to address the hospital market which is now considered non-viable in the short-term and best eliminated from future planning.

This combined "headroom" also allows for payment of the $1.00 per shipped unit to Harold Monroe. A separate line item headed "Royalties" would record these transactions on a formal income statement as standard operating procedure.

Operating Expenses

These have been forecast based on expectations of monthly recurring costs. Throughout the forecast periods, the monthly operating expenses have been increased where appropriate to reflect the natural progression of increased costs to support corresponding growth in sales.

As it is intended to procure the monies necessary to commence operations by way of capital contributions, (sale of stock), no interest expense has been provided for in this forecast.

Interest Expense

This forecast provides for no earnings on retained cash, since it is not possible to determine the necessary cash requirements of increasing various expenditures for rapid expansion.

Interest Income

Income taxes have been provided for at the rate of 25% of the net operating earnings before taxes.

Income Taxes

Depreciation has been computed on the straight-line method over estimated useful lives of five years of operating equipment and office furniture.

Depreciation

SUMMARY OF CASH FLOW ASSUMPTIONS

1) Due to the cash nature of the business, a rapid cash flow is forecast as a direct consequence of sales.
2) Investment cash received: this forecast includes the receipt of $100,000. Received through the sale of company stock.

Cash Receipts

It has been forecast that the direct cost of finished goods, mailings, and telemarketing will be paid in the month incurred. In the case that it is the second month, this in effect means "prior to" for mailing and finished goods.

Cash Disbursements of Direct Costs (Cost of sales)

It has been forecast that all monthly operating costs will be paid in the month incurred.

Cash Disbursements of Operating Costs

The forecast provides for income tax to be paid on a quarterly basis in compliance with Federal & State requirements.

Income Taxes

Media Producer

BUSINESS PLAN

DYNAMIC VIDEO

3470 University Blvd., Ste. 117
Bridgeport MN 27810

August 1994

This plan offers an outline of the steps necessary to launch a successful video production company. This award-winning business plan demonstrates a comprehensive consideration of product design, market, competition, industry, and financing, as well as an understanding of each partner's role. After applying this strategy, the authors revised it to reflect significant changes in the business. The revised version appears following this plan.

- EXECUTIVE SUMMARY

- OUR MISSION

- OUR PRODUCT

- OUR TARGET MARKET

- THE INDUSTRY AND ITS HISTORY

- OUR COMPETITORS

- THE PARTNERSHIP

- THE CHALLENGES

- WHY WE CAN SUCCEED

- OUR PROFESSIONAL RESOURCES

- OUR FINANCIAL PLAN

- APPENDICES

EXECUTIVE SUMMARY

Dynamic Video (DV) is a partnership of three people who produce and distribute videotapes that teach about issues of concern to youth and are marketed primarily to schools.

In our first year of operation, we demonstrated the beginnings of a unique and profitable way of marketing our video on sexual harassment within an educational resources industry seriously lacking in suitable materials.

Dynamic Video handles three types of videotape products—

■ Proprietary: Scripted, produced, owned and marketed by DV;
■ Contract: Produced by DV for another agency, to remain their property;
■ Non-proprietary: Produced and/or owned by another agency, then purchased and/or distributed by DV.

There is an almost unlimited supply of youth issues that DV can use now and in future years to fulfill our mission. Issues that educators have already said they would like DV to treat through the medium of video include—

■ Racial and religious harassment;
■ Girls and abusive relationships;
■ Bullies and gangs.

Since we already have one product, our projected sales estimates are based on the sample of sales achieved early in 1994. Our $20,000 sales for 1994 will increase dramatically during 1995 as we complete our second and third sexual harassment videotapes.

Because of the mix of the partners' skills, we are already able to produce videotapes inexpensively. We are confident that the cost will go down even further as we advance along the learning curve.

With this factor in place, along with our commitment to serving youth and the schools, we believe we have a perfect platform to launch into the educational marketplace of the future.

OUR MISSION

Our mission is to produce fine quality educational videotapes, dealing primarily with health and social issues, to serve the students and teachers of America's schools.

OUR PRODUCT

Sexual harassment (SH) education: The beginning of our partnership

Dynamic Video, a partnership of three people, produces and distributes videotapes that teach about issues of concern to children and youth and are marketed primarily in the schools.

DV was launched one year ago with the purchase of the "Compliance with Sexual Harassment Laws: A Matter of Respect" video script. The script was written by a group of local educators, had been critiqued by professional film producers, and received excellent reviews. DV bought the script in June 1993 and produced the video in the fall and winter, utilizing the talents of students and staff from several school districts as talent. "A Matter of Respect" went on the market to Minnesota schools in February 1994.

So far "A Matter of Respect" shows considerable promise as a money maker:

Our Initial Success

●A single pre-production advertising mailing brought in 65 orders, a 16% percent response rate.

●Since February 1994, DV has finalized sales on 60 tapes with no advertising since pre-production;

●Figuring the cost of production over the first 100 tapes, each tape costs approximately $49 to produce and sells for $99 plus $1.50 for shipping and handling.

●Although other excellent resources now exist for sexual harassment education, "A Matter of Respect" remains one of only a handful of videotapes on the market.

Note: Instructional Videos, Inc., a videotape supplier for librarians, prints a catalogue advertising the videos of 500 distributors nationwide.

Pricing: This year's catalogue includes six (6) SH education videos; price range $19.95 to $199; "A Matter of Respect" is moderately priced at $99 plus $1.50 for shipping.

●The videotape has been praised by teachers for its multicultural images and because it shows "real kids talking to real kids" in everyday school situations. In fact, Holly Selders, a teacher at Moorhead High School, called it "awesome." A high school principal used it the very first day it arrived for "reeducating" a sexual harasser.

●Four school districts have each purchased more than one copy for use in different school buildings.

●The School District of Jackson bought a copy to use in developing its own sexual harassment policy.

●The State Department of Education reviewed "A Matter of Respect" to include it on its list of recommended resources for schools.

Initial Sales of "A Matter of Respect" -- 9/1/93-9/10/94
On Market: 2/94
Price: $99 plus $1.50 shipping
Number Sales to date: 60
Gross Sales to Date: $6,030
Continuing operations/cash balance: $1,487

Encouraged by what we have learned about the educational resources industry, DV plans to least two more videos about sexual harassment over the course of the next two years. This section outlines our reasons, addressing the following points:

Making the Case: More Sexual Harassment Videotapes!

●Across the nation, sexual harassment is perceived as a serious problem in the schools;

●Our state leads the nation in SH education in the schools;

●SH awareness is rising nation-wide. Other states are following our lead;

●Schools around the nation are seeking resources for SH education;

●There is a shortage of SH resources suitable for use with young people;

●Teaching resources are needed for elementary as well as secondary age students.

Sexual harassment among students of all ages has reached alarming proportions in the schools. The use of vulgar language and sexual reference is rampant. Harassing remarks are even printed on clothes. In many schools, harassment happens so often it becomes disruptive to the learning environment. A June 1993 report based on a nationwide study by the American Association of University Women Educational Foundation found that--

- 85% of girls said they were harassed in school
- 76% of boys said they were harassed in school
- 33% of harassed girls said the experience made them not want to go to school and/or not talk in class
- 12% of harassed boys said the experience made them not want to go to school and/or not talk in class

> **Big Enough Sticks?** *In a 1992 landmark case based on Title IX federal antidiscrimination law, the US Supreme Court ruled that there is no limit to the damages awardable to confirmed victims of sexual harassment (Franklin vs Gwinnett County Public Schools).*

In 1989, our state became the first state in the nation to require sexual harassment policies in the schools, ruling that federal law prohibiting discrimination in the schools on the basis of sex applies to sexual harassment as well.

Legislation was passed requiring 400 school districts in this state to put SH policies in place by 1991 and inform staff and students about the policies.

Meanwhile several highly-publicized cases at the national level—such as the Anita Hill hearings—have fostered a rising SH consciousness throughout the country. Other states are pushing for legislation similar to ours.

Educators are also taking a new look at existing state and federal anti-discrimination laws such as Title IX or Wisconsin Statute 118.13, which prohibits discrimination in the schools based on sex, race, religion, disability, etc., to see how they can be used to combat harassment in the schools.

All over the country, schools are seeking resources to help educate young people about sexual harassment. So far they are finding very few. Although workplace-oriented resources for adults do exist, before "A Matter of Respect" there was almost nothing on the market suitable for use with youth in the schools.

In most states, education about SH started with junior and senior high school students. However, beginning in 1994, the emphasis is on reaching young children in elementary grades. DV has already received inquiries from educators seeking SH videos for use in elementary classrooms. Teachers see a need to move early to counteract the negative gender messages children pick up from the surrounding culture and begin to foster healthy, respectful attitudes.

DV's primary target customers through the end of 1996 are the public school districts of Minnesota, Wisconsin and California. Following is the list of products we offer to our customers:

1. "A Matter of Respect" for Minnesota
        Status: Completed
        On market: 2/94
        Tapes sold: 60
        Additional customers: 340
        Projected sales: 205

2. "Respect Across Our Nation" (national version)
        Status: Researching
        On market: 8/95 (Wis & Calif)
        Tapes sold: 0
        Total customers: 1,428
        Projected number of sales: 914

3. "Respect: It's Elementary" (Elementary SH videotape set)
        Status: Scripting
        On market: 3/95 (Minn, Wis & Calif)
        Tapes sold: 0
        Total customers: 1,928
        Projected number of sales: 1,170

OUR TARGET MARKET

Sexual Harassment Videos in DV's Works

New sales projections for the SH education tapes presently in the works (these figures do not reflect sales before 8/1/94).

August 1, 1994 thru December 31, 1996
        3,696   Total customers in Minnesota, Wisconsin & California
        2,289   Projected sales
        $200,211   Projected gross sales

Sales Projections for Sexual Harassment

The projections listed above are based upon the following marketing plan components:

Minnesota Marketing Plan Pertinent Percentages
        100% of our customers personally contacted, offered free preview;
        80% of our customers our experience shows will agree to preview;
        64% of our customers our experience shows will purchase previewed videotape.

Assumptions for Wisconsin and California
        100% of our customers personally contacted, offered free preview;
        66% of customers will buy tapes over 2-year period (first or one of first products on market in these states).

Within the schools themselves, SH education resources are purchased with money from several different sources:

Which Pot the Money Comes From &When the Cash Comes In
●General funds (health curriculum resources); 3-5 weeks
●State violence prevention monies; 3-5 weeks
●State and federal alcohol and drug abuse prevention monies; 3-5 weeks
●Staff development funds. 3-5 weeks

Orders for DV's first tape, "A Matter of Respect" came from faculty and staff from a variety of departments within the schools:

Who Is Using Our SH Videotapes
●Health Teachers
●Staff development committees
●Counselors
●Principals
●Media supervisors

DV Sexual Harassment Videos: The Details

1. "A Matter of Respect" for Minnesota. Our experience with preliminary marketing of our first proprietary videotape, has left us feeling confident about our product. "Respect" in spite of its flaws, is a valuable resource, one of few on the national market which meet the needs of America's secondary schools. We believe our marketing plan should generate sales to more than half the school districts in Minnesota. During the four-month period from September-December 1994, it is the goal of the DV marketing team to have personally contacted every school district in the state and received a yes or no answer.

2. "Respect" Across the Nation. Nationwide there is unquestionably a rising consciousness on the subject of sexual harassment. It is creating a good market for our videotapes, one that we believe will last for at least two years. In fact, a national distributor of educational videotapes called DV to express an interest in distributing the national version of "A Matter of Respect." For this reason, while we do have plans to expand our video catalogue to include other topics, our main emphasis will be SH through most of 1996.

Note: There are about 16,000 school districts across the nation.

Presently we are expanding our market research to California and Wisconsin. California enacted an SH education statute Similar to Minnesota's in 1992. Here is also a push for special legislation. Until it succeeds, Equity Team officials at the Department of Public Instruction are encouraging schools to use existing anti-discrimination legislation to enforce SH policies in the schools.

We plan to revise "Respect" for the national market in spring and summer of 1995, beginning our national marketing campaign with Wisconsin and California. We have set a high sales goal of 2/3 of the market because we are one of the first—if not the very first—resources of our type to hit these state markets. We also believe this issue will continue to gain importance during the next year.

3. "Respect"-It's Elementary. Already DV has received requests for a SH video for elementary-age students. To our knowledge, there is as yet nothing available to fill this need. DV is eager to take advantage of this prime market. We have two elementary videos (to be sold as a set) already in the works. The elementary videos are scheduled to hit the market in early spring of 1995. Beginning with Minnesota, Wisconsin and California, our two-year sales goal is about 2,000 videotapes sets for the three states combined.

Ongoing research from now through the end of 1996 will point DV in the direction of other states and schools standing in need of our SH products.

Although sexual harassment is a "hot" issue in schools across the nation right now, DV recognizes that the market for SH resources in finite. There is, however, a practically unlimited supply of youth and children's issues that DV can use now and in future years to fulfill our mission-albeit not always with the luxury of laws to stimulate our market.

Down the Road: Future Topics for Proprietary Videotapes

Other issues that educators have already said they would like DV to treat through the medium of video are the following:
● Racial and religious harassment
● Girls and abusive relationships
● Bullies and gangs: What it means to be male in the age of equality;
● Mothers who are children (teen parenting).

Here are some other issues that are hot in the schools right now and that would lend themselves to video:
● Violence-free schools
● Being yourself/coping with peer pressure
● Sexual abstinence/AIDS
● Compulsive gambling
● Tobacco, drug and alcohol abuse prevention
● The special emotional perils to girls at adolescence
● Taking the challenge—excelling with disabilities

DV handles three types of videotape products:

Not Just for Ourselves: Contract Production Jobs

1. **Proprietary**: Scripted, produced, owned and marketed by DV (for example, "Respect");
2. **Contract**: Produced by DV for another agency, to remain its property;
3. **Non-proprietary:** Produced and/or owned by another agency then purchased and/or distributed by DV.

The preceding section detailed the proprietary component. This section describes contract-type videos that are already—or almost—in the works. Contract videos in the works:

1. "A Practical History of the Jackson Area Community Center."
Contracting agency: Jackson, MN, school district
Status: Researching
Target completion date: 12/94
Services provided: Scriptwriting production

Anticipated fee: $3,500 total
$1,000 deposit in August

2. "Bi-Racial Dating and Relationships" (tentative)
Contracting agency: Young Adult Network
Status: Contractor investigating grant funding
Target completion date: Unknown
Services provided: Scriptwriting, production, marketing—cooperatively with students
Anticipated fee: Unknown

1. A Practical History of the Jackson Area Community Center (JACC). The JACC is a school reform project founded on school/community partnerships. The Jackson school district has asked DV to produce a videotape which will be useful to schools and communities interested in school reform, student entrepreneurship, and co-location of social and health services to sites within the local community. The video will include an overview on foundations and other funding agencies with tips on how to successfully pursue grant funding.

2. Bi-Racial Dating and Relationships. This is a grant-funded project to be produced in cooperation with teen mothers from Young Adult Network, who initiated the idea themselves. DV has been approached by Young Adult Network which is researching grant funding for the project. DV is interested in helping Young Adult Network find a way to use the videotape project as a learning resource for the teen mothers and possibly to turn it into a student entrepreneurship venture.

Non-Proprietary Videotapes

Potential to date: 2 contracts
Status: Investigating
DV terms: 40% off retail

DV has been approached by two different companies with requests to distribute their educational videotapes. DV is investigating this apparent demand for a local videotape distributor.

THE INDUSTRY AND ITS HISTORY

Since videotape was first introduced in the 1950s, it has been perceived as "flipping through society with hurricane force, uprooting conventional ways and sweeping aside anyone who resists" (Charlene Canape, *How to Capitalize on the Video Revolution*). Initially used only for broadcast television, professional videography equipment dropped dramatically in price in the 1980s, making videos a practical alternative for everything from resumes to fund drives. Its relative cheapness compared to film gave rise to a bumper crop of video entrepreneurs and made visual recordings accessible to the average person in the street.

According to an advertising publication of Karol Media, a Pennsylvania videotape distribution company, the home video industry "had dramatic effects on the information and education business . . . Schools and organizations . . . that never owned 16mm projectors now own VCRs."

Karol goes on, "The strongest audience remains the schools, particularly grades 6 through 12. And what an audience! The needs of our beleaguered schools have been widely publicized. They are eager for the right materials . . . Curriculum tie-ins, teacher-led discussion, follow-up activity, take-away literature, all are possible."

Video is a natural medium for teaching. As an audiovisual tool, it is instantly absorbable by today's generation, young people who "cut their teeth" on television and live and breathe it every day. Because videos can be produced so cheaply, they make excellent "how-to" demonstrators for everything from cutting a square corner to learning to speak in public. Video is especially useful at depicting interactions between people-for example, to illustrate incidence of sexual harassment, or to show effective responses students can make to harassment.

In the schools, a videotape ensures a consistent message from class to class and can serve as an excellent springboard for discussion. A video reaches its maximum potential if its demonstrations are followed up with practice and role playing among members of the audience, turning a passive learning experience into an active one.

Companies such as Beckley-Cardy, which specialize in supplying educational resources to the schools, now have burgeoning catalogues of videotapes for use in the classroom. For example, Beckley-Cardy's catalogue includes listings for hundreds of videos for use in the various academic subject areas and for teaching about values, self esteem, and interpersonal relationships.

Although the issues of concern to educators come and go with the seasons, the reliance on audiovisual resources like video to bring those issues to life in the classroom is here to stay.

Today there are 12 educational videotape producers in this state and more than 1,000 producers and/or distributors throughout the nation. Some of the major suppliers distribute products for three or four academic areas only. In addition to videos and films, these companies deal in print materials, equipment and a wide assortment of "manipulatives" (everything from math counters to CPR dummies).

OUR COMPETITORS

Listed below is some of what DV learned by talking with people representing these supply companies:

Beckley-Cardy
National supplier of teaching resources, including the videos of United Learning Videos (see below);
•Regional office located in Duluth
•# Educational videos in current catalogue: hundreds
•# Sexual harassment videos in catalogue: zero (0)

United Learning Videos
•A video publisher company located in Niles, Illinois
•Deals in videos for all academic areas
•Advertises 60 titles in a 64-page full-color catalogue
•Purchases sole proprietary rights to all tapes

●Has facilities to warehouse thousands of videotapes

●Maintains a national dealer network

●Presently is considering only CD-ROM and laser disc products on non-proprietary basis

●SH videos in current catalogue: zero (0)

●Called DV earlier this month and asked to review our sexual harassment tape with an eye to purchasing sole distribution rights

Educational Videos Group

●A video producer/publisher located in Greenwood, Indiana

●Specializes in the academic areas of social studies, science, English and communications

●No health or guidance tapes (the areas which typically include sexual harassment education)

●According to contact person, 75% of catalogue titles are property of the company, produced by independent video producers on contract to Educational Videos Group

●Videos are curriculum-based, in many cases created to support the basic course textbook

Instructional Videos, Inc.

●National video supplier for librarians; located in Lincoln, Nebraska

●Acts as "jobber" for 500 video distributors

●Purchases videotapes 50% off retail

●Only advertising done is title listing in catalogue

●Big catalogue printed in January, supplement in June

●# Sexual harassment tapes in catalogue: six (6)

●Price range for SH tapes listed: $19.95-199

Cambridge Educational Videos

●Located in Charlottesville, West Virginia

●Major video supplier printing 11 catalogues both for secondary and postsecondary schools

●Areas include home ec, careers/job search, vocational/technical, phy ed and health

●350 proprietary titles

●400 titles as sole distributor (50% off retail);

●Produced "Crossing the Line" sexual harassment curriculum which is widely used in schools (price going down from original $1200)

●Recently completed a companion video (with workbook) which utilizes role play to help students practice responses to sexual harassment

●Price of this video: $89.95

●Other SH videos in catalogue: two (2) tailored for the workplace (DV reviewed one of these)

Master Video

●Located in Minneapolis

●Producer of educational and industrial videotapes on contract to outside agencies

●No catalogue; has produced one educational video on contract to local schools

●14 years old, 10 employees

DV's conversations with suppliers reinforced some of our beliefs about our business's potential. We are encouraged, for example, to learn that--

- The market is definitely there for educational videotapes of all kinds;
- With effective marketing and distribution, there is a bright future for the small, independent producer who can afford to create videos inexpensively;
- Suppliers agree that sexual harassment is currently a topic of concern to educators nationwide;
- As yet, there are few videotapes on this subject directed at young people in the schools;
- DV would not have any problem finding a distributor for non-state-specific sexual harassment videos at either the elementary or secondary level.

On the other hand, it is clear that--
The challenge lies with the marketing and distribution.

Being able to produce good videos and being able to sell enough good videos to put lots of money in one's pocket are two very different skills. Our impression is that it is rare to find a company with the talents and the time to do both well.

A representative of Karol Media told DV that we should figure on spending between $6-$12 on marketing for each dollar spent in production. It is hard for us to see right now where that kind of money would come from. However, we take this remark as a word to the wise. It presents an image of the vastness of the American market and the challenge of communicating with the busy hoard of strangers out there who will someday be our customers.

The Partners--in Brief. Dynamic Video is a partnership formed in June 1993 by Andrea Sheldon and Dedria Johnson for the purpose of producing the "A Matter of Respect" videotape. For the first year, DV operated out of Dedria Johnson's office in her home. This spring the original partners recognized that the business is at a crossroads. It needs to expand in order to realize its potential. They invited Kevin Hill, an accountant with experience in business, to join the partnership. Here are a few facts about each of the partners:

THE PARTNERSHIP

Andrea Sheldon

BS degree in Mass Communications;
6 years professional videography producer;
Owns her own business, in Duluth;
Member of Leadership Superior/Douglas County;
Theatre background, many connections in theatre;
Former promotion manager for KBJR-TRV6.

Dedria Johnson

BS degree in English;
Freelance wirter specializing in education;
8 years experience in the schools as newsletter journalist/
   public relations writer;
Skilled at design and production of promotional materials.

Kevin Hill
BA degree in Accounting;
Experienced in sales;
Owned and operated architectural drafting business for 10 years.

Since Kevin came on board, DV has concentrated on finding an office, creating a business plan, and setting up an accounting system. Presently we are undergoing management education counseling with representatives from both the Small Business Development Center and the Business Incubation Center.

Plans and Personnel

Presently we are applying for an office in the Business Incubation Center. After we get our office—probably sometime during September—we expect to serve the partnership as follows for the first six months:

Andrea Sheldon
Work half-time for DV;
Continue to operate her other business from her Duluth office until her lease expires at the end of the year;
Move into the DV office in January 1995 and operate her other business from there half-time;
Be responsible for coordinating and supervising all video production activities;
Edit all videotapes;
Serve as member of marketing team;
Rent her videography equipment to DV.

Dedria Johnson
Work full-time for DV;
Retain her position as newsletter editor with local district in order to maintain our proprietary position in the schools;
Rent her computer system to DV;
Coordinate contacts with school personnel;
Be responsible for writing and producing promotional materials;
Assist with video shots and editing;
Serve as member of marketing team.

Kevin Hill
Work half-time for DV through November;
Study for CPA exam half-time through November;
Join DV full-time beginning in December;
Be responsible for accounting, shipping and other finance-related activities;
Assist with video shots and production;
Serve as member of marketing team.

	Marketing Plan

●Inexpensive tapes of high-quality content

●Concern with social issues

●Use student actors

●Use educators as script authors

●A partner, Dedria Johnson, involved in education issues and accepted into school districts

●Call-backs to ensure customer satisfaction.

General Strategy

Every sale will include a personal request for an evaluation of the product by the User Teacher and, if possible, the students who viewed the video.

Selected Details
of Marketing Plan

Each partner will contribute to the following phases of the process:

●Obtain state directory of school districts and select a district to call

●Call district and ask for Human Rights Officer (HRO)

●Ask if the school district needs resources and, if so, offer to send free preview tape

●If HRO agrees, send tape, brochures, District Response Form and Student Critique Form for evaluation to HRO or designated person he/she names

●If HRO agrees, send invoice to billing clerk

●If no response in 35 days, phone billing clerk and ask him/her to track down the tape and District Response Form (DRF)

●One week after Classroom Use Date (listed on DRF), contact User Teacher and get verbal evaluation

This evaluation and sales data will enable the marketing team to produce a mailing list and labels for future marketing efforts.

We plan to hire a shipping clerk/secretary in November 1994 for 10 hours per week, increasing the hours to 40/week beginning in January 1995. An assistant to the script writer will also be hired in January, initially for 10 hours per week.

Personnel

Although we expect to increase the size of our organization to include at least two employees, we want to retain our partnership vision of a personalized operation that relies on involvement of all partners in each stage of the process, most especially the video production portion. We are committed to maintaining our direct involvement with the public schools in order to "keep our finger on the pulse" of youth issues and to remind ourselves that education is above all a human endeavor.

As was stated before, our plans for sexual harassment tapes over the upcoming 28 months include a set of two tapes directed at elementary students and a revised version of "A Matter of Respect" which will be generalized for the national market.

Teachers as Authors

Right now we are in the scriptwriting process for the elementary videotapes. An Authors Group of six teachers meets with us weekly on Thursday mornings for a scripting session over brunch. It looks as if this production will include original music, dances and a charming child narrator. The message will work off the theme, "Together boys and girls can make a better, more peaceful world."

One of the tasks of this Authors Group is to define the financial terms for the members' contract with DV. Our intent is to develop a policy which we will use for subsequent videotapes. This contract is still under discussion.

THE CHALLENGES

Although we believe we have many things going for us, DV also faces some real challenges:

1. DV has limited capital for investment and for operational expenses;

2. Since we rely largely on volunteer acting talent from students, the quality and availability of that talent can sometimes be problematic.

3. The time factor continues to be a challenge, especially for Dedria Johnson whose continued presence in the schools is central to the partnership. At present, Dedria will continue her work as newsletter editor for the districts with the help of several writers and production workers.

4. Critiquing our own first product, "A Matter of Respect," we find some technical flaws, such as the poor lighting in the first hallway scene. Some of the acting has been criticized as weak. Some of the scenarios depicting sexual harassment situations in school have been critized as "naive"--not really reflecting the seriousness of the harassment that actually occurs, especially at the senior high level. In addition, students of color are under-represented in the video.

WHY WE CAN SUCCEED

As DV tackles the difficult youth issues of the day, we also take on two other challenges: first, a changeable market and, second, major competitors who are well-established and well-financed and who, like us, market primarily to the schools. We believe DV has the following advantages:

1. Video scripts are written by teachers (and other youth education experts such as counselors and sexual assault advocates) who understand young people and the issues concerning them;

2. Scripts are reviewed by an editorial board of students for authenticity, effectiveness, and "classiness";

3. Marketing plan incorporates critiquing by customer teachers and students in their classrooms;

4. Tapes feature "real kids talking to real kids" in realistic scenarios of school life;

5. DV partner Dedria Johnson is directly involved in the schools as a public relations writer and so is aware of current issues of concern as well as funding opportunities made available to schools for education on specific issues;

6. DV's direct involvement in the schools provides a network of educator colleagues to draw upon for advice and assistance.

7. All three partners have excellent credit records that will serve us well in the event we need to consider borrowing;

8. The mix of skills among the partners allows us to operate all facets of the business with relatively low overhead costs, especially during the startup period;

9. Several teachers who serve as presenter/trainers on sexual harassment to schools in Minnesota and throughout the Midwest have agreed to show the "Respect" videotape and promote it. Workshops are a prime opportunity for selling an issue-oriented product such as "A Matter of Respect." That is because the minds of the educators in attendance are focused on the issue. They are often relieved to be able to find solutions to their resource needs right at hand;

10. Our school connections are already reaping a crop of creative ideas for involving students in videotape production and marketing as a learning experience. This will permit DV to join the ranks of other "school partner" companies.

Creating school/business partnerships is a major focus within the schools these days, not only in Minnesota, but in Wisconsin and other states as well. Such partnerships benefit students, who learn real-world skills and get the jump on an increasingly difficult job market. Over the long run, partnerships benefit business and industry by helping to produce qualified workers.

In the case of a small organization like DV, we would benefit by increased visibility within the schools and also by getting some real, useful help from the "awesome" talent that exists in the schools. One idea we have is to enlist the help of the DECA Club in marketing our videotapes in Wisconsin. This club achieves state and national recognition each year for its outstanding individual and team marketing projects. DV would be fortunate to have DECA's assistance and would be glad to provide learning opportunities to students;

11. Since the market for DV videotapes is the schools, our product is not location sensitive. Videos can be inexpensively mailed to any place in the nation and do not require a retail outlet. In addition, since we do not rely on walk-in customers, we can exist comfortably within a "scaled-down" office environment.

Once a script has been developed and written, it will be reviewed by an Editorial Board comprised of selected students of various ages and backgrounds. To fulfill our mission statement of producing "fine-quality educational videotapes," the script must appeal to our student audience and it must be believable. To achieve this objective, DV needs the input of this valuable board. They will critique the script for its authenticity, effectiveness and "classiness."

Student Editorial Board

Thanks to our counselors at the Small Business Development Center (SBDC) and the Business Incubation Center (BIC), we are getting a glimpse of the amount of labor involved in setting up a successful business. In spite of that, we remain optimistic about our enterprise.

OUR PROFESSIONAL RESOURCES

For one thing, we are encouraged by what we have learned about our industry and about each other as people and as colleagues. In addition, we have discovered a wealth of resource persons to aid us in our venture.

Besides the SBDC counselors and the BIC, these include an Equity Team Member from the Wisconsin Department of Public Instruction and her Minnesota counterpart; an attorney from the School District of Superior; a CPA volunteer consultant; a volunteer attorney consultant; a professional writer and producer; and school faculty and staff too numerous to mention.

We include in that list our bankers, with whom we each separately have good financial relationships, and, last but not least, the talented students in our schools.

We also appreciate the fact that the business development climate is positive in our County and that the timing is opportune. Many agencies and individuals stand poised to assist us in the interest of fostering the economic well-being of our community.

Finally, we partners of DV sincerely value the opportunity to contribute to that economic well-being by putting forth our best combined professional effort.

OUR FINANCIAL PLAN

For Years ended December 31: 1994, 1995, and 1996

Dynamic Video Projected Income Statement

	AUG	SEPT	OCT	NOV	DEC	1994	1995	1996
REVENUE	1	2	3	4	5	YR1	YR2	YR3
Revenue-MN Respect	603	603	2010	3015	3015	9246	11357	0
Revenue-JACC	1000	0		1000	1500	3500	0	0
Revenue-MN Elementary	0	0	975	975	975	2925	16275	0
Revenue-Wisc Elementary	0	0	525	525	525	1575	8700	10275
Revenue-Wisc Secondary	0	0	704	704	704	2111	11658	13769
Revenue-Calif. Elementary	0	0	0	0	0	0	24000	24000
Revenue-Calif. Secondary	0	0	0	0	0	0	32160	32160
Total Revenue	1603	603	4510	4515	6015	19357	104150	80204

Cost of Goods Sold

Video Production Costs	0	0	390	190	590	1170	1380	340
Video Production-Labor	0	0	700	400	400	1500	800	250
Payments to writers	0	0	0	0	0	0	1695	1695
Video Equip. Rental	50	50	50	50	50	250	600	600
Video Copying	0	0	720	0	0	720	2790	3405
Total	50	50	1860	640	1040	3640	7265	6290
Gross Profit	1553	553	2650	3875	4975	15717	96885	73914

Expenses

Telephone Expense	200	200	450	150	200	1200	2400	2400
Office Rent	0	0	100	100	100	300	1800	1800
Meeting Facilities	280	20	0	0	0	300	600	600
Office Supplies	0	0	50	50	50	150	600	600
Interest Expense	0	30	0	0	24	54	39	0
Shipping of Tapes	9	9	30	45	45	138	1755	1371
Brochure Mailing	0	125	20	20	20	185	300	500
Shipping clerk/ Receptionist				200	200	400	10400	10400
Assistant Script Writer							4160	4160
Payroll Tax Expense				19	19	38	1456	1456
Total Expenses	489	384	650	584	658	2765	23510	23287
Operating Profit	1064	169	2000	3291	4317	12952	73375	50627

**Dynamic Video
Projected Cash Flow**

For Years Ended December 31: 1994, 1995, 1996

	AUG	SEPT	OCT	NOV	DEC	1994	1995	1996
	1	2	3	4	5	YR1	YR2	YR3
Cash Bal. Beginning	1487	2551	1003	1003	2294	1487	6499	21422
Revenue-MN Respect	603	603	2010	3015	3015	9246	11357	0
Revenue-JACC	1000	0	1000	0	1500	3500	0	0
Revenue-MN Elementary	0	0	975	975	975	2925	16275	0
Revenue-Wisc Elementary	0	0	525	525	525	1575	8700	10275
Revenue-Wisc Secondary	0	0	704	704	704	2111	11658	13769
Revenue-Calif. Elementary	0	0	0	0	0	0	24000	24000
Revenue-Calif. Secondary	0	0	0	0	0	0	32160	32160
Total Cash Available	3090	3154	5513	5518	8309	20844	110648	101626
Less Disbursements:								
Partners' Draws	0	1500	2000	2000	2000	7500	57600	57600
Telephone Expense	200	200	450	150	200	1200	2400	2400
Office Rent	0	0	100	100	100	300	1800	1800
Meeting Facilities	280	20	0	0	0	300	600	600
Video Equip. Rental	50	50	50	50	50	250	600	600
Office Supplies	0	0	50	50	50	150	600	600
Loan Payable-DR	0	217	0	0	223	440	851	0
Writers--Payments	0	0	0	0	0	0	1695	1695
Shipping of Tapes	9	9	30	45	45	138	1755	1371
Interest Expense	0	30	0	0	24	54	39	0
Video Production-Labor	0	0	700	400	400	1500	800	250
Video Production Costs	0	0	390	190	590	1170	1380	340
Brochure Mailing	0	125	20	20	20	185	300	500
Video Copying	0	0	720	0	0	720	2790	3405
Shipping Clerk/ Receptionist				200	200	400	10400	10400
Assistant Script Writer							4160	4160
Payroll Tax Expense				19	19	38	1456	1456
Total Disbursements	539	2151	4510	3224	3921	14345	89226	87177
Cash Surplus (DEF)	2551	1003	1003	2294	4388	6499	21422	14449
Bank Loan Required	0	0	0	0	0	0	0	0
Cash Balance Ending	2551	1003	1003	2294	4388	6499	21422	14449

The Projected Cash Flow Budget and Income Statement are based on the following assumptions:

Our estimates of total units sold are based on records of our sales during the last quarter of 1993 and early 1994. Of the 400 districts in Minnesota, we have found that 80% (320) will accept a preview of our tape. Of those previews, 64% (205) will subsequently purchase the tape. We use this formula in determining the market for our other tapes, also.

1. Cash receipts for the Minnesota "A Matter of Respect" are estimated as follows: Projected total units: 205 @ $100.50=$20,603.

We do not expect substantial sales beyond June 1995 as all districts will have been covered by this time. These estimates are based on the telephoning done in Spring 94, as well as in July and August to promote the tape. Individual school payment cycles vary, but this assumes approximately 60 days turnaround on the sale. During August, Human Rights Officers (our targets) return to school. We expect most of the cash from this tape to be received by June 95.

2. Cash receipts for the Metro Area Community Center as follows:

Down payment in August 94:	1000
Payment in October 94:	1000
Final payment December 94:	1500
Total Contract:	3500 MACC intends to market the tape themselves.

3. Cash receipts for Elementary Tape sold in Minnesota

Telephone calls in August and September 94, and brochures sent in September will stimulate sales. Pre-production cash receipts are estimated at 13 tapes each in October, November and December. At $75 per unit, the cash receipts for the last quarter of 94 are $2,925. The balance of the cash receipts for this tape will be in Spring and Fall 95. We expect this to be 217 units during 1995. Total revenue for this tape is expected to be $19,200.

4. Cash receipts for Elementary Tape to be sold in Wisconsin and California

Similar to the Minnesota Elementary Tape, telephone calls and brochures mailed to Wisconsin in October will attract pre-production cash receipts estimated at 7 units at $75 for each of October, November and December 94. Total revenue for Wisconsin Elementary tape sales is expected to be $20,550.

The Elementary Tape is expected to produce $48,000 in California during 1995 and 1996.

5. Cash receipts for National "A Matter of Respect" to be sold in Wisconsin and California Following the pattern of soliciting pre-production deposits, this tape is expected to gather cash for October through December at 7 units per months in Wisconsin. This tape retails for $99 plus $1.50 shipping and handling, and will sell throughout 1995 as well as 1996. Total revenue for Wisconsin is expected to be $27,537.

We will begin marketing tapes in the one thousand California school districts in spring 1995, and will sell through 1996.
        1995 sales-320 units @ $100.50=$32,160
        1996 sales-320 units @ $100.50=$32,160   Total: $64,320

Cash Receipts

Disbursements

1. During 1994, the partners will withdraw minimum amounts from the business. Dedria will receive 50 percent of the amount designated for draws: Kevin and Andrea will each receive 25 percent of the designated amount.

In 1995 and 1996, each partner will receive one-third of the $57,600 designated for draws each year.

2. Video equipment rental will be paid to Andrea at the rate of $50 per month. This will provide for us the use of her equipment for copying and editing of the tapes.

3. Payments to each of the six writers' are calculated at the rate of $1.13 per tape sold up to a maximum of 500 tapes. Writers will be paid quarterly beginning in September, 1995. This agreement applies to the Minnesota elementary tape and serves as a model for future agreements with outside script writers.

4. We plan to hire a Shipping Clerk/Receptionist in November 1994 for ten hours per week at the rate of $5.00 per hour. Hours will be increased to 40 hours per week in 1995.

5. The Assistant Script Writer will be hired at $8.00 per hour for ten hours per week.

Summary of Tape Labor/Production Costs

Labor Production Costs: 1994

Elementary Tape	1200	970
JACC	300	200
Total 1994 Costs	1500	1170

Labor Production Costs: 1995

Elementary Tape	0	180
National "A Matter of Respect"	800	1200
Total 1995 Costs	800	1380

Elementary Tape

1994/95	Aug	Sept	Oct	Nov	Dec	Jan	Feb	Totals
Labor								
Cameraman			200	200	200			
Audio & grips			200	200	200			
Total Labor Costs	0	0	400	400	400			1200
Production Costs								
Equipment rental			50	50	50	50	50	
Music					200			
Materials			100	100				
Special Effects					300			
Miscellaneous Expense			40	40	40	40	40	
Total Production Costs	0	0	190	190	590	90	90	1150
Total Costs								$2,350

1994	Oct
Labor Costs	300
Production Costs	200
Total Costs	$500

Jackson Community
Center Tape

1995	Aug	Sept	Oct	Nov	Dec	Total
Labor						
Cameraman			200	200		
Audio & grips			200	200		
Total Labor Costs	0	0	400	400		800
Production Costs						
Equipment rental		83	167			
Music			200			
Materials		200				
Special Effects			300			
Miscellaneous Expense		125	125			
Total Production Costs	0	408	792	0	0	1200
Total Costs						$2,000

National "A Matter
of Respect" Tape

For Years Ending December 31: 1994, 1995, and 1996

Projected Balance Sheet

	August 1994	December 1994	December 1995	December 1996
Assets				
Current Assets				
Cash	1487	6499	21422	14449
Total Current Assets	1487	6499	21422	14449
Fixed Assets				
Office Equipment	98	98	98	98
Total Assets	1585	6597	21520	14547
Liabilities and Net Worth				
Loan Payable	1291	851	0	0
Total Liabilities	1291	851		
Dedria Johnson, Capital	98	666	5924	3599
Andrea Sheldon, Capital	98	2540	7798	5474
Kevin Hill, Capital	98	2540	7798	5474
Total Liabilities and Equity	1585	6597	21520	14547

Additional Information about the Projected Balance Sheet

1. Office equipment includes a desk, two 8-foot tables, chairs, file cabinet. We would like to invest in a 486-type computer and some additional video production equipment in the future.
2. Loan Payable to lender is repayment of a loan to start production of "A Matter of Respect."
3. Capital Account Summaries

Dedria Johnson		
	Beginning Balance	$98
	1994 Profit (one-third)	4317
	Less 1994 Draws	3750
	Total	$665

Andrea Sheldon		
	Beginning Balance	$98
	1994 Profit (one-Third)	4317
	Less 1994 Draws	1875
	Total	$2540

Kevin Hill		
	Beginning Balance	$98
	1994 Profit (one-third)	4317
	Less 1994 Draws	1875
	Total	$2540

Each partner will receive one-third of the profits over the lifetime of the partnership; however, in 1994, Dedria Johnson will receive 50 percent of dolls designated for draws since she is devoting a greater amount of her time to the start-up of the business.

APPENDICES

Job Description: Andrea Sheldon

1. Supervise videotape shooting and production.
   a. Procure talent with Dedria and Kevin.
   b. Supervise staff to schedule shoots.
   c. Supervise/assist with gripping.
   d. Edit tapes with Dedria and Kevin.
   e. Supervise/coordinate copying of videotapes.
   f. Secure talent releases.
2. Responsible for marketing as member of marketing team.
   a. Develop marketing strategies with Dedria and Kevin.
   b. Assist with development of production materials.
   c. With Dedria and Kevin, make phone calls and perform/supervise mailings.
3. Responsible for personnel decisions as member of personnel team.
   a. Create and place advertisement for office and other staff.
   b. With Dedria and Kevin interview candidates and make hiring/firing decisions.
4. Responsible for inventory and ordering.
5. Responsible for billing for videography services.
6. Responsible for physical plant issues.
   a. Equipment installation.
   b. Rental contracts.

c. Appliance/equipment research and purchasing.

d. Furniture/research and purchasing.

1. Responsible for all written materials.
    a. Supervise script and publication writers/production staff.
    b. Produce promotional materials.
2. Coordinate script authors.
    a. Procure authors.
    b. Facilitate scripting groups or procure facilitator.
    c. Draft scripts with staff writers.
3. Assist with video shooting and production.
    a. Procure talent and other personnel with Andrea and Kevin.
    b. Schedule auditions and other shoot-related meetings.
    c. Assist with scheduling shoots.
    d. Secure permission/keys/etc for shoot sites.
    e. Assist with gripping.
    f. Edit tapes with Andrea and Kevin.
4. Develop new videotape projects.
    a. Solicit ideas from school workers and other youth program workers.
    b. Develop worker contracts with Kevin's assistance.
    c. With Andrea and Kevin, help maintain positive communications with schools and communities by participation and service.
5. Responsible for marketing as member of marketing team.
    a. Develop marketing strategies with Andrea and Kevin.
    b. Produce promotional materials.
    c. With Andrea and Kevin, make phone calls and perform/supervise mailings.
6. Responsible for personnel decisions as member of personnel team.
    a. Create and place advertisements for office and other staff.
    b. With Andrea and Kevin, interview candidates and make hiring/firing decisions.
    c. Supervise office staff (i.e. time cards, reporting).
7. Member of Management Team.
    a. Responsible for calling meetings as needed.
    b. Establish agenda for meetings.

1. Responsible for accounting and financial controls for the partnership
    a. Set up accounting system and install computerized accounting program. Maintain this system.
    b. Prepare all bookkeeping entries and prepare monthly finance reports.
    c. Track cash flow.
    d. Track and report on receivables, payables and costs.
    e. Prepare all local, state and federal tax reports.
    f. Contribute to purchasing of supplies, materials and other services.
2. Contribute to preparation of Articles of Co-Partnership.
3. Marketing of Videotapes.
    a. Contribute to creation of sales structure, which includes customer contact, follow-up, close of sale, and customer feedback after sale.
    b. Contribute to creation of database of customers for use in subsequent video productions.

**Articles of
Co-Partnership**

This Contract made and entered into this first day of June, 1994, between Andrea Sheldon of Lake Neawtawaka, Wisconsin, Dedria Johnson of Upper Sentinel, Wisconsin, and Kevin Hill of Brendan, Minnesota.

Witnesseth:

One. The parties, Andrea Sheldon, Dedria Johnson, and Kevin Hill agree to become partners in the video production and distribution business.

Two. The business of the partnership shall be conducted under the name of Dynamic Video, currently at 123 North Main Street, Northville, Wisconsin.

Three. The partnership shall begin on June 1, 1994, and shall continue for an indefinite period.

Four. Each partner shall contribute to the capital of the partnership the sum of ninety-eight dollars ($98.00). This sum shall be without interest.

Five. All profits resulting from the business shall be divided equally between the partners and all losses incurred by the business also shall be borne equally by them.

Six. Proper books of account shall be kept of all transactions relating to the business of the partnership.
At the end of each calendar year, a statement of the business made; the books closed; and the account of each partner credited or debited, as the case may be, with his proportionate share of the net income of loss. A statement of the business may be made to such other times as the partners agree on.

Seven. Each month, each partner may withdraw from the business, for his own use, a sum not exceeding the amounts listed below:

	Dedria	Andrea	Kevin
September 1994	$750	$375	$375
October 1994	1000	500	500
November 1994	1000	500	500
December 1994	1000	500	500
Jan. 1995 and after	1600	1600	1600

The distribution of additional profits will be determined as the need arises.

Eight. All three partners must agree on major purchases, contracts, hiring/firing employees.

Nine. At the termination of this partnership, a full inventory and balance sheet shall be prepared; the debts of the business shall be discharged; and all property then remaining shall be divided equally between the partners.

Ten. During the operations of this partnership, no partner is to become surety or bondsman for anyone without the written consent of the other partners.

Eleven. No partner is to withdraw assets in excess of his salary, any part of the assets invested, or assets in anticipation of net income to be earned, without the written consent of the other partners.

Twelve. In the case of the death or the legal disability of any partner, the other partners will continue the operations of the business until the close of the annual fiscal period on the following December 31. At that time the continuing partners are to be given an option to buy the interest of the departed partner at not more than the departed partner's proprietary interest as shown by the balance of his capital account after the books are closed on December 31. This purchase price is to be paid in four equal installments, payable quarterly.

In Witness Whereof, the parties have hereunto set their hands and seals on the day and year above written.

**Articles of
Co-Partnership**
...continued

Media Producer*

BUSINESS PLAN

DYNAMIC VIDEO

3470 University Blvd., Ste. 117
Bridgeport, MN 27810

Revised June 1995

This revised business plan reflects adjustments in the strategy that Dynamic Video employs due to several major changes in the business. Look for sections detailing changes in perspective and personnel and the impact these had on projects underway. The original plan appears previous to this one.

●A GREAT ATMOSPHERE HELPS MAKE IT EASY

●WE'VE HAD SOME SUCCESS

●WE'RE INCORPORATED

●WE FOUND NEW TALENT

●JOB DESCRIPTIONS MATTER

●HOCUS POCUS, WE GOT NEW FOCUS

●A CHANGE IN PERSONNEL

●THE LEAVING PARTNER

●OUR CURRENT PROJECTS

●RESOURCES OLD AND NEW

●EXPLANATIONS OF REVENUE AND EXPENSE ESTIMATES FOR 1995

●ARTICLES OF INCORPORATION

●JOB DESCRIPTIONS

Dynamic Video: The changes we have gone through since our first Business Plan.

A GREAT ATMOSPHERE HELPS MAKE IT EASY

We have discovered the enjoyment of working in the Incubation Center on the UMS Campus. It's a pleasure to come to work thanks to a very supportive atmosphere. Another positive feature is that Andrea and Kevin no longer work out of separate offices--ideas are shared and business is conducted together under one roof!

WE'VE HAD SOME SUCCESS

We've covered the cost of operations, through sales, in 1994. Important alliances were created with others in education, in business and in the video industry. These assets add promise for a profitable and rewarding 1995.

WE'RE INCORPORATED

Effective January 1, 1995, we are incorporated in the State of Minnesota. Andrea Sheldon has been elected President of the company, and Kevin Hill is Secretary/Treasurer. Andrea has also been elected Chair of the Board of Directors. Kevin Hill is another Board member. Copies of the filed Articles of Incorporation and the Bylaws of the Corporation are attached. All appropriate Federal and State tax identification numbers have been applied for.

WE FOUND NEW TALENT

At a time when we needed a writer, we contracted with Dean Carter to finish writing one of our elementary scripts. We are very fortunate to have him work with us. Dean is a videographer, and he is also able to write specifically for video projects. He has good crossover abilities between writing for paper and writing for video. Knowledge and acceptance of this difference is important to our business.

Dean completed our script in a short time, and it is ready to be broken down into a shooting script for video production. Dean has agreed to work with us as an independent contractor on current and future projects. We do not expect him to become involved in the ownership of the company.

JOB DESCRIPTIONS MATTER

Andrea and Kevin learned the importance of job descriptions. Much of what the partners did for the partnership loosely followed our written format. Vague assumptions and confusion arose from the lack of adherence to the written standards. We are currently defining our roles in the corporation, and putting those ideas into a set of useable job descriptions.

HOCUS POCUS, WE GOT NEW FOCUS

A most important change comes in the form of a revised Mission Statement: "Our mission is to produce and sell informational and educational videotapes for schools and businesses in the United States and abroad."

We found that we were on the right track. We discovered that our work with the schools held important financial value for us, as well as social benefits for us and others. However, we also noted that our company needed sound financial footing that could only be achieved through work with educational and business sources. In this early stage of our growth, the schools alone could not support our fiscal needs. Some partners perceived the complete reliance on the education field as being too limiting and a potential hazard for our company.

As a corporation, we recognize the need to work with business and industry as well as with the educational groups and will continue to do so.

A CHANGE IN PERSONNEL

We do not include Dedria Johnson in this updated Business Plan. She announced her intention to leave the partnership Dynamic Video on December 13, 1994. Dedria is not involved in any way in the ownership or operation of Dynamic Video.

The partnership is to be dissolved effective December 31, 1994. Lewis Peterson, of the law firm MacGregor, Campbell, and Watson, has worked with Andrea and Kevin to prepare the partnership dissolution agreement. A draft of this agreement is currently being negotiated with Dedria.

In step with this change, Andrea and Kevin prepared for the Incubation Center a letter of intent to continue in business.

This Business Plan reflects the several assumptions by the management of Dynamic Video. We believe the corporation will end up with full ownership of current video projects, and Dedria will accept royalty payments on certain projects she worked on for the partnership.

In the event Dedria does not relinquish her share of control of these assets, Dynamic Video is prepared to move forward with alternative plans.

THE LEAVING PARTNER

Dedria produced monthly newsletters for various school districts, which severely limited the amount of time she had available to write the script for our important elementary videotape. Production of the script fell behind schedule, as did work on the Metro Area Community Center (MACC) tape. While video work progressed in jumps and starts, conflicts arose as to how other partnership decisions should be made. Despite a lack of business skills and video production background, Dedria insisted she be considered the final voice in partnership decisions. This unacceptable ultimatum led to the dissolution process.

During this period, the three partners met as a group many times to address this lack of consensus. Our contacts at the Business Incubator were consulted by the group in efforts to clear up this matter. As noted above, the results of these efforts would lead to dissolution.

OUR CURRENT PROJECTS

JACC

We are in the final stages of the JACC tape. Andrea estimates it will take about a week's editing to finish. We intend to deliver the tape before the end of January 1995, and be paid the $1500 balance by February 17. The partnership dissolution will not affect this outcome. Andrea and Kevin want to continue to be in good standing with the education community, and Dedria feels compelled to complete this job as she works with JACC personnel on a regular basis.

**"A Matter of Respect"
(Minnesota)**

This is the tape that started the whole thing rolling. In 1993, eleven tapes were sold. In the calendar year ended December 31, 1994, ninety tapes were sold. Fifty-three tapes are currently being previewed by school districts in Minnesota. The disposition of these tapes will become known in January and February 1995. Each school district varies as to how quickly it views a tape, and subsequently sends payment (or returns the tape.)

During the year Andrea and Kevin marketed the tape via telephone contact with Human Resource Officers in Minnesota school districts. Office telephone logs indicate approximately forty yet to be contacted. As demand for this tape in Minnesota high schools winds down, several issues become apparent:

There is obviously a need for this type of product in schools; thus, we have plans to develop a tape for nationwide coverage

Many of the sexual harassment officers we contacted requested quick delivery of elementary-age versions of the tape

Some college contacts have indicated interest in this tape for women's issues curriculum. We have yet to try this idea.

A sale to the Local Area Juvenile Center perhaps could lead to additional juvenile center sales.

**English as a Second
Language Videotapes**

Dynamic Video has entered into an agreement with Alyshia Cavanaugh of Forward Inc. as equal partners to produce a series of videotapes and written curriculum to teach English as spoken in the United States. Demand is high for tapes that do not involve British English. The initial market areas for these tapes are the southern U.S. and Argentina.

These tapes will feature how holidays such as Christmas and the Fourth of July are celebrated in the U.S. The first of these tapes, based on an American Christmas, is currently being scripted by Alyshia and her staff, and DV has shot most of the scenes needed. Our target completion date is June 1995. We are in the process of researching distribution companies for those products.

Gambling Videotape

Wisconsin Council on compulsive Gambling, Inc., in Duluth has recently contacted us about producing a videotape for their use in Minnesota schools. We will be meeting with this group at the end of January to discuss their needs.

**Highway Safety
Videotapes**

Andrea was contacted by Benny Jansen of the Institute of Driver Behavior to help market a videotape curriculum to truck driving schools and over-the-road freight lines. Benny has many years experience as a truck driver and as a truck safety expert. He is frequently called as an expert witness in suits involving truck and traffic accidents. He invented a method of teaching safe driving habits to stressed drivers.

Benny has produced a series of sixteen high quality videotapes and accompanying written tests which Dynamic Video has begun selling nationwide. Four tapes are directed at experienced truck drivers, as a refresher. The topics are presented in an interesting and memorable format.

A set of twelve tapes are geared for inexperienced drivers. The topics range from proper backing techniques to safeguarding the right side of your rig in traffic.

Andrea and Kevin contact safety directors at trucking companies listed in the AT&T 800 directory. The set of four "experience tapes" and test materials are sent out for a preview. DV boxes and ships tapes and tracks them via a computer program. Any subsequent follow up calls are made by DV.

The sale price of the tapes is $50.00 each. If the trucking company purchases the tapes, DV receives a 40 percent commission. Benny provides the ready-to-mail videotape sets and the written materials. DV pays for the shipping and invoicing costs.

Elementary School Sexual Harassment Videotape

This two-tape set will be marketed nationwide in elementary schools. This tape has the potential to produce a large amount of revenue, as school demand is high and there are few elementary sexual harassment tapes available. The tapes are intended for student audiences which range from kindergarten through sixth grade. For this reason, the first tape in the set covers K through 2, the second tape 3 through 6. One of the scripts has been completed by Dean Carter and is ready to take into the field to shoot. The other script is not finished.

In the event that the two-tape elementary scripts become a point of contention in the partnership dissolution, DV will continue with production of an elementary tape with a new script. Dean has known about the concept of the elementary tape from its earliest stages, and he is prepared to write a script for an elementary sexual harassment tape that would not be a duplicate of the first two-tape set mentioned above. Using Dean's new script, we believe that our spring completion date for the tape would still be feasible.

National Sexual Harassment Videotape

Very little of the original "A Matter of Respect" can be used in the creation of a tape with national sales potential. Again, Dean Carter has expressed interest in creating a script for this topic. DV has not set a schedule for this tape.

RESOURCES OLD AND NEW

We continue to rely on the Incubator staff for help in the myriad workings of our company. They are invaluable.

Recently, Andrea and Kevin took time out to introduce themselves to a representative at National Bank. We discussed our incorporation and the zero-interest loan that is available to us. It is likely that we will access that financial tool to upgrade DV's video camera equipment.

Along with the valuable contacts we've made through the Incubator Center, we've kept ties with previous business associates. From this pool of professionals, we have access to a tremendous support network.

EXPLANATIONS OF REVENUE AND EXPENSE ESTIMATES FOR 1995

Please refer to the following Projected Cash Flow Budget, Projected Income Statement and Projected Balance Sheet for 1995.

"A Matter of Respect" Videotape

We currently have 53 tapes out on preview and approximately 40 districts yet to contact. We estimate 40 of the outstanding 93 will become revenue in the first quarter of 1995. Based on past experience, we believe that revenue will be received at the rate of approximately 13 tapes per month for the first quarter of 1995.

Sales for May through December represent occasional school interest in this tape. Potential sales to juvenile centers in Minnesota and to women's issues curriculums in colleges are not included in these projects.

Trucking and Highway Safety Videotape

The January revenue entry of $480 represents the cash received on three sales of the "4 experienced driver tapes," and an additional sale to one of those companies that ordered the set of "12 training tapes for inexperienced drivers." These tapes were sent out for preview during November and December 1994. The February entry of $1600 indicates receipts for twenty sets of tapes previewed in December and January. During January, we will send out 80 sets of previews to truck companies. We estimate that a minimum of twenty companies will purchase the tapes in February. We currently have no data on the preview-to-sales ratio.

During January and February we intend to find the preview-to-sales ratio that will result in the sales of fifteen "experienced" tape sets per week. This will not include sales of the 12 "inexperienced" tapes. Sales at this level will require a great deal of telephone activity and likely will entail the addition of a person familiar with this type of marketing. The inventory, storage, shipment and tracking details for this project are in place.

The largest expense in this project involves the cost of shipping these tapes by UPS. Other expenses include an hourly worker (with taxes) and marketing costs for materials such as tape and boxes. Use of 800 numbers to access customers will keep telephone costs at a minimum. No other methods will be used to market these products.

The Elementary School Sexual Harassment Videotape (National K-6)

This tape is scheduled for production during the first quarter of 1995 and will sell for $75 each. Initially, brochures mailed in March will create interest, and we conservatively estimate sales at ten tapes per month in May and June. Sales for the last quarter are estimated at 20 units per month. We believe these revenue estimates are low.

Initially, we may do our own marketing of this tape in Minnesota and Wisconsin, using the many contacts made through "A Matter of Respect." Summer and early fall are typically difficult times to reach our school prospects. During this period, we will contact distribution companies which have the ability to market this tape nationally. The expenses Writing--Carter, Production Costs K-6, and Marketing pertain to this vide.

In the event Dedria receives the rights to this project, we will have Dean create a new script and we will produce our version of this tape. Our income and expense estimates would not change appreciably.

Our responsibility in this venture is to produce the scenes called for in Forward's curriculum. Our exposure is limited to $500 against high potential gains. We estimate sales at $500 per month.

We have begun research in an effort to group the 50 states according to enforcement of harassment laws in schools. For example, Minnesota and California would be together at one end of the spectrum, and Mississippi and Alabama would be at the other. Our videotape script would be generic to a point, with a section tailored to suit a group of states. There would be 4 or 5 of these special sections available to tag onto the main part of the tape. Revenue is estimated at $75 per tape and sales of 20 per month. Production costs would be $3000.

Payments made to Dedria Johnson are estimated at $1380 for the year; we do not know how the partnership dissolution will finally turn out.

We likely will access the no-interest loan and purchase $5000 in video production equipment.

The English as a Second Language Videotape

The National 7-12 Videotape

Other Notes

PROJECTED CASH FLOW BUDGET FOR DYNAMIC VIDEO 1995

	4	4	5	4	4	5	4	4	5	4	4	5			
	Jan	Feb	Mar	Apr	May	Jun	Jul	Aug	Sep	Oct	Nov	Dec	1995	1996	1997
Cash Balance Beginning															
	2500	1168	1199	4152	2317	502	3207	4742	6627	11132	15867	20764	2500	27401	34305
Revenue--Matter of Respect															
	1308	1308	1308	100	100	100	100	100	100	100	100	100	4824		
Revenue--Truck tapes															
	480	1600	6000	4800	4800	6000	4800	4800	6000	4800	4800	6000	54880	57600	57600
Revenue--JACC															
		1500											1500	0	0
Revenue--ESL									500	500	500	500	500	2500	6000	6000
Revenue--National K-6				750	750	300	150	150	1500	1500	1500	6600	18000	18000
Revenue--National 7-12								1500	1500	1500	1500	6000	18000	18000
Total Cash Available															
	4288	5576	8507	9052	7967	7352	8407	10292	14877	19532	24267	30364	78804	127001	133905
Less Disbursements:															
Officers Salaries															
	1500	1500	1500	1500	1500	1500	1500	1500	1500	1500	1500	1500	18000	54000	54000
Employee wages															
	0	0	0	300	300	300	300	300	300	300	300	300	2700	3600	3600
Health Insurance															
	0	0	0	300	300	300	300	300	300	300	300	300	2700	3600	3600
Payroll taxes @ 10%															
	150	150	150	180	180	180	180	180	180	180	180	180	2070	5760	5760
Computer payments															
	162	162	162	162	162	162	162	162	162	162	0	0	1620	0	0
Telephone expense															
	150	145	150	150	150	150	150	150	150	150	150	150	1795	1800	1800
Office rent															
	203	203	203	203	203	203	203	203	203	203	203	203	2436	2436	2436
Office expense															
	25	50	50	50	50	50	50	50	50	50	50	50	575	600	600
Travel & Entertainment															
	0	0	0	50	50	50	50	50	50	5050	50	450	600	600	
Loan pmt vid eq															
	150	150	150	150	150	150	150	150	150	150	1500	3500	0		
Video equip rental															
	50	50	50	50	50	50	50	50	50	50	50	50	600	600	600
Loan pay															
	0	0	0	780	0	0	0	0	0	0	0	780	0	0	
Writing--Carter															
	200	300	0	0	0	0	0	0	0	0	0	0	500	2400	2400

	4	4	5	4	4	5	4	4	5	4	4	5			
	Jan	Feb	Mar	Apr	May	Jun	Jul	Aug	Sep	Oct	Nov	Dec	995	1996	1997
UPS-truck tapes															
	680	800	400	320	320	400	320	320	400	320	320	400	000	7200	7200
Attorney fees															
	0	100	100	100	0	0	0	0	0	0	0	0	300	1200	1200
Production costs 7-12															
	0	0	0	0	0	0	0	0	0	0	0	0	0	3000	0
Production costs K-6															
	0	150	300	1500	3500	150	0	0	0	0	0	0	600	0	0
Marketing-trucks															
	0	167	500	100	100	100	100	100	100	100	100	100	567	1200	1200
Marketing National K-6															
	0	0	0	200	200	150	150	150	150	150	150	150	450	1200	1200
Dedria Johnson payments															
	0	600	390	390	0	0	0	0	0	0	0	0	380	0	0
Additional tape															
	0	0	250	250	250	250	0	0	0	0	0	0	000	0	0
Total Disbursements															
	3120	4377	4355	6735	7465	4145	3665	3665	3745	3665	3503	3583	023	92696	86196
Cash Surplus (DEF)															
	1168	1199	4152	2317	502	3207	4742	6627	11132	15867	20764	26781	781	34305	47709
Bank Loan Required															
Cash Balance Ending															
	1168	1199	4152	2317	502	3207	4742	6627	11132	15867	20764	26781	781	34305	47709

PROJECTED INCOME STATEMENT FOR DYNAMIC VIDEO 1995

	4	4	5	4	4	5	4	4	5	4	4	5			
	Jan	Feb	Mar	Apr	May	Jun	Jul	Aug	Sep	Oct	Nov	Dec	1995	1996	1997
Revenue															
Revenue--Matter of Respect															
	1308	1308	1308	100	100	100	100	100	100	100	100	100	4824	0	0
Revenue--Truck tapes															
	480	1600	6000	4800	4800	6000	4800	4800	6000	4800	4800	6000	54880	57600	57600
Revenue--JACC															
		1500											1500	0	0
Revenue--ESL								500	500	500	500	500	2500	6000	6000
Revenue--National K-6				750	750	300	150	150	1500	1500	1500		6600	18000	18000
Revenue--National 7-12								1500	1500	1500	1500		6000	18000	18000
Total Revenue															
	1788	4408	7308	4900	5650	6850	5200	5550	8250	8400	8400	9600	76304	99600	99600
Less Expenses															
Officers Salaries															
	1500	1500	1500	1500	1500	1500	1500	1500	1500	1500	1500	1500	18000	54000	54000
Employee wages															
	0	0	0	300	300	300	300	300	300	300	300	300	2700	3600	3600
Health Insurance															
	0	0	0	300	300	300	300	300	300	300	300	300	2700	3600	3600
Payroll taxes @ 10%															
	150	150	150	180	180	180	180	180	180	180	180	180	2070	5760	5760
Telephone expense															
	150	145	150	150	150	150	150	150	150	150	150	150	1795	1800	1800
Office rent															
	203	203	203	203	203	203	203	203	203	203	203	203	2436	3600	3600
Office supplies															
	25	50	50	50	50	50	50	50	50	50	50	50	575	600	600
Travel & Entertainment															
	0	0	0	50	50	50	50	50	50	50	50	50	450	600	600
Video equipment rental															
	50	50	50	50	50	50	50	50	50	50	50	50	600	600	600
Interest expense															
	0	0	20	0	0	0	0	0	0	0	0	0	20	100	100
Writing-Carter															
	200	300	0	0	0	0	0	0	0	0	0	0	500	2400	2400

PROJECTED INCOME STATEMENT FOR DYNAMIC VIDEO 1995

...continued

	Jan	Feb	Mar	Apr	May	Jun	Jul	Aug	Sep	Oct	Nov	Dec	1995	1996	1997
	4	4	5	4	4	5	4	4	5	4	4	5			
UPS-truck tapes	680	800	400	320	320	400	320	320	400	320	320	400	5000	7200	7200
Attorney fees	0	100	100	100	0	0	0	0	0	0	0	0	300	1000	1000
Production costs K-6	0	150	300	1500	3500	150	0	0	0	0	0	0	5600	0	0
Production costs 7-12	0	0	0	0	0	0	0	0	0	0	0	0	0	3000	0
Marketing-trucks	0	167	500	100	100	100	100	100	100	100	100	100	1567	1200	1200
Marketing--National K-6	0	0	0	200	200	150	150	150	150	150	150	150	1450	1200	1200
Dedria Johnson payments	0	600	390	390	0	0	0	0	0	0	0	0	1380	0	0
Insurance-Office	25	25	25	25	25	25	25	25	25	25	25	25	300	500	500
Total Expenses	2983	4240	3838	5418	6928	3608	3378	3458	3378	3458			47443	90760	88760
Net Income (Loss)	-1195	168	3470	-518	-1278	3242	1822	2172	4792	5022	5022	6142	28861	8840	11840

Projected Balance Sheet for Dynamic Video January 1, 1995 and December 31, 1995

1/1/95 12/31/95

Assets

		1/1/95	12/31/95
	Cash	2500	28901
	Equipment	2249	7249
	Other assets	317	500
Total		5066	36650

Liabilities

	Payables	2185	4283
	Computer	1615	0
	Video Camera		3500
Total Liabilities		3800	7783
Stockholders' Equity		1266	28867
Total Liabilities and Stockholders Equity		5066	36650

Balance Sheet As of 12/31/94

Account	Account Name	Detail Acct
11011	Petty Cash	15.00
11012	Training Account	30.00
11021	Checking Account	2582.50
11051	Accounts Receiv. Module	5125.50
11052	Allow. For Doubtful Acct.	-5326.50
11061	Dedria's Newsletter Exp.	0.00
12021	Office Eq-Original Value	311.00
12041	Computer-Original Value	1938.00
13011	Leasehold Improvement	30.00
13021	Original Value Inc Fee	0.00
13031	Insurance	175.00
14012	Lease Deposit	185.58
	Total Assets	5066.08

Account	Account Name	Detail Acct		**Balance Sheet II**
				As of 12/31/94
2101	Accounts Payable Module	1447.10		
2102	Notes Payable	737.48		
21031	Note Payable--Computer	1615.00		
	Total Liabilities	3799.58		
31011	D. Johnson-Investment	-675.46		
31012	D. Johnson-Withdrawals	-650.62		
31021	A. Sheldon-Investment	-675.47		
31022	A. Sheldon-Withdrawal	-765.66		
31031	K. Hill-Investment	575.00		
31033	K. Hill-Withdrawal	-465.67		
	Current Year Earnings	3924.38		
	Total Equity	1266.50		
	Total Liabilities plus Equity	5066.08		

Account	Account Name	This Period General Acct Detail Acct	Year to Date General Acct Detail Acct	**Income Statement** From 1/1/94 to 12/31/94
4101	Sales Matt. Resp	2376.00	21505.70	
41012	Respect Previews Out	-402.00	-5326.50	
4103	Sales-JACC	0.00	2000.00	
4201	Returns Respect	-693.00	-7426.50	
4301	Shipping Revenue Respect	25.50	142.50	
4403	Dividends	6.13	25.00	
4503	Miscellaneous Revenues	0.00	1000.00	
	Total Revenue	1312.63	11920.20	
5101	COGS Matt. Resp	1000.00	2249.36	
5102	COGS-Elementary	207.10	693.37	
5103	COGS-JACC	235.00	570.00	
52024	Equipment Maintenance	0.00	48.00	
52053	Office Lease	185.58	628.70	
52054	Video Eq. Lease	60.00	160.00	
52062	General Business Ins.	50.00	125.00	
52072	Transportation	0.00	8.85	
52073	Conference--General	0.00	44.22	
52091	Sales Tax/Purchases	17.76	17.76	
52102	Accountants	368.75	568.75	

**Income Statement
From 1/1/94 to 12/31/94**
...continued

52103	Legal	240.00	280.00
52111	Office Supplies	56.89	567.05
52112	Telephone & Telegraph	0.00	226.21
52119	Office Equipment	0.00	163.99
5212	Miscellaneous Expenses	59.99	109.99
5302	Interest	-104.17	20.49
5303	Bank Charges	0.00	27.00
55011	Conference-Respect	0.00	238.67
55012	Shipping Out-Respect	12.97	409.69
55013	Telephone-Respect	0.00	474.51
55016	Interest Expense-Respect	128.18	128.18
55021	Conference-Elem	200.00	206.49
55024	Supplies-Elem	0.00	29.54
	Total Expenses	2718.05	7995.82
	Net Income	-1405.42	3924.38

ARTICLES OF INCORPORATION

Written Action in Lieu of
Organizational Meeting of the Board of
Directors of Dynamic Video

The undersigned being all of the Directors named in the Articles of Incorporation of Dynamic Video, a Corporation organized under the laws of Minnesota, Chapter 180, hereby adopts and consents to the following resolutions necessary or appropriate to complete the organization of the Corporation.

Resolved, that the Articles of Incorporation as filed with the Secretary of State be and are hereby accepted and approved and that said Articles of Incorporation, together with the original receipt showing payment of the statutory organization taxes and filing fee be placed in the Minute Book of the Corporation.

Resolved, that the Bylaws in the form of Exhibit A attached (not available for publication) hereto are approved and adopted as the Bylaws of the Corporation.

Resolved, that the Board of Directors on behalf of the Corporation hereby ratifies, approves, confirms, and adopts all action taken by the Incorporator prior to the formation of this Corporation. The Corporation shall hereafter be bound by the activities of the Incorporator and shall accept the benefit of all agreements, arrangements, negotiations, and contracts, which have been negotiated on behalf of the Corporation, by the Incorporator.

Resolved, that the following persons are elected to the offices set forth opposite their names to serve until their successors are elected and qualified:

Andrea Sheldon, President
Kevin Hill, Secretary/Treasurer

Resolved, that the Corporation shall not have a corporate seal.

Resolved, that the stock certificate in the form of Exhibit B attached (not available for publication) hereto is approved and adopted as the common stock certificate for the Corporation.

Resolved, that the fiscal year of the Corporation shall be the calendar year.

Resolved, that the Corporation through its President and Secretary is authorized and directed to issue One Hundred (100) shares of common stock of the Corporation (which stock shall be issued as IRC Section 1244 stock) to Andrea Sheldon in consideration of the payment by Andrea Sheldon of Two Hundred Fifty dollars and 00/100 ($250.00).

Resolved, that the Corporation through its President and Secretary is authorized and directed to issue One Hundred (100) shares of common stock of the Corporation (which stock shall be issued as IRC Section 1244 stock) to Kevin Hill in consideration of payment by Kevin Hill of Two Hundred Fifty dollars and 00/100 ($250.00).

Resolved, that the officers of the corporation are authorized and directed to procure all corporation books required necessary in connection with the business of the corporation and are further authorized and directed to pay all fees and expenses incident to and necessary for the organization of the corporation and to reimburse those persons who have advanced said fees and expenses on behalf of the corporation.

Resolved, that the funds of the Corporation be deposited in National Bank.

Resolved, that the officers of the Corporation be authorized and directed to qualify the Corporation as a foreign corporation and in connection therewith to appoint all necessary agents in other states and such other attorneys for service of process and to take all other action which may be deemed necessary or advisable to qualify the Corporation as a foreign corporation.

When signed by the Directors named in the Articles of Incorporation the Resolutions contained in here shall be effective as of the 2nd day of January, 1995.

Andrea Sheldon (Signature) _____

Kevin Hill (Signature) _____

Being all of the Directors named in the Articles of Incorporation

JOB DESCRIPTIONS

Andrea Sheldon

- Videotape Production
- Maintain and increase network of video industry contacts
- Note changes in video production technology and how those changes affect DV
- On a specific project: make sure script is ready to be shot; secure talent, equipment and crew

Kevin Hill

- Accounting and financial controls
- Maintain and increase network of business contacts
- Set up system to ship and track tapes

Shared Duties

- Marketing of products
- Research and Development of video project ideas
- Prioritization of current and future projects
- Agreement on purchase of major assets
- Periodically discuss and review sales of products
- Employees and subcontractors--interviews, hiring, supervision and releasing

Media Producer

BUSINESS PLAN

SHALIMAR FILMS, LTD.

805 Sugarbush Ln.
Pittsburgh, PA 30215

March 1995

This plan for a television and entertainment programming company demonstrates how partnerships with others in the field can help ensure success in this rapidly moving industry. Coverage includes financing, products, marketing, facilities, management, and other elements of a well-developed plan.

● EXECUTIVE SUMMARY

● THE GENERAL PARTNERS

● DIRECTORS AND ADVISORS

● MARKET ANALYSIS

● BUDGET DETAIL

● CONCLUSIONS/SUMMARY

EXECUTIVE
SUMMARY

Overview

In the rapidly expanding market for home entertainment, quality programming is a valuable commodity. Shalimar Films, Ltd. was formed to produce a broad range of proprietary new products for the Television and Home Entertainment industry. The company is now applying their resources to building a successful television production enterprise based in Pennsylvania.

The General Partners of Shalimar Films have earned a solid reputation in the film and video production industry. Major distributors and program buyers, including but not limited to: Capital Cities/ABC, Time-Life Video, Wood Knapp & Company, QVC, Columbia House, Unapix Entertainment, Doubleday, Book of the Month Club, Saturday Matinee, Library Video, Rivertown Trading, Pentrex Publishing, Baker & Taylor, Ingram, Time Warner, Borders Books, The Learning Smith, Transworld, Music, ATA Trading Corp., and PBS Home Video are marketing and distributing programs produced by Shalimar Films.

Shalimar Films has consistently received favorable reviews for their products from national, regional, and local media such as Entertainment Weekly, Video Business, Video Librarian, Billboard Magazine, The Dolans'—Straight Talk on Your Money, Inventor's Digest, Entrepreneur Magazine, Knight Ridder Newspaper Syndicate, and Newsday.

Programs produced by Shalimar Films have also been featured on national television programs such as The Joan Rivers Show and on Fox Television Network's national cable network, FX.

With its highly qualified management team, marketing resources, and progressive business relationships, Shalimar Films is well-positioned to take full advantage of the industry's phenomenal on-going growth. In order to assure the success of their products Shalimar Films has prudently enlisted the resources and capabilities of major corporations, secured by contractual commitments, to market and distribute their programs to the worldwide marketplace.

The proven track record of the industry, combined with its current evolution and strong positive forecast for future growth, offers significant potential for highly rewarding investment opportunities. The demonstrated expertise and entrepreneurial temperament of Shalimar Films provides an attractive opportunity for investors to profit from a truly innovative emerging growth company with tremendous potential.

Concept

Shalimar Films recently signed several pre-sale distribution and marketing contracts that guarantee distribution of their original programs to Home Entertainment and Television markets worldwide. These contracts have been signed with Capital Cities/ABC, Pentrex Publishing, Unapix Entertainment, Time-Life Video, and ATA Trading Corporation. The programs are based on a variety of popular, interesting, and entertaining topics. Each program is designed to capitalize on prevailing trends that have demonstrated commercial success within the industry.

Negotiations are also in progress with Mega Books for a series of illustrated books based on our original children's television programming. These book versions will feature an audio cassette with narration, sound EFX, and original music in order to provide children with a more unique, entertaining, and interactive product that will enhance their learning experience and enjoyment.

A diverse assortment of original television and home video programs will be developed and produced by Shalimar films in four (4) individual phases. Each phase will result in the completion and delivery of several commercially viable, revenue producing products for worldwide distribution. The diversity and quantity of programs produced in each phase will dramatically reduce risk typically associated with dependency on the success of just one program or genre.

Shalimar Films plans to create a high yield "catalog of products" (consisting of a collection of successful "hit" programs proven to generate high revenues) by combining the most commercially successful programs from earlier phases with the development and production of commercially viable new products in each successive phase. Over a period of time, this "catalog" will primarily consist of the most highly profitable and successful products produced by the company. This approach will offer incredible long term profit potential to equity investors and partners.

The entire project, representative of all phases, consists of approximately ninety (90) original programs to be developed and completed over a period of approximately six (6) years.

Production

The first phase of the project requires production of approximately twelve (12) original programs over a period of approximately twelve (12) months at a total cost of $800,000. The second phase of the project requires production of approximately twenty (20) programs over a period of eighteen (18) months at a cost of $1,700,000. The third phase of the project requires production of approximately twenty-six (26) programs over a period of twenty-four (24) months at a cost of $2,225,000. The final phase of the project requires production of approximately thirty-two (32) programs over a period of thirty (30) months at a cost of $3,500,000.

The company anticipates continued and successful growth well beyond these initial phases. New programs will be funded by "factoring" credit lines, income, and existing capital against distribution contracts for short periods of time. This will allow the company to develop new programming and ancillary products well into the future by continuously cycling cash flow and lines of credit.

Highly successful programs will be produced as an on-going television or video series with advance funding provided by major distributors. Products developed in this manner will serve to provide Shalimar Films with properties (programs) that substantially increase the company's cash value while providing a significant source of additional revenue. The company will also continue to develop new programming in order to provide steady and equity growth in their "catalog."

Objectives

Shalimar Films plans to produce interesting, entertaining, and educational programs on a variety of well-researched topics proven to be commercially viable in the industry. The company only produces those programs guaranteed distribution to a widespread audience through pre-sale contracts with Major Distributors. By spreading the product line across several different worldwide markets, and releasing them through multiple windows of distribution, the Company will effectively minimize risk and increase the potential success for each series of programs they produce. Approximately forty percent (40%) of the programs produced by Shalimar Films are targeted towards the children's television marketplace. Another forty percent (40%) focus on popular subject matter as is targeted for distribution via Broadcast Television and Cable. The remaining twenty percent (20%) of the Company's programming is a mix of special interest and home video programming targeted for distribution via direct to consumer markets as well as the retail and catalog trade.

The management team of Shalimar Films plans to invest a substantial share of the actual cost for creative services as well as a smaller share of the cost for product development and production through reduced fees for creative services, professional services, and production services. The Company has also arranged for their distributors and suppliers to be solely responsible for specific costs as well. In most cases, these costs will include manufacturing, duplication, packaging, warehousing, fulfillment, public relations, advertising, promotion, marketing and distribution of programs developed, produced, and/or sourced by Shalimar Films.

Management

The management team consists of the General Partners, a Board of Directors and a Board of Advisors with over seventy-five (75) years of combined experience in the industry. This experience consists of:

Television Program Development
Television Program Distribution
Television Facility Design
Creative Artist Management
Business Management & Finance
Entertainment Law & Contracts
Direct to Consumer Sales & Marketing
Television Program Production
Television Facility Management
Legal & Business Management
Business Development & Administration
Contract Negotiations & Distribution
Home Entertainment Video Sales & Distribution
Retail, & Catalog Distribution

Marketing

Shalimar Films has a unique relationship with major distributors that provides an in-depth view of the market that informs our management decisions and focuses our creativity. By utilizing the distributors' extensive knowledge and resources, Shalimar Films is able to produce programs that meet consumer demands and have the pre-approved support of a major distribution network.

The fundamental thrust of Shalimar Film's marketing strategy consists of producing only those programs that have already acquired pre-sale agreements, advance payments, and a commitment from distributors to utilize their resources for manufacturing, promotion, marketing and distribution. The reputation and proven ability of Shalimar Films and their management team plays a key role in securing these pre-sale distribution agreements from major distributors.

Shalimar Films focuses on marketing their products through the largest and best suited distributors in the industry. These distributors not only have the advantage of substantial capital resources for funding promotion and advertising campaigns, but also have the ability to obtain better positioning and shelf space in catalogs and retail outlets.

The original programs produced by Shalimar Films will be distributed through, but not limited to, Home Video, Retail Stores, Mass Merchants, Educational Institutions, Libraries, Catalogs, Direct to Consumer Sales, Direct Mail, Broadcast/Cable Television, Interactive Television, New Media Technologies, Laser Disc, and CD-ROM.

Shalimar Films will only produce programs that have received a solid pre-sale commitment through a signed licensing or distribution contract with a major label, studio, or distributor.

Distribution

A licensing contract commits the distributor to the marketing, distribution and sale of a specific series of programs being produced by the Company. A typical licensing contract warranties that the distributor will provide and pay for all packaging, duplication, warehousing, marketing, advertising, sales, shipping, collection, returns and all other costs related to the marketing, distribution, and sale of programs produced by Shalimar Films. Under this licensing contract, a percentage of all gross sales, referred to as a royalty payment, is earned by the Company.

A licensing contract offers several advantages to the smaller independent producer, especially when a program is targeted to a large demographic audience or has widespread audience appeal. A major distributor has the ability to roll out a program on a national basis and feed the pipeline far more effectively and quickly than an independent producer. They also have the ability to promote, on a very large scale, consumer and trade awareness for the program. Additionally, certain classes of trade such as Rack Jobbers, Distribution Outlets, and larger Retailers are better served by a major label, studio or distributor. When a program is projected to have major potential and widespread appeal, a licensing contract is the preferred method of distribution used by the Company.

In some cases, when it makes economic sense, Shalimar Films will sign a distribution agreement rather than a licensing contract. A distribution agreement tends to yield a much higher profit margin for the Company. The downside is that these agreements do not always provide the same level of marketing and sales support as a licensing contract. However this is not always the case and in some situations this approach is more viable than a licensing contract. Instances where this theory holds true is with programming sold through only one or two distributors that represent 75% plus of the entire marketplace for that specific genre of programming.

Distribution
...continued

Another case where distribution agreements are economically viable is when a program or genre is targeted to a specific class of trade. Certain accounts such as Catalogs, Direct to Consumer Marketing companies and certain Retailers are logical clients for direct sales by the Company. This approach requires a small but highly experienced inside sales staff and a promotional budget to market the programming effectively. Shalimar Films will be hiring such a staff to sell certain products on a distribution basis to these accounts. Under a distribution agreement Shalimar Films sells finished goods to the distributor earning an average profit of 100% to 300% per unit.

For example, as part of a licensing deal with Sunshine Videos, Inc., Shalimar Films will produce several children's television programs scheduled for release and distribution in 1995. The first series of children's programs being produced are entitled: "Kids Pick-Up and Go—Video Travel for Children." These programs are pre-sold for distribution through Sunshine Videos, Inc. in the United States and Canada and Atlantis Exporting Corp. for overseas markets. This series of programs will generate royalty income for the company under an existing licensing contract with these distributors.

Sunshine Videos, Inc. is a major player in the marketplace with considerable financial resources for marketing, promotion and advertising of television and video programs. The "Kids Pick-Up and Go—Video Travel for Children" is a timely original concept that is well positioned for significant success. Production is already underway and most of the preparation and pre-production work has already been completed by the Company.

In another example, as part of a distribution deal with Pentrex Publishing, Shalimar Films produce several "Train Trax" video programs also scheduled for release and worldwide distribution in 1995. Pentrex Publishing dominates the "Train Trax" marketplace and is by far the largest distributor of Railroad Videos in the world. These ancillary programs are being produced in an exceptionally cost efficient manner. By exploiting the same footage shot during production of the first two (2) television episodes of "Kids Pick-Up and Go—Exploring Trains," the cost of completion and delivery of these "Train Trax" programs are dramatically reduced thereby substantially increasing profitability of this product line for the Company.

Since we are manufacturing and delivering the completed "Train Trax" video programs to Pentrex Publishing under a direct marketing distribution agreement, the profit margin per video is significantly higher than with a licensing deal. The Company is selling these "Train Trax" video programs to Pentrex Publishing for $8.00 per unit. Since manufacturing costs are less than $2.00 per unit, the Company will realize a profit of over $6.00 for each unit sold.

In addition, with many of the programs produced by the Company, ancillary products will be licensed or distributed through deals with book publishers, music & record companies, toy manufacturers, clothing manufacturers, and major corporations looking for a promotional tie-in with the television/video series. These contracts will provide additional income and increased consumer awareness through cross promotion and advertising.

For example, Shalimar Films is currently in negotiation with Mega Books for an illustrated children's book based on "The Kids Pick-Up and Go Series" concept. This children's book series will include an audio cassette featuring narration, sound effects, and music from the television program to make the product more unique, fun, interactive, and profitable. Obviously, sales of "The Kids Pick-Up and Go Series" programs will benefit from the cross promotion of ancillary products that are being advertised and distributed in the marketplace.

Additionally, with the funding from this offering, the Company plans to produce a variety of programs for major distributors such as Time-Life Video, Inc., Time Warner, A-Vision, Unapix Entertainment, Inc., Guthy Renker Corporation, National Syndication's, Inc. Media Syndication's Inc. and Mega Books.

A substantial commitment of resources and a large financial investment are required by the distributor to manufacture, market, and distribute a new series of programs. Consequently, major distributors are not inclined to sign these types of distribution contracts without good reason. Distributors must have a firm belief that the Producer is reputable, and that the product is one that will meet with a reasonably large degree of success before signing a pre-sale contract.

Shalimar Films, through their reputation, expertise, and creativity, meets the requirements of Major Distributors and have already successfully secured worldwide distribution contracts for several of their original television and home video programs.

Shalimar Films will be producing several finished products that are pre-sold to major distributors. However, in order to protect the confidentiality of the company, the list of programs is not included in this plan.

Products/Phase 1

To accomplish our goals, we have developed a comprehensive plan to intensify and accelerate the creative development, production, marketing and distribution of these programs. To begin the first phase of development, production, and delivery of our pre-sold programs to distributors, Shalimar Films requires immediate funding in the amount of $800,000.

Finance

With realistic projections based on average industry performance, sales income would be generated within the first nine (9) months from capitalization of the company. The estimated average total return on investment for a typical program would range from a low of four-to-one to a high of twelve-to-one. Equity investors and partners will also benefit from the value being compounded in the "mutual fund" and the long term income from a highly successful or "hit" program. Return of the original capital investment should take a maximum of eighteen (18) months to twenty-four (24) months from the date of release for each program on an average case.

The management and directors of Shalimar Films have extensive practical experience in the production, marketing and distribution of television programs. Over the past 15 years, the Company's management has maintained the practice of utilizing outside facilities for the technical production of their programs. Technical production, for example, would include Principal Photography, Sound Recording, Computer Graphics, Editing, Audio Mixing and Post Production. In addition, a majority of production management services and creative services are being provided by the Company's management, directors, and in-house staff. Production management and creative services include program development, pre-production, production planning, project supervision, sales, marketing, public relations, legal and business affairs.

Facilities

By continuing this practice, Shalimar Films will be able to maintain a lower overhead while producing finished programs of the highest quality and commercial value. Shalimar Films will use outside services, freelance staff, and outside equipment rentals to reduce the Company's overheads, staffing, and office space requirements. During the creative development stages, very little production staff is required. By bringing in outside production companies and facilities when needed, a more cost efficient method of operation is realized.

The Company's objective is to focus on a finished program's overall quality of presentation, information content, style, and format with commercial viability and the targeted audience being the principal determining factors. Elements of quality and style include, but are not limited to, nature of content and information, production values, and presentation format.

Most important of all, the Company is committed to delivering commercially viable programming that meets the requirements of their distributors. Utilizing in-house staff for management, creative development, and production supervision, the Company is better able to control the finished quality of the programming they produce.

Shalimar Films currently manages their operation with a full-time and part-time staff of five (5) people. The Company currently operates out of a 1000 square foot office located in Pittsburgh, PA. The Company directors' also maintain smaller offices located in Harrisburg and Philadelphia, PA. An independent sales office is located in New Mexico.

With the realization of financing, the Company plans to move their operations into a larger office space in the PA area. The Company will increase staff to a total of twelve (12) people, including management and directors, and will consolidate their operations into approximately 3,400 to 3,800 square feet of office space. In addition, an off-line editing system will be purchased and utilized in-house to further improve cost control and finished program quality. Off-line editing is considered to be a key factor in reducing on-line editing costs at outside facilities.

Overall, the experience and expertise of the Company's management team and their approach to structuring their organization, provides for a more streamlined, efficient, and effective operation. The practical experience of management provides for tighter controls over the cost of production and also results in a well planned strategy that is ultimately designed to be more lucrative and profitable.

Conclusion

The management team of Shalimar Films enjoys an established track-record in the entertainment industry with past involvement in numerous programs for the Television and Home Entertainment markets, as well as music videos.

In addition, Gerald M. Callens, one of the General Partners in Shalimar Films, was announced as the First Place Winner in Computing Industry Magazine's Best Business Awards Contest. The article on Shalimar Films is part of a feature cover story in the magazine's May 1995 issue.

The experience and commitment of Shalimar Films, combined with the unique working relationships they have established with distributors, and their focus on developing only those programs with strong commercial potential, make this venture a solid opportunity for investors to become part of a winning team. Our distributor's expressions of satisfaction and encouragement are numerous, and we intend to expand our efforts upon funding. This is a major growth industry filled with exciting opportunities. Shalimar Films invites you to join them in their efforts and the rewards that they bring.

Gerald M. Callens - President

Gerald M. Callens - (Producer/Director/Writer) - has over 18 years of professional experience in the film and television industry. His expertise includes television program development, producing, writing, and directing. He has also gained valuable experience in advertising, public relations, marketing, and sales. Additionally, Mr. Callens has several engineering and technical achievements to his credit including the design and construction of several television studios, remote television broadcast units, and high end commercial audio/video installations utilizing unique and innovative original designs.

René S. Porter - Vice President - Business & Legal Affairs

René S. Porter - (Business & Legal Affairs) - A former musician and artist, Mr. Porter is an entertainment attorney who established his private practice in 1987 to represent creative people and companies involved in entertainment, sports and the fine arts. His practice is the culmination of a varied career in law, writing, public speaking, academia, the arts, and politics.

Sylvia A. Cole - Vice President - Program Development & Acquisitions

Sylvia A. Cole - (Director/Writer) has 10 years of experience in the film and television industry. Her expertise includes television program development, screenwriting, directing marketing and advertising. Additionally, Ms. Cole has had a number of stories and articles published in national and regional magazines.

THE GENERAL PARTNERS

Callens, Porter, and Cole bring over 40 years of industry experience to the firm. The company also taps the skills of a large network of experts. These media specialists serve the needs of a varied client base. The General Partners of Shalimar Films have built a solid reputation and are well known for their impressive record and professional results. More recently, the Pittsburgh video company has focused on providing original television programming and software video products for Broadcast/Cable Television, Home Video Cassette, Interactive Television, Laser Disc, and CD-ROM. Its innovative programs help meet consumer demands for high-impact, high quality material. Through their alliances, Shalimar Films brings more than seventy-five years of experience to the management team. This background draws from specialties in television program development, artist management, business affairs, accounting, entertainment law, marketing, and distribution. Shalimar Films specifically targets the home video and broadcast television markets. In this area, the company is producing programs from Depace Productions, JRD Development Corporation, Wood Knapp & Company, Time-Life Video, Pentrex Publishing, ATA Trading Corporation, and Capital Cities/ABC Video Publishing.

Overview

DIRECTORS AND ADVISORS

Peter Gomez - Director - Marketing & Sales

A 16-year veteran of the entertainment industry, Peter Gomez has spent the last ten years focused on the sales and marketing of prerecorded video cassettes, specifically concentrating on the Special-Interest programming segment. Peter is currently the Vice President, Consumer Products Division of one of the world's largest distributors of Television and Video programming. Peter holds a B.A. in Sociology from Long Island University. Peter brings us knowledge of the supply chain—from wholesale acquisitions through the distribution pipeline to the retail market. His experience in bringing programs to market is a source of essential information.

Margaret Powell - Advisor - Marketing & Sales

Currently the Manager, Music & Video Marketing for Doubleday Book and Music Clubs, Margaret Powell is an entertainment software Direct Marketing specialist. Her creditials include five previous years in the video industry. Prior to entering the field, Margaret worked in Advertising and Marketing. She is currently completing an M.B.A. at New York University and holds a B.S. in Journalism from West Virginia University. Margaret brings with her a deep-seated knowledge of the complex world of direct marketing and catalog sales, a resource of insight into the rapidly expanding mail order industry, and its relationship to entertainment software.

MARKET ANALYSIS

Market Environment

The entire telecommunications industry is exploding with new, highly advanced methods of television program distribution. CD-ROM, 3DO, CDI, Stragazer Systems, Full Service Networks, Interactive Cable, Multimedia, and On-Demand Television are joining a large and still growing cable and broadcast television base to create a home entertainment behemoth with an insatiable appetite for new, high-quality programming. Now, establishing an entity to produce this much-needed programming on modest budgets is a more attractive and viable proposition than ever before. Realizing the potential of this market, Shalimar Films has positioned itself to produce a variety of new programs in order to capitalize on this growing demand.

Customers

There are more than 92 million U.S. homes (98% of all homes) with television sets, about 65% of which have more than one set. It is estimated that more than 80% of these homes are also equipped with a VCR, and that more than 60% are linked with cable systems. The combined advertising revenues of broadcast and cable television exceeded $40 billion dollars in 1992. Conservative estimates suggest advertising revenues in the broadcast and cable television industry exceeding $50 billion in 1994.

Home video consumer spending (for purchase and rental of video programming) reached over $12 billion in 1993. Industry reports project a nationwide market for home video products to be approximately $13.5 billion by the end of 1994 and projections estimate an increase to almost $18 billion per year by 1997.

The average American home watches TV seven hours a day, according to Neilsen Media Research statistics for the 1991-1992 season. Add to this growing market the promise of new technologies and the demand for quality programming becomes practically unlimited.

With the rise of new and fiercely competitive windows of distribution, program buyers are hard pressed to find quality products that they require to fill increasing demand. There is plenty of room for growth and expansion in the industry. Since the majority of its products are proprietary, competition is not seen as a major obstacle to the development and success of Shalimar Films and the products it will produce.

Competition

The markets for our products are worldwide and include cable television, network television, independent stations, on-demand television, Pay-Per-View, videocassette, direct broadcast satellite, wireless cable, interactive television, CD-ROM, 3DO, CDI, laserdisc, optical media, and Video CD to name a few. Shalimar Films plans to optimize programming wherever possible to take maximum advantage of these windows of distribution.

A steady history of growth in the industry, the steady increase in consumer demand for home entertainment programming, and the promise of increasing growth for the future due to new windows of distribution are some of the industry's most promising features. This chart will help to illustrate the steady growth of the Television and Home Video markets.

Strengths

Market Forecast

Direct Consumer
Entertainment Expenditure

Market Forecast				Revenues in Billions
Consumer Markets	*1985	*1992	*1997	1992-1997 % Increase
Theatrical Box Office	3.50	5.00	5.90	18.00%
Home Video - Rentals	0.30	8.30	7.00	-15.70%
Home Video - Sales	0.00	5.00	7.00	40.00%
Pre-Recorded Music	3.30	8.20	10.00	22.00%
Cable Television	4.80	19.90	26.90	35.20%
Pay-Per-View	0.00	0.40	3.60	800.00%
Electronic Shopping	0.00	2.30	8.10	252.20%
Total Consumer	11.90	49.10	68.50	39.50%
Per Capita	53.00	194.00	263.00	35.60%

Advertising Revenue

Market Forecast				Revenues in Billions
Advertising Markets	*1985	*1992	*1997	1992-1997 % Increase
Broadcast Television	14.40	27.10	34.00	25.50%
Cable Television	.10	3.40	6.10	79.40%
Total Consumer	14.50	30.50	40.10	39.50%
Per Capita	53.00	194.00	263.00	35.60%

BUDGET DETAIL

Original Television Programming

Production Budget

Overview: Total estimated production budget for each phase of production—Original Television Programs

Assumptions: Based on producing approximately ninety (90) Television Programs. Contributions are being made by Shalimar Films in the area of creative services and production services. Distributors will be making contributions in the areas of celebrity talent, manufacturing, packaging, promotion, advertising, and distribution services.

Production Category	Phase #1	Phase #2	Phase #3	Phase #4	Prod. Cost
Executive Producer	52,000	95,000	150,000	225,000	522,000
Accounting/ Business Affairs	37,500	67,500	125,000	180,000	410,000
Producer/Director	42,000	90,000	180,000	240,000	552,000
Script Writers/AD's	36,000	90,000	180,000	240,000	546,000
Insurance Policies	24,000	36,000	75,000	90,000	225,000
Production Design	18,000	36,000	90,000	140,000	284,000
Site Visits	7,500	18,000	50,000	75,000	150,500
Casting	6,000	25,000	36,000	72,000	139,000
Choreography/ Rehearsals	4,500	18,000	32,000	48,000	102,500
Transportation	12,000	36,000	60,000	90,000	198,000
Studio/Location	9,000	30,000	45,000	90,000	174,000
Equipment Rental	40,000	120,000	180,000	240,000	580,000
Production Staff	40,000	120,000	240,000	360,000	760,000
Sets/Props	18,000	36,000	72,000	144,000	270,000
Talent/Buyouts	24,000	90,000	180,000	360,000	654,000
Production Expenses	24,000	60,000	120,000	180,000	384,000
Insurance	8,000	18,000	24,000	32,000	82,000
Contingency	25,000	40,000	60,000	90,000	215,000
Titles/Graphics	24,000	36,000	72,000	144,000	276,000
Music/Licensing	18,000	36,000	72,000	144,000	270,000
ADR/Narr./Layback	9,000	24,000	36,000	48,000	117,000
Audio Sweetening/Mix	7,500	24,000	36,000	48,000	115,000
Screening/Off-Line Edit	36,000	60,000	100,000	120,000	316,000
On-Line Editing	60,000	90,000	200,000	240,000	590,000
Post Production Exp	7,500	145,000	32,000	60,000	114,500
Mastering/Air Masters	5,000	10,000	20,000	30,000	65,000
Trademarks/Copyrights	3,000	5,000	9,000	15,000	32,000
Salaries/Benefits	112,000	225,000	300,000	450,000	1,087,000
Supplies	5,000	7,500	12,000	18,000	42,500
Off./Rent Util	18,000	32,000	48,000	60,000	158,000
Rentals/Lease	12,500	25,000	36,000	48,000	121,500
Shipping/Mssgs	4,000	7,000	12,000	18,000	41,000
Maintenance/Srv	9,000	12,000	18,000	24,000	63,000
Phones/Comms	12,000	24,000	36,000	48,000	120,000
Vehicle Expenses	15,000	22,500	30,000	38,000	105,500
Property Insur	3,000	4,500	8,000	15,000	30,500
Petty Cash	12,000	15,000	24,000	36,000	87,000
Duplication/Manufacturing	*	*	*	*	0
Marketing/Promotion	*	*	*	*	0
Celebrity/Talent	*	*	*	*	0
Press/Advertising	*	*	*	*	0
Totals	$800,000	$1,700,000	$3,000,000	$4,500,000	$10,000,000

*Distributor

Original Television Programming

...continued

Cash Flow Projections

Overview: Average projected income from each individual phase of production-Original
Television Programs

Assumption: Shalimar Films, Ltd. will produce approximately ninety (90) Television Programs over a five year period on a guaranteed pre-sale basis. The projections illustrated
represent total income over the average life cycle of a program. The return per program
increases in each phase since production of programs that have proven successful are
continued in the next phase.

Distribution Category	Phase #1	Phase #2	Phase #3	Phase #4
Video Cassette				
Retail	1,200,000	1,500,000	2,250,000	2,800,000
Catalog	0	750,000	1,200,000	1,500,000
Library	90,000	180,000	360,000	600,000
Jobbers	150,000	240,000	400,000	760,000
DR Markets	750,000	1,200,000	1,500,000	3,200,000
Television Syndication	250,000	1,125,000	1,800,000	3,200,000
Overseas Markets	115,000	450,000	650,000	1,250,000
Ancillary Markets	100,000	400,000	750,000	1,200,000
On-Demand Television	90,000	212,500	472,000	725,000
New Media/Other Markets	75,000	192,500	368,000	600,000
Estimated Sales Projs	Projected	Projected	Projected	Projected
Totals	2,820,000	6,250,000	9,750,000	14,400,000
Approximate No. of Programs	12	20	26	32
Approximate Revenue/Prog	235,000	312,500	375,000	450,000

Cash Flow Projections

Overview: Average projected income from all phases of production—Original Television
Programs.

Assumption: Shalimar Films will produce approximately ninety (90)Television Programs
over a five year period. The projection illustrated here represent total average income over
the average life cycle of a program.

Distribution Category	Projected Total
Video Cassette	
Retail	7,750,000
Catalog	3,450,000
Library	1,230,000
Jobbers	1,550,000
DR Markets	5,215,000
Television Syndication	6,375,000
Overseas Markets	2,465,000

Ancillary Markets	2,450,000
On-Demand Television	1,499,500
New Media/Other Markets	1,235,500
Projected Total Gross Income	33,220,000
Projected Total Gross Profit	23,220,000
Projected Return On Investment	232.20%

1) Programs will only be produced based on signed pre-sale agreements with Major Worldwide Distributors.

2) Production costs are not to exceed the figures quoted. Contributions are being made by Shalimar Films and Distributors.

3) Projections based on industry averages. Successful programs will exceed quoted projects, especially over the long term.

4) Projections are calculated using market research and information provided by distributors - Based on average performance.

CONCLUSIONS/ SUMMARY

The television and home entertainment industry has a proven track record of phenomenal growth. Market demand is growing each and every day. People are hungry for entertainment and they are more than willing to pay for it. The explosive arrival of the VCR merely set the stage for the quantum leap in programming consumption that we will soon experience as the new technologies make our televisions an ever more important part of our daily lives.

Shalimar Films understands that this is an opportunity of vast potential. We are positioned to take full advantage of the industry's on-going growth. The combined experience of the management team for Shalimar Films equals 75 years of providing quality entertainment and educational programming. This experience has taught us how to produce programming with an extremely high rate of efficiency and success. In addition, Shalimar Films enjoys key working relationships with some of the largest distributors for the home video and television markets. These relationships offer us information about market needs and trends that is factored into all our decisions regarding the development of new programming. Before we produce a program, we have a good indicator of how well it will be received. And we know the programs will be handled by organizations that will provide the most comprehensive distribution, marketing and promotion expertise in the industry.

This offering has been structured in such a way as to provide the limited partners with the most attractive investment opportunity possible with the right of fist recoupment, a generous share of the profits and greatly reduced risks due to the number of projects; the tailoring of these projects to large, identifiable segments of the viewing public; and the assurance that pre-sale agreements are in place with major distributors before production begins.

Enormous potential exists in this offering and the General Partners are fully committed to the task of transforming your investment dollars into a package of high-quality properties that will generate a substantial revenue stream for years to come.

Microbrewery

BUSINESS PLAN

HARBOR BREWING COMPANY

114-118 East Bay St.
South Harbor, MI 48840

January 1995

This business plan illustrates the author's intention to purchase and renovate the assets and leases of an existing business and then establish and operate a microbrewery restaurant in its place. Look for a variety of financial information, including forecasts of operating costs, income, balance sheets, and cash flow, in addition to discussions of taxes and the history of brewing, and a listing of the menu contents and beers.

- SUMMARY OF MEMORANDUM

- INDUSTRY BACKGROUND

- GENERAL DESCRIPTION

- DEMOGRAPHICS

- LOCATION

- COMPETITION

- MANAGEMENT TEAM

- PERSONNEL

- MARKETING STRATEGY

- FEDERAL TAX DISCUSSION

- FINANCIAL DATA

- SUPPORTING DOCUMENTS

- SOURCES CITED

SUMMARY OF
MEMORANDUM

The Company: Harbor Brewing Company, LLC, a Michigan Limited Liability Company (the "Company") has been formed pursuant to the Operating Agreement attached hereto and to Michigan laws by filing articles of organization with the Michigan Department of Commerce. The Company will hold the lease on the properties at 114 through 118 East Bay Street in downtown South Harbor, Michigan. The initial mailing address of the Company will be Harbor Brewing Company, LLC, 711 Oak Street, South Harbor, MI 48840.

The sole business of the Company is to acquire the business assets (the "Business") from Lincoln Street Station (the "Seller") and the leases at 114 through 118 East Bay Street, South Harbor, MI, and to construct and operate a restaurant and brewery (the "brew-pub") to be called Harbor Brewing Company.

Managing Member: Olson Brewing Services, LLC (OGS) will be the Managing Member of the Company. Linnea and Mark Olson are the Managing Members of OBS which was formed on 10/17/94.

Company Duration: The Company shall continue until December 31, 2025, unless sooner terminated in accordance with the Dissolution Guidelines described in the Operating Agreement.

The Project: The project entails renovating, staffing, and operating a restaurant with an on-premise brewing facility. The Company intends to make necessary improvements to the existing restaurant, to build a brewery and two secondary fermentation rooms and to complete other Property renovations including, but not limited to, adding a second "show" bar and upgrading toilet facilities. See Section 1 for a description of the brew-pub concept and state of the industry.

Units Offered: The Managing Member is offering 21 units at $20,000 each to be paid at the time of execution of the Subscription Agreement.

Minimum Purchase per Investor: 1 Unit ($20,000), or at the sole discretion of the Managing Member, 1/2 Unit ($10,000).

Payment: Each Investing Member will pay $20,000 per Unit purchased upon execution of the Subscription Agreement.

Use of Proceeds: The estimated net proceeds of this offering ($420,000 including the Managing Member's Investment Capital of $10,000) will be used in conjunction with a loan from an Investing Member ($200,000) to purchase the Business, acquire the leases, construct the brewery, make necessary leasehold improvements, acquire operating assets, and finance the initial brew-pub operations (including, but not limited to, licensing, staffing, training, marketing, and working capital).

Other Anticipated Indebtedness: A note payable of $200,000 will be due an investing member of Harbor Brewing Company, LLC. The note will be secured by various unencumbered assets belonging to the Company. The note term is 60 months at a stated interest rate of 15%. Total monthly principal and interest payments are $4,758. Their first payment is not due until April 1, 1995.

Time Limit of Offering: The Partnership Offering will be terminated on February 15, 1995 if fewer than 21 units have been sold or if the Investing Member's loan cannot be secured. This termination data may be extended at the sole discretion of the Managing Member.

Management Fee: The Managing Member will receive as a management fee in 1995 5% of "gross sales revenue" in return for the Managing Member's management of the project. The management fee will increase to 6.5% in 1996, 7.5% in 1997, and 8.0% in 1998 and thereafter. (See Management Team section for a description of the Managing Member's roles and responsibilities in the daily operation of the brew-pub.)

Allocation of Partner Interest: The Investing Members shall be allocated 60% of the Company's Profits and Losses pro rata based on their Units, and the Managing Member shall be allocated 40% of the Company's Profits and Losses.

Any Distributable Income shall be distributed with the Investing Members receiving 99% of such Distributable Income, pro rata, based on their Capital Ratios, and the remaining 1% to be distributed to the Managing Member until the Change Date.

The Change Date occurs when the Investing Members have received distributions of a) an amount equal to 15% per annum of the Capital Contributions and b) an amount equal their Capital Contributions. After the Change Date, Distributable Income shall be distributed with the Investing Members receiving 60% of such Distributable Income and the Managing Member receiving the remaining 40%. After 5 years, the Investing Member has the option to Put and the Managing Member has the option to Call the Units.

All cash and profit distributions will be made out of Distributable Funds, which will come from net income from brew-pub operations and other cash available from non-cash expenses (deductions) relating to amortization and depreciation.

Net income (loss) allocated to each Investing Member will constitute taxable income to said Investing Member, except as to any portion of Distributable Income which may not be taxable owing to deductions for amortization, depreciation and similar noncash tax deduction items.

INDUSTRY BACKGROUND

Brewing in America: A Brief Recent History

Before Prohibition began in 1920, the quality and variety of beer brewed in America rivaled that of the great brewing nations of Europe. With thousands of breweries in operation across the country supplying each region with its own distinctive styles, almost every town had a beer it could call its own.

Unfortunately for the American beer drinker, the only breweries to survive Prohibition were the very large commercial breweries that could convert their existing operations to the production of non-alcoholic malt products. When they resumed brewery operations in 1933, they went in search of a single beer style that was cheap to make, easy to drink, and would appeal to the greatest number of people. The variety, character (and some would argue, quality) was gone from the American beer market.

The tide began to turn in 1979 when a law was passed that legalized the home brewing of beer. This touched off the beer renaissance that is currently sweeping the country. Then in 1983, California passed a law permitting breweries to brew and sell beer directly to the customer (without going through a distributor).

Since that time, home brewers, micro breweries, and brew-pubs have been reintroducing to the American palate the wide variety of styles and flavors available through the small scale production of high quality, hand-crafted beers, brewed naturally, and served fresh. As more and more Americans have come to demand this variety and quality, microbrewers have found an expanding and lucrative niche in an otherwise stagnant beer market.

Attitudes towards beer drinking have also undergone major changes over the couple of decades. Today's craft beer drinkers are not attracted to loud, smoke-filled, cheap-beer bars, but are instead looking for a comfortable, conversational pub atmosphere where they can take their families, meet their friends, and have a good conversation over a great pint of beer.

Michigan is somewhat of a late-comer to the brew-pub scene, since brew-pubs were legalized here only two years ago. Brew-pubs are just now beginning to pop up throughout the state, with facilities currently in operation in Grand Rapids and Detroit.

The wide selection of microbrewed beers available in bars, restaurants, and liquor stores throughout the South Harbor area, together with the growing home-brew supply industry in the area, is a testament to the strong local demand for good, fresh beer that is really brewed the old-fashioned way. For the past two years, South Harbor has been anxiously awaiting the grand-opening of its first brew-pub. Harbor Brewing Company hopes to meet that demand by opening its doors within the next six months.

Brewing in America: Current State of the Industry

1993 (the most recent year for which statistics are available) was a record-breaking year for brew-pubs and micro-breweries across the country. The craft-brewing industry produced over 1.6 million barrels in '93 which is a 40% increase in total taxable output from the previous year. This increased the market share for this segment from .6% to .9% of total beer consumption (Edgar, 1994).

The Institute for Brewing Studies' (IBS) 1994 Industry Review (Edgar, 1994) predicts that 1994 figures will show another banner year with a 30% to 40% increase in craft-brewing industry sales. The number of craft-breweries has grown from 30 to 382 since 1985. The majority of the early growth took place on the West Coast, with the East Coast following close behind. In recent years, the establishment of brew-pubs has followed new legislation through the Mountain and Plains states and finally, into the North Central (or Midwest) region which has enjoyed a period of incredible growth over the past several years.

The table below illustrates growth in sales for craft-brewers in the North Central Region during 1993.

1993 Sales Growth Percentages for the North Central Region

Location	Brewery Name (Micro or Pub)	% Growth in 1993
Iowa	Brandevor/Dubuque Brewing Co. (Micro)	(5)
Iowa	Millstream Brewing Co. (Micro)	(20)
Michigan	Frankenmuth Brewery (Micro)	20
Michigan	Kalamazoo Brewing Co. (Micro)	106
Minnesota	Sherlock's Home (Pub)	16
Minnesota	Summit Brewing Co. (Micro)	42
Minnesota	James Page Brewing Co. (Micro)	15
Ohio	Great Lakes Brewing Company (Pub)	69
Ohio	Hoster Brewing Co. (Pub)	29
Ohio	Columbus Brewing Co. (Micro)	31
Wisconsin	Water Street Brewery (Pub)	196
Wisconsin	The Brewmaster's Pub (Pub)	1
Wisconsin	Appleton Brewing Co. (Pub)	13
Wisconsin	Cherryland Brewing Co. (Pub)	17
Wisconsin	Rowland's Calumet Brewery (Pub)	46
Wisconsin	Lakefront Brewery (Micro)	68

Average Growth in the Region   34

(Adapted with permission from The New Brewer May/June 1994. Copyright held by The Institute for Brewing Studies, Boulder, CO.)

Given this incredible growth, it is not surprising that restaurant sales for beer have been increasing in the 1990s. In fact, a recent study published by the National Restaurant Association (Chapdelaine, 1994) states that the number of restaurant patrons drinking beer with food is increasing, despite a decline in overall alcohol consumption.

Specifically, the Restaurant Association study found that the beers being ordered are expensive, premium-quality craft-brewed beers. According to the National Restaurant Association (Chapdelaine, 1994), consumers will not only order, but also tend to be willing to pay more for menu items that they perceive to be new, popular, or of premium quality. The heightened demand for this product can be explained by the fact that micro-brewed beer meets all three of these criteria:

O Locally produced, hand-crafted beers are still a novelty in many areas (like South Harbor) that do not yet have any brew-pubs or micro-breweries.
O A 1993 Roper Starch Worldwide Study (cited by Chapdelaine, 1994) found that half of all adult consumers believe that locally brewed beer is "in."
O According to the National Restaurant Association (Chapdelaine, 1994), locally brewed beer is perceived as fresher and of higher quality.

According to the IBS, "the boom is happening for micro and specialty brewers and it may be a decade or two before it begins to level off." (Edgar, 1994).

GENERAL DESCRIPTION

Atmosphere and Decor

Harbor Brewing Company hopes to be South Harbor's first brew-pub--serving up a hearty bistro pub menu and five varieties of house-brewed beer on tap. Its spacious and unique interior will offer the warm familiarity and rustic charm of a British pub.

The brew-pub will be located in two beautiful old buildings with hardwood floors, brick walls, high tin ceilings, and large front windows. The space is currently divided by the buildings' original brick wall into a large restaurant area and a smaller bar area.

The large restaurant side will be called the "Brew Room." It will be an airy, open non-smoking space focused around the brewery itself. It will have hardwood floors and will be decorated with antique brewery posters, oak barrels, and other paraphernalia from breweries and brew-pubs, and a large mural of the Harbor Brewing Company's logo on the back wall. It will have seating for 100 including 20 bar seats.

The "Tap Room" will be a smaller, darker, cozier space with hardwood floors, dart boards, several TVs and a traditional English pub atmosphere. One wall will be painted with a large storyboard depicting the brewing process. Smoking will be permitted in the Tap Room. It will seat 50, including 12 bar seats.

Focus on Brewing

The focal point of the brew-pub will be the brewing process and the brewery itself. This 400 square foot glass and wood encased room will be built in the center of the Brew Room. It will be flanked by a full service bar and surrounded by tables. The brewery will house seven stainless steel vessels whose shiny finish will be highlighted by amber-colored floodlights on the ceiling. Customers will be able to observe the brewer at work during the day and will be offered guided educational tours of the brewing facility in the evening.

Harbor Brewing Company plans to offer more than just a great place to eat and drink. Its goal is to be a gathering place for all beer lovers--from the connoisseur to the curious. The Managing Member plans on tapping into the growing market of home-brewers by sponsoring a monthly home-brewers meeting to be held at the Pub. It also plans on entering the brew-pub's beer in local and national competitions to boost name recognition and reputation in the industry.

For the more casual beer enthusiast, the brew-pub will provide a variety of entertaining and educational events like regular brewery tours, bi-weekly lunch with the brewer, weekly beer classes, regularly scheduled tastings, and a variety of special events on famous "beer-drinking holidays" like Oktoberfest and St. Patrick's Day.

Menu

The menu (found in Supporting Documents) offers a terrific balance of interesting appetizers, traditional bar food, hearty entrees, vegetarian and vegan fare, and some unique dishes with a gourmet touch. There is something for every taste, including low fat appetizers and salads (like a fresh fruit and veggie tray, garlic toast with diced peppers and tomatoes, or strawberry marinated chicken salad) as well as vegetarian dishes (all pasta and salad entrees will be available with or without meat).

In addition to the five pub-brewed beers, the brew-pub plans to offer at least 10 other micro-brewed draught beers from around the country to cover styles of beer that it does not produce in-house. It also plans to carry an extensive array of bottled hand-crafted and imported beers, representing the classic styles from around the world. It plans to offer a varied wine list, gourmet coffees, and an extensive selection of top-of-the-line liquors.

The proposed hours for the brew-pub are 11 a.m. to midnight Monday through Wednesday, 11 a.m. to 2 a.m. Thursday through Saturday, and noon to midnight on Sunday. The kitchen is expected to serve items from the bar menu from opening time until one hour before closing time, entree items from 5 p.m. to 10 p.m., and all other items from opening to 10 p.m.

Hours of Operation

Background music will be provided by a stereo system controlled from behind the bar. The Managing Member has begun collecting an assortment of blues, jazz, and new age music.

Entertainment

The Tap Room will air sporting events on a large screen and two ceiling-mounted televisions. During major events, the music will be turned off and the television sound turned up in the Tap Room. The brew-pub plans to stay open until midnight to accommodate the Sunday and Monday night football crowd.

On special occasions, the brew-pub may feature traditional live acoustic music (like Irish folk music on St. Patrick's Day). The Managing Member does not envision a stage but rather plans on providing live acoustic music in the Irish/British tradition of seating musicians at a large table among the patrons.

There will be real dart boards in the pub which will be used for leagues and tournaments.

And of course, Harbor Brewing Company will feature the master brewer in action Monday through Saturday from 10 a.m. to 4 p.m.

The age, education, and affluence of South Harbor's diverse population makes it an ideal market for a brew-pub. Consumer Reports on Eating Share Trends (CREST) data (cited by Chapdelaine, 1994) reveal that affluent and educated Americans eat out more frequently, are more likely to order beer at restaurants, and are more likely to drink regular (non-light) beer than other consumers. This group is also more likely to order beer than wine, liquor, or sparkling wine.

DEMOGRAPHICS

According to the 1990 census report, South Harbor is comprised largely of students, professionals, and service industry employees. The University of South Harbor provides the city with a large pre- and post-graduate student population. The University is also the largest employer in the city with more than 16,000 employees. The University Medical Center employs another 9,600 doctors and professional medical staff. South Harbor is also home to major corporations.

The 1990 census reports that almost half of South Harbor's employed population hold professional or managerial positions: 24% are clerical or in sales; 17% have blue collar jobs; and .5% are in agriculture. Only 3.6% of South Harborites are unemployed. The median family income is $50,192 with the effective buying income (personal income minus tax and non-tax payments) at $29,515 (versus $27,912 nationally). $246 million dollars a year of this buying income is spent in bars and restaurants in the South Harbor area.

South Harbor's education level also ranks well above the national average. 94% of the population has a high school diploma and 66% have four or more years of college (compared to 20% nationally).

The median age of South Harborites is 27.3 (compared to the national median of 33.0) and 35% of the population is between the ages of 25 to 44, the target age group of micro and pub-breweries.

According to a recent study by the National Restaurant Association, these demographics are ideal for supporting a brew-pub. The study (Chapdelaine, 1994) found that higher incomes and higher educational levels were a major factor in determining who orders beer at restaurants. From 1989 to 1993, the percentage of individuals with annual household incomes of $60,000 or more who ordered beers at restaurants rose from 15% to 25%. The study also found that the largest group of beer drinkers (40%) hold some sort of professional or managerial job while only 22% are blue collar workers.

Given these statistics, South Harbor is sure to attract a growing number of craft brewers. The area's ideal demographics easily could -- and most likely will -- support multiple brew-pubs. Harbor Brewing Company's goal is to be the one that opens it doors first and sets the high standard for those that will follow.

LOCATION

Harbor Brewing Company will be ideally located on the waterfront in downtown South Harbor, allowing it to draw from the downtown merchants, diners, shoppers, area businesses, the student population, art fair traffic, and the many sports fans, conventioneers, and business visitors who come to the area.

The downtown area is a very exciting location for a brew-pub. The trend in South Harbor, as in many other towns and cities across the country, is for retail to gradually move from the downtown area out to local malls and shopping strips. In some cities, this leads to the decline of the downtown. In others, like South Harbor, the newly vacated shops are gobbled up by restaurants, night-clubs, and other entertainment-style tenants creating a thriving destination location that can draw from a much wider population radius.

According to a recent article in the South Harbor News, "Restaurants, coffee houses, art galleries, and other non-clothing retailers are the major drawing card these days." However, the article continues, "[l]oss of vitality isn't an issue, because people -- including many customers from outside of the county -- continue to flock downtown." The recent addition of new restaurants like the Barbecue Pit and an expressed interest from clubs like the Harbor Music Cafe should also help to draw precisely the market segment the brew-pub is targeting.

In addition to an overall downtown growth trend, the brew-pub's specific location (East Bay St. between Main and Fifth) has recently benefitted from a $2.7 million Downtown Development Authority (DDA) project which replaced the old gray concrete sidewalks in front of the proposed brew-pub site with wider brick walkways. The project also included planting new trees and installing new street lights. Rachel Berg, DDA coordinator for the project, pointed out that "restaurants in the area will be able to set up tables on the widened sidewalks in the spring and summer for a cafe atmosphere." Harbor Brewing Company's location has already received permission from the city to set up outdoor seating along East Bay Street.

Those familiar with South Harbor know that one of the most frequently cited complaints regarding downtown establishments is the lack of convenient parking nearby. Harbor Brewing Company is located directly across the street from a 245-space parking structure, and three blocks away from 199-space and 883-space ramps (at Lincoln & First and Fourth & Adams respectively). (Parking data is from the October 1992 South Harbor City Administrator resolution Agreement for Management of the South Harbor Municipal Parking System.)

COMPETITION

The Managing Member views the competition to be the local bistro/bar business. The South Harbor restaurant market is extremely competitive, and success is dependent on many factors including, but not limited to, location, price, food, quality, beer quality, consistency, service, ambiance, general concept, and management.

Although the South Harbor market is quite competitive, the Managing Member believes that Harbor Brewing Company should have a huge advantage over existing area restaurants in that it offers a very popular item not currently available anywhere in the South Harbor area -- premium quality, hand-crafted beer brewed, lagered, and served on the premises.

MANAGEMENT TEAM

The Managing Member, OBS, will be providing full-time management and brewing services for the Company.

Linnea Olson - General Manager is a Managing Member of OBS. She will be responsible for the restaurant operations and promotional and marketing activities.

While working as a consultant in the computer industry, Linnea designed and implemented decision support software systems to track and analyze employee effectiveness, monitor and control the quality and cost of long-term care services, and offer timely project status reports to systems management.

She also has five years of experience in technical writing, desktop publishing and graphic design and will further contribute to the project by handling the design and layout of menus, T-shirts, print ads, and promotional materials.

Linnea also brings to the project five years of experience in the food service industry including managing a 30-person staff at a student dining facility which served over 2,000 meals a day.

Mark Olson - Brewery Manager is a Managing Member and Treasurer of OBS. He will be responsible for brewery operations and all financial aspects of the project.

Mark has five years of experience in the healthcare consulting industry with the MED Group. As the Data Center Team Leader, Mark is responsible for managing the delivery of contracted client services within budgetary constraints and the development of the Data Center staff reporting to him. Mark also acts as Account Manager for two large clients with ultimate responsibility for customer satisfaction, service delivery, margins, and contract renewals.

Mark has traveled extensively throughout Europe and the U.S. touring breweries and brew-pubs. He has been a student of beer styles and the brewing process since 1988.

Mark has been brewing for four years and is a member of the IBS. In September, he completed the Pub and Micro-Brewery Operations course at the Siebel Institute of Technology in Chicago. This consisted of hands-on training with a brewmaster as well as instructors from the Siebel Institute in a high-output suburban Chicago brew-pub. Mark will also be receiving training through the equipment supplier for the Company on the equipment that is being purchased.

Lynn Rogers - Operations Manager -- Lynn has accepted a position "at will" with the Company to serve as operations consultant during the planning and start-up phase of the project and as Operations Manager thereafter. She will be responsible for planning, stocking, staffing, and managing both bars. She will also hire, train, and schedule waitstaff.

Lynn brings to the project 25 years of restaurant experience including several new restaurant openings, 13 years of management experience, and the successful implementation of specialized menus, tastings, and staff seminars at establishments including The Harbor Hotel and C.J.'s. She also brings a proven and professional management style and a wealth of knowledge in the area of fine wines and liquor.

Matthew Hewit - Executive Chef/Kitchen Manager-- Matthew has accepted a position "at will" with the Company to serve as menu and kitchen consultant during the planning and start-up phase of the project and as Kitchen Manager/Executive Chef thereafter. He will be responsible for designing, costing, and implementing the menu; working with contractors to redesign and equip the kitchen and storage areas; hiring, training, managing and scheduling the kitchen staff; and managing all ordering and inventory for the kitchen.

Matthew brings to the project over 15 years of experience cooking and managing in the South Harbor restaurant market. During this time he has served as Chef and/or Kitchen Manager in successful restaurants and food service operations including Heritage Inn, the Corktown Bistro, and Babette's Feast. In addition to his good name and experience, Matthew brings to the project a great deal of professionalism and knowledge of the local market and competition.

PERSONNEL

The personnel in the restaurant business is a critical factor in the eventual success or failure of the business. With this in mind, the management staff will be bringing proven individuals with them to fill key service positions such as bartending and cooking.

Beyond these positions, the Company will be looking to hire a more mature, professional waitstaff that will team with management to ensure success by providing an excellent environment and service to the customers. The Managing Member hopes to achieve this "buy-in" from the staff by involving them in the decision-making process, implementing an employee suggestion program to get input on marketing, promotions, and specials, and by treating the staff like the important asset they are in making this business a success.

For the kitchen staff, the Managing Member plans to contact the South Harbor Area Chef's Association and local culinary programs to find young people who plan to make a career in the restaurant business. By drawing from this personnel pool, it would be able to hire people who are enthusiastic, eager to learn, and concerned with establishing a good employment record in the area.

People who have spent time in South Harbor know that the most interesting, and perhaps most important characteristics of the local population are not measured by the census bureau's reports. South Harbor offers a unique blend of the cosmopolitan and the collegiate that draws community-oriented residents who are interested in education, the environment, history, and culture.

MARKETING STRATEGY

Harbor Brewing Company will attempt to cater to these interests by offering more than a great brew-pub where people can come to relax and converse over great food and beer. It will also offer a place where people can come to learn more about beer and the brewing process. It will offer a variety of tours and tasting events where people can learns about the styles and the history of beer. In addition to beer tastings, the brew-pub plans to offer find wine and Scotch tastings.

The Managing Member also hopes to establish the brew-pub in the local market by becoming part of the fabric of South Harbor. It intends to make the brew-pub a "local" pub in every sense of the word: a place that the community will be proud to call its own. It believes that by opening the first brew-pub in town, owned and operated by local entrepreneurs, the Company will have a great advantage over subsequent brew-pub operations.

There has been much talk and anticipation of a brew-pub opening in South Harbor during the past two years. Advertising before the opening will primarily be by word of mouth and should require only very limited capital output.

The South Harbor restaurant market is undergoing a renaissance with the recent openings of the Barbecue Pit and C.J.'s and the anticipated (and two years overdue) opening of the Grizzly Bear Brewing Company. New restaurants have attracted a great deal of attention and anticipation during the past two years. Harbor Brewing Company should attract the same attention if not more so because South Harbor is anxiously awaiting a brew-pub and many rumors are already circulating through the restaurant and patron community as to alleged brew-pubs in progress.

To enhance this excitement, as soon as the Company has secured the building and contracted the appropriate licensing bodies, T-shirts will be printed up with "coming soon..." on the front and Harbor Brewing Company logo on the back. These will be sold at cost to friends, co-workers, neighbors, and supporters. Renovations should also be visible from the street outside the restaurant to involve passers-by with the project and its progress, thereby further heightening the excitement.

The Managing Member plans to open the brew-pub without a lot of formal fanfare and expects it to be extremely busy in the early going due to local anticipation. After approximately two months, when the initial novelty has worn off and the staff is experienced and confident, the Managing Member plans to begin an aggressive marketing campaign including a formal Grand Opening.

**MARKETING
STRATEGY**
...continued

In preparation for the Grand Opening, postcards promoting the Grand Opening will be sent to friends, neighbors, co-workers, Ultimate Frisbee teams, home-brewers, the Company's professional team, and to households in the area. These postcards will be redeemable at the Grand Opening for a discount on a Beer Sampler Set. Flyers will also be printed up and posted around area campuses. To reach a good portion of the target market while integrating with the community, the Company anticipates donating part of the Grand Opening proceeds to WUSH-FM public radio in South Harbor, in return for two weeks of advertisement time.

The Grand Opening will be an Opening Weekend rather than just a single day. The opening will span a Friday, Saturday, and Sunday. The Thursday before the opening, the brew-pub will sponsor a media event targeting radio, newspapers, and TV in and around South Harbor and nearby Chicago. Two weeks prior to the Media Event, the Managing Member plans to send Media Kits containing fact sheets, bios, industry background and the history of brewing in South Harbor. The kits will also contain coasters or T-shirts with the Harbor Brewing Company logo, press releases, sidebar copy, and tables and graphs related to the industry. The media will be invited to schedule times on Thursday to come in and receive a full brewery tour and complimentary tasting with the Brewer. The Managing Member and the kitchen and operations managers also plan to be available for interviews following the tasting.

Ongoing advertising strategies to ensure long-term success are to advertise through local media outlets (like The South Harbor News and WUSH-FM public radio), join the South Harbor Convention and Visitors Bureau, place brochures with coupons in all area hotels, send flyers with coupons advertising lunch specials to businesses in South Harbor and advertise in alternative media.

Harbor Brewing Company will also be promoting several special events throughout the year such as beer tastings, seasonal festivals, brewer's lunches, etc. It may offer one monthly charity tank where non-profit clubs and organizations (like sports teams, travel clubs, home-brewers clubs) could keep a specified percentage of the revenue earned on a specific tank of beer during an evening. They would be encouraged to bring in as many customers as possible to help support their cause. This would boost business on slow nights and introduce more people to the pub.

Other promotional campaigns include sponsoring one men's and one women's softball team by providing them with uniforms bearing the Harbor Brewing Company logo in return for their business and support; and sponsoring a bar dart league and a dart team to compete in the South Harbor Dart Association. These are ways of bringing patrons to the restaurant on nights that are traditionally slower while at the same time building community affiliations.

**FEDERAL TAX
DISCUSSION**

The Company will be taxed as a partnership. Instead of corporation income taxes, the members of the Company will be taxed on their proportionate share of the Company's taxable income. Therefore, no provision or liability for Federal income taxes has been included in these forecasted financial statements.

The Company is expected to distribute, at a minimum, an estimated amount of cash necessary to cover income taxes incurred by the individual members on taxable profits of the Company. It is anticipated that the Company will distribute 99% of distributable income to investing members and 1% to the organizing member, Olson Brewing Services, until such time that the investors have received all of their original capital back plus an effective 15% annual rate of return. Michigan single business tax is included in the forecast as an administrative expense.

The State Bar of Michigan has submitted the Michigan Limited Liability Company Act to the national office of the Internal Revenue Service with a request for a published ruling as to the classification for tax purposes of Michigan LLCs. A published ruling has not been provided by the IRS. The IRS has informally expressed concern regarding the continuity of life provisions of the Michigan statute. It is contemplated that a technical correction to the Michigan statute will be proposed to alleviate the IRS's concern, which could be incorporated into the Operating Agreement of the Company. The risk of forming an LLC prior to the IRS resolving its concern is that if the LLC is formed and it is determined to be taxed as a corporation, liquidating and distributing corporate assets could cause adverse tax consequences. Lack of an IRS ruling has not delayed action by many businesses in forming and operating LLCs under the Michigan law.

The discussion set forth above does not address the state, local, or foreign tax aspects of an investment in the Units. The discussion is based on currently existing provisions of the code, existing and proposed Treasury regulations thereunder and current Administrative rulings and court decisions. All of the foregoing are subject to change and any such changes could affect the continuing validity of this discussion. Each prospective investor should consult his or her own tax advisor with respect to the specific tax consequences of an investment in the Units to such person, including the application and effect of state, local, and foreign tax laws and possible effects of changes in federal laws or other tax laws.

FINANCIAL DATA

Forecasted Balance Sheets

	1999	1998	1997	1996	8 Months 1995
Assets					
Current Assets					
Cash	$108,144	$144,469	$135,876	$127,810	$114,490
Accounts Receivable	12,572	12,085	11,653	11,222	7,380
Inventory	19,509	18,941	18,264	18,288	13,898
Prepayments	12,049	11,519	11,185	10,731	7,748
Total Current Assets	152,274	187,014	176,979	168,051	143,517
Fixed Assets					
Restaurant Equipment	273,123	258,123	243,123	228,123	213,123
Furniture & Fixtures	36,997	31,997	26,997	21,997	16,997
Lease Improvements	175,000	175,000	175,000	175,000	175,000
	485,120	465,120	445,120	425,120	405,120
Less Accum. Depr.	(181,834)	(139,155)	(98,476)	(59,798)	(23,119)
	303,286	325,965	346,644	365,322	382,001
Other Assets					
Deferred Charge Net	64,067	70,267	76,467	82,667	88,867
Liquor License	20,000	20,000	20,000	20,000	20,000

Forecasted **Balance Sheets** *...continued*	Deposits	5,000	5,000	5,000	5,000	5,000
		89,067	95,267	101,467	107,667	113,867
	Total Assets	$544,627	$608,245	$625,089	$641,040	$639,384

		1999	1998	1997	1996	8 Months 1995
	Liabilities & Capital					
	Current Liabilities					
	Accounts Payable	$30,210	$29,386	$28,405	$27,456	$20,446
	Accrued Expenses	38,084	36,661	34,757	32,312	19,702
	C/P L-T Debt	13,924	50,787	43,753	37,694	32,474
	Total Current Liab.	82,218	116,834	106,915	97,462	72,621
	Long-Term Liabilities					
	Note Payable Member	0	13,924	64,711	108,464	146,158
	Total L-T Debt	0	13,924	64,711	108,464	146,158
	Total Liabilities	82,218	130,758	171,626	205,926	218,779
	Members Capital	462,409	477,487	453,463	435,114	420,605
	Total Liabs & Capital	$544,627	$608,245	$625,089	$641,040	$639,384

Forecasted Statement **of Income**		1999	1998	1997	1996	8 Months 1995
	Sales					
	Food	1,037,175	996,996	961,389	925,782	608,850
	Beverage	848,598	815,724	786,591	757,458	498,150
		1,885,773	1,812,720	1,747,980	1,683,240	1,107,000
	Cost of Sales	1,292,128	1,246,963	1,196,899	1,144,815	776,654
	Gross Profit	593,644	565,757	551,081	538,425	330,346
	Other Operating Expenses					
	Controllable	177,477	172,757	167,384	158,927	103,936
	Noncontrollable Costs	206,256	199,047	192,128	184,585	127,278
		383,733	371,805	359,512	343,512	231,214
	Operating Income	209,911	193,953	191,569	194,913	99,132
	Nonoperating Income (Expense)					
	Retail Sales Commissions	7,468	7,251	6,992	6,733	4,428
	Interest, Net	(1,976)	(9,009)	(15,069)	(20,289)	(17,120)
		5,493	(1,758)	(8,077)	(13,556)	(12,692)
	Net Income	$215,404	$192,194	$183,492	$181,357	$86,440

	1999	1998	1997	1996	8 Months 1995

Forecasted Statement of Cash Flows

Cash Flow From Operating Activities

Net Income (Loss)	$215,404	$192,194	$183,492	$181,357	$86,440

Items in net income not requiring (providing) cash from operations in the current period:

Depreciation	42,679	40,679	38,679	36,679	23,119
Amortization	6,200	6,200	6,200	6,200	4,133

Cash provided by (used for) working capital

Accounts Receivable	(487)	(432)	(432)	(3,842)	7,380)
Inventory	(568)	(676)	24	(4,390)	(13,898)
Prepayments	(531)	(334)	(454)	(2,983)	(7,748)
Accounts Payable	824	981	949	7,010	20,446
Accrued Liabilities	1,423	1,904	2,445	12,611	19,702
Net cash provided by operations					
	264,944	240,516	230,903	232,642	124,813

Cash Flows From Investment Activities

Purchase of PPE	(20,000)	(20,000)	(20,000)	(20,000)	(405,120)
Purch. Liq. Lic.	0	0	0	0	(20,000)
Purch. of Intangibles	0	0	0	0	(65,000)
Pay't of Deposits	0	0	0	0	(5,000)
Repay't of Deposit	0	0	0	0	0
Pay't of Deferred Charges	0	0	0	0	(28,000)

Net cash (used by) provided for investment

	(20,000)	(20,000)	(20,000)	(20,000)	(523,120)

Cash Flow from Financing Activities

Long-Term Borrowing	0	0	0	0	200,000
Repay't of l-t debt	(50,787)	(43,753)	(37,694)	(32,474)	(21,368)
Capital Contributions - Cash	0	0	0	0	420,000
Distribution to investor members					
	(129,243)	(166,488)	(163,491)	(165,180)	(84,976)
Distribution to management members					
	(101,240)	(1,682)	(1,651)	(1,668)	(858)
Net cash provided for (used by) financing					
	(281,269)	(211,923)	(202,837)	(199,322)	512,797
Increase (decrease) in cash					
	(36,325)	8,592	8,066	13,320	114,490
Beg Cash Balance	144,469	135,876	127,810	114,490	0
Ending Cash Balance	$108,144	$144,469	$135,876	$127,810	114,490

Supplemental Disclosure of Cash Flow Information

Cash paid during the year for

Interest	$6,309	$13,343	$19,402	$24,622	$21,454
State Taxes	18,661	17,999	17,343	16,897	10,438

Disclosure of Accounting Policies

For purposes of the Statement of Cash Flows, the Company considers cash on hand, funds on deposit in banks, money market funds, certificates of deposit and similar types of deposits to be as equivalents.

Forecasted Changes in Members' Contributed Capital

	1999	1998	1997	1996	8 Months 1995
Beginning Balance	$477,487	$453,463	$435,114	$420,605	$0
Capital Cont'n Cash	0	0	0	0	420,000
Net Income	215,404	192,194	183,492	181,357	86,440
Distributions	(230,482)	(168,170)	(165,143)	(166,849)	(85,835)
Ending Balance	$462,409	$477,487	$453,463	$435,114	$420,605

Forecasted Sales & Cost of Sales

	1999	1998	1997	1996	8 Months 1995
Sales					
Food	$1,037,175	$996,996	$961,389	$925,782	$608,850
Beverage - beer	527,828	507,380	489,260	471,139	309,849
Beverage - other	320,770	308,344	297,331	286,319	188,301
Total	1,885,773	1,812,720	1,747,980	1,683,240	1,107,000
Cost of Sales					
Purchases					
Food	349,148	338,979	326,872	314,766	239,210
House Brew	37,889	36,785	35,471	34,158	25,958
Purchased Beverages	63,519	61,669	59,466	57,264	43,518
Total	450,555	437,432	421,810	406,187	308,687
Labor					
Front of House - hrly	269,277	261,434	252,097	242,760	164,443
Kitchen - hrly	128,067	124,337	119,896	120,953	79,546
Management	95,388	92,610	88,200	84,000	41,538
Bonuses	28,007	27,191	26,220	25,249	16,605
Benefits & Taxes	94,541	84,257	85,561	83,707	60,004
Total	615,280	589,828	571,974	556,669	362,137

	1999	1998	1997	1996	8 Months 1995	
Direct Variable Costs						**Forecasted Direct Variable Costs & Operating Costs**
Cleaning Supplies	18,671	18,127	17,480	16,832	11,070	
China & Expendable	13,070	12,689	12,236	11,783	7,749	
Operating Supplies	14,003	13,595	13,110	12,624	8,303	
Laundry	11,203	10,876	10,488	10,099	7,306	
Menus	9,336	9,064	8,740	8,416	5,535	
Credit Card Charges	10,642	10,333	9,963	12,793	10,517	
Management Fees	149,368	145,018	131,099	109,411	55,350	
Total	226,293	219,702	203,115	181,958	105,829	
Operating Costs						
Controllable						
Telephone	3,726	3,621	3,515	3,380	2,492	
Pager	745	724	703	676	141	
Utilities - Gas	20,725	20,121	19,403	18,645	11,070	
Utilities - Electric	60,681	58,913	56,809	54,705	35,978	
Utilities - Water	4,099	3,983	3,867	3,718	2,375	
Waste Control	5,008	4,866	4,724	4,543	3,024	
Promotion & Advert	12,509	12,509	12,509	9,828	6,750	
Mystery Diner	1,300	1,300	1,300	1,300	900	
Office Supplies	1,165	1,141	1,112	1,082	723	
Gift Certificates	2,236	2,172	2,109	2,028	1,350	
Building - R&M	18,671	18,127	17,480	16,832	11,070	
Equipment - R&M	16,804	16,314	15,732	15,149	9,963	
Miscellaneous	29,809	28,965	28,122	27,040	18,000	
Total	177,477	172,757	167,384	158,927	103,936	

	1999	1998	1997	1996	8 Months 1995	
						Forecasted Noncontrollable Fixed Costs
Noncontrollable Fixed Costs						
Rent	92,124	88,712	85,300	82,310	59,577	
Liability Ins. - Liquor	8,929	8,677	8,424	8,112	4,985	
Liability Ins. - General	14,900	14,478	14,056	13,516	9,997	
Bank Charges	745	703	703	676	500	
Alarm Expense	1,043	1,014	984	946	630	
Prof'l Service - Other	3,000	3,000	3,000	3,000	1,500	
Prof'l Service - Acctg	4,800	4,800	4,800	4,800	3,692	
Prof'l Service - Legal	1,248	1,248	1,248	1,248	828	
Dues & Subs	230	217	217	217	150	
Licenses & Permits	3,183	3,003	3,003	3,003	2,079	
Pers. Property Tax	3,445	3,250	3,250	3,250	2,500	
Real Property Tax	5,069	5,069	4,921	4,732	3,150	
Single Business Tax	18,661	17,999	17,343	16,897	10,438	
Amortization	6,200	6,200	6,200	6,200	4,133	
Depreciation	42,679	40,679	38,679	36,679	23,119	
Total	206,256	199,047	192,128	184,585	127,278	

Other Income (Expenses)					
Retail Sales Commissions	7,468	7,251	6,992	6,733	4,428
Interest Income	4,333	4,333	4,333	4,333	4,333
Interest - Member Note	(6,309)	(13,343)	(19,402)	(24,622)	(21,454)
Total	11,802	11,584	11,325	11,066	8,761

Forecasted Property and Equipment Purchases

	1999	1998	1997	1996	8 Months 1995
Property Purchases					
Furniture & Fixtures	5,000	5,000	5,000	5,000	16,997
Kitch. & Brew. Equip.	15,000	15,000	15,000	15,000	213,123
Leasehold Improvements	0	0	0	0	175,000
Total	20,000	20,000	20,000	20,000	405,120

Forecasted Financial Ratios

	1999	1998	1997	1996	8 Months 1995
Solvency Indicators					
Debt/Equity Ratio	0.18	0.27	0.38	0.47	0.52
Debt/Asset Ratio	0.15	0.21	0.27	0.32	0.34
Liquidity Indicators					
Net Working Capital	$70,056	$70,180	$70,064	$70,589	$70,896
Current Ratio	1.85	1.60	1.66	1.72	1.98
Quick Ratio	1.47	1.34	1.38	1.43	1.68
Funds Management Ratios and Days					
Accts Recv Turnover	153.0	152.7	152.8	181.0	150.0
Days in Accts. Rec.	2	2	2	2	2
Inventory Turnover	18.2	18.2	17.9	19.6	17.2
Days in Inventory	20	20	20	19	16
Accts Pay Turnover	15.9	16.0	15.9	18.0	15.7
Days in Accts Payable	23	23	23	20	18
Profitability Ratios					
Return on Sales	11.42%	10.60%	10.50%	10.77%	7.81%
Return on Assets	37.37%	31.17%	28.98%	28.33%	27.04%
Return on Equity	45.84%	41.29%	41.30%	42.39%	41.10%
Growth Ratios					
Sales	4.03%	3.70%	3.85%	52.05%	#N/A
Profits	12.08%	4.74%	1.18%	109.81%	#N/A
Assets	-10.46%	-2.69%	-2.49%	0.26%	#N/A

Sources of Funds

Capital Contributed by Investing members	410,000
Capital Contributed by Managing member (Olson Brewing Services)	10,000
Note Payable	200,000
	620,000

Use of Funds

Purchase of East Bay Street Station	185,000
Brewing Equipment	140,000
Leasehold Improvements	125,000
Additional Working Capital	50,000
Kitchen Equipment Improvements	45,000
Inventory	15,000
Legal and Accounting	11,000
Deposits	10,500
Training Expenses	10,000
Furniture & Fixture Upgrade	5,000
Consulting	5,000
Operating Expenses	2,000
Appraisal Fee	1,500
Contingency	15,000
	620,000

Forecasted Sources and Uses of Funds

	1999	1998	1997	1996	8 Months 1995
One Unit Investment					
Cash Return of Capital (4)	0	2496	2605	2750	1615
Cash distrib's of profit (4)	6305	5625	5370	5308	2530
Total pretax cash flow	6305	8121	7975	8058	4145
Tax (cost) (3)	(2232)	(1991)	(1901)	(1879)	(896)
Total after-tax cash flow	4073	6130	6074	6179	3250
Pretax cash on cash					
Return on invest. (2)	59.85%	43.17%	34.35%	28.87%	12.65%
After-tax cash on cash					
Return on invest. (2)	57.66%	46.61%	38.85%	33.61%	16.25%

Forecasted Annual Pretax and After-tax Cash Return on Investment per investor

Memo:

Total forecasted pretax distribution per investor unit is:	$34,604
Total forecasted after-tax cash distribution per investor unit is:	25,705
Total forecasted return of capital cash distribution per investor unit is:	9,466
Forecasted capital account balance as of December 31, 1999 is:	10,534

Notes:

1 Assumes a total of 21 units of which 20.5 units will be offered to investors

2 Cash on cash return on investment is equal to the total cash flow divided by the inital investment less any return of capital.

3 Assumes a 31% federal income tax rate and a 4.4% state tax rate.

4 Assumes a 60% profit sharing ratio and a 99% cash distribution ratio until investors receive a total cash distribution equal to their capital investment plus an effective 15% annual return.

Upon receipt of cash equal to investment plus an effective 15% retun on annual return, the cash sharing ratio will be in proportion to the 60% profit sharing ratio. The forecast tyhis will occur in the last quarter of 1998.

SUPPORTING DOCUMENTS

Standard House Beer List

Prussian Pilsner

Ever since studying in Germany, our brewmaster has had a love affair with Pilsner style beers. Pilsners are the hardest to make and (in his opinion) the most rewarding to taste. Our Prussian Pilsner is actually modeled after Pilsner Urquell, the original Pilsner from the city of Plzen in the Czech Republic. The Prussian Pilsner has a light golden color and rich maltiness, which separates it from the less malty German Pilsners. The best way to describe the Czech style is to say that it has a little more of everything - sweetness, bitterness, and hop nose - than the more commonplace German and North American pilsners.

Red Dragon Special Bitter

The Red Dragon is brewed after the British "Special Bitter" style. This is a truly memorable bitter with a depth of hop taste and acidity in the palate and finish. The Dragon is a clear, deep red brew with medium carbonation and a well-balanced, understated bouquet.

Bavara-Weiss

This fresh, sunny wheat beer is made with 50% wheat and 50% barley, giving it a clean light body and clove-like aroma. In addition to being a great thirst quencher and attitude adjuster, Weiss beer (the breakfast beer of Bavaria) has long been heralded by Germans for its health benefits. The special wheat beer yeast suspended in every pint contains a wealth of vitamin B complexes, trace mineral elements and protein compounds.

O'Faolain-Fest Irish Stout

You'll be surprised by this smooth, easy drinking Irish Stout. Like a true Irish Stout, the O'Faolain-Fest is light bodied, low in alcohol, and very, very creamy. It has a hop bitterness in the nose and taste and a rich coffee-like roasted barley flavor. Our Stout is a sociable brew that lubricates the wit. After a couple of pints of the O'Faolain-Fest, you'll realize that it's the Stout, not the Blarney Stone, that gives the Irish their gift for storytelling.

Spring Bock

Brewing tradition holds that when the weather is uncertain, stronger beers are made. Thus it is customary to bring in the tumultuous Spring season with a good Bock beer. For centuries, Bock beer was also served in European monasteries as a food supplement during Lent while the Monks were fasting. While Bocks cover a wide range of colors and characteristics, our Spring Bock is a strong, pale, malty beer with a hint of sweetness. The Spring Bock makes a wonderful dessert beer.

Bamberg Beer is the perfect drink to go with summertime smoked barbecue fare. The tradition of smoked beer started in the small brewing town of Bamberg, Germany. The maltings in Bamberg actually use beechwood fires to kiln the malt. The smoke from the beechwood saturates the malt which gives the final beer a very mellow smoky flavor. This beer goes great with food, but is also enjoyed as a stand-alone experience. | Bamberg Beer

Our Oktoberfest is a Marzen style beer. Marzen (or March) beer dates back to the time in Germany when March was the last month for brewing before the warmth of summer would bring out the wild yeasts and higher temperatures, wreaking havoc on developing beers. The March batch would be consumed during the summer months and whatever was left in storage would be ceremonially consumed in the fall. | Oktoberfest

The Oktoberfest celebration itself was conceived in 1810 to celebrate the betrothal of the Crown Prince of Bavaria. The "weekend" get-together was so enjoyable and the beer so fabulous, that the reception ran for 16 days.

Beware the Brewmeister! A Doppelbock is first and foremost a strong beer. The strongest beer produced in German breweries, it is likely to have an alcohol content of greater than 6.8% by volume. The first Doppelbock was brewed by the monks of St. Francis of Paula in 1634 to serve as "liquid bread" during lent. This original Doppelbock is called the Paulaner Salvator. This style of beer is full, round, and malty. It boasts a dense head, a powerful aroma, a rich start, and a long, chewy, malty finish. This one is sure to keep you warm during the long, cold, South Harbor winter. | Brewmeister Doppelbock

Sample Menu

Appetizers

Caponato Crostini
Spicy eggplant and caper salsa on crisp garlic Italian bread rounds.
Beerhall Pretzel
Fresh hot pretzel with beerradish mustard and melted cheese.
Chips and Homemade Salsa
A great starter, add $1.00 for guacamole or black bean dip.
Crunchy Fruit and Veggie Plate
Assorted fresh fruits and veggies and homemade dips.
Beer Battered Chicken Wings
Crispy golden brown with ranch, BBQ, or honey mustard sauce.
New Orleans Style BBQ Shrimp
Tangy peel-and-eat shrimp served with plenty of crusty bread.
Jamaican Jerk
A unique spicy chicken wing all the way from Jamaica, mon.
New Hampshire Codfish Cakes
Potatoes, cod fillets and onion rolled in pancake flour and browned.

Veggie Nachos
Smothered with black beans, scallions, peppers, salsa, and cheese.
Brewer's Beer Rocks
Potato dough stuffed with cabbage and sausage and baked to a golden brown.
Bread and Cheese Plate
McDougal Style served with Tempeh Pate, Curried Bean Spread, Indian Lentil Spread, and Tofu Scallion Cream Cheese. *Traditional Style* served with Crusty breads and stinky cheeses.

Side Dishes

Garlic Fries
Crisp thin fries tossed with fresh garlic.
Classic Pub Fries
Straight from the Isles, sliced thick and served hot.
McDougal Baked Potato Patties
Herbed potato patties breaded and baked to a golden brown.
Onion Rings
Homemade and hand-dipped in our own beer batter.

Soups and Stews

Brewhouse Chili
Southwestern style chili with black beans and shredded beef.
McDougal's Bean & Rice
Spicy, garlicky black beans and brown rice.
Beer & Onion Soup
This hearty, zesty soup is made with our own famous Red Dragon.
White Bean & Shredded Chicken Chili
A brewhouse favorite. Try it with a crisp cold lager.
Veggie Noodle
A great warm-me-up made from homemade vegetable stock.
Goulash
An old world favorite with sausage, tomatoes, and spices.

Pasta

Porcini Pepper Pasta
Cognac, Parmesan cheese, pepper and parsley combined in a creamy porcini sauce and tossed with linguini.
Pasta Bolognese
A zesty Italian tomato sauce with hot Italian sausage, served over corkscrew pasta with freshly grated parmesan cheese.
Chicken Pepper Pesto
Traditional garlic and basil pesto, sauteed green peppers and onions, grilled chicken breast served over a bed of linguini.
McDougal's Pesto Pasta Salad
Firm fettucini tossed in delicious pesto sauce made without the oil.

Salads

Spinach Tortellini Salad
We toss a bushel of steamed vegetables in a zesty orange and thyme balsamic vinaigrette, and heap over a platter of spinach tortellini.
Strawberry Marinated Chicken Salad
Crisp romaine lettuce tossed with grapes, green apples, cheddar cheese, red onions, and scallions and topped with grilled marinated chicken breast, fresh strawberries, and our own strawberry poppyseed dressing.

Trail Mix Salad

A garden variety of greens tossed with sweet red onions, red and green peppers, grapes, raisins, pinenuts, dried cherries and cranberries. Served with raspberry vinaigrette.

Fajita Salad

Grilled chicken or beef, onions, peppers, black beans, and tomatoes served on a crisp bed of lettuce in an edible bowl.

Caesar Salad

Tossed fresh, served with crunchy garlic croutons. Add marinated shrimp, chicken, or steak for a delicious main course.

NOTE: All salads available with shrimp, chicken, or steak.

Smothered Turkey

Thin-sliced turkey breast piled high on a sourdough baguette and smothered in a creamy Havarti and scallion cream cheese.

Dilled Roast Beef

Roast Beef, sweet pickles, sweet red onions, topped with cucumber dill sauce and served on a caraway rye roll.

The Club

Turkey, ham, bacon, lettuce, and tomato served on your choice of toasted white, wheat, or rye.

Grilled Chicken Breast

Tender chicken breast marinated and grilled to perfection, served with your choice of toppings.

Chicken Pesto

Onions and peppers sauteed in homemade pesto sauce and served on a grilled chicken breast with parmesan cheese.

Grilled Veggies

Mushrooms, onions, peppers, zucchini, and tomatoes - marinated, grilled and served in a hollowed baguette.

Hamburger

1/4 or 1/2 pound of fresh ground beef, grilled to order and served with any 3 of our delicious toppings.

Friendly Burger

Meatless patty made with soy grains, nuts, and spices, and served with any three toppings.

BBQ Beef

Hot shredded beef smothered n tangy BBQ sauce and served on a warm sourdough baguette.

Smoked Chicken with Brie

Roasted red peppers, smoked chicken and brie on baguette.

Tuna Caponata

Chunk tuna and caponata salsa served on crusty bread.

Italian Caponata Submarine

Italian Cold cuts, lettuce, tomatoes, and caponata salsa served on fresh Italian bread.

Fish 'n' Chips

A pub classic. Beer battered cod fillets served with fries.

Beer Boiled Corned Beef

Juicy, tender, and delicious, served with our famous horseradish and garlic mashed potatoes and a side salad.

Sandwiches

Entrees

Garbanzo Shepherd's Pie
This lighter interpretation of an old pub favorite leaves more room for beer!
Greek Tavern Chicken and Rice
Pennsylvania Dutch Stuffed Onions
Whole sweet Vidalias, stuffed with spicy sausage and baked in a house lager sauce.
Red Snapper Fish Tacos
Tender red snapper on a soft taco with all the trimmings.
Turkeyless a la King
This is a delicious McDougal interpretation with only 6g of fat.
Veggie Quiche
Ask your server about today's fresh veggie quiche.
Corned Beef Hash Bash
Sure to be a South Harbor favorite, homemade, and served with bread and a side salad.
Creole Stuffed Chicken Breasts
Sausage Sampler
Authentic German bratwurst and Italian sausage marinated in our secret blend of onions, garlic, Stout and spices. Grilled and served with a sourdough baguette and 3 of your favorite toppings.

Desserts

Chocolate Mocha Stout Cake
The O'Faolain-Fest Irish Stout gives this cake a rich texture and smooth coffee flavor. Try it with a stout or a specialty coffee drink!
New York Style Cheesecake
With or without strawberries, this rich and creamy cheesecake is the brewer's choice - no menu is complete without it.
McDougal's Apple Crisp
Baked tart apples and sweet brown sugar and cinnamon. If you prefer your desserts a little more sinful, add a scoop of silky French vanilla ice cream.

Or Try One of Our Dessert Drinks!

SOURCES CITED

Aidells, B. and Kelly, D. 1992. *Real Beer and Good Eats: The Rebirth of America's Beer and Food Traditions*. New York: Alfred A. Knopf, Inc.

Chapdelaine, S. *Premium Beer on the Menu Can Brew Up Business*. Restaurants USA vol. 14 no. 7 (August 1994) 42-44.

Edgar, D. 1994 *Industry Review: Out-of-This-World Growth*. The New Brewer vol. 11 no. 3 (May-June 1994) 11-40.

--------. 1994 ed. *North American Brewers Resource Directory*. Boulder: Brewers Publications.

FIU. *The Real Failure Rate of Restaurants*. Hospitality Review Fall 1991.

University of Michigan and Cornell Researchers. *Failure Rate Better than Expected*. Restaurant Hospitality March 1992.

Microbrewery

BUSINESS PLAN

JUNIPER CREEK BREWING COMPANY

777 Main St.
Troy, MI 48333

February 1995

This business plan for a microbrewery explains the development of a brewery from the ground up. It explains elements of the brewing process, including the brewhouse, barrels, keg filler, and malt, hops, and other supplies; the necessary machinery and laboratory equipment; expenses, such as start-up, insurance, rent, and overhead; the need for a skilled brewmaster and the attendant costs; and the other crucial components of production. It also features considerations of market segment, competition, and regulations.

- STATEMENT OF PURPOSE

- COMPANY DESCRIPTION

- FUNDING

- PRODUCTS

- MARKET SEGMENT

- COMPETITION

- LOCATION

- MARKETING

- MANAGEMENT

- FINANCE

- PRODUCTION

- REGULATIONS

STATEMENT OF PURPOSE

The Juniper Creek Brewing Company is a small scale microbrewery that will be located in Troy, Michigan. The brewery will occupy the back 3600 square feet of 777 Main Street. This is a new business in the start-up phase. Recent changes in Michigan law have made microbrewing legal. Due to certain tax advantages available only to microbrewers, it is profitable as well. By definition a microbrewer is one that brews less than 20,000 barrels per year. Juniper Creek Brewery plans to start production at 3120 barrels and with phased expansion grow to 7500 barrels over five years.

Initial plans are to produce one product that shall be an amber-style ale. This beer will be sold in kegs to a local distributor for resale to the tri-county draught beer market. In-house sales of beer as well as take-out sales are also planned. Tours and sampling will be offered.

The long-term goals of the Juniper Creek Brewing Company are to slowly add capacity up to the constraints of the site (7500 BBL). A second product is planned once the market has accepted the initial ale offering. This second product will be a lager beer. Specialty and seasonal brews will also be crafted once the business is up and running. These types of beers sell quickly and are usually quite popular. In addition, specialty "house" beers will be brewed and labeled for local taverns.

COMPANY DESCRIPTION

Juniper Creek Brewing Company is a small scale microbrewery located in Troy, Michigan. It occupies a one-floor, light-industrial building at 777 Main Street. The building is divided into three business sections. Juniper Creek Brewery will occupy the back section, which is approximately 3600 square feet and faces Water Street. The brewery will produce up to 3120 barrels of beer per year in its initial design. There are the capacity and space available to expand to 7500 barrels per year. Initial plans are to produce one product that shall be an amber-style ale.

The Juniper Creek Brewing Company is incorporated in the State of Michigan as a sub-chapter S Corporation. The Internal Revenue Service has officially accepted Juniper Creek Brewery's election as an S-Corporation as of January 10, 1994. The corporation is currently in the investigation stage by the State Liquor Control Commission. In addition, application materials have been sent to the Bureau of Alcohol, Tobacco, and Firearms. Their investigation has yet to commence. These two investigations, once complete will result in the issuance of a Brewers License and a Brewers Notice respectively.

Key vendors have been identified and quotes obtained. Cost figures for equipment, inventory, building renovation, and labor have been identified and figured into the business plan. Production costs have been calculated, product pricing has been estimated, and profit potential has been approximated. A tentative lease has been written up, but it is not yet signed.

The legal name of the corporation is Juniper Creek Brewing Company. The company was incorporated in the State of Michigan in 1993. The corporation has also registered a DBA or "Doing Business As" under "Juniper Creek Brewery". The Internal Revenue Service has issued an Employer Identification Number which is 67-2488907, issued 10/5/93.

The project will be funded with primarily debt financing. A loan will be sought through First of Michigan Bank, Troy. First of Michigan will finance approximately 75% of the project, with Juniper Creek Brewery financing the remainder. The start-up project costs, which includes capital equipment, initial inventory, building renovations, and working capital, total approximately $250,000.

> **Amount of Funds Sought**: $250,000
>
> **Basic Use of Funds Sought**:
>
> ☐ To acquire brewing equipment, supplies, and inventory
> ☐ To reconstruct portions of the building and bring in the necessary utilities.
> ☐ To make the building meet local zoning requirements.
> ☐ To provide working capital.
> ☐ To purchase initial inventory (1 month supply or 60 barrels).

The Juniper Creek Brewing Company will initially produce one product. This will be an ale product, along the lines of an Amber Ale. The beer will be produced continuously throughout the year, with a targeted weekly production of 60 barrels. This will result in two weekly batch runs of 30 barrels each. Bottling and kegging operations will be done on non-brewing days. The initial yearly volume of the brewery will be 3120 BBL with room for expansion to 7500.

The brewery will be open to the public for tours and sampling. The hours of operation will be from 9:00 a.m. to 5:00 p.m. Beer will be offered for sale on the premises as well as take-out. Kegged beer will be sold to Johnson & Sons Distributors for further sale to retail outlets. Sales will be in half barrels, quarter barrels, cases of bottles, and six-packs.

The brewery has targeted the tri-county area surrounding Troy (Oakland, Macomb, and Wayne) as the main market area for sales. The population demographic of this area is well-suited to beer sales.

It is important to note that the microbrewing industry is now in its second decade. As of June 1993 there were more than 320 micro- and pub-breweries in the United States. The breakdown more precisely is 110 microbreweries and 210 brewpubs. These combined producers of craft-brewed beer account for only 0.6% of domestic beer sales. Total U.S. beer sales were 180,770,000 barrels of which 1,204,000 barrels were from microbreweries, reflecting growth of 41% for the microbreweries over the large domestic brewers. It is important to note the failure rate for microbreweries is 1 in 4 whereas for small business start-ups it is 1 in 2.

In a ranking of the top five U.S. counties with populations of 1 million or more, based on per capita income, Oakland county ranks third highest. The per capita income for Oakland county is $21,125. In addition, Oakland county is ranked first in Michigan in per capita income. Oakland county is ranked as the 28th largest county in the United States with a population of 1,083,592, according to the 1990 census.

Beer keg sales of domestic beer from the large breweries, specifically Anheuser-Busch, Miller Brewing, and Coors vary in price, as often beer specials and promotions are underway as these companies vie for the mass market consumer. Their sales prices reflect this in generally a lower price than a microbrewed beer.

Miller Brewing Company commonly sells 1/2 barrels for $50.00 a piece. This includes their flagship brands, Miller and Miller Lite, as well as Genuine Draft. Beer prices have increased in 1994 with half-kegs of Budweiser now selling at $63.00 per half barrel.

"Old Detroit," a microbrewed beer from Detroit-Mackinac, is selling for $62.00 per half-keg, while Frankenmuth's Pilsner is at $76.00 per half-barrel. Frankenmuth is Michigan's largest and most well-known microbrewery. The Juniper Creek Brewery is targeting the bar/ restaurant draught beer sales.

COMPETITION

The largest competitive advantage for the microbrewery is the demographic population shift to Oakland county, coupled with the rise of the Troy area as a retail and dining magnet. The Troy area boasts some of the areas finest eating and drinking establishments with more of the same coming into the area. Juniper Creek Brewing Company will be highly visible with its product in most area bars and nightclubs, as well as in retail stores.

The sheer uniqueness of the business coupled with the great superiority of the product quality and flavor all contribute towards a winning formula for success. On either coast of the United States brewpubs and microbreweries are growing and succeeding at a rapid clip due to demands of the public, which is looking for superior flavor, high quality, and moderate price.

LOCATION

The microbrewery has decided to locate in Troy, in the heart of Oakland county. This was a purposeful decision. In Oakland County, in 1993, 19,000 jobs were created, representing 2 out of every 3 new jobs in the state. In addition, 60% of all foreign money invested in Michigan is in Oakland county. One third of all the research and development money is in this county. There are 36,000 businesses in Oakland county, including 200 of the Fortune 500. The population shift and pursuant demand for goods and services is in full swing in the Troy area.

The Chrysler Tech Center alone has 7000 jobs, with General Motors putting 4000 jobs into Pontiac. The I-75 corridor is becoming know as "Automation alley" with all the robotics, plastics, computers, and R&D companies located there. Over 51% of state robotic sales emanate from Oakland county.

The business success here is due to the diversity of government services, the availability of land and office space, and the competitive costs to do business. Michigan is leading all northern industrial states in terms of economic growth as well.

Oakland University is investing 38.5 million dollars in their new science and technology center. Oakland Community College will design tailor-made training programs for existing and newly-created high tech businesses to attract them. There are 53,000 students currently enrolled in Oakland University.

The quality of life here is highly sought after, with over 450 lakes; 100 golf courses; 87,000 acres of parkland; ski resorts; the Pistons; the Lions; and Cranbrook & museums.

Major firms represented in Oakland County

Michigan National Corp.
Kmart Corp.
Handleman Company
Alexander Hamilton
Dupont Automotive
General Motors
Perry Drugs Stores
Kelly Services
Thorn Apple Valley
PMH Corp.
Ameritech Publishing
Masco
Chrysler Corp.
Arbor Drugs
The Budd Company
Guardian Alarm
ACO Hardware

MARKETING

Juniper Creek Brewing Company will market their products through two different avenues. The first will focus on the sales of kegged beer to draught accounts throughout the Metro Detroit area. The marketing in this area involves the use of Point-of-Sale (POS) materials such as posters, table tents, tap handles, buttons, tee-shirts, etc. In the initial product roll-out, extensive use of our distributor Johnson & Sons Inc.'s experience and account knowledge will be made.

Area bars and restaurants will be provided POS materials appropriate to their ability to sell the product. Tap handles will also be provided. Tap handles cost approximately $10 each, and will be purchased through Taps 'R' Us, Window Lake, Wisconsin. Posters and table tents range in price based on quantities ordered. These will be procured through a local printer.

The second marketing thrust will be for sales of bottled beer through retail outlets. Once again, POS materials are necessary, although with differing needs. Posters and shelf markers, as well as posters and vinyl stickers will be used. These will also be procured through a local printer.

MANAGEMENT

The microbrewery will be managed by Kate Bannister. Ms. Bannister will be in charge of production planning, purchasing, inventory control, quality control and accounts payable. Ms. Bannister has experience in all of the above areas through her working background in business. She will be assisted by Patrick O'Connor, her spouse.

Sales will be handled by Patrick O'Connor, who has extensive management experience. Mr. O'Connor has a B.S. degree in Engineering from Boston University as well as a Masters degree in Business Administration from Michigan State University. He is also a member of the Institute for Brewing Studies. The I.B.S. is an educational association for micro- and pub-brewers. He has attended the Siebel Institute of Technology's "Microbrewery and Pub Brewery Operations Course" Nov. 15-19, 1993, in Chicago. This class was given in a working brewery for an entire week.

Operations will be handled jointly by management and the brewmaster. The brewmaster will be hired in the near future. The person for the job will be a graduate from one of the nations brewing schools who has worked under a Master brewmaster for 2-4 years. Candidates are always available, as there are more brewers looking for work than there are openings. Juniper Creek Brewery will have the luxury of being very selective to identify the perfect candidate for the job and for the right price. The brewhouse supplier has offered to assist in the interviewing process. Candidates are available through a resume service offered by the Institute for Brewing Studies and through trade journal advertising.

FINANCE

Cash Requirements

Cash requirements for start-up include the following elements

- Working Capital
- Percentage of capitalization costs
- Initial Inventories

Overhead Costs

Overhead costs are made up of the following elements

Rent

The brewery is renting a portion of an 11,000 square foot building located at 777 Main St., Troy, Michigan. The brewery will rent 3600 square feet of the available floor space on a single floor. The building is semi-industrial in nature with the proper utilities necessary for the successful operation of a microbrewery.

The brewery will share the building with two other established businesses. In the first third of the building, which fronts Main Street, is occupied by Troy Hardware. The middle section of the building is occupied by The High Rise Bakery. It is anticipated that brewery operations will not be affected by any of the other businesses' operations, nor will the brewery affect the other businesses.

The lease is intended to function and operate as a triple net lease, with the brewery responsible for its pro rata portion of real estate taxes, insurance, and operating expenses. The approximate cost of the lease is $2,000 per month inclusive.

Insurance

In addition to the insurance included in the lease, the brewery is responsible for certain business insurances. These additional insurances are liability (includes State mandated liquor liability), workmans' compensation, and contents insurance. The policy will through the Sheister & Sheister Agency, Troy, Michigan at a yearly cost of $6,000.

Start-up costs include improvements made to the building which are necessary for brewing operations. This includes bringing water, electric, and natural gas into the building to where the brewhouse equipment will be located. In addition, floor drains and waste water handling improvements are necessary. The build-out costs are broken down into a labor component and a supply component.

Initial inventories for one month of brewing are also included in the start-up costs. Malt, hops, yeast, and cleaning supplies are included in this amount. After start-up, inventory costs will be handled on a month-to-month basis.

Electrical: For wiring of pumps, solenoids, temperature controller, natural gas burner control panel, and refrigeration unit. Calvin Electrical, Oakland, Michigan will be used. Approximate cost is under $1,000.

Natural Gas: Installation of a natural gas line to the Mash/Brew Kettle at a flow rate of 12 cubic feet per minute at minimum 5 inch water column. Westchester Mechanical, Oakland, Michigan will be used at an approximate cost under $500.

Water: Bring in city water to brewhouse at a flow rate of 25 gallons per minute at a minimum of 30 PSI. Westchester Mechanical will do this at the same time as the gas line is installed.

Rigger: Material handling equipment to unload and set tanks in place. Cambridge Supplies, Oak Park, Michigan will provide these services for under $1,000.

Gas: Oxygen, carbon dioxide, and controls need to be provided. The gas canisters and controls will be provided by CJO Gas. Oxygen tanks are for lease for $100 plus $11 per fill (50lb). Carbon dioxide tanks are for lease at $160 plus $18 per fill (50lb.)

HVAC: The burner exhaust and steam vents must be vented to the outside through the roof. This work will be done by Martin Heating and Cooling at an approximate cost of $1,000.

Refrigeration System: A walk-in refrigeration system is necessary for keeping the kegged beer cold. The walk-in is 20' by 25', 10.5' tall., and cooled by a 4 HP 230 V three phase motor. This includes an 84" door. Glycol is used to chill the unit. The entire system will be installed by Pontiac Refrigeration, Pontiac, Michigan.

Start-up Costs

Skilled Trades

Start-Up Cost Summary

Build-Out

Electrical	$1000
Plumbing	$1000
HVAC	$1000
Rigger	$1000
Refrigeration	$2000
Walk-in	$10,000
Total	$16,000

Start-Up Cost Summary
...continued

Capital Equipment

Brewhouse	$175,000
Barrels	$13,950
Keg Filler	$13,750
Lab Equipment	$2,000
Total	$204,700

Starting Inventory

Barley Malt (1 month supply)	$3600
Hops (1 month supply)	$240
Yeast	$500
Total	$4340

Malt 60 bags/wk x 4 weeks @ $15.00 per 50 lb bag
Hops 1.25 boxes/wk x 4 weeks @ $45.00 per 44 lb box

Wage costs: Brewmaster
Base pay $30,000 year

FICA (7.65%)	$2,295
FUTA (3.80%)	$1,140
W/C (5.25%)	$1,575
Total	$35,010

Brewmaster will cost approximately $3000 per month.

PRODUCTION

The beer will be produced in a 15 barrel brewhouse supplied by JV Northwest, Wilsonville, Oregon. The various parts of the brewhouse are described as follows:

The first step in brewing is to mix the cracked malted barley with hot water in the mash/lauter tun, which produces "mash." The mash tun is a double-walled vessel crafted from polished stainless steel with fiberglass insulation and a top double door. A side manway makes grain removal easy. Standard features include a vee wire screen, complete drainage, a temperature well and sparging fittings. A sweet, clear liquid called "wort" is filtered out of the mash and transferred to the brewkettle.

The brewkettle is constructed similarly to the mash tun, featuring double-wall stainless steel with fiberglass insulation. The wort in the kettle is brought to a rolling boil and some hops are added early to provide a mild bitterness. Other hops (finishing hops) are added later to give a fine aroma. The hot wort is cooled to fermentation temperature through a heat exchanger. The heat removed from the wort is transferred to water, which is stored in a large tank called a hot liquor tank. This hot water is used constantly over and over again, either in cleaning, sterilization, or to fill the mash tun.

The cold wort is transferred to the fermented. Yeast is added and fermentation begins. Fermenters are also know as uni-tanks. The fermenters Juniper Creek Brewery will use are double-wall stainless steel with dished heads and conical bottoms. The cooling jacket has automatic temperature control. The uni-tanks have sample ports as well as temperature controls, a pressure manifold, and adjustable legs. During fermentation the brewers yeast transforms the sweet wort into a flavorful solution containing alcohol and carbon dioxide. After fermentation, the green beer is aged to develop its final smooth taste.

Once the beer is aged properly, in our case after 14 days, it is filtered to remove yeast and to clarify the beer. After filtration the finished beer is stored in a bright beer tank (serving tank or tax tank) until it is ready to be served, bottled, or kegged. At this point the beer is at the height of its freshness and full of flavor.

Capital Equipment

The brewhouse is supplied by JV Northwest, Wilsonville, Oregon. JV Northwest is one of the leading suppliers of brewing equipment throughout the United States and Canada. The brewhouse will be a 15-barrel turnkey system complete with all tanks, hoses, fittings, controls, and gauges to brew 3120 barrels of ale per year. Each additional fermentation tank adds 780 barrels more production. Expansion can reach 7500 barrels per year with the 15 barrel brewkettle. Juniper Creek Brewery plans expansion in year 2 as well as year 3. The initial cost of the brewhouse is $175,000.

Brewhouse

JV Northwest includes in their sales price extensive consultation services. These services include working with all trade groups by phone as well as a site visit. In addition, in consultation with our brewmaster, JVNW will provide formulation for up to four brands of beer or ale. Formulation will include instructions for wort production, yeasting, control of fermentation, aging of beer, etc. Additionally, up to five days of start-up assistance by a qualified brewer will be provided.

Barrels

Barrels will be bought from SABCO Industries, Toledo, Ohio. Initial plans are to buy 500 barrels, which will provide a four-week barrel supply when brewing to capacity. Cost per barrel is $27.90 for a standard Hoff-Stevens keg. Total barrel cost is $13,950.

Keg Filler

A semi-automatic single valve keg washing, sanitizing, and filling machine will be bought from I.D. Distributions, Thousand Oaks, California. Called the Mini-King, it is a complete washer/sterilizing/racking machine complete with detergent and water supply system, include dual compartment tank, stainless steel pumps, heater dosing system, and controls. The machine can fill up to 30 half kegs per hour, therefore it is estimated kegging operations for 60 barrels weekly production will take a minimum of 4 hours, and most likely complete in one working day. The cost of the Mini-King is $13,750.

Laboratory Equipment

The laboratory equipment necessary for proper testing and evaluation of the beer throughout the brewing and fermentation process includes the following items:

Microscope, for counting yeast cells.
Hydrometer, for measuring specific gravity.
PH meter, accurate to 0.01 of a unit, plus combination electrode suitable for use with wort and fermentation products.
Air tester

These will be purchased from Cole-Parmer Instrument Company, Niles, Illinois. Cost for the above, plus any incidental supplies, is approximately $2000.

Supplies

Malt

Malted barley is the primary ingredient by which beer is produced. The malt will be supplied by Briess Malting Company, Chilton, Wisconsin. Briess is one of the national premier maltsters, with the ability to ensure timely delivery and consistent quality of the mal product.

Malt one packaged in 50 lb. bags. Each brew will consume 15 bags. 60 bags will be used weekly at a cost of $900/week, or in other terms, $225 per brew.

Hops

Hops will be bought from John I. Haas and Company, Yakima, Washington. Like Briess maltsters, Haas and Company enjoys the reputation of being a national leader in hop production. The ingredient suppliers were chosen for their known reputations of timely delivery as well as consistent and known quality.

Each brew will use 7.5 lbs. of hops at a cost of $15.00 per brew or $60 per week.

Yeast & Additives

Yeast, beer clarifiers, stabilizers, finings, cleaning supplies, as well as laboratory and technical services will be purchased from J.E. Siebel Sons, Chicago, Illinois.

Cleansing and Sanitation

The proper cleaning and sanitation levels necessary to meet strict health department guidelines will be achieved through the use of Orasan, (previously Huwa-San). Orasan is a new, complex compound of highly concentrated oxygen carriers, stabilizing agents on an acid base, and synergistically acting trace elements. It is superior to chlorine in its ability to kill germs, is completely safe for human and animal consumption, and will not create adverse environmental conditions. The advantages to using Orasan is no unpleasant taste; no odor; disinfects by separation of oxygen; assisted by trace elements; long-term effect; single application for long distance water conduits; not harmful to pipes and installations; water doesn't foam in it; and it is heat resistant and efficacious in hot water. Orasan is supplied by International Connection, Inc., Kewaskum, Wiscosin.

Filters

Sheet filters will be used to filter the fresh beer. From one to two pad filters are used per barrel brewed, resulting in a cost of approximately $0.80 - $1.20 per barrel. This type of filtering is easy to operate, easy to clean and sanitize. It leaves no particulate matter in the beer and is suitable for aseptic filtration. Sheet filters will be obtained from Siebel Company, Chicago, Illinois.

REGULATIONS

Regulation of microbreweries is done in many ways. The Department of the Treasury through the Bureau of Alcohol, Tobacco, and Firearms regulates and collects Federal excise tax. The State of Michigan Liquor Control Commission collects state excise tax. In addition, the state Department of Agriculture inspects and licenses facilities. Local ordinances must be followed as well.

Labels

Michigan label requirements state that the brewery must adopt Federal Alcohol Administration labeling regulations. In Michigan this means the label cannot state the alcohol content. In addition, the product label must have federal approval. Product samples must be analyzed and a registration number of approval assigned before the product can be sold in the state. Once the label has federal approval, two samples of 12-ounce bottles must be submitted as well as one set of loose labels. A special provision requires the refund value of the container and the name of the state to be clearly indicated on the label.

Taxes & Deposits

A keg deposit is required upon sale of the keg. The deposit for Michigan is $10. Bottle deposits are $.10 per bottle.

The state beer tax rate for Michigan is $6.30 per 31 gallon barrel. In-state brewers receive a rebate of tax on beer shipped outside of the state. The tax per case of 24 12oz. bottles is $.4645.

Shipping Requirements

Beer may only be shipped from the brewery to a licensed wholesaler. If beer sales are made out-of-state, then a special seller's license is required. It costs $1000. A bond is required of the brewery of either $1000 or 1/2 of the total excise taxes paid in the last calendar year, whichever is greater. Shipping brewers must pay taxes twice monthly. In addition, a monthly report of shipments is required.

Wholesaler Relations

The brewery shall grant each wholesaler with a written agreement and designate a specific sales territory. The brewery may not fix, maintain, or establish the resale price. The wholesaler may not sell outside his sales territory. The brewery may not terminate, cancel, refuse to renew, or discontinue an agreement, except for good cause, and must afford the wholesaler 30 days in which to submit a plan of corrective action to comply with the agreement and an additional 90 days to cure such noncompliance.

Mobile Studio

BUSINESS PLAN

CRS MOBILE STUDIO

427 Longman Blvd.
Donnar Park, MI 48269

November 1994

This business plan describes a traditional business that takes advantage of mobility to create a niche for itself. This twist on a photography studio serves as an example of how an entrepreneur can compete in a field once thought too competitive. Look for a discussion of market potential and an easy way to perform demographic research.

MOBILE STUDIO BUSINESS PLAN

EXECUTIVE SUMMARY

The purpose of this report is to determine the feasibility of opening a mobile portrait studio tentatively named CRS Mobile Studio, in the predetermined area of Donnar Park, Michigan. An extensive study of area demographics, equipment cost, and expenses was performed to determine if the sales potential out weighs the breakeven point. Also, a sampling of the target market was taken to determine how consumers in the chosen trading area felt about a proposed traveling studio.

Secondary Highlights

Market potential for the chosen area was determined through a demographic study. Statistics that were closely considered included 1994 total population and the number of competitors. These figures were then applied to a number of formulas to determine total market potential, total sales potential, capital needs, and sales volume needed to meet the breakeven point. All ending figures are based on a time period of one year. These secondary resources yielded the following results:

⊃Total market potential of 550 houses
⊃Total sales potential of $154,550
⊃Breakeven point of $109,292.64
⊃Jobs needed to breakeven: 388
⊃Capital needed for start-up: $54,646.32

Primary Highlights

A sampling of the Donnar Park area was taken by conducting a survey of 100 parents at Donnar Park Nursery School. Results were used to asses the potential market, and can be considered an accurate account of the target market's photography needs and wants. The most pertinent question posed to those surveyed was, "Does the idea of having a competitively-priced, professional portrait done in your home appeal to you?" The results proved more than satisfactory with 81% responding yes, and a mere 19% answering no. Other questions on the survey dealt with specifics such as types of backgrounds and portrait packages. These results were of great help in planning the equipment and retail strategy for CRS Mobile Studio.

Conclusion/ Recommendations

A considerable amount of time and effort went into assessing the true market potential of Donnar Park and the capability of it supporting another photography studio. After closely examining all the data compiled, and looking at what it would take for CRS Mobile Studio to succeed, it is the conservative opinion of this writer the CRS Mobile Studio would have a reasonable chance for success.

INTRODUCTION

From as early as the mid 1800's, people have had their portraits taken in order to document themselves and their loved ones. This desire outweighed the personal discomfort often involved in having a portrait taken including wearing a head brace and sitting still for several minutes in the bright sun, without blinking. (Upton and Upton 10). This longing for personal documentation is still alive and thriving today, especially in households with young children. According to American Demographics, families with young children are avid picture takers. Eighty percent of households with children aged two and under are involved in regularly obtaining portraits. While this percentage does decrease as children age, seventy-five percent of families with three to eleven year-olds and seventy percent of households with teenagers still habitually solicit photographic services. (Judith Waldrop p10). The following is an in-depth business plan for a mobil portrait studio designed to capitalize on those households involved in picture taking.

The purpose of this document is to determine the feasibility of successfully opening a portable photography studio in the are of Donnar Park, Michigan. It closely examines the demographics of this area and determines possible market potential, sales potential, capital needed for start-up, and the breakeven point in dollars and jobs. Although extensive primary and secondary research and analysis of this target area has been conducted, this report is limited to some extent by lack of knowledge of certain formulas used to give a precise accounting of a market's potential. To overcome this limitation, certain figures have been conservatively applied to these formulas so as not to exaggerate the market's true potential.

Purpose, Scope, and Limitations

In the preparation of this report, three secondary sources were reviewed and cited. Specific area demographics were gathered from Metropolitan Neighborhood Market Information, distributed by Ameritech Pages Plus. In addition, 54 surveys out of 100 were totaled and analyzed to gain additional information on the want and need for this type of service. Together, these sources have been used to reach a "go or no go" decision for the mobile photography studio. Distinct figures have been readied to aid in the understanding and verification of the final decision.

Sources and Methods

This report will begin with a description of the service to be offered. It will be followed by a look at the chosen community, including demographics and competitive pressures. From this examination of the targeted area, a complete market potential analysis will be formed, and will conclude with recommendations on how to proceed.

Report Organization

The business chosen for study is a mobile portrait studio referred to as CRS Mobile Studio or simply CRS. The basic operations of CRS Mobile Studio will be to travel to homes in the Donnar Park area, photograph household members, and then approximately three weeks later, furnish customers with finished portraits. CRS will travel with a complete studio that will provide the customer with a diverse choice of portrait style (formal or informal) and background.

DESCRIPTION OF THE PROPOSED BUSINESS

CUSTOMER ANALYSIS

Since the beginning of portrait photography people have been enthralled with the ability to document their lives through the use of portraits. This is especially true for families who

Customer Motivations

want to chart the growth of their children. The capability of having a seemingly permanent record of themselves, and those close to them, is the main motivation of the consumer seeking the services of a portrait studio. In most cases this means picking up the phone, making an appointment with a studio, getting the portrait subjects, usually children, to the studio without getting their clothes dirty, and approximately two to six weeks later picking up and paying for portraits.

CRS proposes to eliminate most of this hassle by providing the Donnar Park consumer with an in-home portrait studio. Results for the primary research revealed that out of those surveyed, 81% like the idea of a portrait studio coming to their homes, as opposed to a mere 19% who did not like such a concept.

Buying Habits

The desire to document family history through photography leads directly to the buying habits of the portrait consumer. For example, a family with one child, seeking a record of his/her growth will have their child's portrait taken as early as the day he/she is born. This is soon followed by portraits taken when the child reaches three and/or six months, one year, eighteen months, and two years. The average consumer will follow with a yearly portrait of the child normally taken on or near a birthday or major holiday. As the child grows, the number of portraits decrease, but not to the detriment of the portrait studio. With age comes change, and new opportunities for the studio photographer. These would include school portraits, team pictures, dance class pictures, prom pictures, and the list goes on. Being a mobile studio, CRS could easily follow this progression.

The Community

The area chosen to open the mobile photography studio is Donnar Park, Michigan. Many factors entered into this decision. To begin with, it will be the chosen residence of the photographer. Knowing that just because you live in an area isn't reason enough for opening a business there, many other factors have been considered. These include demographics, such as population by households, income and total retail sales captured on photographic finishing and supplies in the area. According to *1994/1995 Metropolitan Neighborhood Market Information*, published by Ameritech Pages Plus, the total population of the Donnar Park area is 47,952 persons, with 18,357 households. Dollars spent on photography finishing and supplies top out at 5,158,000 (12). These statistics alone are encouraging, and are the basis for further investigation.

Competitive Pressures

A list of competitors within Donnar Park dealing with portrait photography are as follows:

- BF Collins
- Carol Carter Photography
- Glamour Portrait Photography
- JT Kennedy Photography

With the $5,158,000 total dollars being spent on photography in the area, (Ameritech 12), divided by the four existing studios, gives an estimated sales volume per existing studio of $1,289,500. With the addition of CRS Mobile Studio, the estimated sales volume (5,158,000/5) is $1,031,600 per studio.

The main advantage the existing studios have is their established customer base. However, after contacting them on the phone, it was discovered that when they do travel to peoples' homes, three out of four do not bring a complete studio. The main reason cited for this was the difficulty in bringing different backgrounds and lighting systems into individual homes. Contrary to what the competition said, this problem is easily solved at a minimal cost by purchasing a collapsible background specifically designed for on-the-road photography.

Retail Strategy

For a new studio to succeed in this community, it has to differentiate itself from the existing studios. CRS will offer the advantages of total mobility, multiple backgrounds, and start-up specials.

Capitalizing on the current studios' inability to travel with a complete studio, CRS will offer a collapsible background, specifically designed for on-the-road photography (refer to equipment list). The need for traveling with a complete studio is supported by the primary research conducted. The results revealed that the consumer likes the flexibility to choose among different backgrounds or simply a room in their home. Complete results can be found below.

CRS will also differentiate itself from its competitors by offering start-up specials that customers expect will accompany the opening of a new business. The logical choice for an opening special would be a portrait sale. Knowing that the price of printing a portrait decreases with each additional portrait purchased, the start-up special would offer a free 8 x 10 portrait to each first time customer. The initial cost of giving a free 8 x 10 portrait to each first time customer, would be $4.36, with the price decreasing to $2.37 after the first three ordered. The cost of this offer will be easily offset by the sale of additional portraits. For example, the average market value of 8 x 10 portrait is $35.00. This figure was obtained by calling 15 different studios within the metropolitan area. Some studios quoted prices as high as $65.00 for one 8 x 10. The bottom line for success in the photography field is the ability to capture the "perfect" image on a negative. This is only achieved through knowledge, experience, and a love for the art form. All the specials in the world won't help if the studio does not have the ability to fill this very basic, but all important task.

MEASURE OF POTENTIAL MARKET

Trade Area

The trading area, Donnar Park, Michigan, is a community of people whose average household income is $63,853 (Ameritech p. 12). The total household (i.e., residential) expenditure in photographic finishing and supplies is $5,158,000 (Ameritech p. 12). Taking this figure and dividing it by the number of households in the area ($5,158,000/18.357) reveals that each household spends an average of $281.00 a year in this classification. Taking the total number of households and dividing them by five (the four existing studios plus CRS), reveals a market share for each studio of 3,671 homes.

Market Potential for CRS Mobile Studio

Based on Demographics of Trading Area
Donnar Park, Michigan
1994

Total Dollars Spent On Photography in Trade Area	$5,158,000
Total Houses In Trade Area	18,357
Dollars Spent Per Household	$281.00
Total Houses In Trade Area	18,357
No. of Studios in Trade Area	5
Total Market Potential in Households for CRS Mobil Studio	3671
Total Houses in Trade Area	3671
Dollars Spent per Household	$281.00
Total Market Potential in Dollars	**$1,031,551**

Sales Potential

Realistically, it would not possible for CRS to adequately service 3,671 homes initially. Also, leakage to other studios outside the selected trading area needs to be considered. Therefore, taking into account the probability of efficient service and the consideration of leakage, CRS's realistic market share will be based on 15 percent of the 3,671 homes or 550 homes. Using this figure, and multiplying it by $281.00 (expenditure per household) reveals a potential earning of $154,550 per year.

To realize annual earnings of $154,550, the new studio would need to visit eleven houses a week. This figure is based on a fifty week year as opposed to a fifty-two week year.

One Year Sales Potential for CRS Mobile Studio

Based on Demographics of Trading Area
Donnar Park, Michigan
1994

Total No. of Houses in Trade Area	3671
Total Dollars Spent per Household	$281.00
Total Potential Sales Volume for CRS Mobile Studio	$1,031,551
Total No. of Houses in Trade Area	3671
% of Capable Coverage & Leakage Allowance	15%
No. of Remaining Houses for Basis of Sales Potential	550
No. of Remaining Households	550
Dollars Spent per Household	$281.00
Total Sales Potential for CRS Mobile Studio	**$154,550**

To obtain the goal of eleven houses per week, CRS will have to be creative in its approach. As previously stated, primary research revealed that 81 percent of those surveyed liked the idea of a fully equipped traveling studio. Therefore, this will be one of CRS's main selling points. Survey results also show holidays and birthdays as the time of greatest consumer demand. Armed with this information and knowledge that these occasions are hot sellers for most retailers, CRS will focus marketing strategies accordingly.

Advertising in the beginning will be done through direct mail campaigns, initially targeted at the 48269 ZIP code area. Also, advertisements will be posted in the local newsletters of area churches. In addition to the above, CRS will make its services known to new parents at local hospitals by including in the baby packages distributed to these parents, coupons for 20 percent off portraits taken within the first six months of the babies life. The object of capturing this specific segment of the target market will be to create and foster a loyalty between CRS and the new family in hopes of achieving repeat business as the baby and/or family grows.

Detailed below is a complete list of equipment, supplies, and expenses. Normally, these three would be separated into more specific categories to obtain a true breakeven point. However due to the limitations mentioned earlier (see "Purpose, Scope, and Limitations"), they have been compiled into one group, Expenses, on the Breakeven Point chart.

Capturing the Market

BREAKEVEN SALES VOLUME

Estimated First Year Sales Volume

Equipment

Hasselblad 501c 2 1/4 Camera	$2400.00
Polaroid Back	440.00
Westcott Specialty Collapsible Backdrops	
1-Blue, 1-Grey	200.00
Paper 9ft. Backdrop	29.00
Backdrop Stand-Westcott	29.00
Novatron Pro Light Kit (1040)	1569.99
Minolta Flash Meter	329.00
Bogen Tripod No. 3036	209.00
Bogen Panhead No. 3047	72.99
FH-1 Universal Filter Holder	53.99
Smith Victor 12 x 12 Jells	17.99
Multi-Dome Soft Box	70.99
Camera ag	100.00
TOTAL EQUIPMENT	**$5623.93**

Supplies and Expenses Based on One Years Needs

Account at North American Lab	$2000.00
Film—negative (576 rolls)	2016.00
Film—polaroid	619.20
Gas ($20 a week)	960.00
Answering Service Inc. ($55 a week)	660.00
Advertising Expense	5000.00
Salaries	35,000.00
Insurance—Car	1754.00
Insurance—Equipment	36.00
Maintenance—Equipment	300.00
Depreciation—Equipment	100.00
Business License	100.00
Phone	100.00
Phone Line	600.00
Taxes	496.39

TOTAL SUPPLIES AND EXPENSES $49,122.39

Total equipment, sales, and expenses equals $54,746.32. As previously stated, these have been compiled under the grouping of Total Expenses. This figure was then divided by the sales-to-expense ratio of 50%, yielding a breakeven point of $109,292.64. The breakeven point was then divided by $281.00 (expenditure per household) to reveal a total 388 jobs needed in the first year of operations in order to breakeven. For a clear breakdown of these figures, refer to the Breakeven Point for CRS Mobile Studio on the table below.

First Year Capital Requirements

The total equipment plus total supplies and expenses equals $54,746.32. CRS Mobile Studio will obtain this through the use of a private backer.

CONCLUSIONS AND RECOMMENDATIONS

This plan has attempted to analyze the market potential of Donnar Park, Michigan and assess its capability of supporting a fifth portrait studio, CRS Mobile Studio. A considerable amount of time and effort has gone into a close examination of the market, and what it would take for a new studio to succeed in said area.

The decision to proceed with this venture has not been made lightly. After carefully assessing the market and examining what it would take for CRS to succeed, it is the opinion of this writer that the said studio could breakeven in the first of operation. Even taking into consideration the difficulty of capturing the market share needed to succeed, this studio has the necessary drive, commitment, and the education to venture out on its own.

Based on 1994 Expense Figure

Total Expenses	$54,646.32
Expense to Sales Ratio	50%
Breakeven Point	$109,292.64
Breakeven Point	$109,292.64
Dollars Spent per Household	$281.00
Total No. of Jobs in First Year Needed to Break Even	**388**

WORKS CITED

Upton, Barbra and John Upton. *Photography*. Boston: Brown and Company, 1976.
Waldrop, Judith. "Photography of Children." *American Demographics*. 14 April 1992: 10.

Newsletter

BUSINESS PLAN

NETWORK JOURNAL

117 Munson Ave.
Eunice, LA 70677

November 1994

This plan provides insight into the planning, production, and distribution of a periodical publication conceived and written by one person. Equipment, cost, and procedures are covered. The revised version of this plan immediately follows.

●STATEMENT OF PURPOSE

●THE BUSINESS

●SUMMARY

●DESIGN

●GOALS AND OBJECTIVES

●METHODS FOR OBTAINING GOALS

●MARKET

●READER PROFILE

●PROJECT MANAGEMENT—COMPONENTS

●PROJECT MANAGEMENT—PHASE I

●PROJECT MANAGEMENT—PHASE II

●PRODUCTION SCHEDULE

●ADDENDA

NEWSLETTER BUSINESS PLAN

STATEMENT OF PURPOSE

This plan will be an operating and policy guide for Network Journal, as well as a proposal to be submitted for the purpose of obtaining a grant for starting a small home-based business.

Janice K. McGraw, sole proprietor and operator of Network Journal, is requesting a $20,000 grant to purchase the computer, printer, supplies, and services necessary to create an environment conducive to immediate business start-up. A list of items, services, and costs is included in this proposal.

This grant will allow this publication to go online within three months of receipt of funds.

THE BUSINESS

Description of Business

Network Journal will be a solely-owned and operated publication, producing and distributing quarterly newsletters pertaining to personal and planetary enlightenment, free at distribution points and by subscription for a fee.

The beginning target market areas will be Lafayette, Baton Rouge, New Orleans, and Lake Charles, Louisiana, with minimal interspersion in the continental United States.

Network Journal has an anticipated distribution start-up date of January 1, 1995. Initial contacts are currently being made for advertising and distribution commitments. All advertisements, directory listings, and events listings will be paid with submission of information by money order or certified check.

The publisher is currently researching copyright and trademark acquisition.

Product and Service

The primary product offered will be a several-page newsletter offering in-depth interviews with a featured person (holistic practitioners, authors, teachers, philosophers, spiritual leaders, futurists, etc.); book, audio, and video reviews; calendar of events—local and national; guest writers of articles; directory listings; and advertisements from persons or businesses that fit into the scope of the publication.

The Market

Network Journal will provide quality, informal journalistic newsletters to all readers in pursuit of persons, services, and/or products promoting enlightenment and self-empowerment as it relates to the individual and his planetary symbiosis by means of free distribution and subscriptions to the public on a quarterly basis.

The goal is to provide a newsletter, paid for by advertising, directory listings, and events listings, beginning in the Lafayette, Baton Rouge, New Orleans, and Lake Charles, Louisiana areas, with initial minimal distribution to other areas of the United States. This market has an approximate population of 1,209,939. Figuring a 1% minimum interested population results in an initial start up market of approximately 12,099.

Approximately two hundred potential initial advertisers have been targeted.

Customers will be approached through distribution points and subscriptions, then in the future through advertising in local and national magazines and newspapers. Word-of-mouth advertising is expected.

Network Journal will be located and operated at the publishers's residence at 117 Munson Ave., Eunice, Louisiana. Production of the publication requires proper computer equipment, desktop publishing capabilities, a laser printer, supplies, telephone, fax machine, and an answering machine. Physical location is important to the extent of having a space for equipment and supplies. Printing, assembly, and sorting of the publication will take place off-site. The publication will be delivered to Lafayette distribution points by the publisher. All other distribution points will receive their copies via a competent shipping service or the United States Post Office, based on the least expensive rate of shipping.

Location of Business

Subscriptions will be mailed first class through the United States Postal Service.

At present there are only four newsletters being published in the South that are similar to the scope of Network Journal. One is being published in Mississippi, one in New Orleans, and a new health-based publication in Baton Rouge. One Lafayette publication offers some holistic contributions, but is primarily targeted at business women. Two charge for publication, and two are free at distribution points.

Competition

Similarities exist in the areas of articles, listing of events, and advertising availability. None, however, are currently offering the full range of featured interviews or comprehensive directory listings that will allow Network Journal to appeal to a large audience beyond the immediate area. The majority of articles in each currently published newsletter represent editorial-styled articles by the same contributors each month. Network Journal will present in-depth interviews with local as well as national, and in some cases, international persons involved in body, mind, spiritual, and futurists paths, as well as articles from these same persons and others, giving great variety of information—two reasons that will make Network Journal stand apart from the current format of newsletters being published.

Janice K. McGraw, publisher and manager of Network Journal, has a degree from the University of Louisiana in Office Administration; twenty years of various experiences in bookkeeping, computer operations, and management with a local Certified Public Accounting firm; one year experience as an art editor, contributing editor, and co-publisher of a monthly newsletter for the local chapter of the Sierra Club; and two years experience publishing a monthly in-house newsletter for a sales and consulting business she owned and operated. She was a co-developer of a $20,000,000 proposed museum of science and industry, having been involved in the project's development for six years in the capacity of researcher, editor, and project coordinator. Additionally, she has been involved in the local literacy program for adults; co-implementer of the first recycling program in her region; and co-producer of the County Solid Waste program.

Management

The publisher will initially receive a monthly part-time salary of $300, increasing to a full-time salary parallel to the growth of the publication. Ms. McGraw is currently employed full-time at Michaels & Affiliates, Ltd., A Professional Corporation of Certified Public Accountants, and will continue to work there until the publication of Network Journal warrants her full-time attention. The owner of Michaels & Affiliates, Ltd. is, at present, negotiating the sale of his business in anticipation of retirement at some point within the next two to three years. Full-time operation of the publication is being targeted to coincide with this transition.

Network Journal will begin as a small publication for a focused area, with expansion planned for the near future. Being published and distributed quarterly, the schedule required will allow Ms. Shafer to operate it while she remains employed full-time.

The accounting firm for Network Journal is Michaels & Affiliates, Ltd., 1066 Norman Rd., Scott, Louisiana. The attorney is Robert E. Crenshaw, 1193 Norman Rd., Scott, Louisiana.

Personnel

Network Journal will remain solely operated by Janice K. McGraw until such time as additional staff is required.

Application and Expected Effect of Grant

The $20,000 will be used as follows:

Micro 486DX2-66 Computer	$2,000
Laser Master WinPrinter 1,000/dpi	1,095
Supplies	600
Occupational License	70
Postage and Shipping	500
Printing, Sorting and Assembly—5,000	625
Telephone	500
Utilities	100
Auto expense	100
Desktop Publishing program-—PageMaker	452
WordPerfect for Windows	289
Post office box	50
Secretary of State	50
Subscriptions	300
Part-time salary	300
Trademark Acquisition	345
Shipping-Computer, Printer, Fax Machine	300
Fax Machine	300
UPS System (Surge and Battery Protector)	300
Total	$8,276

Network Journal will purchase the equipment and supplies on a cash basis from funds provided by the grant.

The vehicle used for the business is in good working order and bears no mortgage or lien. Other vehicles are available.

The computer, desktop publishing program, laser printer, additional equipment, and supplies will allow for in-house publication to produce a product ready for printing by the off-site printer.

The balance of the funds, which will remain in a bank account established solely for the purpose of operating the newsletter, will provide a monthly part-time compensation to the publisher, as well as operating funds including printing, telephone, utilities, auto expense, postage and shipping, and any other expenses involved in start-up and initial operation of the publication. This balance will act as a reserve line of credit to be used in taking advantage of special opportunities or to meet emergencies.

SUMMARY

Network Journal is a sole-proprietorship. It publishes and distributes, for free as well as by subscription, a quarterly newsletter under the premise of being "the forum for like-minded individuals." It also provides space for advertising for persons and businesses who fit the scope of the newsletter.

Production will occur at the publisher's residence at 117 Munson Ave., Eunice, Louisiana, with distribution focus beginning in Lafayette, Baton Rouge, New Orleans, and Lake Charles, Louisiana.

The owner, Janice K. McGraw, is seeking $20,000 to purchase the necessary equipment, supplies, and adequate working capital to provide for start-up and operating costs, with some funds to be placed in reserve for expansion purposes. This amount will sufficiently finance publication and enable it to be delivered by January 1, 1995, so that the business may begin as a profitable venture. It will also provide for enhancement of primarily local and some national businesses.

Market response, to date, has indicated an unfilled demand for a method of networking between people who offer services and products in self-enlightenment, holistic, and planetary areas and those who seek them. Ms. McGraw's managerial and sales experience, and the assistance of legal and accounting associations, assures the entire operation will be carefully controlled.

The funds sought will result in the immediate production and controlled expansion of the business as Ms. McGraw will be performing the production, distribution, deliveries and shipping until such time as expansion warrants additional personnel. The additional reserve and working capital will enable Network Quarterly to substantially increase its sales while maintaining profitability.

DESIGN

8 1/2" x 11" (To be printed on 11" x 17")
White or cream paper (to be determined) [Recycled]
Stapled in center to form booklet
Black ink
Printing on front and back of sheets
Margins: 1" on all sides
Copies for distribution will remain flat
Subscriptions will be folded into thirds, secured with small tab

DESIGN

...continued

Self-mailer on bottom third of back page
Grid: Two columns

Body Text:	Style for Banner (to be determined)
	Banner in Bold
	Style for Text (to be determined)
	Flush left
	Indents (to be determined)
Captions:	Flush left
	Slant
	Width of photo or centered, depending
	1/2 pica beneath photo or drawing
Lead article headline:	Point (to be determine)
	Semi-bold
	Flush left
	Underline (to be determined)
Column heads:	Point (to be determined)
	Style same as text
	Semi-bold
	Flush left
Pull quotes:	Point (to be determined)
	Slanted
	Flush left or centered, depending
	Match to column width, depending

GOALS AND OBJECTIVES

Network Journal is a newsletter published quarterly by a sole-proprietor. Its purpose is to inform interested readers about events, individuals, and materials available in the holistic, spiritual, and metaphysical fields, as well as to provide a place for advertising for persons and businesses that fit the scope of the publication.

Goals

To provide income for myself.
To provide information to readers about current and existing holistic events and fields.
To recognize practitioners, authors, teachers, philosophers, etc., for their contributions to the evolution of the individual, and thereby, humanity as a whole.

Message Strategies

Content
Regular features on local, state, national, and international practitioners, authors, teachers, spiritual leaders, et al, book and video reviews, directory listings, calendar of events, articles by practitioners, authors, etc., advertisements.

Style of Message
Informal news style, supplemented with informational content to appear in journalistic form.

Style Sheet - Format
Number of pages depending on available material and number of ads and listings.
8 1/2" x 11" on either white or cream paper.
2 column grid
All elements to combine into informal, tasteful, contemporary style to appeal to readers.

Frequency of Distribution
Quarterly
Unfolded for free distribution
Folded in thirds for subscriptions, mailing labels, first class

Printing Method
Personal computer using desktop publishing
Copies to be made at local print shop

METHODS FOR OBTAINING GOALS

Target all practitioners, authors, philosophers, psychics, etc., who are involved in disseminating information to the public. Receive paid-in-advance monies (money orders or certified checks only) for advertisements and listings, starting local, with some others areas of the country included.
Expand advertisers and distribution points as publication grows. Provide part-time income starting at $300 per month, increasing as publication grows.
Allow one year from start-up for part-time income to be established.
Allow two years from start-up for full-time income to be established.

Goals—A

Target all businesses and teachers involved in holistic, spiritual, or metaphysical practices.
Demonstrate increased awareness of services and events available.
Allow businesses and individuals to communicate with readers.
Increase contact between business people and readers
Begins with first newsletter.

Goals—B

Target all patrons or clients of advertised businesses and/or distribution points.
Inform readers about the background of practitioners, authors, teachers, philosophers, etc.
Inform readers about the various holistic, spiritual, and metaphysical services available.
Give readers sufficient information to allow choice of path for self-empowerment.
Begins with first newsletter.

Goals—C

Readers
Individuals involved in the pursuit or distribution of physical, mental, emotional, spiritual, metaphysical, and symbiotic planetary information and/or practices.

MARKET

MARKET
...continued

Where
Starting in Lafayette, Baton Rouge, New Orleans, and Lake Charles, Louisiana, with small distribution to other parts of the country. Eventual expansion throughout the state, later, throughout the country.

What the readers know
The readers are either teaching and serving in a business capacity or are looking for services and products that serve their holistic pursuits.

Where they currently get information
Readers currently get information by word-of-mouth, physically traveling to various locations that have business cards, pamphlets, or other publications. Little to no telephone directory access is available.

Why they want Network Journal
Businesses and individuals resort to handouts, word-of-mouth advertising, and minimal public advertising for information. This publication would provide strong local and statewide support of businesses and provide seekers with more information than normally given, through the vehicle of in-depth interviews and articles rather than solely through advertisements and directory listings. A need for this "network" has been expressed to the publisher by business persons and the public.

What my goal is
To affect readers and advertisers in a positive manner by providing a source of predominantly local and state, with a future expansion into national areas, information to facilitate connecting, thereby enhancing business for advertisers and each individual's pursuit of personal and planetary enlightenment.

The Goal simplified
To provide a vehicle for connecting or networking for like-minded individuals seeking personal and planetary enlightenment.

Definition of Purpose
To provide insights and information about new and existing holistic, spiritual, metaphysical, and planetary services and products to interested individuals as well as provide a place for advertising for practitioners, authors, teachers, and all other persons or businesses fitting into the scope of the publication.

To Achieve this Purpose
Network Journal will provide a compilation of information, easy to access through either free distribution at businesses or through subscription of $10 per year.

Why a newsletter
Several years ago, a need was expressed locally for a directory listing holistic practitioners, bookstores, persons and or businesses that offered services and or products within this scope. A directory was printed, distributed once a year, and ceased operations after the second year because it was not cost-effective.

When this need was expressed recently, it was expressed in the context that perhaps a newsletter that contained a directory was needed. Combining a vehicle for business listings with in-depth articles about and by practitioners, authors, philosophers, Think-tank participants, etc., will provide the readers with more information than usually given for choosing an appealing holistic personal and planetary path, providing readers a reason for wanting to read the publication each quarter, and thereby, a reason for people to continue to advertise in the publication.

Individuals, practitioners, authors, philosophers, Think-tank participants, and all like-minded persons or businesses desiring to either inform or become informed about practices, events, or books, audios, and videos relating to self-empowerment in the areas of nutrition, physical well-being, emotional balance, spiritual evolution, and their relationship to planetary responsibility.

READER PROFILE

Demographics:
>   Age: 13 and over
>   Gender: Both
>   Marital Status: Not applicable
>   Education: Around 12th grade reading level and above
>   Business: All fields
>   Income Average: $10,000 and above

Geographic:
>   Cities of and Parishes surrounding
>>   Lafayette
>>   Baton Rouge
>>   New Orleans
>>   Lake Charles
>   Expanding to
>>   Remainder of state of Louisiana
>>   With some other areas of the United States involved
>>   Eventually expanding to the continental United States

Population: (1990 Figures)
>   Lafayette: 94,440
>   Lafayette Parish: 164,762
>   Baton Rouge: 219,531
>   East Baton Rouge Parish: 380,105
>   New Orleans: 496,938
>   Orleans Parish: 496,938
>   Lake Charles: 70,580
>   Calcasieu Parish: 168,134

Total Population of the Four Parishes: 1,209,939

PROJECT MANAGEMENT: COMPONENTS

Feature

Holistic practitioners, spiritual leaders, authors, philosophers, futurists, and those of similar ilk—local and non-local. Interviews to be conducted by publisher and those who wish to contribute.

Book, Audio, and Video Reviews

New and existing books, audios, and videos reviewed by the publisher and others who wish to contribute.

Calendar

List of events, seminars, and meetings to occur within the three-month period. Local and non-local. Occasional listings of events far in advance. $5 for 20 words, $.25 for each additional word per quarter.

Guest Writers/Contributors

Contribute articles on holistic practices, spiritual studies, philosophy, and any topic fitting the scope of the publication. A small biography will serve as free advertising for contributors of articles.

Directory

Lists all holistic practitioners, psychics, teachers, and businesses that fit into the scope of the publication. $5 for 20 words, $.25 for each additional word per quarter.

Advertisements

All businesses, services, and products that fit into the scope of the publication.

Business Card	$40.00 per quarter
1/4 page	$85.00 per quarter
1/2 page	$160.00 per quarter
Full page	$325.00 per quarter

Camera-ready copy is requested.
Non-camera ready copy to be negotiated between publisher and advertiser.

Additional Components
        Table of Contents
        Editorial (optional)
        In the Next Issue

PROJECT MANAGEMENT: PHASE I

1. Contact federal government for grant applications/Apply for federal grant(s). (6-13-94)
2. Verify that Word Perfect 5.0 can be used for presentable desktop publishing (Done)
If not:
        a. Research and price alternative programs (Complement: PageMaker—$452)
        b. Research cost of transferring by diskette to local computer store.
3. Determine if label program (mlist) can be accessed on home computer (Done-Yes) and add it to the menu. (Done)
4. Determine how much room is on the hard drive/Determine what can be deleted, if necessary.
5. Go through all WP 5.0 material.

6. Do rough draft on home computer.
    a. Do interview with local practitioner, write article.
    b. Do book, audio, and video reviews.
    c. Use practitioner's business card and some made up ads, directory listings, and events.
    d. Ask contributor for an article on a spiritual topic.
    e. Include disclaimers and subscription.
7. Get all expenses listed.
    a. Call printer and ask for price list for copying from computer original, batch sizes, assembly charges, paper, delivery, etc. (Done)
    b. Ask for cost of computer, laser printer. (Done)
    c. Ask if desktop publishing is included with programs. (Access C:\WP50\NEWSPAPR.WPG)
    d. Research cost effective desktop publishing available that will fit on computer.
    f. Prepare low-end start up costs. (Done.)
8. Check information on self-incorporating.
    a. Check library first
    b. Check business supply store (Reserve for when necessary.)
9. Check on Secretary of State requirements and availability of name for publication.
10. Make a comprehensive list in mlist, if available, for contacts.
    a. Need names, business name, address, phone. (Nearly done)
    b. Categorize for ads, directory, interviews, guest writers.
11. Create forms for meetings, ads, directory, articles, subscriptions, events (Done)
12. Create and send out feasibility survey.
13. Order telephone books for Baton Rouge, New Orleans, and Lake Charles—business only, if available. (Alternative: go to library and write them down.)
14. Get population of Lafayette, Baton Rouge, New Orleans, Lake Charles and surrounding parishes. (Done)

1. When surveys are returned:
    a. Organize into categories.
    b. Make contacts.
    c. Meet with Michaels for start-up procedures, taxes, etc.
2. Fine-tune publication process (Make copy on laser printer at computer store, if not yet purchased.)
3. Set up interviews.
4. Arrange for articles, book reviews, etc.
5. Open a bank account.
6. Produce first newsletter.
7. Distribute first newsletter.
8. Send several free copies of first issue to family and friends.

**PROJECT
MANAGEMENT:
PHASE II**

**PRODUCTION
SCHEDULE**

1. Weeks One and Two:
    a. Target featured individual(s).
    b. Make contact(s).
    c. Submit forms for articles, reviews, events, etc.
2. Weeks Three and Four:
    a. Schedule and conduct interviews.
    b. Write and edit articles.
    c. Collect articles, reviews, etc.
    d. Select and edit articles.
3. Weeks Five and Six:
    a. Put all information into computer.
    b. Create format.
    c. Run rough draft.
    d. Edit.
    f. Rough draft.
    g. Edit.
    h. Run final.
    i. Cut and paste.
    j. Run laser copy.
    k. Edit.
    l. Make corrections and additions to addresses.
4. Weeks Seven and Eight:
    a. Bring to Vendor for printing, assembly, sorting.
    b. Proof copy.
    c. Pick up from vendor or have them deliver.
    d. If necessary, make address changes or additions.
5. Weeks Nine and Ten:
    a. Run labels.
    b. Affix labels.
    c. Prepare for mailing, shipping, and delivery.
6. Week Eleven: Deliver, mail and ship.
7. Week Twelve:
    a. Take a one-week deep breath.
    b. Start all over.

The following Addenda represent forms used by the plan author for everyday use in conducting her business.

ADDENDA

Reader Survey Form

Network Journal
117 Munson Ave.
Eunice, LA 70677
Janice K. McGraw, Publisher

Contact:
Company:
Address: Phone:

Network Journal is a quarterly newsletter. The goal of the newsletter is to establish a "paper forum" where holistic practitioners, teachers, philosophers, futurists, authors, and so forth, can connect with people seeking this information, infusing new information as it becomes available.

Please take a few moments to respond, then return this form in the envelope provided. Your prompt response is appreciated.

1. I am interested in being interviewed as one of the people to be featured each quarter.
                    Yes   No
2. I am interested in contributing articles; book, audio, and/or video reviews for publication.
                    Yes   No
3. I am interested in advertising in Network Journal.
                    Yes   No
4. I am interested in being listed in the Directory.
                    Yes   No
5. I am interested in listing events; seminars; and/or books, audio tapes, and video tapes I have produced/published.
                    Yes   No
6. I am interested in being a distributor for Network Journal.
                    Yes   No
7. You may contact me in the future:
Date:
Phone:
                         Thank you for your response. JKM

Features, Reviews, and Guest Articles provide free advertising through brief biographies.

Events and Directory Listings
$5 for 20 words; $.25 for each additional word—per quarter

Advertisements
Business Cards: $40 per quarter
1/4 Page: $85 per quarter
1/2 Page: $160 per quarter
Full Page: $325 per quarter
Please feel free to call or write for more information.

Advertisements

Please use one form for each advertisement

Please attach business card or camera-ready art to this form along with money order or check. Advertisements cannot be published without payment. Thank you.

☐ Business Card:　$40 per quarter
☐ 1/4 Page:　$85 per quarter
☐ 1/2 Page:　$160 per quarter
☐ Full Page:　$325 per quarter

Total Attached $ _____

Note to Advertiser:
If you do not have camera-ready art, please contact me. There is a $10 fee for advertisements that need to be set up.

This form and payment must be received no later than _____ for the _____ issue.

First Quarter:　　January - March
Second Quarter:　　April - June
Third Quarter:　　July - September
Fourth Quarter: October - December

Network Journal
117 Munson Ave.
Eunice, LA 70677

Janice K. McGraw, Publisher

Directory Listings

Please use one form per listing

Please print or type information and check spellings. Rates are $5 for 20 words; $.25 for each additional word. Please attach money order or check for amount required to this form. Listings cannot be published without payment. Thank you.

1-20 Words: $5.00
Additional Words ___ X $.25
Total

Please use this space to print or type listing. _____

Please be sure to include your name and/or business name, service or product offered, telephone number and/or address, and any additional information you deem necessary.

This form and payment must be received no later than _____ for the _____ issue.

First Quarter:　　January - March
Second Quarter:　　April - June
Third Quarter:　　July - September
Fourth Quarter: October - December

Articles/Interviews

Please use one form for each article/interview submitted

Note to Submitter:
Please attach this form to the article/interview and mail in no later than ___ for the __ issue.

First Quarter:	January - March
Second Quarter:	April - June
Third Quarter:	July - September
Fourth Quarter:	October - December

Title of Article:
Submitter:
Topic:
Brief Biography of Submitter:

All articles must be either printer or typed. Thank you.

Network Journal
117 Munson Ave.
Eunice, LA 70677
Janice K. McGraw, Publisher

Events

Please use one form per event to be listed.

Please print information and check spellings. Rates are $5 for 20 words; $.25 for each additional word. Please attach money order or check for the amount required to this form. Listings cannot be published without payment. Thank you.

1-20 Words: $5.00
Additional Words ___ X $.25
Total

Please use this space to print or type event.

Please be sure you have included the day, date, name of event, time, address where event will be held, your name and/or affiliation name, attendance cost, any items required, phone number, and any explanation necessary.

This form and payment must be received no later than _____ for the _____ issue.

First Quarter:	January - March
Second Quarter	April - June
Third Quarter	July - September
Fourth Quarter	October - December

Newsletter*

BUSINESS PLAN

NETWORK JOURNAL

117 Munson Ave.
Eunice, LA 70677

Revised April 1995

The original plan appears previous to this one. This updated version reflects the author's adjustments in business strategy as a result of her real-life test of the original plan. Look for plans to expand, as well as changes in the format, content, and production schedule of the newsletter.

- STATEMENT OF PURPOSE

- THE BUSINESS

- COMMENTS

- SUMMARY

- DESIGN

- PROJECT MANAGEMENT—COMPONENTS

- MARKET

- PRODUCTION SCHEDULE

NEWSLETTER BUSINESS PLAN	
STATEMENT OF PURPOSE	This plan is an operating and policy guide for Network Journal, a quarterly newsletter designed as "A Forum for the Like-Minded Seeking Enlightenment," and is a home-based business.
THE BUSINESS	
Description of Business	Network Journal is a solely-owned and operated publication, producing and distributing quarterly newsletters pertaining to personal and planetary enlightenment. It is distributed free to distribution points and by annual subscription for $10 inside the United States, $11 outside the U.S.
	The target market area is primarily the United States with interspersion into other countries.
	Network Journal had a start-up date of January 6, 1995. Continuous contacts are being made for advertising, subscriptions and distribution commitments. Advertisements, directory listings and events listings are paid by money order, check or cash with submission of information.
	The publisher has been granted an occupational license.
Product and Service	The primary product is a multiple-page newsletter offering interviews with holistic practitioners, authors, teachers, philosophers, spiritual leaders, futurists, etc.; book, audio and video reviews; a calendar of events—local, state, some national, and in the near future, international; guest writers of articles and reviews; directory listings and advertisements from persons or businesses that offer products or services that fit the scope of the publication.
The Market	Network Journal provides quality, informal journalistic newsletters to readers in pursuit of connection with persons, services, and/or products promoting enlightenment and self-empowerment as it relates to the individual and his planetary symbiosis by means of free distribution at some locations and by subscriptions, and is offered on a quarterly basis.
	The goal is to provide a newsletter, paid for through advertising, subscriptions, directory listings, and events listings, throughout the United States and to other countries.
	There are currently 1,000 potential and active advertisers, subscribers, submitters and distributors being targeted and reached.
	Readers and contributors are approached via complimentary copies at distribution points and mail, and in the near future through the Louisiana Women's Business Directory. Future advertising in local and national publications is in consideration. Word-of-mouth advertising is occurring.

Network Journal is located and operated at the publisher's residence at 117 Munson Ave, Eunice, Louisiana. Production of the publication requires proper computer equipment, desktop publishing capabilities, laser printer, supplies, telephone, fax machine, and an answering machine. Physical location is important to the extent of having space for equipment and supplies. Printing, assembly, and sorting takes place off-site. Some phases of the publishing process occur offsite until all the equipment needed is acquired by the publisher. The publication is delivered to local distribution points by the publisher. Other distribution points receive copies via a competent shipping service with cost of shipping reduced through use of a discount card granted as part of the South Central Bell Work at Home Connection project. Subscriptions and complimentary copies are mailed using a U.S. Postal Service mail permit for bulk mail, offering a reduction in mailing costs.

Location of Business

At present, there are only four readily-available newsletters being published in the South that are similar to the scope of Network Quarterly. One newsletter is primarily a health-based publication, while another is primarily targeted at business women. Two charge for publications; two are free at distribution points.

Competition

Similarities exist in the areas of articles, directory and events listings, reviews, and advertising availability. Currently, none are offering interviews with national as well as local persons, as is the Network Journal. Also, as the Network Journal is targeting a market area of the United States and other countries rather than primarily local areas, articles and interviews are currently being sought and obtained from persons around the united States who are world-renown authors, teachers, and lecturers—as well as persons who operate on a smaller scale. International participants are being contacted.

A significant change has occurred in the format of Network Journal. The publication is arranged so that the reader can start at the beginning and read through each segment without the interruption of moving to another area of the newsletter to finish the segment. Advertising is located in one area of the newsletter in order to assist in the reading flow. White, partially-recycled bond paper is used instead of newsprint paper. The newsletter is printed on 11" X 17" paper, folded and stapled into an 8 1/2" X 11" booklet.

The broader range of interviews and articles published, the larger area targeted for directory, events, and advertising, and the non-typical format of the newsletter allow the Network Quarterly to stand apart from other currently published newsletters.

J. K. McGraw, publisher and manager of Network Journal, has a degree from the University of Louisiana in Office Administration; twenty years of various experiences in bookkeeping, computer operations, and management with a local certified public accounting firm; one year experience as an art editor, contributing editor, and co-publisher of a monthly newsletter for the local chapter of the Sierra Club; and two years experience of publishing a monthly in-house newsletter for a sales and consulting business she owned and operated.

Management

She was a co-developer of a $20,000,000 proposed museum of science and industry, having been involved in project development for six years in the capacity of researcher, editor, and project coordinator. She has also been involved in the local literacy program for adults, co-implementor of the first recycling program in her region, and co-producer of the County Solid Waste program.

Affiliations and studies relating to the scope of Network Journal include Silva Mind Control, Reiki (Level I), The Rosicrucian Order, Unity Church Worldwide, and the International New Thought Alliance.

The publisher will not receive a salary until the publication supports one. When a salary can be supported, it will be parallel to the growth of the publication. Ms. McGraw is currently employed full-time with Michaels and Affiliates, Ltd., A Professional Service Corporation of Certified Public Accountants. She will continue working full-time until the publication of Network Journal warrants her full-time attention.

Network Journal is a small publication with expansion planned and occurring to date. Being published and distributed quarterly, the time required allows Ms. McGraw to operate the business while remaining employed full-time.

The accounting firm for Network Journal is Michaels and Affiliates, Ltd., P.O. Box 10, Scott, Louisiana. The attorney is Robert E. Crenshaw, 1193 Norman Rd., Scott Louisiana.

Personnel

Network Journal will remain solely operated by J. K. McGraw until such time as additional staff is required.

Financial Comparison: First and Second Quarters

	First Qtr.	Second Qtr.
Income		
Ads & Subscriptions	$456.50	$487.00
Loan - JKM	368.02	534.89
	$824.52	$1,021.89
Expenses		
Shipping	$10.41	$31.46
Postage	104.68	229.38
Licenses	10.00	0
Miscellaneous	27.80	0
Sales Tax	43.59 55.75	
Telephone	7.44	25.90
Office Supplies	43.16	20.22
Subscriptions	14.00	0
Publishing	526.78	638.83
Marketing	0	88.03
Bank Service Charge	0	32.95
	$787.86	$1,133.03

Cost Per Copy: First Quarter

1,200 12-page copies = 14,400 pages @ .055/page X 12 = .66/issue to produce and distribute.

Cost Per Copy: Second Quarter

1,000 16-page copies = 16,000 pages @ .071/page X 16 = $1.14/issue to produce and distribute.

Although the second quarter indicates a small increase in income compared to the first quarter, with an increase in expenses, the second quarter issue has resulted in advertisements and subscriptions being received from various parts of the United States. Authors of renown that were contacted have expressed an interest in submitting articles or having their books reviewed in the Network Journal. Additional practitioners and spiritual leaders have contacted the publication expressing a desire to advertise or participate in other ways. Local advertisers are experiencing an increase in sales and services, with buyers and clients stating they are responding to information seen in the publication. Distributors of the newsletter are reporting patrons are coming to their shops ahead of the new release date, looking for the next issue. Although the increase dollar-wise in ads from the first to the second quarter was not substantial, more ads were placed.

The mailing list indicates which copies are complimentary and the beginning date. At the end of one year, receivers will be notified that to continue to receive issues, a subscription needs to be sent in. Also, most of the distribution point has been established in Albuquerque, New Mexico.

COMMENTS

SUMMARY

Network Journal is a sole-proprietorship. It publishes and distributes, for free as well as by subscription, a quarterly newsletter under the premise of being a forum for like-minded individuals. It also provides space for advertising for persons and businesses who fit the scope of the newsletter.

Production occurs at the publisher's residence at 117 Munson Ave., Eunice, Louisiana, with distribution in nearly all of the United States, with interspersion into England, Canada, Nova Scotia, Sweden, Peru, Mexico, and Ecuador.

Market Response to date, has indicated an unfilled demand for a method of networking between people who offer services and products in self-enlightenment, holistic and planetary areas, and those who seek them. Ms. McGraw's managerial and sales experience and the assistance of legal and accounting associations, assures the entire operation will be carefully controlled.

Ms. McGraw will be performing the production and distribution until such time as expansion warrants additional personnel.

DESIGN

- 8 1/2" X 11" (printed on 11" X 17")
- White partially-recycled paper
- Stapled in Center to form Booklet
- Black ink
- Printed on Front and back of sheets
- Even numbered sheets-ascending order on left,
   odd numbered sheets-ascending order on right
- Margins: 1" on all sides
- Copies for mailing & distribution are sealed with tab label and remain flat
- Self-mailer on bottom third of back page, includes "Address Correction Requested"
- Grid: Two columns

DESIGN
...continued

Body Text:	Style for Banner - Present, Size 30
	Bold
	Headline - Present, Size 12
	Style for Text - Courier 12 (8 & 10 where needed)
	Indent first line of each paragraph, no space between paragraphs
	Three spaces between segments
Lead Article Headline:	Point - Courier 14
	Bold
	Flush Left
	Underlined
Column Heads:	Point - Courier 14 or larger
	Style same as text
	Bold
	Flush left
	Underlined
Back Page:	Disclaimer - Helvetica Black, Size 6
	Bold
	Return Address - Present
	NQ size 10 or larger
	Address, phone, name - Size 6 or 4
	Subscription - Present, Size 6, Bold

PROJECT MANAGEMENT: COMPONENTS

Feature
Interviews with holistic practitioners, spiritual leaders, authors, philosophers, futurists, and those of similar ilk—local and non-local. Interviews to be conducted by publisher and those who wish to contribute.

Book, Audio, & Video Reviews
New and existing books, audios, and videos reviewed by publisher and those who wish to contribute.

Calendar
List of events, seminars, and meetings—local and non-local. $5 for 20 words, $.25 for each additional word per quarter.

Guest Writers/Contributors
Contribute articles on holistic practices, spiritual studies, philosophy, and any topic fitting the scope of the publication. A brief biography serves as free advertising for contributors of articles.

Directory
Listing of persons or businesses offering services or products that fit the scope of the publication. $5 for 20 words, $.20 for each additional word per quarter.

Advertisements

Businesses, services, and products that fit the scope of the publication.

Business Card:	$40.00 per quarter
1/4 Page:	$85.00 per quarter
1/2 Page:	$160.00 per quarter
Full Page:	$325.00 per quarter

Camera-ready copy is requested. Non-camera ready ads to be discussed. $10 fee for production or alteration of ad by publisher. Listings and ads to be submitted according to deadline with payment by money order, check, or cash.

Readers

MARKET

Individuals involved in the pursuit or distribution of physical, mental, emotional, spiritual, metaphysical, and symbiotic planetary information and or practices.

Where

Currently reaching most of the United States with interspersion into England, Canada, Sweden, Peru, Ecuador, and Mexico.

What the Readers Know

The readers are either teaching and/or serving in a business capacity or, are looking for services and products that serve their holistic and planetary pursuits.

Where They Currently Get Their Information

Teachers, businesses, and individuals receive information from flyers, word-of-mouth advertising, publications, and minimal advertising. This publication provides strong local, statewide, and national (with some international expected), support of teachers and businesses and provides seekers with more information than normally given through articles, interviews, and reviews rather than solely through advertisements and directory listings. A need for this "network" has been expressed to the publisher by teachers, business persons, and the public.

What My Goal Is

To affect readers and advertisers in a positive manner by providing a source of information to facilitate connection on a global scale, thereby enhancing business for advertisers and each individual's pursuit of personal and planetary enlightenment.

The Goal Simplified

To provide a vehicle for connecting or networking for like-minded individuals seeking enlightenment.

Definition of Purpose

To provide insights and information about new and existing holistic, spiritual, metaphysical, and planetary services and products to interested individuals as well as provide a place for advertising for practitioners, authors, teachers, and all other persons or businesses fitting into the scope of the publication.

To Achieve This Purpose
Network Journal will provide a compilation of information, easy to access through either free distribution at businesses or through subscription for $10 per year inside the U.S., $11 per year outside the U.S. At present, one local public library offers copies for distribution.

Why a Newsletter
Several years ago, a need was expressed locally for a directory listing holistic practitioners, bookstores, persons and/or businesses that offered services and/or products within this scope. A directory was printed and distributed once a year. It ceased operation after the second year because it was not cost-effective.

When this need was expressed to the publisher, it was expressed in the context that perhaps a newsletter that contained a directory was needed. Combining a vehicle for business listings with interviews and articles about and by practitioners, authors, philosophers, teachers, etc., provides readers with more information than usually given for choosing a appealing holistic personal and planetary path, providing the readers with a reason for wanting to read the publication each quarter. This, and the locally noted increase in business as a result of advertisements and reviews in the newsletter, promote continued support of the publication by advertisers and others.

Reader Profile
Individuals, practitioners, authors, philosophers, and like-minded persons or businesses desiring to either inform or become informed about practices, events, or books, audios, and videos relating to self-empowerment in the areas of nutrition, physical well-being, emotional balance, spiritual evolution, and their relationship with planetary responsibility.

Demographics:
    Age: 13 and over
    Gender: Both
    Marital Status: Not Applicable
    Education: Ninth grade reading level and above
    Business: All Fields
    Income Average: Not Applicable
Geographic:
    United States
    Expanding to other countries now including England, Canada, Sweden, Peru, Ecuador, and Mexico

PRODUCTION SCHEDULE

Week One
    a. Make sure all subscriptions & complimentary copies are mailed.
    b. Get copies delivered & shipped to distributors.
Week Two
    a. Prepare Action Grid: Interviews, ads, listings, distributors & number of copies, etc.
    b. Get copies of all forms required for above list.
Week Three
    a. Fill out and mail forms for submissions to publication according to Action Grid.

        b. Schedule interviews.
Week Four
        a. Make contact with local advertisers to determine ad needs, etc.
Week Five
        a. Begin collecting ads, listings, etc.
        b. Conduct interviews.
Week Seven
        a. Begin rough draft.
        b. Edit.
Week Eight
        a. Do final edit.
        b. Do mock-up of ad lay-out.
        c. Get mailing supplies.
Week Nine
        a. Bring final copy to printer.
        b. Make mailing list adds and changes.
        c. Print mailing labels in zip code order.
        d. Get mailing supplies.
Week Ten
        a. Begin targeting interviews, ads, reviews for next issue.
Week Eleven
        a. Receive newsletter from printer.
        b. Begin applying labels.
Week Twelve
        a. Sort mailings and shipping.
        b. Mail and ship newsletter.
        c. Begin distributions.

**PRODUCTION
SCHEDULE**...*continued*

Photo Framing

BUSINESS PLAN

TALKING PHOTO TECHNOLOGY

17351 Sunset Blvd. #404
Pacific Palisades, CA 90272
(310)573-9898

October 1992

This business plan for a mulitmedia application for photo displays outlines how extensive market research and an advanced product launch can create a profitable place in the booming photograph frame industry. The plan features discussions of the company's two products and its marketing strategy. This business plan has not been disguised, but the product names have been changed.

PHOTO FRAMING BUSINESS PLAN

SUMMARY

Talking Photo Technology is focused on the manufacturing and marketing of patentable products that integrate multiple pictures with sound or speech at an affordable price. The simplicity of the technology, though designed for the consumer market, can easily be adapted for business applications. The first two products are "PortraiTalk" and "SoundPhoto."

The photo-frame business has doubled every year for the last ten years. We have advanced the current stage of high-tech "talking picture frames" to the next level with our unique multi-photo talking concept. "PortraiTalk" is a wall-mounted eight-picture photo display. Each of the standard size, 3.5" x 5" pictures, is set within a light-illuminating frame. A different 20-second recorded message, synchronized to the lighted plexiglass shell, plays back when that photo frame is illuminated. Each picture can be recorded or rerecorded independently from the others. "PortraiTalk" has a high perceived value so it can easily be sold at the full price of $79.95 or a discounted price of $69.95.

"SoundPhoto," the desktop version, displays photos in a continuous loop. As each picture is displayed within the window, a 20-second synchronized message plays back the message attached to that 3.5" x 5" photo. This smaller version, holding the same number of portrait photos as the wall unit, is ideally suited for an office or coffee table. "SoundPhoto" can be sold at the full price of $49.95 or a discounted price of $39.95.

The company has dramatically broadened the photo frame market by combining multiple pictures with recorded messages. This combination has merged the simplicity of individual photos and the sound recording of a VCR into a visually appealing product. Offering two different but similar products to retailers at two different price points greatly enhances the company's chances of success. Both of these low-tech tape products have distinct advantages over the high-tech digital products in cost, recording longevity, twin channels or simulated stereo, and the adaptability to other markets.

The estimated number of projected sales during the first five full years, through all channels of distribution, could reach two million for the desktop unit and one million for the wall unit. The estimated cost of manufacturing and assembly, in minimum production, is $9.00 for "SoundPhoto" and $15.00 for "PortraiTalk."

Larry Koenig, the CEO and inventor, has over 12 years in cataloging and selling cutting-edge consumer products. Ken Tarlow, the prototype designer and engineer, has over 20 years in product development. Jules Sacks, Bill Adelman and Sam Friedman, the marketing and sales team, have 60 years in the combined fields.

The company is seeking investment capital of $600,000 for tooling and molding, marketing, operations, preliminary orders for 25% of the company's stock. This should return $5.9 million after an IPO at the end of the third full year, representing a 9.8% return on investment, based upon a 10 to 1 ratio.

Larry Koenig, CEO and creator of the products in Talking Photo Technology, has over 12 years of experience in selecting, marketing, and selling high and low tech products. His knowledge in marketing and promotion came as the founder and president of The Price of His Toys, a nationally known catalog company and retail operation. His use of creative promotions and public relations made his company appear like a giant in the industry to its competitors, suppliers and customers.

Mr. Koenig has been involved with marketing and cataloging since the late 1970s. During this period he occasionally developed and successfully sold original products through his catalog and retail operation. As president of this 30-person company, Mr. Koenig has had to wear many hats from CEO, CFO, and computer programmer to catalog designer and writer.

During and before this period, Mr. Koenig had successfully owned and operated a series of small professional pharmacies in the Southern California area.

Kenneth Tarlow, the prototype designer, has over 20 years experience in the field. He was founder and president of T-2 Design, where for eight years he worked with hundreds of inventors by guiding them through the various stages of product development.

Prior to T-2 Design, Mr. Tarlow was President of Olympic Group, Inc., a full service and product development company. He was responsible for the aesthetic and engineering design of over 15 consumer products, some of which are still on the market today. Mr. Tarlow was directly or indirectly responsible for the design, production and marketing of over 200 successful products. These products resulted in $400 million in retail sales.

Jules Sacks, VP for Sales and Marketing, is thoroughly experienced in sales, marketing and product development. He has recruited, trained and managed a large sales force for several successful companies. Mr. Sacks has developed excellent national contacts among power retailers, discount chains, mass merchandisers, department stores, membership clubs, and home shopping networks. He achieved a marked degree of success as Executive Vice President at Datawave where he increased their business by 230% and reduced their expenses by 30% over a three year span. Before that, he had worked for Sanyo Fisher (USA) for five years, with his last year as a National Sales Manager, Special Markets. He has always managed to increase sales and reduce overhead in the five major companies he has worked for since 1980.

Bill Adelman, National Sales Manager, has spent the last 13 years working as regional manager for Jack Carter Associates, where he has been exposed to all types of consumer electronic and personal care products from manufacturers like Sharp, Nintendo, Maxell, Harmon Kardon, Bell Atlantic, Mitsubishi and Betty Crocker. In many instances, he has managed to increase sales volumes within his territories by improving merchandising concepts and acquiring new accounts. Mr. Adelman has developed a personal relationship with many large and small accounts in California and across the country. He has never worked less than five years with any company since 1970, and has always improved their financial and customer relations positions.

Sam Friedman, computer coordinator, has an extensive background in sales, marketing and computer integration. He was president of Datacon Computer System, a three million dollar marketing and graphic company. He has a degree in advanced programming and systems design, and has worked for a variety of major companies from Coca-Cola Bottling Company and TRW Information Systems Group to Universal Studio/MCA and Ralphs Markets. Mr. Friedman has set up direct sales systems and has worked with a number of sales representatives from various fields.

Rob Frankel, president of Frankel & Anderson, is an experienced marketing/advertising person with a broad range of capabilities. He has worked with a variety of startup companies ranging from computer software to catalogs. He understands their needs and budgets by focusing on strategic planning. Mr. Frankel has run his company since 1986. He has started in the advertising field as an entry level writer and worked his way up to a creative director. He has held that position in several top level firms.

Additional management professionals, ranging from regional managers to financial experts, can be hired from the vast pool of talented people available due to the recession.

THE PRODUCTS

The prototypes stages have evolved from an initial book version to the free standing unit, using eight wallet pictures, to the final version wall unit. The evolution was necessary to determine how the public perceived the product and to finalize the mechanical system. Prototyping is the only effective way to prove the product would work cost effectively. The mechanics and the lighting system work the same in the prototype and the final version of "PortraiTalk."

"PortraiTalk" uses standard size 3.5" x 5" photos that are set within their own light-illuminating frame. Starting with the first of six vertical pictures and ending with two horizontal pictures, the frames light up sequentially. This illumination is synchronized to a 20-second message that can be recorded and/or rerecorded independently from the other pictures, so a total story can be told. The controls are set on the right hand side for easy access while the unit hangs on the wall. The frames are illuminated by separate back lights, which can be clear or in color. The customer can determine this by inserting the desired colored filters.

"SoundPhoto," is the lower priced, desktop version. Eight 3.5" x 5" vertical pictures are set in a continuous loop inside of a cube, measuring 6" x 6" x 7.5". As each photo is displayed in the framed window, a 20-second synchronized message plays back the recorded information attached to that individual picture. The desktop version has a different design, but still takes advantage of the mechanical principle used in the wall unit.

The 20-second record/playback message was chosen based upon testing with shorter and longer play time. A 30-second message is approximately 100 words based upon a prewritten script. A 20-second message equals 60 to 65 words or four to five independent sentences. This will depend on the clarity of thoughts and the speed of speech.

Kodak recently did a test and selected a 30-second record/playback for their single photo based upon a test market survey of over 1,000 people. The company feels that viewers' attention spans are very short. While 30 seconds might work for a single photo it would be too long for multiple pictures. This was further proven after demonstrating multiple photos with either seven or 30 second recording. Four sentences (60 words) was the maximum amount of time that people would stay focused on a picture. The company's initial prototype was seven seconds, which was too short. The second prototype had used 30 seconds (100 words) per photo, and appeared to lose the focus of the audience after two photos.

The company's patentable concept allows for easy recording and rerecording of any of the individual time slots. The tape and pictures can be easily removed and replaced by a new combination. Additionally, as both units use mechanical synchronization, the assembly can be readjusted for a longer or shorter record/playback time for the next generation. This can be done by having an inset gear assembly designed to change speeds. An eight-photo display was chosen for each unit based upon the ratio of perceived value to size and cost.

The twin channel recording capability of the products allows for the overlay of music on one channel while speech can be recorded on another. This concert-hall effect, which is not available with digital technology in this price range, adds to the enjoyment of the products.

The marketing of new products is rapidly changing. The uses of advertising and public relation's editorial copy are the recognized formulas that still work in promoting retail and catalog sales. New methods consist of infomercials, TV shopping services, multi-level marketing, interactive computer sales, and interactive TV. Most of these new ways, though sales oriented themselves, can be uses as a bridge for promoting the retail market, which accounts for 75% of total sales.

INITIAL MARKET PENETRATION

Manufacturers' representatives are the primary sales people that small- and medium-sized companies use to sell their products within the retail and catalog markets. It is important to coordinate with the representative who has major connections and who can meet with top level buyers. The company's sales team can set up a national organization.

The company feels it could have preproduction units within 60 to 90 days from initial funding. If time is available, these units can be used to solicit last minute wholesale orders from the retailers and catalogers for the Christmas season.

TV home shopping can be solicited quite late into the Christmas buying season. The two major TV home shopping companies operate under different premises. Home Shopping Network places an order and buys the product directly on a guaranteed sales basis (they can return what doesn't sell). TV shopping does not have the same time constraints that retailers or catalogers have. They usually expect a 40% discount off of the retail price, with another 10% going for commissions.

The company feels that the direct sales method will be the initial marketing direction for the first Christmas season regardless of wholesale, catalog, or TV home shopping. Direct sales establishes the correct markets, the proper pricing and the initial advertising for retail. Promotions and sales at the end of the first year for these year-round products serve as an excellent jumping-off point for the following year.

The direct marketing promotions will start 60 days before the product is received by using the pre-production models. Brochures can be printed, ads can be designed and placed in magazines, short-form infomercials (one minute spots) can be produced, and TV air time can be bought or bartered.

The brochures for each product will be produced in individual full-color one-page format. These brochures can be used as part of the direct sales campaign, informational public relation pieces, bounce back inserts for selective catalogers, and a wholesale marketing campaign.

The print advertisements consist of a variety of small placement ads inserted in newspapers and magazines. These are more effective than only a few large ones. The company hopes to place as many as possible through barter and PI (per inquiry), with the balance purchased directly.

Direct TV sales for short form (one minute spot) can be produced for under $5,000. The company intends to place as many of these spots through barter and PI as possible. Both items will be tested in different locals, time slot, and prices. A bounce back advertisement could be inserted in the orders for the version not offered in that particular ad.

Bounce back inserts is a method many catalogers use during the fulfillment process. This method of generating extra revenue can be used at the last minute as long as a deal can be structured with certain catalogers.

Life Extensions, a Multi Level Marketing (MLM) company has expressed an interest in the product and in promoting it to their 50,000 downline members.

The company's catalog knowledge and writing skills will aid us in these areas. A public relation campaign will start 30 days before receiving our first shipment and will continue through year end in hope of enticing retailers and direct sales.

ADVANCED MARKETING

Once the products have been launched and the retail and catalog sales force are in place, the next stage will be emphasized. Major resellers from department stores to catalogers will be contacted directly and through trade shows.

To ensure the success in selling to the larger companies, a number of separate deals will have to be worked out. Price and terms are their primary concerns. The negotiations will depend on how successful the products appear to be initially and their perceived value or recognition in the marketplace.

The company's projected sales are driven in the two following ways. The first is through advertising and promotion.

Type	Driven By
Direct Sales	Consumer Advertising
Catalog	Trade Advertising and Sales Marketing
Retailers or Resellers	Trade Advertising and Sales Marketing
Specialty and Premium	Promotions

The second is based on the time of year. The following chart will illustrate the months of the year versus the percentages of sales and the reasons. The last three months of the year are approximately equal to the first nine months in sales volume. The percentages could vary depending on promotions and seasonal events.

Month	%	Reasons
January	4	Year end sales/Christmas bonus purchases
February	6	Valentines Day
March	4	Winter Vacations
April	4	Spring Break/Income tax refunds
May	8	Mothers Day
June	8	Fathers Day/Weddings/Graduations
July	6	Summer Vacations/Weddings
August	6	Summer Vacations/Weddings
September	5	Back to School/Beginning Catalog Season
October	12	Catalog Season and Start of Christmas Buying
November	15	Strong Christmas Buying
December	22	Christmas

Total Percentage 100

Media Results

The price of a direct sales ad is related to size, media circulation, and use of four-color printing. A small ad (2" x 2" or 1/12 page for a magazine) will probably average $500, based upon a 500,000 circulation. This should return ten orders for the desktop or five orders for the wall unit in the base months of January, March or April (4%). February (the 6% month) will show a 50% increase for the same amount of advertising. These assumptions are based upon a quality ad placed in a receptive media.

Wholesale and catalog sales are more difficult to measure when matched against trade advertising. These ads usually just open doors for sales reps to close the deals. The sales of retail versus catalog have a ratio of 4 to 1. Therefore 20% of every trade advertisement will be devoted to catalog sales and 80% to retail. These trade expenses are listed as a single entry but drive the combination of both products, since many companies are active in both fields. Direct mail is the optimum method of solicitation to this industry. Every $500 spent should generate 1,000 direct mail pieces. This should produce a 0.75% return or 7.5 orders per 1,000, especially if some form of telemarketing was used as reenforcement. The average order should be ten desktop units and five wall units per order. The same seasonality that affects direct sales also affects wholesale and catalog sales.

The company will initially focus on the prestigious resellers. These resellers set a pricing standard and have customers who can afford the higher perceived value of the products. These non-discount retail stores and premium catalogs should establish and retain the full price for the first year or two. It is important to keep that level of distribution because once the discounters enter the market the price will drop. If that happens a majority of the initial resellers either cannot or will not sell the product. Additionally, the discounters do not want a product that either is not well recognized or is priced higher than they feel their customers will pay.

Catalogers may have several other requirements besides the lowest wholesale cost. They sometimes request a product placement fee and/or an exclusive. The exclusive can only be done within the first partial year, and only if a large enough order is received. A product placement fee will depend on the following:

Media Results
...continued

❑Size of the order
❑Amount of the fee
❑The success of other similarly priced products
❑Time of year
❑Size of the picture
❑Location within the catalog
❑Final negotiated price
❑The number of insertions into additional issues

Locating Resellers

The simplest way to access the numerous resellers are through CD-ROM databases like Marketplace Business or American Business. Specific business types can be located with an 8-digit classification called Standard Industrial Classification, which is commonly known as the SIC code. Telemarketers can contact the best qualified companies by overlaying specific classifications over Scan/US, a database mapping program that contains multiple income levels and census statistics for the area.

Catalogers can be cross-referenced with the same systems if they maintain retail locations. Additionally, the company is more concerned with the quality of the catalogs and products in them.

ADDITIONAL MARKETS

The wall unit is ideally suited for commercial applications such as the following:

❑Point-of-purchase displays in retail locations
❑Promotional information pieces in hotels
❑Product promotions at trade shows
❑Sales promotions at seminars or special events

This product will probably have to be modified and reinforced to withstand the constant use for these applications.

The patentable technology can be used to reconfigure either unit for the children's market, ages four to ten. Each frame will act as a separate stage setting where characters and scenery from cut-out books can be displayed. This combination of pictures and words are set as scenes within a play. Kids can use their imagination to tell an unlimited number of stories.

The singles and related industries are also ideally suited for this product. Individuals can present themselves in pictures while voicing their description.

The premium markets range from photographic and film companies promoting photo development to pharmaceutical manufacturers demonstrating new drugs to doctors. Kodak has recently entered the consumer field and has an Imagining Division designed for developing new products. Motion picture companies are always looking for new ways to promote their latest entry. Either of the units can be customized by placing company logos in key locations on the frame.

The company will use manufacturers representatives and will hire specialized sales people called "in-house" sales reps. The "in-house" reps will be divided between "outside" and "inside" sales.

The average commission will be 15% of sales based upon paid invoices by the resellers. The commissions will range from 10% for quantity and catalog orders to 15% and 20% for small orders. The Consumer Electronic representatives usually receive 10% while the Gift representatives range from 15 to 20%. This also depends on services and trade shows where the products are displayed. The income statements use 15% as an average. Direct expenses will be reimbursed, especially for "in-house" reps. The reps must fill out their itinerary, the amount spent, the results and the reasons.

Telemarketers can be employed as either lead generators or closers. As lead generators they will receive a small portion of the sales rep commission, usually 20% of it. The sales refer to wholesale and/or direct sale retail. In response to growing direct sales or problems that arise a verifier can be used for spot verifications. The company's outside and inside sales reps and telemarketers will receive a starting salary against commissions for 60 days and then straight commissions. The management team, in addition to their salary, will receive a yearly bonus based upon gross profit, starting with the first full year.

The photo picture frame industry is a booming industry in a niche marketplace. Major manufacturers are reporting profits in a down economy. The price, an increase in amateur photography, and an upgrade in design contributed to the photo and picture frame industry's 4.6 percent growth from 1991 to 1992, industry sources said. These factors, along with mass merchants' increasing control of overall market share, helped lift wholesale dollar volume to $730.8 million in 1992, and will assure growth of 1993 sales, vendors said.

Summary of report: Photo frame vendors have unveiled a diverse assortment of products this spring. From trendy theme offerings to the juvenile market to sophisticated woods, manufacturers have managed to present fresh collections of frames and albums for summer and fall delivery.

Talking picture frames have been available for several years. Almost all the focus has been on digital and solid state technology. Sharper Image sold a ten-second version in their June 1993 catalog at $39.95. The starting prices for wallet-size digital picture frames are $19.95 with a ten-second recorded message.

Hallmark Cards recently marketed a line of greeting cards at $14.00 that allows a person to record and playback a ten-second message with each card. Hallmark claims that the four batteries can be replaced without loss of memory. A backup system stays active for a limited period for battery replacement probably by keeping a capacitor charged. As the batteries drain from constant use, the effect of this method is extremely questionable.

Kodak is testing a true non-volatile (no loss of memory) photo card as a joint venture with Information Storage Devices (ISD). ISD sells non-volatile 14-second chip at $3.00. Their 90-second non-volatile chip is selling for $10.00 and they expect the introduce a 300-second non-volatile chip for $25.00 by the middle of 1995.

SALES PLAN AND COMMISSIONS

THE INDUSTRY

Picture Frame Market

Talking Picture Frames

Several Taiwan companies have recently introduced a four-picture frame unit wholesaling from $29.00 to $32.00 FOB, with a suggested retail of $99.00. The disadvantages are that this product has no way of distinguishing which picture is talking and the volatile memory chip will eventually lose its memory. A new volatile chip was recently introduced by a Taiwan company with a 600-second recording time for $2.00. All prices are for quantity orders in the millions over several years.

Regardless of the chip used, it still has to be integrated through hardware and software with a microphone and a speaker, plus an on/off, a play/record, and a start/stop button. This integration can probably be configured for $3.00 per unit plus the initial R & D. Therefore, an eight-photo frame using eight non-volatile chips and the same set of buttons would cost $27.00 plus the costs of the individual frame holders and some form of photo recognition such as lights. This would probably drive the manufactured price above $32.00. The chips with longer recording time do not appear to have any price advantage. They also have to be integrated with a "location access" feature for the recorded messages. Volatile chips are really not suitable for this application even with battery backup, unless the company wants to explain to grandmothers, parents, and lovers why those precious voice recordings were suddenly lost after several years.

Based upon the five to one formula of retail sales to manufactured cost, the cost of using solid state non-volatile technology is still too expensive for home use. However, it would probably work in business applications such as point-of-purchase displays.

MARKET SIZE AND LONGEVITY

The company's product line appears to be in a niche market by bridging the easy viewing of separate photos with the full viewing of multiple sound pictures on a VCR recording. This hybrid market is almost unlimited as indicated by the fact that the standard photo frame market is rapidly expanding, along with the video camera market.

Summary of report: Picture frames had double-digit growth for almost ten years, and as the economy recovers, picture frames are expected to be even stronger sellers, according to Bill Johnson of Intercraft Industries. The frame market is dominated by discount stores, which account for 24% of all sales, while drug stores account for 15%. Of frames sold, 2% are through supermarkets, with the rest sold through photography dealers, card and gift stores, variety stores, and arts and craft's shops. According to Popular Photography's "The Wolfman Report," 66% of shoppers buy more than one frame at a time and 33% of consumers buy frames as gifts. Frame suppliers say that it is essential to position the products near a main aisle in the front of the store. The move toward fashion frames is also focused.

The talking photo business is in its infancy. This was demonstrated by a recent sale on QVC of several thousand single-photo talking frames that sold at $39.95 in less than 10 minutes. As the variations increase the market will expand. Basic single photo frames start under $10.00 and a number of decorator frames are priced over $50.00.

The bridging of sound with photos will change the way people look at and remember those special pictures. It will also expand the concept of perceived value for a photo frame, especially one with talking multiple photos.

Retailers prefer companies with two or more products in different price points, especially if they start under $49.95. This price point appeals to a larger customer base than those over $49.95. The $79.95 wall unit fits that slightly higher marketplace of people who prefer a product with more aesthetic value.

It is just as easy for these retailers to enter a new company in their computers with one SKU as it is with two or more SKUs. Additionally, the retailers have the benefits of stock balancing and market testing.

Retailers feel that people could easily use multiples of this product either for special events like weddings, family celebrations, or vacations. Desktop and wall units expand the consumer line dramatically. The longevity of this product should greatly exceed the norm for new products, which is usually three to five years.

Both products are made using standard tape recorders and a patentable drive and display mechanism. This low-tech method is much less expensive than the high-tech solid state format. In addition, the patent should slow or prevent other companies from entering the field from this direction.

A utility patent will be applied when all the engineering drawings are completed. A patent search has shown that no competitive product using the same or even similar technology currently exists. The patent laws provide a 12-month "window of protection" for well documented products. The final patent should protect the products since these laws have become greatly strengthened over the years. The patents will remain with Larry Koenig but will be fully assigned to the corporation. The investors can secure their investments with the rights to the patents. This will remain in effect until the investors have received a reasonable return on their investment.

Both products will probably have to be manufactured overseas to save on tooling, molding, and assembly. The company has contacted a manufacturer who lives in the U.S. but has a factory in Indonesia, where the daily labor costs are less than the hourly labor costs in the United States. China is another potential place for manufacturing. China would like to gain larger inroads in the U.S. as compared with Taiwan, Hong Kong, or Korea. Mexico is also a distinct possibility.

The advantage of manufacturing in these countries is price. The disadvantage is the lack of control, potential for mistakes, and problems with shipping.

The company would prefer to locate a manufacturer in this country if the final cost of production is within 5% of the offshore counterpart. Mr. Tarlow has used manufacturers in Utah and Arizona where the labor costs are less.

The completed engineering drawings will be sent out to bid when they are finished. Based on Mr. Tarlow's 20 years of experience, the final costs should not exceed $15.00 for the wall unit and $9.00 for the desktop version. He also believes the tooling and molding for the wall unit should not exceed $85,000 offshore or $125,000 in the United States. The desktop unit should be less than one-half of the wall unit based upon its size.

Retailers' Preference

PROTECTION OF PRODUCTS

MANUFACTURING

The actual tooling and molding will be probably take eight weeks, once all agreements are completed. Production will take 30 days and shipping by boat will also take 30 days.

Prior to production the preproduction units can be shipped by air for evaluation, corrections, initial sales through wholesale channels, brochure pictures, and short-form infomercial production.

For several select retailers and catalogers initial shipments can be shipped by air. Usually these companies want only a few hundred for testing. The reorders can be fulfilled from the main shipment arriving by boat.

If the product is very successful the company may experience a problem of short supply. Short supply has the following advantages:

- The creation of an over demand
- Elimination on overstocking
- Elimination of stock balancing
- Prompt payment of bills

History has shown where companies with successful products became even more successful when they kept their products scarce. The classic case is Nintendo. Successful products, where the supply eventually caught up with and passed the demand, demonstrate how these products quickly fell from desire. The best examples are The Rubik Cube, Trivial Pursuit, and the original hand-held electronic games. The theory of short supply is not the company's intention but it feels that if handled correctly it could be a decided advantage.

COMPETITION

The competition will come from photo picture frame manufacturers who produce singular or multiple picture frames and consumer electronic manufacturers who want to enter the talking picture frame field.

The company feels that most if not all of these competitors will attack the marketplace using solid state technology. Currently, as was explained earlier, that form of technology does not appear to poise a threat until the prices drop.

Companies like Kodak would probably prefer a joint venture or licensing agreement with Talking Photo Technology rather than producing a similar product, as indicated through conversation with the division involved with photo frames.

RESELLERS

The following is a list of potential resellers compiled from Dun & Bradstreet and Hayes Druggist Guide:

Name	Numbers
Beauty Salons	127,988
Bridal Shops	5,885
Catalog and mail-order houses	3,205
Catalog sales	2,460

Catalog Showroom stores	689
Children's and infant's wear stores	2,827
Children's wear	7,159
Consumer Electronic resellers	6,192
Department Stores	7,251
Department Stores, discount	5,961
Department Stores, non-discount	3,737
Drug Store Chains	24,574
Drug Store Independents	27,085
Gift Stores (all types)	74,851
Luggage and Leather Goods stores	1,617
Men's Clothing and boy's clothing stores	14,184
Party planning services	1,306
Photographers, still and video	10,323
Photographic services	2,469
Photographic Stores	1,650
Photography Studios	14,592
Pre-school & Private Kindergarten	1,366
Stationery and Office Supplies	3,388
Women's accessory and specialty stores	3,735
Women's and children wear	6,316
Women's Clothing Stores	23,618

RESELLERS...continued

For clarity purposes and to remove overlapping SIC codes, certain categories have been combined. The numbers represent the number of businesses (except for drug stores) not locations. These numbers serve to illustrate the number of potential resellers.

END USERS

The following is a partial list of the type of consumers who would be targeted initially:

- Parents with children
- Grandparents
- Newlyweds
- Single mothers
- Single women (21 to 39)
- Teenage girls (13 to 18)

Based upon a demographic and statistical analysis of the U.S. supplied by Scan/US, there are 32.8 million households with children. The highest concentrations are the northeastern section of the U.S. The second heaviest concentrations are in the southeast, California and Texas, followed by the South and the Midwest. The highest income levels are in California, New York, and Pennsylvania.

PRICING

Price is based upon three factors. The first is perceived value or what the market will bear. The second is the manufacturing cost. The last is the desired profit structure of the company balanced against what the resellers need.

The final price is usually five times the final production cost including boxing and landing charges in the U.S. There is some room since most of today's retailers work on margins of 30 to 40% for smaller and 50% for larger quantities. Catalogers usually work on 50%. Sales rep's commissions range from 10% in the consumer electronic field to 15 to 20% for the gift industry. A stocking distributor usually buys the product for 50% and an additional 10% off the retail. A master distributor's discount is negotiable but could be an extra 10 to 20% off the retail.

Each level of discount requires a larger initial and continued commitment from that particular buyer. The company feels that $79.95 for the wall unit and $49.95 for the desktop is reasonable, based upon the cost to manufacture, box, and ship. We may find by doing final test evaluations through direct sales and short-form infomercial that the market may accept a higher retail than what we indicated. The final suggested retail price will be the one determined during test with preproduction units. Test marketing and focus groups can be used but they do not always convey what people will actually spend. The wall unit could be retailed at $69.95 and the desktop at $39.95, without any significant loss in revenue.

INCENTIVES

Resellers

Incentives for advertising and promotion range from a cash discount to free goods included within the order. These incentives are usually designed for the major customers and catalogers. They are based upon either larger orders or proof of performance such as print advertisements or catalog inserts. Three to five percent is acceptable but each deal may have to be negotiated separately provided the company stays within the legality of the law.

Some companies also want exclusives for a period of time. Considering the size of the order, the particular marketplace and the length of the exclusive and the starting time, this is possible.

In addition, certain retailers will only place orders on a "guaranteed sales" basis where units not sold can be returned for cash refunds. Talking Photo Technology feels that by having two products "stock balancing" will be an alternative. For the important retailers who insist on this mode, Talking Photo Technology will require a minimum test purchase with a larger non-returnable backup purchase order, if the test is successful.

The company will produce its own point-of-purchase (POP) display to aid in the selling of the products to consumers. These POP displays will be sold to the retailers and offset with free goods. The POP is a modified unit, designed for continuous AC operation.

Consumer

Direct sales and short form TV infomercials will also help to drive the retail sales. Additionally, the company will investigate the use of cross promotion incentives with photo companies for film discounts, and photo developers for processing discounts.

A direct sales promotion targeted to grandparents, new parents, and newlyweds can be accomplished by mail and telemarketing. The campaign can include photo discounts with the product purchase, discounts off the second units of equal or lesser value, and a joint venture promotion with a particular retail chain or group of catalogs.

The key personnel are the members of the management team. Securing additional management personnel who can help advance the company along each level should not be difficult with the current state of the economy. Many qualified people are either looking for work or working in low paying positions.

As the company advances beyond the start-up phase it will need a Chief Financial Officer. Larry Koenig has worn many hats in the past and in the initial stages is fully capable of handling or assisting in many areas for a portion of the first year or longer if necessary.

The company will contract out many of the services during the initial year or two, including direct sales, fulfillment, and telemarketing.

As the company grows and the product line increases it may be more beneficial to bring these various services within one facility. The following is a partial list of prospective employees and department types, the numbers, and the estimated monthly salaries that could be brought in at various stages:

Name	Number	Estimated Monthly Salary
Accounting Department	1	$2,000
Customer Service	1	2,500
In-house Sales Department	3	7,500
Product Development	1	3,000
Regional Sales Managers	2	8,000
Repair Department	1	3,000
Secretaries	2	6,000
Telemarketers	3	6,000
Total in a fully staffed company	15	38,000

The company would prefer not to store or ship the majority of the product. It would be cheaper to let the manufacturer ship FOB to our larger customers. Talking Photo Technology prefers to conserve capital by starting in smaller or shared quarters. Products would be sent directly to our contracted fulfillment center except for a smaller quantity that can be stored in a local warehouse. For the next stage of the company's growth it can relocate to a larger facility where it can do local shipping, set up an accounting department, and handle returns. Additional departments can be added with each stage of growth.

The company intends to set up a series of controls starting by using only manufacturers with proven performances. Dealing directly with the owner of the manufacturing facility and not going through an agent is a advantage. The initial preproduction run should expose most problems.

The company will institute a series of quality control check points at various stages of production, shipping, and receiving, and not depend on the manufacturers' guarantee. The cost of verification and spot checking will be more intensive in the early stages of growth. This is important because resellers will not give the company a second chance if they receive a large number of defective products.

The company will source a second manufacturer in case the first one is unable to maintain production or for reasons beyond his control he can not produce. In theory, the two products can be manufactured by two manufacturers. Once the tooling is paid for, and becomes the property of Talking Photo Technology it can be relocated to another facility. This would be difficult but not impossible.

INSURANCE

Besides standard insurance, our intention is to bond key manufacturers against production problems, at least on the onset, if possible. The company will pay for business interruption insurance, where feasible. Key personnel will have special insurance. Product liability should not be a problem since everything is battery operated. Since we are not doing manufacturing we don't expect labor or union problems.

ADDITIONAL PRODUCTS

"PortraiTalk" and "SoundPhoto" are the first in a series of high-profile products that the company will produce. Multiple versions of the wall unit can be produced so they can be interconnected. Volatile digital technology is probably best suited for the premium, point-of-purchase and area where memory loss is not essential. The non-volatile chips should be in the usable price range in 18 to 24 months.

Price versus performance is always the key factor. Incorporating digital technology with long term memory on a magnetic media at an affordable price would be ideal. If made small enough, these pieces can be retrofitted to existing photo albums or attached to store shelves as a sales tool.

Another area of exploration is the health industry. Some elderly people take a number of different prescriptions. In cases where a patient may become confused as to which prescription they took, their next dose, and when they should get the medication refilled, a voice memory product with a possible picture of the particular medication can inform the patients on the status of their drug intake.

The multiple talking photo concept can be used with coffee mugs, daily notepads, and phone dialers.

Any product or idea that appears to have potential will be test marketed before and after prototyping. Only then will the company invest time or money into the concept. Product potential will be rated on the following 12 areas:

☑Exciting patentable feature	☑Simple to understand
☑Fills a real need	☑No new parts to reinvent
☑Easily manufacturable	☑Center of attraction in retail environments
☑Aesthetically appealing	☑No safety problems
☑Simple to operate	☑Great price to value ratio
☑Psychologically fulfilling	☑Excellent gift idea

The sales of the company are driven by advertising, marketing, promotion, and time of year. Breaking even in December is not the same as breaking even in March. Additionally, direct sales produce a higher gross profit than wholesale sales. Therefore, by comparing the income statements of 1995 and 1996 of slow months versus better months, it is safe to assume that a break-even position will not occur until the last quarter of 1995. This assumes that the products were sold at the ratio of two desktop units to one wall unit and that the majority of orders would come through the wholesale route.

Based upon the estimate of the first year the company feels that 15,000 total units would be required as an initial inventory consisting of 10,000 desktop and 5,000 wall units. This initial revolving inventory should prevent any normal out-of-stock situation from occurring in the start up year, especially since merchandise could take 60 to 90 days from purchase order to actual receipt.

The company can use purchase order financing and factoring as a means of handling cash flow problems for its second Christmas.

The following is a list of how the funds will be used and allocated to reach a positive cash flow:

Use	Amount
Final Prototyping and Design Work	$24,000
Capital Equipment, Computers/Software	12,000
Contingency money	85,000
Losses until a positive cash flow	175,000
Furniture and Fixtures	8,000
Initial Inventory Desktop Unit (10,000)	90,000
Initial Inventory Wall Units (5,000)	75,000
Legal and Accounting startup	6,000
Tooling and Molding Desktop Unit	40,000
Tooling and Molding Wall Unit	85,000
Total	$600,000

BREAK EVEN ANALYSIS

USE OF FUNDS

ECONOMIC FORECAST

The Economy in 1993

A brief review of economic developments in 1993 provides a helpful introduction to the projections of 1994. As of late October 1993, it appeared that growth in 1993 would be somewhat less than was projected in Outlook '93, not only in the United States, but also in the rest of the industrial world generally. Following strong growth in the United States during late 1992 (some of which stemmed from reconstruction associated with hurricane damages earlier in the year) the nation's economic activity slowed considerably during the first half of 1993. The annual rate of growth in real gross domestic product (GDP) fell below 1 percent in the first quarter, partly reflecting a record decline in defense spending and disruptions caused by a severe storm along the Eastern seaboard. Growth then rose to an annual rate of approximately 2 percent in the second quarter, and was expected to average approximately 3 percent during the second half of 1993.

Economic Outlook for 1994

Commerce Department analysts developed their industry projections for 1994 against the background of expected overall growth of close to 3 percent-the Blue Chip consensus as of July 1993. In September, forecasts of real GDP growth for 1994 over 1993 remained in that range: the International Monetary Fund (IMF) projected a 2.6 percent growth for the United States; the Blue Chip consensus was shaded to 2.7 percent (the same as that of the Congressional Budget Office); and the Administration's mid-session forecast called for a 3 percent increase. As the analysis below suggests, the economy is likely to expand moderately-in the range of 2.5 to 3 percent-in 1994. On the policy side, the Budget Act of 1993 is expected to restrain growth modestly in 1994. The estimated deficit reduction is about $47 billion or 0.7 percent of projected current-dollar GDP. However, the deficit-reduction program has contributed to a decrease in long-term interest rates to their lowest levels in many years. The stimulus provided by these low rates will tend to offset the fiscal restraint. Several other factors may continue to contain growth in the United States. These include the following:

○ Further corporate restructuring, limiting growth in employment and wages (related to this are uncertainties about the costs to businesses associated with the proposed health care reform package)
○ Continued weakness in the commercial real estate market, which was heavily overbuilt during the 1980s
○ Continued cutbacks in defense purchases, possibly on an accelerated basis, and limitations on spending by governments at all levels due to budget constraints
○ Weaker-than-expected recoveries in the economies of some major U.S. trading partners, especially Japan and Western Europe

No single sector stands out as the principal engine of growth in 1994, though gross private domestic investment is projected to increase twice as fast as overall GDP (much less, however, than in 1993). In general, interest-sensitive components of spending are expected to provide much of the impetus to overall growth. Consumer purchases of durable goods, producers' durable equipment, and residential investment all are expected to show fairly good growth in 1994. State and local government expenditures, also interest-sensitive to some extent, grow much faster in 1994 after a modest gain in 1993.

Total personal consumption expenditures are projected to increase a little faster than disposable personal income. Sales of new cars and light trucks, which are reflected in both consumer durables and producers' equipment, are expected to rise approximately 6 percent in 1994. Vehicles built in North America (considered to be domestically produced) account for all of the gain. The sharp decline in the value of the dollar against the yen during 1993 increased prices of imported Japanese models relative to prices of domestic U.S. cars, while consumers began to perceive quality improvements in U.S. models. This development is expected to reduce further exports of Japanese motor vehicles to the United States in 1994.

On the investment side, another healthy gain expected for corporate profits in 1994 will help to sustain solid growth in private nonresidential fixed investment. The rate of increase in investment in producers' equipment will slow in 1994, while investment in nonresidential structures should undergo little change. Ongoing weakness in the construction of office buildings, hotels and motels, and other commercial structures should be largely offset by modest gains in construction of most other nonresidential structures. Housing is expected to post another moderate increase in 1994, primarily in the construction of single-family units and in remodeling. Growth in multi-family housing will remain modest, given the continuation of high vacancy rates in rental housing during 1993.

Exports of goods and services are expected to increase in line with overall GDP in 1994, weakening slightly from their growth in 1993. These developments stand in sharp contrast to the strong U.S. export performance from 1985 to 1992, when the dollar was declining and real exports of goods and services rose five times as fast as GDP. The dollar showed little change during 1993. Although it weakened considerably in relation to the yen, it appreciated against most European currencies.

Economic Outlook for 1994...*continued*

Table 1: Gross Domestic Product 1992-1994

Category	Actual 1992	Estimate 1993	Forecast 1994
Gross Domestic Product	2.6	2.6	2.9
Personal consumption expenditures	2.6	2.7	2.9
Durable goods	7.0	6.8	6.8
Nondurable goods	1.4	1.3	1.5

Note: Projections for 1993 and 1994 were made in August 1993. For an updated official forecast, refer to the Administration's economic outlook, published in the annual budget document and The Economic Report of the President, February 1994.

Table 2: Key Economic Indicators 1992-94

Category	Actual 1992	Estimate 1993	Forecast 1994
Before-tax corporate profits	9.1%	11.8%	8.2%
Real disposable personal income	2.9%	2.3%	1.9%
Consumer price index	3.0%	3.3%	3.2%
Producer price index for finished goods	1.2%	2.2%	3.3%

The financials are structured in a calendar year format because of the influence that Christmas has upon yearly sales. The sales after the startup partial year should dramatically increase in the first full year. The second full year should increase by a minimum of three times the previous year. This is the year that the mass merchants, discounters, and large chains start to sell the product. By the end of the third year the sales should reach 15 times the original investment. The projected financials are for three years plus the initial startup year. These factors, along with the economy and technology, really prevent long range forecasts. The company also feels that the end of the third year would be an ideal time for either an IPO, investor buyout, merger, or sale to a larger company. Any of these avenues would present an exit for the investor.

FINANCIALS

CONTINGENCIES

Potential Problems

The company wants to get the products on the market quickly yet it is imperative that it keeps mistakes to a minimum. Though these products will sell better at Christmas they are also year-round items for weddings, special events, graduations, holiday vacations, Valentines Day, Mother's Day, and Father's Day. On some of these occasions multiples can be purchased. If the Christmas season is missed the break-even time will take longer but the company should not be seriously affected.

Copy-cat products will arrive on the scene usually 12 to 18 months after our product is launched provided it is successful. Some will even attempt to circumvent the patent laws, but most will use digital technology and some method of picture synchronization. A few may even foster a margin of success. Their major problem will be the retention of memory after the batteries wear out for the products using volatile memory or the higher cost of the products using non-volatile memory. The company intends to use solid state technology for point-of-purchase displays. This research should enable it to stay in the forefront of technology and switch over to solid state when feasible.

New Products

Traditionally, within 18 to 24 months the company should be ready to launch the next series of products and open up additional markets. These products should be more advanced versions of the original products, different but similar products for other markets (health industry), and modifications of the original for other markets (point-of-purchase display). New products should keep the company in the forefront.

The success and longevity of our current products will determine the amount of resources placed on any new products. It takes from six to twelve months to place a new product on the market. The company does not believe in the shot gun approach of new products. Marketing is too expensive; therefore an initial and a secondary evaluation must decide if a product is viable.

If the perceived value is not as apparent with the current models or the solid state technology advances faster than expected, then the company will have to incorporate digital technology into the product more rapidly than expected.

Alternative Marketing Concept

After 12 months, if the company feels is has not penetrated the market successfully using conventional methods of direct sales and wholesales then it could opt to go in the direction of multi-level marketing (MLM) or network marketing. It would have to bring in experienced people in that arena or merge with a current company. MLM companies require products with high appeal, easily sold on a one-to-one method, and a minimum of a 5 to 1 ratio. In addition, the company would produce a catalog of available high and low-tech products. This formula has been accomplished very successfully by a company called Quorum. Talking Photo Technology would need at least 10,000 but preferably 20,000 multi-level sales people called its downline.

The company would produce a standard size 64-page catalog with products ranging from it own line of proprietary products to other consumer electronics. It would also include the areas of computers and/or accessories, children's toys, health, beauty, kitchen, dietary and food items, plus recreational products. The catalog would have a minimum of 150 products besides its own. The only requirements are that the acquired selections must be shippable, and have a minimum of 50% margins (a $50.00 retail item would cost $25.00).

The main thrust of the catalog would be its line of proprietary products that it could produce or acquire from investors on a royalty basis. The downline people would receive a similar profit structure that would have been set up for resellers and commissioned sales people.

The cost for producing one million catalogs including product selection, copy writing, layout and design, photography, models, color separation, order form, printing, and binding is estimated at $400,000. The shipping of the catalog, based on 20,000 members with 50 catalogs per person, is approximately $0.19 each, which is paid for by the people. In addition, they would be charged a fee of $.0.75 per catalog, equating to a $350,000 net profit for your company.

The people would be allowed to buy a maximum of one of each of the products in the catalog at a 40% discount for their use. Regular orders would start with a profit structure of 20% to the seller followed by 5% for the next in line and ending at 1%. Let's take an example of a product with a wholesale of $50.00 and a retail of $100.00. Here is a possible way distribution could work with the individual profit margins.

Seller	1st in Line	2nd in Line	3rd in Line	4th in Line	5th in Line
$20.00	$5.00	$4.00	$3.00	$2.00	$1.00

This leaves a gross profit of 15%, or in this example $15.00. The cost of order processing and fulfillment, by an outside company, should not exceed 5% or $5.00 in this example. There will some additional operating expenses (credit card processing) and/or overhead, estimated to be 3%, leaving a 7% or $7.00 per $100.00 per order.

Assuming the average retail sale is $100.00 and the number of unit sold per product is 200, then a catalog containing 150 products should gross $3,000,000. This would produce a net profit of $210,000 for the company per season.

These estimates and catalog pricing are based upon the Quorum catalog and their items selected and initial returns. The net profit could increase by three to four times that amount for Christmas, based upon conventional catalog sales. The main income for the multi-level people and the company would come from its proprietary product line. Successful MLM companies make millions. An original product company not in the health and beauty field could do exceptionally well.

Another source of revenue is a product placement fee which Larry Koenig accomplished very successfully in his previous catalogs, The Price of His Toys. Within several years the company should be able to receive $300,000 or equivalent from product placement.

A major source of revenue that Sharper Image had ($1,000,000 per year) was from its list name rental.

The success of any catalog requires the correct product selection, good design, selling copy and a quality customer base. The company either has or can acquire people with that expertise.

It would take a minimum of six months to set up the MLM organization provided it did not have to start from the beginning. The major expense would be the catalog that should be prepaid by the downline people.

Product ordering is a little tricky and requires a certain amount of expertise in this area. If the company is not careful a portion of its profit can be sitting in some warehouse as inventory. There are ways of disposing of extra inventory with minimum risk, especially through its downline.

Within several years the company could be generating four to five million as net profit on the catalog and outside product alone. This method has been proven successful by Quorum and they just focus on consumer electronics. A multi-style catalog should out-perform a single style, especially since half the people in MLM are women who do not buy electronics.

THE DEAL
Desired Method

The company is seeking an investment of $600,000 and is offering 25% of its stock for this money. The investment can be made in several payments. The repayment options are explained under the EXIT section. The company plans to operate in Southern California but can be incorporated in any state. This will be done after the first round of capital is raised and all the investors are in place, thereby saving on legal fees.

ALTERNATIVE DEAL
Purchase Order Financing and Factoring

The following is a list of how the funds will be used and allocated to reach break even if the company uses purchase order financing (POF) and factoring:

Use	Amount
Tooling and Molding Wall Unit -- Balance from Profits	$60,000
Tooling and Molding Desktop Unit -- Balance from Profits	$30,000
Losses prior to cash flow	175,000
Contingency money	25,000
First Payment Prototyping/Design Products balance over time	5,000
POF/Factoring on Wall Units (4,500)	9,000
POF/Factoring on Desktop Unit (8,500)	11,000
Total	315,000

The company has arranged for purchase order financing and factoring. The manufacturer should cooperate, provided money is received from the purchase orders. This method is not the first choice but can be accomplished. The company would only be willing to offer 15% of its stock based upon this proposal. The other 10% would be needed for a second round of financing in case projected results are not achieved.

The company would prefer to go public sometime after the third full year or sooner if the profits can attract a substantial IPO. this will depend on the economy, the public market, and the company's perceived potential.

The first alternative to a normal IPO would be a SCOR (Small Company Offering Registration) offering. This is a limited public offering done on at the State level for a registration fee of $2,500 in California (other states may be different). Attorneys charge $5,000 to $15,000. The company must sell its own stock initially. The state approval is somewhat difficult unless the company is profitable and has a two-year track record. The company can raise a maximum of $1,000,000 per year by selling its shares of stock at a fixed price of $5.00 per share. The company can not use any of this money to payoff investors unless the money came from a financial institution (bank) as a loan.

The company feels that the potential stock purchasers in this case would be resellers of its product line, end users, and other interested parties who feel that the company is a prudent investment. The company can solicit a market marker from a major investment house when it has a minimum number of stock holders (estimated to be 500 or more).

The SCOR idea would work exceptionally well with the MLM format described under Contingencies.

Based upon the above premise the investors could lend the money to the company through a bank secured by a CD. After two or three years the investors would receive their initial investment back, yet still retain an interest in the company.

The second alternative would entail a straight pay back over a period of years with a substantial return on investment.

The third alternative would consist of a merger or buyout with a larger company.

The rights to patents (assigned to the investors until their investment is recovered) should generate enough income on a royalty basis if they sold to another company.

EXIT

The retail price for the wall unit is $79.95 with an average wholesale price of $48.00 for retailers and $40.00 for catalogers. The retail price for the desktop unit is $49.95 with an average wholesale price of $30.00 for retailers and $25.00 for catalogers. The company assumes Christmas sales will be minimal for the initial year but direct sales could sustain it until the resellers come on board.

The company did not allocate funds for use of purchase order financing (POF) in the Income Statements. Factoring is used at the end of the first full year. POF can only be used for orders over $50,000 by a qualified buyer, which has been approved by a factor. This is an alternative method.

The company assumes sales of 13,000 units for the balance of the first year in all fields. This is very conservative as the company feels that if it had at least 50 preproduction models of each unit (before the end of the third quarter) it could set up a national marketing campaign throughout the country.

ASSUMPTIONS

ASSUMPTIONS
...continued

The company assumes total sales of just under 100,000 units for the first full year for both models, 200,000 for the second year and 360,000 for the third year. This is very conservative based upon the average market potential of 2,000,000 sales for a five-year period for a single good product.

The company feels that "SoundPhoto" (the desktop version) will outsell "PortraiTalk" (the wall model) by a ratio of 2 to 1, provided both units are available and shown. The company also feels that the sales of both will be higher when both are shown. As the products go into wider distribution, the percentages of consumer and trade advertising dollars will rise from less than 0.5% to over 1% in sales.

An extensive patent search was performed by Macro-Search on 2/9/94 to determine the feasibility of proceeding with a patent. No conflicting patents were shown. This does not guarantee that either a similar product was in the pending stage or a patent had expired. Due to the length of the patent search, it is not included in this plan.

Units Sales 1994

Months	July	Aug	Sept	Oct	Nov	Dec	Total	% of Total
Adjustment				3	3.75	5.5		
Desktop Units								
Retail Price				$50	$50	$50		
Low Wholesale				$25	$25	$25		
High Wholesale				$30	$30	$30		
Direct	0	0	0	150	563	1,650	2,363	18.85%
Specialty	0	0	0	150	563	825	1,538	12.27%
Catalog	0	0	0	99	248	545	891	7.11%
Retail	0	0	0	396	990	2,178	3,564	28.44%
Total Sold			0	795	2,363	5,198	8,355	66.67%
Units Ordered			10,000	0	0	0		
Balance On Hand			10,000	9,205	6,843	1,645		
Wall Units								
Retail				$79.95	$79.95	$79.95		
Low Wholesale				$40	$40	$40		
High Wholesale				$48	$48	$48		
Direct	0	0	0	75	281	825	1,181	9.43%
Specialty	0	0	0	75	281	413	769	6.13%
Catalog	0	0	0	50	124	272	446	3.55%
Retail	0	0	0	198	495	1,089	1,782	14.22%
Total Sold				398	1,181	2,599	4,178	33.33%
Units Ordered			5,000	0	0	0		
Balance On Hand			5,000	4,603	3,421	823		
Total Products				1,119	3,544	7,796	12,533	
Total Cost			$165,000	$13,118	$38,981	$85,759		

Month	1st Qtr	Oct	Nov	Dec	Total	% of Sales	**Income 1994**
Income							
Direct Sales at $49.95	$0	$7,493	$28,097	$82,418	$118,007	22.54%	
Direct Sales at $79.95	$0	$5,996	$22,486	$65,959	$94,441	18.04%	
Specialty Sales &							
Home Shopping	$0	$8,093	$30,350	$44,513	$82,956	15.85%	
Wholesale Catalogs	$0	$4,451	$11,128	$24,482	$40,062	7.65%	
Wholesale Retail							
Outlets	$0	$19,586	$48,964	$107,721	$176,271	33.67%	
Shipping/Handling	$0	$749	$2,810	$8,243	$11,802	2.25%	
Total	$0	$46,368	$143,835	$333,335	$523,539	100.00%	
Cost of Goods	$0	$12,977	$38,714	$84,726	$136,417	26.06%	
Gross Profit	$0	$33,392	$105,121	$248,610	$387,122		
Expenses							
Advertising - Consumer	$0	$5,000	$15,000	$30,000	$50,000	9.55%	
Advertising - Trade	$0	$5,000	$10,000	$15,000	$30,000	5.73%	
Advertising Allowances	$0	$0	$556	$1,224	$1,781	0.34%	
Bad Debt	$0	$0	$2,877	$6,667	$9,543	1.82%	
Commissions:							
Specialty Sales	$0	$0	$4,552	$6,677	$11,229	2.14%	
Wholesale Sales	$0	$0	$9,014	$19,830	$28,844	5.51%	
Depreciation	$7,500	$2,500	$2,500	$2,500	$15,000	2.87%	
Direct Sales Credit Cards	$0	$225	$843	$2,473	$3,540	0.68%	
Customer Returns	$0	$0	$4,315	$10,000	$14,315	2.73%	
Customer Service	$0	$0	$2,000	$2,000	$4,000	0.76%	
Fulfillment	$0	$647	$2,428	$5,787	$8,862	1.69%	
Insurance	0	$1,000	$1,000	$1,000	$3,000	0.57%	
Legal/Acct	$1,500	$2,000	$500	$500	$4,500	0.86%	
Management CEO	$15,000	$5,000	$5,000	$5,000	$30,000	5.73%	
Miscellaneous	$1,000	$500	$1,000	$1,000	$3,500	0.67%	
Natl Sales Manager	$12,000	$4,000	$4,000	$4,000	$24,000	4.58%	
Phone	$2,000	$1,000	$2,000	$2,000	$7,000	1.34%	
Promotions	$2,000	$1,000	$3,000	$3,000	$9,000	1.72%	
Publicist/Promotions	$0	$1,500	$1,500	$1,500	$4,500	0.86%	
Rent	$2,000	$1,000	$1,000	$1,000	$5,000	0.96%	
Royalty to Proto Des.	$0	$668	$2,102	$4,972	$7,742	1.48%	
Salaries	$3,000	$1,500	$1,500	$1,500	$7,500	1.43%	
Sales & Mrkt VP	$15,000	$5,000	$5,000	$5,000	$30,000	5.73%	
Taxes - Payroll	$5,400	$1,860	$1,860	$1,860	$10,980	2.10%	
Trade Shows	$0	$0	$2,500	$0	$2,500	0.48%	
Travel/Prod Promo	$4,000	$4,000	$2,500	$1,000	$11,500	2.20%	
Utilities	$600	$200	$200	$200	$1,200	0.23%	
Total Expenses	$71,000	$43,600	$88,748	$135,690	$339,038	64.76%	
Net Profit							
before taxes	($71,000)	($10,208)	$16,373	$112,920	$48,085	9.18%	
Taxes Due					$16,830		
Net Profit							
after taxes		($10,208)	$16,373	$112,920	$31,255		

Balance Sheet 1994

	Opening	Jul	Aug	Sep	Oct	Nov	Dec
Assets							
Cash	$430,000	$413,620	$393,060	$201,500	$182,872	$204,671	$333,739
Accts Rec	$0	$0	$0	$0	$24,037	$60,092	$132,203
Inventory	$0	$0	$0	$165,000	$151,883	$112,901	$27,143
Current							
Assets	$430,000	$413,620	$393,060	$366,500	$358,792	$377,665	$493,085
Deposits	$25,000	$25,000	$25,000	$25,000	$25,000	$25,000	$25,000
Fixed Assets							
Gross	$150,000	$150,000	$150,000	$150,000	$150,000	$150,000	$150,000
Accum Depr	$0	($2,500)	($5,000)	($7,500)	($10,000)	($12,500)	($15,000)
Net	$150,000	$147,500	$145,000	$142,500	$140,000	$137,500	$135,000
Total							
Assets	$605,000	$586,120	$563,060	$534,000	$523,792	$540,165	$653,085
Liabilities							
Accts Pay	$0	$0	$0	$0	$0	$0	$0
Current Liabs	$0	$0	$0	$0	$0	$0	$0
Debt	$600,000	$600,000	$600,000	$600,000	$600,000	$600,000	$600,000
Equity	$5,000	($13,880)	($36,940)	($66,000)	($76,208)	($59,835)	$53,085
Total							
L & E	$605,000	$586,120	$563,060	$534,000	$523,792	$540,165	$653,085

Cash Flow 1994

	Jul	Aug	Sep	Oct	Nov	Dec
Cash from Operating Activity						
Beginning Profit						
After Tax	($18,880)	($23,060)	($29,060)	($10,208)	$16,373	$112,920
Deprec	$2,500	$2,500	$2,500	$2,500	$2,500	$2,500
Decr/(Incr) in A/R	$0	$0	$0	$24,037	$36,055	$72,111
Decr/(Incr) in Inv	$0	$0	$165,000	($13,118)	($38,981)	($85,759)
Incr/(Decr) in A/P	$0	$0	$0	$0	$0	$0
Cash						
from Ops	($16,380)	($20,560)	$138,440	$3,211	$15,947	$101,772
Incr/(Decr)						
in Debt	$0	$0	$0	$0	$0	$0
Net						
Cash Flow	($16,380)	($20,560)	$138,440	$3,211	$15,947	$101,772
Beginning						
Cash Bal	$430,000	$413,620	$393,060	$201,500	$182,872	$204,671
Net						
Cash Flow	($16,380)	($20,560)	$138,440	$3,211	$15,947	$101,772
Ending						
Cash Flow	$413,620	$393,060	$531,500	$204,711	$198,819	$306,443

Months	1st Qtr	2nd Qtr	3rd Qtr	4th Qtr	Grand Total	% of Total	Units Sales 1995
Desktop Units							
Direct	325	850	788	4,813	6,775	6.90%	
Specialty	638	1,125	956	3,675	6,394	6.51%	
Catalog	638	1,050	1,275	7,500	10,463	10.65%	
Retail	2,550	4,200	5,100	30,000	41,850	42.61%	
Total	4,150	7,225	8,119	45,988	65,481	66.67%	
Units Ordered	10,000	10,000	10,000	40,000	70,000	71.27%	
Balance On Hand	7,495	10,270	12,151	6,164			
Wall Units							
Direct	163	425	394	2,406	3,388	3.45%	
Specialty	319	563	478	1,838	3,197	3.25%	
Catalog	319	525	638	3,750	5,231	5.33%	
Retail	1,275	2,100	2,550	15,000	20,925	21.30%	
Total	2,075	3,613	4,059	22,994	32,741	33.33%	
Units Ordered	5,000	5,000	5,000	20,000	35,000		
Balance On Hand	3,748	5,135	6,076	3,082			
Total Products	6,225	10,838	12,178	68,981	98,222		
Total Costs	68,475	119,213	133,959	758,794			

	1st Qtr	2nd Qtr	3rd Qtr	4th Qtr	Total	% of Sales	Income 1995
Income							
Direct Sales							
@ $49.95	$16,234	$42,458	$39,336	$240,384	$338,411	9.59%	
@ $79.95	$12,992	$33,979	$31,480	$192,380	$270,831	7.67%	
Specialty Sale &							
Home Shopping	$34,415	$60,733	$51,623	$198,395	$345,167	9.78%	
Wholesale							
Catalogs	$28,664	$47,211	$57,327	$337,219	$470,420	13.33%	
Retail Outlets	$126,158	$207,790	$252,316	$1,484,213	$2,070,476	58.67%	
Ship/Hndl	$1,624	$4,246	$3,934	$24,042	$33,846	0.96%	
Total	$220,086	$396,416	$436,017	$2,476,632	$3,529,151	100.00%	
COG	$67,536	$117,626	$131,792	$744,475	$1,061,429	30.08%	
Gross Profit	$152,550	$278,790	$304,225	$1,732,157	$2,467,722		
Expenses							
Accounting Dept	$6,000	$6,000	$6,000	$6,000	$24,000	0.68%	
Advertising							
Consumer	$25,000	$45,000	$55,000	$110,000	$235,000	6.66%	
Trade	$35,000	$40,000	$60,000	$115,000	$250,000	7.08%	
Advertising Allows	$1,433	$2,361	$2,866	$16,861	$23,521	0.67%	
Bad Debt	$4,402	$7,928	$8,720	$49,533	$70,583	2.000%	
Commissions							
Specialty Sales	$3,442	$6,073	$5,162	$19,839	$34,517	0.98%	
Wholesale Sales	$23,223	$38,250	$46,446	$273,215	$381,134	10.08%	
Cost: Dir Sales Cr Crds	$877	$2,293	$2,124	$12,983	$18,277	0.52%	
Customer Returns	$6,603	$11,892	$13,080	$74,299	$105,875	3.00%	

Income 1995...*continued*

	1st Qtr	2nd Qtr	3rd Qtr	4th Qtr	Total	% of Sales
Customer Service	$7,500	$7,500	$7,500	$7,500	$30,000	0.85%
Depreciation	$7,500	$7,500	$7,500	$7,500	$30,000	0.85%
PO Finance/Factoring	$0	$0	$0	$5,009	$5,009	0.14%
Fulfillment	$877	$2,293	$2,124	$12,983	$18,277	0.52%
Insurance	$3,000	$3,000	$3,000	$3,000	$12,000	0.34%
Legal/Acct	$1,500	$1,500	$1,500	$1,500	$6,000	0.17%
Management/CEO	$15,000	$15,000	$15,000	$63,049	$108,049	3.06%
Management/CFO	$0	$0	$0	$0	$0	0.00%
Miscellaneous	$3,000	$3,000	$3,000	$3,000	$12,000	0.34%
Natl Sales Mgr	$12,000	$12,000	$12,000	$44,033	$80,033	2.27%
Phone	$7,500	$9,500	$15,000	$22,500	$54,500	1.54%
Promotions	$7,000	$9,000	$9,000	$12,000	$37,000	1.05%
Publicist/Promos						
Inhouse	$4,500	$4,500	$9,000	$9,000	$27,000	0.77%
Rent	$3,000	$3,000	$3,000	$3,000	$12,000	0.34%
Reg Sales Mgrs	$0	$0	$12,000	$12,000	$24,000	0.68%
Repair	$0	$0	$9,000	$9,000	$18,000	51%
Salaries/Secretaries	$9,000	$9,000	$18,000	$18,000	$54,000	1.53%
Sales & Mrktg VP	$15,000	$15,000	$15,000	$55,041	$100,041	2.83%
Taxes - Payroll	$5,580	$5,580	$7,200	$15,849	$34,209	0.97%
Telemarketing	$6,000	$6,000	$12,000	$12,000	$36,000	1.02%
Trade Shows	$12,500	$7,500	$12,500	$6,000	$38,500	1.09%
Travel	$4,500	$4,500	$4,500	$4,500	$18,000	0.51%
Utilities	$1,500	$1,500	$1,500	$1,500	$6,000	0.17%
Total Expenses	$226,436	$280,671	$372,725	$999,694	$1,879,525	53.26%
Net Profit						
before taxes	($73,886)	($1,881)	($68,500)	$732,464	$588,197	
Taxes Due					$205,869	
Net Profit						
after taxes	($73,886)	($11,459)	($68,500)	$476,101	$322,256	

Balance Sheet 1995

	1st Qtr	2nd Qtr	3rd Qtr	4th Qtr
Assets				
Cash	$266,603	$143,998	$70,172	$71,851
Accts Receivable	$36,429	$109,286	$91,072	$1,001,787
Inventory	$123,668	$169,455	$200,496	$101,702
Current Assets	$426,699	$422,739	$361,739	$1,175,340
Deposits	$25,000	$25,000	$25,000	$25,000
Fixed Assets	$0	$0	$0	$0
Gross	$150,000	$150,000	$150,000	$150,000
Accum Depr	($22,500)	($30,000)	($37,500)	($45,000)
Net	$127,500	$120,000	$112,500	$105,000
Total Assets	$579,199	$567,739	$449,239	$1,305,340
	$0	$0	$0	$0

Liabilities	$0	$0	$0	$0	**Balance Sheet 1995**
Accts Payable	$0	$0	$0	$330,000	*...continued*
Current Liabilities	$0	$0	$0	$330,000	
Debt	$600,000	$600,000	$600,000	$600,000	
Equity	($20,801)	($32,261)	($100,761)	($375,340)	
Total L&E	$579,199	$567,739	$499,239	$1,305,340	

	1st Qtr	2nd Qtr	3rd Qtr	4th Qtr	Total	**Cash Flow 1995**
Cash from Operating Activity						
Beginning						
Profit After Tax	($73,886)	($11,459)	($68,500)	$476,101	$322,256	
Depreciation	$7,500	$7,500	$7,500	$7,500	$30,000	
Decr/(Incr) in A/R	($95,775)	$72,857	($18,214)	$910,716	$869,584	
Decr/(Incr) in Inv	$96,525	$45,788	$31,041	($98,794)	$74,559	
Incr/(Decr) in A/P	$0	$0	$0	$330,000	$330,000	
	$0	$0	$0	$0	$0	
Cash From Ops	($65,635)	$114,685	($48,174)	$1,625,523	$1,626,399	
	$0	$0	$0	$0	$0	
Beginning Cash Bal	$899,319	$604,823	$524,124	$321,204	$2,349,470	
Net Cash Flow	($65,635)	$114,685	($48,174)	$1,625,523	$1,626,399	
	$0	$0	$0	$0	$0	
Ending Cash Bal	$833,684	$719,508	$475,950	$1,946,727	$3,975,869	

	1st Qtr	2nd Qtr	3rd Qtr	4th Qtr	Grand Total	% of Total	**Units Sales 1996**
Desktop Units							
Direct	906	1,500	1,063	8,344	11,813	5.77%	
Specialty	1,200	1,900	1,275	7,050	11,425	5.58%	
Catalog	2,000	3,700	3,150	13,350	22,200	10.83%	
Retail	8,000	14,800	12,600	53,400	88,800	43.34%	
Total	12,106	21,900	18,088	82,144	134,238	65.51%	
Units Ordered	10,000	25,000	20,000	80,000	135,000		
Balance On Hand	4,058	7,158	9,070	6,926			
Wall Units							
Direct	725	1,200	850	6,675	9,450	4.61%	
Specialty	600	950	638	3,525	5,713	2.79%	
Catalog	1,00	1,850	1,575	6,675	11,100	5.42%	
Retail	4,000	7,400	6,300	26,700	44,400	21.67%	
Total	6,325	11,400	9,363	43,575	70,663	34.49%	
Units Ordered	5,000	12,500	15,000	40,000	72,500		
Balance On Hand	1,757	2,857	8,494	4,919			
Total Products	18,431	33,300	27,450	125,719	204,900		
Total Cost	203,831	368,100	303,225	1,392,919			

Income 1996

	1st Qtr	2nd Qtr	3rd Qtr	4th Qtr	Total	% of Sales
Income						
Direct Sales						
@ $49.95	$45,267	$74,925	$53,072	$416,770	$590,034	6.26%
@ $79.95	$57,964	$95,940	$67,958	$533,666	$755,528	8.02%
Specialty Sales &						
Home Shopping	$64,746	$102,515	$68,793	$380,383	$616,436	6.54%
Wholesale						
Catalogs	$89,925	$166,361	$141,632	$600,249	$998,168	10.59%
Retail Outlets	$575,520	$1,064,712	$906,444	$3,841,596	$6,388,272	67.80%
Ship/Hndlg	$5,614	$9,293	$6,582	$51,690	$73,178	0.78%
Total	$839,036	$1,513,745	$1,244,480	$5,824,354	$9,421,616	100.00%
COG	$257,638	$467,485	$387,681	$1,750,207	$2,863,011	30.39%
Gross Profit	$581,398	$1,046,260	$856,799	$4,074,148	$6,558,604	
Expenses						
Accounting Dept	$9,000	$9,000	$9,000	$9,000	$36,000	0.38%
Advertising						
Consumer	$60,000	$70,000	$60,000	$160,000	$350,000	3.71%
Trade	$85,000	$105,000	$110,000	$160,000	$460,000	4.88%
Adv Allowances	$4,496	$8,318	$7,082	$30,012	$49,908	0.53%
Bad Debt	$16,781	$30,275	$24,890	$116,487	$188,432	2.00%
Commissions						
Specialty Sales	$6,475	$10,251	$6,879	$38,038	$61,644	0.65%
Whlsl Sales	$99,817	$184,661	$157,211	$666,277	$1,107,966	11.76%
Cost of Direct Sales						
Credit Cards	$3,097	$5,126	$3,631	$28,513	$40,367	0.43%
Customer Returns	$25,171	$45,412	$37,334	$174,731	$282,648	3.00%
Customer Service	$7,500	$7,500	$7,500	$7,500	$30,000	0.32%
Depreciation	$7,500	$7,500	$7,500	$7,500	$30,000	0.32%
PO Finance/Factoring	$0	$0	$0	$22,209	$22,209	0.24%
Fulfillment	$3,097	$5,126	$3,631	$28,513	$40,367	0.43%
Insurance	$3,000	$3,000	$3,000	$3,000	$12,000	0.13%
Legal/Acct	$1,500	$1,500	$1,500	$1,500	$6,000	0.06%
Management/CEO	$15,000	$15,000	$15,000	$150,646	$195,646	2.08%
Management/CFO	$15,000	$15,000	$15,000	$15,000	$60,000	0.64%
Miscellaneous	$3,000	$3,000	$3,000	$3,000	$12,000	0.13%
Natl Sales Mgr	$12,000	$12,000	$12,000	$102,431	$138,431	1.47%
Phone	$15,000	$20,000	$22,500	$22,500	$80,000	0.85%
Promotions	$10,000	$11,000	$9,000	$17,000	$47,000	0.50%
Publicist/Promotions						
Inhouse	$6,000	$6,000	$6,000	$6,000	$24,000	0.25%
Rent	$7,500	$7,500	$7,500	$7,500	$30,000	0.32%
Reg Sales Mgrs	$12,000	$12,000	$24,000	$24,000	$72,000	0.76%
Repair	$9,000	$9,000	$9,000	$9,000	$36,000	0.38%
Salaries/Secretaries	$25,171	$45,412	$37,334	$174,731	$282,648	3.00%
Sales & Mktg VP	$15,000	$15,000	$15,000	$128,038	$173,038	1.84%
Taxes - Payroll	$10,341	$12,889	$11,680	$53,544	$88,454	0.94%
Telemarketing	$18,000	$18,000	$27,000	$36,000	$99,000	1.05%

	1st Qtr	2nd Qtr	3rd Qtr	4th Qtr	Total	% of Sales	
							Income 1996...*continued*
Trade Shows	$12,500	$10,000	$12,500	$6,000	$41,000	0.44%	
Travel	$4,500	$4,500	$4,500	$4,500	$18,000	0.19%	
Utilities	$3,600	$3,600	$3,600	$3,600	$14,400	0.15%	
Total Expenses	$517,045	$703,572	$644,773	$2,207,770	$4,093,159	43.44%	
Net Profit							
before taxes	$64,353	$342,688	$192,026	$1,866,378	$2,465,445		
Taxes Due					$862,906		
Net Profit							
after taxes	$40,397	$221,315	$133,386	$1,213,145	$1,608,243		

	1st Qtr	2nd Qtr	3rd Qtr	4th Qtr	
					Balance Sheet 1996
Assets					
Cash	$334,006	$894,926	$556,851	$908,988	
Accts Recvble	$166,361	$532,356	$249,542	$2,195,969	
Inventory	$62,871	$107,271	$209,046	$136,127	
Current Assets	$563,237	$1,534,552	$1,015,438	$3,241,084	
Deposits	$25,000	$25,000	$25,000	$25,000	
Fixed Assets	$0	$0	$0	$0	
Gross	$150,000	$150,000	$150,000	$150,000	
Accum Depr	($52,500)	($60,000	($67,500)	($75,000)	
Net	$97,500	$90,000	$82,500	$75,000	
Total Assets	$685,737	$1,649,552	$1,122,938	$3,341,084	
	$0	$0	$0	$0	
Liabilities	$0	$0	$0	$0	
Accts Payable	($330,000)	$412,400	($247,500)	$757,500	
Current Liabs	($330,000)	$412,500	($247,500)	$757,500	
Debt	$600,000	$600,000	$600,000	$600,000	
Equity	$415,737	$637,052	$770,438	$1,983,584	
Total L&E	$685,737	$1,649,552	$1,122,938	$3,341,084	

Cash Flow 1996

	1st Qtr	2nd Qtr	3rd Qtr	4th Qtr	Total
Cash from Operating Activity					
Beginning					
Profit After Tax	$40,397	$221,315	$133,386	$1,213,145	$1,608,243
Depreciation	$7,500	$7,500	$7,500	$7,500	$30,000
Decr/(Incr) in A/R	($835,426)	$365,995	($282,814)	$1,946,427	$1,194,181
Decr/(Incr) in Inv	($38,831)	$44,400	$101,775	($72,919)	$34,425
Incr/(Decr) in A/P	$660,000	($742,500)	$660,000	($1,005,000)	($427,500)
Cash from Ops	($166,360)	($103,290)	$619,847	$2,089,153	$2,439,349
Incr/(Decr) in Debt	$0	$0	$0	$0	$0
Net Cash Flow	($166,360)	($103,290)	$619,847	$2,089,153	$2,439,349
Beg Cash Balance	$637,432	$604,823	$524,124	$321,204	$2,087,582
Net Cash Flow	($166,360)	($103,290)	$619,847	$2,089,153	$2,439,349
End Cash Balance	$471,071	$501,532	$1,143,971	$2,410,357	$4,526,932

Units Sales 1997

	1st Qtr	2nd Qtr	3rd Qtr	4th Qtr	Grand Total	% of Total
Desktop Units						
Direct	1,375	2,813	2,125	13,203	19,516	5.42%
Specialty	1,500	2,875	2,125	12,875	19,375	5.39%
Catalog	2,625	5,750	4,625	26,406	39,406	10.95%
Retail	10,500	23,000	18,500	105,625	157,625	43.82%
Total	16,000	34,438	27,375	158,109	235,922	65.58%
Units Ordered	15,000	35,000	30,000	155,000	235,000	65.33%
Balance On Hand	5,926	6,489	9,114	6,004		
Wall Units						
Direct	1,100	2,250	1,700	10,563	15,613	4.34%
Specialty	750	1,438	1,063	6,438	9,688	2.69%
Catalog	1,313	2,875	2,313	13,203	19,703	5.48%
Retail	5,250	11,500	9,250	52,813	78,813	21.91%
Total	8,413	18,063	14,325	83,016	123,816	34.42%
Units Ordered	10,000	17,500	15,000	80,000	122,500	
Balance On Hand	4,669	4,107	4,782	1,766		
Total Products	24,413	52,500	41,700	241,125	359,738	
Total Cost	$270,188	$580,875	$461,250	$2,668,219	$3,980,531	

	1st Qtr	2nd Qtr	3rd Qtr	4th Qtr	Total	% of Sales	Income 1997
Income							
Direct Sales							
@ $49.95	$68,681	$140,484	$106,144	$659,496	$974,805	7.52%	
@ $79.95	$87,945	$179,888	$135,915	$844,472	$1,248,219	9.63%	
Specialty Sales &							
Home Shop	$80,933	$155,121	$114,654	$694,671	$1,771,804	8.07%	
Wholesale							
Catalogs	$118,027	$258,534	$207,952	$1,187,291	$1,771,804	13.67%	
Retail Outlets	$519,317	$1,137,551	$914,987	$5,224,080	$7,795,935	60.17%	
Ship/Hndl	$8,518	$17,423	$13,164	$81,793	$120,899	0.93%	
Total	$883,420	$1,889,002	$1,492,816	$8,691,803	$12,957,041	100.00%	
COG	$265,123	$569,565	$452,077	$2,615,885	$3,902,650	30.12%	
Gross Profit	$618,298	$1,319,437	$1,040,739	$6,075,918	$9,054,391		
Expenses							
Accounting Dept	$9,000	$9,000	$9,000	$9,000	$36,000	0.28%	
Advertising							
Consumer	$90,000	$125,000	$120,000	$250,000	$585,000	4.51%	
Trade	$90,000	$130,000	$130,000	$250,000	$600,000	4.63%	
Adv Allowances	$5,901	$12,927	$10,398	$59,365	$88,590	0.68%	
Bad Debt	$17,668	$37,780	$29,856	$173,836	$259,141	2.00%	
Commissions							
Specialty Sales	$8,093	$15,512	$11,465	$69,467	$104,538	0.81%	
Commissions							
Whlsl Sales	$95,602	$209,413	$168,441	$961,706	$1,435,161	11.08%	
Cost of Direct Sales							
Credit Cards	$4,699	$9,611	$7,262	$45,119	$66,691	0.51%	
Customer Returns	$26,503	$56,670	$44,784	$260,754	$388,711	3.00%	
Customer Service	$10,500	$10,500	$10,500	$10,500	$42,000	0.32%	
Depreciation	$7,500	$7,500	$7,500	$7,500	$30,000	0.23%	
PO Finance/Factoring	$0	$0	$0	$32,057	$32,057	0.25%	
Fulfillment	$4,699	$9,611	$7,262	$45,119	$66,691	0.51%	
Insurance	$3,000	$3,000	$3,000	$3,000	$12,000	0.09%	
Legal/Acct	$1,500	$1,500	$1,500	$1,500	$6,000	0.05%	
Management/CEO	$15,000	$15,000	$15,000	$195,493	$240,493	1.86%	
Management/CFO	$15,000	$15,000	$15,000	$15,000	$60,000	0.46%	
Miscellaneous	$3,000	$3,000	$3,000	$3,000	$12,000	0.09%	
Natl Sales Mgr	$12,000	$12,000	$12,000	$132,329	$168,329	1.30%	
Phone	$22,500	$22,500	$22,500	$22,500	$90,000	0.69%	
Promotions	$10,000	$13,000	$12,000	$24,000	$59,000	0.46%	
Publicist/Promotions							
Inhouse	$9,000	$9,000	$9,000	$9,000	$36,000	0.28%	
Rent	$15,000	$15,000	$15,000	$15,000	$60,000	0.46%	
Reg Sales Mgrs	$30,000	$30,000	$30,000	$30,000	$120,000	0.93%	
Repair	$9,000	$9,000	$9,000	$9,000	$36,000	0.28%	
Salaries/Secretaries	$26,503	$56,670	$44,784	$260,754	$388,711	3.00%	
Sales & Mrkt VP	$15,000	$15,000	$15,000	$165,411	$210,411	1.62%	
Taxes - Payroll	$10,500	$14,480	$12,934	$72,779	$110,694	0.85%	

Income 1997...*continued*	Telemarketing	$18,000	$24,000	$36,000	$36,000	$114,000	0.88%
	Trade Shows	$12,500	$17,500	$30,000	$20,000	$80,000	0.62%
	Travel	$9,000	$9,000	$9,000	$9,000	$36,000	0.28%
	Utilities $6,000	$6,000	$6,000	$6,000	$24,400	0.19%	
	Total Expenses	$603,668	$915,174	$848,187	$3,195,188	$5,562,217	42.93%
	Net Profit						
	before taxes	$14,630	$404,262	$192,552	$2,880,730	$3,492,174	
	Taxes Due					$1,222,261	
	Net Profit						
	after taxes	($2,863)	$257,022	$125,159	$1,872,475	$2,251,792	

Balance Sheet 1997

	1st Qtr	2nd Qtr	3rd Qtr	4th Qtr
Assets				
Cash	$1,470,245	$2,895,746	$1,723,152	$3,146,376
Accts Recv	$182,098	$606,994	$303,497	$3,338,466
Inventory	$125,377	$120,002	$153,752	$80,533
Current Assets	$1,775,720	$3,622,742	$2,180,401	$6,565,375
Deposits	$25,000	$25,000	$25,000	$25,000
Fixed Assets	$0	$0	$0	$0
Gross	$150,000	$150,000	$150,000	$150,000
Accum Depr	($82,500)	($90,000)	($97,500)	($105,000)
Net	$67,500	$60,000	$52,500	$45,000
Total Assets	$1,868,220	$3,707,742	$2,257,901	$6,635,375
Liabilities	$0	$0	$0	$0
Accts Payable	($712,500)	$870,000	($705,000)	$1,800,000
Current Liabilities	($712,500)	$870,000	($705,000)	$1,800,000
Debt	$600,001	$600,004	$600,007	$600,010
Equity	$1,980,720	$2,237,742	$2,362,901	$4,235,375
Total L&E	$1,868,221	$3,707,746	$2,257,908	$6,635,385

Cash Flow 1997

	1st Qtr	2nd Qtr	3rd Qtr	4th Qtr	Total
Cash from Operating Activity					
Beginning					
Profit After Tax	($2,863)	$257,022	$125,159	$1,872,475	$2,251,792
Depreciation	$7,500	$7,500	$7,500	$7,500	$30,000
Decr/(Incr) in A/R	($2,013,870)	$424,896	($303,497)	$3,034,969	$0
Decr/(Incr) in Inv	$42,844	($3,375)	$33,750	($73,219)	$1,142,497
Incr/(Decr) in A/P	$1,470,000	($1,582,500)	$1,575,000	($2,505,000)	($1,042,500)
Cash from Ops	($496,360)	($896,458)	$1,437,912	$2,336,725	$2,381,789
Incr/(Decr) in Debt	$0	$0	$0	$0	$0
Net Cash Flow	($496,360)	($896,458)	$1,437,912	$2,336,725	$2,381,789
Beg Cash Balance	$1,996,627	$1,505,078	$2,309,711	$1,763,985	$7,575,401
Net Cash Flow	($496,360)	($896,458)	$1,437,912	$2,336,725	$2,381,789
End Cash Balance	$1,500,237	$608,620	$3,747,623	$4,100,710	$9,957,190

Public Relations Firm
BUSINESS PLAN

SHP & ASSOCIATES BUSINESS COMMUNICATIONS

757 N. Main Street
Morgan MI 48104

April 1, 1987

This business plan is for a public relations firm offering both traditional and non-traditional public relations services. It features highly-developed goals, strategies for networking, a detailed discussion of the competition in the area, and comments from experts in the field.

- PURPOSE
- EXECUTIVE SUMMARY
- COMMENTS ON THE MARKET
- THE OPPORTUNITY
- THE MARKET
- DEFINITION OF THE BUSINESS
- OBJECTIVES, GOALS AND STRATEGIES
- COMMENTS ON THE BUSINESS

- HISTORY
- MANAGEMENT AND BOARD OF ADVISORS
- COMPETITION
- COMMENTS ON COMPETITION
- PLAN FOR DEVELOPMENT
- POTENTIAL WEAKNESSES OF THE BUSINESS
- ADDITIONAL RESOURCES
- FINANCIAL INFORMATION

PUBLIC RELATIONS
BUSINESS PLAN

SHP and Associates serves the needs of companies for quality business communications. It has the ability to help clients formulate and enunciate their information to important audiences in a controlled and professional manner. Its principals are practiced business professionals and communicators. Its associates are able business analysts, writers, trainers, designers and graphic specialists.

PURPOSE

This Business Plan indicates that the principals and those associated with the business have defined the business as well as possible using available information and judgment. Further, that they have thought through the issues and created practical, workable strategies; that they have reasonable, prudent and achievable goals; and that they have a realistic assessment of the probability of success for the business and a sound plan to build it.

This plan is to be a living document that we will revisit regularly, especially in the first year of development.

EXECUTIVE SUMMARY

SHP and Associates (SHP) is a business communications firm. It was formed by two experienced business and public relations executives to work in the areas of corporate, financial, marketing and management communication. It serves the corporate relations needs of emerging and operating technology and industrial businesses in the southeastern Michigan region, particularly Morgan.

The firm has operated on a part-time consulting basis with a few clients since 1984. Its principals are seasoned businessmen who have served in executive marketing, communications and financial management positions for a number of large international concerns.

The firm is similar in concept to other traditional marketing or public relations firms. However, it differs from such firms in several important aspects:

It has sound relationships with executives at many operating businesses in its market area, as well as with senior partners in the region's leading legal and accounting firms and senior executives of financial institutions. These relationships with influences and venture capitalists are important to the business because they can provide SHP with immediate awareness and exposure with a large core of influential peers.

A Board of Advisors composed of industrial, marketing and financial executives of business and financial institutions and universities has been assembled. This Board serves as a consulting and directive body to assist the firm in securing and conducting its basic business.

SHP offers independent professional counsel and expertise that can be used by clients on an "as needed" basis. This means clients can benefit from such expertise when they require it, on a project or continuing basis. Clients need not retain an expensive house staff.

SHP has close working relationships with specialty firms to get the best work for clients. These specialists are in existing and established firms that maintain selected areas of expertise in video, art and design, training, and typography. This permits SHP principals to concentrate on developing clients rather than building staff and facilities.

Its principals, Mr. John Smith and Mr. Mike Johnson, have industrial operating business experience, thereby giving them a very real understanding of the kinds of tough business and marketing issues faced by corporate or divisional operating managers. SHP principals are not mere communications professionals; rather they are experienced and accomplished business executives who bring business acumen to any company's requirement to communicate its product, people, and related messages in a disciplined and planned way to its chosen audiences. Mr. Smith and Mr. Johnson have held the following positions: Director of Communications, Controller, Vice President of Advertising and Public Relations, Vice President of Marketing, Vice President of Sales, and Vice President of Corporate Operations.

SHP is developing complementary marketing relationships with a network of existing communications firms in Boston, New York, Chicago, and San Francisco. These enable SHP to conduct research or implement activities in those areas on a cost-effective basis.

COMMENTS ON THE MARKET

"This area is well into the phase of requiring a sound infrastructure to support all the excellent area entrepreneurial businesses that have moved out of the start-up phase and into the operational phase. Your kind of business, which can help with market positioning and pinpointing these companies communications, is the key to that infrastructure."

Tom Porter
Partner, Enterprise Management Inc.
Chairman, New Enterprise Forum

The Morgan area "is improving for your kind of business because many companies need help but not necessarily on a regular basis. They don't have resources to staff up, but they do have the needs and resources to expend for major projects."

Dr. John Psarouthakis
Founder, Chairman and President
J. P. Industries

"I know several banks and companies that need your kind of service and will use you-- assuming you do quality work at reasonable cost--on an as-needed basis."

George H. Cress
President
Citizens Trust Co.

THE OPPORTUNITY

"Communications, especially public relations, is growing in every phase of business. An entire redefinition of business communications is taking place and all kinds of companies are looking at how they can communicate most effectively with their audiences, be they investors, customers, communities or employers."

Robert Strayton
President, Advanced Technology Division
Hill and Knowlton

SHP's role is to serve the needs of clients in the newest way--by putting senior executives with broad skills and sound judgment to work on every account.

The Morgan area "is much like the Silicon Valley in California was 12-15 years ago. That is, the infrastructure is now developing here to support the growing number of successful technology businesses as well as the solid operating companies that already exist in the area. That infrastructure includes communications, law and accounting firms. It also includes the general growing awareness the commercial businesses are finding the area a good place to be."

Mike Johnson
Partner
SHP & Associates

THE MARKET

The geographic marketplace for SHP is primarily southeastern Michigan, with the highest concentration of effort initially aimed at the Morgan area. It has several substantial existing businesses as well as numerous smaller ones and others spawned by University of Michigan work. Also, the Morgan area is best known to SHP principals; Mr. Smith has worked and resided in the area for most of the past 20 years; Mr. Johnson for the past seven.

Two additional target areas for the business are Toledo and Grand Rapids, both excellent industrial sites. These areas will be explored through complementary relationships with existing communications firms, or with legal or accounting firms or printers.

In the primary target market of southeastern Michigan and northern Ohio, there are approximately 600 businesses that are included in the industrial technology areas. Of these, it is estimated that about 100 now use services in the marketing or financial communication areas; another 50-75 could use such services but do not at this time. These estimates are based on the known number of public companies, client lists of the approximate 30 firms now conducting such business, directories of business from chambers of commerce and Crain's Detroit Business and the Michigan's 100 Leading Securities book of First of Michigan Securities.

In terms of market size, SHP's competitive analysis shows that the approximate 30 firms doing business in this region had a combined total of $10 to $11 million net fee income in 1986, up from about $6 million in 1981. (Figures based on firms' reports published in Crain's Detroit Business and Jack O'Dwyer's newsletter, the leading PR industry trade publication.)

SHP believes it will build its business in two years. First by gaining accounts from businesses that do not now employ outside communications counsel. Second, over time by gaining accounts from businesses now employing competitive firms.

Further, some five of the 30 firms have been started in the past year, thus indicating decent success at opening this type of business. While this has added to the competition, the five new firms have not been directly in the financial and marketing segment served by SHP.

The type of firms SHP has targeted are:

•Public, with need for financial relations work
•Private and positioning to go public
•Public or private with clear need to communicate with customers and prospects in a controlled, direct manner

Annual revenue in range of $2 to $150 million, and particularly in the $25 - $75 million range. Larger firms are also targets although most have in-house staffs to conduct such communications work and are not, therefore, deemed primary targets at the early stage of SHP's business.

This is being created in Phase I through use of the business leaders' network, meetings and presentations with principals of targeted accounts and a mailing to targeted and secondary accounts. It will be broadened in June by official announcement of the business.	**Awareness**
In the four county area, which is the initial phase focus of SHP, there are the following businesses: 105 public companies, 100 private, 33 service, 36 manufacturing, 15 bank holding, 14 savings and loans, 31 wholesale and retail, 15 large accounting, 25 large advertising agencies, 15 large law firms, 15 engineering firms, 10 health maintenance organizations, 15 general contractors, 25 large hospitals, 24 divisions or subsidiaries of larger corporations, and 1 major governmental research agency.	**Focus**

The focus of SHP for its three business segments will be:

100 private firms, 105 public firms. Especially those in the $1-5 million revenue range whose markets are unclear and that are run by technically-oriented entrepreneurs.	Marketing Positioning
We are directing our marketing efforts toward them through affiliation with the 1600-member Michigan Technology Council, through venture capitalists who have funded such firms, and through our executive network.	
36 manufacturing firms, 1 governmental research agency, 33 service firms. Our marketing efforts are being directed through the executive network, mailing to target accounts, affiliation with Human Resource Development Systems and one key start up reference account.	Training
105 public companies, 100 private firms, firms which recently went public. We are directing our marketing effort through affiliation with an existing PR firm which does not do corporate/financial work, and the executive network.	Communications

DEFINITION OF THE BUSINESS

SHP and Associates is a partnership of professional business executives with expertise in specific areas of marketing, financial and management communications and special events.

SHP and Associates offers professional expertise in areas often needed by industrial and technology businesses on a project or interim basis.

This practice means clients can use SHP for its expertise on an as-needed basis. clients do not have to retain internal staff and they gain the benefit of having experienced counsel to meet needs as they arise. Such services are also available under ongoing programs.

SHP offers these communications services and products.

Corporate/Financial

- Media relations
- Corporate identity programs
- Annual and quarterly reports
- Private and public offerings
- Annual meetings
- Company positioning
- Speeches and presentations
- Security analyst relations

Marketing

- Business and trade articles, news releases
- Market research - focus groups and surveys
- Customer newsletters and videos
- Marketing plans and presentations
- Product and market segmentation and positioning
- Sales training/incentive programs
- Product introductions
- Seminars and employee training/motivational programs
- Telemarketing

OBJECTIVES, GOALS AND STRATEGIES

This section outlines the reasons why SHP and Associates can be built into a successful firm. The section contains the non-changing objectives, 1987 goals and 1987 strategies as to how those goals will be achieved.

Objective

The objectives of SHP are:
Be a profitable, recognized, respected and authoritative professional leader in its field and market area, as judged by the amount and quality of business it has.

Provide a range of business communications services that are a positive benefit to clients we serve.

	Goals and Strategies for 1987
Be a successful start up, emerging from the year with sufficient business to insure profitable operation in 1988. This net fee income base for 1987 will be $125,000 by year end.	Goal 1
Secure sufficient business to insure that we meet plan. Do this by gaining a minimum of eight accounts by year end.	Strategy
Establish the firm's reputation and awareness among the entire prospect base, the media, the financial community and in the trade, thus helping to position it in order to be able to secure reasonable growth planned for years two and three. Basis of judgement here to be eight clients by year end.	Goal 2
Successfully complete all work for clients and build awareness and credibility of the firm by marketing these results. Provide communications products, thus directing the business to the areas for which it desires to become known. Provide the benefits of the firm's accumulated knowledge and expertise in marketing and communications to counsel and guide where there is apparent client need.	Strategies
Attract sufficient investment to insure the ability to direct attention to building the business successfully and not diverting attention to fund raising or other ancillary activities.	Goal 3
Work with investors, banks or other appropriate financial institutions. Do not give up any ownership in the business by raising capital via other private investors. Establish separate corporations which will work together under the joint venture of SHP & Associates.	Strategy
"98 percent of all businesses that fail do so because of the lack of expertise of management in the business, or management's incompetence." --The Business Plan Price Waterhouse "Any consulting business must never try to be all things to all people. You must direct your work and be able to perform better than your competitors in those certain select segments." --Dr. John Psarouthakis Founder, Chairman and President, J. P. Industries	**COMMENTS ON THE BUSINESS**

COMMENTS ON THE BUSINESS
...continued

"Three things are needed for an entrepreneurial business to succeed: the best people, the resources those people need and the environment they need."
--John Barfield
Founder, Barfield Companies

"The best things a good businessman has going for him are his integrity and reputation."
--John Daly
Vice Chairman, Johnson Controls

HISTORY

The firm began partial operations in 1984 as a consulting business serving different computer and software companies.

It functioned as Michael Johnson Associates and was run on a part-time basis. The firm's primary area of business was the preparation of marketing and communications plans, with some implementation work. Clients of the firm in this period included JM Systems Corporation, DataLogic Systems, Dynagraphic Systems Corporation, and others.

In the summer of 1986, Johnson became associated with John Smith. They produced a 50th anniversary celebration plan for Huge Firm International, a division of Huge Conglomerate Inc., in addition to developing other marketing and public relations activities, projects and programs for industrial and technology companies.

Mr. Smith and Mr. Johnson direct the business. In addition, SHP uses business and technical writers, designers, graphics specialists and other support staff to conduct assignments. Also, the firm has a business relationship with an 11-employee professional design and production firm that has been in business since 1975, and a management and sales training firm, Resource Development Systems. Additional business relationships will be structured in 1987 that are complementary to the nature of SHP's business. That is, with existing established communications and marketing firms that offer services synergistic to SHP's. This will include complementary marketing agreements with existing communications firms in New York, Minneapolis, Chicago and Boston, as well as agreements with an audio-visual firm. Freelance researchers and writers will be employed on an as-needed basis throughout 1987; there are no present plans to employ additional staff.

MANAGEMENT AND BOARD OF ADVISORS

SHP and Associates is a business partnership with Michael Johnson and John Smith as principals. The goal is to incorporate as separate businesses and form the joint ventures of SHP & Associates. The firm also has Board of Advisors, as follows:

♦T. Randall Macintosh, Group Vice President and Director, Inc., $70 million computer software firm.
♦George Coswell, President, Big Insurance Co.
♦Joseph Gerald, President, Huge Firm International, a Huge Conglomerate Company.
♦Dr. Thomas Kennedy, Associate Dean and Professor of Marketing, Graduate School of Business Administration, University of Minnesota.

The above individuals are available for references, also. Additional references and a current client listing are available upon request.

There are some 30 general and specialized public relations and communications firms already in the marketplace in which SHP operates. These include large, established firms with substantial financial, people and customer resources; smaller general and specialty firms that have unique market niches; and individuals who perform freelance work. In general, many of these firms are run by former newspaper or broadcast people ("communicators") whose business experience, understanding and acumen is not high.

It is estimated that these firms have net fee income of approximately $10-11 million annually, and that this number has increased from $5-6 million annually five years ago. These estimates are based on published figures for firms in the attached competitive analysis. Another relevant factor is the number of start ups that have been successful and have thus added to the total market size.

Competition also includes in-house staffs, although this is primarily confined to the larger companies in the area. Also, such larger firms tend to have larger budgets and therefore use outside resources to augment their own capabilities.

Another element of competition is commonly overlooked, but certainly ever-possible. That is... not doing this type of marketing and communications work at all. The reasoning, although believed specious by SHP, is that this type of work is optional to a company, that is does not contribute to the bottom line, to product development, or to sales.

And that may well be... for firms that have a unique and solo market niche, ever satisfied customers, no desire to create awareness or generate business leads, or for other reasons.

But for those majority that do not fit such categories, SHP has several differentiators which set it apart from its competition. Those are listed below.

Business Relationship: a network of known industrial, community and academic leaders.

Industrial Operations Experience: first hand knowledge of business operations due to the principals breadth of experience.

Product Specialization: in financial, marketing and management communications areas.

Board of Advisors: of high level business leaders.

Complementary Marketing Agreements: with sound established firms whose skills, geographic range and goals are complementary.

Following is a summary of area firms with which SHP and Associates competes...

Frederick Marshall, Detroit	A large firm in the midwest with an annual net fee income in the millions. Specialized in financial and marketing PR and has numerous clients covered by its numerous employees. Has very professional brochures and capabilities book and lists many large companies as clients. Has high fees ($4000 monthly retainer is common at low end). Its market is primarily larger companies with substantial promotional budgets.
DP & Associates, Detroit	DPA has 37 employees and $2.5 million net fee income, double that of four years ago. Much lower visibility than Marshall, but has solid client list in Coopers and Lybrand. Owner is a creative and independent person, known for crisis-type guidance to clients as opposed to the strategy planning and counsel of Marshall. DPA is well regarded for special projects, general publicity and brainstorming ideas with clients. Does much community and charity work and has good ties with the Michigan Commerce Department and area ad firms which do not have PR units.
The Hutchinson Group, Ypsilanti	High competition. Smart people, good work and reputation. Five years old and run by Terrie Hutchinson, a well known promotion woman who created a noted and successful Michigan university fund-raiser. She is well connected and does work for the Chamber of Commerce, accounting firms, Ann Arbor News, Private Industry Council and some 15 other clients. Billings in 1986 said to be $500K; seven employees, all bright. Not much financial, corporate or marketing work, but deemed to be a primary competitor because of established base and abilities. Primary emphasis is publicity programs; well known capability is staging special events.
Butler Communications, Jackson	Run by Jeff Lehman, who was general manager of the Business Alliance before starting Quorum in 1981. Does advertising, writing, design. Very good growth in hospital promotions - St. Peter's HMO etc. Did 1985 TL Industries' annual report design. Has some 10 people. Very well tied to the community to get business leads; has capitalized on these relationships to build the business.
Willis Communications, Southfield	Run by Kelly Willis, an ex-Hamilton PR executive. Aims at high tech companies and does all kinds of brochures, annual reports, articles. Irwin Magnetics, La-Z-Boy Chair, Synthetic Vision and Symplex Corporation are or have been significant clients. Probably $100K net fee income in 1986. Willis knows many people and is well liked.
Gabriel Sapetta, Troy	New and aimed at corporate-financial area. One man band with Detroit, Michigan as an account. Has made self known among target audience since he left Hamilton, where he was Director of Press Relations for one year.
COMMENTS ON COMPETITION	None of the firms mentioned are public. Companies of this kind tend to list clients as if they do all the client's work. In fact many, or even most, do project work--not on-going retainer work--except with the larger companies.
	There are many, many competitors--mostly small. Numerous one and two man bands, as well as consultants in select areas who could be competition on some projects.
	Large New York or Chicago headquartered firms have never had much good results in establishing outposts offices in Detroit, Minneapolis, Cleveland, or other midwestern cities.

Their costs and fees are high and they offer the New York mentality of "tell them how to do it" which is not often accepted well by the typical midwestern businessman. Therefore, they are not deemed to be a significant current factor in competition.

Primary competition we are running into are Hutchinson, Willis, and Sapetta.

Two Chicago-based firms currently have clients in SHP market area. Public Relations Board serves Great Lakes Federal Bank and Interface Systems for financial and investor relations. The Investor Relations Company serves Medstat.

SHP's plan is to divide the start up year of 1987 into two phases: April 1 - June 30 and July 1 - December 31. These activities are planned in Phase I.

PLAN FOR DEVELOPMENT

I. Build client base
  - Prospect mailing and meetings with top 5--Ongoing
  - Key influencers list
  - 25 next likely
  - Remainder (100)

Phase I

II. Complete Business Plan--March 31
  - Reviews by selected participants

III. Complete Corporate Structure--April 30
  - Investment
  - Type of structure
  - Establish of Board of Advisors
  - Financial
  - Get reference approvals

IV. Evaluate Complementary Relationships
  - Opportunities April 30
    - --TI Group
    - --Other design firms
    - --Other PR firms

V. Evaluate facilities May 31
  - Company offices
  - Offices at client sites
  - Offices in, or with, other firms

VI. Conduct work for those clients we gain Ongoing

VII. Announce the business June 1

VIII. Complete plan for development for Phase II June 15

IX. Complete Phase III (1988) Plan

POTENTIAL WEAKNESSES OF THE BUSINESS

♦ Too few people to complete work on time, in budget on a consistent basis.

♦ Acceptance of projects that are not within the segment of business SHP desires to build; may be especially true in year 1.

♦ Financial issues
- •Cash flow inadequate to meet necessary goals
- •Clients may desire to pay less for services the SHP desires to charge

♦ Lack of awareness of the firm could cause lack of chance at existing opportunities, especially in first several months.

♦ Could be trying to do too many things

♦ Not absolutely certain of what the market will buy

♦ Competition could beat us out

ADDITIONAL RESOURCES

♦ Freelance writers: Marie Caliski, former Business Week writer; Margaret Dayner, technical writer; Ted Moran, business and technical writer

♦ Freelance Artists: Mega Group--design and graphics work

♦ Management sales and training firm: Resource Development Systems

♦ Law firms

♦ Accounting firms

♦ Family members

♦ Secretary

♦ Board of Advisors

♦ Business executives and others in network

♦ Banks

♦ Printing Firms

♦ University of Michigan Business School

♦ Public Relations firms in other cities, and in local area

♦ Venture capital firms

FINANCIAL INFORMATION

"The central question to any business is: who will buy this service or product?"
John Smith, Partner,
SHP & Associates

"The toughest part of a business plan is the sales forecast. You must do your best to understand the environment, outline assumptions, and list controllables and non-controllables."
Richard David, Partner
Jefferson, Franklin, and Washington

Finance

Philosophy

The plan of SHP is not to spend unless it is absolutely necessary or an opportunity becomes apparent at an earlier time than was planned, thus requiring expenditures earlier. This policy will apply through Phase Ia, at the end of which the policy will be refined to account for expenditures necessary in Phase Ib.

It is the anticipation of the principals of the business that numerous assumptions made in the Business Plan will prove to be wrong, while other unknowns will prove to be a benefit. This is, some planned areas of developing revenue will not work out, while others will arise.

❑Two phases in year 1
- •April 1 - June 30
- •July 1 - December 31

❑No office space paid for until July 1 at least
- •Use TI office
- •Use TI phone answering and message center
- •Use home offices
- •Use offices at client sites

❑No wages until July 1
- •Exception as client engagements are gained individually, or joint projects with work apportioned.

❑Design and production work gratis by TI
- •SHP pays typeset, print costs

❑Probable purchase of used MVI furniture
- •desks, chairs, conference table
- ••files, audio-visual equipment, IBM XI computer, phones easel other sources also available - leasing, etc.

❑No public announcement of the business until it is solidified
- •8 clients
- •Complementary relationships established

Computer
Used IBM XT with hard disk and printer $1500

Furniture
3 desks and 2 chairs
1 conference table and 4 chairs
2 wood book shelves
2 file cabinets
1 computer table
2 credenzas $5000

Office supplies $ 500

Secretarial help $2000
$500/month x 4 months

Telephone $ 75
$25/month x 3 months

Professional fees
Attorney $1000
Accountant $1000

Assumptions

**Start up Costs
(1 year period)**

Start up Costs
(1 year period)
...continued

Printing and mailing	
stationery, brochure, business cards	$1000
Copying	$250
Travel and entertainment	$2000
Auto leases	$2100
2 x $350/month x 3 months	

Second Phase: Year 1
(Ongoing Costs)

Office space (6 months)	$7500
Lease cars (6 x $700/month)	$4200
Professional fees	
Attorney	$ 200
Accountant	$2500
Insurance	$1500
Travel and entertainment	$5000
Wages	$10,000
Secretary (6 months)	
Partners (6 months)	
Benefits	

Note: partners may only take expenses from business in this phase; depends on size of revenues.

SHP & ASSOCIATES,
INC. PROFIT & LOSS

	1st Year	2nd Year	3rd Year
Income			
Partnership Billings	93	144	168
Outside Reps/Contractors Billings	20	40	80
In-house Media/Adv Services			
Creative		20	80
Printing Etc.		30	120
Gross Income	113	234	448
Cost/Services Provided			
Partnership Draws	73	100	120
Outside Reps/Contractor Billings	15	28	55

	1st Year	2nd Year	3rd Year
In-house Media/Adv Services			
Creative		10	40
Printing Etc.		25	100
Gross Margin	25	71	133
G&A & Other			
Rent (includes clerical services - 1st year)	6	5	8
Clerical Payroll & Costs		12	18
Partnership Insurance		5	6
Auto Expenses	8	12	12
Office supplies/Postage	2	5	8
T&E	3	6	12
Telephone	2	6	10
Professional Services, Dues & Subs	3	6	10
Furniture & Fixtures (Expenses)	4	4	4
Other (included adv. promotion, interest exp. & Loan reimb.	7	15	23
Totals	35	76	111
Net Income (Loss)	(10)	(5)	22
Employees (including partners)	2	2 3/4	4 1/2

	I	II	Total
1987 Partners Individual Billings	45.0	48.0	93.0
Outside Reps/Contractors Billings (less costs)	20.5	2.5	5.0
In-House Media/Adv. (less cost)			
Gross Billings/Receipts	47.5	50.5	98.0
Less: Operating Expenses	17.5	17.5	35.0
Net Before Loan	30.0	33.0	63.0
Rates: Loan	5.0	5.0	10.0
Net Draw/Taxable	35.0	38.0	73.0
1988 Partners Individual Billings	80.0	64.0	144.0
Outside Reps etc.	6.0	6.0	12.0
In-House Media etc.	7.5	7.5	15.0

SHP & Associates, Inc. "Samples": Analysis/Draws

SHP & Associates, Inc. "Samples": Analysis/Draws *...continued*

1988 Cont'd...	I	II	Total
Gross Billing/Receipts	93.5	77.5	171.0
Less: Operating Expenses	38.0	38.076.0	
Net Draw/Taxable	55.5	39.5	95.0
1989 Partners Individual Billings	88.0	80.0	168.0
Outside Reps etc.	12.5	12.52	5.0
In-House Media etc.	30.0	30.0	60.0
Gross Billings/Receipts	130.5	122.5	253.0
Less: Operating Expenses	55.5	55.5	111.0
Net Draw/Taxable	75.0	67.0	142.0

SHP & Associates, Inc. Income Analysis

By Income Element	1st Qtr	2nd Qtr	3rd Qtr	4th Qtr	Total
Partner's Billings (Retainer etc.)					
1987	9	28	27	29	93
1988	34	36	35	39	144
1989	40	42	41	45	168
Outside Reps/Contractors Billings					
1987		5	15	20 .	
1988	10	10	10	10	40
1989	20	20	20	20	80
In-House Media/Adv Services					
1987					
1988	5	10	15	20	50
1989	30	50	60	60	200
By Year					
1987--Partner's Billings	9	28	27	29	93
Outside Reps/Contractors			5	15	20
In-House Media/Adv.					
	9	28	32	44	113
1988--Partner's Billings	34	36	35	39	144
Outside Reps/Contractors	10	10	10	10	40

By Year Cont'd...	1st Qtr	2nd Qtr	3rd Qtr	4th Qtr	Total
In-House Media Adv.	5	10	15	20	50
	49	56	60	69	234
1989--Partner's Billings	40	42	41	45	168
Outside Reps/Contractors	20	20	20	20	80
In-House Media Adv.	30	50	60	60	200
	90	112	121	125	448

•Partner's draw equal to individual billings and allocations of outside reps/contractor's services (billings less expenses) less 1/2 operations expenses (in first year of operations - partners will equally share responsibility of $20,000 loan line (by individual investor) and will borrow $10,000 ($5,000 each) against this line).

•Partner's will file corporation papers under sub-chapter "S" and will assume income tax liabilities (Federal and State), FICA, etc. as individual payers.

•Net Income derived from billings for outside contractors and reps, for in-house media services, printing, etc. less expenses for such services will be divided equally among partners.

•All expenses associated with operations will likewise be born equally by the partners.

SHP & Associates, Inc. Expense Analysis--see following page...

Profit & Loss Assumptions

SHP & Associates, Inc.
Expense Analysis

	J	F	M	A	M	J	J	A	S	O	N	D	TTL.	1988	1989
Rent (includes clerical srvs.--1987)							.8	.8	.8	1.0	1.0	1.1	5.5	5.0	8.0
Clerical Payroll & Payroll Costs														12.0	18.0
Partnership Insurance														5.0	6.0
Auto Expenses					1.0	1.0	1.0	1.0	1.0	1.0	1.0	1.0	8.0	12.0	12.0
Office Expenses				.1	.1	.5	.1	.2	.2	.2	.2	.3	1.9	5.0	8.0
Telephone	.1	.1	.1	.2	.2	.2	.2	.2	.2	.3	.3	.3	2.4	6.0	10.0
T & E	.1	.1	.1	.2	.2	.3	.3	.3	.3	.4	.4	.4	3.1	6.0	12.0
Professional Service, Dues & Subs				.6	.3	.7		.2	.8			.5	3.1	6.0	10.0
Furniture & fixtures (expensed)			2.7			1.3							4.0	4.0	4.0
Interest Exp & Loan Repayment												1.0	1.0	6.0	11.0
Other (includes adv/promotion)			.6		.1	.9	.7	.1	.1	.6	1.7	1.2	6.0	9.0	12.0
	.2	.2	3.5	1.1	1.9	4.9	3.1	2.8	3.4	3.5	4.6	5.8	35.0		
			3.9			7.9			9.3			13.9	35.0	76.0	111.0

Restaurant/Bar

BUSINESS PLAN

THE PLUGGED NICKEL BAR

772 S. Cassopolis
Detroit, MI 48222

April 1995

This business plan for a bar with entertainment highlights the advantages and cost benefits of an owner-managed business. The proposed business is in an Economic Empowerment Zone, and notes this as one of the reasons for the request for loan.

- BUSINESS

- TARGET MARKET

- UNIQUENESS

- PURPOSE

- BACKGROUND

- GOALS

- LOGISTICS

- MARKETING

- EXPENSES

RESTAURANT/BAR BUSINESS PLAN

BUSINESS

The Plugged Nickel Bar, on South Cassopolis in Detroit's new Empowerment Zone, will become a high quality venue for original creative arts. Live music, original theatre, performance art, and comedy will be featured, along with displays by local artists. With high quality entertainment and attention to detail, it will become a destination for patrons of the arts. Live recordings of performances will be released on CD and cassette. The diversity of the metro area will be utilized, to provide a greater variety of entertainment currently available anywhere. Well-lit parking will be available, and Chinese food from Wang's Restaurant will be available until 12:00a.m. The business will be open Thursday through Saturday nights.

TARGET MARKET

Original music venues are gaining in popularity due to the past success of alternative rock, and the "back to basics" approach that many musicians are taking. The Plugged Nickel will recreate the energy, experimental feel, and diversity that popularized alternative rock in the first place, before it was homogenized by corporate interests. People want something that is new and different, as what was once avant garde but has become mainstream. Current patrons of clubs would find new excitement, and others would be encouraged.

UNIQUENESS

Most clubs center on one style of music or performance, or perhaps devote different nights to particular styles. Sometimes this works, but other times there are complaints that it all sounds the same. This complaint will never be heard at the Plugged Nickel. On any given night, customers will experience at least two completely different acts. It will be normal to have an evening that might include classical, jazz, latin, rock, blues, bluegrass, folk, or any named or as yet unclassified forms of music. These could be combined with performance art, comedy, poetry or original theatre for a completely new experience.

In order to complete renovation of the building at 772 South Cassopolis in Detroit's Empowerment Zone, I am requesting a loan of $10,000, at an interest rate of 10%, amortized over five years.

PURPOSE

a) To renovate and re-open the Plugged Nickel bar as a premier venue for original creative arts. Live music, original theatre, performance art, and comedy will be welcome, along with exhibits from local artists, most likely from the neighboring universities.

b) Take advantage of renewed interest in original music, and the increasing popularity of the entertainment districts in downtown Detroit.

c) Provide greater exposure for the diverse and innovative music created in the region, through the production of CDs and cassettes recorded "Live at the Plugged Nickel."

d) Utilize the benefits of renovation in the Empowerment Zone.

Building and Bar

The Plugged Nickel bar, at 772 South Cassopolis, was opened in 1936. In 1990, the name was changed, and the business closed in 1993. Over the years, through changes in management and ownership, it has had a wide variety of themes and customers. Despite some damage due to roof leakage and vandalism, classic features remain, including the bar area, mirrors, and indirect lighting. In addition, the stage, stage lights, and dressing rooms are complete and appropriate to the proposed new usage. The bar building, two additional attached storefronts, and an adjacent large storage garage were purchased in March, 1995 by Nigel Y. Mea. There are no mortgages, liens, or back taxes owed on the property.

Nigel Y. Mea

In 1988, Mr. Mea was a student at the Berklee College of Music in Boston, Massachusetts, with the aspiration of eventually making a living as a producer and sound engineer. Upon viewing the difficulties of life as a "starving artist," he returned to the University of Minnesota to finish dual degrees in Mathematics and English, and start his own production company. Metro Productions began in August 1988, as a small recording studio, and soon branched out into live music production, involving booking and promotion of acts, as well as operation of sound reinforcement equipment. It also provided income to help complete the degrees. In 1990, Mr. Mea graduated and moved to the Detroit area for a highly successful career as a Systems Engineer at Corporate Data Systems, and more recently, Midwest Research. Throughout this time, he continued as a performing musician, producer, and sound engineer, scheduling and promoting local shows. As the business will be operating only three or four nights per week, current professional employment will be maintained.

GOALS

a) To establish a profitable venue by providing a greater variety of entertainment than any currently operating establishments by utilizing the diversity of the Detroit area to the fullest potential. Many clubs feature the same kind of music every night: jazz, blues or rock, etc. Some give different nights to different styles. Ideally, the Plugged Nickel will have two or three distinctly different styles on every night of operation. It would be possible, for example, to experience classical, Latin, and alternative rock in one night. The establishment will be open to the public three or four nights per week.

b) Promote original music in the area, particularly at the Plugged Nickel, through the use of the facility for live and studio recording, including the production of a CD featuring music recorded at performances. Mr. Mea currently owns recording studio equipment, and has had live recordings used on locally-released CDs and demo cassettes.

LOGISTICS

a) The Plugged Nickel is located on South Cassopolis Avenue in Detroit, just South of Wang's Restaurant. It is centrally located, less than one mile from Oakland State University, the Center for Fine and Applied Arts, Mexicantown, many revitalized theatres, downtown Detroit, the New Center area, and other music venues.

b) The customer area is approximately 35' by 55', and includes a large stage opposite the bar. Dressing rooms are located at the back of the building, away from the customer area. Capacity is rated at 74 with dancing, and 107 without. Sufficient

Logistics
...continued

parking is available in a paved lot beside the bar.

c) Identifiable customer base:

1. Current patrons of other music bars in Detroit and Hamtramck, looking for a greater variety and higher quality of entertainment.

2. Students of local universities.

3. Audiences of diverse musical styles not represented by the current club scene.

4. Artists and musicians seeking a more supportive and performer-friendly environment.

d) Immediate competition includes the following:

1. Melvin's, located about one mile south on South Cassopolis, and features live music on weekends and some weeknights. Usually alternative rock. Typically draws 150 customers per weekend night.

2. The Old Havana, approximately five blocks south on South Cassopolis featuring alternative and punk rock on weekends. Audience size ranges from 30 to 75.

3. St. Phillip's Hall in Mexicantown. A large club open for dancing and nationally known alternative rock bands. Draws consistently large crowds.

4. The Impressionistic Theatre. Similar in size and clientele to St. Phillip's. It continues to enjoy good crowds, despite complaints of poor sound quality from performers and patrons.

5. Paystubs, Lilian's, and the Hamtramck Corner Bar in Hamtramck, small clubs for local rock bands.

These establishments, though similar in initial appearance, do not feature the diversity that will be unique to the Plugged Nickel.

MARKETING

a) Marketing efforts will center around weekly advertisements in local publications, most likely "Metro Times," "Spirit," and "The Monitor."

b) Regular advertising will be supplemented by occasional advertisements in diverse cultural and ethnic publications such as "Latino World," "National Entertainment Plus," "Jazz Quarterly," and any many others that appear viable and inexpensive.

c) Monthly fliers of scheduled events will be posted in record stores, and at the local universities.

d) A one-page flier, "Guide to Dining and Entertainment in the South Cassopolis District" with a map and very brief reviews of establishments in the vicinity, from the Whitmore, Stu's,

Onion Street, and the others, to Melvin's, The Old Havana, the many theatres, and more. Of course, the Plugged Nickel will be featured prominently. This flier will be distributed at establishments inside and outside the immediate area, to promote the area as an entertainment center.

Plugged Nickel Expenses
ALL already paid by Nigel Y. Mea

Rct	Date	Description	Cost
Y	12/19/94	Re-Key of Plugged Nickel Lock	$55.00
Y	1/4/95	Title Search/Insurance	$120.00
Y	2/10/95	Builders Square: light, lock, misc.	$82.10
Y	2/28/95	MCM: Alarm, wiring	$309.02
Y	3/9/95	Damark Answering Machine	$35.49
Y	3/10/95	Deed: Jack Baxter	$5,000.00
Y	3/10/95	County Tax 1992 (cash)	$246.26
Y	3/10/95	County Tax, 1993, 1994	$425.34
Y	3/10/95	Detroit City Tax, Payment plan	$2,239.00
Y	3/10/95	Tax, filing title Co	$58.00
Y	3/13/95	MCM: Another alarm	$169.77
Y	3/13/95	Colonial: Phone	$16.62
Y	3/14/95	Insurance: 6 Months	$449.00
Y	3/26/95	Murrays: Tools	$4.23
Y	3/27/95	Builders Square: Locks, barrel bolts	$113.16
Y	3/28/95	Fred's: Lock for back of stores	$13.73
Y	3/30/95	Outside Electrical, D. Best	$2,500.00
Y	4/1/95	Saw Chain, cut trees for elec	$13.42
Y	4/3/95	State of Mich: Lic. Investigate	$140.00
Y	4/3/95	License: Downpayment	$2,000.00
Y	4/6/95	Remainder of city taxes	$8,896.77
Y	4/6/95	Builders Square: Plywood, lights (mtn)	$62.59
Y	4/6/95	Siren box, wire, sec. strobe	$34.93
Y	4/9/95	HQ: Roof stuff & paint	$40.67
Y	4/10/95	A-1 Security, setup, apr-june monitor	$120.00
Y	4/10/95	County: SET tax transferred	$122.53
Y	4/10/95	Radio Shack: Smoke detectors, switch	$86.89
Y	4/13/95	State of Mich: Regulation bk.	$5.00
Y	4/16/95	HQ: Roof supplies	$81.58
Y	4/17/95	Builders Square: Return extra lights	($24.96)
Y	4/19/95	HQ: More roof stuff	$71.61
Y	4/21/95	Great Lakes Fence: Barbed Wire	$10.60
Y	4/21/95	Ameritech: Phone setup and bill	$131.10
Y	5/2/95	WSU Small Business Development Center	$5.00
Y	5/3/95	CPI: Passport photos LCC	$15.85
Y	5/23/95	Phone Bill	$22.10
Y	5/23/95	Zoning Hearing	$450.00
Y	5/23/95	HQ: Roofing Stuff	$137.98
Y	5/27/95	Handy Andy: Back door break fix	$21.36

EXPENSES
...continued

Y	5/28/95	Builders Square: Drills, door fix stuff	$64.64
Y	6/1/95	First Edison bill	$17.89
Y	6/2/95	Alarm Sirens (2 more)	$30.62
Y	6/26/95	Alarm Monitoring	$75.00
Y	6/26/95	Edison	$10.65
Y	6/26/95	Phone	$19.62

Year to date sub-total: $24,500.16

Items listed below were previously purchased by Nigel Y. Mea, and will become part of the assets of the Plugged Nickel.

Complete Sound Reinforcement System	$6,000.00
Complete Studio Recording System	$4,000.00
Liquor License Closing (cash on hand)	$4,000.00

Total invested in business by Nigel Y. Mea $38,500.16

Projected Revenue/ Expense

Projected Revenue/Expense — First Month
(3/1/96 to 3/31/96)

Total Projected Revenue	$4,200.00	(1)
Cost of Goods Sold	$1,470.00	
Employee Salaries	$604.80	(2)
Utilities	$350.00	
Maintenance	$100.00	(3)
P & I (5 Yr Amort.)	$212.47	(4)
Insurance	$100.00	(5)
Operating Expense	$2,837.27	
N.P.B.T.	$1,362.73	

Notes:

(1) Anticipated opening March 1996. Payments until that time will be made from current salary. Revenue figure is based on operation of the business initially three nights per week, with 50 customers per night with an average order of $7.00.

(2) There will two employees working 6-hour shifts per night, at $4.20 per hour. Nigel Y. Mea will work 7-hour shifts with no compensation.

(3) Most maintenance will be performed by Nigel Y. Mea, who has experience in these areas.

(4) Figure is based on initial principle of $10,000, 10% interest, and amortization of 5 years.

(5) From quote from Northpoint Insurance.

Cost Breakdown of Additional Monies
(All based on recent estimates)

ITEM	VENDOR	AMOUNT
Roof Repair, 50% complete	Nigel Y. Mea	$400.00
H.V.A.C.	Barton Co.	$1,700.00
Plumbing	Joe Roller	$2,300.00
Furniture	REI or Local	$1,500.00
Glassware, etc.	REI or other	$300.00
Inventory		$500.00
Refrigeration Repair		$1,000.00
Advertising		$500.00
Signage		$400.00
Fence, parking lights	Great Lakes	$800.00
Re-decoration - Labor by local artists		$500.00
Total:		$9,900.00

Note: Nigel Y. Mea currently owns professional sound and stage equipment, for sound reinforcement, lighting, and recording.

Projected Revenue/Expense—Following Year
(4/1/96 to 3/31/97)

Total Projected Revenue	$64,260.00	(1)
Cost of Goods Sold	$21,000.00	(2)
Employee Salaries	$7,711.20	
Utilities	$4,200.00	
Maintenance	$1,200.00	
P & I (5 Yr Amort.)	$2,549.64	
Insurance	$1,200.00	
Operating Expense	$37,860.84	
N.P.B.T.	$26,399.16	

Notes:

(1) Revenue figure is based on operation three nights per week, 51 weeks per year, with 60 customers per night, and an average order of $7.00.

(2) Cost of sales is figured as a percentage of sales, using figures deemed reasonable from similar businesses.

Cost Breakdown

Projected Revenue/ Expense -- Following Year

Restaurant/Bar

BUSINESS PLAN

THE WATERING HOLE

1019 Oak Lane
Galina, IL 34309

May 1995

The following business plan outlines a bar/ restaurant venture that takes advantage of renovations in the surrounding area to help drawn in clientele for itself. The business takes an existing venue and updates it, thereby contributing to the urban renewal taking hold in this previously neglected area.

- PURPOSE

- BACKGROUND

- GOALS

- LOGISTICS

- MARKETING

- PROJECTED REVENUE/EXPENSE

- COST BREAKDOWN

RESTAURANT/BAR BUSINESS PLAN

PURPOSE

First, to renovate and re-open the Watering Hole tavern in the Oak Lane Hotel into an eastern, urban style corner pub that offers a casual environment and bill of fare as well as live acoustic type of music and/or jazz.

Secondly, to take advantage of the increased entertainment business caused by renovation of the Wolfe and Evergreen Theatres. More business will be garnered with the opening of the Galina Centennial Choir in 1996 (additional seasonal business will be derived from the downtown enhancement project it if is implemented). Other immediate sources of business include Artie's Comedy Club patrons as well as Galina University students.

Thirdly, to provide local residents as well as area workers an alternative to existing restaurants and pubs.

Fourthly, to supplement business for the Broadway Cafe, a deli-style restaurant which is currently situated across the lobby from the proposed bar facility.

Finally, to provide additional support to the City of Galina as it strives to attract new business.

BACKGROUND

The Oak Lane Hotel has been a family-owned business since 1967. The hotel is a full-time residential facility consisting of 170 residents. Over the past several years the hotel has enjoyed consistent occupancy in excess of 90%. The owner, S. Lord Properties, (Steven Lord) provides store front space to Luke Lord to own and operate a deli/cafe known as the "Broadway Cafe". The cafe was renovated with family funds in 1992 and has been run profitably for the past 2.5 years. Across the hotel lobby from the cafe is an empty room that is 76.6' x 48' x 13.6' x 23'. As mentioned above, the Lords plan to re-open the bar that used to operate in the now-empty room. As of this writing, the family is seeking funds to renovate and equip this facility. Currently, the Broadway Cafe has a multi-year open-ended lease for $1.00 per month. The same lease provisions will be arranged with the Watering Hole. The Hotel is free and clear of mortgages or any other liens according to a title search by Black Sea Title Co. in December 1994.

GOALS

To recreate and update the original Watering Hole into a profitable business that will benefit both the immediate geographical area and enhance the Oak Lane Hotel's amenities for its residents. The Watering Hole was considered a prominent entertainment spot during the 1940s and 1950s. In short, turn unused street-level space in the Hotel into a profit center.

LOGISTICS

Oak Lane Hotel (hence, The Watering Hole) is located at the corner of Oak Lane and Forrest in Galina. It is located one block west of Goddard Ave., two blocks north of Main St. and one block east of Maple. It is readily visible to pedestrian traffic at street level.

Immediate identifiable customer base:

❑ Cheezy's Pizza corporate headquarters, which is located one block west. Population of approximately 460.
❑ Galina Fire Department, which is located across the street (Oak Lane) and has a population of approximately 125.
❑ Oak Lane Hotel with a population of 170 residents.
❑ Wolfe Theatre (one block west) has a population of approximately 60.
❑ Sundry weekend foot traffic generated by events at the Wolfe Theatre, the Evergreen, Diamond Theatre, Artie's Comedy Club and Restaurant, and in 1996, the Galina Centennial Choir.

Size of facility is approximately 76.6' x 48' x 13.6' x 23' ft. with a maximum planned capacity of approximately 155 persons.

Immediate competition is somewhat limited due to customer focus of this establishment (i.e., pub style). Jake's Bar is located at Patricia and Main, and Strikers is located 4 blocks north on Main. Both are within a 1/2 mile radius. Any other similar establishments are located approximately 1.5 miles north in the University area or approximately 1 mile south in and around Galina's central business district. The key difference between the Watering Hole and immediate competition will be live acoustic/jazz entertainment which will make it a true alternative to other pubs in the area. Parking is readily available in the Wolfe Theatre Garage and on the street.

Marketing efforts will consist of advertisement in entertainment section of local publications such as The Galina Post and The Reader, as well as hand bills when appropriate.

A twenty-foot vertical, neon sign affixed to the southeast corner of the Oak Lane Hotel will be highly visible to immediate residents as well as evening foot traffic on Main St.

MARKETING

(Quarterly Basis)

PROJECTED REVENUE/EXPENSE

	6/1/96 to 6/30/95	
Total Projected Revenue	$3,600	(1)
Cost of Goods Sold	$1,470	(2)
Employee Salaries	$1,008	(3)
Utilities	$1,000	
Maintenance	$250	
Lease/Rent	$1	(4)
P & I (10% @ 15 Yr Amort)	$2,149	(5)
Operating Expense	$5,878	
N.P.B.T.	$(2,278)	

**PROJECTED
REVENUE/EXPENSE**

...continued

Notes:

(1) The Watering Hole anticipated opening by June 1995. This is a one month projection based on average of 25 customers per day (1.67 customers per hour based on a 15 hour day) with an average order of $6.00.

(2) Represents beverage costs only. All food costs will be borne by the Broadway Cafe and calculated into yearly revenue/expense base of that entity.

(3) There will be two employees that will work a 5 hour shift, 6 days per week at $4.20 per hour. Luke Lord will work daily approximately 8 to 10 hours with no compensation.

(4) Lease is $1.00 per month to S. Lord Properties with an indefinite tenor.

(5) Principal and Interest payment is calculated for a $200M note with an interest rate of 10% and amortization of 15 years.

	7/1/95 to 9/30/95		10/1/95 to 12/31/95	
Tot. Proj. Revenue	$27,000	(1)	43,200	(2)
Cost of Goods Sold	$8,820	(3)	14,256	(4)
Employee Salary	$3,024		3,024	
Utilities	$3,000		3,000	
Maintenance	$750		750	
Lease	$3		3	
P & I	$6,447		6,447	
Operating Expense	$22,044		27,480	
N.P.B.T.	$4,956		15,270	

Notes:

(1) Revenue base assumes 50 customers daily avg. (3.3 per hour) spending $6.00 per day over 3 month period.

(2) Revenue base assumes 60 customers daily avg. (4 per hour) spending $8.00 per day over 3 month period.

(3) Cost of Goods Sold represents a 100% increase in dollar volume over June 1995, annualized and totalled over 3 month period.

(4) Cost of Goods represents a 38% increase in dollar volume over pervious quarter (7/1/95 to 9/30/95).

	1/1/96 to 3/31/96		4/1/96 to 6/30/96	
Tot. Proj. Revenue	$43,200	(1)	54,000	(2)
Cost of Goods Sold	$8,798		17,820	(3)
Employees Salary	$3,024		3,024	
Utilities	$3,000		3,000	
Maintenance	$750		750	
Lease	$3		3	
P & I	$6,447		6,447	
Operating Expense	$27,480		31,044	
N.P.B.T.	$ 15,270		22,956	

Notes:

(1) See Notes 1 & 3 for the Previous Quarter

(2) Revenues represent an average of 75 customers on a daily basis (5 customers per hour). These customers can be anticipated to spend approximately $8.00 per day. Increases in spending per customer and daily client base are attributed to familiarity with product and establishment and willingness to spend more time in tavern based on seasonal attitudes.

(3) Cost of Goods Sold is a 50% increase over previous quarter.

	7/1/96 to 9/30/96		10/1/96 to 12/31/96	
Tot. Proj. Revenue	$54,000	(1)	57,600	(2)
Cost of Goods Sold	$17,820	(3)	19,008	(4)
Employee Salaries	$3,024		3,024	
Utilities	$3,000		3,000	
Maintenance	$750		750	
Lease/Rent	$3		3	
P & I	$6,447		6,447	
Operating Expense	$31,044		32,262	
N.P.B.T.	$22,956		25,338	

Notes:

(1) Revenues are based on an average of 75 customers daily (5 per hour) spending an average $8.00 per day.

(2) Revenues are based on an average of 80 customers daily (5.3 per hour) spending an average of $8.00 per day. Estimated increases in customer base for last 6 months of 1996 are predicated on an increased popularity of the Watering Hole. Marginal increase in client base represents a leveling off and steadying of the number of patrons visiting the tavern on a daily basis.

(3) Cost of Goods Sold is same as previous quarter.

(4) Cost of Goods Sold represents only a 7% increase over previous quarter.

(Dimensions of Tavern: 76.6' x 48' x 13.6' x 23')   **COST BREAKDOWN**

Title	$5,000.00
Carpeting	$4,000.00
H.V.A.C.	$21,200.000
Serving Bar and Bar Back	$62,333.00
Plumbing	$5,000.00
Signage	$12,025.00
Bar Equipment	$26,505.00
Bar Furniture	$2,150.00
Electrical	$42,650.00
Ceiling Panels	$15,455.00
China & Flatware	$3,500.00
Total	$199,818.00

(All costs are based on most recent estimates.)

Restaurant Franchise

BUSINESS PLAN

STEPHENSON'S, INC., dba REUBEN'S DELI

413 S. Kraut Ln.
Akron, OH 43905

April 1995

Stephenson's, Inc. operates Reuben's Deli, a franchise delicatessen. This business plan features a discussion of factors unique to a franchise, such as the history of its performance in other areas, the applicability of the concept in the new area, special trademark and image issues, and the advantages of a franchise as opposed to an independently-owned restaurant.

- NARRATIVE

- RISK FACTORS

- COMPANY STATUS

- PROPRIETARY FEATURES

- COMMUNITY BENEFITS

- THE PRODUCT

- COMPETITION

- PLANNED DEVELOPMENT

- SALES AND ADVERTISING PROGRAMS

- MANAGEMENT DUTIES AND RESPONSIBILITIES

- FINANCIAL ESTIMATES

RESTAURANT BUSINESS PLAN

NARRATIVE

The Company

Stephenson's, Inc. was formed as a Delaware Corporation in July of 1995. The Company was formed to establish operating Reuben's Deli restaurants in Akron, OH. The Company will develop this concept, which currently has a time-tested, proven market acceptance of its food and beverage group(s). In addition to other considerations, the Company in its evaluations elected to execute this concept based upon the simplicity of the concept overall, the training by the Franchisor, the support offered by the local area developer group, and the ease and costs of entry and the likelihood of success at the store level under the various market conditions and environments. Initial efforts in this development shall be primarily focused upon the commitment and execution of an initial Reuben's Restaurant located in the Akron, OH area. It is the intention of the company to establish its headquarters in Akron, OH during its first year of operation.

Company History

Stephenson's, Inc. was co-founded by Caren and Eddie Stephenson. Mrs. Stephenson acts as President and Mr. Stephenson acts as Executive Vice President. Both are Directors of the Company. The Company is a start-up situation, however, and it should be recognized that it also represents an extension of a successful 23 year-old chain of more than 400 operating restaurants. Further, the company will have very effective guidance provided by the local Area Developers who will be working day to day with the Company to help insure its success. The Area Developers are Mr. Wilson and Mr. Jones. Mr. Wilson has extensive experience in the food and beverage industry. Mr. Wilson was formerly with Wendy's International Inc. of Columbus, OH and worked for its chairman Mr. Dave Thomas for over five (5) years. He was also Co-Founder and President of Calibre Inc., a publicly held company in the business of building and operating various restaurant concepts. These concepts include Chuck E. Cheese Pizza Time Theaters, RAX Restaurants, and G.D. Ritzy's. In addition, Mr. Wilson began his restaurant career with his family as they owned and operated one of the first Kentucky Fried Chicken restaurants and a full-service family restaurant known as Wilson's Drive-In located in Lima, OH. Mr. Jones has over 15 years' experience in developing start-up and ongoing businesses. Mr. Jones has worked closely with successful entrepreneurs, including the nationally recognized billionaire and insurance magnate Clement Stone; America's leading real estate educator and author, Dr. Albert J. Lowry; and others, including Charles J. Givens, Zig Ziglar, and Mr. Bob Harrington (Chaplin of Bourbon Street). Mr. Jones spent six years doing national platform speaking engagements on investment strategies, business management, and motivational topics. He has extensive experience in formulating and executing start-up businesses for others as well as himself. He has spent the past eight years involved with law firms specializing in tax planning strategies to high net worth individuals and clients of these law firms. Additionally, Mr. Jones taught attorneys and CPAs methods of tax and estate planning with the use of both domestic and off-shore trusts.

Company Objectives

The Company's first priority is to establish its first operating Reuben's Deli restaurant. Prior to opening the first restaurant, the principals shall obtain complete training from both the parent company, Reuben's Inc. of Boise, Idaho, and the local Area Developer, Yukon, Inc.

Second, it will continue to pursue sites for the future development of subsequent restaurants. The Company has entered into an Agreement with Reuben's Inc. to build and develop additional franchise units.

It is the long-term objective of the Company to obtain adequate financing for the project, identify sites, and develop successful Reuben's Deli restaurants. The selection of this specific concept was made as a result of the likelihood of success in a new business venture of this type. Significant risks that are usually inherent in start-up businesses are reasonably mitigated as a result of Reuben's history and track record. Reuben's Inc. has developed a 24-year track record of success and profitability with over 400 operating franchises. The Company believes that the timing of this sector of the food market is most desirable. Food industry experts agree that a specialty sandwich with unique flavors offered at competitive prices will be the fastest growing segment for the next ten (10) years. However, in all events, there are certain risks that need to be addressed appropriately since the Company is directly competing for transactions with other existing restaurant chains as well as independent operations.

RISK FACTORS

Stephenson's, Inc. is in its first year of operation. It has located and established its headquarters in Akron, OH. The Company has submitted a lease proposal on a site located at _____. Further consideration is under evaluation for a site in _____, OH. It is anticipated that construction and completion of the initial company store shall be not later than _____. Stephenson's, Inc. will expedite additional efforts during 1995 and into 1996 to build and operate additional company-owned stores and increase the depth and strength of management of the company.

Operating History

The success of the Company will depend on the ability of management to operate daily. The Company plans upon growing its base of management as needed and when it becomes financially feasible. There is no assurance that management can do this in a timely or profitable manner.

Dependence on Management

All aspects of the retail food industry are highly competitive, but the competition in the quick serve food segment is particularly intense. The Company will be competing with a large number of other quick serve food stores. Some of the competitors have greater financial resources and more established reputations that this company. However, the Reuben's chain does have a 24-year successful operating history.

Competition

The Company's ability to develop and manage franchises will require significant time commitments from management. The Company intends upon staffing two persons by the end of the second year to manage the franchise with its owners. The placement of these persons will be difficult in light of the competition. Therefore, no assurance can be given that the Company will attract or be able to retain qualified individuals to satisfy the Company's requirements for such personnel. In such an event, the management may need to continue to maintain and operate the stores and their growth.

Dependence on Company Support Personnel

Dependence on Manufacturers and Suppliers

The Company has no production facilities for food and equipment and is dependent upon obtaining the services of outside manufacturers. Although the Company anticipates that it will be able to purchase sufficient products, equipment, and agreements with approved manufacturers, no assurance can be given that the Company will be able to always obtain such products, equipment, or agreements.

COMPANY STATUS

The Company has entered its first full year of operations and has started to develop relationships with area professionals to advise the Company in the areas of Real Estate, Banking, Accounting, and Legal needs. Its activities include the establishment of initial store financing. The Company has also recently submitted a proposal to acquire a lease in Akron, OH. Upon obtaining a commitment for financing for its first store, the Company will then execute a Franchise Unit Development Agreement with Reuben's, Inc. Currently, the Company has executed a Unit Development Agreement with Reuben's and has paid $_____.00 in franchise fees to the franchisor. The Company anticipates building a minimum of _____ units.

Capitalization

The Company is currently seeking to obtain a loan of $170,000 to develop the first store. The terms of that loan shall be determined when management has negotiated what is going to be realistic to offer based upon projected earnings. Further, the Company anticipates providing an additional amount of cash between $75,000 and $90,000 towards its first store development.

Use of Proceeds

The amounts set forth in this business plan represent the Company's present intentions with respect to promised expenditures. Actual expenditures may vary substantially, depending upon future developments such as marketing, sales activity, corporate opportunities, and certain other recognized or unforeseen factors. Any change either in the allocation of funds or in the order of priority will be at the discretion of the Company's Board of Directors.

Loans

The Company may utilize trade and other commercial credit, if available. Working capital, lines of credit, secured by orders and accounts receivable, will likely be used during the routine course of its business.

PROPRIETARY FEATURES

The Company and Reuben's Inc. intend to mutually protect all patents, trademarks and other proprietary rights to the extent such action is feasible. The packaged goods, advertising, logos, recipes, local promotions, and any other product, service or idea deemed proprietary will also be protected appropriately. The intent is to preserve the integrity of the concept and to hold the protected property to certain standards and monitor use of these trademarks as they are supposed to apply to certain promotions and products as directed by the parent company. The Company and Reuben's Inc. rely upon certain recipes and proprietary products to present a unique atmosphere, ambiance, aroma, food taste, and overall consistent presentation to the customer. Any representation of these items or trademarks should only be as directed by Reuben's Inc. and the Company as an area developer. The Company primarily relies upon the laws of unfair competition and confidentiality agreements to protect its designs and other proprietary information.

The Company believes it will be an asset within its development area as it will generate new job opportunities for the residents of the respective communities in which it builds stores. The Company plans to hire as many employees as possible from the local community residents for each store. It will also give the cities increased revenues through payroll and sales taxes and increased consumer spending by employing the local residents. The Company believes that as a franchise owner for Reuben's Inc., that Reuben's Deli will become a well-known brand name nationwide and create a company that the local communities will be proud to have. Further, Reuben's has established a tradition that the Company plans on supporting along with other area franchise owners and the Area Developers for the benefit of local charities. For the past several years Reuben's Inc. has sponsored a 5K race to benefit various charities by raising significant dollars through the participation of the public. It is noted to be one of the most successful 5K races in the U.S. Stephenson's Inc., in cooperation with other franchise owners plans on co-sponsoring this race in the greater Akron market.

COMMUNITY BENEFITS

THE PRODUCT

The Need

The Company together with Reuben's Inc. is providing an opportunity designed to fulfill the needs of an active population who find themselves in a busy working environment with schedules that are pressing because of circumstances which cause them to have their time restrained for various reasons. Therefore, this population who appreciates a quality product at a fair price will use their disposable income to eat at a quick service restaurant offering outstanding customer service in an effort to obtain both convenience and entertainment. Reuben's Deli enjoys a base of customers that have traditionally developed during the past 24 years, into a heavy user profile (more than 4 visits per month). This allows for a solid customer base. Therefore a Reuben's franchise fulfills a need for a small business owner of a single unit or a larger business organization which would include multi-unit operations. The franchise provides a time-tested business opportunity with a successful track record and products proven to be widely accepted.

Customer Response

The Company has observed and spoken with customers of other Reuben's Deli franchise units who have indicated their overwhelming acceptance of the products in this market. Indications are strong that as the Reuben's system grows nationally and internationally, the recognition will continue to cause further interest in the concept. Many studies point out that if you're interested in operating a restaurant your odds of success are greatly enhanced with a concept that has been in business for at least 10 years and offers a unique product. In fact, it has been statistically shown that the odds are that if you start your own restaurant without any history, it will fail 85% of the time, while if you develop a franchise with a proven track record, like Reuben's Deli, you will be successful 85% or more of the time. Reuben's Deli certainly is a proven entity. The customer responds for the following reasons:

The wide appeal and the quality of Reuben's Deli products. Reuben's enjoys one of the highest customer responses in the food industry today. The average customer visits a Reuben's Deli 4-6 times per month.

○ The universal acceptance of the old and especially new restaurant designs.
○ The affordable price of the products as compared to other competitive food operations.
○ The cleanliness of the overall operation.

COMPETITION

Any restaurant is certainly considered competition in this industry. However, the food segment that we are in, the specialty deli type sandwich is rapidly becoming the fastest growing segment in the food industry. Reuben's Deli and similar food operators in this category are showing impressive results as featured in various industry publications like "Restaurant News."

Competitive Advantage

The Reuben's restaurant concept has a 24-year operating history which gives it a vast amount of past operating history and proven stability. The products in a Reuben's Deli have stood the test of time. The quality is unequaled and truly unique and that is why so many franchise owners already operating in this system have experienced success. The new updated building layouts and designs, together with the quality of the product and expanded menu is encouraging a very high level of repeat business. The addition of many new store, approximately 15-20 per month, is creating an awareness of Reuben's Deli nationwide and will fuel its popularity through this growth. In 1993, system-wide sales exceeded $71,000,000.00, an increase of over 20% from the previous year. In 1994, sales reached in excess of $100,000,000.00 system-wide. It is anticipated that by 1999, there will be in excess of 3800 stores producing almost two (2) billion in annual sales. The Area Developer program has further enhanced this growth and success of the nationwide development of the Reuben's Deli system due to the increase in support to the local franchise owners by their area developers.

Industry and Market Overview

The Reuben's Deli restaurant concept is involved in one of the largest dollar volume industries in the world. However, those who excel in this category are generously rewarded both personally and financially. The largest cross section of population in the world spends money daily in this industry and those trends are continuing to increase rapidly. Reuben's Deli has a 24-year operating history and has now entered the mature growth stage of their development. This is the time in the development history when restaurant chains historically experience explosive growth and effective market penetration. The markets are growing nationally and internationally, and the specialty sandwich segment is viewed by experts in the industry as the segment clearly offering the most dynamic opportunities. The blended flavors of the sandwich menu and the popular gourmet pizza products, together with the new flavored coffee program, have combined to attract industry attention. "Entrepreneur Magazine" again recently named the Reuben's Deli concept as the Number 1 franchise in the sandwiches, soups, and salads category, representing the second consecutive year that award has been won by Reuben's. This is an impressive list to be on at any level and to be named Number 1 is a tribute to the concept. Reuben's Inc. and Yukon, Inc. (Area Developers) have been the focus of several national and local periodicals.

PLANNED DEVELOPMENT

Yukon, Inc., Area Developer, anticipates and estimates that the territories under their control for development will support over 667 Reuben's Deli restaurants. The minimum development contract demands that at least 317 stores be developed over the next five years. This growth is affected by seasonality, market share achieved, market trends, pricing strategies, and product line strategies. Management has determined that after evaluating all of these criteria and spending valuable due diligence time, that the growth in our respective areas will significantly enhance the credibility and visibility of Stephenson's, Inc. in its efforts to develop.

Stephenson's, Inc. plans on using several methods of local store marketing as suggested by the Reuben's, Inc. marketing department and the area developer. The primary method for obtaining sales is initially contacting surrounding businesses and residents and inviting them to visit the store through special local store promotions. Coupons, radio, and frequency cards will be utilized early as pre-opening sales tools. Reuben's has also contracted a number of national magazines and/or newspapers to continuously prepare and run advertising for exposure of the concept. Stephenson's, Inc. will contribute 1% of total gross store sales to the national marketing fund for the overall corporate wide system marketing program. Additionally, the Company will spend at least 3% annually of its gross revenues of Company-owned stores on local advertising and promotions and will participate with these funds in the area co-op programs. The Company will develop working relationships with various advertising agency's and will receive quality guidance from the co-op members and its area development company, Yukon, Inc., in choosing the most effective advertising.

SALES AND ADVERTISING PROGRAMS

The Company consists of a Board of Directors and two (2) full-time management employees including Mr. Eddie Stephenson and Mrs. Caren Stephenson who are also officers of the Company. The principals will be managers in these stores. The functions of managements are structured according to the operating requirements for the successful execution of the business. These functions include but are not limited to corporate strategic planning, sales and marketing, implementation and updates of operations, advertising and promotions. Additionally, management currently is responsible for the daily operations of Company-owned stores. Outside professional services will support the needs for legal and accounting functions. Also, the Company will utilize the services of a life insurance professional and an advertising and public relations firm based in the greater Akron, OH area.

MANAGEMENT DUTIES AND RESPONSIBILITIES

The Company has outlined as its 1995 major management objectives the following points in order to continue to successfully execute its business plan:

Major Management Objectives

- Complete the Company's need for financing
- Locate, negotiate, obtain, develop, and open store #1
- Complete training in operations at Boise, Idaho, per Reuben's, Inc. requirement
- Increase the depth of knowledge in management of the Company organization
- Participate closely with Reuben's Inc. to further enhance the overall improvement of the Reuben's Deli concept
- Promote awareness of the Reuben's Deli in the local trade area through in-store promotions
- Select and hire quality employees who appropriately represent the image of the success of Reuben's Deli
- Operate a clean profitable store

**FINANCIAL
ESTIMATES**

**Projected Statement of
Earnings**

For years ending December 31, 1996-1998

	Year 1		Year 2		Year 3	
	Dollars	**Percent**	**Dollars**	**Percent**	**Dollars**	**Percent**
Gross Sales	400,000	100.00	450,000	100.00	500,000	100.00
Less: Coupons	4000	1.00	4500	1.00	5000	1.00
Less: Emp. disc./meals	5840	1.45	5570	1.46	7300	1.45
Net Sales	390,160	97.54	438,930	97.54	487,700	97.54
Cost of Sales						
Food & Bev	111,000	27.75	124,875	27.75	138,750	27.75
Paper & Plastic	9000	2.25	10,125	2.25	11,250	2.25
Total Cost of Sales	120,000	30.00	135,000	30.00	150,000	30.00
Gross Profit	270,160	67.54	303,930	67.54	337,700	67.54
Employee Expenses						
Payroll						
Owner	10,632	2.66	5315	1.18	3544	.71
Manager	12,500	3.13	25,750	5.72	26,500	5.30
Hourly	60,000	15.00	61,800	13.73	63,654	12.73
Taxes	10,800	2.70	11,124	2.47	11,458	2.29
Workers Comp	1200	.30	1350	.30	1500	.30
Health Ins.	2400	.60	4800	1.07	4800	.96
Total Emp. Exp.	97,532	24.38	110,140	24.48	111,456	22.29
Other Expenses						
Accounting						
Bookkeeping	3000	.75	3000	.67	3300	.66
Year End Rev & Taxes	5000	1.25	5000	1.11	6000	1.20
Payroll Service	360	.09	2750	.61	2750	.55
Advertising	8000	2.00	8779	1.95	9754	1.95
Amortization						
Franchise Fees	2750	.69	2750	.61	2750	.55
Organizational Costs						
Accounting	500	.13	500	.11	500	.10
Legal	520	.13	520	.12	520	.10
Training Costs	900	.23	900	.20	900	.18
Cash Over/Short & Theft	320	.08	360	.08	400	.08
Depreciation						
Leasehold Imprv	12,500	3.13	12,500	2.78	12,500	2.5
Equipment	18,800	4.7	18,800	4.18	18,800	3,76
Franchise Royalties	23,410	5.85	26,336	5.85	29,262	5.85

	Year 1		Year 2		Year 3		Projected Statement of Earnings ...*continued*
	Dollars	**Percent**	**Dollars**	**Percent**	**Dollars**	**Percent**	
Insurance	2000	.5	2000	.44	2000	.4	
Laundry & Uniforms	1800	.45	1800	.4	1800	.36	
Lease	28,000	7.00	31,500	7.00	3500	7.00	
Lease CAM	8000	2.00	9000	2.00	10,000	2.00	
Lics. & Permits	600	.15	600	.13	600	.12	
Miscellaneous	2000	.5	2250	.5	2500	.5	
NAMF Contribution	4000	1.00	4500	1.00	5000	1.00	
Postage	300	.08	300	.07	300	.06	
Repairs & Maint							
Bldg.	500	.13	500	.11	500	.10	
Equip	2400	.60	2400	.53	2400	.48	
Supplies	4000	1.00	4500	1.00	5000	1.00	
Taxes	0	0	0	0	0	0	
Telephone	900	.23	900	.20	900	.18	
Waste Removal	300	.08	300	.07	300	.06	
Utilities	15,000	3.75	15,000	3.33	15,000	3.00	
Total Other Expenses	145,860	36.46	157,744	35.05	168,378	33.75	
Earnings from Ops	26,758	6.69	36,046	8.01	57,508	11.50	
Other (Income) Expenses							
Interest Income		0.00		0.00		0.00	
Interst Expense	12,616	3.15	11,719	2.60	10,742	2.15	
Total Other (Income)							
Expense	12,616	3.15	11,719	2.60	10,742	2.15	
Net Earnings	14,152	3.54	24,372	5.41	46,766	9.35	
Non-cash Expenses							
Amortization							
Franchise Fees	2750	.69	2750	.61	2750	.55	
Organizational Costs							
Accounting	500	.13	500	.11	500	.10	
Legal	520	.13	520	.12	520	.10	
Training Costs	900	.23	900	.20	900	.18	
Depreciation							
Leasehold Imprv.	12,500	3.13	12,500	2.79	12,500	2.50	
Equipment	18,800	4.70	18,800	4.18	18,800	3.76	
Total Non-cash							
Expenses	35,970	8.99	35,970	7.99	35,970	7.19	
Cash Flow	50,122	12.53	60,297	13.40	82,736	16.55	

Projected Balance Sheet	Assets	Year 1
	Current Assets	
	Cash	5450
	Inventory	6233
	Prepaid Expenses	
	Total Current Assets	11,683
	Property & Equipment	
	Leasehold Improvements	125,000
	Equipment	94,000
	Less: Accumulated Depreciation--Leaseholds	(12,500)
	Less: Accumulated Depreciation--Equipment	(18,800)
	Total property and equipment	187,700
	Other Assets	
	Franchise Fees	27,500
	Deposits	4500
	Organizational Costs--Accounting	2500
	Organizational Costs--Legal	2600
	Training Costs	4500
	Less: Accumulated Amortization--Franchise Fees	(2750)
	Less: Accumulated Amortization--Org. Cost, Accounting	(500)
	Less: Accumulated Amortization--Org. Cost, Legal	(520)
	Less: Accumulated Amortization--Training Costs	(900)
	Total Other Assets	36,930
	Total Assets	236,313
	Liabilities and Stockholders' Equity	
	Current Liabilities	
	Current Maturities of Long-term debt	11,045
	Accounts Payable	
	Accrued Rent Concessions	
	Accrued Liabilities	
	Total Current Liabilities	11,045
	Long-term Debt	142,852
	Less: Current Maturities of Long-term Debt	(11,045)
	Total Long-term Debt	131,807
	Stockholders' Equity	
	Common Stock	1000
	Preferred Stock	
	Contributed Capital	78,309
	Retained Earnings	14,152
	Total Stockholders' Equity	93,461
	Total Liabilities & Stockholders' Equity	236,313
	Cash Requirements	120,283

Leasehold Improvements	125,000
Equipment	94,000
Subtotal	219,000

Start-up Expenses

Opening Cash	5450
Opening Inventory	6233
Franchise Fees	27,500
Deposits	4500
Organizational Costs--Accounting	2500
Organizational Costs--Legal	2600
Training Costs	4500
Common Stock Purchase	1000
Subtotal	54,283

| Less Loan Proceeds | (153,000) |
| **Net Cash Requirements** | 120,283 |

Adjusted Projections: Cash Flow Only

					Percent
Sales Per Month	33333	41666	50000	58333	
Gross Sales	400000	500000	600000	700000	100
Less: Coupons	8000	10000	12000	14000	2
Less: Employee Meals	4000	5000	6000	7000	1
Net Sales	388000	485000	582000	679000	97
Cost of Sales					
Food & Beverage	111000	138750	166500	194250	27.75
Paper & Plastic	9000	11250	13500	15750	2.25
Total Cost of Sales	120000	150000	180000	210000	30
Gross Profit	268000	335000	402000	469000	67
Employee Expenses					
Payroll & P. Tax/Owner	5979	5979	5979	5979	
Payroll & P. Tax/Manager	28118	28118	28118	28118	
Payroll Hourly	76000	95000	114000	133000	19
Payroll Tax/Hourly	6360	7950	9540	11130	1.59
Workers Compensation	1840	2300	2760	3220	0.46
Health Insurance	2400	2400	2400	2400	
Total Employee Expenses	120697	141747	162797	183847	45.95

Adjusted Projections:
Cash Flow Only
 ...continued

Other Expenses

Accounting Year End - Taxes	1500	1500	1500	1500	
Accounting - Payroll	360	360	360	360	
Advertising	11640	14550	17460	20370	2.91
Cash Over/Short - Theft	320	400	480	560	0.08
Franchise Royalties	23400	29250	35100	40950	5.85
Insurance	2000	2000	2000	2000	
Laundry	1800	1800	1800	1800	
Lease	62400	62400	62400	62400	
Licenses & Permits	600	600	600	600	
Miscellaneous	2000	2500	3000	3500	0.5
Muzak	660	660	660	660	
NAMF Contribution	3880	4850	5820	6790	0.97
Repairs & Maint. - Bldg.	1000	1000	1000	1000	
Repairs & Maint. - Equip.	500	500	500	500	
Supplies	4000	5000	6000	7000	1
Taxes					
Telephone & Postage	1200	1200	1200	1200	
Waste Removal	600	600	600	600	
Utilities	15000	15000	15000	15000	
Total Expenses	132860	144170	155480	166790	
Net Earnings from Operations	14443	49083	83723	118363	

Restaurant (Nonprofit)

BUSINESS PLAN

McMurphy's Grill

St. Patrick's Center
1200 6th St.
St Louis, MO 63106
(314) 621-1283

April 1994

*This business plan has not been disguised in any way; references to locations, people, and products are real, not fictional. McMurphy's seeks to give job skills to mentally ill homeless people in order to help them. The contributor has asked that those interested in forming a business of this type contact St. Patrick's Center with their questions during regular business hours prior to instituting any of the suggestions in the plan. **Note**: A number of Appendices to which the plan refers were deliberately excluded due to privacy considerations. This plan has been re-printed from the first volume for the purpose of comparison with its revision. (See next plan.)*

- EXECUTIVE SUMMARY

- THE COMPANY AND THE CONCEPT

- THE INDUSTRY AND MARKET ANALYSIS

- STRATEGIC PLAN

- OPERATIONS AND MANAGEMENT

- MAJOR COMPETITORS: LUNCH BUSINESS

- EMPLOYEE TRAINING COST ANALYSIS

- MENU

- TARGET CUSTOMER ANALYSIS

- MARKETING STRATEGY

- ADVERTISING AND PROMOTIONAL RECOMMENDATIONS

- McMURPHY'S GRILL INCOME STATEMENT

- CASH FLOW CALCULATIONS

- FINANCIAL ASSUMPTIONS AND ANALYSIS

EXECUTIVE SUMMARY

Opening its doors on December 3rd, 1990, McMurphy's Grill has brought a little bit of earth-quaking to the St. Louis community. While operating as a competitive restaurant, McMurphy's has set about the task of making people without homes, but with diagnostic psychiatric labels, into food servers and cooks. This business plan primarily focuses on the operational aspects of McMurphy's Grill, defining McMurphy's as two distinct, but interrelated functional organizational units: one being the restaurant business and the other being the employment training component. A strategic plan is presented for each component and the strategic direction which this operation as a whole should take to achieve growth will be outlined.

With an appealing product, both in terms of its mission and its fare, McMurphy's Grill certainly has an added advantage over its competitors. Located at Eleventh Street and Lucas in downtown St. Louis, McMurphy's, as a restaurant, has been favorably noted by restaurant critics and customers alike. Its mission, of training mentally ill homeless men and women, certainly sets it apart from any other competitive restaurant in the St. Louis area.

The success of this operation depends a great deal on the cohesiveness of the two functional organizational units as well as an aggressive marketing strategy. With this in place and a little "luck of the Irish", McMurphy's will likely reach its optimistic sales goals. If the Celebrity Hosts promotion, a newly initiated program, which will be described in more detail in the Strategic Plan, is any indication, a 30 percent increase in sales over fiscal year 1994 is not unrealistic.

Most of us can only imagine the obstacles people who are homeless and mentally ill must overcome to hold down a job, much less one in the restaurant business. Yet, this innovative employment training program has helped to ease the transition for many. From life on the streets to independence, McMurphy's goals are enthusiastic to say the least.

Perhaps the most compelling concern of this type of endeavor lies with the ability to balance both sides of the coin -- the mission and the business. An organization's focus on its prime business. The delicate balance of maintaining the effectiveness and success of each component requires extra care and effort. However, with a well defined strategic plan, the community support afforded St. Patrick Center, a myriad of volunteers, and a staff with a vision -- this tightrope can be successfully maneuvered.

THE COMPANY AND THE CONCEPT

While operating as a competitive establishment, McMurphy's prime focus is on teaching homeless individuals, many suffering from mental illness, skills in food preparation as well as the restaurant service.

McMurphy's has enjoyed favorable reviews for both its food and its mission. The 80-seat restaurant provides its customers with wholesome, hearty meals and a comfortable, pleasant atmosphere, while its trainees learn on-the-job skills in self-sufficiency. Primarily drawing customers from the downtown lunch business crowd, McMurphy's has a unique advantage in that it also draws people from other areas because of its mission. To support its favorable status, in both categories, McMurphy's Grill is proud to have been the 1992 Winner of the Midwest Living Magazine Hometown Pride Award and Hospitality Awards finalist for the Restaurant of the Year -- Casual category sponsored by the Convention and Visitors Commission. In addition, McMurphy's Grill has been awarded grants from the Share Our Strength Foundation for its efforts in training for self-sufficiency.

Owned and operated by St. Patrick Center, a multi-service nonprofit agency providing a variety of services for homeless and low-income people in St. Louis, this innovation transitional employment program has provided an opportunity for sixty-seven men and women, thus far, to learn valuable employment skills. St. Patrick Center is located at 1200 North Sixth Street, on the near north side of downtown St. Louis. Dedicated in 1983, the Center provides opportunities for homeless and low-income persons to attain self-sufficiency and dignity through programs which effect permanent solutions, including education, counseling, job training, employment, housing assistance, and substance abuse rehabilitation. Special emphasis is placed on those who experience mental illness or chemical dependency.

The concept of a restaurant operation stemmed from a restaurant in Rock Island, Illinois which is run by mentally ill employees. By owning their own business, which serves as a transitional training program, St. Patrick Center is able to provide the flexibility required to allow the clients to move at their own pace.

With a generous grant from McDonnell Douglas Employees Community Fund and the McDonnell Douglas foundation as well as contributions from other private and corporate sources, McMurphy's Grill became a reality. The Pasta House Company provided the management expertise and restaurant operations knowledge in addition to numerous donations of restaurant fixtures and supplies. Through the Neighborhood Assistance Program of the State Department of Economic Development, McMurphy's was able to receive free rent for much of its existence. In 1993, Paric Corporation, the owners of Lucas Place, the building which houses McMurphy's Grill, donated the entire 3-floor building to St. Patrick Center. The top two floors are constructed for office space. This innovative project is truly a community endeavor.

The operation of McMurphy's Grill has provided a challenge to St. Patrick Center, whose primary expertise has been in the social service arena. In addition, McMurphy's is only one of thirteen programs operated by St. Patrick Center and thus does not have the concentrated effort that many small restaurant operators employ. Changes in administration at St. Patrick Center, especially at the Executive Director's level, along with changes in the management at McMurphy's has significantly affected the operations of the restaurant.

THE COMPANY AND THE CONCEPT *...continued*

Under the direction of St. Patrick Center's new Executive Director and the Center's Board of Directors, efforts are underway to develop a long-range strategic plan for the entire agency along with establishing better methods to measure program effectiveness. This business plan will provide the long-range strategic direction for this particular operation, providing target measurements and goals for the business component as well as the employment training component. In addition, this operational plan will help to define management responsibilities, controls and reporting expectations of each component. The strategic plan will also help ensure consistency of operation, despite personnel changes, within each component as well as for the entire McMurphy's Grill operation.

THE INDUSTRY AND MARKET ANALYSIS

McMurphy's Grill falls into two industry classifications. As a competitive restaurant, McMurphy's Grill falls into the foodservice industry. As a facility which provides employment and training for mentally ill homeless persons and those recovering from substance addictions, McMurphy's can also be classified among other vocational rehabilitation programs.

The Foodservice Industry

Description of Product Category

Restaurants are the largest part of the U.S. foodservice industry and according to the National Restaurant Association. They "had an estimated sales of $255 billion in 1992." Fuller-service stand alone restaurants, the category which would include McMurphy's, accounted for "32 percent of all foodservice sales in 1992."

The characteristics of most limited menu tableservice restaurants, of which McMurphy's is a part of, include:

- ❑ 62.7 percent of limited-menu tableservice restaurants are single units (independent).
- ❑ 46.3 percent of these restaurants have a sales volume under $500,000.
- ❑ Over 65 percent serve both food and beverage.
- ❑ The average check per person is usually under $10.00.
- ❑ The average daily seat turnover was 1.8.

The Size of the Market

The foodservice industry is highly fragmented, thus making it an extremely competitive industry. This industry continues to be dominated by small businesses as is evidenced by "average unit sales of $429,000 reported by tableservice restaurants..." McMurphy's Grill has experienced, thus far, a much lower unit sales volume than the average. This is in part due to the limited time

McMurphy's is open on a daily basis. Lack of a comprehensive marketing strategy has also had an impact upon sales.

The foodservice industry continues to experience healthy growth patterns. The National Restaurant Association forecasts an increase of 5.6 percent. Sales for Eating and Drinking places for the City of St. Louis are much higher than for the state as a whole. Total retail sales for the City of St. Louis, of which 18.7 percent are from Eating and Drinking establishments, is expected to increase 45.3 percent over 1992 sales by 1997. With this growth pattern, along with an aggressive marketing strategy, McMurphy's has the potential for significant increases in sales over the next three years.

McMurphy's is located in the extreme northwest section of the downtown core district. Thus, this geographic area represents a huge potential market for McMurphy's lunch business, box lunches, and business functions.

Because McMurphy's is located in the core downtown business district, comprised mainly of white-collar professional persons, its ability to attract a lunch crowd is greater than for many other locations not in the downtown area. Thus, there is a significant potential market for McMurphy's services. It is also important to note that, "Consumers are spending 52 cents out of every dollar at restaurants and bars. This shift reflects the fact that there are more women in the work force and that convenience has become a major decision factor."

Consumer Attitudes and Demographics

McMurphy's Grill has the added attribute in that dining at McMurphy's brings the satisfaction of helping people become self-sufficient. While fast-food operations are marketed as "value" deals, restaurants that are moderately priced, like McMurphy's, are more likely to be considered an overall value by the consumer.

In terms of the business aspect, McMurphy's Grill certainly has a competitive edge that no other restaurant in the St. Louis community has. In addition to providing a quality meal and friendly service, this operation also offers its customer the satisfaction of knowing that they have contributed to helping someone achieve self-sufficiency. While other restaurant operations can compete more effectively by offering lower prices or boasting of quick service or providing a more elaborate atmosphere, none can compete directly with McMurphy's Grill's unique attribute -- its mission.

The Competition

McMurphy's large bright dining area, appealing decor, warm atmosphere, friendly service and homey meals set it apart from many of its competitors. It is also the only restaurant with outside seating, an important consideration among office workers on warm days. After being cooped up in an office all morning, people look for ways to get outside and enjoy the fresh air. The management is making plans to develop the small plot of land in front of the restaurant into a garden, which will add to the attractiveness of eating outside. It is also the only one with celebrity hosts (to be described in the Marketing Plan).

In regard to the private function market, competition is also extremely tight. Eleven facilities, located in the downtown area, advertise under Banquets/ Catering in the Yellow pages. Seven are hotels, three are restaurants and one is a non-traditional facility which has a facility rental of $750.00. This non-traditional facility will be eliminated in the analysis because it competes in an entirely different arena. McMurphy's can compete very effectively in terms of price as it has one of the lowest priced facilities for both a sit down meal and open bar event. Free parking and the privacy of being the only ones in the establishment are other advantages afforded customers of McMurphy's evening functions. Its major limitation is in its capacity limits. It certainly cannot compete with the hotels in that regard. McMurphy's will need to highlight these attributes in its advertising and promotional programs.

McMurphy's is in the position to gain the support of many of its suppliers when promoting a special event or day. This is in large part because of McMurphy's overriding goal of employment and training for people working toward self-sufficiency. Unlike any of its competitors, McMurphy's Grill is a member of the following organizations which gives it credibility as a restaurant and networking capability:

☐ Downtown St. Louis, Inc.
☐ Missouri Restaurant Association
☐ St. Louis Convention & Visitors Commission

Only members of the St. Louis Convention and Visitors Commission will have direct access to scheduled conventions and can directly market to them. Thus McMurphy's can directly target any potentially large conventions through direct mail as well as publicly via material at the Convention Center.

Transitional Training/ Employment Industry

Description and Size of Industry

McMurphy's Grill does not focus on individuals only with mental illness, which alone complicates a person's ability to function independently within the community, but those who are also homeless. It is difficult to assess the number of people who are homeless and mentally-ill. According to the National Resource Center on Homelessness and Mental Illness, "an estimated one-third of single, homeless adults have severe and disabling mental illness, and that as many as half of homeless persons with mental illnesses also have alcohol and/ or drug problems." Many are unemployed and have few or no employment skills that will enable them to earn a living wage. Vocational Rehabilitation Programs and other related agencies tend to inhibit the participation of this population due to their many regulations and lack of models which meet the specific needs of this population.

The continuum of services provided by St. Patrick Center for individuals with mental illness and substance addictions, of which McMurphy's Grill is a key component, is consistent with the psychiatric rehabilitation model. Current research points to the success rate of psychiatric rehabilitation as an effective and cost-efficient treatment for persons with serious and persistent mental illness. The psychiatric rehabilitation model emphasizesactivities which are integrated into the normal life of the individual and the community.

In St. Louis, two other agencies are recognized for their efforts, at the community level, with people suffering from mental illness, Independence Center and Places For People also utilize this general psychiatric rehabilitation model. The need for psychiatric rehabilitation programs is far greater than what the existing programs in St. Louis can address. McMurphy's Grill has provided training and employment skills, along with the other supportive services offered by St. Patrick Center, for sixty-seven individuals since the inception of this program in December of 1990. Thirty percent have been employed in the community in a variety of positions. A total of 36 percent, which includes the 20 individuals employed, have moved into more stabilizing situations. Places for People reports that "21 percent of all clients surveyed worked at sometime during the year examined (July 1, 1992 through June 30, 1993)." Independence Center was not able to track clients beyond the initial supported work environment and so statistics are not available. Thus, from the available data, McMurphy's Grill appears to be the most effective in terms of permanent solutions.	Competition

In comparing the efficiency of McMurphy's Grill Employment Training component with other similar programs, in terms of the cost of the training program, McMurphy's is certainly competitive. The Fountain House program, of which Independence Center is a branch, reports that their cost of training is $30.00 per day, per client. McMurphy's Grill projections for 1995 indicate that the cost of training will be $21.00 per day, per client. By 1997, this number will be significantly reduced as a result of the operating profit from the restaurant business which will be used to offset the training portion of these costs. Appendix B presents this analysis.

There is very little competition among providers of programs for the mentally ill homeless. All providers agree that there is no competition for clients/members. In fact, most would agree that there are more clients than can be served by the existing programs. The two other providers work cooperatively with St. Patrick Center in an effort to deal more effectively with this population. Information and ideas are shared, and collaborative efforts are organized.

The only source of competition is in terms of funding. However, even here the competition is minimal. Independence Center and Places For People rely heavily on the State Department of Mental Health for some of their other programs,

McMurphy's Grill is strictly funded through corporate grants and private contributions. Except for Neighborhood Assistance Tax Credits through the State Department of Economic Development which has been used to offset rental costs at the outset and to help facilitate the contribution of the building which houses McMurphy's Grill, no government funds are used in the operation.

STRATEGIC PLAN

McMurphy's Grill houses two functional organizational units. Each is viewed as distinct, but interrelated. The Restaurant Business component operates to employ persons from the second functional unit, the Employment Training component.

Because of the distinct nature of each component, separate strategic plans have been developed. The close integration of these two units requires a third step which links the two and provides operational guidelines which assist in the efficient and effective management of McMurphy's Grill.

McMurphy's Grill: The Business Unit

Mission: To maintain a viable business operation in order to employ participants of the Employment Training Program.

Description of Product Services

Lunch Business

McMurphy's offers three primary services. First, McMurphy's Grill is a full-service limited menu restaurant located in downtown St. Louis. It is open from 11:00 a.m. to 3:00 p.m. and serves a hearty lunch of traditional American cuisine, with an Irish flair, at a modest price (prices on the menu range from $3.00 to $7.00). The menu, while limited, offers a wide range of soups, sandwiches, salads, entrees, plus daily specials. By offering moderate prices and reasonably quick service (a customer can be in and out within 60 minutes), McMurphy's is attractive to those individuals who like a home-cooked meal, but who are limited somewhat by time. In order to attract more of the business community and improve on McMurphy's "value" image, the menu has been revised. The changes reflect both a surface change in terms of design, but also adds side dishes to some of the entrees. This makes the meals more appealing to the value-oriented consumer.

The same homey, tasty meals are available for carry-out as well, which can be phoned in or faxed prior to being picked up. Takeout remains the driving force behind industry growth and continues to offer expansion opportunities for foodservice operators. Thus, it is extremely important that the carry-outs continue to be emphasized in the marketing efforts since the trend in lunch traffic is away from long lunch hours.

Its appeal as a restaurant have been favorably noted by restaurant critics and customers alike. The large bright dining area, appealing decor, warm atmosphere and homey menu make McMurphy's a far superior dining experience than most of its nearest competition. Because McMurphy's Grill falls into the "moderate" price range, it is considered more of a value by the customer than fast-food operations or those establishments whose price per person is over $10.00.

Box lunches are another service available from McMurphy's Grill. For a reasonable price of $6.50, McMurphy's box lunch menu offers a variety of sandwiches, salads and combo's for business and organizational meetings. The current box lunch menu has previously only included sandwiches. In order to be more attractive to the business community, McMurphy's box lunches now include more options. Recommendations for these changes came from people in the business community whose firms are potential customers. Delivery of both the box lunches and the carryouts is a must in this industry. McMurphy's currently delivers box lunch orders of 10 or more. In the near future, McMurphy's will need to establish a full delivery service for carryouts as well as box lunches.

Box Lunches

Lunch sales, including box lunches, have represented approximately 80 percent of total sales. Box lunches have represented less than one percent of the total sales until in March of 1994 when sales for box lunches skyrocketed because of one very large order. For the first quarter of 1994, box lunch sales represented 5 percent of the total sales and lunch business represented 78 percent.

The restaurant is also available for private functions every evening and on weekends. Cocktail parties, hors d'oeuvres and full-service dinners are offered. Prices for a cocktail party range from $7.95 per person (for up to 3 hours of open bar) to $8.95 per person (for 4 hours or more). Hors d'oeuvres prices range from $4.95 per person to $8.95 per person, depending upon the selection of options. Full course meals range from $11.50 per person to $16.50 per person. Functions with personalized menu items are also welcomed, but prices will vary with items requested. For the first quarter of 1994, sales in this area represented approximately 17 percent of total sales.

Private Functions

The characteristics of McMurphy's customers differ whether we are discussing the lunch business, the boxed lunch business or the party business. Each has its own unique characteristics. However, they all encompass supporters of St. Patrick Center as well as individuals and groups who are unfamiliar with the restaurant's primary mission.

Target Customer

Marketing Plan

The overall goal of McMurphy's Grill marketing strategy is to increase the number of employment training opportunities in order to expand the number of clients participating in and moving through the program. In order to accomplish this goal, however, the restaurant component must be a viable operation so as to employ persons from the employment training component. The following objectives have been identified by management as targets:

❑ Begin realizing an operating profit by the end of 1997 by:
❑ Increasing lunch time customer traffic by 40 percent over a three year period.
❑ Increasing the number of private functions and catering events by 2 1/2 times the current level over the next three years.
❑ Increase dollar sales by:
  ♦ 30 percent in Year 1 (1995)
  ♦ 20 percent in Year 2 (1996)
  ♦ 20 percent in Year 3 (1997)
❑ Institute a motivational compensation program for the restaurant manager and the kitchen manager.

❑ Increase public awareness of McMurphy's Grill and its mission.

The management of McMurphy's Grill has been busily making plans for marketing the various services offered by the restaurant (i.e. lunch, boxed lunches, and parties). At the same time, they have already begun making some changes in the environment to enhance the decor by changing the curtains and adding new tablecloths. In addition, the bar has been reorganized which has improved its appearance and helped the efficiency of the operation. Table groupings have been rearranged so as to increase the number of tables for two. In the past, most of the tables had been set up in groups of four. Since more customers arrive in groups of two, rearranging the tables helps to eliminate wasted space.

Future plans include both short term and long term efforts to assist the Restaurant in achieving its goals of increased sales.

Financial Plan

McMurphy's previous financial history can certainly leave one wondering about its future. Sales have decreased while costs have increased. However, there is much information gleamed from these results that can be channeled into a brighter future.

As one glances at the history and then at the future based on new sales results, it is obvious that much depends upon the level of sales an operation is able to achieve. Most of McMurphy's expenses are fixed, therefore the higher the sales level the better the bottom line.

To achieve the objectives outlined in the marketing plan, it is important to understand some of the financial data and assumptions which led to the arrival of these target levels. A 40 percent increase by the end of year three would increase the average number of customers to 97 per day. This is not unrealistic, considering that the management has made plans to reduce the size of the bar which would increase its capacity of 28 seats. The seating capacity would then be 108 instead of 80.

The current breakdown between lunch sales and sales from private functions is approximately 80 percent lunch and 20 percent parties. This certainly demonstrates the significance of the lunch business. However, growth in the lunch business is not as great as in the private function business, due in part to capacity limits as well as the time frame for lunch. Thus, the future sales breakdown is more likely to resemble: 70 percent lunch and 30 percent parties.

The increase in the number of parties and catering events is expected to more than double. This assumption is based on the fact that sales per party is averaging $750. At a sales level of $150,000, the sales from private functions is approximately $30,000 (maintaining our 80/20 breakdown as explained above). With the average sales per party at $750, the number of parties would be 40 per year. Transferring this analysis to the 1997 estimated sales level, but assuming a 70/30 breakdown, the sales from private functions would be $75,000. Assuming the average sales per party remains the same at $750, the number of parties would increase to 100. This is more than double the current level. Given the potential market of area firms, future convention traffic, and supporters of St. Patrick Center, management feels this is a feasible target. They also realize that a significant marketing effort must take place to achieve this goal.

The financial reports in the future will also reflect more detail. The current accounting procedure for St. Patrick Center will need to be adjusted in order to segregate out more detail, especially in terms of sales, various types of wages, and some operational expenses. The process should be in place for the start of the new fiscal year in July.

Mission: To select and assist appropriate clients in the process of attaining on-the-job skills that will assist them in becoming self-sufficient.

McMurphy's Grill: The Employment Training Unit

Description of Service

Along with other St. Patrick Center programs, McMurphy's Grill provides a continuum of services which moves the client from the street, receiving no services, to competitive employment and independence. The pre-training portion of this program begins with the selection of appropriate mentally ill homeless clients by counselors at Shamrock Club (one of St. Patrick Center's programs). These clients will complete a series of pre-training classes before placement at McMurphy's. Training includes, but is not limited to communication, self-esteem, personal hygiene, accepting criticism, coping with past problems, time management, and problem solving. Usually the first four classes (Self-Image; Behavior (Old and New); Making Choices; and Communication) are required before being placed at the restaurant. During the period in which the client is involved in the On-The-Job-Training portion of the program, the remaining four classes (Problem Solving: Saving Money/Goal Setting: Leisure Time Management/Personal Growth; and Budgeting Priorities) are offered once a week.

After the client has completed the first series of Pre-Employment Classes and before being placed into a position at the restaurant, an orientation is conducted by the Client Case Manager and individualized treatment plans are developed.

Clients are then assigned to an appropriate position at the restaurant and receive proper on-site training. This phase of training includes basic skills such as cleaning and mopping and can lead into more complex positions such as waiting. The client is encouraged to move on to competitive employment only when fully emotionally, psychologically, and socially ready to do so. The initial placement in the community will include careful monitoring by the Case Manager. Hopefully, independent employment is the end result.

Target Market

For the Employment Training component, the customer (or client trainee) is most often homeless and has symptoms of mental illness. Many also are recovering alcoholics or dealing with drug addictions. While most of our trainees are men, which is indicative of this population as a whole, there have been a few women in the program. They suffer from a variety of psychiatric illnesses and have been a part of The Shamrock Club, a day program for mentally ill homeless men and women, operated by St. Patrick Center.

While the prime target for this training program are persons who are homeless and mentally ill, if space is available clients from other programs offered by St. Patrick Center may also participate in this training program. Most are homeless, but without disabling psychiatric illnesses.

The following goals have been set in terms of the number of participants and the number who successfully become self-sufficient:

❑ 25 participants in 1995 with 10 successes
❑ 28 participants in 1996 with 12 successes
❑ 30 participants in 1997 with 14 successes

Financial Plan

The cost of the Employment Training component will be funded in part by the remaining corporate contributions as well as additional solicited funding. By 1997, profits from the restaurant business will help to defer a portion of these costs. Continued profits from the restaurant business segment will reduce these training costs, so that future expansion of this endeavor is likely.

Continued interest in this program from McDonnell Douglas Corporation has been received and the potential for further funding has been expressed. With this possible source of funding, coupled with St. Patrick Center's ability to raise funds, the employment training portion will be covered.

Perhaps the most important aspect of this strategic plan is in the operations and management of the endeavor. The management indirectly involved in the operating of the restaurant business component or the employment training component. It is vital that there be clear reporting relationships and expectations. It is also essential that both components work closely together to ensure the success of the client trainees.

As one of St. Patrick Center's programs, McMurphy's falls under the governance of the St. Patrick Center Board of Directors. The full board meets bi-monthly and the executive committee of the board meets on the odd months when the full board does not meet.

Six task groups have been organized, made up of board and staff members, to look at important issues facing the center in the future:

❑**Mission and Vision**: What should be our continuing mission and vision be for the next five years?
❑**Programs**: What programs will best meet the client needs?
❑**Organization and Staffing**: What are the ideal organization and staffing necessary to effectively serve our clients?
❑**Facilities**: What facilities will be needed to house these services?
❑**Revenue**: How will the revenue needs for the future be met?
❑**Board**: What should be our board composition?

Chosen by the board of directors, the executive director of St. Patrick's Center reports directly to the board and is responsible for the budget of over $1.8 million, a full-time/part-time staff of over 50 people and the effective management of thirteen programs.

The Director of Programs (Mental Health) and the Client Case Manager are responsible for the selection of appropriate clients, conducting the pre-employment classes and the orientation session, preparing individual treatment plans with the client/trainee, and providing support services (budgeting, help with locating housing, clothing, transportation, etc.).

The Client Case Manager directly monitors client progress through the training program, assessing the clients ability to move on. This position reports directly to the Director of Programs (Mental Health).

The Director of Programs (Mental Health) reports directly to the executive director and is involved with selection of appropriate clients. The Director also

OPERATIONS AND MANAGEMENT

supervises the Client Case Manager. A monthly report indicating client progress will be prepared for the executive director by the Director of Programs (Mental Health).

The Business Director is responsible for overseeing the operation of the restaurant business component of McMurphy's Grill. It is essential that this person have a significant background and experience in business. This person works very closely with the restaurant manager in the operation of the restaurant. This position, which reports directly to the executive director, also supervises the Marketing Consultant. Because the foodservice industry is so competitive, it is essential that the marketing effort by carefully monitored and progress noted.

The Restaurant Manager is responsible for the effective and efficient operation of the restaurant business component. This includes the training of client employees in their assigned restaurant positions, hiring other professional staff, as well as all that is involved in the daily operation of this facility. This position will report directly to the business director, who will work closely with the Restaurant Manager and his staff to ensure the viability of the operation.

Assisting the Restaurant Manager the Kitchen Manager. The Kitchen Manager is responsible for the efficient and effective operation of the kitchen facilities. Responsibilities include: ordering food and supplies, training client trainees at the various stations within the kitchen area, quality food preparation, suggesting new menu items, costing out menu items, and monitoring food waste. This position reports directly to the restaurant manager.

The Management Consultant coordinates activities with the restaurant manager and the business manager. The Management Consultant is directly responsible to the business director. Responsibilities include: preparation of a marketing plan along with an annual calendar of events; the organization, coordination and implementation of the marketing activities; establishing measurements to evaluate the effectiveness of various marketing efforts; and networking with various community organizations.

Operations

Weekly and Monthly management reports will be prepared and discussed at weekly and monthly staff meetings of those involved in this program. Problems will be identified and potential solutions discussed. Progress will be highlighted and noted for future plans. Currently, the staff meetings consist of the Restaurant Manager, the Kitchen Manager, the Director of Programs (Mental Health) and the Client Case Manager. In the future these meetings will also include the Business Director and the Marketing Consultant. This will assist in shoring up the fragmentation that exists and improving the communication process, which will help in assessing particular marketing efforts and keep everyone informed of future plans. All involved will have a better understanding of the performance of the entire operation, including the training process and the operations of the business. This will certainly improve the effectiveness and efficiency of the marketing efforts.

In addition, the following procedures need to be incorporated into the operations.

Responsibility of the Restaurant Manager. Inventory should be taken on a weekly basis and maintained via computer so that prices can be updated regularly and will require less time each week. At this time there is not a computer at McMurphy's, but the Executive Director and Director of Development at St. Patrick Center will seek donations of computer equipment.

Inventory

Responsibility of the Kitchen Manager. A listing of each menu item and the ingredients needed for each, along with their costs needs to maintained and updated regularly. This will assist the management in determining prices as well as evaluating cost of sales margin.

Meal Costing

Responsibility of the Restaurant Manager. To be completed on a daily basis and turned into the finance office at St. Patrick Center within two days. The receipts should be deposited daily as well.

Daily Receipts Report

Responsibility of the Restaurant Manager and St. Patrick Center's Finance Office. To be checked against ordered items and then sent over to St. Patrick Center to be paid. Price changes should be noted on the inventory list and entered with the next weeks inventory.

Invoices

Responsibility of the Restaurant Manager. In addition to the sales report, a report should be prepared summarizing the prime costs. A food statistic summary should also be maintained along with a summary of the daily productivity.

Daily Report

Responsibility of the Director of Finance/Administration. They include:

❑**Customer Count** Comparisons with previous years and periods
❑**Inventory Valuations and the determination of Gross Profit**
❑**Income Statement** To include a breakdown of the various products offered (lunch business, box lunches, carry-out, and parties). It should also include comparisons with previous years and prior periods.
❑**Annual Budget** To be compiled with the input of the restaurant manager, the kitchen manager, the Business Manager, and the Marketing Consultant.
❑**Labor Costs** With this item being such a large percentage of the operating costs, this expense needs to be carefully monitored by the restaurant management on daily, weekly, and monthly reports which are to be prepared for the Restaurant Manager and Business Director by the Finance Office.

Management Reports and Variance Report

Calendar of Events

Responsibility of the Marketing Consultant and (indirectly) the Business Director. A plan that includes specific promotional events and advertising efforts by month. An estimated cost of each event and ad should be identified. The plan should be evaluated monthly by the project team along with the Marketing Consultant and revised as necessary. This will help reduce the fragmentation that has existed and served to assist management in the preparation of the annual budget.

McMurphy's Grill Operations Report

Responsibility of the Business Director; to be prepared for the Executive Director. A periodic written report (monthly or quarterly) of progress, problems, and potential solutions for the review and updating of the executive director. Problems that need immediate attention will be dealt with separately and in a timely manner. Variances in budget projections, marketing program expectations, client progress, and specific measurable results of advertising efforts should be included.

MAJOR COMPETITORS: LUNCH BUSINESS

Le Dejeuner Deli & Bakery

Located next door to McMurphy's Grill, this newly opened deli is open Monday through Friday from 7:00 a.m. to 2:30 p.m. This small operation provides a variety of menu items at a somewhat lower price. Services include dining in, carry-out, boxed lunches and catering. However, the dining environment is definitely lacking in appeal and does not seem to draw the professional business person. Its carry-out and boxed lunch business may detract from McMurphy's Grill. The atmosphere prevents a significant competitive threat. It is only the nearness of its location that identifies it as a competitor.

The Shell Cafe

Located at 1221 Locust on the Main Floor of the Shell Building, The Shell Cafe is within four blocks of McMurphy's Grill. Open primarily during the lunch period, the prices are similar. However, the menu items do not have the "homemade" appeal that is characteristic of McMurphy's Irish stew, meatloaf platter, or chicken and noodles. Menu items include dinners (steak, fish, pasta, ham, beef and gyros) and a variety of sandwiches and salads.

The Missouri Bar & Grill

Located on north Tucker (701 N. Tucker), a couple of blocks from McMurphy's Grill, has a menu selection and prices comparable to McMurphy's. It also has a full bar (open until 2 a.m.). The outside of the restaurant has an attractive big, bright red awning, which is visible from far away. While similar in some ways to McMurphy's, The Missouri Bar and Grill primarily attracts people interested in the bar. It has the largest sales volume of any of the competition.

The St. Louis Fish Company

Located 2 blocks from McMurphy's Grill on Locust, the St. Louis Fish Company (a new addition to the downtown area) offers a unique menu listing. Open from

10:30 a.m. until 10:00 p.m. (Monday through Friday), this establishment offers: a lunch buffet for $2.99 per pound, and "All You Can Eat" Special for $5.99, and a Lunch Box Special for $2.50 which includes choice of fish plus one side order. This is in addition to the regular menu. Service is similar to the St. Louis Bread Company and thus does not include the full-service provided at McMurphy's.

The St. Louis Bread Company

The Saint Louis Bread Co. is considered a bakery/cafe that offers authentic breads, as well as croissants, muffins and pastries. Their advertisements usually focus on their "fresh" bread and pastries. However, their menu also includes cold sandwiches, salads and soups. Prices for their sandwiches range from $4.00 to $6.00 and each restaurant has a fax number for ordering. Since their service is similar to that of a fast-food restaurant, they capitalize on the "alternative" to burgers and fries by focusing on a quick and healthy meal.

DEE DEE's Deli

DEE DEE's Deli is an interesting establishment. Located at the corner of 10th Street and Washington Ave, three blocks from McMurphy's, it appears to be a "hole in the wall" from its very unattractive exterior and the interior is very drab and dark. However, it is usually full every working day. What makes it successful is a reputation based on good food, friendly service and a great price. They differ from the Saint Louis Bread Company in that they offer items that come from the grill. Burgers and charbroiled chicken are listed among the hot and cold deli sandwiches. The service makeup is practically identical to the St. Louis Bread Company. An average customer orders from a display menu and pays the cashier. They are then given a number to take back to their table. When the order is ready, an employee will bring it to the table. Everything else, from condiments to utensils, are self-service.

All of these operations are fairly small and (except for The Missouri Bar & Grill), are only open for lunch. They all offer boxed lunches. While specific data is unavailable on these competitor's sales levels and market share, it is reasonable to assume that each possesses less than one percent of the market share and that their annual sales level is well under the industry average of $429,000 for a tableservice operation. It would be safe to assume that most of them realize between $100,000 and $300,000 in sales annually. The Missouri Bar and Grill might be higher because of its longer hours, yet it would be safe to estimate that it recognizes less than the industry average because it is not a high traffic area.

Lastly, but certainly not least among the competitive issues, are those firms which provide an inside cafeteria for their employees. The Post-Dispatch and Mercantile Bank both have international cafeterias available for their employees. This certainly detracts from business as both are large employers within walking distance of McMurphy's Grill. Management will need to reduce the impact by appealing to the employees desire for a home cooked meal and the satisfaction that they are helping someone at the same time.

EMPLOYMENT TRAINING COST ANALYSIS

Financial data for this analysis is taken from the Pro Forma Income Statement found in Appendix P. Using the bottom line figures, which include both the operational profit/loss as well as the training costs involved, a picture of the true training costs can begin to materialize.

1995: Loss of $49,118 divided by 260 days of operation divided by the number of clients per day (which for this analysis we will assume to be 10) would derive a cost per client day of: $18.89

Utilizing a similar analysis, by taking the loss of $49,118 and dividing it by the expected success rate of 10 (success rate = clients/trainees who have completed the program and have gone on to attain self-sufficiency through employment) would derive a cost for each success of: $4,912

Utilizing this same analysis, by taking the loss of $49,118 and dividing it by the number of participants expected for 1995, of 25 would derive a cost per trainee of: $1,965

1996: Loss of $32,595 divided by 260 days of operation divided by 10 clients would derive a cost per client day of: $12.54

- ♦ Cost per success: $2,716 (based on 12 successes)
- ♦ Cost per trainee: $1,087 (based on 30 participants)

1997: Loss of $12,890 divided by 260 days of operation divided by 10 clients would derive a cost per client day of: $4.96

- ♦ Cost per success: $ 921 (based on 14 successes)
- ♦ Cost per trainee: $ 430 (based on 30 participants)

MENU

McMurphy's Grill is owned and operated by St. Patrick Center, a multi-service agency which addresses the needs of poor and homeless people in our community.

Through a generous grant from the McDonnell Douglas Foundation and the McDonnell Douglas Employees' Community Fund, along with the assistance and expertise of The Pasta House Company, McMurphy's Grill opened on Dec. 3, 1990. It serves as a training facility for homeless mentally ill individuals who wish to make positive changes in their lives.

Open Monday through Friday from 11 a.m. to 3 p.m., McMurphy's offers carry out service, box lunches, and private parties any evening or weekend. We invite you to become a part of this endeavor by visiting McMurphy's often and by telling others about us.

Thank you for your patronage.

	MENU...*continued*

Irish Clam Chowder 1.75/2.50	**Soups (Cup/Bowl)**
Soup of the Day 1.50/2.25	
Celtic Chili 1.95/2.95	

Fried Mozzarella Sticks 3.95	**Appetizers**
Toasted Ravioli 2.95	
Chicken Wings 3.95	
Homemade Irish Chips 2.95	
Handcut French Fries 1.25	
Onion Rings 2.95	

Side Salad 1.25	**Salads**
House Salad (Mixed Greens) 2.25	**(Your Choice of Dressing)**
Caesar Salad 3.50	
Caesar Salad w/chicken 4.95	
Chef Salad 4.50	

McMurphy's Deli 4.50	**Sandwiches**
Charcoal Broiled Chicken 4.50	
Hamburger 3.95	
Cheeseburger 4.50	
Sirloin Strip Steak 5.95	
Corned Beef 4.50	
Roast Beef 4.50	
Breaded Fish 4.50	

Meat Loaf with Potatoes and Fresh Vegetables 5.95	**Specialties**
Irish Stew (with Beef) served with Irish Soda Bread 4.95	
Fresh Steamed Vegetables served with Garlic Butter 4.75	

Bowl of the Soup of the Day w/House Salad 3.75	**Soup and Salad**
Cup of Soup of the Day & 1/2 Sandwich	
Choice of Roast Beef or Deli 4.00	
House Salad & 1/2 Sandwich	
Choice of Roast Beef or Deli 4.25	
Low-cal Chicken with Side Salad & Vegetables 6.25	

Ask about our Daily Specials and Light Entrees!	**Daily Specials**

Bailey's Irish Cream Cake 2.75	**Desserts**
Ask about our Daily Dessert Specials!	

TARGET CUSTOMER ANALYSIS

Lunch Business

The lunch customer tends to be a professional person, approximately equal distribution between men and women, who work within walking distance of McMurphy's Grill. Observation by the management points to the speculation that most are in mid-level management positions. Three factors support this observation. First, most are wearing business suits or dresses that reflect a professional position. Secondly, they have the leeway to enjoy a more leisurely lunch and are not bound by a time clock. Thirdly, their incomes or expense accounts seem to equate with mid-level positions since McMurphy's Grill is a medium-priced establishment. Numerous other nearby options, which are much lower priced, are available. While not in the direct vicinity, higher priced establishments that are equated with a higher status are also easily accessible from anywhere in the downtown arena and usually have better parking facilities.

A much smaller portion of the lunch business are customers who come to support St. Patrick Center and the Mission of McMurphy's Grill. This group includes professional people working in the area, employees of other nonprofit or religious organizations, and other individuals who are either downtown shopping or in the area for a business appointment.

McMurphy's carry-out service tends to draw mostly business workers in the local area. Usually, the order is for more than one person. It is a growing business segment and certainly consistent with the lunch time trend of shorter lunch periods. By offering free delivery and soliciting orders through a series of discount coupons, McMurphy's expects to significantly increase this portion of the lunch business. Previously, McMurphy's has not tracked this aspect of the lunch business, but will do so in the future.

Other groups and individuals that McMurphy's Grill hopes to target more effectively in the future include:

❑ Tour guides and their groups.

❑ People attending special events (i.e. St. Patrick Day parade, Olympic Festival and Cardinal Baseball games).

❑ Convention and Tourist Traffic. With the Cervantes Convention Center only two blocks away, this market seems to be a perfect opportunity to increase business. However, to be able to do this, McMurphy's Grill needs to be open when it is compatible with the particular convention's schedule. This may not be feasible or profitable for every convention.

The boxed lunch business usually attracts the following groups:

❑Nonprofit and other charitable organizations. Groups that have consistently ordered from McMurphy's Grill are United Way, Cardinal Glennon Hospital and the Girl Scouts of America.

❑Religious organizations, including churches, religious congregations and schools.

❑Business Meetings. An area that McMurphy's would like to increase.

The boxed lunch business needs to be more aggressively marketed to all of the above target markets, especially to the business community. Appendix F depicts a possible advertisement for the box lunches along with the revised menu which has been recommended. These revisions reflect additional options which make it more appealing to those in the business community as well as other organizational groups.

This particular segment of the operation has the most diverse customer base and realizes the largest contribution margin. McMurphy's Grill has been the site of wedding rehearsal parties, birthday parties, anniversaries, holiday parties (especially during the Christmas season), business meetings, art shows, fund raisers, and a variety of other gatherings. Customers learn about McMurphy's Grill from a variety of sources, most however are familiar with the restaurant's mission and desire to support its efforts. There have been other groups who were looking for space to have a party and have been steered to McMurphy's Grill by supporters or other people familiar with McMurphy's quality, service and lower cost. Management intends to focus more on this segment of its operation, recognizing that the private party business is the aspect of the business which will most help the operation research, or at least come much closer, to its break-even point.

Private Parties

MARKETING STRATEGY

Remodeling

In order to increase capacity, so as not to discourage those coming for lunch on days that the restaurant is full and to improve McMurphy's ability to attract lunch business meetings, McMurphy's Grill is planning to reduce the size of its bar. The bar business at McMurphy's is negligible during the lunch hour. By cutting the bar in half, which leaves sufficient space in which to service small group meetings, a new room could be created which would increase capacity by 28 seats. The benefits of this improvement, aside from those mentioned above, are additional party seating and/or cocktail area. Bar area will be easier to maintain and more inviting for customers to sit at. In addition, there is the potential for two groups to use McMurphy's Grill in the evening. The estimated cost for this, including reorganizing the serving area, would be $5,300. The restaurant manager has already solicited bids for some of the work.

Improvements to the kitchen area which would help to make the operation more efficient and the service better, include the addition of a six burner stove, a 48-inch grill, shelving, a salad window, and improvements to the dishwashing area. The cost of these changes would be approximately $1,850.

Note: The benefits are hard to estimate for items 1 & 2 above, however, in terms of the lunch business alone this increase in capacity could potentially realize a gross profit of $33,124 (based on an average check of $7.00 and full capacity every day). The assumption of full capacity is probably unreasonable considering that currently the restaurant is only filling, on the average, 69 seats per day or 86 percent of its current capacity. However, if other marketing efforts continue to improve the customer traffic, as has the Celebrity Hosts Program (sales are up 20 percent over 1993), then this assumption is not totally unrealistic.

Advertising

A large sign or printed awning that would better identify the location of McMurphy's Grill from Eleventh Street. Currently, the name is not visible until you have already passed the location. This issue is currently under consideration.

Marketing

Parking, which has been a headache from the beginning, has a significant impact upon sales. The Executive Director, the Board of Directors and the staff of this program have been working on this problem. Thus far, McMurphy's Grill has succeeded in getting the City of St. Louis to add additional parking meters along Eleventh and Lucas Streets. Management is in the process of talking with lot owners in the vicinity (of which there are several) and negotiating an arrangement whereby customers from McMurphy's can park at a reduced rate and that we can be guaranteed a particular number of parking spaces.

Develop a customer evaluation/survey for all of various services offered by McMurphy's. A recommended customer evaluation/survey for McMurphy's lunch business has been included in Appendix H. Request suggestions for improvements from customers or potential customers. Periodically invite members of the Board of Directors or other interested supporters to have lunch at McMurphy's to evaluate the quality of the food and service.

ADVERTISING AND PROMOTION RECOMMENDATIONS

McMurphy's Grill has had an added advantage in this area as the operation receives a lot of free coverage, which has been beneficial. From articles on the restaurant by the *Post-Dispatch* to being featured on local radio and television McMurphy's has received a lot of free publicity. The most recent coverage in the February 1994 edition of *St. Louis Commerce*, continues to keep St. Patrick

Center and McMurphy's Grill in the mind of the St. Louis community. These efforts certainly help to increase the scope of McMurphy's Market potential by educating people as to its mission and location.

McMurphy's has recently implemented a Celebrity Hosts Promotion strategy, which has been extremely successful. Various local and state celebrities are featured each Wednesday at McMurphy's where they become the Celebrity Host for the day. Each is asked to provide names of guests to whom we can send a special invitation. This has the added advantage of increasing the restaurants mailing list for all major promotional events.

It is important that McMurphy's continue to keep its name in the forefront, both in terms of getting the message of what its mission is all about and to dispel some of the myths that may surface when discussing a project that involves the homeless mentally ill. It also doesn't hurt the bottom line by encouraging people to participate in this endeavor.

However, McMurphy's Grill long ago realized that it would never survive based solely on this type of exposure and so has aggressively advertised from the beginning. Except for a period of time after the founding Executive Director left and until the arrival of the newest Executive Director, advertising and promotion of the restaurant business has been on the forefront.

McMurphy's advertises regularly in Downtown Dollars, which is a flyer with a distribution of over 20,000 published on a monthly basis. In addition, McMurphy's occasionally advertises in the *St. Louis Business Journal* and *St. Louis Commerce*. Sometimes these are complementary adds. As a member of the St. Louis Convention & Visitors Commission, McMurphy's Grill can promote the restaurant business directly to convention traffic and tourists. McMurphy's is also listed in the National Restaurant Association Membership directory as well as among the members of Downtown St. Louis., Inc. Occasionally, an ad is run in the *St. Louis Review*, the Catholic newspaper of the Archdiocese of St. Louis. Finally, but certainly not least, is that McMurphy's Grill is usually cited in the *St. Patrick Center Chronicles*, a publication of St. Patrick Center published three times a year.

Direct mail is often used to notify supporters or other people on our mailing list about various promotional events at McMurphy's Grill. The mailings often focus on businesses downtown, supporters of St. Patrick Center, nonprofit organizations and other patrons of McMurphy's Grill. Postcards were sent out, for instance, promoting the Celebrity Hosts program. Appendix I provides a sample of what was sent out.

This effort has increased sales by 20 percent over last year during the same period. The list of willing celebrities continues to grow with the addition of a nationally known St. Louis artist. Recently, we have begun to get phone calls from leaders in the community interested in becoming a celebrity host. And this is only after two months of operation.

Continue the Celebrity Hosts Program

Add to the list of Celebrity Hosts, CEOs of major firms located in downtown St. Louis. This can have a significant impact sales from the business community. By inviting the top executives, who are likely to invite other significant people within their organization as well as other employees, McMurphy's reputation as a quality restaurant will spread. The business community will become better informed as to what McMurphy's Grill is all about.

Reinstitute Lunch of the Month Club

Set up a calendar of events and identify advertising and promotional efforts needed. Appendix K is a sample of some recommendations for the next year.

Make personal contacts with key personnel at local firms that are within walking distance to invite them to McMurphy's Grill for lunch. Offer free menu items to motivate them. The best person to identify within these local organizations are the secretaries.

Offer Sales Promotions for Frequent Diners

Revise boxed lunch menu to offer an upscale version to groups seeking a higher quality boxed lunch and who are willing to pay for it.

Offer special promotions for Secretaries Day, Boss's Day, Birthday's, etc.

Promote the anniversary of McMurphy's Grill through specials on the menu, printed advertisement, articles in a local publication, and a featured article in the St. Patrick Center Chronicles.

Advertise the availability of McMurphy's Grill for private functions in the evening or on weekends, by focusing on various wedding supply places, churches, local publications, with musicians or mobile DJ's, membership organizations (such as fraternities and sororities) and business firms in the downtown area.

Continue Responding to Convention and Visitor Commission Leads

Continual evaluation and re-focusing of these efforts is a must. By regular monthly meeting with the Marketing Consultant and better communication efforts regarding the business side of the operation, these efforts should prove to be effective and more efficient than past efforts.

	Final FY92	Final FY93	FY94 YTD
Sales:			
Food & Beverage	$167,369	$146,392	$88,203
Cost of Sales:			
Food & Beverage	65,170	52,422	34,175
% Of Sales	39%	36%	39%
Gross Profit Margin	102,199	93,970	54,028
Operating Expenses:			
Salaries	81,79	177,929	59,246
P/R Taxes/Benefits	21,948	20,732	13,611
Utilities/Bldg Exp	9,707	22,79	29,068
Telephone	1,857	1,910	1,468
Supplies	12,713	16,900	69,452
Postage	266	0	856
Stationery/Pstg	912	195	792
Equip Purchases	879	1,169	411
Depreciation	0	4,775	9,550
Repairs/Rent Equip	5,027	3,560	1,144
Local Transport	457	464	507
Advertising/Publicity	8,940	8,170	5,394
Business Svc's & Fees	7,820	13,845	3,985
Insurance	2,825	3,290	2,670
Membership Dues	125	325	275
Licenses & Permits	949	675	858
Aid to Individuals	0	250	20
Total Expenses	156,216	176,987	119,307
Net Profit (Loss)	($54,017)	($83,017)	($65,279)

**MCMURPHY'S GRILL
INCOME STATEMENT:
Fiscal Years 1992 - 1994**

Cash Flow: Designated Funds*

Balance as of 6/30/93	$142,648
Estimated loss for 1994	-97,919
Depreciation	+9,550
Balance as of 6/30/94	$54,279
Estimated loss for 1995	-49,118
Depreciation	+9,550
Balance as of 6/30/95	$14,711
Estimated loss for 1996	-43,095
Depreciation	+9,550
Balance as of 6/30/96	$(8,334)
Estimated loss for 1997	-25,390
Depreciation	+9,550
Balance as of 6/30/97	$(11,674)

CASH FLOW CALCULATIONS

This assumes no increase in grant dollars.

FINANCIAL ASSUMPTIONS AND ANALYSIS

Pricing Strategy

McMurphy's Grill has a twofold pricing strategy. First, since McMurphy's prime objectives is its training opportunities, the flow of customers through the restaurant is essential. Customer volume is also important to the bottom line. Thus, the price must remain reasonable in order to attract customers. Many restaurant patrons, according to the National Restaurant Association sfudy, thought that medium priced restaurants provided the most value for their money. McMurphy's Grill falls into this category and thus is seen as a provider of value. It must also be competitive with other similar (limited menu tableservice) establishments.

Secondly, the prices must be at a level to cover variable operational costs as well as allow enough margin to cover fixed operational costs and help to defray the training costs involved. The training aspect incurs increases in personnel, employee benefits, food waste, and supply costs as a result of the learning curve -- which is likely to be higher than in other cases because of the turnover of trainees and their disability.

For the limited-menu tableservice establishment, the cost of food sold should be about 35 percent. The cost of food and beverage (wine, beer and other liquor) is usually around 29 to 32 percent. We can assume that 30 percent is a good average cost that McMurphy's should attempt to target. Reviewing the Income Statement for Fiscal Years 1992, 1993, 1994, which can be found in Appendix L, it can be seen that McMurphy's is higher than the average. Better inventory and waste control will assist with maintaining lower margins. The cost of sales will decrease as the party volume increases and more liquor is sold.

Thus, it is the goal of McMurphy's Grill to maintain a 30-32 percent cost of sales so that at least 68-70 percent of total sales goes toward operating expenses. Operating expenses, for foodservice establishments, tend to be rather high because of the amount of fixed assets involved. McMurphy's Grill is running high in this area, but management is in the process of assessing where the problems lie.

The kitchen manager and a volunteer at St. Patrick Center are also in the process of conducting a food cost analysis. Once this has been completed, it will be maintained and evaluated periodically with the restaurant manager. To facilitate this process, the analysis will be computerized so that it can be updated as prices change.

Sales

While sales levels have fallen since FY 1992, much can be attributed to the change in management at St. Patrick Center. Initially, the original Executive Director was heavily involved in marketing McMurphy's Grill and had become rather successful. After she moved from St. Louis, her predecessor was not very active in the marketing of the restaurant business. In fact, during his stay as Executive Director, very little marketing was done. The Marketing Consultant was rarely communicated with and at that time, the Executive Director was the only one who could direct her activity.

In addition, very little financial reporting or control was taking place. With the recent change in the Executive Director position, these areas are being highlighted more intensely. It is recommended that responsibility for the marketing and business aspect of McMurphy's Grill be handed to a newly defined position of Business Director. This will be a new position and is currently not filled, but the responsibility for the Restaurant business should fall to the Finance and Administration Department in the mean time. Such an approach reflects a more effective business approach, rather than laying the responsibility for running a business to a Director of Programs. Just as it would be inappropriate to assign the responsibility of coordinating the training program to the Director of Finance/Administration, so the current approach does not reflect a strategic orientation toward growth. This is a key consideration for implementing an effectivestrategic plan which will realize growth in the business component.

Since the start of the Celebrity Hosts promotion, sales for the past two months are higher, by 20 percent, than for the same two months of 1993. The increase in sales from January and February, as is depicted in Appendix M (Calendar Year 1994 Sales Breakdown), is also significant. It is obvious from this picture that liquor is not a priority item during the lunch period, but is a significant portion of the total sales of private parties.

The customer count is also a significant factor as is illustrated in both Appendix M and Appendix N (Calendar Year 1994 Customer Count). Appendix N is a little more detailed and shows that the average number of customers per day is under the 80-seat capacity that currently exists. For a restaurant like McMurphy's, the average daily seat turnover was 1.8 (this includes operations that are open for both lunch and dinner) and the median check was $6.48. McMurphy's daily seat turnover, using the data from the last two months, is .86 and the average check amount is $7.11. The large jump in the number of customers per day from January to February reflect growth as well. This picture also shows that Wednesday is by far the biggest day. This is not surprising as this is the day the celebrity hosts are with us. Thursdays and Fridays seem to also be good days. This is helpful information when considering other promotional activity.

Information such as in Appendix M and N are not available for the prior years so as to better make comparisons. In the future, however, this type of information will be maintained and reviewed on a regular basis. The usefulness of this information is beyond saying in making day-to-day decisions in any business environment.

Pro Forma projections of sales are based on the marketing goals of a 30 percent increase in the first year; a 20 percent increase in the second year; and a 20 percent increase in the third year. Also taken into consideration has been the breakeven point. For the 1995, 1996 and 1997 sales projections, the following breakeven points exist:

♦ 1995: $198,197
♦ 1996: $203,298
♦ 1997: $208,058

The variable costs used in calculating these breakeven points includes cost of sales, supplies and advertising. All other items are assumed to be fixed. The costs involved in the training component have not been included in this analysis. It is anticipated that McMurphy's Grill will breakeven after year two (1996). It is well on its way to success. Refer to Appendix S for the complete Breakeven Analysis.

Cost of Sales

The Historical Income Statement reflects that McMurphy's Grill is achieving a 39 percent Cost of Sales, which is higher than the industry's average of about 35 percent. It must be noted that these numbers do not reflect inventory changes. For the past year and a half no inventory records have been kept and until very recently inventories had not been taken for some time. For many food operations this is a major issue. In the future, management will ensure that inventories are taken on a regular basis. Thus, in the future, it is reasonable to assume that McMurphy's Grill will be able to maintain the industry average of 35 percent cost of food and an overall cost of sales in the range of 30 percent.

Operating Expenses

It is rather obvious, when looking at Appendix L (Historical Income Statement), that the Operating Expenses are where much of the problem is. The high level of operating expenses can in part be attributed to the high salaries/wages. The number of employees working is far more than a regular operation would utilize. In fact, an operation the size of McMurphy's might have four people working in addition to the Manager and the Kitchen Manager. For McMurphy's, the number is usually around ten people. Thus, in the Pro Forma Income Statements (Appendix O and P) the cost of training has been deducted from the Operating Expenses and noted separately to give a better reflection of the restaurant operation's performance.

In reviewing some of the operating expenses for 1993 and 1994 it was obvious that expenses for the entire building had been charged to McMurphy's Grill. The building, which had been donated in 1993, has two other floors (one of which had been occupied for a part of 1993) which can be rented out for office space. This practice, of charging the entire building's expenses to McMurphy's, had been at the direction of the Executive Director. This practice has been reversed with the arrival of a new Executive Director and so for FY 1994 an attempt was made to deduct expenses, or a portion of them, that did not directly relate to the operation of the restaurant.

An attempt has also been made to better organize these categories for the sake of industry comparisons in the Pro Forma statements. In the preparation of the Pro Forma Income Statements, an attempt was also made to review expense items with industry averages and as a result reduce some line items. In the past,

budgets have been prepared based solely on historical data without consideration for what might be reasonable for a restaurant operation the size of
McMurphy's Grill. Appendix P depicts line items as a percentage of sales, which
will be useful in making future decisions. For the most part, the Pro Forma
Projections are in line with the industry averages or are at least heading that
direction. Appendix P (Pro Forma Income Statements -- 3 year summary)
highlights this point when looking at the Operating Expenses as a whole. As
a percentage of sales, these expenses are decreasing significantly over the next
three years. The industry average indicates that Operating Expenses usually
average about 53.4 percent of sales. At least now, McMurphy's is heading in
the right direction. It is recommended that management continue to review
industry averages in the future for a better understanding of its performance and
to stay ahead of its competition.

One last note, most of the fixed expense projections reflect an inflation rate of
approximately 3.5 percent. Variable expenses are somewhat less that the
expected changes in sales, but much higher than the 3.5 increase per year applied
to most of the fixed expenses.

Income Taxes

Because McMurphy's Grill is a part of a nonprofit entity and any profit that is
reaped will be channeled back into the program or into the programs at St. Patrick
Center, no income taxes will need to be paid. This assumption flows throughout
all the financial analyses.

Balance Sheet Cash Flow

Finally, a few notes about the Balance Sheet and a further explanation of
McMurphy's Cash Flow assumptions. Appendix Q presents the Pro Forma
Balance Sheet. Because McMurphy's Grill is categorized as a nonprofit
operation, things are presented in a somewhat different manner. Fund Balances
reflect what a for-profit organization would consider Owners Equity.

The Balance Sheet reflects very little activity because the accounting procedures for St. Patrick Center and McMurphy's Grill implement a cash-based
system. While some of the parties are on a receivable basis, they are usually
collected within a month. The same can be said about the payables. Invoices
are paid as they are received. Cash flow is not a significant issue for St. Patrick
Center or McMurphy's because of its large resource base and so the timing of
receivables and payables is not a problem.

On the balance sheet, the cash reflects the balance of a grant received from
McDonnell Douglas as well as other smaller contributions at the outset of this
project. Further contributions will be solicited as these funds run out, primarily
to cover the cost of training. The property and equipment line reflect a portion
of the contribution of the Lucas Plaza building. Thus is seen as an asset for the
restaurant as no rental payments must be paid out, thus it is important that it be
documented. This valuation is one-third of the total value of the building, land
and equipment that had been contributed. Depreciation has been deducted for
the building and the equipment.

Balance Sheet Cash Flow
...continued

The cash flow, as seen in the cash line, takes into consideration the declining designated fund balance as a result of restaurant losses. Keep in mind that St. Patrick Center has been extremely successful at fund-raising and is confident that it can receive corporate support to cover the cost of training. However, because we have included depreciation in the expenses, which is not a cash item, it has been added back in to reflect a non-cash item. The loss which was used in this calculation was the Operating Loss and thus does not include the reduction of the loss by the amount of the training costs. Refer to Appendix R for a review of Cash Flow projections.

Restaurant (Nonprofit)*

BUSINESS PLAN

McMurphy's* Grill

St. Patrick's Center
1200 6th St.
St. Louis MO 63106
(314)621-1283

*Revised September 1995

This business plan has not been disguised in any way. It is the revised version of the plan that appears before it. Due to its nonprofit nature, this business is subject to different stresses than the average restaurant. However, it has achieved significant strides and is an example of a venture whose success is due in part to the clarity of the original strategic business plan. Successes resulting from initiatives outlined in the previous plan are discussed here.

- ●EXECUTIVE SUMMARY

- ●THE COMPANY AND THE CONCEPT: A YEAR IN REVIEW

- ●HIGHLIGHTS OF YEAR ONE

- ●THE EMPLOYMENT TRAINING UNIT

- ●MCMURPHY'S GRILL INCOME STATEMENT

EXECUTIVE
SUMMARY

With the fifth anniversary of the opening of McMurphy's Grill fast approaching, there is much reason to celebrate. As a result of a successful implementation of the Strategic Business Plan, developed in the Spring of 1994, sales are up over 42 percent and the number of customers per day has increased 21 percent. In addition, cost of sales (as a percentage of sales) has declined 4 percentage points. While operating expenses increased 18 percent, primarily as a result of efforts to increase sales revenue, it did not increase at the same rate as sales, thus contributing to the improvement in the profitability of the operation.

Opening its doors on December 3rd, 1990, McMurphy's has set about the task of making people without homes, but with diagnostic psychiatric labels, into food servers and cooks. Without a profitable business, or at least reasonable loss, the mission of McMurphy's will not be achieved. Prior to the development of this Strategic Business Plan, the business was experiencing a serious trend over the previous few years of declining sales and increasing costs. Over the past year, significant strides have been made to reverse these trends and improve the viability of the operation.

Perhaps the most difficult task an endeavor of this kind faces is to be able to balance both sides of the coin -- the mission and the business. An organization's focus on its prime objective can easily be lost in the day to day operation of the business. While the business aspect has experienced significant growth, the Employment Training component has not achieved desired results. A better balance will be the focus of the coming year.

The staff of both McMurphy's Grill and St. Patrick Center have worked closely to successfully implement many of the components of the original Strategic Business Plan as well as initiate other ideas. A review Fiscal Year 1995 reflects the initiative, creativity, and dedication of the staff.

THE COMPANY AND
THE CONCEPT: A
YEAR IN REVIEW

McMurphy's Grill, a restaurant located at the corner of Lucas and Eleventh streets in downtown St. Louis, will celebrate five years in operation on December 3rd, 1995. Considering the significant decline in sales and continual increase in costs during the three years prior to 1994, management recognized the need to develop a plan of action aimed at reversing these trends. In the Spring of 1994 a comprehensive strategic business plan was developed with implementation beginning with the start of the new fiscal period, July 1, 1994. After one year the results of the successfully implemented plan have far exceeded most of the goals originally established in the plan:

❑ A 42 percent increase in total dollar sales -- compared with a projected increase for year one of 30 percent

❑ A 4 point actual drop {a 10% improvement} in cost of sales

❑ Operating expense increased only 18 percent over Fiscal Year 1994 compared with the 42 percent increase in sales

While operating as a competitive establishment, McMurphy's prime focus is on teaching homeless individuals, many suffering from mental illness, skills in food preparation as well as the restaurant service. Owned and operated by St. Patrick Center, a multi-service nonprofit agency providing a variety of services for homeless and low-income people in St. Louis. This innovative transitional employment program has provided an opportunity for 86 men and women, thus far, to learn valuable employment skills.

This first year of implementation of the strategic business plan has noted significant improvements in the profitability of the restaurant business. The operation of McMurphy's Grill provided a major challenge to the staff of St. Patrick Center, whose primary expertise has been in the social service arena. Several factors have contributed to this challenge, including changes in the management personnel at McMurphy's and the administration at St. Patrick Center, prior to the written strategic plan. These personnel changes, without a written direction, had a significant impact on the operations of the restaurant. In addition, the Restaurant Business component lacked the involvement of someone with business knowledge in the day-to-day operation of the facility. This resulted in a lack of emphasis on the business aspect of McMurphy's. Another major factor affecting the operation of the restaurant was the reality that McMurphy's Grill is only one of St. Patrick Center's 14 programs and thus does not have the concentrated effort that many small restaurant operators employ.

While not totally eliminating the challenges faced by St. Patrick Center in its operation of McMurphy's Grill, the in-depth strategic business plan has made them manageable. This business plan focused primarily on the operational aspects of McMurphy's Grill, defining McMurphy's as two distinct, but interrelated functional organizational units: one being the Restaurant Business component and the other being the Employment Training component. This separation has helped to get a clearer picture of each component, but most especially the restaurant business. The revised organizational structure has improved communication and shored-up reporting procedures, thus contributing to better management of the restaurant business component. Clearly defined marketing and financial objectives have generated creative initiatives which have resulted in expanded opportunities.

Lacking in emphasis during this past year, however, has been the Employment Training component. An incentive program developed for the manager and kitchen manager, focuses on improved sales, reductions in cost of sales and the overall profitability of the operation. This has resulted in less effort being extended to the training process and a slower movement of trainees through the program in order to maintain a more stable and efficient workforce -- resulting in personal financial gains for McMurphy's manager and kitchen manager. Recognizing the problem presented by the newly established incentive program, an added dimension to the incentive program being developed for the coming fiscal year will encompass the training aspect. It is hoped that this will achieve a better balance, thus ensuring that the mission of McMurphy's Grill is maintained.

THE COMPANY AND THE CONCEPT: A YEAR IN REVIEW
...continued

**HIGHLIGHTS OF
YEAR ONE
Industry and Market
Analysis**

McMurphy's Grill falls into two major industry classifications. As a competitive restaurant, McMurphy's Grill falls into the foodservice industry. As a facility which provides employment and training for mentally ill homeless persons and those recovering from substance addictions, McMurphy's can be classified among the vocational rehabilitation programs.

Both industries have remained fairly consistent over the past year, with little changes in either market. Three points which have possible future impacts, however, are worth noting:

1. With a football team having been secured and completion of the new football stadium in sight, prospects of opening on Sunday during home games is under serious consideration. Being located within three blocks of the new football stadium gives McMurphy's an added advantage over many of its competitors.

2. The LeDejeuner Deli and Bakery, McMurphy's closest competitor, has closed its doors. This facility has assumed many names and been operated by various business operators, without success. This reduces, to some degree, the direct competition for both the lunch time business as well as for box lunches.

3. With the threat of funding cuts looming at the federal level, McMurphy's Grill is in a better position than most of its competitors in respect to its Employment Training component. With not having to rely on federal or state funds, McMurphy's is in a position to survive the ax. The endeavor may face, however, increased competition for private resources which may have a significant impact on its continued survival.

**Strategic Plan:
A Year in Review**

McMurphy's Grill, as previously noted, houses two functional organizational units: the Restaurant Business component and the Employment Training component. Each is viewed as distinct, but interrelated. As defined in the original strategic business plan, the mission of the Business component is:

To maintain a viable business operation in order to employ participants of the Employment Training Program.

Because of the distinct nature, however, of each component, separate strategic plans were developed. However, the Operations and Management section has served to link the units, providing operation guidelines which have resulted in improved management and efficiency. Successful implementation of the plans have achieved enormous results, however, some of the planned actions have been revised while others have been delayed or eliminated.

**The Restaurant
Business Unit**

The results of the past year have been tremendous:

❑ A 21 percent increase in the number of lunch customers per day from 69 customers per day to 83; strategic plan calls for averaging 97 per day by the end of year three
❑ Significant increases in revenue (over fiscal year 1994) derived from all three service areas:

LUNCH:	20 percent
BOX LUNCHES:	152 percent
PRIVATE FUNCTIONS:	76 percent

Specific actions which led to the successful accomplishment of the established goals and objectives flowed out of the targeted goals and action steps outlined in the written strategic business plan.

Attractive New Menus were prepared for both the Lunch and Box Lunch business. With a new attractive cover, for which a donation of the design was secured, the menu depicts a few new items and selective increases in the prices.

Marketing

The Celebrity Host Program continues to expand with an increase in the number of CEO's and other top level executives joining the ranks. Being given much of the credit for the reversal of the prior trends in Lunch revenue, the Celebrity Host program has had the additional impact of increasing the revenue derived from Box Lunches and Private Functions. There has been an increase of 50 percent in lunch business on Wednesdays, which is the day designated for Celebrity Hosts.

Regular Marketing Meetings are now conducted every other week to discuss upcoming events and strategies as well as to assess the previous two weeks marketing efforts. Personnel involved in these meetings include:

• McMurphy's Grill manager and kitchen manager
• St. Patrick Center's Business Director (who is now responsible for the supervision of the Restaurant Business operation).
• A member of St. Patrick Center's Board of Directors (and former Executive Director of St. Patrick Center)

Significant Increases In Revenue Derived From Private Functions can be attributed to:

Marketing Consultant

1. An increase in direct-mail efforts targeted at specific audiences, particularly church groups and lists of friends and co-workers submitted by each Celebrity Host.

2. A "Show-Me" party, held in the fall, which provided an opportunity for potential patrons to experience the food, atmosphere, and service offered by McMurphy's Grill. A second "Show-Me" party is planned for this fall.

The Schedule of Events (Marketing Efforts) was reduced to focus on specific areas each Quarter:

Quarter 1 of FY 1995:	Focused on Celebrity Hosts program
Quarter 2 of FY 1994:	Focused on Private Functions; resulted in an increase of 80% over 1993 calendar year
Quarter 3 of FY 1995:	Focused on Box Lunches
Quarter 4 of FY 1995:	Physical plant

Customer Evaluation Surveys have been used on occasion with very positive responses. They will continue to be used periodically in order to maintain a high level of customer satisfaction.

Advertising Media has remained fairly constant with articles being strategically placed in Downtown St. Louis Inc. A major source of free advertising during the past year has come about from press releases announcing each week's Celebrity Host.

Sales Promotions for Secretary's Day, St. Patrick's Day; special promotions welcoming employees of new businesses locating in the area and other special promotions continue to attract new business. A means of measuring response to specific promotions has not yet been developed, but observation suggests a positive reaction, although not coming close to the success that the Celebrity Host program has achieved.

Operations/Management

An Incentive System was developed and implemented during this first year. This system has been attributed with increasing the cooperation, efficiency and creative flow of ideas from McMurphy's manager and kitchen manager. The system is outlined below:

Incentive Compensation System

A competitive incentive compensation program was developed during fiscal year 1995 for the manager and kitchen manager of McMurphy's Grill. The system is a two-tier system based on increased Private Function business as well as improved overall results:

LEVEL 1: Both the manager and kitchen manager receive a percentage of the gross receipts from a Private Function (Private Parties).
      ○ The Manager receives 5 percent
      ○ The Kitchen Manager receives 4 percent
LEVEL 2: Overall Operations: This part of the compensation program was partitioned based on two components:
      ○ Sales (60%)
      ○ Expense (40%)

The incentive ranged from 0 percent up to 15+ percent for "Outstanding" performance, which was based on specific levels of sales and expense measurements. Thus, achieving the Outstanding level of sales would provide a 9 percent (15% x 60%) bonus of base salary. Similarly, Outstanding in Operating Costs (for the Restaurant Manager) or Food Costs (for the Kitchen Manager) would provide an additional 6 percent (15% x 40%) bonus based on the base salary. The incentive was paid quarterly based on projected annual performance.

Note: The fiscal year 1995 performance exceeded Outstanding overall for both managers.

Kitchen Facilities Reorganized in order to improve the efficiency and productivity of the operation. It also facilitates the increase in the number of customers served, especially on days when Celebrity Hosts are present.

McMurphy's Grill Staff Involved in the Budgeting Process. They are responsible for helping to establish financial targets in addition to defining action steps toward their accomplishment.

A Computerized Inventory System, along with other incentives, has helped to reduce the cost-of goods sold.

Supervision of the Restaurant Business has shifted to the Business Director which has helped to focus attention on the business side of things.

Increased Staffing for McMurphy's, in terms of management personnel, is another consideration faced by McMurphy's as business continues to increase. A full-time position has been added in order to meet increased demand for McMurphy's various services and to assist in the training of program participants.

Reduction of the Bar Area was completed in March. It provided a 20 percent increase in seating capacity (from 80 seats to 96 seats).

Plaza Upgrade is currently in process. Expanded outside seating in the plaza area will further increase the seating capacity on clement days.

A rough draft of a Meal Costing Report was developed prior to the new menu being printed. The Business Director has plans to computerize this task, in the future, so that it can be accurately and efficiently maintained.

Financial

Cost of Goods Sold goal will be set at 35% of sales, rather than the original estimate of 30%. While it is hoped that the 35% ratio can be reduced, it is not expected to reach much below 33 or 34%. The computerized inventory system will help in the management of food costs, but it is not expected to reduce costs to the original goal of 30%.

Significant increases in promotion expenses is a part of the efforts to increase sales, particularly the Celebrity Host program. This particular line item will be carefully monitored by the Business Director, Manager of McMurphy's Grill, and the Marketing Consultant. Daily Receipts Report, Invoices, and other Daily Reports are maintained on a regular basis with management of both McMurphy's Grill and St. Patrick Center receiving regularly detailed sales reports, monthly income statement, and explanation of cost variances.

Sales are expected to reach $220,000 during FY 1996. This is $10,000 above what was originally projected.

A Large Sign or Printed Awning is still under consideration but is not a high priority considering McMurphy's recent success. At this time management does not feel this outlay of financial resources will result in equal benefits.

Future Considerations

Parking remains an issue and has become an even more severe problem with increased commercial business in the nearby area. Due to the increased demand for parking, lot owners are not very receptive to reduced rate arrangements. However, it apparently has not resulted in a loss of business as originally anticipated.

Lunch Of The Month Club and Sales Promotions For Frequent Diners has not been instituted considering the level of success McMurphy's has attained during the past year. Management has determined that, at this time, it is not necessary to expend resources for this type of promotion. However, should business begin to trail off this particular promotion will be considered in order to attract return customers.

Corporate sponsorship to maintain the training portion of the program is yet to be established since funds have continued to be available to cover the shortfall. However, funds are anticipated to be depleted by the end of FY 1996. Thus, this effort will be a top priority for St. Patrick Center administration and Board of Directors for the coming year.

THE EMPLOYMENT TRAINING UNIT

Along with other St. Patrick Center programs, McMurphy's Grill provides a continuum of services which moves the client from the street and receiving no services, to competitive employment and independence. The process includes a pre-training portion which begins with the selection of appropriate mentally ill or recovering substance abuse clients by a counselor. These clients complete a series of pre-training classes before placement at McMurphy's. Clients are then assigned to an appropriate position at the restaurant and are to receive proper on-site training. This phase of the training includes basic skills such as washing dishes and busing tables, but hopefully lead into more complex positions such as waiting tables. The client is encouraged to move on to competitive employment only when fully emotionally, psychologically, and socially ready to do so.

As has previously been identified, the Training process has been somewhat weak during the past year. While the pre-training aspect of the program has been continuing to operate in much the same way, the on-the-job training has been extremely limited. With the focus on increasing sales, training has not received the attention it should. The end results reflect this fact. Instead of the estimated 25 participants for 1995 with 10 successfully moving out of the program, there were only 19 new employees with four attaining permanent employment and three others entering another training program.

While the results are not devastating, they do reflect a lack of balanced emphasis. By including a measurement of successful outcomes as part of the Incentive program, the Employment Training segment should gain the appropriate attention. The Business Director and the Executive Director of St. Patrick Center will continue to assess this situation and work toward a more equal balance of emphasis among both segments of the operation.

	Final FY92	Final FY93	Final FY94	Final FY95
Sales:				
Food & Beverage	$167,369	$146,392	$136,197	$193,954
Cost of Sales:				
Food & Beverage	65,170	52,422	56,707	73,647
% of Sales	39%	36%	42%	38%
Gross Profit Margin	102,199	93,970	79,490	120,307
Operating Expenses:				
Salaries	81,791	77,929	100,616	115,524
P/R Taxes/benefits	21,948	20,732	21,522	18,394
Utilities/Bldg Exp	9,707	22,792	22,172	23,579
Telephone	1,857	1,910	2,392	2,019
Supplies	12,713	16,906	17,514	20,394
Postage	266	0	1,555	3,666
Stationary/Prtg	912	195	2,037	8,147
Equip Purchases	879	1,169	411	2,940
Repairs/Rent Equip	5,027	3,560	2,169	3,031
Local Transport	457	464	565	428
Advertising/Publ	8,940	8,170	9,811	10,873
Business Svc's/Fee	7,820	13,845	6,545	10,140
Insurance	2,825	3,290	2,670	2,995
Membership Dues	125	325	315	789
Licenses & Permits	949	675	1,439	3,519
Aid to Individuals	0	250	20	0
Total Expenses	156,216	172,212	191,753	226,438
Operating Profit	-54,017	-78,242	-112,263	-106,131
Other Income:				
Restricted Contrib	38,496	44,135	0	3,354
Special collection	0	8,866	0	0
Grant Revenue	4,063	2,229	25,000	41,300
Miscellaneous	0	180	943	757
Rent Revenue	0	2,000	0	0
Total	42,559	57,410	25,943	45,411
Other Expenses:				
Legal Services	0	47,945	3,272	0
Net Profit (Loss)	($11,458)	($68,777)	($89,592)	($60,720)
Designated Funds:				
End of Period	$142,465	$142,648	$126,578	$97,681

MCMURPHY'S GRILL INCOME STATEMENT

Search Service

BUSINESS PLAN

THE SEARCHERS

9876 S.W. 17th St.
Alexandria, VA 22209

April 1994

This business plan is for a search and retrieval service providing clients with online transmission of data. This established business is seeking minority shareholder investors to contribute needed capital. Look for discussions on offering unique services to remain competitive and positioning oneself in a competitive market.

- EXECUTIVE SUMMARY

- NATURE OF VENTURE

- DESCRIPTION OF THE MARKET

- DESCRIPTION OF SERVICES

- MANAGEMENT TEAM AND OWNERSHIP

- GOALS AND OBJECTIVES

- BUSINESS STRATEGIES

- FINANCIAL DATA

EXECUTIVE
SUMMARY

The Searchers will be a multi-service public record search, document retrieval and business information services company with corporate offices located in Alexandria, Virginia. The corporate mission of the Searchers will be delivery of prompt, accurate, high quality, cost-efficient services on a consistent basis backed by excellent customer service. These services will be delivered through a highly automated computer system that features PC to PC communication for timely ordering and information reporting. Our client base will consist of financial institutions (banks, thrift), mortgage companies, credit unions, finance companies, legal services companies and small to middle market size corporations located throughout the market area defined as Delmarva--Delaware, Maryland, and Virginia.

The Searchers offers a unique opportunity to become part of a business that does not require a huge investment and that provides a variety of search, retrieval and business information services that are in continuous demand from a large established client base. Our client base is in constant need of public record and business information services in order to verify the credit and collateral status of commercial and retail customers in connection with new financing/loan requests, refinancing and ongoing credit maintenance. As a result, by the end of the Searchers' second year the company is expected to have a consistent cash flow that strengthens as revenues and earnings steadily improve. The Searchers' financial goal is to reach revenues of $600M + generating after-tax profits of $65M + by the end of year five. The Searchers will be adequately capitalized by the end of year five allowing for investors to benefit from distributions via dividends, management fees or bonuses. The Searchers will achieve these goals by:

■Concentrating sales efforts on providing services where volume, demand and margins are highest.

■Providing a wide selection of basic and custom services through the use of state-of-the-art computer systems that feature electronic ordering, transmission and payment of search and information services.

■Replacing competitors that have become order-takers with a sophisticated and dynamic sales and marketing organization that is customer driven. The Searchers will provide:

◆a consistent calling effort via personal selling

◆a monthly newsletter to inform clients of new services and improvements to existing services

◆free seminars to educate clients on services offered, how they work and why they are important to the clients.

■Building long-term and loyal customer relationships through the implementation of the Searchers' relationship management selling approach. This approach emphasizes consultative selling that focuses on rapport-building and gaining a thorough understanding of the clients business and needs in order to increase selling opportunities.

■Fully utilizing the experience, skills and industry contacts of Mr. Smiley to build and develop a strong client base. Moreover, the Searchers will have a strong sales, management and support staff by recruiting talented, hard-working, dedicated employees.

■Offering additional services as the company grows such as title insurance, residential real estate appraisals, financial structuring/loan brokering, bank telemarketing programs and loan document preparation in order to maximize cross-selling opportunities with existing clients. This will diversify the revenue mix, improve margins and lead to increased profitability. The Searchers strategy is to eventually market itself as a "one stop provider" of certain business services to the financial marketplace.

The Searchers will be Delaware corporation in which George D. Smiley will maintain a majority ownership interest. Mr. Smiley will initially invest $20,000. This business plan seeks an additional infusion of approximately $254,000 in equity to underwrite start-up costs and provide needed working capital.

NATURE OF VENTURE

Background

The search and business information services industry is an established industry which has historically been slow to address and adapt to changes within the credit and lending environments with respect to market trends, regulation and technology. The primary competitors are mature companies that have developed into order takers relying on repeat business rather than aggressive sales and marketing companies that provide innovative, accurate, high quality search and business information services and prompt customer service on a consistent basis. There is a need for a sales oriented, professional, high-tech information services company that provides a wide selection of competitively priced services and is customer driven.

Nature of Services

The Searchers will provide a wide selection of services including public record searches, business information and miscellaneous document search and retrieval services. Public record searches include UCC-secured transaction searches, real property, deed information, legal descriptions, judgments, federal liens, environmental liens, litigation, assignment and bankruptcy searches, U.S. District Court searches, Superior Court searches and flood hazard reports. Business information services includes corporate status reports, incorporation searches, patent/trademark searches and fictitious names searches. Miscellaneous document search and retrieval services include copies of mortgages, motor vehicle record services, resume checks, social security number traces, criminal records reports, employment verification, and delinquent tax information. Business hours will be Monday through Friday 8:30 a.m. to 5:00 p.m.

Location of Venture

The Searchers will be located in the Town Square, Alexandria, VA. The office is centrally located to provide easy access to all the major surrounding county courthouses.

DESCRIPTION OF THE MARKET

The Searchers will target financial institutions (bank/thrift), mortgage companies, credit unions, finance companies, legal services companies, and middle market size corporations in the tri-state area. However, the Searchers will initially concentrate its sales and marketing efforts in the Chesapeake Bay area. The company will seek to develop a highly qualified network of correspondents to support client needs within the outside the market area. The Searchers will focus on developing relationships will the corporate and consumer lending, credit support, and collection departments of financial institutions, credit unions, and finance company clients. In addition, the Searchers will target the underwriting and processing departments of mortgage company clients. The company will seek to develop client relationships with legal service companies (attorneys/law firms/paralegals) and the accounting, accounts receivable and legal departments of corporate clients.

Market Trends

The growth in the number of regionally located financial institutions, credit unions, and finance companies within the market area is expected to be modest through the remainder of the 1990s. Major factors effecting growth include (1) the mature nature of the market and large number of competition (2) industry consolidation via verger and acquisitions (3) barriers to entry are high i.e. capital requirements (4) highly regulated by federal, state and local government (5) current recessionary environment. Merger and acquisition activity among financial institutions is expected to continue throughout the remainder of the 1990s according to the Standard and Poor Industry Survey Guide. The Guide indicates that from 1975 to 1992 the number of FDIC insured banks nationwide fell from 14,628 to 11,900 as a result of bank mergers, acquisitions and failures. By the year 2000, the number of banks in the U.S. could be reduced another 25%-50%. This consolidation is expected to continue within the Searchers target market area as the large money center and super-regional banks continue to grow through merger and acquisitions. From 1991 to 1992 the number of national and state-chartered commercial banks within the market area fell from approximately 475 to 449. Nevertheless, this decline is not expected to have a major impact on the Searchers' expected growth since much of the decline is due to consolidation via merger and acquisition. As a result, the client base will shrink, but the order volume is expected to remain consistent. Additionally, competition from non-bank corporations such as insurance companies and investment banks that are eager to enter the bank field may expand the target market.

The thrift industry (savings and loans/savings banks) has gone through a difficult period through the late 1980s and into the early 1990s. The industry has undergone significant shrinkage nationwide as a result of the many failed banks and continues to go through the final stage of a longstanding consolidation. However, the number of thrifts remained relatively stable at 275 between 1991 and 1992 within the market area. Nevertheless, their long term prospects are contingent upon their ability to profitably compete in increasingly open mortgage markets. Despite the consolidation and shrinkage among banks and thrifts, the high volume of potential business from the financially sound institutions makes them very attractive clients.

The mortgage company market includes primary and secondary mortgage bank and broker companies. The mortgage company industry realized substantial growth in the late 1980s as a result of strong economic conditions and again over the past several years due to the attractive interest rate environment. Between 1991 and 1992, the number of mortgage companies increased from 1,393 to 1,523. The Searchers will target established, financially sound medium to large size companies in order to take advantage of high volume.

The credit union market over the past decade has consolidated with over 300 voluntary mergers nationwide due primarily to the presence of more competition from banks and non-banks providers of financial services. Within the market area, the number of credit unions decreased from 540 in 1990 to 527 in 1992. In order to compete more effectively, credit unions are merging to form larger institutions which will enable them to offer more services. Nevertheless, their market share for long term loans has declined over the past ten years due to increased competition. Despite the decline in long term lending, the strength of the credit union industry and their strong niche in the consumer residential mortgage market make them attractive clients for the Searchers in which loan term, profitable relationships can be established.

The finance company market is expected to continue to gradually decline as a result of industry consolidation and from intense competition. There are over 1,000 consumer discount and sales finance companies in the market are. The Searchers will focus on high volume industry leaders such as GE, ITT, Sears, American Express and Prudential because of their large branch networks, as well as small-medium size companies where client relationships can be developed more quickly.

The legal service market is expected to grow due to growth among paralegals and the opening of paralegal firms. Independent paralegals have increased from about 200 individuals in 1985 to an estimated 6,000 in 1992 nationwide. The attorney market is expected to remain relatively stable despite some decline from mergers and consolidations. Nevertheless, receipts in 1994 are projected to increase 5%-6% as the demand for legal services increases. There are approximately 131,000 attorneys within the market area. Both paralegals and attorneys are candidates for real property and UCC searches/filing information, bankruptcy, litigation, judgement and lien searches.

The Searchers will target small to middle market size companies (generally sales of $2MM-$100MM) in the market area. Within this sales range there are approximately 49,000 businesses in Virginia, 2,500 in Delaware and 47,000 in Maryland. This large market provides the Searchers with significant opportunities to provide business information and search services to the accounting, accounts receivable and legal departments of these companies.

Changing demographics are not expected to have a large scale impact on the target market. The Searchers will deal primarily with business clients, thus demographic changes within the market area will have a minimal impact. However, population and income levels do effect the Bank's market, particularly from the consumer lending standpoint. The Searchers will be somewhat insulated due to the fact that the majority of clients will be business clients spread over a broad geographical area. However, economic trends can significantly impact credit standards, lending practices, interest rates and loan demand. The low interest rate environment over the past three years has spurred loan demand and the need for increased public record searches, document retrieval and business information services. The changing regulatory environment along with increasing interest rates could have an impact on the commercial and consumer lending practices of banks, thrifts, mortgage and finance companies which will ultimately impact commercial and consumer loan demand.

Demographics and Economic Trends

Current Competitors

There are several primary competitors in the Delmarva area. The principal competition of the Searchers will come from five to six established companies. They include Delmarva Abstracts Inc., Chesapeake Search and Abstract Co., Alexandrian Search Inc., ABC Credit Co., Bay Watch, and Virginia Research Inc. The most significant Alexandria-based competitor is Alexandrian Search, the leading provider of public record searches to banks, thrifts, mortgage companies and law firms in Alexandria and surrounding areas. Delmarva Abstracts employs approximately 140 people and maintains six branch offices in neighboring regions. The dominant competitor in Maryland is Bay Watch which employs 150 people with two offices. Additionally, both companies provide title agent and real estate appraisal services. ABC Credit and Virginia Research are smaller Alexandria-based firms covering the same marketplace as the larger competition but offering fewer services. Chesapeake Search and Abstract is a Delaware-based competitor with 10 offices nationwide and is the dominant provider in the Delaware, Maryland, and Washington, DC area. Chesapeake was recently purchased by Information Inc., a Dallas-based information retrieval service company with over $15 billion in annual revenues. The company offers a wider selection of services than any of the aforementioned competitors and competes effectively on price and service.

All of the primary competitors are established and experienced providers of the services offered by the Searchers. However, Alexandrian Search and Chesapeake Search and Abstract are the only competition with a relatively consistent sales effort and marketing programs. Nevertheless, they lack a relationship management strategy that builds loyal customers and increases selling opportunities. The remaining competitors rely on repeat business from established customers.

DESCRIPTION OF SERVICES

Uniqueness of The Services

Since many of the search and business information services provided by the Searchers will be the same as the primary competition, the uniqueness of the services offered will come from how they are provided and delivered. The Searchers will highlight the electronic ordering, transmission and payment of information services from PC to PC which will appeal to those clients who have made substantial investments in computer systems and technology and demand more timely, efficient service. However, the most significant aspect of the Searchers will be the manner in which the company sells and markets its services. The concept of relationship management selling will appeal to those clients who demand accurate, high quality, prompt, cost-efficient search and information services backed with excellent customer service. By gaining a thorough understanding of the clients needs, miscommunication and mistakes are minimized, rapport building and customer loyalty is enhanced and additional selling opportunities are realized. Our highly knowledgeable and well-trained staff will provide seminars to educate clients regarding available services, industry information and terminology.

Advantages Over Competing Products

The Searchers' principal competitive advantage will come from its relationship management selling approach which will distinguish the company from competitors who have become order takers. Additionally, delivery of services through PC-to-PC communication will set the Searchers apart from the competition.

George D. Smiley will maintain a majority ownership interest in the Searchers and will serve as President. He will be primarily responsible for sales, marketing and finance. Mr. Smiley had been a corporate lender for TriState Financial Inc. serving as Vice President in the regional lending area for the past 10 years. He brings extensive knowledge and experience in the field of banking, finance and credit. Specifically, he has a thorough understanding of the public record search and business information needs of the company's clients.

Mr. Smiley plans to hire an office/accounting manager who will be responsible for office operations and administration. This person will have prior office management/administration experience and an accounting/computer operations background. Three part-time computer operators/customer service/administrative employees will be hired to process, search and document retrieval requests, as well as handle customer questions and problems. These individuals will have prior computer operations experience and backgrounds in customer services. In addition, two document/information searchers will be hired on a part-time/as needed basis to physically search document sources not available on databases. One additional experienced salesperson is expected to be hired by the end of the base year to strengthen revenues by providing improved and expanded market coverage. A second experienced salesperson will be hired by the end of year two.

MANAGEMENT TEAM AND OWNERSHIP

GOALS AND OBJECTIVES

Short Term Goals

The initial major short-term goal of the Searchers is to obtain financing to launch the venture and provide adequate liquidity to fund ongoing working capital needs and support future growth. The Searchers' short-term financial goal is to generate a small profit by the end of the base year. The company will emphasize sales volume growth, strong cost controls and consistent improvement in cash flow and profitability. Profits will be retained to finance operations, pay off investor debt (if applicable) and support future growth.

Long Term Goals

The long-term of the Searchers is to become the leading provider of public record search and business information services within the market area. The Searchers will strive to increase profitability and cash flow and improve capitalization to support regional expansion of operations in the future.

BUSINESS STRATEGIES

The Searchers will employ a differentiation strategy that focuses on providing cost-effective, high quality, prompt and accurate search and business information services that features a state-of-the-art information collection, delivery and payment system. Moveover, the company's relationship management strategy, which focuses on rapport building, understanding of the client's business and needs, communication, client satisfaction and superior service will distinguish the Searchers from its order-taker competitors.

Marketing Plan and Supporting Strategies

The Searchers will support its differentiation strategy by effective execution of its marketing plan which contains supporting strategies including promotional, service, pricing and distribution.

The Searchers will use multiple media sources which effectively utilize allocated promotional dollars while focusing on relatively short time periods. Although the primary competition does little in the way of advertising, the Searchers will need to have a well organized promotional strategy to make inroads and generate new business. The Searchers' target client base will be attracted primarily through personal selling. The Searchers' personal selling efforts will be supported by marketing brochures and pamphlets that provide company background information and highlight the features and benefits of our services. The effectiveness of personal selling will rely on the use of industry contacts, referrals and a consistent calling effort. This will be supported by advertisements in industry publications (i.e. Maryland Business Journal, American Banker) and yellow page advertisements. The Searchers will highlight specific services such as the ability of the client to order and receive information electronically. Other future promotional strategies will include a direct mail and telemarketing program to focus on specific client groups and market area. For example, most corporate clients are not aware that there are search services available that can help them with collection problems and provide judgement, lien and collateral information. A well designed and implemented direct mail and telemarketing program would target the best potential clients and create the most selling opportunities.

The Searchers will offer certain promotional items in conjunction with the company's personal selling strategy, such as cups, pens, golf balls and calendars. The company will also join certain industry associations such as the American Banker's Association, Mortgage Bankers Association, National Association of Credit Management and various local Chambers of Commerce. These associations provide a good way to develop industry contacts and create marketing and selling opportunities for the Searchers as well as build good community relations. Additionally, these associations are often times willing to sell mailing lists of members and subscribers. The Searchers will also seek referrals from industry contracts and consistently network to develop new referral sources.

The Searchers' service strategy will entail providing certain services such as real property, UCC, lien and judgement searchers as well as flood reports where demand and volume tend to be high, margins are strong and services are repeatedly ordered. The Searchers estimates that 75% of its revenues will be derived from these services because they are required by the bulk of the company's client base in connection with the approval and ongoing maintenance of corporate and consumer loans and mortgages.

The Searchers will utilize a competitor based pricing strategy that prices its services in line with the leading competitors. The company's strategy will be to position itself among the leading price. This strategy will allow the Searchers to be on the high-end of the pricing scale which will help to maintain targeted margins and profitability levels. By developing a high quality image and reputation, the Searchers will be a price leader within the industry. This will enable the company to command premium prices for special and customer services. In addition, the Searchers introduces new services (i.e. title insurance, real estate appraisals, document preparation) it can leverage off its quality image and maintain high-end pricing.

The average client is expected to request several types of services with each other, especially among financial institutions, mortgage companies, finance companies and credit union clients. These client generally need several specific types of information to complete a new loan request and/or refinancing as well as for ongoing credit maintenance.

The average order is expected to be $30.00. The Searchers will group services together into four or give types of service packages. The price will be dependent on the type of service package ordered. The more services offered within a package, the higher the price. Prices are expected range from $10.00 to $60.00.

The Searchers will provide services and information as requested an forward the results via mail, fax or through PC-to-PC transmission. The client need only have a modem and basic communication software such as CrossTalk or ProComm. This software can be purchased easily and is relatively inexpensive at about $100-$150.

The Searchers will need an excellent support staff of well trained, knowledgeable, motivated and dedicated employees who can interact well with customers. Therefore, the Searchers will hire an office/accounting manager who is experienced with a strong office management/administrative/computer operations background and excellent customer services skills. Additionally, three part-time computer operator/customer service/administrative employees will be hired. These employees will have good computer operations, administrative, telephone and excellent customer service skills. The Searchers will also hire two document/information searchers on a part-time/as needed basis. The Searchers will hire only experienced searchers who have backgrounds in the area of public records, business information and archival research and are detail oriented. An additional salesperson is not expected to be hired until the end of the first year. The Searchers will look for experienced salespeople who are professional, self-starters, motivated and aggressive. The company will pay the prevailing rate for good computer operator/customer service employees. However for key positions such as office/accounting manager, searchers, and salespeople, the Searchers will pay higher than prevailing rates to attract and retain the best employees.

Human Resources Strategy

The Searchers will be owned by George Smiley who prefers to retain financial and managerial control. Mr. Smiley desires to maintain a controlling interest of no less than 51% of the company's capital stock. The Searchers will require $254,000 in equity funding to finance initial start-up costs and working capital needs. Equity financing will be sought from informal investors via venture capital networks, exchanges and clearinghouses. Growth stage funding will be provided from the retention of earnings as well as from SBA/ bank financing and possibly subordinated debt from informal investors.

Financial Strategy

The Searchers expects to realize strong consistent sales and earnings growth over the next five years. This growth will be principally attributable to the development of new and existing which will come at the expense of competitors. The Searchers expects to develop five to ten new clients by the end of the base year. TriState Financial is expected to be the primary client generating the bulk of sales. TriState Financial purchase volume of public record searches is approximately $300M-$350M annually. The remainder of new clients will be developed through a consistent and effective personal selling, telemarketing and advertising program and from the use of industry contacts and effective networking to develop good referral sources. Additionally, the Searchers will benefit from cross-selling of new services through its expanded sales force over the five year period. Management will effectively control labor expense and profitability. Additionally, operating expenses

Overall Growth Strategy

will be carefully managed to insure that the majority of incremented revenue growth results in increased bottom line profitability.

FINANCIAL DATA

Estimated Start-Up Costs and First Year Operating Costs

DESIRED MINIMUM CASH BALANCE		**$75,000**
Deposits		4,500
Prepaid Rent Insurance		12,000
Salaries and Wages (Year One)		28,500
Officer	$50,000	
Office Manager	25,000	
Support Staff	30,700	
Searchers	23,000	
TOTAL SALARY AND WAGES		$128,700
Miscellaneous Prepaid Expenses		
Advertising	$3,500	
Legal	1,000	
Office Supplies	500	
TOTAL MISCELLANEOUS EXPENSE		$5,000
Building and Equipment		
Leaseholds	$2,000	
Equipment	13,200	
Furniture & Fixtures	5,000	
TOTAL BUILDING AND EQUIPMENT		$20,200
TOTAL START-UP COSTS		**273,900**
OWNERS EQUITY INVESTMENT		**20,000**
ADDITIONAL FUNDING REQUESTED		**$253,900**

	12/31/95	
	Balance Sheet	

ASSETS	($)	($)
Cash & Equivalents	227,500	
Accts Receivable Trade (net)	39,400	
A/R Prog Billings	0	
A/R Cur. Retention	0	
Merchandise Inventory	0	
Cost & Est. Earnings in Excess of Billing	0	
Prepaid Expenses	12,000	
Other Current Assets	0	
TOTAL CURRENT ASSETS		278,950
Fixtures	5,000	
Vehicles	0	
Equipment	13,200	
Leasehold Improvements	2,000	
Buildings	0	
Land	0	
Accumulated Depreciation	(6,100)	
TOTAL FIXED ASSETS		14,100
JOINT VENTURES & INVEST		0
INTANGIBLES		0
OTHER NON-CURRENT ASSETS		4,500
TOTAL ASSETS		**297,550**

LIABILITIES & OWNERS EQUITY		
Accounts Payable (Trade)	13,000	
Accounts Payable (Retention)	0	
Current Portion LTD	0	
Notes Payable (Short Term)	0	
Billings in excess of Estimated Earnings	0	
Accrued Expenses	3,000	
Income Taxes Payable	0	
Other Current Liabilities	0	
TOTAL CURRENT LIABILITIES		16,000
Notes Payable (Long Term)	0	
Bank Loans Payable	0	
Deferred Taxes	0	
Other Loans Payable	0	
Other Long Term Liabilities	0	
TOTAL LONG TERM LIABILITIES		0
TOTAL LIABILITIES		**16,000**
Retained Earnings	7,550	
Capital Stock	274,000	
NET WORTH		**281,550**
TOTAL LIABILITIES & STOCKHOLDERS EQUITY		**297,550**

Income Statement

Period Ended 12/31/95

	PERIOD DATA 100% OF ANNUAL ($)	ANNUAL ($)
GROSS SALES/REVENUES	315,000	315,000
Less: Discounts & Returns	0	0
NET SALES/REVENUES	315,000	315,000
Less: COST OF GOODS SOLD/COST OF CONTR.	151,100	151,100
GROSS PROFIT	163,900	163,900
OTHER INCOME	0	0
TOTAL RECEIPTS	163,900	163,900
OPERATING EXPENSES		
Advertising & Promotion	5,000	5,000
Bad Debts	0	0
Bank Services Charges	300	300
Car & Delivery	2,000	2,000
Commissions	0	0
Amortization of Intangs	0	0
Depreciation/Depletion	6,100	6,100
Dues & Publications	250	250
Employee Benefit Program	1,500	1,500
Freight	0	0
Insurance	12,100	12,100
Laundry & Cleaning	0	0
Leased Equipment	0	0
Legal/Professional	6,000	6,000
Office Expense	1,000	1,000
Outside Labor	0	0
Pension/P.S./Payroll Taxes	7,500	7,500
Rent	28,500	28,500
Repairs & Maintenance	0	0
Operating Supplies	0	0
Taxes & Licenses	0	0
Travel & Entertainment	1,500	1,500
Utilities & Telephone	9,600	9,600
WAGES		
Salaries—Officers	50,000	50,000
Payroll	25,000	25,000
TOTAL OPERATING EXPENSES	156,350	156,350
INTEREST	0	0
MISCELLANEOUS EXPENSES	0	0
TOTAL EXPENSES	156,350	156,350
PROFIT (LOSS) BEFORE TAXES	7,550	7,550
TAXES	0	0
NET PROFIT (LOSS) AFTER TAXES	7,550	7,550
DIVIDEND/DISTRIBUTION	0	0
RETAINED EARNINGS	7,550	7,550

Analysis Processed on 4/26/1994 for Income/Balance on 12/31/95

Breakeven Analysis

	($)	(%)
SALES/REVENUE	**315,000**	**100.00**
VARIABLE DISBURSEMENTS		
Cost of Goods Sold/Cost of Contracts	151,100	47.97
Advertising	5,000	1.59
Bad Debts	0	0.00
Car/Delivery	2,000	0.63
Commissions	0	0.00
Freight	0	0.00
Taxes/Licenses	0	0.00
Travel and Entertainment	1,500	0.48
TOTAL VARIABLE DISBURSEMENTS	**159,600**	**50.67**
CONTRIBUTION	**155,400**	**49.33**
FIXED DISBURSEMENTS		
Bank Services Charges	300	0.10
Amortization of Intangs	0	0.00
Depreciation/Depletion	6,100	1.94
Dues & Publications	250	0.08
Employee Benefit Program	1,500	0.48
Insurance	12,100	3.84
Laundry & Cleaning	0	0.00
Leased Equipment	0	0.00
Legal/Professional	6,000	1.90
Office Expense	1,000	0.32
Outside Labor	0	0.00
Pension/P.S./Payroll Taxes	7,500	2.38
Rent	28.500	9.05
Repairs & Maintenance	0	0.00
Supplies, Operating	0	0.00
Utilities	9,600	3.05
Salaries–Officers	50,000	15.87
Payroll	25,000	7.94
Interest	0	0.00
Miscellaneous Expenses/(Income)	0	0.00
TOTAL FIXED DISBURSEMENTS	**147,850**	**46.94**
PRETAX PROFIT	**7,550**	**2.40**
DOLLAR SALES BREAKEVEN	**299,696**	

DEGREE OF OPERATING LEVERAGE -3.20
Z-SCORE PREDICTOR 12.80

**12/31/95 Financial
Projection Assumptions**

■Sales are expected to reach $315M of which TriState Financial will represent approximately $50M. The remainder will be from the development of five to ten new clients throughout the year. This Figure also assumes $0 sales during months one and two and an average of $31.5M each month thereafter.

■The gross margin is expected to be strong at 52%. The margin is expected to remain strong going forward since the bulk of COS is comprised of labor. The Searchers will control labor expense carefully and will maximize usage of its labor force in order to realize increased operating efficiencies by the second half of the year.

■Operating expenses will appear high as a percentage of sales at 48.6% in year one. This is because these expenses will be comprised primarily of fixed costs such as salaries, rent and insurance. However, as sales grow the incremental increase will fall to the bottom line because the Searchers fixed cost structure can support significant volume increases with only minimal increases in operating expense dollars.

■Liquidity, as measured by the current ratio is strong at 17.4:1 as is working capital of $263M. This is principally due to strong initial capitalization of the company.

■Accounts receivable turnover is projected at 45 days although the Searchers' terms will be net 30. However, A/R quality is expected to be high and bad debts are expected to be minimal. The Searchers expects to improve A/R turnover going forward by encouraging payment through the electronic funds transfer system.

■Accounts payable turnover will be approximately 30 days. Payable will be comprised primarily of correspondent fees and computer access time costs. The Searchers will pay promptly and discount where possible to establish a strong credit history with major vendors.

■Equipment will consist of computer hardware and software, a telephone system, fax machine modem and printer. Equipment will be depreciated over three years. Furniture and fixtures will be depreciated over five years and leaseholds over the expected life of the lease which is projected to be three years. All items are depreciated assuming straight line depreciation.

■Leverage is minimal since the Searchers has been funded by the equity investments of the shareholders. As a result, net worth comprises 94.6% of total capitalization.

Financial Statement Projection

Income Statement

Historical Cases: Base Study Case

DATE	12/31/95	YEAR+1	YEAR+2	YEAR+3	YEAR+4	YEAR+5
NET SALES	**315.0**	**330.8**	**363.9**	**418.5**	**502.2**	**603.0**
Cost of Goods	151.1	158.7	174.7	200.8	241.1	289.4
Gross Profit	163.9	172.1	189.2	217.7	261.1	313.6
Other Income	0.0	0.0	0.0	0.0	0.0	0.0
TOTAL RCPTS	**163.9**	**172.1**	**189.2**	**217.7**	**261.1**	**313.6**
Var Costs	8.5	15.0	18.0	21.0	24.0	27.0
Contrib (GP-VC)	155.4	157.1	171.2	196.7	237.1	286.6
Depr/Depl/Amort	6.1	6.1	6.1	1.9	0.0	0.0
Other Fixed Costs	147.9	174.3	179.3	184.3	214.3	221.8
TOTAL EXPENSES	**162.5**	**195.4**	**203.4**	**207.2**	**238.3**	**248.8**
Bef Tax Prof	7.6	-23.3	-14.2	10.5	22.8	64.8
Income Taxes	0.0	0.0	0.0	0.0	0.0	0.0
AFTER TAX PROFIT	**7.6**	**-23.3**	**-14.2**	**10.5**	**22.8**	**64.8**
DIVIDENDS	**0.0**	**0.0**	**0.0**	**0.0**	**0.0**	**0.0**
RET EARNINGS	**7.6**	**-23.3**	**-14.2**	**10.5**	**22.8**	**64.8**

Balance Sheet

Historical Cases: Base Study Case

DATE	12/31/95	YEAR+1	YEAR+2	YEAR+3	YEAR+4	YEAR +5
ASSETS						
Cash	227.6	238.9	262.9	302.3	362.8	435.6
Accts Rcvbl	39.4	41.4	45.5	52.3	62.8	75.4
Inventory	0.0	0.0	0.0	0.0	0.0	0.0
Prepaid Expenses	12.0	15.0	15.6	15.9	18.3	19.1
Other Curr	0.0	0.0	0.0	0.0	0.0	0.0
Fix Assests Net	14.1	8.0	1.9	0.0	0.0	0.0
Other N-Curr	4.5	4.5	4.5	4.5	4.5	4.5
TOTAL ASSETS	**297.6**	**307.8**	**330.4**	**375.1**	**448.4**	**534.6**
LIABILITIES						
Accts Pay	13.0	13.7	15.0	17.3	20.7	24.9
Curr Port Ltd	0.0	0.0	0.0	0.0	0.0	0.0
Accrued Exp	3.0	3.7	3.8	3.9	4.5	4.7
Inc Tax Pay	0.0	0.0	0.0	0.0	0.0	0.0
N/P Short Term	0.0	32.2	67.5	99.4	145.8	162.9
Other Curr	0.0	0.0	0.0	0.0	0.0	0.0
Other Long Term	0.0	0.0	0.0	0.0	0.0	0.0
TOTAL LIAB	**16.0**	**49.5**	**86.4**	**120.5**	**171.0**	**192.5**
NET WORTH						
Ret Earnings	7.6	-15.8	-30.0	-19.5	3.3	68.1
Capital Stock	274.0	274.0	274.0	274.0	274.0	274.0
TOTAL LIAB & NW	**197.6**	**307.8**	**330.4**	**375.1**	**448.4**	**534.6**

**Projected Cash Flow
Analysis**

Base Date 12/31/95

	Year 1	Year 2	Year 3	Year 4	Year 5
<u>CASH FLOW FROM OPERATIONS</u>	$000	$000	$000	$000	$000
PROFIT AFTER TAXES	**-23.3**	**-14.2**	**10.5**	**22.8**	**64.8**
Plus:					
Depr/Depl/Amort Expense	6.1	6.1	1.9	0.0	0.0
WORKING CAPITAL FROM OPERS	**-17.2**	**-8.2**	**12.4**	**22.8**	**64.8**
Plus:					
INC (DEC) VS. PREV IN					
Accounts Payable	0.7	1.4	2.2	3.5	4.2
Accrued Expenses	0.7	0.2	0.1	0.6	0.2
Other Current Liabilities	0.0	0.0	0.0	0.0	0.0
Plus:					
DEC (INC) VS. PREV PER IN					
Accounts Receivable	-2.0	-4.0	-6.8	-10.5	-12.6
Inventory	0.0	0.0	0.0	0.0	0.0
Prepaid Expenses	-3.0	-0.6	-0.3	-2.4	-0.8
Other Current Assets	0.0	0.0	0.0	0.0	0.0
NET CASH FLOW FROM OPERS	**-20.9**	**-11.3**	**7.6**	**14.0**	**55.7**
<u>CASH FLOW FROM INVESTING ACTIVITIES</u>					
DEC (INC) VS. PREV PER IN					
Fixed Assets	0.0	0.0	0.0	0.0	0.0
Other Non-Current Assets	0.0	0.0	0.0	0.0	0.0
NET CASH FLOW FROM INVSTING	**0.0**	**0.0**	**0.0**	**0.0**	**0.0**
<u>CASH FLOW FROM FINANCING</u>					
INC (DEC) VS. PREV PER IN					
Short Term Debt	32.3	35.3	31.8	46.5	17.1
Long Term Debt	0.0	0.0	0.0	0.0	0.0
Other Long Term Liabilities	0.0	0.0	0.0	0.0	0.0
Cap Stock Add/Ret Earnings Adj.	0.0	0.0	0.0	0.0	0.0
Less: Dividends Paid	**0.0**	**0.0**	**0.0**	**0.0**	**0.0**
NET CASH FLOW FROM FINANCING	**32.2**	**35.3**	**31.8**	**46.5**	**17.1**
TOTAL CASH FLOWS	**11.4**	**23.9**	**39.4**	**60.5**	**72.8**

■Sales are expected to increase by 5% in Year 1 as additional clients are developed. Year 2 sales increase 10% and Year 3 sales by 15%. The addition of a new salesperson in each year will result in development of new and existing clients are expanded market coverage. Years 4 and 5 sales increase by 20% due to an increase among existing clients, additional new clients and from cross-selling of new services.

■Cost of Sales are expected to remain relatively constant at 48%. The Searchers will continue to manage labor expenses carefully and will maximize usage of its labor force to realize operating efficiencies as revenues grow.

■Operating expenses will be high in Year 1 at 59% of sales. However, operating expenses will decline each year thereafter to 41.3% as a percentage of sales by Year 5. Operating expenses are comprised largely of fixed costs such as salaries, rent and insurance. The Searcher's fixed cost structure can support significant volume increases with only minimal increases in operating expense dollars. During Years 4 and 5 operating expenses dollars increase more quickly due primarily to salary increases.

■Liquidity and Working Capital as measured by the current ratio remains strong through the projection period despite losses in years 1 and 2. This is principally attributed to strong initial capitalization of the company.

■Accounts payable turnover will be approximately 30 days. Payable will be comprised primarily of correspondent fees and computer access time costs. The Searchers will pay promptly and discount where possible to establish a strong credit history with major vendors.

■Equipment will consist of computer hardware and software, a telephone system, fax machine, modem and printer. Equipment will be depreciated over three years. Furniture and fixtures will be depreciated over five years and leaseholds over the expected life of the lease which is projected to be three years. All items are depreciated assuming straight line depreciation.

■Leverage is minimal since the Searchers has been funded by the equity investments of the shareholders. As a result, net worth comprises 94.6% of total capitalization.

Five-Year Financial Statement Projections

Sports Collectibles

BUSINESS PLAN

THE DIAMOND CONNECTION, INC. ET AL

6740 10 Mile Rd.
Center Line, MI 48015
(313)885-0140

February 1992

This plan introduces a collaborative business venture to produce a limited production artwork series featuring members of the Hockey Hall of Fame. The plan features an overview of the history of sports collectibles, a comprehensive product description, and discussions of production, marketing, distribution, personnel, and financing to substantiate the viability of this venture. This business plan has not been disguised in any way; references to locations, people, and products are real, not fictional.

- STATEMENT OF PURPOSE

- HISTORY OF SPORTS COLLECTIBLES

- PHYSICAL PRODUCT

- DESCRIPTION OF PROJECT CONCEPT AND CRITERIA

- QUALIFICATIONS

- PRODUCTION

- MARKETING

- DISTRIBUTION

- PRO FORMA FINANCIAL PROJECTION

STATEMENT OF PURPOSE

The purpose of this presentation is to review the potential for a project involving the production of a limited production artwork set featuring members of the Hockey Hall of Fame. The project would involve the joint efforts of the Diamond Connection, Inc., Sports Gallery of Art and the Hockey Hall of Fame. The results of this project will provide many benefits to the participants. Significant among these are the following:

Hockey Hall of Fame:

O Ability for financial gain from royalties generated by the project.
O Favorable marketing and awareness of the Hall of Fame as a result of advertising and publicity from the project.
O Education of hockey fans about the Hall of Fame who purchase the product.
O The potential for added attendance at the Hall of Fame as a result of the project.

The Diamond Connection, Inc. and Sports Gallery of Art:

O Financial gain from the revenues granted by sales of the product.
O The opportunity to further validate their position as leaders in the field of Sports Art and collectibles.
O The benefit of marketing and publicity to a wide spectrum of sports collectors throughout the United States and Canada.

We intend to present the following at this meeting:

1. Introduce the individuals from the Diamond Connection, Inc. ("DC") and Sports Gallery of Art ("SGA") to the Hockey Hall of Fame.
2. Review the history and status of the sports collectibles industry.
3. Review the project concept and comparable projects from other sports.
4. Review the credentials of DC and SGA to successfully complete the project.
5. Review the proposed Marketing, Production and Distribution plans.
6. Review the financial projections.

At the conclusion of our meeting we hope to be able to address the following questions:

Does the Hockey Hall of Fame approve of the concept?
Does the Hall of Fame have an interest in participating in the project?
When can the Hall commit to a decision regarding participation?
What involvement might be required of the NHL, the NHL Players Association and individual members of the Hall of Fame to allow the project to proceed?
What is the next logical step for all involved to commit in order to move forward?

The sports collectibles hobby came into existence in the 1880's with the introduction of artistic portrayals of 19th century baseball players. These portrayals were often on cords included in boxes containing tobacco and caramel products. The cards were meant as an enhancement to the product being sold.

These cards were collected by many individuals over the following 90 years. However, no sophisticated secondary market existed until approximately 1970. By that time, sports cards had been produced to varying degrees for all of the major sports, including hockey. Significant production of hockey cards began in the early 1950's when both Parkhurst and Topps produced trading cards.

Beginning in the early 1970's, significant interest on the part of collectors in old sports cards resulted in the creation of hobby trade shows. The purpose of these events were to gather collecting enthusiasts together to buy, sell, or trade sports cards. All of the participants were true collectors whose primary incomes were derived outside of the hobby. Throughout the decade these trade shows steadily increased in both frequency and size.

By the early 1980's, the sports collecting hobby had grown to significant enough proportions to be no longer regarded as a "kid's hobby". A number of hobbyists were able to participate in the hobby on a full time basis while living off of income from their activities. This decade saw a tremendous growth within the sports collectibles industry as significant numbers of people began collecting.

The present day finds the industry as a legitimate full time business for many individuals. Estimates suggest that as many as $6 billion is spent annually on sports collectibles. The hobby's annual convention now hosts over 100,000 collectors over a four day period every year. An individual T-206 Honus Wagner baseball card (circa 1910) was purchased last year by Wayne Gretzky and Bruce McNeil for over $400,000. In summary, due to the vast number of collectors, the hobby has now become big business.

The collecting public's appetite has also caused the hobby to become increasingly more sophisticated over the last ten years. A major portion of this sophisticated has involved authentic hand signatures by athletes as well as limited production, high quality collectibles.

Two significant areas of the hobby have evolved as a result of this demand for increased sophistication. Sports figurines and plates were introduced to the hobby in the mid to late 1980's. These products involve limited production items (usually 500 to 10,000 pieces), many of which are also hand autographed. Sports art, while in existence since the introduction of the first sports card in the 1880's, has now become increasingly popular with upscale hobby collectors. There are now many naturally recognized sports artists who have received national recognition and are highly sought after by hobby collectors. These include, but are not limited to, Christopher Paluso, Ron Lewis, Mike Petronella, Joseph Catalano, Michael Taylor, Richard Perez, Ed LePere and Doug West.

The hobby can expect to continue to grow in the 1990's as it has in previous decades. One of the attributes that we expect in this decade is that collectors will continue to request truly unique collectibles that are both limited and are of high quality. This brief is a cornerstone behind our desire to undertake The Hall of Fame project.

HISTORY OF SPORTS COLLECTIBLES

PHYSICAL PRODUCT

The following describes certain significant attributes regarding the project product.

Product

Individual postcard sized artistic portrayals of all the members of the Hockey Hall of Fame produced on a very high quality stock.

Total Production

10,000 full sets will be produced and the cards in each set will be individually numbered.

Packaging

The cards will be issued and sold in "series". Each series will consist of between 14 and 20 cards. Typically, a series will include 12 to 14 players and between 2 and 6 "builders" and/ or game officials.

Series Frequency

Series will be released every 4 months until all members of the Hall have been depicted. At that time, annual update series will be released for new inductees into the Hall.

Pricing

Each series will be priced at $5 (U.S.) per player card. Founders and game officials will not be priced. Accordingly, a typical series will cost approximately $75 (U.S.). Various accessories, including protector sheets and educational data about the Hall, etc., will be included at no extra charge.

Accessories

As part of the base cost of the set, purchasers will be entitled to other accessories as part of the package. For instance, the first series would include a storage box (much like the Perez-Steele example) as well as an informational booklet about the Hockey Hall of Fame.

DESCRIPTION OF PROJECT CONCEPT AND CRITERIA

The project concept is to produce a high quality artwork set depicting members of the Hockey Hall of Fame. The set would be limited to 10,000 full sets. Each artist's rendering would be sized approximately the same as a postcard and be presented artistically in both an action and portrait format on high quality stock paper.

There is historical precedence for such a project. There are Hall of Fame sets in the marketplace showcasing both the Baseball Hall of Fame as well as the Football Hall of Fame. Both sets have been well received by the collecting public as a result of their uniqueness and quality.

The project concept, when successfully introduced, will address all of the benefits to the participating parties that were described in the introduction. In order to be successfully introduced, the following criteria also needs to be considered:

1. Is there a sufficiently sized marketplace to absorb the product?

Hockey is the fastest growing area in today's sports collectible industry. The marketing success of the San Jose Sharks suggests that, perhaps in contrast to the situation a decade ago, hockey interest is being established throughout both Canada and the United States. The season ticket sales in Ottawa, Hamilton and Tampa Bay, prior to the most recent expansion franchise awards by the NFL, further confirms this high level of interest. In our opinion, hockey today takes a back seat only to baseball on an overall basis in the industry. There are many devoted hockey fans presently spending large sums of money for hockey related items. Our Red Wings lithograph project enjoyed rapid absorption with only regionally based marketing.

2. Is the price point of the product likely to be attractive to the potential customer?

As will be described in a later section, our proposed price point is slightly less than the current introductory price for the Perez-Steele baseball products. We feel that this price point will be satisfactory to our target customers. The baseball and football sets have now been fully absorbed by the collecting public. The baseball version was produced by a private company named Perez-Steele, who worked in conjunction with the Baseball Hall of Fame. The set depicts all makes of the Baseball Hall of Fame and was circulated in an issue of 10,000 total sets. The football set was produced by a company named Goal Line Art in conjunction with the Football Hall of Fame. The total issue size of the product amounted to 5,000 sets.

The Perez-Steele product has been so successful that a number of follow-up products have been created in conjunction with the Baseball Hall of Fame.

The football venture was initially released in 1990 and has just recently been fully absorbed into the marketplace.

There are a number of reasons why these projects have been successful. First, the boom within the sports collectibles industry has resulted in a corresponding demand for hand autographs from famous retired athletes. The baseball and football issues have been extremely popular with autograph collectors. This group represents a significant portion of the purchases of this type of product. Another reason for project success has been the set's affiliation with the Hall of Fame for each respective sport. It is our firm opinion that there is a significant "legitimacy" given to the product as a result. Lastly, the projects were carried out by private entrepreneurs who had a solid combination of artistic expertise and hands on knowledge of production and distribution.

3. Is the quality of the product sufficient to satisfy the standards of a sophisticated sports hobbyist?

We fully intend to have the Hockey Hall of Fame product be superior in quality to both the baseball and football products.

4. Can the majority of potential customers be reached via a comprehensive marketing program?

As will be described in a later section, we feel that a combination of certain marketing releases will be sufficient to reach our potential customers.

QUALIFICATIONS

In addition to creating a valid concept for this type of project, it is also critical to combine joint venture partners capable of getting the job done. The Hockey Hall of Fame is an important partner in this project because of the legitimacy and marketing benefits that it would be able to contribute.

We believe that The Diamond Connection and Sports Gallery of Art also bring important benefits to the project. These qualifications include:

Personnel

Doug West
Nationally recognized sports artist with a proven track record.

Dave Sell
Extensive marketing and retail background with international experience.

Dave Schulte
Significant sports collectibles hobby experience.

John Moore
Significant sports collectibles hobby experience. Extensive financial background including familiarity with multi-million dollar financings, sales and lease transactions.

Steve Graus
Significant sports collectibles hobby experience. Related experience in retail, marketing and distribution areas.

Sports Hobby Experience

Sports Gallery of Art and Doug West have been producing sports art for over 10 years.

The principals of The Diamond Connection have been involved in the retail side of the industry for over 5 years.

Similar Project Experience

We have successfully negotiated a project in conjunction with The Detroit Red Wings distributing lithographs of selected Red Wings players. This project has been extremely effective and we have demonstrated proficiency in production, marketing and distribution of this project. We are about to launch a similar project in terms of both concept and execution with the Chicago Black Hawks.

Financial Expertise

We have the capabilities to bring forth from either owners, past project equity investors or bank financing sources, sufficient funds to allow the project to occur. It is an integral part of our proposal that the Hall of Fame not be involved in project investment. At the present time, we only contemplate that the Hall of Fame will derive free income from the gross revenues.

Marketing Expenses

We have a track record indicating our ability to procure publicity via print and video. We would continue to use these methods to create sufficient publicity for the project as well.

In short, we believe that the joint venture relationship, as proposed, will bring all of the required talents and capabilities needed to successfully implement this project.

PRODUCTION

The original artwork will be created by Doug West. The color separation process and other technical aspects of converting the original artwork to cards will be performed by the Sports Gallery of Art. All media advertising layouts will be created by Sports Gallery of Art. The actual printed production of cards will be subcontracted to an appropriately qualified printing company. Other production aspects of the project, including the production of a

Hall of Fame information booklet, leather binder and other storage materials relating to the project will also be subcontracted. The Sports Gallery of Art will responsible for all artistic design of the entire project inclusive of work performed on an in-house, as well as outsourced, basis.

We propose to use both print and broadcast advertising for marketing. This has worked successfully in our previous projects. We would utilize the following

MARKETING

Print Publications
O The Hockey News
O Sports Collectors Digest
O Tuff Stuff
O Legends Magazine
O NHL Game Programs

Broadcast Media
O Hockey Night in Canada
O Sports Channel USA

This would represent a more comprehensive marketing effort than either the baseball or football project. The timing of the marketing program will be "front loaded" so as to create adequate publicity at the time of project introduction. Adequate initial marketing will create steady market absorption until the product is fully absorbed into the marketplace.

The distribution would only occur from either of two sources:

DISTRIBUTION

1. Hockey Hall of Fame
2. The Diamond Connection, Inc.

The primary source of distribution will be on a mail order basis. The reason for utilizing this sort of arrangement would be twofold. First, inventory control of the product is much easier with only two outlets. Secondly, there is a market negative to a product such as this by not making it readily available on a retail basis. This feature leads to the perception of its exclusivity and helps to spur demand. The Hall of Fame would be entitled to an additional sales commission for all sets sold at its location.

PRO FORMA FINANCIAL PROJECTION
FEBRUARY 1992

	1992	1993	1994	1995	1996	1997	1998	1999	2000	Totals
Revenues:										
Sales	65,000	600,000	1,400,000	1,900,000	2,000,000	1,935,000	1,400,000	600,000	100,000	10,000,000
Total Revenues	65,000	600,000	1,400,000	1,900,000	2,000,000	1,935,000	1,400,000	600,000	100,000	10,000,000
Expenses:										
Production Costs	100,000	200,000	600,000	700,000	800,000	800,000	600,000	200,000	0	4,000,000
Marketing Costs	100,000	250,000	100,000	100,000	50,000	0	0	0	0	600,000
Legal and Financial	40,000	15,000	15,750	16,538	17,364	18,233	19,144	20,101	21,870	184,000
Hall of Fame Royalties	6,500	60,000	140,000	190,000	200,000	193,500	140,000	60,000	10,000	1,000,000
Other Royalties	6,500	60,000	140,000	190,000	200,000	193,500	140,000	60,000	10,000	1,000,000
Personnel Costs	30,000	31,500	33,075	34,729	36,465	38,288	40,203	42,213	43,527	330,000
Insurance	5,000	5,250	5,513	5,788	6,078	6,381	6,700	7,036	7,254	55,000
Contingency and General	12,000	23,250	35,788	40,827	43,368	40,912	30,957	11,005	1,094	239,200
Total Expenses:	300,000	645,000	1,070,125	1,277,881	1,353,275	1,290,814	977,005	400,355	93,744	7,408,200
Net Cash Flow	(235,000)	(45,000)	329,875	622,119	646,725	644,186	422,995	199,645	6,256	2,591,800
Cash Flows to Participants:										
Hockey Hall of Fame	6,500	60,000	140,000	190,000	200,000	193,500	140,000	60,000	10,000	1,000,000
Other Royalty Sources	6,500	60,000	140,000	190,000	200,000	193,500	140,000	60,000	10,000	1,000,000
Diamond Connection/Sports Gallery of Art:										
Gross Cash Flow	(235,000)	(45,000)	329,875	622,119	646,725	644,186	422,995	199,645	6,256	2,591,800
Tax Effected (30%)	82,250	15,750	(115,456)	(217,742)	(226,354)	(225,465)	(148,048)	(69,876)	(2,189)	(907,130)
Net Cash Flow	(152,750)	(29,250)	214,419	404,377	420,371	418,721	274,947	129,769	4,066	1,684,670

Net Present Value of Project to DC/SGA: at 15% rate 867,339

Note: A 15% rate was used because it is comparable to returns from other industry projects. Additionally, any debt or equity sources used for the project would evaluate the project in a similar manner as venture capital projects.

<u>Line Item Assumptions:</u>
Sales

Detailed compilation of sales can be found under the table subheading Revenue Calculations.

Production Costs

Detailed compilation of production costs can be found under the table subheading Production Calculations.

It is assumed that each card will cost $2 to produce. The production costs include the following:

- ◆ Printing
- ◆ Shipping
- ◆ Artwork Production
- ◆ Layout and Design
- ◆ Accessory Products mentioned in this presentation

Marketing Costs

Include estimated costs for all media advertising, promotional costs and travel expenses associated with execution of the project.

Legal and Financial

Include estimated costs for the formation of legal entities, execution of royalty agreements and filing of required financial statements and tax returns.

Hall of Fame Royalties

Are assumed to be 10% of gross sales.

Other Royalties

Are assumed to be 10% of gross sales. This line item could potentially include The National Hockey League and/or the NHL Alumni Players Association.

Personnel Costs

Assumed to be the cost of one full time administrator/clerk with some fringes.

Insurance

Related to general liability and property insurance requirements of the project.

Contingency and General

Is calculated as 5% of Production, Marketing, Legal and Financial costs. This line item would offset any budget overruns in any other expense lines.

Other Assumptions:

All financial data in this pro forma are stated in U.S. dollars.

There will be approximately 200 player members of the Hall by 1995.

The three annual series will depict about 40 players per year.

The project will take about 5 years to complete the portrayal of all Hall members.

The project will be initiated in the fall of 1992 with the first series.

All subscribers to the project will be offered subsequent series at four month intervals commencing with the purchase of the first series.

The absorption estimates for purchase of the initial series are as follows:

- ◆ 1992   1,000 sets (333 per month)
- ◆ 1993   4,000 sets (333 per month)
- ◆ 1994   4,000 sets (333 per month)
- ◆ 1995   1,000 sets (333 per month)

Footnotes to Pro Forma

Footnotes to Pro Forma
...continued

Any sales and/or use taxes will be assumed by the purchaser.

Production of series will be accomplished in increments of 50,000 cards at a time in order to efficiently balance production and holding costs.

Any inflation affected line assumptions in the pro forma assume inflation at a 5% rate per annum.

Revenue Calculations

	1992	1993	1994	1995	1996	1997	1998	1999	2000	Totals
1992 Issuances:										
Cards per Year	13	40	40	40	40	27				200
# of sets	1,000	1,000	1,000	1,000	1,000	1,000				1,000
Price per Card	$5	$5	$5	$5	$5	$5				$5
Revenues	65,000	200,000	200,000	200,000	200,000	135,000				1,000,000
1993 Issuances:										
Cards per Year		20	40	40	40	40	20			200
# of sets		4,000	4,000	4,000	4,000	4,000	4,000			4,000
Price per Card		$5	$5	$5	$5	$5	$5			$5
Revenues		400,000	800,000	800,000	800,000	800,000	400,000			4,000,000
1994 Issuances:										
Cards per Year			20	40	40	40	40	20		200
# of sets			4,000	4,000	4,000	4,000	4,000	4,000		4,000
Price per Card			$5	$5	$5	$5	$5	$5		$5
Revenues			400,000	800,000	800,000	800,000	800,000	400,000		4,000,000
1995 Issuances:										
Cards per Year				20	40	40	40	40	20	200
# of sets				1,000	1,000	1,000	1,000	1,000	1,000	1,000
Price per Card				$5	$5	$5	$5	$5	$5	$5
Revenues				100,000	200,000	200,000	200,000	200,000	100,000	1,000,000
Total Revenues	65,000	600,000	1,400,000	1,900,000	2,000,000	1,935,000	1,400,000	600,000	100,000	10,000,000

Production Calculations

Absorption									
1992	1993	1994	1995	1996	1997	1998	1999	2000	Totals
1992 issuance cards									
13,000	40,000	40,000	40,000	40,000	27,000	0	0	0	200,000
1993 issuance cards									
0	80,000	160,000	160,000	160,000	160,000	80,000	0	0	800,000
1994 issuance cards									
0	0	80,000	160,000	160,000	160,000	160,000	80,000	0	800,000
1995 issuance cards									
0	0	0	20,000	40,000	40,000	40,000	40,000	20,000	200,000
Total Sales									
13,000	120,000	280,000	380,000	400,000	387,000	280,000	120,000	20,000	2,000,000
Total Production									
50,000	100,000	300,000	350,000	400,000	400,000	300,000	100,000	0	2,000,000
Production Cost per									
2.00	2.00	2.00	2.00	2.00	2.00	2.00	2.00	2.00	2.00
Total Production Costs									
100,000	200,000	600,000	700,000	800,000	800,000	600,000	200,000	0	4,000,000

Television Childproofer

BUSINESS PLAN

TELEVISION FOR KIDS

903 Bennington Rd.
Syracuse, NY 98239

November 1994

Television for Kids was created by a small team of professionals to market and distribute a unique and highly effective television childproofing system called SafeViewing. This plan studies current markets, demographics, competition, and the skills and equipment needed to successfully build a business in a multi-billion dollar industry.

- EXECUTIVE SUMMARY

- NATURE OF VENTURE

- MARKET DESCRIPTION AND ANALYSIS

- DESCRIPTION OF THE PRODUCT

- MANAGEMENT

- BUSINESS STRATEGIES

- FINANCIAL DATA

- PATENTS, TRADEMARKS AND REGULATORY APPROVAL

- EXHIBIT

Television for Kids (TK) was formed to market and distribute SafeViewing, a new product that represents a breakthrough in television childproofing. SafeViewing offers parents, grandparents, and other concerned caregivers a simple but fully effective method of screening the television programming available for viewing by children. The system enables adults to selectively eliminate violent or explicit programming from their children's viewing choices with the push of a button. At the same time, this user-friendly system makes it easy for adults to restore full program viewer capability to their television by simply entering a Personal Identification Number (PIN). SafeViewing is compatible with all televisions. Two models are available for basic cable systems and for systems with premium channel or pay-per-view cable descramblers.

The development of SafeViewing was prompted by the widely publicized need for a television parental control device that would be available to the general public and would be applicable to most if not all the different cable systems throughout the country. The goal of Television for Kids' SafeViewing project is to provide a comprehensive control system which is operator friendly, universally adaptable to all television and cable systems, and priced within the reach of the average middle income household. In addition, SafeViewing's development has been based on the belief that parents have the responsibility to monitor and provide guidance to their children through the formative years. SafeViewing allows parents to determine which programming content is acceptable for their children's viewing in lieu of the outside control methods presently being developed.

TK's corporate mission is to provide a highly effective, high quality, affordable childproofing system which gives parents a secure means of selecting specific television programming which they judge to be acceptable for viewing by their children while blocking out programming which they judge to be unacceptable. TK intends to market and distribute SafeViewing nationwide through a well designed and coordinated marketing plan. This plan will include the executive of a comprehensive multi-channel direct response marketing program featuring mass media advertising, direct response television, mail order, direct mail, and public relations. TK's customer base will consist of several million households with parents ages 25 to 55 and/ or grandparents with children and/or grandchildren ages two through 13.

TK offers a unique opportunity to become part of a business that does not require an enormous capital investment. In addition, the company has developed a unique product which effectively protects children from violent and explicit television programming in response to a growing demand from a large number of concerned parents nationwide. TK expects to realize a steady increase in revenue and earnings in year one, along with a consistent improvement in cash flow. The company's financial goal is to reach revenues of $20 million, generating after-tax profits of $3.6 million by the end of year four.

	1994	1995	1996	1997	1998
Sales	0	1,790	10,000	20,000	15,000
Gross Profit	0	624	4,413	8,825	6,620
Gross Margin (%)	0	34.96	44.13	44.13	44.13
Pre-Tax Profit	(25)	171	2,802	5,949	3,870
Total Assets	12	99.7	2,873	6,907	9,002
Total Liabilities	1	281	477	942	715
Net Worth	11	715	2,396	5,965	8,287

TK will achieve these goals by:

O Execution of a coordinated and comprehensive sales and marketing effort designed to maximize selling opportunities.

O Offering a unique and highly effective television childproofing system.

Safe Viewing features:

O Easy operation and programming

O Lets parents, grandparents and other responsible caregivers control what their children/ grandchildren watch on television, tunes out violent or explicit television programming at the touch of a button

O Non-restrictive to adult users with easy PIN # release of the television to full channel capability

O Automatic lock function insures secure operation

O Full function remote control for channel and volume control

O Connects easily to all television sets

O Two models available for all cable systems

       ☑ SJS100 for use with basic cable systems

       ☑ SJS200 for systems using channel descramblers

O Registered with the Federal Communications Commission

O UL listed and approved

O Full 90 day warranty

O Mastercard, Visa and American Express acceptance

Fully utilizing the experience, skills and industry contacts of Thomas Martin, Celeste Harding, and Casey Williams. TK's management team provides strong engineering and technical skills in combination with strong sales/marketing, financial, and administrative skills.

Offering high margin component parts including coaxial cables and connector head covers which will generate additional revenue and increase profitability.

The initial major short term goal for TK is to obtain start-up and early stage financing to provide adequate liquidity necessary to fund working capital needs and support growth. TK's short term financial goal is to realize strong revenue growth and increase profits through the projection period. The company will emphasize sales volume growth along with strong cost and inventory controls in order to achieve consistent cash flow and profitability improvement. Profits will be retained to finance operations, pay off investor debt and/or bank debt, and support future growth.

The long term goal of TK is to make SafeViewing the number one selling television childproofing system in the nation. TK will strive to substantially increase revenue, profitability, and cash flow as well as improve capitalization to support national and international distribution and future operations.

TK is currently seeking to raise capital through a private placement of securities. The company is initially seeking $625,000 by placing 416,667 shares of common stock representing an approximate 20.8% ownership interest. TK intends to use the proceeds of the offering to complete technical improvements, purchase inventory, establish sales, marketing and promotional programs, and for working capital purposes.

NATURE OF VENTURE

Background

The multi-billion dollar television and television products industry is undergoing continuous change due to changing consumer preferences, buying habits, social trends, and technological advancements. More recently, television programming has come under close scrutiny by the general public, parent groups, associations, coalitions, and the federal government. The principal concerns regard programs containing excessive violence, language, behavior, and explicit sexual content. In fact, an increasing number of Americans have expressed so much concern regarding the nature and content of much of the programming to which children--particularly their young children aged two through 13--are exposed that Federal lawmakers have drafted new legislation.

This new legislation would restrict violent and sexually explicit programming to times when children are unlikely to be in the audience. Additionally, cable television companies have agreed to develop a plan which would include a new program rating system (V-Chip Technology). In the meantime, parents continue to try to monitor their children's television viewing. Violence, sexual activity, language and behavior that many parents find unacceptable are graphically portrayed during all parts of the day, including afternoon and early evening hours that have traditionally been considered to be "family viewing time." However, no parent can be on guard all day, every day, to monitor every moment of television viewing by their children and the caregivers who are with them when the parents are not. Many so-called experts simply advise parents to "just turn off the set." But, when the parent is not at home, that advice is easier to give than it is to actually enforce. Therefore, many parents are looking for ways to ensure that their children have access only to programming that they judge to be valuable or, at the very least, acceptable in terms of personal task, judgment, and communication of moral values. At present, there are several devices available to parents who wish to pre-select the programming to which their children have access. These devices either control the flow of electricity to the television (leaving the parent to decide whether the set is to be "on" or "off") or work on a timing system which shuts the television completely off after a pre-determined period of time. None of these devices allow the parent to pre-select specific stations and "lock out" others.

Nature of the Product

SafeViewing represents a breakthrough in television childproofing. It offers parents a simple yet fully effective method of screening television programming and enabling them to selectively eliminate violent or explicit programming from their children's viewing choices without the loss of choices available to more mature audiences. Unlike any other device available on the market today, this system allows parents to select the stations to which they wish their children to have access and lock out those they judge to be unacceptable--all with just the touch of a button. Because there is no timing system, SafeViewing remains programmed until the adult enters a Personal Identification Number (PIN) which immediately unlocks the system and releases the television to full channel capability.

Extremely user-friendly, SafeViewing is easy to operate and program. After it is programmed by the adult, it may be operated by a child without compromising its security function. A full function remote control allows channel selection (pre-programmed channels when activated, full range of channels when de-activated) and volume control. SafeViewing is compatible with all televisions and comes in two models, one for basic cable systems and one for systems with descramblers.

TK will initially operate out of the home-based office of Tom Martin and Celeste Harding, Syracuse, NY. The office is fully equipped and functional and will allow for cost-effective management of the operation.

Location of Venture

TK's target market for SafeViewing will be households with basic cable service consisting of parents ages 25 to 55 or grandparents with children and/or grandchildren ages two through 13. The company will initially focus its sales and marketing efforts in the U.S. with the expectation of expanding internationally.

MARKET DESCRIPTION AND ANALYSIS

The concern of the general public regarding the types of programming on television is expected to heighten as more attention is drawn to issues such as excessive violence, language, behavior and explicit content by parents and lawmakers. Numerous studies by respected groups such as the American Medical Association, National Institute of Mental Health, American Psychological Association, and American Academy of Pediatrics have concluded that television violence is harmful to children and that viewing violence increases violent activity. These studies indicated that by the age of 18 the average American has viewed 200,000 acts of violence on television, including 40,000 murders. One study by the American Psychological Associates (APA) found "a significant relationship between exposure to television violence at eight years of age and antisocial acts--including serious, violent criminal offenses and spouse abuse--22 years later." Furthermore, studies have found that violence desensitizes the viewer, making him/her less likely to intervene on behalf of a victim when violence occurs in real life. These conclusions are not surprising when we consider that during prime time hours television portrays five to six violent acts per hour. Saturday morning children's programs are saturated with 20 to 25 violent acts per hour. In 1990, the American Academy of Pediatrics recommended pediatricians to advise "parents to limit their children's viewing to between one and two hours per day" because exposure to television violence was proven to increase a child's physical aggressiveness. Nevertheless, children between the ages of two and 11 watch television for an average of 28 hours each week.

Market Trends and Customer Buying Habits

The television networks and cable companies have been reluctant to address the problem of television violence aggressively although a plan has been drafted to create a new program rating system. The Federal government has proposed legislation to help control and restrict

TV violence, however, a great deal of debate is expected before passage of any new legislation. In the event such legislation is enacted, most parents are likely to be less than comfortable with a programming rating system in which levels of programming acceptability are determined and established by sources outside the home. As such, parents are still faced with the responsibility of monitoring their children's television viewing. SafeViewing provides parents with an affordable, high quality television childproofing system that ensures children have access to programming their parents determine as being acceptable.

TK's direct response marketing strategy is expected to be highly effective based on the buying habits of the target market. According to the Direct Marketing Association's 1993/1994 Statistical Fact Book (DMA Book), of the 102 million buyers ordering merchandise by mail or phone in 1992, approximately 35 million or 34.3% were adults from households with children between the ages of two and 11. The majority of these buyers are married females between the ages of 25 and 55 who are high school graduates with household incomes of $30,000 or more living and owning homes in the south.

The buying habits of the target market are further segmented by the following direct response programs: direct mail, catalog, print and television. According to the DMA Book, of the 19 million total buyers ordering from direct mail in 1992, 7.4 million were adults from households with children between the ages two and 11. Again, the largest numbers of buyers were married females, 25 to 55, high school educated with household incomes of $30,000 or more, living in the south. Overall, the statistics reveal an increase in respondents ordering from direct mail offers.

The buying habits of catalog buyers corresponds nicely with TK's profile customer. According to the DMA Book, of the 85.7 million adults who purchased from catalogs in 1992, 29.8 million were adults from households with children between ages two and 11. Most of the purchases are made by mail, despite the increase in the number of catalogues offering an 800 number for service, and are paid for by check.

The buying habits of those buyers ordering merchandise from advertisements in print media (newspaper and magazines) also reveals a large segment who fit TK's profile of the target market customer. Of the 48.5 million total adult buyers in 1992 ordering from magazines and newspapers, 14.1 million were adults from households with children between ages two and 11.

Television continues to be one of the most effective media alternatives influencing buyer purchases. According to Paul Kagen Associates, Inc., a respected market research firm, in 1993 there were approximately 94 million television households of which approximately 57 million were basic cable system subscribers. Consequently, home shopping programs (HSP's) have continued to become popular. In 1992, 5.5% of U.S. adults reported buying from a HSP, up from 3.7% in 1991. In 1992, more than 12 million U.S. adults watched the Home Shopping Network (HSN) and more than 11 million tuned into QVC. Of the 22.8 million adults watching home shopping programs in 1992, approximately 8.8 million were adults from households with children between the ages of two and 11. Of the 8.8 million, 3.4 million bought items from home shopping programs within the last three months of 1992.

Changing demographics could have a large-scale impact on the target market. A significant change in the demographic profile or buying habits of TK's target market customer could impact revenue growth in future years. However, statistics reveal a large target market spread over a broad geographical area. Furthermore, a large percentage of buyers ordering merchandise from direct response programs match the demographic profile of TK's target market customer. Additionally, the demographic profile is expected to change slowly over time and have only a minimal effect on TK's target market. The median age of the U.S. population is forecasted to increase from age 33 in 1990 to 36 in the year 2000. In addition, population growth is expected to continue in the south and midwest. Median household income levels are projected to remain in the $15,000 to $50,000 range.

A change in economic conditions can influence the demographics and buying habits of the target market. The most recent recession and moderate economic recovery has caused consumer spending to be inconsistent despite modest inflation and an increase in per capita disposable personal income over the last 14 years.

Changing social trends can have significant implications as evidenced by the heightened attention given to excessive violence, language, behavior, and explicit content of television programming. This increased level of concern, in conjunction with the timely introduction of SafeViewing, is expected to create a strong demand for the product. Nevertheless, TK's management realizes social trends can quickly change, causing demand to decline sharply in a short period of time. Furthermore, management realizes the "window of opportunity" could be relatively short in duration.

TK faces the additional problem of changing technology and the subsequent impact on the window of opportunity. A limited number of television manufacturers are now including some form of parental blocking capability in higher-end televisions. In addition, Congress is pushing for passage of legislation which would require the inclusion of a "V-chip" in all new television sets to give viewers the option to block out violent and explicit programming. In the future, if forced by this new legislation, all televisions could have this capability. These expected technological changes could substantially impact demand for SafeViewing and quickly erode market opportunities. TK plans to act swiftly to capitalize on existing opportunities.

There are a variety of competitive products available throughout the U.S. which offer varying methods for regulating programming access. These devices are manufactured specifically for local cable broadcast systems by manufacturers such as General Instrument or Scientific Atlanta. The type of television converter offered by these companies is an addressable descrambling converter utilized for premium channel reception or "pay per view" applications. This type of converter, depending on which model is chosen for use by the cable system operator, may or may not have parental control as an integral part of its operating software.

The above systems allow the operator to preclude access to individual channels by programming them out of the standard channel selection sequence. Channels which are eliminated must be added back into the programming sequence on an individual basis each time the operator chooses to view that particular "restricted" channel. In addition, many of

Demographic and Economic Trends

Social and Technological Changes and Trends

Current Competitors and Competitive Products

the converters offered have a parental control time limitation. Channels which are programmed in and restricted become available to the operator after a predetermined period of time. This time expiration feature is built into the software of the converter and cannot be eliminated by the operator/parent, thus requiring re-programming of the restricted channels when the time period has expired.

V-Chip technology, now in the development stages, will offer parents a method for precluding channel or programming availability by utilizing a rating system for channel programming. The parent would program the limits of programming acceptability based on a predetermined rating system into the device. Programs which are broadcast will initiate a coded signal to the receiving unit prior to airing of the program. This coded signal will be interpreted by the receiver at the owners home as either acceptable or rejected based on the viewer's selection. The inherent problem with this method is that the level of acceptability or rating system is determined at the broadcast center and that the system may or may not allow the parent a degree of restriction narrow enough to remain within the guidelines of acceptability as determined by the parent.

Alternate devices offer parental control by allowing a parent to program available channels into a grid on their television screen. Grimaldi Inc. based in Pittsburgh, Pennsylvania, has developed a computer chip known as the C-chip which is used in their cable box called Q-TV. The Q-TV box is expected to be introduced in 1995. The Q-TV system requires the parent fill in a grid with both channel selection and time slot which is accessible while in the lock mode. This method allows a parent to pick out specific programs which are available to a child at any given time. While this method is effective it requires that the grid be reviewed and reprogrammed on a weekly basis.

Several smaller companies provide competitive products with channel blocking and/or television monitoring capability. Stewart Research Inc. located in Alton, Illinois, developed "The Button" which is basically a childproof lock designed to prevent the child from turning on the television. Suntrex, Inc., based in Ft. Lauderdale, Florida, developed "Kid Watch." This timing device allows parents to program how long their children can watch television. When the designated time has elapsed, the TV shuts off. "Advantage" developed by Teck Associates based in Carmel, California, turns the TV on and off for two different time periods each day.

DESCRIPTION OF THE PRODUCT

Uniqueness of the Product

SafeViewing is a television childproofing system which is unlike any other device available on the market today. The system employs a unique technique for which the developer has acquired a patent pending status. This technique allows the user to easily change modes from "restricted" to "full access." Because there is no timing system, SafeViewing can be operated by the child without compromising its security function and is easy for the adult to program and operate. In addition to providing a unique childproofing system, TK will differentiate itself from the competition through execution of a sales and marketing plan designed to maximize selling opportunities. Unlike the competition, TK will market SafeViewing through many distribution networks including retailers, commissioned sales representatives, mail order houses, and directly to consumers. This multi-channel distribution will give the product significant exposure and brand name recognition. Most of the company's competitors rely on mail order to generate sales.

Advantages Over Competing Products

SafeViewing has several distinct advantages over the competition. The unique system, for which a patent is pending, is difficult for the competition to duplicate. The advantage of the parental control method as offered by the SafeViewing system is the ability to easily regulate the availability of selected channel programming. SafeViewing's primary function is to operate as a parental television control device and has been designed to be easily operated by both the adult and child user. The device puts the control of available programming in the hands of the parent. The system is designed to be usable in conjunction with the many different cable television broadcast systems and is non-restrictive to the adult user. The system is secure by virtue of the baseband converter technology incorporated in the design, as well as by the use of default programs which assure the user that the device remains in the locked mode when not in use by the adult operator. Competitive products do not incorporate a channel blocking system, using instead a lock-out feature based on television access time. Consequently, they are less secure and less effective than SafeViewing. However, the aforementioned products are also less expensive than SafeViewing and will compete on price rather than on security and effectiveness. The Q-TV cable box containing the C-chip offers channel blocking capability but is more difficult to program and does not permit the user to switch easily to full channel capability. Furthermore, the device is priced approximately $70 higher than the SafeViewing SJS100 model and is approximately four times as large. The channel blocking feature offered by cable companies and by competitors are effective. However, these systems do not give the user the ability to easily change modes from restricted to full access and, when available, must be rented from the local cable company.

Some of the devices discussed above remain in the development stages. Others are only available through local cable networks and would be cost prohibitive to the average user if they were available to the general public. The SafeViewing design, effective on all types of cable television broadcast systems, is designed to be extremely user friendly as well as affordable. These comprehensive features and its availability to the general public are the advantages to this system. No single system has yet become available on the market which offers the features available in SafeViewing.

MANAGEMENT

TK's management team is comprised of three highly focused, hard working, energetic and broadly experienced individuals whose combined talents provide a strong and qualified management team. Thomas Martin provides strong technical and engineering expertise and will be responsible for product development refinement, purchasing and operations, as well as overall company management. Celeste Harding provides strong administrative and organizational skills and is experienced and knowledgeable in the area of marketing and advertising production and programs. Casey Williams provides the needed experience and knowledge in the areas of office administration, finance and sales/marketing. His extensive business background and academic credentials compliment the strengths and talents of the other management team members.

BUSINESS STRATEGIES

TK will employ a strategy that will focus on providing a high quality, affordable television childproofing system which will be easier to operate and program, as well as more effective and less costly than comparable competitive products.

Production and Operations Strategy

The basic prototype design of SafeViewing parental control system is complete. TK will offer two distinct models of SafeViewing for use with basic cable systems or for systems with channel descramblers. Both models are registered with the Federal Communications Commission and are listed and approved by Underwriters Laboratories.

The methods of production associated with the SafeViewing products are intended to be kept within the Television for Kids, Inc. organization. The component parts for both the remote control and the baseband television converter associated with the system are available from numerous manufacturers within the United States. Customization of the base components is available from each of the manufacturers with pricing directly related to the quantity purchased. Base units will be purchased from the respective vendors. Remote control units are also available from a number of manufacturers.

Contec, L.P. has been contracted by Television for Kids, Inc. to provide both prototype design and testing as well as interfacing of the new design with existing baseband converter box control technology. Short term manufacturing requirements will be met by utilizing Contec, L.P. for short production runs of the remote control units. Contec, L.P. is a major manufacturer of television and converter box remote control devices in the United States and provides warranty and design services for the major cable converter box manufacturers for such clients as Zenith, General Instrument and Scientific Atlanta. Contec is based in Schenectady, New York and has engineering and manufacturing facilities in seven states, Mexico and overseas. The design work consisted of modifying a baseband television converter. Contec, L.P. has electronic design facilities for prototype hardware design development and testing as well as software development in their Schenectady facility. Contec was chosen for the base design work based on their ability to design, test and incorporate all aspects of the required project scope as well as their thorough knowledge of the equipment and practices of the cable converter industry.

Gemini Industries of Clifton, New Jersey has been contracted by TK to furnish "off the shelf" converter boxes. Gemini Industries represents the largest U.S. manufacturer of video accessory products available. The units will be customized, tested and repackaged by Television for Kids, Inc, at our facility in Syracuse, New York.

Long term production requirements will require firm contractual agreements between Television for Kids, Inc. and vendors for both remote control and baseband converter manufacture. Television for Kids, Inc. is presently in negotiations with Gemini Industries and Contec, L.P. to acquire fixed pricing and delivery schedules for large quantity purchases of the required component parts. Customization of both the remote control and the baseband converter boxes will be incorporated into large quantity purchases of the component parts. Each component will be tested at its respective factory for initial quality assurance.

Final quality assurance testing of the completed units will be performed by Television for Kids prior to packaging. Each unit will be tested for proper operation and assembly and then packaged for shipment at our Syracuse facility.

Television for Kids, Inc. is presently having discussions with Gemini Industries, Inc. with regard to a licensing agreement for the SafeViewing system. Gemini's large size and strong market penetration make them a desired candidate for an alliance with Television for Kids, Inc. for national distribution of this product. Gemini Industries is a vendor to many of the nations largest distribution outlets for this type of video product including: Circuit City, QVC Network, Wal Mart, Kmart, Rickel Home Center, Best Products, and Channel Home Center.

TK will support its differentiation strategy by effective execution of its marketing plan which contains several integral supporting strategies including promotional/sales, pricing, and distribution strategies.

Marketing Plan and Supporting Strategies

TK will employ several well organized and effective promotional and sales strategies to target qualified potential buyers and generate new business and selling opportunities in the U.S. and abroad. SafeViewing will be positioned in the market as a highly effective, high quality, affordable television childproofing system which will distinguish it from those competitors providing less effective, more expensive alternatives. The principal marketing strategy will involve a comprehensive direct response marketing plan which will include mass media advertising, direct response television, direct mail, mail order, and public relations programs. Management plans to hire a professional direct marketing consultant to assist in the development and execution of the company's marketing plans and strategies, with specific emphasis on multi-channel direct response mass marketing programs. TK will also attract new business through personal selling and tradeshows.

The company's mass media advertising program will include the use of multiple media sources. Media sources will be selected to maximize the return on allocated advertising dollars. TK will utilize the resources of a professional public relations firm to assist in creating awareness of and demand for SafeViewing among concerned parents locally and nationally. Public relations activities will include press release and product information placement in local and national general interest print (newspapers, magazines) and broadcast media [television news (local and national), features ("talk" shows) and selected radio programs] and retail industry and trade media. A media kit will be developed to provide background for interested editors, reporters, and distributors. The kit will include a product information sheet, photograph, press release, news articles, and a biographical profile of the principals. Following distribution of the media kit, the public relations firm will telephone key media personnel to gauge interest and intent to use the information as a basis for a news story. TK plans to aggressively promote the product through direct response television advertising on home shopping channels such as QVC and Home Shopping Network. In addition, TK's future promotional plans include the hiring of a professional advertising firm to assist in the development of local and national direct response television spot advertisements and/or an infomercial. This will provide instant product awareness and immediate national exposure to the target audience.

TK will complement its mass media advertising program with a direct response mail program to target specific potential user groups. These include parents groups and organizations, day care centers, elementary schools, and associations such as the National PTA, National Association for the Education of Young Children, Coalition for the Code, and National Coalition on Television Violence. TK has received the endorsement of The National Coalition on Television Violence and will seek the endorsement of these associations to enhance credibility. Other groups include community organizations as well as religious groups. The direct response mail program will include monthly mailings to targeted user groups. TK expects to obtain the member and subscriber lists of those associations, organizations and/or parents groups who endorse the product. TK will investigate oppor-

**Marketing Plan and
Supporting Strategies**

...continued

tunities to purchase or rent targeted lists of potential customers if necessary. In addition, mailing lists of specific potential user groups will be purchased or rented from reputable list management companies. These lists will be used to create the company's database of customers and future customer prospects. A professional database management company will be hired to assist in the development, management and enhancement of the TK database.

The marketing program will include a professionally designed brochure intended to create awareness, educate the consumer and provide product information. In conjunction with the brochure, TK intends to create a professionally produced informative sales videotape on the SafeViewing childproofing system. The video will be made available to all potential customers who have responded to our direct mail advertisement by having them contact our Toll Free 800 number or request the free video. The video is intended to lower sales resistance, educate and inform potential buyers, build perceived value in the product and deliver a powerful sales message. Follow up telephone calls will be made to all video recipients to provide additional information, answer questions, and to close each sale.

The marketing plan will also feature a direct response mail order program. This program will target specific national and international catalogues and magazines, thus giving SafeViewing wide national and international exposure.

TK will also seek to develop sales through distribution to retail chains such as Circuit City, Silo, BEST, Sears, and Walmart. The company will also consider licensing agreements with cable networks for use of SafeViewing as rental equipment. The technology could also be licensed to television manufacturers as a built-in feature. In addition, TK will explore licensing opportunities with marketing companies and will consider joint venture opportunities with childproofing companies. TK will also seek to develop sales through personal selling via commissioned sales representatives and house-to-house salesmen. Other promotional strategies will include the use of resident buyers, dealers, and national trade show promotions. Additionally, management plans to join certain industry groups such as the National Cable Television Association, Direct Marketing Association and Mail Order Association of America, as well as various local chambers of Commerce in order to build good community relations. These associations provide valuable market information and are often willing to sell or rent mailing lists of members and subscribers.

TK will utilize a combination of competitor-based pricing and penetration pricing. This will ensure pricing is in line with leading competitors and will enable the company to maximize market share gains. The company's strategy will be to position itself among existing competitors and compete on quality, performance, and effectiveness while offering value-based pricing. By developing a high quality image and reputation for security and effectiveness, TK will become an industry leader. Furthermore, this will enable the company to increase pricing over time as new and improved models are introduced. The suggested retail price is expected to be $129.95 for the SJS100 model and $149.95 for the SJS200 model. TK expects to offer wholesale pricing to allow for mark-ups of 40-50% against the suggested retail pricing.

SafeViewing will be produced and assembled by several manufacturers located in the northeastern U.S. The product will be shipped to the corporate office/warehouse location via UPS and orders shipped via UPS to specific buyer locations.

TK will provide a complete and detailed operating instruction booklet which will include an 800 number to call with problems and questions. In addition, the company will provide a 90 day limited warranty against defective material or workmanship. TK will also enclose a customer satisfaction response card with every unit to test for feedback on product quality and customer satisfaction.

TK will initially maintain a small employee base of non-management personnel which is expected to modestly increase despite strong anticipation revenue growth. Management will maintain a lean full-time staff by subcontracting for certain services such as fulfillment services, marketing specialists, and administrative support. Customer service representatives will be used for order taking, processing, and support services. In addition, TK will outsource for certain professional marketing, public relations, market research, testing, and analysis services.

Human Resources Strategy

TK will be owned and operated by Tom Martin and Celeste Harding who prefer to retain financial and managerial control.

Financial Strategy

The details of the financing sought and the risk of investment will be described in the Company's Subscription Agreement. All potential investors should read and thoroughly understand that Document.

TK is offering a maximum of 416,667 shares a Common Stock at a purchase price of $1.50 per share representing approximately 20.8% of the company's equity. Use of the proceeds will include ongoing product and technical development, product re-design and upgrades, general and administrative expenses, including salaries for existing employees and working capital through initial product launch. The company plans to use up to $96,918 to meet the costs of compensating its two key employees during the months June through December 1995 following the Private Offering. In addition, expenses related to the offering are estimated to be $10,000 to $20,000 which will be paid out of proceeds. TK expects that it will use the balance of the proceeds for market research and testing, sales and marketing programs and to support accounts receivable and inventory growth.

TK expects to realize strong sales and earnings growth in year one which will increase significantly by year five. This growth will be principally attributable to the development of new customers nationally and internationally. Growing demand for SafeViewing is expected in response to TK's comprehensive multi-channel direct response marketing programs. Additionally, TK will benefit from sales of high margin component parts. Through the five year period, management will effectively control purchases and inventory and improve operating efficiency and profitability. In addition, operating expenses will be carefully managed to ensure incremental revenue growth results in increased bottom line profitability.

Overall Growth Strategy

FINANCIAL DATA

Financial Statements

TK began operations on a very limited basis in early 1994. Expenses, particularly for development have increased throughout 1994. The company has not yet produced revenue and has experienced losses in each month as indicated in the 1994 monthly financial statements. A brief analysis of the actual results for 1994 are as follows:

1994 Income Statement

Sales

Because the company was still in a development stage, no sales were recorded in 1994 and therefore no costs were included in cost of goods sold.

Salaries

Management did not take salaries in 1994. Salaries are anticipated to begin in fiscal 1995. Salaries will be paid to full-time management only and are expected to cover living expenses.

Selling, General & Administrative Expenses

This included primarily legal expenses for both patent and general counsel as well as consultant fees and normal office operating expenditures.

Market Research

The principals of the company have conducted the majority of the market research to date. However, management may choose to use professional marketing research assistance to obtain an independent assessment of the target market.

Research and Development

All development costs are expenses as incurred and consist principally of prototype costs for software development and hardware configuration.

1994 Balance Sheet

Paid-In-Capital

There have been approximately $36 million in equity investments through December 1994. Management believes additional equity will be generated through the proceeds collected from additional investors; however, that is not reflected in this projection.

Inventory

Inventory as of 12/31/94 represents 100 SafeViewing units which have been tested and packaged and are ready to be sold.

Accounts Payable

This represents manufacturer and component supplier credit terms extended to TK through such companies as Contec and Gemini Industries.

Notes Payable

This represents the remaining balance of a note payable to Fred and JoAnne Dillard. The Dillards initially provided funding for the company in anticipation of becoming equity investors. Subsequently, they decided not to become equity investors and their investment was converted to a note payable. The principals are repaying the note from their personal cash investments into TK.

Financial Projects and Assumptions

The financial projections included are based on estimates and assumptions set forth therein, and have been delivered for the information and convience of persons who wish to evaluate the feasibility of the company's strategy and goals. Each such person who has received them realizes that financial projections are inherently speculative. The financial projections are based upon the company's assumptions reflecting conditions it expects to exist or the course of action it expects to take. As the company is in the late development to start-up stage and as such has limited operating experience, these projections are based on estimates and not on the company's historical results. Because events and circumstances do not occur as anticipated, there will be differences between the financial projections and actual results, and those differences may be material. The financial projections are based upon detailed underlying assumptions. Interested parties should consult their own professional advisors regarding the validity and reasonableness of the assumptions contained herein.

1994 Balance Sheet

	Actual Jan	Feb*	Mar*	Apr*	May*	Jun*	Jul*	Aug*	Sep*	Oct*	Nov*	Budget Dec
Assets												
Cash	7,025	12,017	9,984	7,951	5,918	3,885	35,598	32,047	19,409	14,994	10,913	2,364
Accts Receivable	0	0	0	0	0	0	0	0	0	0	0	0
Inventory	0	0	0	0	0	0	0	0	7,879	8,947	9,437	9,537
Current Assets	7,025	12,017	9,984	7,951	5,918	3,885	35,598	32,047	27,288	23,941	20,450	11,901
Gross Fixed	0	0	0	0	0	0	0	0	0	0	130	130
Accumulated Depreciation	0	0	0	0	0	0	0	0	0	0	0	0
Net Fixed Assets	0	0	0	0	0	0	0	0	0	0	130	130
Prepaid	0	0	0	0	0	0	0	0	0	0	0	0
Other Assets	0	0	0	0	0	0	0	0	0	0	0	0
Total Assets	7,025	12,017	9,984	7,951	5,918	3,885	35,598	32,047	27,288	23,941	20,580	12,031
Liabilities	0	0	0	0	0	0	0	0	0	0	0	0
Accounts Payable	0	0	0	0	0	0	0	0	0	0	0	0
Short Term Debt	0	0	0	0	0	0	0	0	0	0	0	0
Notes Payable	0	0	0	0	0	0	14,050	11,499	8,948	6,397	3,846	1,295
Accruals	0	0	0	0	0	0	0	0	0	0	0	0
Current Port Long Term Debt	0	0	0	0	0	0	0	0	0	0	0	0
Current Liabilities	0	0	0	0	0	0	14,050	11,499	8,948	6,397	3,846	1,295

1994 Balance Sheet
...continued

Actual Jan	Feb*	Mar*	Apr*	May*	Jun*	Jul*	Aug*	Sep*	Oct*	Nov*	Budget Dec
Long Term Debt											
0	0	0	0	0	0	0	0	0	0	0	0
Total Liabilities											
0	0	0	0	0	0	14,050	11,499	8,948	6,397	3,846	1,295
Net Worth											
Paid in Capital											
7,025	14,050	14,050	14,050	14,050	14,050	35,691	35,691	35,691	35,691	35,691	35,691
Retained Earnings											
0	(2,033)	(4,06)	(6,099)	(8,132)	(10,165)	(14,143)	(15,143)	(17,351)	(18,147)	(18,957)	(24,955)
Total Net Worth											
7,025	12,017	9,984	7,951	5,918	3,885	21,548	20,548	18,340	17,544	16,734	10,736
Total Liabilities & Net Worth											
7,025	12,017	9,984	7,951	5,918	3,885	35,598	32,047	27,288	23,941	20,580	12,031

1995 Income Statement

Sales

Sales in each month equal the number of units sold multiplied by the sale price. All sales in 1995 are projected to be model SJS100 (sales cost and unit price would increase proportionally if there is a greater mix of SJS200 units). The sales price is primarily driven by the selling price of competitive products currently on the market which range from $29.00 to $250.00. The list price of the SJS100 model will be $129.95 and the SJS200 model will be $149.95. The wholesale price is expected to be $90.00 for the SJS100 and $109.00 for the SJS200 which will allow for mark-ups of 40% to 45% against the retail price.

Sales are projected to begin in May and are segmented as: Catalog and Other (Wholesale) and Direct Response Retail (Retail). Sales are projected to increase monthly in conjunction with the execution of TK's targeted sales and marketing programs. The companies direct marketing/video program will fuel retail sales which are projected to reach $1,195,540 (or 9200 units) and comprise 67% of total sales. The Catalog and Other sales segment will consist principally of wholesale sales and will comprise the remaining $594,000 in sales (or 6600 units).

Costs of Goods Sold

Per unit costs to produce are derived from firm component supplier quotes which are based on minimum purchasing requirements and include estimated costs for assembly, packaging and shipping. The total cost for the SJS100 is projected to average $81.68 per unit through July of 1995. Costs of Goods Sold are expected to decline to $71.68 per unit thereafter as a result of more favorable pricing from cable box and remote control suppliers due to an increase in minimum purchase quantities from 1500 units to 3600 units. The cost structure will vary depending on the sales mix of wholesale and retail units. Retail units will carry a slightly higher cost per unit but will maintain a significantly higher gross margin as compared to wholesale units.

	Operating Expenses

Management salaries are projected to begin in July of 1995. The remaining salaries will be for part-time assembly and packaging employees.

Salaries

The principal SG & A items include advertising and promotional costs, insurance, legal, consultants and postage. Advertising and promotional costs includes general and product liability expenses. Legal includes expenses for both patent and general council. Postage expenses correlate to the increasing level of the monthly mailing program.

Selling, General and Administrative Expenses

Includes expenses for focus groups, market testing and analysis.

Market Research

Includes expenses relative to product refinement and enhancement.

Research and Development

The effective tax rate is projected to be 40%. For the purposes of this projection, available tax losses are not carried forward but are available to be used in future periods to reduce taxable income.

Taxes

1995 Balance Sheet

TK will be moving from a development stage to an early stage company in 1995 and as such will require significant capital. Projections are based on an investment of $625,000 into the company during 1995. Capital infusions are currently projected to occur from February to October. The capital infustions may be in the form of government grants, government backed or independently arranged long or short term debt, or some other form. However, it will must likely be in the form of equity, and for the purpose of these projections, will be shown that way.

Paid-in-Capital

TK will offer terms of 2%/10 net 30 day terms to all wholesale clients. The company expects collection of receivables between 30 to 50 days from the invoice date. Receivable levels are calculated to be the current months sales plus 70% of the previous months sales.

Accounts Receivable

The projected sales levels assume a need for a 45 to 50 day inventory of completed units.

Inventory

A minimum of fixed assets are expected to be purchased. Necessary items will include computer hardware and software, telephone system, fax machine, modem and printer. These items will be purchased or leased on an as needed basis. Equipment will be depreciated over two years assuming straight line depreciation.

Fixed Assets

TK has negotiated terms with most suppliers including Contec. TK expects to negotiate 30 day terms with Gemini Industries by August.

Accounts Payable

Upon achieving profitability in the late months of 1995, TK will attempt to establish a line of credit from a financial institution, however, no availability of funds is expected prior to year end.

Short Term Debt

The equipment needs for 1995 are projected to be financed by the proceeds provided by the principals and investors.

Long Term Debt

1995 Income Statement

	Jan	Feb	Mar	Apr	May	Jun	Jul	Aug	Sep	Oct	Nov	Dec	Total
Sales	0	0	0	0	87,980	96,980	157,960	166,960	227,940	297,920	367,900	385,900	1,789,540
Costs of Goods Sold	0	0	0	0	63,111	73,344	114,688	107,688	144,032	187,376	230,720	244,720	1,165,679
Depreciation	0	0	0	0	11	11	11	11	11	11	11	11	88
Gross Profit	0	0	0	0	24,858	23,625	43,261	59,261	83,897	110,533	137,169	141,169	623,773
Gross Profit %	0.0	0.0	0.0	0.0	28.3	24.4	27.4	35.5	36.8	37.1	37.3	36.6	34.9
Operating Expenses													
Salaries & Benefits	0	0	0	0	0	0	12,684	13,284	13,284	13,284	13,884	13,884	80,304
Payroll Taxes	0	0	0	0	0	0	1,395	1,461	1,461	1,461	1,527	1,527	8,833
SG & A Expenses													
Advertising & Promotion	0	0	0	4,700	34,000	5,400	9,400	9,400	12,800	17,200	19,100	19,100	131,100
Bank Charges	0	0	0	0	650	650	1,040	1,040	1,559	1,559	1,949	1,949	10,396
Car/Delivery	0	0	0	50	100	100	100	100	100	100	100	100	850
Depreciation/Amortization	0	0	0	0	0	146	146	146	146	146	146	146	876
Insurance	0	0	0	0	4,532	4,532	4,532	4,532	4,532	4,532	4,532	4,532	36,258
Telephone	100	100	100	150	300	300	400	400	400	500	500	600	3,850
Utilities	50	50	50	50	50	50	50	50	50	50	50	50	600
Legal/Accounting	0	2,000	2,250	8,777	8,777	777	777	777	777	777	777	777	27,243
Consultants	600	1,555	1,555	1,555	1,555	1,555	1,555	1,555	1,555	1,555	1,555	1,555	17,705
Office Supplies	0	0	0	50	440	330	790	835	1,140	1,490	1,840	1,930	8,845
Office Expenses	0	0	0	100	100	100	100	100	100	100	100	100	900
Taxes & Licenses	8	8	8	8	8	8	8	8	8	8	8	8	96

1995 Income Statement
...continued

	Jan	Feb	Mar	Apr	May	Jun	Jul	Aug	Sep	Oct	Nov	Dec	Total
Travel & Entertainment													
	0	0	200	100	100	100	150	150	200	200	200	200	1,600
Dues/Subscriptions													
	0	0	0	50	50	50	50	50	50	50	50	50	450
Rent													
	0	0	0	0	250	250	250	250	250	250	250	250	2,000
Equipment Rent													
	0	0	0	75	75	100	100	800	800	800	800	800	4,350
Postage													
	0	0	30	50	5,000	5,000	10,000	10,000	15,000	20,000	25,000	25,000	115,080
Market Research													
	0	0	0	5,000	0	0	0	0	0	0	0	0	5,000
R & D													
	0	0	0	200	200	200	200	200	200	200	200	200	1,800
Total Operating Expenses													
	758	3,713	4,193	20,915	56,187	19,502	43,728	45,138	54,412	64,263	72,568	72,758	458,136
Operating Profit Loss													
	(758)	(3,713)	(4,193)	(20,915)	(31,329)	4,123	(467)	14,123	29,485	46,270	64,601	68,411	165,637
Operating Profit/Loss %													
	0%	0%	0%	0%	0%	4%	0%	8%	14%	16%	18%	18%	9%
Interest Income													
	0	50	100	50	250	300	550	850	700	1,300	1,200	1,300	6,650
Pre-Tax Loss/Income													
	(758)	(3,663)	(4,093)	(20,865)	(31,079)	4,423	83	14,973	30,185	47,570	65,801	69,711	172,287
Taxes													
	0	0	0	0	0	1,769	19	5,886	11,971	18,925	26,306	27,870	92,746
Net Income/Loss													
	(758)	(3,663)	(4,093)	(20,865)	(31,079)	2,654	64	9,087	18,214	28,645	39,495	41,841	79,541
Units Sold													
	0	0	0	0	800	900	1400	1500	2000	2600	3200	3400	15,800
Average Price Per Unit													
	0.00	0.00	0.00	0.00	109.98	107.76	112.83	111.31	113.97	114.58	114.97	113.50	113.26

Annual Projections

Income Statement

Sales from 1996 to 1998 equal the number of units sold multiplied by the average sale price. TK expects sales to increase significantly through the projection period due to the success of the company's multi-level mass marketing programs. Approximately 70% of the company's sales are projected to be retail sales to the consumer as a result of orders generated primarily from the company's direct response mail/video program. Due to the changing technology and anticipated increase in competition, sales are projected to decline approximately 25% beginning in mid 1998.

Cost of Goods Sold

TK expects to realize improvement in the cost of goods in 1996 and thereafter due to improved pricing from component suppliers of both remote control units and converter boxes. Management believes that more favorable prices will be attainable as a result of design improvements and quantity purchase discounts.

Operating Expenses

Salaries

Salaries are anticipated to begin in July of 1995. Salaries will be paid to full time management and part time personnel. Management salaries are expected to be at the minimum level required to cover living expenses.

Selling, General and Administrative Expenses

Due to substantial sales growth from 1996 through 1998, selling, general and administrative expenses are forecast to increase due principally to the higher level of expenditures related to the company's mass marketing programs. In addition, SG & A expenses decline as a percentage of sales during 1996 (14.2%) and 1997 (12.9%) due to tight expense controls. These expenses are projected to increase slightly in 1998 (16.2%) due to anticipated sales declines.

Market Research

These expenditures remain steady through the projection period and include expenses for market testing and analysis.

Research and Development

These expenses will continue as the company invests in new product development as well as product refinement and enhancement.

Balance Sheet

Accounts Receivable

The company expects to generate accounts receivable from wholesale customers including catalog and mail order companies. Management projects collections to average 50 days despite sales terms of 2% 10 days net 30 days.

Inventory

These estimates are driven by the annual costs of goods sold projections. Management projects a need for a 45 to 50 day inventory of finished product to fulfill customer requirements.

Fixed Assets

Fixed asset purchases will include primarily computer and office equipment. The bulk of equipment will be purchased or leased on an as needed basis and will be depreciated over two years assuming straight line depreciation.

Component suppliers are expected to extend 30 day terms and TK will generally pay within these terms.

No short term debt is expected, however, the company expects to establish a bank line of credit by mid-1996 to support accounts receivable and inventory if required prior to year end.

TK is expected to achieve profitability in 1996 and thereafter. The company expects to finance its growth out of cash flow from operations. No additional equity will be required after 1995.

	12/31/94	12/31/95	12/31/96	12/31/97	12/31/98
Sales	0	1,789,540	10,000,000	20,000,000	15,000,000
Costs of Goods Sold	0	1,165,679	5,587,120	11,174,849	8,380,500
Depreciation	0	88	42	0	0
Gross Profit	0	623,773	4,412,838	8,825,151	6,619,500
Gross Profit%	0.0	34.9	44.13	44.13	44.13
Operating Expenses					
Salaries & Benefits	0	81,090	185,320	280,200	288,680
Payroll Taxes	0	8,920	20,385	30,822	31,754
SG & A Expenses					
Advertising & Promotion	343	131,100	478,400	1,027,600	1,027,600
Bank Charges	0	10,396	45,000	105,000	75,000
Car/Delivery	0	850	2,000	4,000	5,000
Depreciation/Amortization	0	876	4,252	3,372	0
Insurance	0	36,258	201,000	401,000	301,000
Telephone	285	3,850	10,000	20,000	25,000
Utilities	0	600	1,000	1,500	1,300
Legal/Accounting	14,517	27,243	22,000	35,00	25,000
Consultants	1,850	17,705	12,200	15,000	15,000
Office Supplies	401	8,845	18,000	24,000	21,000
Office Expenses	361	900	2,000	4,000	5,000
Taxes & Licenses	240	96	200	900	500
Travel & Entertainment	93	1,600	8,000	15,000	15,000
Dues/Subscriptions	0	450	500	600	600
Rent	0	2,000	5,000	7,500	7,500
Equipment Rent	228	4,350	9,600	9,600	9,600
Postage	389	115,080	600,000	900,000	900,000
Market Research	0	5,000	5,000	5,000	5,000
R & D	6,248	1,800	2,000	2,000	2,000

Sidebar labels (right column):

Accounts Payable

Short Term Debt

Net Worth

**Annual Projections
Income Statement**

Annual Projections Income Statement
...continued

Total Op Expenses	24,955	459,009	1,620,857	2,891,594	2,761,534
Operating Profit Loss	(24,955)	164,764	2,791,981	5,933,557	3,857,966
Operating Profit/Loss %	0%	9.21%	27.92%	29.77%	25.72%
Interest Income	0	6,650	10,000	15,000	12,000
Pre-Tax Loss/Income	(24,955)	171,414	2,801,981	5,948,557	3,869,966
Taxes	0	68,566	1,120,792	2,379,423	1,547,986
Net Income/Loss	(24,955)	102,848	1,681,189	3,567,134	2,321,980
Units Sold	0	15,800	87,200	174,401	132,508
Average Price Per Unit	0.00	113.26	114.68	114.68	113.20

Annual Projections Balance Sheet

	12/31/94	12/31/95	12/31/96	12/31/97	12/31/98
Assets					
Cash	2,364	426,058	1,716,652	4,602,567	7,203,369
Accounts Receivable	0	302,857	410,959	821,918	684,932
Inventory	9,537	259,496	688,823	1,377,721	1,033,212
Current Assets	11,901	988,411	2,816,434	6,802,206	8,921,513
Gross Fixed	130	3,630	8,630	8,630	8,630
Accumulated Depreciation	0	964	5,258	8,630	8,630
Net Fixed Assets	130	2,666	3,372	0	0
Prepaid	0	4,533	51,000	101,000	76,000
Other Current Assets	0	1,000	2,000	4,000	4,000
Total Assets	12,031	996,610	2,872,806	6,907,206	9,001,513
Liabilities					
Accounts Payable	0	274,332	459,215	918,481	688,808
Short Term Debt	0	0	0	0	0
Notes Payable	1,295	0	0	0	0
Accruals	0	7,000	18,000	24,000	26,000
Curr. Port Long Term Debt	0	0	0	0	0
Current Liabilities	1,295	281,332	477,215	942,481	714,808
Long Term Debt	0	0	0	0	0
Total Liabilities	1,295	281,332	477,215	942,481	714,808
Net Worth					
Paid in Capital	35,691	660,691	660,691	660,691	660,691
Retained Earnings	(24,955)	54,587	1,734,900	5,304,034	7,626,014
Total Net Worth	10,736	715,278	2,395,591	5,964,725	8,286,705
Total Liabilities & Net Worth					
	12,031	996,610	2,872,806	6,907,206	9,001,513

	12/31/94	12/31/95	12/31/96	12/31/97	12/31/98

Annual Projections Cash Flow Analysis

Cash Flow From Operating Activities

	12/31/94	12/31/95	12/31/96	12/31/97	12/31/98
Net Income (Loss)	24,955	79,541	1,681,189	3,569,134	2,321,980
Depreciation	0	964	4,294	3,372	0
(Incr)/Decrease in Trade Receivables	0	(302,854)	(108,102)	(410,959)	136,986
(Incr)/Decrease in Inventory	(9,537)	(249,959)	(429,327)	(688,898)	344,509
Incr/(Decrease) in Accounts Payable	0	274,332	184,833	459,266	(229,673)
Incr/(Decrease) in Accruals	0	7,000	11,000	6,000	2,000
(Incr)/Decrease in other Assets	0	(5,533)	(47,467)	(52,000)	25,000
Net Cash Used in Operating Activities	(34,492)	(196,512)	1,296,470	2,885,915	2,600,802

Cash Flows from Investment Activities

	12/31/94	12/31/95	12/31/96	12/31/97	12/31/98
Purchase of Equipment	(130)	(3,500)	(5,000)	0	0
(Incr)/Decrease in other Assets	0	0	0	0	0
Net Cash Used in Investment Activities	(130)	(3,500)	(5,000)	0	0

Cash Flow from Financing Activities

	12/31/94	12/31/95	12/31/96	12/31/97	12/31/98
Incr/(Decrease) in Notes Payable	1,295	(1,295)	0	0	0
Increase-Paid in Capital	35,691	625,000	0	0	0
Net Cash Provided by Financing Activities	36,986	623,705	0	0	0
Net Change in Cash	2,364	423,694	1,291,470	2,885,915	2,600,802
Beginning Cash	0	2,364	426,058	1,717,528	4,603,443
Ending Cash	2,364	426,058	1,717,528	4,603,443	7,204,245

**Annual Projections
Salary Budget**

	12/31/95	12/31/96	12/31/97	12/31/98
Compensation and Benefits				
President	53,334	90,000	90,000	100,000
Vice President	43,584	65,000	75,000	85,000
Assembly & Production1	14,400	80,640	115,200	103,680
Assembly & Production2				
Assembly & Production3				
Total	81,090	225,640	280,200	288,680
Management Head Count	2	2	2	2
Assembly & Prod. Head Count	3	8	10	8
Total	5	10	12	10

**Annual Projections
Ratios**

	12/31/94	12/31/95	12/31/96	12/31/97	12/31/98
Liquidity					
Working Capital	10,606	707,079	2,339,219	5,859,725	8,206,705
Quick Ratio	1.83	2.59	4.46	5.76	11.04
Current Ratio	9.19	3.51	5.90	7.22	12.48
Growth %					
Net Sales	n/a	n/a	458.80%	100.00%	-25.00%
Total Assets	n/a	8183.68%	188.36%	140.43%	30.32%
Total Liabilities	n/a	21624.50%	69.63%	97.50%	-24.16%
Profitability %					
Return on Assets	n/a	10.32%	58.52%	51.67%	25.80%
Return on Equity	n/a	14.38%	70.18%	59.84%	28.02%
Gross Margin	n/a	34.96%	44.13%	44.13%	44.13%
Operating Margin	n/a	9.21%	27.92%	29.77%	25.72%
Effective Tax Rate	n/a	40.00%	40.00%	40.00%	40.00%
Activity					
Receivable Days	n/a	124.92	50.00	50.00	50.00
Inventory Days	n/a	54.54	45.00	45.00	45.00
Payable Days	n/a	57.66	30.00	30.00	30.00

The design and incorporation of the specific means and methods of incorporating intelligence into the base remote control design of the SafeViewing parental control system is the subject matter of a pending patent application filed with the U.S. Patent and Trademark Office on October 23, 1993. All materials issued with regard to the SafeViewing unit are clearly marked as U.S. Patent Pending indicative of the rights associated with a potential patent. Ownership of the patent will be in the name of Thomas P. Martin with exclusive licensing to Television for Kids, Inc. All contributory parties are subject to Confidentiality and Non Disclosure Agreements signed prior to all contractual agreements for both services and ownership of all designs, hardware and software associated with this project.

The components of the SafeViewing parental control system are derivatives of existing component parts which have been approved by both Underwriters Laboratories and the Federal Communications Commission. Modifications to the existing components for this product do not undermine the integrity of the basic designs and therefore do not require additional regulatory approvals. We are at this time investigating the requirement for an additional FCC approval for the addition of a video signaling switching network to be incorporated into a second generation of the base product. This switching network is being designed by Contec L.P. and will be incorporated within the FCC guidelines for the specific application. Regulatory approval will be acquired by Contec, L.P. on behalf of Television of Kids, Inc.

The Safeviewing control system is based on a standard microprocessor control system for both its remote control unit and baseband tuning converter. The remote control unit transmits a pulsed infrared beam to a receiver in the baseband converter whose microprocessor initiates a predetermined control sequence for the tuning of specific frequencies associated with broadband coaxial cable television transmission. The receiving converter box converts the broadband signal to a single frequency which is relayed to the television tuner for specific channel reception. The use of a baseband converter unit allows for regulating both the audio and video signal characteristics of the specified frequency. The advantage to utilizing the baseband control method over other standard cable signal control or tuning converters is that the signal control window is extremely narrow and as such does not allow for overlap of received signals. This control method and converter will not allow a television tuner to deviate from the baseband broadcast frequency as sent out by the converter box and any such deviation will result in an audio and video signal loss at the television set. This feature results in a secure method of regulating the signal or channel available at the television.

SafeViewing takes advantage of the narrow window signal control offered in base band converter design and further enhances its control method. Standard infrared remote control devices utilize application specific microprocessors, commonplace technology, to transmit a specific infrared signal which is interpreted by the microprocessor within the receiving converter boxes which in turn intiates a specific program sequence. The remote control unit which drives the SafeViewing parental control system has been upgraded to incorporate not only the basic remote control features of channel selection, channel memory and volume control but has the added feature of on-board nonvolatile memory. The addition of this memory to the basic remote control design enables the SafeViewing remote control to be programmed by the user to "lock out" specific transmission sequences. A user program-

PATENTS, TRADEMARKS AND REGULATORY APPROVAL

EXHIBIT

SafeViewing Description and Operation

**SafeViewing Description
and Operation**
...continued

mable Personal Identification Number (PIN) is utilized to provide access to the programming sequences.

The "lock out" feature of the SafeViewing operates by disabling the control keypad of the remote control unit. While in the locked mode only specific transmissions sequences are available to the operator. Those transmissions include: power on/off, channel memory scan, volume control, and sleep timer activation. The keypad of the SafeViewing remote control unit is enhanced to indicate to a child which functions are operable while locked. This allows for easily teaching a child how to use the device. Operation of the device is limited to selection of channels preporgrammed into memory by an adult user prior to locking of the unit. The unit is also preprogrammed to tune the television to a user programmed reference channel when it is turned on or off.

Virtual Shopping

BUSINESS PLAN

CLICK 'N SHOP INC.

425 Loop Rd., Ste. 14
Chicago, IL 60060

March 1995

This business plan for a virtual reality application is an example of how state-of-the-art technology can become the basis for a popular start-up business. It discusses the use of a virtual shopping kiosk that allows customers to connect via video teleconference to retailers whose products are displayed in the booth. The plan features considerations of strategy and technology as well as a comparative balance sheet and other financial details.

- EXECUTIVE SUMMARY

- BUSINESS DESCRIPTION

- THE MARKET

- MARKETING

- TECHNOLOGY/SYSTEM SUMMARY

- THE MANAGEMENT TEAM

- COMPETITION

- FUTURE PLANS

- SUMMARY

- FINANCIAL INFORMATION

EXECUTIVE
SUMMARY

Click 'n Shop Inc. is a Delaware corporation which is looking to secure expansion capital to begin the roll out of its Point 'n Click Booths and to provide working capital to fully exploit the opportunities presented by using its proprietary technology to enable retailers to visually communicate with their customers using a videoconferencing connection.

The Company

Click 'n Shop Inc. (CSI) utilizes video compression technology (video teleconferencing) to create an alternative retail distribution channel which will enable America's premier retailers an opportunity to market and sell their products directly to consumers using tomorrow's "electronic superhighway" ...today.

CSI will build, install and operate a series of Point 'n Click Booths (PCB). The PCB is an 18 square foot kiosk that permits a user to sit down and have a face-to-face conversation with any retailer equipped to receive videoconference calls. The PCB, in an effort to minimize risk, capitalizes on off-the-shelf proven technology and uses proprietary CSI software to create a point-of-sale location which can be used efficiently by a multitude of retailers.

The PCB is a complete marketing system which will be placed in high-traffic areas, such as airline lounges, hotel lobbies, superstores, office buildings, etc. The video monitor on the front of the unit is used to draw customers to the PCB by advertising retailer's products on the screen. Once inside the PCB, the customer encounters an electronic browsing screen that enables him to use interactive touch-screens to preview retailer's products and generate manufacturer's discount coupons.

While browsing retailer's product offerings, the customer can press "connect" at any point they have a question or would like to place an order. For example, a customer who is interacting with the system regarding a Hawaiian vacation and has a question would touch the "connect" button on the monitor. At that instant, the PCB establishes an automatic two-way live videoconference directly between the customer and the retailer. This customer would be instantly connected to the American Express Travelways Travel Center, where an AMEX travel expert would assist the customer in making a selection.

This new retailing concept provides a hybrid environment in which today's sophisticated customers can easily manipulate information in concert with assistance from a sales expert to efficiently make a purchase decision. Both the customer and sales person can simultaneously view the product information screen and each other, thus enabling the sales person to add both visual and audio input into the sales process, while at the same time maintaining a human element. The end result of this innovative process is a fresh retailing climate which will facilitate the goals of both the consumer and the retailer.

From the customer's viewpoint, the PCB is indeed a virtual mall. While standing in one spot, the customer can contact, talk to, discuss with, and shop from literally hundreds of retailers selling every different kind of product and/or service, and the customer is always in control of the shopping and selection process. The PCB has created exactly what today's consumers are looking for--a convenient, high information sales process that still maintains the "human touch."

To retailers, the PCB represents a tremendous opportunity to add hundreds of new distribution outlets without incurring the hard costs of building stores, carrying inventory, and staffing stores with salespeople. A retail tenant in the PCB has combined the best of both "store" and "non-store" distribution--the ability of an "expert" salesperson to provide information to the consumer and "close" the sale, as well as the benefits of minimal inventory and staffing costs which enable the retailer to price their products more competitively.

To CSI and its investors, the PCB represents an immediate application of technology to take advantage of, and profit from, the American retailer's stated desire to "sell outside of their walls." The introduction of the PCB will position CSI as the first company to advocate and market the use of video conferencing in a direct business to consumer application. By being in front of the "electronic tidal wave," CSI will be positioned to profit handsomely as the nations first "virtual landlords."

The July 26, 1993 cover of Business Week declared "Retailing will Never Be the Same." The cover story deals with the merging of entertainment, telecommunications and electronics into the "electronic superhighway." Major conglomerates have aired television commercials explaining the benefits of 500 channels and interactive TV. Emerging technologies, like Virtual Reality, are beginning to make their way into real-world business applications. From an investment standpoint, it seems clear that the electronic tidal wave is coming, and those best positioned when it hits will benefit the most.

Strategy

CSI has the opportunity to be enormously successful in its endeavor, due primarily to its unique approach to implementing its products and services. The continuous onslaught of such technological developments as hand-held computers, interactive TV, and the video dial tone are changing the way American consumers shop. The electronic superhighway is creating a new digital pipeline that will directly connect retailers with consumers.

The corporate giants are all jockeying to build the consumer end of this pipeline. While these elephants fight for the rights to equip every American household with interactive consumer shopping capabilities, CSI believes that minimal effort has been expended towards developing the retail end of this pipeline. Even if millions of American households were equipped with interactive TV's today, most retailers in most industries are incapable of distributing their products via an electronic format.

America's most powerful retailers have recognized that in order to gain market share and thrive in the future, they must be positioned to market their products and services using this new technology. There is tremendous media attention being focused on the coming "electronic superhighway." CSI will enable business to take advantage of retailing's future today. In developing the PCB, CSI has recognized that today's retailers and telemarketers do not have the hardware, software, or training necessary to sell their products through electronic and video formats. Therefore, CSI has designed and built the Retailer's Point 'n Click Desktop (RPCD). The RPCD is a combination of state-of-the-art, yet off the shelf, hardware components and a US Patent Pending unit that is connected and operated by CSI's proprietary software and companies in the country to offer the necessary technology to convert any company in any industry into a video/virtual retailer, filling the untapped end of the pipeline.

CSI believes that the home consumer market will ultimately be the most lucrative. CSI also believes its strategic positioning is the best fit for the current state of affairs in the electronics industry. In the short term, CSI will build and operate PCB's all around the country, providing a real, practical application of the associated technologies during the years it will take for the corporate conglomerates to implement the grand scheme that enables every household to shop interactively. In the long term, regardless of who (Cable TV, Cellular, Telco, etc.) ultimately prevails, when home shopping becomes a reality, CSI will market the RPCD, and will equip the retail end of the pipeline to feed the product-hungry consumer end. CSI will be profiting from the new method of retailing via its virtual malls long before the home consumer market becomes reality.

Status

CSI completed the development and construction of the first Point 'n Click Shopping Center (PCSC) and began the initial live revenue generating application in February 1994, to prove the concept and shorten the learning curve required for future PCSCs. With the information gathered during the beta test, CSI has developed the PCB) which will allow consumers a smaller footprint, in which they can have a more private interaction with the retailer.

CSI currently has Danmark International (a $500 million in sales electronics cataloger) and American Express Travelways as the first two anchor tenants slated for the 20 PCB roll-out scheduled for May 1995. The PCB roll-out will be concentrated in two fantastic consumer markets; Minneapolis/St. Paul and Houston. The initial locations include the Northwest Airlines Frequent Flyer Lounges, The Hyatt Hotel lobbies in each city, Rice University and several premier office towers.

CSI is also engaged in discussions with several other major retailers that have expressed an interest in the PCB, including Best Buy (a retailer of home electronics), Dayton's (Department Stores), NordicTrak (a retailer of home exercise equipment) and Sky Mall (Department Stores). Moreover, Recycle to New, Inc. (an international clothing recycler) has placed an order for the first Private Network PCB to be delivered in May 1995.

Financial Requirements

Click 'n Shop Inc. has completed the successful development and installation of the nation's first Point 'n Click Shopping Center. Due to the initial positive reactions from shoppers at the Bob's Grocery PCSC (an overwhelming 89.6% responded that they will shop this way in the future), CSI intends to implement its business plan with the systematic proliferation of PCBs around the country.

CSI expects to raise $2.5 million to initiate the operating phase of this revolutionary retailing concept. With 50 corporate owned PCBs slated for 1995 and an additional 7 Private Network PCBs targeted for 1995, the Company will have the inertia to capitalize on its preeminent position as the nation's first virtual landlord. The body and financial projections of this business plan detail the exciting opportunity presented by this innovative company. With the videoconferencing industry expected to grow to over $7 billion by 1998, CSI and its investors are well positioned to capitalize on this burgeoning market.

CSI is a Delaware corporation that utilizes video compression technology to provide an alternate distribution channel for today's retailers. In addition to creating an alternate means of retailing CSI has developed a complete marketing system with the introduction of the Point 'n Click Shopping Center (PCSC). CSIs primary business is to be a full service "virtual landlord." A virtual landlord leases access and connect time to retailers, to market and distribute their products through a PCSC or Point 'n Click booth (PCB). A full service virtual landlord provides retailers with the tools with which to market their products in this new format: The Retailer's Point 'n Click Desktop (RPCD).

CSI believes that the development of the PCB fills an important need for both retailers and consumers. With the availability of new video compression technology, CSI has developed a cost effective means for retailers to broaden their distribution capacity through additional point-of-sale locations at dramatically reduced costs. CSI will charge "tenant" retailers a monthly "rental rate" per PCB location in which they wish to enable consumers the ability to establish a video link on shop on-line with the selected retailer. The retailer will derive the benefit of maintaining a full service retail location for the equivalent cost of only leasing a 200 square foot store. Moreover, as part of the lease rate, tenants will also be able to use full motion video to advertise their products and services and draw consumers to the point-of-sale kiosk. Each tenant will have four 30 second spots per hour on the exterior video monitor included in their lease rate.

In addition to the rent that CSI will charge its tenants, CSI will also charge a monthly lease fee for the RPCD which will be deployed at the tenants telemarketing center. The RPCD is the combined hardware and software necessary for our tenants to interact with their customers at a PCB location. The RPCD includes CSI's US Patent Pending software, as well as an extremely user friendly graphical user interface. Moreover, the RPCD is designed to permit the retailer to use their existing order entry and inventory management software in conjunction with the RPCD operating system. The RPCD software was designed for use with Microsoft Windows and as a result, the retailer's existing software can simply be pulled through a new window to create an easy to use one page interface.

CSI believes that the ownership and operation of America's first Point 'n Click Shopping Centers and Point 'n Click Booths is, and will become, an extremely viable and profitable business. The attributes that make a landlord successful today and attractive to potential tenants are; 1) Location, location, location, 2) Complementary tenants, 3) "Value" lease rates and 4) The capability to assist tenants in the marketing of their products and the attraction of consumers to the location. CSI will be able to deliver on all of these counts. Most importantly, however, the PCB will provide the best "value" in many locations that are now considered too costly to establish a retail store.

The 50 largest retailers in America racked up $478 billion in 1992 sales, a growth of 6.1% over 1991. Retailing is big business. Retailing is also a profitable business. The Service 500 published by Fortune marked "Retailing" as one of the top industries in the service category in total return to investors (19.2%) between 1982-1992. Return on assets for 1992 ranked first at 5.3%. Retailing was number one with $5.51 of sales per dollar of shareholder's equity. Return on Shareholder's equity for 1992 was the highest at 14.0%. Sales per retail employee averaged $122,740. Wal-Mart ranked number one in service sector profits with almost $2.0

BUSINESS DESCRIPTION

THE MARKET

The Retailer/Tenant Market

billion. Retailing has demonstrated profit potential. CSI is targeting a large and lucrative group of tenants.

Business Week proclaimed on its cover that "Retailing Will Never Be The Same." As indicated in the previous paragraph, America's retailers are a large and profitable group. However, the business of retailing is going to change forever with the emergence of the "electronic superhighway." Changes in retailing are not new to the American public (see chart below), but the magnitude of the "Electronic Distribution Era" will have a profound effect on the business.

Modern American Shopping

1940-1960 - Department Store Era

Downtown	Neighborhood	Home
•Department Store	•"Full Service" Gas	•Milkman
•Full "Retail" Pricing	•Grocery	•Fuller Brush
•High Service	•Shoe Repair	•Avon
•Home Delivery	•Drug Store	•Handyman

1960-1980 - Mall Era

From Downtown to Suburbs	Neighborhood	Home
•Shopping Mall	•"Fast Service"	•Tupperware
•Discount Stores	•"Self-Service" Gas	•Catalog Sales
•Low Service	•Direct Mail	•Pyramid Sales
•Self Service	•Telemarketing	•"Do It Yourself"

1980-Present - Super Discount Era

Suburbs	Neighborhood	Home
•"Category Killer" Stores	•Video Stores	•Cable TV Shopping
•Warehouse Shopping	•Coffee Shops	•Automated
•Outlet Malls	•Gas/Convenience Stores	•Telemarketing
•More Franchises	•Pizza	•Home Pizza

Future - Electronic Distribution Era

Suburb & Downtown	Neighborhood	Home
•High Service/Low Price	•2-Way Video Shopping Malls	•2-Way Video Shopping Anytime/ Everywhere
•2-Way Video Shopping Kiosks		
•2-Way Video Stores in Office Buildings	•Neighborhood Convenience Stores	

The media hype that surrounded the proposed QVC/Paramount acquisition is a foreshadowing of things to come. Every retailer in America has seen not only the $3 billion in "Home Shopping" TV sales, but the speed and efficiency with which that retailing environment allows companies to operate. CSI has developed exactly what key retailing executives are looking for: 1) Additional retail distribution outlets ("outside of their walls"); 2) Utilization of technology to reduce costs; 3) Reduction in Sales personnel/Increase in sales per employee; 4) Better inventory management and cost control; 5) The ability to provide high service and low prices to their consumers. With the introduction of the PCB and the RPCD, CSI has created exactly what the market has been looking for.

CSI's target market for retailer/tenants will be those companies whose products and/or services are information intensive. The ideal product or service to market through the PCB is one which has a high gross margin and a low "close time" (see chart below). The industries which are best suited for this retailing environment include, but are not limited to, travel, financial services, and consumer electronics. However, CSI believes that a number of retailers which currently market their products through catalogs would benefit from the PCB. In any event, one of the overriding factors effecting the tenant market that CSI targets will be the location of each of the PCBs.

A key to CSI's ultimate success will be the site locations of the PCSCs. The initial test PCSC will be located inside Bob's Grocery, a 106,000 square foot grocery superstore that has 25,000 customers weekly. The agreement with Bob's Grocery includes a provision, upon the success of the initial live test, to move forward with a joint venture which will enable CSI to locate PCSCs in additional stores. CSI's management team is keenly aware of the need to locate the PCSCs in the proper locations. In addition to grocery chains, CSI intends to pursue large regional malls, high traffic downtown locations such as high rise office buildings, and public use areas such as airports and train stations.

The Landlord Market

The immediate benefits to the company of the grocery store location is the high traffic count which is extremely attractive to tenants as well as non-tenant advertisers. It is also an extremely large market with the 30 largest chains accounting for over 6,000 stores of 30,000 square feet or larger.

The benefit to Bob's Grocery as well as any other grocery store location will be increased traffic. Unlike most marketing companies that are soliciting grocery chains to permit the installation of video walls and monitors on which to advertise consumer goods, the PCSC will not simply advertise to the existing customers, but will bring additional traffic into the store. Eventually, shoppers will visit Bob's Grocery with the primary goal being to pick up their airline tickets from the PCSC, but they will most likely make ancillary purchases during their visit to the PCSC.

The other Landlord locations that CSI will pursue can benefit from some of the same factors that make this appealing to Bob's Grocery. Future PCSC and PCB sites will eventually use the kiosk as an amenity to attract commercial tenants. This is particularly true in the case of large downtown office buildings. In addition, with the PCB only occupying 18 square feet, CSI, with the advantage of multiple tenants paying rent in the 18 square feet, can offer significant compensation to the Landlord relative to the amount of space that is necessary. If the market rent for major retail or commercial space is $25 per square foot, CSI will be able to offer landlords the equivalent of $100 per foot for the amount of space that the kiosk will occupy.

The initial rollout of PCBs will be concentrated in the Atlanta and Chicago markets. The company has the ability to monitor the units closely and with a significant concentration in a single metropolitan area, the benefits of media exposure and advertising are very significant. To date, the company has secured locations in some of the premiere office buildings in these markets, at Northwestern University, and at both Mega hotel locations. Several more landlord locations are in the final contract process.

MARKETING

There are three distinct markets that CSI must gear its marketing efforts towards: 1) The Tenant/Retailer, 2) The Landlord, and 3) The Consumer. CSI intends to segment its marketing approach to insure that all of the necessary groups are getting adequate marketing attention.

The Tenant/Retailer Market

The $2 trillion retail market consists of both store and non-store retailers. Store retailing accounts for 95% ($1.9 trillion). The $100 billion of non-store retailing consists of catalog sales ($65 billion), direct sales ($11 billion), television retailing ($3 billion) and direct mail/outbound telemarketing ($21 billion). The non-store market is growing at a significantly higher rate than the store market. The growth, however, is primarily from store retailers looking at the benefits and potential of the non-store market. Two good examples are J.C. Penny creating its own video catalog and Macy's developing its own "Home Shopping" cable TV channel.

After evaluating the trends in the market, CSI will target its efforts towards traditional store retailers that are considering, or should be considering, retailing in a non-store environment. CSI will also focus on store and/or non-store retailers that have an existing telemarketing operation, such as Dayton Hudson, J.C. Penney, The Sharper Image, etc.. Those retailers with both an existing telemarketing operation as well as retail store locations will immediately understand the economic benefits of this proposed retailing concept. CSI will more easily convert existing telemarketing operations, with the use of the RPCD, to video telemarketing oprations.

A.Y. Cook, CSI's President, will be the point person in the company's marketing efforts toward these potential tenants. Ms. Cook has demonstrated that she can sign major tenants as is evidenced by the DAMARK and AMEX contracts. Her primary marketing strategy will be one of direct contact. Whether direct mail or telephone, Ms. Cook will make contact with the appropriate management at the target retailer to present the Point 'n Click Shopping concept. This method has been well received thus far, as Ms. Cook has been extremely adept at gaining access to the decision makers at IBM, Dayton Hudson, and Best Buy. CSI also intends to display and demonstrate its products at various trade shows sponsored by the Direct Marketing Association and the Catalog Conference.

The Landlord Market

The marketing plan regarding the landlord market is two-fold. First, CSI will identify those locations that will be attractive to existing and future tenants. Second, CSI will identfy the "landlords" located in those locations that will be potential strategic capital partners. The company's objective, with respect to soliciting landlord or site locations, is to provide an ample qualified traffic count, while at the same time identifying a corporate partner with multiple "like" locations.

James Watt will have the primary responsibility for locating and securing future PCB sites. Mr. Watt will use the initial Bob's site as a marketing tool with which to attract new landlord partners.

Mr. Watt will gather statistical information regarding increased traffic, free publicity for the landlord and customer acceptance/approval of the PCB to bolster his marketing presentation. He will also bring prospective landlords to the test site to witness the entire operations.

Upon identification and prioritization of future landlord sites, CSI will initiate a direct marketing campaign to solicit additional landlord locations. The company has also developed a Joint Venture financial model that demonstrates extremely attractive economic returns to the landlord of a partnership with CSI. The combination of a live operating site with the economic incentive package should greatly aid in the proliferation of future landlord locations.

Based upon research from the consumers at the Bob's facility and various catalog retailers who have been introduced to the concept, it has been suggested that CSI target four primary landlord locations: 1) Airline Frequent Flyer Lounges, 2) Hotel Lobbies, 3) Large Multi-Tenant and Single Tenant Office Complexes and 4) Universities. The company is now aggressively pursuing these locations and has several under contract in both the Chicago and Atlanta markets.

The Consumer Market

The ultimate success of this venture is predicated upon CSI's ability to attract consumers to use the PCB. The demographics of the early locations must be consistent with the data that suggests "Early Adapters," people most comfortable with new technology, will be the first group to use the PCB. CSI intends to use the PCB itself to advertise to this target group of consumers. CSI will prepare a series of full motion broadcast quality ads to run on the Video Monitor that demonstrate the PCB and what Point n' Click Shopping is all about. CSI's primary goal is to raise consumer confidence and comfort with the PCB as a distribution outlet for goods and services.

In addition to the ad campaign on the video monitor, CSI will seek outside media coverage for additional credibility and publicity. The "Grand Opening" of the inaugural 20 PCB locations will be designed as a media event. The company is currently working with different advertising and public relations firms to craft a well executed PR campaign. CSI will also solicit interest from the local media by sending direct mail announcing the event. The company will also continue to employ various media groups to assist in the promotion of the PCB through the use of news releases and article submissions. CSI intents to pursue like strategies in subsequent markets in which the company establishes additional PCB sites.

CSI has also begun the groundwork of developing a customer affinity program. The Shopper Tracker (ST) will enable CSI to capture customer demographics for our tenant retailers. More importantly, it will provide the customer with an accumulated point system which will encourage repeat business through our Point 'n Click Network. We will communicate directly with customers who have access to a PCB via our Bi-Monthly newsletter to our ST members. It is through this communication that we can announce various promotions and new tenants, thereby creating a direct link to our most important customers.

TECHNOLOGY/ SYSTEM SUMMARY

The Point 'n Click Shopping Center could not exist before now. The convergence of disparate technologies creates the opportunity for the video retailing revolution. The PCSC seizes the opportunity by integrating the following technologies into a new type of shopping experience. Each PCSC and PCB has three advanced systems that deliver the complete Point 'n Click Shopping experience.

> 1) Interactive Information System
>> (Consumer Controlled Interactive, "touch screen"
> 2) Expert Information System
>> (Multimedia information remotely controlled by video communications slaes expert through the RPCD)
> 3) Two-Way Video Communications System
>> (Consumer at the PCB to Sales Expert at RPCD)

Interactive Information System

Located inside the PCB is a 17" interactive touch screen monitor on which customers can browse through the system looking for information on goods or services available at the PCB. The purpose of this interactive system is to allow the shopper to discover for himself/herself, using interactive "touch screen" computer technology, information and advice on items of interest. The system features buying guides, prices and detailed descriptions (e.g. infomercials). This interactive framework is housed in a proprietary CSI software system, the Video Enabled Catalog (VECAT).

The June 22, 1992 issue of Business Week reported that approximately 60,000 interactive computer "kiosks" are now in use nationwide replacing the old electronic data boxes. An estimated 2 million interactive systems are expected to be in use by 1996. The new touch screen systems have colorful graphics, video, and sound.

American consumers are becoming very accustomed to this technology. The PCB incorporates the interactive browsing screens as a means to attract additional consumers. The benefit, in the case of the PCB, is that the customer will be both entertained and informed. Thus, once the consumer does select to be connected to the retailer via a videoconference, due to the earlier use of the interactive "touch screen," they are more informed and the video connect time may be reduced. Eventually, the Interactive Information System will allow the consumer to print out information or record on tape to take home as desired.

Expert Information System

IBM researchers report that we have short term rentention rate of 20% of what we hear, compared to 40% of what we see and hear, compared to 75% of what we see, hear, and do. Effective communication is multi-dimensional. The Point 'n Click Booth's use of multimedia systms creates a multi-dimensional shopping experience.

The Expert Information System (EIS) is a more comprehensive multimedia version of the Interactive Information System. The EIS is remotely controlled from the Retailer's Point 'n Click Desktop by a sales expert who:

> 1) Guides consumers through information and answer questions.
> 2) Takes orders and provides shopping information.
> 3) Captures the customer profile for data base manipulation.

Both the Interactive and Expert Information Systmes use state of the art touch screen interaction and multimedia technology. By combining computer and television technology it is possible to express information to consumers in a more intuitive manner. These systems are designed with a Multimedia object-oriented data base management system used to store and manipulate text, graphics, digitized photos, animation and full motion video. These can easily be updated with new product information. Outlined below is the connection between the RPCD and the multimedia equipment in the PCB.

To say advances in compresion technology have been dramatic is to seriously understate the facts. In 1985 the electronic devices used to code and decode video (CODEC) cost $70,000 and produced, by today's standards, rudimentary picture quality. Today CODEC chips are being introduced by the AT&T microelectronics division at a cost of $400 to the video conference manufacturers. Complete office systems currently start at $15,000 (Hitachi) and personal computer CODEC systems (albeit lower quality, jerky motion images) were recently introduced and priced at $995.

Two-Way Video Communications System

Video compression, the ability to send full motion, broadcast quality video over phone lines, is the heart of this new shopping experience. Two-way video communications puts the consumer in control of the shopping process. Each video conferencing station in the PCB features a wall mounted 17" "touch screen" monitor. The monitor is for both a live face-to-face videoconference with the product or service expert of the shopper's choice as well as the interactive browsing.

Using a picture-in-picture feature, the monitor is used by the retail sales expert for multimedia presentations that answer the shopper's questions.

Many individuals are put off by an aggressive sales clerk rushing over to ask, "How may I help you?" when shopping in a retail store. A customer in the Point 'n Click Booth is never asked "How may I help you?" until the customer touches "CONNECT" on the monitor. The shopper is free to shop independently by following a simple touch screen menu that leads the shopper to increasingly complex information made possible by the new multimedia systems. However, at any time, the shopper can press "CONNECT" or "HELP" and a live expert will instantly appear on the monitor. Giving the shopper total control of the shopping and buying experience is truly revolutionary.

The PCB is one half of the videoconference sales channel. To come to life the center must be able to connect consumers to a wide variety of retailers equipped with videoconferencing equipment. CSI's Point 'n Click Private Web will act as an electronic switch that will route PCB calls to the appropriate Retailer's Point 'n Click Desktop. The RPCD allows the expert sales agent to deliver multimedia presentations to the consumer (Expert Information System) as well as to check inventory positions and enter customer orders all from one terminal. The devleopment of the properitary software which enables the RPCD to fucntion and deliver a seamless presentation to customers is critical to the ultimate success of the shopping experience.

The confluence of these technologies is unique. Prior to "now," each piece of the technology puzzle was awaiting inventor or refinement that would produce a cost acceptable solution. The year 1993 produced video codec chips, multimedia PC's, new tariffs that dramatically reduce the cost of video cummunication via broadband services and new video production

Summary

tools. With these systems in place and the proprietary software to tie them together to function as one entity, the Point 'n Click Booth is a reality. Each PCB delivers service that stimulates the imagination and self-image aspect of the consumers mind. The PCB network does not seek "shelf space," it seeks "mind space." Skilled video sales experts will use multimedia to feed the mind answers on a wide range of information intensive products and services. Both the consumer and the retailer win in this environment.

THE MANAGEMENT TEAM

CSI's senior management currently consists of three members:

A.Y. Cook is the original founder of CSI and is the current President and a Director of the company. Prior to starting CSI, Ms. Cook owned and operated a large travel & tour packaging company. At its peak, that company's sales exceeded $39 million and passenger volume reached more than 150,000 per year. She has been dedicating 100% of her time to CSI since 1992.

Ms. Cook's primary responsibility at CSI is to market the company's services to potential tenants. The concept of allocating the cost of video retailing across several tenants in a Point 'n Click Shopping Center is Ms. Cook's idea. She first embarked upon this trail in 1986, when she was searching for a new retailing method which would enable her to gain greater personnel efficiency. The ability to gain telemarketing efficiency (roughly 67% of a telemarketer's time is spent talking directly to customers) was extremely attractive given the inordinate amount of "down time" experienced by retail sales agents. The use of videoconferencing, which was just becoming reality at the time, would be an extraordinary system with which to market travel services and gain greater efficiency. However, at the time, the video quality was poor and the costs were too prohibitive to utilize this new technology. Just recently, with the improvements in picture quality and the dramatic reduction in costs, this new method of retailing can become a reality. More over, when the cost is allocated across several retailers at the consumer end of the systems, this new retailing mode becomes extremely cost effective.

Ms. Cook's intimate involvement with this project since its inception ideally suits her to be the point person for CSI's marketing efforts. Furthermore, it was Ms. Cook that signed CSI's first tenant, AAA Travel, and her experience and success to date in marketing this novel retailing concept are invaluable in this position. She has also been involved with a variety of vendors and technical experts in designing the PCSC. The knowledge that has been gained throughout this process is a key attribute for the individual charged with overseeing the sales process.

James Winchester is the Chairman, Chief Executive Officer, and director of the company. Mr. Winchester's primary responsibilities include marketing and promotion of the company and its products and services, raising funds for continued company growth, and participation in the technical development of software and systems.

Prior to joining the company, Mr. Winchester was the President and Chief Operating Officer of a private technology venture developing a nationwide network of electronic ticketing machines for machines for airline tickets and other types of documents. Mr. Winchester's experience in building electronic distribution networks will be a direct benefit to the company in achieving its plan quickly and profitably.

Mr. Winchester will play an instrumental role in moving the company from a start-up venture to a production operation. Mr. Winchester has a demonstrated track record of success with moving technology companies from the initial concept stage to the profitable operating stage. His most notable success was a company which has since been acquired by MasterCard.

James Watt is the Executive Vice President, Chief Financial Officer, and a Director of the Company. Mr. Watt has been involved with as a Director of the Company since October 1993 and joined the company full time in January 1994. Upon joining CSI, Mr. Watt assumed responsibility for the financial operations of the company and the future site selection for the company's PCSCs. Mr. Watt's educational background and previous experience in the investment banking field make him an ideal candidate for these positions. More importantly, his familiarity with retail real estate financing and management should provide an excellent background as CSI embarks upon its course as the nationsl first virtual landlord.

Prior to his position with CSI, Mr. Watt was employed by Jones & Associates as a Vice President in their Investment Banking Department. Mr. Watt joined Jones & Associates in 1989 after his graduation from The Wharton School at the University of Pennsylvania with an MBA in Finance. His primary responsibility at Jones & Associates was the underwriting and marketing of private real estate investments.

In addition to Cook, Winchester, and Watt, the company has six permanent employees. Ms. Sharon Cloyd oversees the technical operations of the company as its Director of Development. Ms. Cloyd manages three software and hardware engineers whose primary expertise and responsibility are the software development and integration at the PCB and the RPCD. The other full-time employees are engaged in sales and administrative roles. As the company becomes more firmly established, additional full-time personnel will be employed in areas of responsiblity where they can be economically justified.

CSI believes that it has assembled an excellent management team to guide the company from a start-up venture to a profitable operating concern. With the assistance of outside advisors, consultants, and relationships such as that with Telecom, as well as outsourcing such operational tasks as routine PCB maintenance to Park Service Inc., CSI is adequately staffed to handle finance, operations, site selection, marketing & sales, and technical operations. Included in the Appendix are brief biographies on the key manangement team members.

COMPETITION

CSI will be competing in two primary arenas:
> 1) Competing for Consumer Purchase Dollars.
> 2) Competing for Retailer Distribution Dollars.

Consumer Purchase Dollars

The Point 'n Click Shopping Center is a hybrid: both a store and a non-store that will be competing with other "stores" and "non-stores." Stores include any retail location that sells goods and/or services. "Non-Store" covers all other forms of retail sales including catalog, direct mail, direct sales, broadcast sales and telemarketing. The benefit of a store, in the case of merchandise, is the ability to "kick the tires" or "touch the merchandise." In fact, many types of stores shipping experiences involve "seeing" only. Touching the merchandise does not take place until the customer is at home and opens the box. Video communications can simulate, and in the case of information intensive products, surpass the "touch the merchandise" experience. A far greater choice of merchandise can be stored in CD-ROM files or recordable optical disks for visual display and manipulation than can be stored on a shelf. Seeing and touching consumer electronic products in a no service, discount warehouse may ultimately be less satisfying than "seeing" consumer electronic products, accompanied by a live consumer electronics expert's detailed explanation of the benefits and features of competing models and brands.

The growth in non-store sales has been fueled by the 13.6 billion catalogs that were mailed in 1990 compared with 5.8 billion in 1980. Over 98.6 million adults (54.4% of the adult population) made a "non-store" purchase in 1990. The non-store purchasing experience through catalog stores or direct sales provides a combination of quality, price, service and convenience. To capture sales from store retailers, non-store marketers generally emphasize one or more of these benefits. With catalog and telemarketing sales the consumer is usually limited to a single product image and brief description. When the customer calls for more information he or she must trust a disembodied voice to answer questions and paint verbal pictures that describe additional features and product benefits.

The Point 'n Click Booth monitors allow the customer to "see" all sides of a product and "see" the selling agent. More critically, the selling agent "sees" the client. The ability of the selling agent and client to see each other is vital. According to a recent study, only 7% of what we communicate in face-to-face conversations in conveyed by the meaning of the words themselves. Another 38% of our communiation is based on how we say words -- the intonation we use. The remaining 55% of our communication is based on non-verbal messages. The selling agent's reliance on visual clues helps make the sale. Using the PCB, a client receives the best a store and non-store can offer...personal service, expert information, visual product presentation, shopping entertainment, and convenience at the most competitive price.

Retailer Distribution Dollars

The above discussion dealt with the consumer benefits associated with the PCSC and PCB. There is a strong case to be made that consumers will be drawn to this retailing environment because of the "best of both worlds" benefits. Retailers, however, must make decisions regrading the allocation of limited resourxes to accomplish their goals. CSI believes that the PCB provides an extremely attractive alternative distribution outlet when compared to its competition.

The PCB offers a cost efficient means for marketing and distributing retail productions and services, much like most non-store techniques, including reduced real estate costs, reduced inventory carrying costs, and reduced labor costs due to better efficiency of sales personnel (centralized sales force with approximately 67% of time spent interacting with customers). Because using the PCB will create a cost advantage over its competitors, tenants can price more aggressively and still maintain higher margins. Notwithstanding the above, the one major difference (benefit) between the PCB and other non-store distribution outlets is the high level of customer service and the sales agent's ability to "close" the sale. The 1990s consumer demands low prices and high service. The PCB has finally given retailers a means to deliver on both of those demands.

With one exception, CSI is currently unaware of any other companies attempting to create a Point 'n Click Booth, Retailer's Point 'n Click Desktop or to use video conferencing in a busines to consumer application to retail goods and/or services. The only exception is in the banking industry where two companies, have begun to solicit banks to use videoconverencing technology with their customers. CSI significantly differentiates itself from those firms in two distinct ways: 1) Neither of the two banking companies have developed the systems necessary to use this technology in a virtual mall concept with multiple retailers, and 2) CSI built is products from the ground up with the consumer sales presentation in mind. Our Patent Pending Software gives the retailer a significant advantage over simply using desktop video systems to interact with their customers. Moreover, our software is designed to overlay the retailers existing system which creates a one screen interface and is extremely user friendly.

CSI believes that being "first" in this market will provide a competitive advantage over future entrants. The company believes that it has an approximate eighteen month lead over potential future competitors. The time involved in determining exactly what equipment is necessary and the development of the essential software to tie it together has given CSI a commanding lead in this arena. The ability to continue to sign major companies as tenants and to secure high profile locations as PCB sites will insure CSI's preeminent position as the leader in this industry. Furthermore, when the eventuality arrives that the "electronic superhighway" is feeding 500 channels into every American home, the Retailer's Point 'n Click Desktop will grant CSI a virtual franchise on the "turn key" business of providing America's retailers with the capabilities to market their products and services interactively.

CSI intends to develop the Point 'n Click Shopping Center concept to its fullest potential. In addition to the PCSC and PCB, this plan has also detailed the Retailer's Point 'n Click Desktop (RPCD). Initially, the RPCD will be leased to customers who are tenants in the company's PCBs. In the future, CSI envisions marketing the RPCD as a stand alone system that will enable any retailer to become a video retailer. The implementation of this logical business extension (installing RPCDs for direct to consumer retail sales) is predicated on the successful installation of additional interactive video conference outlets located in homes, offices, or future virtual landlord's kiosks. The company also believes that a market currently exists for the RPCD in a dedicated multi-store retailing environment.

FUTURE PLANS

CSI has had interst from large multi-store retailers in the development of an in-store Expert Information Provider network. The concept behind this service is to provide customers with a high level of service/information while they are shopping. The current problem is that in order for a multi-store retailer to provide knowledgeable "expert" sales staff in each department at each location, the retailer must incur all of the associated costs with maintaining an enormous staff. The benefit of maintaining an information videoconference kiosk in each location is that customers can access an "expert" at any time they wish while shopping. The retailer has provided what customers are looking for: high customer service and information. The retailer can centralize its "expert" staff in one location and deliver services to all of its retail outlets. The efficiency of a video telemarketing center will greatly reduce the necessary personnel while still delivering exemplary service and thus save the retailer significantly on the associated cost of the previously excess personnel.

The RPCD will be necessary for retailers considering the option of developing an in-store information network. CSI will market the RPCD separately as a turnkey service to multi-store retailers who have decided to pursue this effective service alternative. CSI's existing use of the RPCS in conjunction with its PCB tenants makes the "In-Store Information Provider" market a viable business to pursue in the near future.

The future applications of videoconference technology are too numerous to mention here. It has been estimated that the videoconference industry will grow from its current $1 billion to over $7 billion by 1998. CSI's unique approach to the use of videoconference technology in a direct business-to-consumer application is thus far unprecedented in the industry. CSI intends to vigorously pursue those applications of the technology that logically lend themselves to a direct consumer contact as opposed to a strictly business-to-business use. The benefits to retailers of this technology (lower "real estate" costs, improved sales staff efficiency, and lower inventory carrying costs) will also entice other multi-location service providers. For example, a large hotel chain could employ this concept (centralized expert staff) in a Virtual Concierge, thereby reducing the costs associated with maintaining a staff at each location.

In an effort to realize its potential, CSI will first focus on the Point 'n Click Booth and the Retailer's Point 'n Click Desktop. Subsequent to developing this market place into an economically profitable business unit, CSI will devote excess capital to R&D projects designed to enhance the PCB and RPCD and explore the products necessary to exploit additional subsequent markets for this technology. In an effort to supplement its internally generated cash flow, CSI intends to seek additional capital for growth via an initial public offering of the company's common stock within the next 5 years.

SUMMARY

Click 'n Shop Inc. is poised to embark upon a pioneering new business opportunity as the nation's first virtual landlord. The convergence of several different technologies has made the Point 'n Click Shopping Center not only a viable retail distribution outlet, but a complete marketing and sales system. With the video conferencing business expected to grow seven fold over the next three years, CSI is entering an industry at the bottom of its growth curve. CSI has taken a unique approach to this business by positioning its products and services in a direct business-to-consumer market, as opposed to the business-to-business strategies that are currently employed in other sectors of this industry. The combination of a growth industry and a distinctive application of the technology will produce rich rewards for CSI and its investors.

The development of the PCSC, the Point 'n Click Booth and the Retailer's Point 'n Click Desktop fill a well defined need of America's retailers. This exceptional retailing environment will permit the PCB tenant retailers to deliver exactly what customers are demanding, high service and low price, while reducing the typically associated costs with such a retailing climate. This new hybrid store/non-store retailing strategy will allow retailers to directly benefit from:

1) Low or no inventory carrying costs
2) Additional point-of sale locations without the hard costs of real estate development and rent
3) Reduced employment costs/More efficient sales staff and
4) Technological experience that will position them for the future (The ultimate "Home Shopping" network of fully interactive television).

The management team at CSI has ample experience, education, and desire to successfully guide the company from its start up stage to becoming a profitable operating concern. By continuing to select the correct strategic corporate partners coupled with a captial infusion of $2,500,000, CSI will be adequately prepared to embark on this journey. As the market for its products and services, like the RPCD, grows, CSI will seek to tap the public equity markets to fuel this growth and to enable the company's investors to realize the full potential of their initial equity investment.

"Retailing Will Never Be the Same" proclaimed Business Week. Click 'n Shop Inc. will help redesign the business of retailing with the introduction of the Point 'n Click Shopping Center and the Retailer's Point 'n Click Desktop. And with these innovative introductions, CSI will flourish as this retailing revolution gains momentum.

FINANCIAL INFORMATION

Sources & Uses of Investment Proceeds

Sources

Proceeds of Offering	$2,500,000
Total Sources	**$2,500,000**

Uses

Point 'n Click Booth	
Development & Construction of 50 PCBs	750,000
PCB R&D	50,000
Total for PCB	**$800,000**
Retailer's Point 'n Click Desktop	
RPCD Lease Units (50)	625,000
RPCD R&D	50,000
Total for RPCD	**$675,000**
Office Equipment	50,000
Retire A/P & Short Term Debt	102,000
Legal & Professional Fees	25,000
Supplement Working Capital	848,000
Total Uses	**$2,500,000**

**Point 'n Click Booth
Unit Economics**

Cost	15,000

Revenue

Tenant Lease Revenue	33,000	(10 Tenants @ $275/month)

Total Revenue 33,000

Direct Expenses

PCB Service Expense	4,800	($400 per PCB/month)
PCB Rent	3,300	(Rent @ $100/sq. ft. or 10% of Rev.)

Total Direct Expenses 8,100

Gross Margin 24,900

**Break Even
Analysis - PCB**

	Std. Rev. Assumptions	*Lower Case Assumptions	**Better Case Assumptions
FY 1995 SG&A	$1,045,000	$1,045,000	$1,045,000
PCB Net Contribution	$24,900	$8,400	$41,400
Number of PCB's Installed to B/E	42	124	25

*Assumes PCB tenant revenue drops to 50% of base assumption.
**Assumes PCB tenant revenue is 150% of base assumption.

**Profit and Loss:
April through
December 1994**

Income	
Software Unit Sales	2,200.00
Interest Income	2,852.23
Tenant Lease Revenue	6,000.00
Total Income	11,052.23
Cost of Goods Sold	
Software Unit Cost	2,200.00
Total COGS	2,200.00
Gross Profit	8,852.23

Expense

Communications			7,751.43
Depreciation Expense			27,073.35
Independent Con			1,644.00
Insurance			125.20
Interest Expense			5,876.82
Location Service			2,801.01
R&D			
PCBC		1,000.00	
R&D - Other		19,691.75	
Total R&D			20,691.75

SG&A

Ads & PROM	6,188.28	
Bank Charge	470.69	
Freight	886.87	
L&P Fees	23,520.61	
Office	14,605.24	
Payroll Expenses		
Employee Benefits	1,047.14	
Gross Wages	250,991.63	
Total Payroll Expenses	252,038.77	
Payroll Service	726.51	
Payroll Taxes		
FICA	16,099.79	
FUTA	182.40	
SUI	795.15	
Total Payroll Taxes	17,077.34	
Rent Paid	15,566.11	
Secretarial SVC	1,471.11	
Telephone Exp.	20,673.97	
Trade Associations	745.00	
Trade Shows	6,257.10	
Travel		
Dining	4,196.98	
Travel - Other	38,192.93	
Total Travel	42,389.91	

Total SG&A   402,617.51

Software Exp.	3,693.59
Tax	100.00
Video Wall Exp.	1,211.28
RPCD Service	409.00

Total Expense   473,994.94

Net Income   -465,142.71

Profit and Loss: April through December 1994
...continued

Balance Sheet as of December 31, 1994

Assets

Current Assets

    Checking/Savings

Checking	5,101.72
Firstar Chkg.	14,633.61
Firstar MM	23,407.48

Total Checking/Savings	43,142.81

    Other Current Assets

Deposits	13,736.65
Undeposited Funds	23.90

Total Other Current Assets	13,760.55

Total Current Assets	56,903.36

Fixed Assets

Accumulated Depreciation	-40,019.35
Equipment	229,121.22

Total Fixed Assets	189,101.87

Other Assets

Loan to Officers	10,500.00
Pre-Paid interest	3,472.17

Total Other Assets	13,972.17

Total Assets	**259,977.40**

Liabilities & Equity

Liabilities

    Current Liabilities

        Accounts Payable

Accounts Payable	12,197.96

Total Accounts Payable	12,197.96

        Credit Cards

Comp USA	596.48
OfficeMax	10.80
Staples	44.53

Total Credit Cards	651.81

Other Current Liabilities		
Deferred Compensation	20,833.29	
JDH Bridge Loan	54,975.93	
Payroll Liabilities	<u>788.36</u>	
Total Other Current Liabilities	<u>76,597.58</u>	
Total Current Liabilities	89,447.35	
Long Term Liabilities		
Lease Obligations	<u>11,722.93</u>	
Total Long Term Liabilities	<u>11,722.93</u>	
Total Liabilities	101,170.28	
Equity		
Equity CS	6,250.00	
Preferred Stock	4,000.00	
Retained Earnings	-237,250.17	
Net Income	-465,142.71	
Surplus Capital	<u>850,950.00</u>	
Total Equity	<u>158,807.12</u>	
Total Liabilities & Equity	**259,977.40**	

Balance Sheet as of December 31, 1994
...continued

Balance Sheet Comparison As of December 31, 1994

	Dec 31, '94	Dec 31, '93	$ Change	% Change
Assets				
Current Assets				
Checking/Savings				
Checking	5,101.72	88,573.25	-83,471.53	-94.2%
Firstar Chkg.	14,633.61	0.00	14,633.61	100.0%
Firstar MM	23,407.48	0.00	23,407.48	100.0%
Total Checking/Savings	43,142.81	88,573.25	-45.430.44	-51.3%
Other Current Assets				
Deposits	13,736.65	0.00	13,736.65	100.0%
Undeposited Funds	23.90	0.00	23.90	100.0%
Total Other Current Assets	13,760.55	0.00	13,760.55	100.0%
Total Current Assets	56,903.36	88,573.25	-31,669.89	-35.8%
Fixed Assets				
Accumulated Depreciation	-40,019.35	0.00	-40,019.35	-100.0%
Equipment	229,121.22	103,865.20	125,256.02	120.6%
Total Fixed Assets	189,101.87	103,865.20	85,236.67	82.1%
Other Assets				
Loan to Officers	10,500.00	0.00	10,500.00	100.0%
Pre-Paid interest	3,472.17	0.00	3,472.17	100.0%
Total Other Assets	13,972.17	0.00	13,972.17	100.0%
Total Assets	259,977.40	192,438.45	67,583.95	35.1%
Liabilities & Equity				
Liabilities				
Current Liabilities				
Accounts Payable				
Accounts Pay.	12,197.96	0.00	12,197.96	100.0%
Total Accs Pay.	12,197.96	0.00	12,197.96	100.0%
Credit Cards				
Comp USA	596.48	0.00	596.48	100.0%
OfficeMax	10.80	0.00	10.80	100.0%
Staples	44.53	0.00	44.53	100.0%
Total Credit Cards	651.81	0.00	651.81	100.0%

Other Current Liabilities				
Accounts Payable	0.00	4,452.59	-4,452.59	-100.0%
Deferred Comp.	20,833.29	0.00	20,833.29	100.0%
JDH Bridge Loan	54,975.93	0.00	54,975.93	100.0%
Payroll Liabilities	788.36	99.07	689.29	695.8%
Total Other Current Liabilities	76,597.58	4,551.66	72,045.92	1,582.9%
Total Current Liabilities	89,447.35	4,551.66	84,895.69	1,865.2%
Long Term Liabilities				
Lease Obligations	11,722.93	0.00	11,722.93	100.0%
Total Long Term Liabilities	11,722.93	0.00	11,722.93	100.0%
Total Liabilities	101,170.28	4,551.66	96,618.62	2,122.7%
Equity				
Equity CS	6,250.00	5,250.00	1,000.00	19.1%
Preferred Stock	4,000.00	2,500.00	1,500.00	60.0%
Retained Earnings	-237,250.17	0.00	237.250.17	-100.0%
Net Income	-465,142.71	-72,313.21	-392,829.50	-543.2%
Surplus Capital	850,950.00	252,450.00	598,500.00	237.1%
Total Equity	158,807.12	187,886.79	-29,079.67	-15.5%
Total Liabilities & Equity	259,977.40	192,438.45	67,538.95	35.1%

Balance Sheet Comparison As of December 31, 1994
...continued

Business Plan Template

Business Plan Template

USING THIS TEMPLATE

A business plan carefully spells out a company's projected course of action over a period of time, usually the first two to three years after the start-up. In addition, banks, lenders, and other investors examine the information and financial documentation before deciding whether or not to finance a new business venture. Therefore, a business plan is an essential tool in obtaining financing and should describe the business itself in detail as well as all important factors influencing the company, including the market, industry, competition, operations and management policies, problem solving strategies, financial resources and needs, and other vital information. The plan enables the business owner to anticipate costs, plan for difficulties, and take advantage of opportunities, as well as design and implement strategies that keep the company running as smoothly as possible.

This template has been provided as a model to help you construct your own business plan. Please keep in mind that there is no single acceptable format for a business plan, and that this template is in no way comprehensive, but serves as an example.

The business plans provided in this section are fictional and have been used by small business agencies as models for clients to use in compiling their own business plans.

GENERIC BUSINESS PLAN

Main headings included below are topics that should be covered in a comprehensive business plan. They include:

Business Summary

Purpose
Provides a brief overview of your business, succinctly highlighting the main ideas of your plan.

Includes

- ○ Name and Type of Business
- ○ Description of Product/Service
- ○ Business History and Development
- ○ Location
- ○ Market
- ○ Competition
- ○ Management
- ○ Financial Information
- ○ Business Strengths and Weaknesses
- ○ Business Growth

Table of Contents

Purpose

Organized in an Outline Format, the Table of Contents illustrates the selection and arrangement of information contained in your plan.

Includes

     ○ Topic Headings and Subheadings
     ○ Page Number References

Business History and Industry Outlook

Purpose

Examines the conception and subsequent development of your business within an industry specific context.

Includes

     ○ Start-up Information
     ○ Owner/Key Personnel Experience
     ○ Location
     ○ Development Problems and Solutions
     ○ Investment/Funding Information
     ○ Future Plans and Goals
     ○ Market Trends and Statistics
     ○ Major Competitors
     ○ Product/Service Advantages
     ○ National, Regional, and Local Economic Impact

Product/Service

Purpose

Introduces, defines, and details the product and/or service that inspired the information of your business.

Includes

     ○ Unique Features
     ○ Niche Served
     ○ Market Comparison
     ○ Stage of Product/Service Development
     ○ Production
     ○ Facilities, Equipment, and Labor
     ○ Financial Requirements
     ○ Product/Service Life Cycle
     ○ Future Growth

Market Examination

Purpose

Assessment of product/service applications in relation to consumer buying cycles.

Includes

- Target Market
- Consumer Buying Habits
- Product/Service Applications
- Consumer Reactions
- Market Factors and Trends
- Penetration of the Market
- Market Share
- Research and Studies
- Cost
- Sales Volume and Goals

Competition

Purpose

Analysis of Competitors in the Marketplace.

Includes

- Competitor Information
- Product/Service Comparison
- Market Niche
- Product/Service Strengths and Weaknesses
- Future Product/Service Development

Marketing

Purpose

Identifies promotion and sales strategies for your product/service.

Includes

- Product/Service Sales Appeal
- Special and Unique Features
- Identification of Customers
- Sales and Marketing Staff
- Sales Cycles
- Type of Advertising/Promotion
- Pricing
- Competition
- Customer Services

Operations

Purpose
Traces product/service development from production/inception to the market environment.

Includes

○ Cost Effective Production Methods
○ Facility
○ Location
○ Equipment
○ Labor
○ Future Expansion

Administration and Management

Purpose
Offers a statement of your management philosophy with an in-depth focus on processes and procedures.

Includes

○ Management Philosophy
○ Structure of Organization
○ Reporting System
○ Methods of Communication
○ Employee Skills and Training
○ Employee Needs and Compensation
○ Work Environment
○ Management Policies and Procedures
○ Roles and Responsibilities

Key Personnel

Purpose
Describes the unique backgrounds of principle employees involved in business.

Includes

○ Owner(s)/Employee Education and Experience
○ Positions and Roles
○ Benefits and Salary
○ Duties and Responsibilities
○ Objectives and Goals

Potential Problems and Solutions

Purpose
Discussion of problem solving strategies that change issues into opportunities.

Includes

- Risks
- Litigation
- Future Competition
- Economic Impact
- Problem Solving Skills

Financial Information

Purpose
Secures needed funding and assistance through worksheets and projections detailing financial plans, methods of repayment, and future growth opportunities.

Includes

- Financial Statements
- Bank Loans
- Methods of Repayment
- Tax Returns
- Start-up Costs
- Projected Income (3 years)
- Projected Cash Flow (3 Years)
- Projected Balance Statements (3 years)

Appendices

Purpose
Supporting documents used to enhance your business proposal.

Includes

- Photographs of product, equipment, facilities, etc.
- Copyright/Trademark Documents
- Legal Agreements
- Marketing Materials
- Research and or Studies
- Operation Schedules
- Organizational Charts
- Job Descriptions
- Resumes
- Additional Financial Documentation

Food Distributor

FICTIONAL BUSINESS PLAN

COMMERCIAL FOODS, INC.

3003 Avondale Ave.
Knoxville, TN 37920

October 1992

This fictional plan demonstrates how a partnership can have a positive impact on a new business. It demonstrates how two individuals can carve a niche in the specialty foods market by offering gourmet foods to upscale restaurants and fine hotels. This plan is fictional and has not been used to gain funding from a bank or other lending institution.

- STATEMENT OF PURPOSE

- DESCRIPTION OF THE BUSINESS

- MANAGEMENT

- PERSONNEL

- LOCATION

- PRODUCTS AND SERVICES

- THE MARKET

- COMPETITION

- SUMMARY

- PRO FORMA INCOME STATEMENT

- FINANCIAL STATEMENTS

FOOD DISTRIBUTOR BUSINESS PLAN

STATEMENT OF PURPOSE

Commercial Food, Inc. seeks a loan of $75,000 to establish a new business. This sum together with $5,000 equity investment by the principals will be used as follows:

Merchandise inventory	$25,000
Office fixture/equipment	12,000
Warehouse equipment	14,000
One delivery truck	10,000
Working capital	39,000
	$100,000

DESCRIPTION OF THE BUSINESS

Commercial Foods, Inc. will be a distributor of specialty food service products to hotels and upscale restaurants in the geographical area in a 50-mile radius of Knoxville. Richard Roberts will direct the sales effort and John Williams will manage the warehouse operation and the office. One delivery truck will be used initially with a second truck added in the third year.

We expect to begin operation of the business within 30 days after securing the requested financing.

MANAGEMENT

A. Richard Roberts is a native of Memphis, Tennessee. He is a graduate of Memphis State University with a Bachelor's degree from the School of Business. After graduation, he worked for a major manufacturer of specialty food service products as a detail sales person for five years and for the past three years, he has served as a product sales manager for this firm.

B. John Williams is a native of Nashville, Tennessee. He holds a B.S. Degree in Food Technology from the University of Tennessee. His career includes five years as a product development chemist in gourmet food products and five years as operations manager for a food service distributor.

Both men are healthy and energetic. Their backgrounds complement each other which will ensure the success of Commercial Foods, Inc. They will set policies together and personnel decisions will be made jointly. Initial salaries for the owners will be $1,000 per month for the first few years. The spouses of both principals are successful in the business world and earn enough to support the families.

They have engaged the services of Foster Jones, CPA, and William Hale, Attorney to assist them in an advisory capacity.

PERSONNEL

The firm will employ one delivery truck driver at a wage of $8.00 per hour. One office worker will be employed at $7.50 per hour. One part-time employee will be used in the office at $5.00 per hour. The driver will load and unload his own trucks. Mr. Williams will assist in the warehouse operation as needed to assist one stock person at $7.00 per hour. An additional delivery truck and driver will be added the third year.

The firm will lease a 20,000 square foot building at 3003 Avondale Ave., in Knoxville, which contains warehouse and office areas equipped with two-door truck docks. The annual rental is $9,000. The building was previously used as a food service warehouse and very little modification to the building will be required.

LOCATION

The firm will offer specialty food service products such as soup bases, dessert mixes, sauce bases, pastry mixes, spices, and flavors, normally used by upscale restaurants and nice hotels. We are going after a niche in the market with high quality gourmet products. There is much less competition in this market than in standard run of the mill food service products. Through their work experiences, the principals have contacts with supply sources and with local chefs.

PRODUCTS AND SERVICES

We know from our market survey that there are over 200 hotels and upscale restaurants in the area we plan to serve. Customers will be attracted by a direct sales approach. We will offer samples of our products and product application data on use of our products in the finished prepared foods. We will cultivate the chefs in these establishments. The technical background of John Williams will be especially useful here.

THE MARKET

We find that we will be only distributor in the area offering a full line of gourmet food service products. Other foodservice distributors offer only a few such items in conjunction with their standard product line. Our survey shows that many of the chefs are ordering products from Atlanta and Memphis because of lack of adequate local supply.

COMPETITION

Commercial Foods, Inc. will be established as a foodservice distributor of specialty food in Knoxville. The principals, with excellent experience in the industry are seeking a $75,000 loan to establish the business. The principals are investing $25,000 as equity capital.

SUMMARY

The business will be set up as an "S" Corporation with each principal owning 50% of the common stock in the corporation.

Attached is a three year pro forma income statement we believe to be conservative. Also attached are personal financial statements of the principals and a projected cash flow statement for the first year.

	1st Year	2nd Year	3rd Year
Gross Sales	300,000	400,000	500,000
Less Allowances	1,000	1,000	2,000
Net Sales	299,000	399,000	498,000
Cost of Goods Sold	179,400	239,400	298,800
Gross Margin	119,600	159,600	199,200

PRO FORMA INCOME STATEMENT

Operating Expenses			
Utilities	1,200	1,500	1,700
Salaries	76,000	79,000	102,000
Payroll Taxes/Benefits	9,100	9,500	13,200
Advertising	3,000	4,500	5,000
Office Supplies	1,500	2,000	2,500
Insurance	1,200	1,500	1,800
Maintenance	1,000	1,500	2,000
Outside Services	3,000	3,000	3,000
Whse Supplies/Trucks	6,000	7,000	10,000
Telephone	900	1,000	1,200
Rent	9,000	9,500	9,900
Depreciation	2,500	2,000	3,000
Total Expenses	114,400	122,000	155,300
Other Expenses			
Bank Loan Payment		15,000	15,000
Bank Loan Interest	6,000	5,000	4,000
Total Expenses	120,400	142,000	174,300
Net Profit (Loss)	(800)	17,600	24,900

FINANCIAL STATEMENT I

Assets		Liabilities	
Cash	15,000		
1991 Olds	11,000	Unpaid Balance	8,000
Residence	140,000	Mortgage	105,000
Mutual Funds	12,000	Credit Cards	500
Furniture	5,000	Note Payable	4,000
Merck Stock	10,000		
	182,200		117,500
Net Worth			64,700
	182,200		182,200

FINANCIAL STATEMENT II

Assets		Liabilities	
Cash	5,000		
1992 Buick Auto	15,000	Unpaid Balance	12,000
Residence	120,000	Mortgage	100,000
U.S. Treasury Bonds	5,000	Credit Cards	500
Home Furniture	4,000	Note Payable	2,500
AT&T Stock	3,000		
	147,000		115,000
Net Worth			32,000
	147,000		147,000

Hardware Store

FICTIONAL BUSINESS PLAN

OSHKOSH HARDWARE, INC

123 Main St.
Oshkosh, WI 54901

June 1994

The following fictional plan outlines how a small hardware store can survive competition from large discount chains by offering products and providing expert advice in the use of any product it sells. This plan is fictional and has not been used to gain funding from a bank or other lending institution.

- EXECUTIVE SUMMARY

- THE BUSINESS

- THE MARKET

- SALES

- MANAGEMENT

- GOALS IMPLEMENTATION

- FINANCE

- JOB DESCRIPTION-GENERAL MANAGER

- QUARTERLY FORECASTED BALANCE SHEETS

- QUARTERLY FORECASTED STATEMENTS OF EARNINGS AND RETAINED EARNINGS

- QUARTERLY FORECASTED STATEMENTS OF CHANGES IN FINANCIAL POSITION

- FINANCIAL RATIO ANALYSIS

- DETAILS FOR QUARTERLY STATEMENTS OF EARNINGS

EXECUTIVE SUMMARY

Oshkosh Hardware, Inc. is a new corporation which is going to establish a retail hardware store in a strip mall in Oshkosh, Wisconsin. The store will sell hardware of all kinds, quality tools, paint and housewares. The business will make revenue and a profit by servicing its customers not only with needed hardware but also with expert advice in the use of any product it sells.

Oshkosh Hardware, Inc. will be operated by its sole shareholder, James Smith. The company will have a total of four employees. It will sell its products in the local market. Customers will buy our products because we will provide free advice on the use of all of our products and will also furnish a full refund warranty.

Oshkosh Hardware, Inc. will sell its products in the Oshkosh store staffed by three sales representatives. No additional employees will be needed to achieve its short and long range goals. The primary short range goal is to open the store by October 1, 1994. In order to achieve this goal a lease must be signed by July 1, 1994 and the complete inventory ordered by August 1, 1994.

James Smith will invest $30,000 in the business. In addition the company will have to borrow $150,000 during the first year to cover the investment in inventory, accounts receivable, and furniture and equipment. The company will be profitable after six months of operation and should be able to start repayment of the loan in the second year.

THE BUSINESS

The business will sell hardware of all kinds, quality tools, paint, and housewares. We will purchase our products from three large wholesale buying groups.

In general our customers are homeowners who do their own repair and maintenance, hobbyists, and housewives. Our business is unique in that we will have a complete line of all hardware items and will be able to get special orders by overnight delivery. The business makes revenue and profits by servicing our customers not only with needed hardware but also with expert advice in the use of any product we sell. Our major costs for bringing our products to market are cost of merchandise of 36%, salaries of $45,000, and occupancy costs of $60,000.

Oshkosh Hardware, Inc.'s retail outlet will be located at 1524 Frontage Road, which is in a newly developed retail center of Oshkosh. Our location helps facilitate accessibility from all parts of town and reduces our delivery costs. The store will occupy 7500 square feet of space. The major equipment involved in our business is counters and shelving, a computer, a paint mixing machine, and a truck.

THE MARKET

Oshkosh Hardware, Inc. will operate in the local market. There are 15,000 potential customers in this market area. We have three competitors who control approximately 98% of the market at present. We feel we can capture 25% of the market within the next four years. Our major reason for believing this is that our staff is technically competent to advise our customers in the correct use of all products we sell.

After a careful market analysis we have determined that approximately 60% of our customers are men and 40% are women. The percentage of customers that fall into the following age categories are:

Under 16	0%
17-21	5%
22-30	30%
31-40	30%
41-50	20%
51-60	10%
61-70	5%
Over 70	0%

The reasons our customers prefer our products is our complete knowledge of their use and our full refund warranty.

We get our information about what products our customers want by talking to existing customers. There seems to be an increasing demand for our product. The demand for our product is increasing in size based on the change in population characteristics.

SALES

At Oshkosh Hardware, Inc. we will employ three sales people and will not need any additional personnel to achieve our sales goals. These salespeople will need several years experience in home repair and power tool usage. We expect to attract 30% of our customers from newspaper ads, 5% of our customers from local directories, 5% of our customers from the yellow pages, 10% of our customers from family and friends and 50% of our customers from current customers. The most cost-effective source will be current customers. In general, our industry is growing.

MANAGEMENT

We would evaluate the quality of our management staff as being excellent. Our manager is experienced and very motivated to achieve the various sales and quality assurance objectives we have set. We will use a management information system which produces key inventory, quality assurance and sales data on a weekly basis. All data is compared to previously established goals for that week and deviations are the primary focus of the management staff.

GOALS IMPLEMENTATION

The short term goals of our business are:
1. Open the store by October 1, 1994
2. Reach our breakeven point in two months
3. Have sales of $100,000 in the first six months

In order to achieve our first short term goal we must:
1. Sign the lease by July 1, 1994
2. Order a complete inventory by August 1, 1994

In order to achieve our second short term goal we must:
1. Advertise extensively in September and October
2. Keep expenses to a minimum

In order to achieve our third short term goal we must:

1. Promote power tool sales for the Christmas season
2. Keep good customer traffic in January and February

The long term goals for our business are:

1. Obtain sales volume of $600,000 in three years
2. Become the largest hardware dealer in the city
3. Open a second store in Fond du Lac

The most important thing we must do in order to achieve the long term goals for our business is to develop a highly profitable business with excellent cash flow.

FINANCE

Oshkosh Hardware, Inc. Faces some potential threats or risks to our business. They are discount house competition. We believe we can avoid or compensate for this by providing quality products complimented by quality advice on the use of every product we sell. The financial projections we have prepared are located at the end of this document.

JOB DESCRIPTION: GENERAL MANAGER

The General Manager of the business of the corporation will be the president of the corporation. He will be responsible for the complete operation of the retail hardware store which is owned by the corporation. A detailed description of his duties and responsibilities is as follows:

Sales

Train and supervise the three sales people. Develop programs to motivate and compensate these employees. Coordinate advertising and sales promotion effects to achieve sales totals as outlined in budget. Oversee purchasing function and inventory control procedures to insure adequate merchandise at all times at a reasonable cost.

Finance

Prepare monthly and annual budgets. Secure adequate line of credit from local banks. Supervise office personnel to insure timely preparation of records, statements, all government reports, control of receivables and payables and monthly financial statements.

Administration

Perform duties as required in the areas of personnel, building leasing and maintenance, licenses and permits and public relations.

QUARTERLY FORECASTED BALANCE SHEETS

	Beg Bal	1st Qtr	2nd Qtr	3rd Qtr	4th Qtr
Assets					
Cash	30,000	418	(463)	(3,574)	4,781
Accounts Receivable	0	20,000	13,333	33,333	33,333
Inventory	0	48,000	32,000	80,000	80,000
Other Current Assets	0	0	0	0	0
Total Current Assets	30,000	68,418	44,870	109,759	118,114

	Beg Bal	1st Qtr	2nd Qtr	3rd Qtr	4th Qtr
Land	0	0	0	0	0
Building & Improvements	0	0	0	0	0
Furniture & Equipment	0	75,000	75,000	75,000	75,000
Total Fixed Assets	0	75,000	75,000	75,000	75,000
Less Accum. Depreciation	0	1,875	3,750	5,625	7,500
Net Fixed Assets	0	73,125	71,250	69,375	67,500
Intangible Assets	0	0	0	0	0
Less Amortization	0	0	0	0	0
Net Intangible Assets	0	0	0	0	0
Other Assets	0	0	0	0	0
Total Assets	30,000	141,543	116,120	179,134	185,614

Liabilities and Shareholders' Equity

	Beg Bal	1st Qtr	2nd Qtr	3rd Qtr	4th Qtr
Short-Term Debt	0	0	0	0	0
Accounts Payable	0	12,721	10,543	17,077	17,077
Dividends Payable	0	0	0	0	0
Income Taxes Payable	0	(1,031)	(2,867)	(2,355)	(1,843)
Accured Compensation	0	1,867	1,867	1,867	1,867
Other Current Liabilities	0	0	0	0	0
Total Current Liabilities	0	13,557	9,543	16,589	17,101
Long-Term Debt	0	110,000	110,000	160,000	160,000
Other Non-Current Liabilities	0	0	0	0	0
Total Liabilities	0	123,557	119,543	176,589	177,101
Common Stock	30,000	30,000	30,000	30,000	30,000
Retained Earnings	0	(12,014)	(33,423)	(27,455)	(21,487)
Shareholders' Equity	30,000	17,986	(3,423)	2,545	8,513
Total Liabilities & Shareholders' Equity	30,000	141,543	116,120	179,134	185,614

QUARTERLY FORECASTED BALANCE SHEETS

...continued

BUSINESS PLAN TEMPLATE

QUARTERLY FORECASTED STATEMENTS OF EARNINGS AND RETAINED EARNINGS

	Beg Actual	1st Qtr	2nd Qtr	3rd Qtr	4th Qtr	Total
Total Sales	0	60,000	40,000	100,000	100,000	300,000
Goods/Services	0	21,600	14,400	36,000	36,000	108,000
Gross Profit	0	38,400	25,600	64,000	64,000	192,000
Operating Expenses	0	47,645	45,045	52,845	52,845	198,380
Fixed Expenses						
Interest	0	1,925	1,925	2,800	2,800	9,450
Depreciation	0	1,875	1,875	1,875	1,875	7,500
Amortization	0	0	0	0	0	0
Total Fixed Expenses	0	3,800	3,800	4,675	4,675	16,950
Operating Profit						
(Loss)	0	(13,045)	(23,245)	6,480	6,480	(23,330)
Other Income						
(Expense)	0	0	0	0	0	0
Interest Income	0	0	0	0	0	0
Earnings (Loss)						
Before Taxes	0	(13,045)	(23,245)	6,480	6,480	(23,330)
Income Taxes	0	(1,031)	(1,836)	512	512	(1,843)
Net Earnings	0	(12,014)	(21,409)	5,968	5,968	(21,487)
Retained Earnings,						
Beginning	0	0	(12,014)	(33,423)	(27,455)	0
Less Dividends	0	0	0	0	0	0
Retained Earnings,						
Ending	0	(12,014)	(33,423)	(27,455)	(21,487)	(21,487)

QUARTERLY FORECASTED STATEMENTS OF CHANGES IN FINANCIAL POSITION

	Beg Bal	1st Qtr	2nd Qtr	3rd Qtr	4th Qtr	Total
Sources (Uses) of Cash						
Net Earnings						
(Loss)	0	(12,014)	(21,409)	5,968	5,968	(21,487)
Depreciation						
& Amortization	0	1,875	1,875	1,875	1,875	7,500
Cash Provided						
by Operations	0	(10,139)	(19,534)	7,834	7,834	(13,987)
Dividends	0	0	0	0	0	0
Cash Provided by (Used For) Changes in						
Accounts Receivable	0	(20,000)	6,667	(20,000)	0	(33,333)
Inventory	0	(48,000)	16,000	(48,000)	0	(80,000)
Other Current Assets	0	0	0	0	0	0

	Beg Bal	1st Qtr	2nd Qtr	3rd Qtr	4th Qtr	Total
Accounts Payable	0	12,	721	(2,178)	6,5340	17,077
Income Taxes	0	(1,031)	(1,836)	512	512	(1,843)
Accrued						
Compensation	0	1,867	0	0	0	1,867
Dividends Payable	0	0	0	0	0	0
Other Current						
Liabilities	0	0	0	0	0	0
Other Assests	0	0	0	0	0	0
Net Cash Provided by (Used For)						
Operating Activities	0	(54,443)	18,653	(60,954)	512	(96,233)
Investment Transactions						
Furniture &						
Equipment	0	(75,000)	0	0	0	(75,000)
Land	0	0	0	0	0	0
Building &						
Improvements	0	0	0	0	0	0
Intangible Assets	0	0	0	0	0	0
Net Cash From						
Investment						
Transactions	0	(75,000)	0	0	0	(75,000)
Financing Transactions						
Short-Term Debt	0	0	0	0	0	0
Long-Term Debt	0	110,000	0	50,000	0	160,000
Other Non-Current						
Liabilities	0	0	0	0	0	0
Sale of Common						
Stock	30,000	0	0	0	0	0
Net Cash from Financing						
Transactions	30,000	110,000	0	50,000	0	160,000
Net Increase (Decrease)						
in Cash	30,000	(29,582)	(881)	(3,111)	8,355	(25,219)
Cash-Beginning						
of Period	0	30,000	418	(463)	(3,574)	30,000
Cash-End						
of Period	30,000	418	(463)	(3,574)	4,781	4,781

QUARTERLY FORECASTED STATEMENTS OF CHANGES IN FINANCIAL POSITION

...continued

FINANCIAL RATIO ANALYSIS

	Beg Act	1st Qtr	2nd Qtr	3rd Qtr	4th Qtr
Overall Performance					
Return on Equity	0.00	(66.80)	625.45	234.50	70.10
Return on Total Assets	0.00	(8.49)	(18.44)	3.33	3.22
Operating Return	0.00	(9.22)	(20.02)	3.62	3.49
Profitability Measures					
Gross Profit Percent	0.00	64.00	64.00	64.00	64.00
Profit Margin (AIT)	0.00	(20.02)	(53.52)	5.97	5.97
Operating Income					
per Share	0.00	0.00	0.00	0.00	0.00
Earnings per Share	0.00	0.00	0.00	0.00	0.00
Test of Investment Utilization					
Asset Turnover	0.00	0.42	0.34	0.56	0.54
Equity Turnover	0.00	3.34	(11.69)	39.29	11.75
Fixed Asset Turnover	0.00	0.82	0.56	1.44	1.48
Average Collection					
Period	0.00	30.00	30.00	30.00	30.00
Days Inventory	0.00	200.00	200.00	200.00	200.00
Inventory Turnover	0.00	0.45	0.45	0.45	0.45
Working Capital Turns	0.00	1.09	1.13	1.07	0.99
Test of Financial Condition					
Current Ratio	0.00	5.05	4.70	6.62	6.91
Quick Ratio	0.00	1.51	1.35	1.79	2.23
Working Capital Ratio	1.00	0.43	0.33	0.57	0.60
Dividend Payout	0.00	0.00	0.00	0.00	0.00
Financial Leverage					
Total Assets	1.00	7.87	(33.92)	70.39	21.80
Debt/Equity	0.00	6.87	(34.92)	69.39	20.80
Debt to Total Assets	0.00	0.87	1.03	0.99	0.95
Year-End Equity History					
Shares Outstanding	0	0	0	0	0
Market Price per Share	0.00	0.00	0.00	0.00	0.00
(@20x's earnings)					
Book Value per Share	0.00	0.00	0.00	0.00	0.00
Altman Analysis Ratio					
1.2x(1)	1.20	0.47	0.37	0.62	0.65
1.4x(2)	0.00	(0.12)	(0.40)	(0.21)	(0.16)
3.3x(3)	0.00	(0.35)	(0.72)	0.07	0.07
0.6x(4)	0.00	0.00	0.00	0.00	0.00
1.0x(5)	0.00	0.42	0.34	0.56	0.54
Z Value	1.20	.042	(.041)	1.04	1.10

	Beg Act	1st Qtr	2nd Qtr	3rd Qtr	4th Qtr	Total	%Sales	Fixed
Sales								
Dollars Sales Forecasted								
Product 1	0	60,000	40,000	100,000	100,000	300,000		
Product 2	0	0	0	0	0	0		
Product 3	0	0	0	0	0	0		
Product 4	0	0	0	0	0	0		
Product 5	0	0	0	0	0	0		
Product 6	0	0	0	0	0	0		
Total Sales	0	60,000	40,000	100,000	100,000	300,000		
Cost of Sales								
Dollar Cost Forecasted								
Product 1	0	21,600	14,400	36,000	36,000	108,000	36.00%	0
Product 2	0	0	0	0	0	0	0.00%	0
Product 3	0	0	0	0	0	0	0.00%	0
Product 4	0	0	0	0	0	0	0.00%	0
Product 5	0	0	0	0	0	0	0.00%	0
Product 6	0	0	0	0	0	0	0.00%	0
Total Cost of Sales	0	21,600	14,400	36,000	36,000	108,000		
Operating Expenses								
Payroll	0	12,000	12,000	12,000	12,000	48,000	0.00%	12,000
Paroll Taxes	0	950	950	950	950	3,800	0.00%	950
Advertising	0	4,800	3,200	8,000	8,000	24,000	8.00%	0
Automobile Expenses	0	0	0	0	0		0.00%	0
Bad Debts	0	0	0	0	0	0	0.00%	0
Commissions	0	3,000	2,000	5,000	5,000	15,000	5.00%	0
Computer Rental	0	1,200	1,200	1,200	1,200	4,800	0.00%	1,200
Computer Supplies	0	220	220	220	220	880	0.00%	220
Computer Maintenance	0	100	100	100	100	400	0.00%	100
Dealer Training	0	1,000	1,000	1,000	1,000	4,000	0.00%	1,000
Electricity	0	3,000	3,000	3,000	3,000	12,000	0.00%	3,000
Employment Ads and Fees	0	0	0	0	0	0	0.00%	0
Entertainment: Business	0	1,500	1,500	1,500	1,500	6,000	0.00%	1,500
General Insurance	0	800	800	800	800	32,000	0.00%	800
Health & W/C Insurance	0	0	0	0	0	0	.00%	0
Interest-LT Debt	0	2,500	2,500	2,500	2,500	10,000	0.00%	2,500
Legal & Accounting	0	1,500	1,500	1,500	1,500	6,000	0.00%	1,500
Maintenance & Repairs	0	460	460	460	460	1,840	0.00%	460

DETAILS FOR QUARTERLY STATEMENTS OF EARNINGS

**DETAILS FOR
QUARTERLY
STATEMENTS OF
EARNINGS**
...continued

	Beg Act	1st Qtr	2nd Qtr	3rd Qtr	4th Qtr	Total	%Sales	Fixed
Office Supplies	0	270	270	270	270	1,080	0.00%	270
Postage	0	85	85	85	85	340	0.00%	85
Prof. Development	0	0	0	0	0	0	0.00%	0
Professional Fees	0	1,000	1,000	1,000	1,000	4,000	0.00%	1,000
Rent	0	8,000	8,000	8,000	8,0003	2,000	0.00%	8,000
Shows & Conferences	0	0	0	0	0	0	0.00%	0
Subscriptions & Dues	0	285	285	285	285	1,140	0.00%	285
Telephone	0	1,225	1,225	1,225	1,225	4,900	0.00%	1,225
Temporary Employees	0	0	0	0	0	0	0.00%	0
Travel Expenses	0	750	750	750	750	3,000	0.00%	750
Utilities	0	3,000	3,000	3,000	3,000	12,000	0.00%	3,000
Research & Devlpmnt.	0	0	0	0	0	0	0.00%	0
Royalties	0	0	0	0	0	0	0.00%	0
Other 1	0	0	0	0	0	0	0.00%	0
Other 2	0	0	0	0	0	0	0.00%	0
Other 3	0	0	0	0	0	0	0.00%	0
Total Operating Expenses	0	47,645	45,045	52,845	52,845	198,380		
Percent of Sales	0.00	79.41	112.61	52.85	52.85	66.13		

Organizations, Agencies and Consultants

Organizations, Agencies, & Consultants

A listing of Associations and Consultants of interest to entrepreneurs, followed by the 10 Small Business Administration Regional Offices and all Small Business Development Centers.

ASSOCIATIONS

This section contains a listing of associations and other agencies of interest to the small business owner. Entries are listed alphabetically by organization name.

Alliance of Minority Women for
Business and Political Development
c/o Brenda Alford
PO Box 13858
Silver Spring, MD 20911-3858 United States
Phone: (301)230-5583

American Association for Consumer Benefits (AACB)
PO Box 100279
Fort Worth, TX 76185 United States
Fax: (817)735-1726
Toll Free: 800-872-8896
Primary Contact: William D. Abbott

American Business Association (ABA)
292 Madison Ave., 4th Fl.
New York, NY 10017 United States
Phone: (212)949-5900
Fax: (212)949-5910
Toll Free: 800-221-2168
Primary Contact: Ms. Pat Arden - Exec.Dir.

American Business Women's Association (ABWA)
9100 Ward Pky.
PO Box 8728
Kansas City, MO 64114 United States
Phone: (816)361-6621
Fax: (816)361-4991
Primary Contact: Carolyn B. Elman - Exec.Dir.

American Small Businesses Association (ASBA)
1800 N. Kent St., Ste. 910
Arlington, VA 22209 United States
Toll Free: 800-235-3298
Primary Contact: Vernon Castle - Exec.Dir.

American Woman's Economic
Development Corporation (AWED)
71 Vanderbilt Ave., 3rd Fl.
New York, NY 10169 United States
Phone: (212)692-9100
Fax: (212)692-9296
Primary Contact: Rosalind Paaswell - CEO

Asian Business League of San Francisco (ABL-SF)
233 Sansome St., Ste. 1102
San Francisco, CA 94104 United States
Phone: (415)788-4664
Fax: (415)788-4756
Primary Contact: Julia Hsiao - Exec.Dir.

Association for Corporate Growth (ACG)
4350 DiPaolo Center, Ste. C
Dearlove Rd.
Glenview, IL 60025 United States
Phone: (708)699-1331
Fax: (708)699-6369
Primary Contact: Carl A. Wangman CAE - Exec.Dir.

Association for University Business
and Economic Research (AUBER)
c/o Terry Creeth, IBRC
801 W. Michigan, BS 4015
Indianapolis, IN 46202-5151 United States
Phone: (317)274-2204
Primary Contact: Terry Creeth

Association of African-American
Women Business Owners (AAA-WBO)
c/o Brenda Alford
Brasman Research
PO Box 13858
Silver Spring, MD 20911-3858 United States
Phone: (301)585-8051
Primary Contact: Tracy Mason - Pres.

Association of Business Products Manufacturers (ABPM)
1001 Connecticut Ave. NW, Ste. 1035
Washington, DC 20036 United States
Phone: (202)296-7400
Fax: (202)296-7565
Primary Contact: John C. Vickerman - Exec.Dir.

Association of Collegiate Entrepreneurs (ACE)
Wichita State University
Center for Entrepreneurship
1845 Fairmount
Wichita, KS 67260-0147 United States
Phone: (316)689-3000
Fax: (316)689-3687
Primary Contact: Scott Schulz - Dir. of Marketing

Association of Master of Business
Administration Executives (AMBA)
AMBA Center
277 Commerce St.
East Haven, CT 06512 United States
Phone: (203)467-8870
Primary Contact: Albert P. Hegyi - Pres.

Association of Small Business
Development Centers (ASBDC)
1313 Farnam, Ste. 132
Omaha, NE 68182 United States
Phone: (402)595-2387
Fax: (402)595-2388
Primary Contact: Jacquelyn Johnston -
          Membership Services Dir.

BEST Employers Association (BEA)
4201 Birch St.
Newport Beach, CA 92660 United States
Phone: (714)756-1000
Fax: (714)553-0883
Toll Free: 800-854-7417
Primary Contact: Donald R. Lawrenz Jr. - Exec.Sec.

Booker T. Washington Foundation (BTWF)
4324 Georgia Ave. NW
Washington, DC 20011 United States
Phone: (202)882-7100
Fax: (202)882-4354
Primary Contact: Charles E. Tate - Pres.

Business Coalition for Fair Competition (BCFC)
1101 King St.
Alexandria, VA 22314 United States
Phone: (703)739-2782
Primary Contact: Art Davis

Business Enterprise Trust
204 Junipero Serra Blvd.
Stanford, CA 94305 United States
Phone: (415)321-5100
Fax: (415)321-5774
Primary Contact: Kathleen A. Meyer - Exec.Dir.

Business for Social Responsibility
1850 M St. NW, Ste. 750
Washington, DC 20036 United States
Phone: (202)872-5206
Fax: (202)872-5227
Primary Contact: Michael Levett - Pres.

Business Market Association
4131 N. Central Expy., Ste. 720
Dallas, TX 75204 United States
Phone: (214)559-3900
Fax: (214)559-4143
Primary Contact: R. Mark King - Pres.

Canada-United States Business Association
150 W. Jefferson, Ste. 2500
Detroit, MI 48226 United States
Phone: (313)496-7579
Fax: (313)496-8451
Primary Contact: Dennis K. Loy - Pres.

Center for Entrepreneurial Management (CEM)
180 Varick St., Penthouse Ste.
New York, NY 10014 United States
Phone: (212)633-0060
Fax: (212)633-0063
Primary Contact: Joseph R. Mancuso - Pres.

Center for Family Business (CFB)
5862 Mayfield Rd.
PO Box 24268
Cleveland, OH 44124 United States
Phone: (216)442-0800
Fax: (216)442-0178
Primary Contact: Leon A. Danco Ph.D. - Pres.

Center for International Private Enterprise (CIPE)
1615 H St. NW
Washington, DC 20062 United States
Phone: (202)463-5901
Fax: (202)887-3447
Telex: 277559 CIPE UR
Primary Contact: Wally Workman - VP

Chief Executives Organization (CEO)
5430 Grosvenor Ln., Ste. 210
Bethesda, MD 20814 United States
Phone: (301)564-9614
Fax: (301)564-0060
Primary Contact: Terry Mooney - Exec.Dir.

Christian Chamber of Commerce (CCC)
PO Box 267
Silver Springs, NV 89429-0267 United States
Primary Contact: Rev. John P. Hansen - Founder

Coalition of Americans to Save the Economy (CASE)
1100 Connecticut Ave. NW, Ste. 1200
Washington, DC 20036 United States
Fax: (202)293-1702
Toll Free: 800-752-4111
Primary Contact: Bob Schwarze

Committee of 200 (C200)
625 N. Michigan Ave., Ste. 500
Chicago, IL 60611-3108 United States
Phone: (312)751-3477
Fax: (312)943-9401
Primary Contact: Lydia Lewis - Exec.Dir.

Deaf and Hard of Hearing
Entrepreneurs Council (DHHEC)
817 Silver Spring Ave., Ste. 305-F
Silver Spring, MD 20910 United States
Phone: (301)587-8596
Fax: (301)587-5997
Primary Contact: Louis J. Schwarz CFP - Pres.

Dealer Management Association (DMA)
239 Drakeside Rd.
Hampton, NH 03842 United States
Phone: (603)926-8000
Fax: (603)926-4505
Toll Free: 800-370-3362
Primary Contact: R. M. Caravati

EDGES Group (EDGES)
Amerada Hess Corp.
1 Hess Plz.
Woodbridge, NJ 07095 United States
Phone: (908)750-6408
Primary Contact: Walter Vertreace - Pres.

Entrepreneurship Institute, The (TEI)
3592 Corporate Dr., Ste. 101
Columbus, OH 43231 United States
Phone: (614)895-1153
Fax: (614)895-1473
Primary Contact: Mr. Jan W. Zupnick - Exec. Officer

Executive Leadership Council (ELC)
444 N. Capitol St., Ste. 715
Washington, DC 20001 United States
Phone: (202)783-6339
Primary Contact: Earl S. Washington - Pres.

Hispanic Organization of Professionals and Executives (HOPE)
87 Catoctin Ct.
Silver Spring, MD 20906 United States
Phone: (301)598-2535
Primary Contact: Stanley Valadez - Exec.Dir.

Home Executives National Networking Association (HENNA)
PO Box 6223
Bloomingdale, IL 60108 United States
Phone: (708)307-7130
Primary Contact: Laura M. Vaughn - Exec.Dir.

Independent Cash Register Dealers Association (ICRDA)
1897 I-85 South
Charlotte, NC 28202 United States
Phone: (704)392-3951
Fax: (704)394-8400
Primary Contact: Bill Bussard - Mgt.Exec.

Independent Small Business Employers of America (ISBE)
520 S. Pierce, Ste. 224
Mason City, IA 50401 United States
Phone: (515)424-3187
Fax: (515)424-1673
Toll Free: 800-728-3187
Primary Contact: Jim Collison - Pres.

Institute of Certified Business Counselors (ICBC)
PO Box 70326
Eugene, OR 97401 United States
Phone: (503)345-8064
Fax: (503)726-2402
Primary Contact: Wally Stabbert - Pres.

International Association for
Business Organizations (INAFBO)
PO Box 30149
Baltimore, MD 21270 United States
Phone: (410)581-1373
Primary Contact: Rudolph Lewis - Exec. Officer

International Association of African and American Black
Business People (IAAABBP)
18900 Schoolcraft
Detroit, MI 48223 United States
Primary Contact: William Bert Johnson - Pres.

International Association of Business (IAB)
701 Highlander Blvd.
Arlington, TX 76015 United States
Phone: (817)465-2922
Fax: (817)467-5920
Primary Contact: Paula Rainey - Dir.

International Association of Business Forecasting (IABF)
Loyola College
Jenkins Hall, Rm. 211
4501 N. Charles St.
Baltimore, MD 21210-2699 United States
Phone: (410)617-2892
Fax: (410)617-2104
Primary Contact: LeRoy R. Simmons Ph.D. - Pres.

International Association of Merger and Acquisition
Consultants (INTERMAC)
60 Revere Dr., Ste. 500
Northbrook, IL 60062-1577 United States
Phone: (708)480-9037
Fax: (708)480-9282
Primary Contact: Alison C. Brown - Exec.Dir.

International Council for Small Business (ICSB)
c/o Jefferson Smurfit Center for Entrepreneurial Studies
St. Louis University
3674 Lindell Blvd.

St. Louis, MO 63108 United States
Phone: (314)658-3896
Fax: (314)658-3897
Primary Contact: Ken O'Neill - Pres.

International Downtown Association (IDA)
915 15th St. NW, Ste. 600
Washington, DC 20005 United States
Phone: (202)783-4963
Fax: (202)347-2161
Primary Contact: Richard H. Bradley - Pres.

International Executive Service Corps (IESC)
333 Ludlow St.
PO Box 10005
Stamford, CT 06904-2005 United States
Phone: (203)967-6000
Fax: (203)324-2531
Primary Contact: Hobart C. Gardiner - Pres.

The International Alliance, An Association of Executive
and Professional Women (TIA)
8600 LaSalle Rd., Ste. 617
Baltimore, MD 21286 United States
Phone: (410)472-4221
Fax: (410)472-2920
Primary Contact: Marian E. Goetze - Exec.VP

Interracial Council for Business Opportunity (ICBO)
51 Madison Ave., Ste. 2212
New York, NY 10010 United States
Phone: (212)779-4360
Fax: (212)779-4365
Primary Contact: Lorraine Kelsey - Exec. Officer

Invest to Compete Alliance (ITCA)
1010 Pennsylvania Ave. SE
Washington, DC 20003 United States
Phone: (202)546-4991
Fax: (202)544-7926
Primary Contact: Jeanne Campbell - Coord.

Latin American Management Association (LAMA)
419 New Jersey Ave. SE
Washington, DC 20003 United States
Phone: (202)546-3803
Fax: (202)546-3807
Primary Contact: Luz A. Hopewell - Exec.VP

Latin Business Association
5400 E. Olympic Blvd., No. 3130
Los Angeles, CA 90022 United States
Phone: (213)721-4000
Fax: (213)722-5050
Primary Contact: Diana Sanchez Roberson - Exec.Dir.

Majestic Eagles (ME)
2029 Rhode Island Ave. NE
Washington, DC 20018 United States
Phone: (202)635-0154
Fax: (202)635-1086
Primary Contact: Col. Jim Dicks - Exec.Dir.

MCAP Group (MCAP)
89-50 164th St., Ste. 2B
Jamaica, NY 11432 United States
Phone: (718)657-6444
Fax: (718)523-2063
Primary Contact: Sherman L. Brown - Pres.

Minority Business Enterprise Legal
Defense and Education Fund (MBELDEF)
220 Eye St. NE, Ste. 240
Washington, DC 20002 United States
Phone: (202)543-0040
Fax: (202)543-4135
Primary Contact: Anthony W. Robinson - Pres.

Mothers' Home Business Network (MHBN)
PO Box 423
East Meadow, NY 11554 United States
Phone: (516)997-7394
Fax: (516)997-0839
Primary Contact: Georganne Fiumara - Dir.

National Alliance for Fair Competition (NAFC)
3 Bethesda Metro Center, Ste. 1100
Bethesda, MD 20814 United States
Phone: (410)235-7116
Fax: (410)235-7116
Primary Contact: Tony Ponticelli - Exec.Dir.

National Association for Business Organizations (NAFBO)
PO Box 30149
Baltimore, MD 21270 United States
Phone: (410)581-1373
Primary Contact: Rudolph Lewis - Pres.

National Association for Female Executives (NAFE)
30 Irving Pl., 5th Fl.
New York, NY 10003 United States
Phone: (212)477-2200
Fax: (212)477-8215
Toll Free: 800-927-6233
Primary Contact: Wendy Reid-Crisp - Dir.

National Association for the Cottage Industry (NACI)
PO Box 14850
Chicago, IL 60614 United States
Phone: (312)472-8116

National Association for the Self-Employed (NASE)
PO Box 612067
Dallas, TX 75261-2067 United States
Phone: (202)466-2100
Fax: (800)551-4446
Toll Free: 800-232-NASE
Primary Contact: Bennie Thayer - Pres. & CEO

National Association of Black Women Entrepreneurs (NABWE)
PO Box 1375
Detroit, MI 48231 United States
Phone: (313)559-9255
Fax: (313)559-9256
Primary Contact: Marilyn French-Hubbard - Founder

National Association of Home Based Businesses (NAHBB)
PO Box 30220
Baltimore, MD 21270 United States
Phone: (410)363-3698
Primary Contact: Rudolph Lewis - Pres.

National Association of Investment Companies (NAIC)
1111 14th St. NW, Ste. 700
Washington, DC 20005 United States
Phone: (202)289-4336
Fax: (202)289-4329
Primary Contact: Bruce Gamble - Pres.

National Association of Minority Automobile Dealers (NAMAD)
1250 Connectucut Ave. NW
Washington, DC 20036 United States
Phone: (202)637-9095
Fax: (202)637-9195
Primary Contact: Cynthia Burns - Exec.Dir.

ORGANIZATIONS, AGENCIES, & CONSULTANTS

National Association of Minority
Women in Business (NAMWIB)
906 Grand Ave., Ste. 200
Kansas City, MO 64106 United States
Phone: (816)421-3335
Fax: (816)421-3336
Primary Contact: Inez Kaiser - Pres.

National Association of Private Enterprise (NAPE)
PO Box 612147
Dallas, TX 75261-2147 United States
Fax: (817)332-4525
Toll Free: 800-223-6273
Primary Contact: Heidi Williams - Acct.Exec.

National Association of Small Business
Investment Companies (NASBIC)
1199 N. Fairfax St., Ste. 200
Alexandria, VA 22314 United States
Phone: (703)683-1601
Fax: (703)683-1605
Primary Contact: Jeanette D. Smith

National Association of Women
Business Owners (NAWBO)
1010 Wayne Ave., Ste. 900
Silver Spring, MD 20910 United States
Phone: (301)608-2596
Fax: (301)608-2596
Toll Free: 800-55-NAWBO
Primary Contact: Patty DeDominic - Pres.

National Black Business Alliance (NBBA)
PO Box 26443
Baltimore, MD 21207 United States
Phone: (410)752-3682
Fax: (410)752-3593
Primary Contact: Willie H. Scott - CEO

National Business Association (NBA)
5025 Arapaho, Ste. 515
Dallas, TX 75248 United States
Phone: (214)458-0900
Fax: (214)960-9149
Toll Free: 800-456-0440
Primary Contact: Robert G. Allen - Pres.

National Business Incubation Association (NBIA)
20 E. Circle Dr., Ste. 190
Athens, OH 45701 United States
Phone: (614)593-4331
Fax: (614)593-1996
Primary Contact: Dinah Adkins - Exec.Dir.

National Business League (NBL)
1511 K St. NW, Ste. 432
Washington, DC 20005 United States
Phone: (202)737-4430
Fax: (202)466-5487
Primary Contact: Sherman Copilin - Pres.

National Business Owners Association (NBOA)
1200 18th St. NW, Ste. 500
Washington, DC 20036 United States
Phone: (202)737-6501
Fax: (202)737-3909
Primary Contact: J. Drew Hiatt - Exec.VP

National Executive Service Corps (NESC)
257 Park Ave. S.
New York, NY 10010-7304 United States
Phone: (212)529-6660
Fax: (212)228-3958
Primary Contact: Robert S. Hatfield - Chm.

National Family Business Council (NFBC)
1640 W. Kennedy Rd.
Lake Forest, IL 60045 United States
Phone: (708)295-1040
Fax: (708)295-1898
Primary Contact: John E. Messervey - Dir.

National Federation of Independent Business (NFIB)
53 Century Blvd., Ste. 300
Nashville, TN 37214 United States
Phone: (615)872-5800
Fax: (615)872-5899
Primary Contact: Fred Holladay - VP & CFO

National Hispanic Corporate Council (NHCC)
2323 N. 3rd St., Ste. 101
Phoenix, AZ 85004 United States
Phone: (602)495-1988
Fax: (602)495-9085
Primary Contact: Joanne Samora - Dir.

National Minority Business Council (NMBC)
235 E. 42nd St.
New York, NY 10017 United States
Phone: (212)573-2385, (212)573-2301
Fax: (212)573-4462
Primary Contact: John F. Robinson - CEO & Pres.

National Minority Supplier Development
Council (NMSDC)
15 W. 39th St., 9th Fl.
New York, NY 10018 United States
Phone: (212)944-2430
Fax: (212)719-9611
Primary Contact: Harriet Michel - Pres.

National Nurses in Business Association (NNBA)
1000 Burnett Ave., Ste 450
Concord, CA 94520 United States
Phone: (510)356-2642
Fax: (510)356-2654
Primary Contact: Kay Davis M.N. - Pres.

National Small Business Benefits Association (NSBBA)
2244 N. Grand Ave. E.
Springfield, IL 62702 United States
Phone: (217)753-2558
Fax: (217)753-2558
Primary Contact: Les Brewer - Exec.VP

National Small Business United (NSBU)
1155 15th St. NW, Ste. 710
Washington, DC 20005 United States
Phone: (202)293-8830
Fax: (202)872-8543
Toll Free: 800-345-6728
Primary Contact: John Paul Galles - Exec.VP

National Society of Hispanic MBAs (NSHMBA)
PO Box 2903
Chicago, IL 60690-2903 United States
Phone: (512)472-5545
Primary Contact: Jeanette Esquivel - Pres.

National Women's Economic Alliance Foundation
(NWEAF)
1440 New York Ave. NW, Ste. 300
Washington, DC 20005 United States
Phone: (202)393-5257
Fax: (202)639-8685
Telex: 756546
Primary Contact: Patricia Harrison - Pres.

Ombudsman Association (TOA)
PO Box 7700
Arlington, VA 22207 United States
Phone: (703)532-2795
Fax: (703)532-2795
Primary Contact: Vincent J. Riley - Exec. Officer

POWERLUNCH!
c/o The Employment Support Center
5 Thomar Cir. NW
Washington, DC 20005 United States
Phone: (202)462-8004
Fax: (202)462-8448
Primary Contact: Ellie Wegener - Exec. Officer

Presidents Association (PA)
135 W. 50th St.
New York, NY 10020 United States
Phone: (212)586-8100
Fax: (212)903-8168
Primary Contact: Virginia L. O'Connor

Service Business Marketing Association (SBMA)
PO Box 909, Department EA
Buena Vista, CO 81211 United States
Phone: (719)395-2459
Fax: (719)395-8374
Primary Contact: Marilyn Ross

Service Corps of Retired Executives Association (SCORE)
409 3rd St. SW, Ste. 5900
Washington, DC 20024 United States
Phone: (202)205-6762
Fax: (202)205-7636
Primary Contact: W. Kenneth Yancey Jr. - Exec.Dir.

Small Business Assistance Center (SBAC)
554 Main St.
PO Box 1441
Worcester, MA 01601 United States
Phone: (508)756-3513
Fax: (508)791-4709
Primary Contact: Francis R. Carroll - Pres.

Small Business Exporters Association (SBEA)
4603 John Tyler Ct., Ste. 203
Annandale, VA 22003 United States
Phone: (703)642-2490
Fax: (703)750-9655
Primary Contact: E. Martin Duggan - Exec.Dir.

Small Business Foundation of America (SBFA)
1155 15th St.
Washington, DC 20005 United States
Phone: (202)223-1103
Fax: (202)872-8543
Primary Contact: Regina Tracy - Exec.Dir.

Small Business Legislative Council (SBLC)
1156 15th St. NW, Ste. 510
Washington, DC 20005 United States
Phone: (202)639-8500
Primary Contact: John Satagaj - Pres.

Small Business Network (SBN)
PO Box 30149
Baltimore, MD 21270 United States
Phone: (410)581-1373
Primary Contact: Rudolph Lewis - CEO

Small Business Service Bureau (SBSB)
554 Main St.
PO Box 1441
Worcester, MA 01601-1441 United States
Phone: (508)756-3513
Fax: (508)791-4709
Primary Contact: Francis R. Carroll - Pres.

Support Services Alliance (SSA)
PO Box 130
Schoharie, NY 12157-0130 United States
Phone: (518)295-7966
Fax: (518)295-8556
Toll Free: 800-322-3920
Primary Contact: Robert M. Marquardt - Pres.

Try Us Resources
2105 Central Ave. NE
Minneapolis, MN 55418 United States
Phone: (612)781-6819
Fax: (612)781-0109
Primary Contact: Liz Kahnk - Exec.Dir.

United States Council for International Business (USCIB)
1212 Ave. of the Americas, 21st Fl.
New York, NY 10036 United States
Phone: (212)354-4480
Fax: (212)575-0327
Primary Contact: Abraham Katz - Pres.

Washington Chinese Business Association (WCBA)
8131 Heatherton Ln., Ste. 304
Vienna, VA 22180 United States
Phone: (703)560-8001
Fax: (703)560-7445
Primary Contact: Gang Ke - Pres.

World Presidents Organization (WPO)
North Bldg., Ste. 520
601 Pennsylvania Ave. NW
Washington, DC 20004-2660 United States
Phone: (202)508-0100
Fax: (202)737-0654
Primary Contact: Rachael M. Lowder - Exec.VP

Young Entrepreneurs Organization (YEO)
1010 N. Glebe Rd., Ste. 600
Arlington, VA 22201 United States
Phone: (703)527-4500
Fax: (703)527-1274
Primary Contact: Mohamed Fathelbab - Exec.Dir.

Young Presidents' Organization (YPO)
451 S. Decker, Ste. 200
Irving, TX 75062 United States
Phone: (214)650-4600
Fax: (214)650-4777
Primary Contact: David E. Stahl - Exec.Dir.

CONSULTANTS

This section contains a listing of consultants specializing in small business development. It is arranged alphabetically by country (Canada, then United States), then by state or province within country, then by city, and where there is more than one entry for a city, by the firm's name.

CANADA

BRITISH COLUMBIA

Syspo Consulting
371 Delta Ave.
Burnaby, BC V5B 3C7
Phone: (604)291-9545

DeBoda & DeBoda
1523 Milford Ave.
Coquitlam, BC V3J 2V9
Phone: (604)936-4527
Fax: (604)936-4527

The Sage Group Ltd.
980 355 Burrard St.
Vancouver, BC V6C 3H2
Phone: (604)669-9269
Fax: (604)681-4938

Expense Reduction Consultants
3444 Karger Terr.
Victoria, BC V9C 3K5
Phone: (604)478-0457

ONTARIO

Cynton Company
17 Massey St.
Bramalea, ON L6S 2V6
Phone: (905)792-7769
Fax: (905)792-8116

JPL Business Consultants
Box 1587
Niagara-on-the-Lake, ON L0S 1J0
Phone: (905)935-2648
Fax: (905)935-2648

The ARA Consulting Group Inc.
116 Albert St., Ste. 303
Ottawa, ON K1P 5G3
Phone: (613)238-7400

HST Group Ltd.
430 Gilmour St.
Ottawa, ON K2P 0R8
Phone: (613)236-7303
Fax: (613)236-9893

Harrison Associates
111 Richmond St. W, Ste. 308
Toronto, ON M5H 2G4
Phone: (416)364-5441
Fax: (416)364-2875

Ken Wyman & Associates Inc.
64B Shuter St., Ste. 200
Toronto, ON M5B 1B1
Phone: (416)362-2926
Fax: (416)362-3039

QUEBEC

The Zimmar Consulting Partnership Inc.
PO Box 95
Westmount, Montreal, PQ H3Z 2T1
Phone: (514)484-1459
Fax: (514)484-3063

SASKATCHEWAN

Randall Marketing Group Inc.
PO Box 197
Regina, SK S4P 2Z6
Phone: (306)586-0870

UNITED STATES

ALABAMA

Business Planning Inc.
300 Office Park Dr.
Birmingham, AL 35223
Phone: (205)870-7090
Fax: (205)870-7103

ALASKA

Alaska Business Development Center
3335 Arctic Blvd., Ste. 203
Anchorage, AK 99503
Phone: (907)562-0335
Fax: (907)562-6988

Financial Concepts
449 No. 18 Dailey
Anchorage, AK 99515
Phone: (907)349-4458
Fax: (907)349-4458

Business Matters
PO Box 287
Fairbanks, AK 99707
Phone: (907)452-5650

ARIZONA

Greenwich Direct Marketing Corp.
8001 E. Serene St.
PO Box 3737
Carefree, AZ 85377
Phone: (602)488-4227
Fax: (602)488-2841

Thomas B. Galitski
5540 W. Glendale Ave., Ste. A101
Glendale, AZ 85301
Phone: (602)842-0656
Fax: (602)931-3174

Arthur Aschauer & Co., Inc.
4520 E. Indian School Rd., Ste. 1
Phoenix, AZ 85018
Phone: (602)840-0066

Computer & Management Advisory Services
1625 E. Northern, Ste. 201
Phoenix, AZ 85020
Phone: (602)395-1001

Advanced Franchising Worldwide, Inc.
7950 E. Redfield, Ste. 120
Scottsdale, AZ 85260
Phone: (602)443-0432
Fax: (602)991-1418

Ceekay Consultants
4919 N. Granite Reef Rd.
Scottsdale, AZ 85251
Phone: (602)946-1474

Gary L. McLeod
PO Box 230
Sonoita, AZ 85637
Phone: (602)455-5661

Trans Energy Corporation
219 S. Siesta Ln., Ste. 101
Tempe, AZ 85281
Phone: (602)921-0433
Fax: (602)967-6601

Van Cleve Associates
6932 E. 2nd St.
Tucson, AZ 85710
Phone: (602)296-2587

CALIFORNIA

Lindquist Consultants
225 Arlington
Berkeley, CA 94707
Phone: (510)524-6685
Fax: (510)527-6604

Larson Associates
PO Box 9005
Brea, CA 92621
Phone: (714)529-4121
Fax: (714)572-3606

Louis V. O'Brien,
Management Consultant
1060 Whitwell Rd.
Burlingame, CA 94010
Phone: (415)347-4504

Kremer Management Consulting
PO Box 500
Carmel, CA 93921
Phone: (408)626-8311
Fax: (408)624-2663

Hunter G. Jackson, Jr.
Consulting Environmental Physicist
P.O. Drawer 880
Cupertino, CA 95015
Phone: (408)446-4097

Northwest Consulting Group
317 Third St., Ste. 3
Eureka, CA 95501
Phone: (707)443-0030
Fax: (707)443-5683

Burnes Consulting Group
930 Cedar St.
Fort Bragg, CA 95437
Phone: (707)964-1459
Fax: (707)964-1458
Toll Free: 800-949-9021

Strategic Business Group
800 Cienaga Dr.
Fullerton, CA 92635
Phone: (714)449-1040
Fax: (714)449-1040

Pioneer Business Consultants
9042 Garfield Ave., Ste. 312
Huntington Beach, CA 92646
Phone: (714)964-7600
Fax: (714)962-6585

MCS Associates
18300 Von Karman, Ste. 1100
Irvine, CA 92715
Phone: (714)263-8700
Fax: (714)553-0168

Kris Dean
PO Box 214
La Honda, CA 94020
Phone: (415)747-0979

RCL & Co.
PO Box 1143
La Jolla, CA 92038
Phone: (619)454-8883
Fax: (619)454-8880

General Business Services
3201 Lucas Cir.
Lafayette, CA 94549
Phone: (510)283-8272

The Ribble Group
27601 Forbes Rd., Ste. 52
Laguna Niguel, CA 92677
Phone: (714)582-1085
Fax: (714)582-6420

Bell Springs Publishing
Bell Springs Rd.
Box 640
Laytonville, CA 95454
Phone: (707)984-6746

Norris Bernstein
9309 Marina Pacifica Dr. N
Long Beach, CA 90803
Phone: (310)493-5458
Fax: (310)493-5459

Horizon Consulting Services
1315 Garthwick Dr.
Los Altos, CA 94024
Phone: (415)967-0906
Fax: (415)967-0906

Brincko Associates, Inc.
1801 Ave. of the Stars
Los Angeles, CA 90067
Phone: (310)553-4523
Fax: (310)553-6782

Business Expansions International
210 S. Anita Ave.
Los Angeles, CA 90049
Phone: (310)476-5262
Fax: (310)478-1876

Hutchinson Consulting and Appraisals
11966 Woodbine St.
Los Angeles, CA 90066
Phone: (310)391-7086
Fax: (310)391-7086

F.J. Schroeder & Associates
1926 Westholme Ave.
Los Angeles, CA 90025
Phone: (310)470-2655
Fax: (310)470-6378

Leslie J. Zambo
3355 Michael Dr.
Marina, CA 93933
Phone: (408)384-7086

Marketing Services Management
PO Box 1377
Martinez, CA 94553
Phone: (510)370-8527
Fax: (510)370-8527

Keck & Company Business Consultants
410 Walsh Rd.
Menlo Park, CA 94027
Phone: (415)854-9588
Phone: (415)854-9589
Fax: (415)854-7240

W & J Partnership
17211 Quail Ct.
Morgan Hill, CA 95037
Phone: (408)779-1714
Fax: (408)778-1305

Palo Alto Management Group, Inc.
2672 Bayshore Pkwy., Ste. 700
Mountain View, CA 94043
Phone: (415)968-4374
Fax: (415)968-4245

Market Connection
4020 Birch St.
Newport Beach, CA 92660
Phone: (714)851-6313
Fax: (714)833-0253

Muller Associates
PO Box 7264
Newport Beach, CA 92658
Phone: (714)646-1169
Fax: (714)646-1169

NEXUS - Consultants to Management
PO Box 1531
Novato, CA 94948
Phone: (415)897-4400
Fax: (415)898-2252

Adelphi Communications Incorporated
1300 Clay St., Ste. 600
Oakland, CA 94612
Phone: (510)464-8076
Fax: (510)530-3411

Creston Financial Group
1800 Harrison St., 18th Fl.
Oakland, CA 94612
Phone: (510)987-8500
Fax: (510)893-1321

Metropolis Communications
5546 Fremont St.
Oakland, CA 94608
Phone: (510)652-4558
Fax: (510)658-9846

Gerber Business Development
1135 N. McDowell Blvd.
Petaluma, CA 94954
Phone: (707)778-2900
Fax: (707)778-2999

Western Management Associates
8640 Gulana Ave., Ste. J 3015
Playa Del Rey, CA 90293
Phone: (310)823-4752
Fax: (310)823-4756

Management Seminars
2639 Hurricane Cove
Port Hueneme, CA 93041

Business Research Consultants, Inc.
PO Box 1646
Rancho Mirage, CA 92270
Phone: (619)328-3700
Fax: (619)328-2474

RECO Management Consulting
3084 Woodley Ct.
Rosamond, CA 93560
Phone: (805)256-6666

Business Incubation Development Associates
225 Broadway, Ste. 2250
San Diego, CA 92101
Phone: (619)237-0559
Fax: (619)237-0521

G.R. Gordetsky Consultants Inc.
11414 Windy Summit Pl.
San Diego, CA 92127
Phone: (619)487-4939
Fax: (619)487-5587

Wilson Associates
PO Box 126704
San Diego, CA 92112
Phone: (619)423-7772
Phone: (619)294-2141

Freeman, Sullivan & Co.
131 Steuart St., Ste. 520
San Francisco, CA 94105
Phone: (415)777-0707
Fax: (415)777-2420

Ideas Unlimited
2151 California St., Ste. 7
San Francisco, CA 94115
Phone: (415)931-0641
Fax: (415)931-0641

PKF Consulting
425 California St., Ste. 1650
San Francisco, CA 94104
Phone: (415)421-5378
Fax: (415)956-7708

Russell Miller Inc.
300 Montgomery St.
San Francisco, CA 94104
Phone: (415)956-7474
Fax: (415)398-0620

WEH Corporation
PO Box 470038
San Francisco, CA 94147
Phone: (415)567-3340
Fax: (415)567-3340

Welling & Woodard, Inc.
1067 Broadway
San Francisco, CA 94133
Phone: (415)776-4500
Fax: (415)776-5067

Quincy Yu
3300 Laguna St., Ste. 6
San Francisco, CA 94123
Phone: (415)567-1746

ORDIS, Inc.
6815 Trinidad Dr.
San Jose, CA 95120
Phone: (408)268-3321
Fax: (408)268-3582

Stanford Resources, Inc.
3150 Almaden Expy., Ste. 229
PO Box 20324
San Jose, CA 95160
Phone: (408)448-4440
Fax: (408)448-4445

Productivity Computing Services
1625 Waverly Rd.
San Marino, CA 91108
Phone: (818)281-7079

Helfert Associates
1777 Borel Pl., Ste. 508
San Mateo, CA 94402
Phone: (415)377-0540
Fax: (415)377-0472

RB Consultants
720 9th Ave.
San Mateo, CA 94402
Phone: (415)348-1619
Fax: (415)348-1619

The Information Group, Inc.
PO Box Q
Santa Clara, CA 95055
Phone: (408)985-7877
Fax: (408)985-2945

Cast Management Consultants
1620 26th St., Ste. 2040N
Santa Monica, CA 90404
Phone: (310)828-7511
Fax: (310)453-6831

Abrams Thompson Inc.
PO Box 14549
Santa Rosa, CA 95402
Phone: (707)575-9890
Fax: (707)575-5933

Cuma Consulting Management
Box 724
Santa Rosa, CA 95402
Phone: (707)785-2477
Fax: (707)785-2478

Goodrich Associates
20622 Russell Ln.
Saratoga, CA 95070
Phone: (408)867-5126

RJR Associates
1639 Lewiston Dr.
Sunnyvale, CA 94087
Phone: (408)737-7720
Fax: (408)737-7720

Schwafel Associates
790 Lucerne Dr., Ste. 10
Sunnyvale, CA 94086
Phone: (408)720-0649
Fax: (408)732-3507

Out of Your Mind
...and Into the Marketplace
13381 White Sand Dr.
Tustin, CA 92680
Phone: (714)544-0248
Fax: (714)730-1414

Independent Research Services
PO Box 2426
Van Nuys, CA 91404
Phone: (818)986-2927

Ingman Company Incorporated
16005 Sherman Way, Ste. 206
Van Nuys, CA 91406
Phone: (818)375-5027
Fax: (818)894-5820

Innovative Technology Associates
3639 E. Harbor Blvd., Ste. 203E
Ventura, CA 93001
Phone: (805)650-9353
Fax: (805)984-2979

Whittelsey Associates
180 Fox Hollow Rd.
Woodside, CA 94062
Phone: (415)851-8313
Fax: (415)851-2064

J.H. Robinson & Associates
20695 Deodar Dr., Ste. 100
PO Box 351
Yorba Linda, CA 92686
Phone: (714)970-1279

COLORADO

GVNW, Inc./Management
PO Box 25969
Colorado Springs, CO 80936
Phone: (719)594-5800
Fax: (719)599-0968

M-Squared, Inc.
755 San Gabriel Pl.
Colorado Springs, CO 80906
Phone: (719)576-2554
Fax: (719)576-2554

The Crosstern Corp.
670 Grant St.
Denver, CO 80203
Phone: (303)832-2546

Western Capital Holdings, Inc.
7500 E. Arapahoe Rd., Ste. 395
Englewood, CO 80112
Phone: (303)290-8482
Fax: (303)770-1945

Thornton Financial FNIC
1024 Centre Ave., Bldg. E
Fort Collins, CO 80526
Phone: (303)221-2089

Tactical Technology Inc.
287 Arlington Dr.
Grand Junction, CO 81503
Phone: (303)241-9707
Fax: (303)241-9707

TenEyck Associates
1760 Cherryville Rd.
Greenwood Village, CO 80121
Phone: (303)758-6129
Fax: (303)761-8286

Associated Enterprises Ltd.
8725 W. 14th Ave., Ste. 110
Lakewood, CO 80215
Phone: (303)274-2783
Fax: (303)274-5429

GSI Consulting Group
28 Red Fox Ln.
Littleton, CO 80127
Phone: (303)979-9033
Fax: (303)979-2870

Johnson & West Management Consultants, Inc.
PO Box 2364
Littleton, CO 80161
Phone: (303)730-6002
Fax: (303)694-3364

Janus Healthcare Consultants Inc.
18780 Deerfield Rd.
Monument, CO 80132
Phone: (303)660-2039
Fax: (303)688-8027

Business Associates
PO Box 3552
Vail, CO 81658
Phone: (303)479-9046

CONNECTICUT

Stratman Group Inc.
40 Tower Ln., Ste. 3
Avon, CT 06001
Phone: (203)677-2898
Fax: (203)677-8210

Cowherd Consulting Group, Inc.
106 Stephen Mather Rd.
Darien, CT 06820
Phone: (203)655-2150
Fax: (609)584-3523

Greenwich Associates
8 Greenwich Office Pk.
Greenwich, CT 06831
Phone: (203)629-1200
Fax: (203)629-1229

JC Ventures, Inc.
88 Field Point Rd.
Greenwich, CT 06830
Phone: (203)698-1990
Fax: (203)661-6143
Toll Free: 800-969-3680

Lead Brokers
185 Pine St., Ste. 818
Manchester, CT 06040
Phone: (203)647-7542
Fax: (203)646-6544

Shoreline Business Consulting
92 Knollwood Dr.
Old Saybrook, CT 06475
Phone: (203)388-9903
Fax: (203)388-9903

Charles L. Hornung
52 Ned's Mountain Rd.
Ridgefield, CT 06877
Phone: (203)431-0297

William M. Shine Consulting Service
Heritage Village
PO Box 2069
Southbury, CT 06488
Phone: (203)264-4024

Gerald S. Gilligan and Associates Inc.
One Strawberry Hill
Stamford, CT 06902
Phone: (203)325-3935

Manus Associates
100 Prospect St., S. Tower
Stamford, CT 06901
Phone: (203)326-3880
Fax: (203)326-3890
Toll Free: 800-445-0942

Rhinesmith and Associates
Palmer Landing 506
123 Harbor Dr.
Stamford, CT 06902
Phone: (203)327-7988
Fax: (203)327-5688

Sternbach Associates International
16 Tamarac Rd.
Westport, CT 06880
Phone: (203)227-2059
Fax: (203)454-7341

DELAWARE

Daedalus Ventures, Ltd.
PO Box 1474
Hockessin, DE 19707
Phone: (302)239-6758
Fax: (302)239-3755
Toll Free: 800-666-6216

Selden Enterprises Inc.
2055 Limestone Rd., Ste. 213
Wilmington, DE 19808
Phone: (302)999-1888
Fax: (302)999-9520

DISTRICT OF COLUMBIA

Enterprise Consulting, Inc.
2806 36th Pl. NW
PO Box 32273
Washington, DC 20007
Phone: (202)342-7640
Fax: (703)751-9240

Bruce W. McGee and Associates
7826 Eastern Ave. NW, Ste. 300
Washington, DC 20012
Phone: (202)726-7272

McManis Associates Inc.
2000 K St. N.W.
Washington, DC 20006
Phone: (202)466-7680
Fax: (202)872-1898

FLORIDA

H.P. Bieber and Associates
4800 Bayview Dr.
PO Box 030458
Fort Lauderdale, FL 33303
Phone: (305)771-6373

Eric Sands Consulting Services
6193 Rock Island Rd., Ste. 412
Fort Lauderdale, FL 33319
Phone: (305)721-4767

Bridge-It
3704 Broadway, Unit 313
Fort Myers, FL 33901
Phone: (813)278-4218
Fax: (813)936-6380

Host Media Corp.
3948 S. Third St., Ste. 191
Jacksonville Beach, FL 32250
Phone: (904)285-3239
Fax: (904)285-5618

The Bracken Group
233 E. New Haven Ave., 2nd Fl.
Melbourne, FL 32901
Phone: (407)725-0796
Fax: (407)724-0736

Corporate Business Computer Services Inc.
7458 SW 48th St.
Miami, FL 33155
Phone: (305)666-2225
Fax: (305)666-2254

William V. Hall
1925 Brickell, Ste. D-701
Miami, FL 33129
Phone: (305)856-9622
Fax: (305)856-4113

Taxplan, Inc.
134 National Professional Center
2699 Collins Ave.
Miami Beach, FL 33140
Phone: (305)538-3303
Phone: (305)531-6222

T.C. Brown & Associates
8415 Excalibur Cir., Ste. B-1
Naples, FL 33963
Phone: (813)594-1949

Comprehensive Franchising, Inc.
2465 Ridgecrest Ave.
Orange Park, FL 32065
Phone: (904)272-6567
Fax: (904)272-6750
Toll Free: 800-321-6567

F.A. McGee, Inc.
2810 Ocean Shore Blvd., Ste. 8
Ormond Beach, FL 32176
Phone: (904)441-6349

F. Newton Parks
210 El Brillo Way
Palm Beach, FL 33480
Phone: (407)833-1727
Fax: (407)833-4541

Avery Business Development Services
2506 St. Michel Ct.
Ponte Vedra, FL 32082
Phone: (904)285-6033

Focus Marketing
PO Box 4161
St. Petersburg, FL 33731
Phone: (813)527-0503

Dufresne Consulting Group, Inc.
10014 N. Dale Marby, Ste. 101
Tampa, FL 33618
Phone: (813)264-4775
Fax: (813)961-2395

Todd Organization
PO Box 552
Tampa, FL 33601

The Apogee Group, Inc.
PO Box 3907
Tequesta, FL 33469
Phone: (407)575-0299
Fax: (407)575-4542

Holton Associates
50 Beach Rd., Ste. 301
Tequesta, FL 33469
Phone: (407)744-9314

Center for Simplified Strategic Planning, Inc.
PO Box 3324
Vero Beach, FL 32964
Phone: (407)231-3636
Fax: (407)231-1099

GEORGIA

Bock, Center, Garber and Long
2 Piedmont Ctr.
Atlanta, GA 30305
Phone: (404)231-9011
Fax: (404)233-3756

Marketing Spectrum Inc.
990 Hammond Dr.
Atlanta, GA 30328
Phone: (404)395-7244
Fax: (404)393-4071

Nucifora Consulting Group
2859 Paces Ferry
Atlanta, GA 30339
Phone: (404)432-1072
Fax: (404)432-3528

Richard Siedlecki Marketing & Management
2996 Grandview Ave., Ste. 305
Atlanta, GA 30305
Phone: (404)816-4040

J. Charles Hulsey Consulting & Assistance Corp.
PO Box 43
Gainesville, GA 30503
Phone: (404)534-3142

Business Ventures Corp.
6030 Dawson Blvd.
Norcross, GA 30093
Phone: (404)729-8000
Fax: (404)729-8028

E. Peter Kite, Management Consulting Services
18 Coventry Close
Skidaway Island
Savannah, GA 31411
Phone: (912)598-1730
Fax: (912)598-0369

ILLINOIS

TWD and Associates
431 S. Patton
Arlington Heights, IL 60005
Phone: (708)398-6410
Fax: (708)437-1901

Management Planning Associates, Inc.
2275 Half Day Rd., Ste. 350
Bannockburn, IL 60015
Phone: (708)945-2421
Fax: (708)945-4917

Phil Faris Associates
86 Old Mill Ct.
Barrington, IL 60010

Minarich Group Inc.
200 N. Northwest Hwy., 1st Fl.
Barrington, IL 60010
Phone: (708)382-1453
Fax: (708)540-9585

Seven Continents Technology
787 Stonebridge
Buffalo Grove, IL 60089
Phone: (708)577-9653
Fax: (708)870-1220

Robetta Corporation
Professional Executive Center
1817 S. Neil St.
Champaign, IL 61820
Phone: (217)359-0641
Fax: (217)356-7050

ACE Accounting Service, Inc.
3128 N. Bernard St.
Chicago, IL 60618
Phone: (312)463-7854

FMS Consultants
5801 N. Sheridan Rd., Ste. 3D
Chicago, IL 60660
Phone: (312)561-7362
Fax: (312)561-6274

Miller, Mason & Dickenson
123 N. Wacker Dr.
Chicago, IL 60606
Phone: (312)701-4800
Fax: (312)701-2347

James C. Osburn, Ltd.
2701 W. Howard St.
Chicago, IL 60645
Phone: (312)262-4428
Fax: (312)262-6755

James B. Peterson & Associates
3 First National Plaza
70 W. Madison St., Ste. 1400
Chicago, IL 60602
Phone: (312)214-3172
Fax: (312)214-3110

Tarifero & Tazewell Inc.
211 S. Clark
PO Box 2130
Chicago, IL 60690
Phone: (312)665-9714
Fax: (312)665-9716

William J. Igoe
3949 Earlston Rd.
Downers Grove, IL 60515
Phone: (708)960-1418

Human Energy Design Systems
620 Roosevelt Dr.
Edwardsville, IL 62025
Phone: (618)692-0258

The Organizational Consulting Group, Ltd.
PO Box 54
Glenwood, IL 60425

BioLabs, Inc.
15 Sheffield Ct.
Lincolnshire, IL 60069
Phone: (708)945-2767

Clyde R. Goodheart
15 Sheffield Ct.
Lincolnshire, IL 60069
Phone: (708)945-2767
Fax: (708)945-4382

Profit Growth, Inc.
2705 Walters Ave.
Northbrook, IL 60062
Phone: (708)498-9043

Smith Associates
1320 White Mountain Dr.
Northbrook, IL 60062
Phone: (708)480-7200
Fax: (708)480-9828

Francorp Inc.
20200 Governors Dr.
Olympia Fields, IL 60461
Phone: (708)481-2900
Fax: (708)481-5885
Toll Free: 800-877-1103

Camber Business Strategy Consultants
PO Box 986
Palatine, IL 60078
Phone: (708)202-0101
Fax: (708)705-0101

McGladrey & Pullen
1699 E. Woodfield Rd., Ste. 300
Schaumburg, IL 60173
Phone: (708)517-7070
Toll Free: 800-365-8353

Koch International, Inc.
1040 S. Milwaukee Ave.
Wheeling, IL 60090
Phone: (708)459-1100
Fax: (708)459-0471
Toll Free: 800-323-7597

A.D. Star Consulting
320 Euclid
Winnetka, IL 60093
Phone: (708)446-7827
Fax: (708)446-7827

Indiana

Midwest Marketing Research
PO Box 1077
Goshen, IN 46526
Phone: (219)533-0548
Fax: (219)533-0540

Crosby & Associates
5699 E. 71st, Ste. 4-A
Indianapolis, IN 46220
Phone: (317)841-3300
Fax: (317)841-3300

JMG Associates
4437 N. Franklin Rd., Ste. D
Indianapolis, IN 46226
Phone: (317)546-5780

Ketchum Consulting Group
8021 Knue Rd., Ste. 112
Indianapolis, IN 46250
Phone: (317)845-5411
Fax: (317)842-9941

Marketing Department Inc.
3390 W. 86th, Ste. 2-F
Indianapolis, IN 46268
Phone: (317)876-5780
Fax: (317)876-5770

MDI Management Consulting
1519 Park Dr.
Munster, IN 46321
Phone: (219)838-7909
Fax: (219)838-7909

Lee Andreae
Research Associates
56420 Butternut Rd.
South Bend, IN 46619-1541
(219)289-5880

Iowa

Management Solutions
PO Box 7004
Des Moines, IA 50311
Phone: (515)277-6408
Fax: (515)277-3506

Grandview Marketing
117 Pierce St., Ste. 230
Sioux City, IA 51101
Phone: (712)258-8989
Fax: (712)258-7578
Toll Free: 800-475-8989

Kansas

Strategic Planning Management Associates, Inc.
6201 College Blvd., Ste. 210
Overland Park, KS 66211
Phone: (913)339-9001
Fax: (913)339-6226

Kentucky

New Horizons Planning Group, Inc.
PO Box 2616
Paducah, KY 42002
Phone: (502)443-6467

Maine

Edgemont Enterprises
PO Box 8354
Portland, ME 04104
Phone: (207)871-8964
Fax: (207)871-8964

Pan Atlantic Consultants
148 Middle St.
Portland, ME 04101
Phone: (207)871-8622
Fax: (207)772-4842

John E. Webster, Jr.
PO Box 979
Wells, ME 04090
Phone: (207)646-5878
Fax: (207)646-5516

Maryland

Imperial Group, Limited
305 Washington Ave., Ste. 501
8600 LaSalle Rd.
Baltimore, MD 21204
Phone: (410)337-7575
Fax: (410)337-7641

Kamanitz, Uhlfelder and
Permison Professional Association
4 Reservoir Cir.
Baltimore, MD 21208
Phone: (410)484-8700

Burdeshaw Associates Ltd.
4701 Sangamore Rd. N.
Bethesda, MD 20816
Phone: (301)229-5800
Fax: (301)229-5045

Michael E. Cohen
5225 Pooks Hill Rd., Ste. 1119 S
Bethesda, MD 20814
Phone: (301)530-5738
Fax: (301)493-9147

Federal Market Development
6111 Massachusetts Ave.
Bethesda, MD 20816
Phone: (301)229-5003
Fax: (301)229-3036

James K. McCracken & Co.
9211 Holly Oak Dr.
Bethesda, MD 20817
Phone: (301)365-9188
Toll Free: 800-365-9188

World Development Group, Inc.
5101 River Rd., Ste. 1913
Bethesda, MD 20816
Phone: (301)656-5070
Fax: (301)907-6630

Swartz Consulting
PO Box 4301
Crofton, MD 21114
Phone: (301)262-6728

Software Solutions International Inc.
9633 Duffer Way
Gaithersburg, MD 20879
Phone: (301)330-4136

Strategies, Inc.
8 Park Center Ct., Ste. 200
Owings Mills, MD 21117
Phone: (410)363-6669
Fax: (410)356-0602

Hammer Marketing Resources
179 Inverness Rd.
Severna Park, MD 21146
Phone: (410)544-9191
Fax: (410)544-9189

Andrew Sussman & Associates
13731 Kretsinger
Smithsburg, MD 21783
Phone: (301)824-2943

Energetics Development Inc.
109 Post Office Rd.
PO Box 966
Waldorf, MD 20604
Phone: (301)934-8875
Toll Free: 800-377-7049

MASSACHUSETTS

Geibel Marketing Consulting
PO Box 611
Belmont, MA 02178
Phone: (617)484-8285
Fax: (617)489-3567

Bain and Co.
2 Copley Pl.
Boston, MA 02116
Phone: (617)572-2000
Fax: (617)572-2427

Center for Strategy Research, Inc.
101 Arch St., Ste. 1700
Boston, MA 02110
Phone: (617)345-9500
Fax: (617)345-0207

Boston Computer Society
Consultants' and Entrepreneurs' Group
1 Kendall Sq.
Cambridge, MA 02139
Phone: (617)252-0600
Fax: (617)577-9365

Financial/Management Solutions, Inc.
180 Magazine St.
Cambridge, MA 02139
Phone: (617)876-4946
Fax: (617)547-5283

Mehr & Company
62 Kinnaird St.
Cambridge, MA 02139
Phone: (617)876-3311
Fax: (617)876-3023

Monitor Co.
25 First St.
Cambridge, MA 02141
Phone: (617)252-2000
Fax: (617)252-2100

IEEE Consultants' Network
614 Hammond St.
Chestnut Hill, MA 02167
Phone: (617)893-8379

Data and Strategies Group, Inc.
463 Worcester Rd.
Framingham, MA 01701
Phone: (508)820-2500
Fax: (508)820-1626

Information & Research Associates
PO Box 3121
Framingham, MA 01701
Phone: (508)788-0784

Easton Consultants Inc.
252 Pond St.
Hopkinton, MA 01748
Phone: (508)435-4882
Fax: (508)435-3971

Jeffrey D. Marshall
102 Mitchell Rd.
Ipswich, MA 01938
Phone: (508)356-1113
Fax: (508)356-2989

B.L. Livas Associates
620 Essex St.
Lawrence, MA 01841
Phone: (508)686-6195
Fax: (508)688-8027

Consulting Resources Corporation
6 Northbrook Park
Lexington, MA 02173
Phone: (617)863-1222
Fax: (617)863-1441

Planning Technologies Group
1840 Massachusetts Ave.
Lexington, MA 02173
Phone: (617)861-0999
Fax: (617)861-1099

Coordinated Service, Inc.
531 King St.
Littleton, MA 01460
Phone: (508)486-0388
Fax: (508)486-0120

VMB Associates, Inc.
115 Ashland St.
Melrose, MA 02176
Phone: (617)665-0623

The Company Doctor
14 Pudding Stone Ln.
Mendon, MA 01756
Phone: (508)478-1747

The Enterprise Group
73 Parker Rd.
Needham, MA 02194
Phone: (617)444-6631
Fax: (617)444-6757

Practice Management Associates Ltd.
10 Midland Ave.
Newton, MA 02158
Phone: (617)965-0055
Fax: (617)965-5152
Toll Free: 800-537-7765

Business Planning and Consulting Services
20 Beechwood Terr.
Wellesley, MA 02181
Phone: (617)237-9151
Fax: (617)237-9151

Cooper, McPhee & Associates, Inc.
70 Walnut St.
Wellesley, MA 02181

Interim Management Associates
21 Avon Rd.
Wellesley, MA 02181
Phone: (617)237-0024

Pendergast & Co.
70 Walnut St.
Wellesley, MA 02181
Phone: (617)720-0400
Fax: (617)484-2496

MICHIGAN

Birmingham Consultants
31625 Nixon
Birmingham, MI 48025
Phone: (313)644-2700

G.G.W. and Associates
1213 Hampton
Jackson, MI 49203
Phone: (517)782-2255
Fax: (517)784-1256

Altamar Group Ltd.
6810 S. Cedar, Ste. 2-B
Lansing, MI 48911
Phone: (517)694-0910
Fax: (517)694-1377
Toll Free: 800-443-2627

Sheffieck Consultants, Inc.
23610 Greening Dr.
Novi, MI 48375
Phone: (810)347-3545
Fax: (810)347-3530

Rehmann, Robson and Company,
The Consulting Group
5800 Gratiot
PO Box 2025
Saginaw, MI 48605
Phone: (517)799-9580

Francis & Company
17200 W. Ten Mile Rd., Ste. 207
Southfield, MI 48075
Phone: (313)559-7600
Fax: (313)559-5249

JGK Associates
14464 Kerner Dr.
Sterling Heights, MI 48313
Phone: (810)247-9055

MINNESOTA

Gieseke Management Works
PO Box 21097
Eagan, MN 55121
Phone: (612)456-0757
Fax: (612)456-9138
Toll Free: 800-848-4912

Robert F. Knotek
14960 Ironwood Ct.
Eden Prairie, MN 55346
Phone: (612)949-2875

Kinnon Lilligren Associates Incorporated
6211 Oakgreen Ave. S
Denmark Township
Hastings, MN 55033
Phone: (612)436-6530

Decker Business Consulting
6837 Booth Ave.
Inver Grove Heights, MN 55076
Phone: (612)451-6600

Family Business Group
Division of McGladrey & Pullen
1300 Midwest Plaza E
800 Marquette Ave.
Minneapolis, MN 55402
Phone: (612)376-9376
Fax: (612)376-9876
Toll Free: 800-831-1272

Franchise Business Systems Inc.
4200 Dahlborg Dr.
Minneapolis, MN 55422
Phone: (612)520-8403
Fax: (612)520-8410
Toll Free: 800-433-2540

Health Fitness Corp.
3600 W. 80th St., Ste. 235
Minneapolis, MN 55431
Phone: (612)831-6830
Fax: (612)831-7264

ORGANIZATIONS, AGENCIES, & CONSULTANTS

Minnesota Cooperation Office for
Small Business & Job Creation, Inc.
5001 W. 80th St., Ste. 1005
Minneapolis, MN 55437
Phone: (612)830-1230
Fax: (612)830-1232

Consatech Inc.
1 Capital Centre, Ste. 1500
St. Paul, MN 55102
Phone: (612)222-3700
Fax: (612)222-1313

Power Systems Research
1301 Corporate Center Dr., Ste. 113
St. Paul, MN 55121
Phone: (612)454-0144
Fax: (612)454-0760
Toll Free: 800-433-7746

MISSOURI

Business Planning and
Development Incorporated
4030 Charlotte St.
Kansas City, MO 64110
Phone: (816)753-0495

MED Image, Inc.
The Frances Vandivort Center
305 E. Walnut, Ste. 110LL
Springfield, MO 65806
Phone: (417)831-0110
Fax: (417)831-0288
Toll Free: 800-879-2357

NEBRASKA

Chandler & Associates Ltd.
4220 Pratt St.
Omaha, NE 68111
Phone: (402)453-4560

Heartland Management Consulting Group
PO Box 3453
Omaha, NE 68103
Phone: (402)291-0136

NEW HAMPSHIRE

Wolff Consultants
10 Buck Rd.
PO Box 1003
Hanover, NH 03755
Phone: (603)643-6015

King MacRury Associates
Box 215
Rye, NH 03870
Phone: (603)439-7975

NEW JERSEY

ConMar International, Ltd.
283 Dayton-Jamesburg Rd.
PO Box 437
Dayton, NJ 08810
Phone: (908)274--1100
Fax: (908)274-1199

Realty Asset Services, Inc.
Meridian Center 3
6 Industrial Way W
Eatontown, NJ 07724
Phone: (908)531-2944
Fax: (908)517-0422

Kumar Associates, Inc.
260 Columbia Ave.
Fort Lee, NJ 07024
Phone: (201)224-9480
Fax: (201)585-2343

Louw's Management Corp.
PO Box 1508
Fort Lee, NJ 07024
Phone: (201)585-8368

John Hall & Company, Inc.
PO Box 187
Glen Ridge, NJ 07028
Phone: (201)680-4449
Fax: (201)680-4449

PA Consulting Group
279 Princeton Rd.
Hightstown, NJ 08520
Phone: (609)426-4700
Fax: (609)426-4046

Strategic Management Group
PO Box 402
Maplewood, NJ 07040
Phone: (201)378-2470

Vanguard Communications Corp.
100 American Rd.
Morris Plains, NJ 07950
Phone: (201)605-8000
Fax: (201)605-8329

Thomas S. Adubato Associates
PO Box 89
Pequannock, NJ 07440
Phone: (201)835-3566
Fax: (201)835-6470

Strategic Innovations International
544 W. 8th St.
Plainfield, NJ 07060
Phone: (908)755-7357
Fax: (908)755-4244

Aurora Marketing Management, Inc.
210 Carnegie Center, Ste. 101
Princeton, NJ 08540
Phone: (609)520-8863

HYTECH Development
PO Box 2003
Princeton, NJ 08543

Tracelin Associates
1171 Main St., Ste. 6K
Rahway, NJ 07065
Phone: (908)381-3288

Schkeeper Inc.
130-6 Bodman Pl.
Red Bank, NJ 07701
Phone: (908)219-1965
Phone: (908)530-3703

Henry Branch Associates
2502 Harmon Cove Tower
Secaucus, NJ 07094
Phone: (201)866-2008
Fax: (201)601-0101

Worldwide Marketing Service, Inc.
503 E. Revere Way
Smithville, NJ 08201
Phone: (609)748-1983

Gibbons & Co.
46 Knoll Rd.
Tenafly, NJ 07670
Phone: (201)871-3933
Fax: (201)871-2173

PMC Management Consultants, Inc.
11 Thistle Ln.
Three Bridges, NJ 08887
Phone: (908)788-1014
Fax: (908)806-7287

Mitchell Brian & Associates
5 Carlton Ln.
Voorhees, NJ 08043
Phone: (609)751-3224
Fax: (609)751-3225

R.W. Bankart & Associates
20 Valley Ave., Ste. D-2
Westwood, NJ 07675
Phone: (201)664-7672

Albert L. Emmons
580 Jackson Ave.
Westwood, NJ 07675
Phone: (201)666-0225

New Mexico

Vondle & Associates, Inc.
4926 Calle de Terra NE
Albuquerque, NM 87111
Phone: (505)292-8961
Fax: (505)296-2790

NEW YORK

Powers Research and Training Institute
PO Box 78
Bayville, NY 11709
Phone: (516)628-2250
Fax: (516)628-2252

Consortium House
139 Wittenberg Rd.
Bearsville, NY 12409
Phone: (914)679-8867
Fax: (914)679-9248

Progressive Finance Corporation
3549 Tiemann Ave.
Bronx, NY 10469
Phone: (718)405-9029
Toll Free: 800-225-8381

Wave Hill Associates
2621 Palisade Ave., Ste. 15-C
Riverdale
Bronx, NY 10463
Phone: (718)549-7368
Fax: (718)884-1856

Marketing Resources Group
71-58 Austin St.
Forest Hills, NY 11375
Phone: (718)261-8882

Group I Financial Services
PO Box 922
Highland, NY 12528
Phone: (914)883-9356
Fax: (914)883-9356

North Star Enterprises
670 N. Terrace Ave.
Mount Vernon, NY 10552
Phone: (914)668-9433

E.N. Rysso & Associates
21 Jordan Rd.
New Hartford, NY 13413
Phone: (315)732-2206
Fax: (315)732-2206

Atlantic Venture International Inc.
745 5th Ave.
New York, NY 10151
Phone: (212)593-0266
Fax: (212)319-4128

Boice Dunham Group
437 Madison Ave.
New York, NY 10022
Phone: (212)752-5550
Fax: (212)752-7055

Brancato Fritsch & Co.
45 W. 60 St., Ste. 25D
New York, NY 10023
Phone: (212)315-4155
Fax: (212)315-2950

Elizabeth Capen
27 E. 95th St.
New York, NY 10128
Phone: (212)427-7654

Cypress International, Inc.
2413 Bayshore Blvd., Ste. 2102
New York, NY 10169
Phone: (212)254-0051

Dunham & Marcus International
575 Madison Ave., Ste. 1006
New York, NY 10022
Phone: (212)605-0571

Growth Dynamics, Inc.
595 Madison Ave.
New York, NY 10022
Phone: (212)758-3379
Fax: (212)753-0314

Haver Analytics Inc.
60 E.42nd St.
New York, NY 10017
Phone: (212)986-9300
Fax: (212)986-5857

Jordan Edmiston Group
885 Third Ave.
New York, NY 10022
Phone: (212)754-0710
Fax: (212)754-0337

KPMG Peat Marwick - Management Consultants
767 5th Ave.
New York, NY 10153
Phone: (212)909-5000
Fax: (212)909-5070

Mahoney Cohen and Co.
111 W. 40th St.
New York, NY 10018
Phone: (212)490-8000
Fax: (212)398-0267

Management Practice, Inc.
342 Madison Ave.
New York, NY 10173
Phone: (212)867-7948
Fax: (212)972-5188

Moseley Associates, Inc.
270 Madison Ave., Ste. 1207
New York, NY 10016
Phone: (212)213-6673
Fax: (212)213-6675

Pofcher Company
825 3rd Ave., Ste. 2320
New York, NY 10022
Phone: (212)355-1390
Fax: (212)755-3061

Practice Development Counsel
60 Sutton Pl. S
New York, NY 10022
Phone: (212)593-1549
Fax: (212)980-7940

RRA Consulting Services, Inc.
166 E. 34th St.
New York, NY 10016
Phone: (212)686-4614

Vencon Management, Incorporated
301 W. 53rd St.
New York, NY 10019
Phone: (212)581-8787
Fax: (212)397-4126

R.A. Walsh Consultants
429 E. 52nd St.
New York, NY 10022
Phone: (212)688-6047
Fax: (212)535-4075

Werner International Inc.
111 W. 40th St.
New York, NY 10018
Phone: (212)642-6092
Fax: (212)642-6084
Toll Free: 800-333-7816

Zimmerman Business Consulting
44 E. 92nd St., Ste. 5-B
New York, NY 10128
Phone: (212)860-3107
Fax: (212)860-7730

Command Communications, Inc.
2500 Westchester Ave.
Purchase, NY 10577
Phone: (914)251-1515
Fax: (914)251-1562

J.F. Kenney Consultants, Inc.
Executive Office Bldg., Ste. 330
Rochester, NY 14614
Phone: (716)232-6898
Fax: (716)454-1289

David Lang Wardle
101 Birchwood Dr.
Schenectady, NY 12303
Phone: (518)355-9172

ComputerEase Company
Hachaliah Brown Dr.
Somers, NY 10589
Phone: (914)277-5317
Fax: (914)335-7971

Executive Extra, Inc.
PO Box 6036
Syracuse, NY 13217
Phone: (315)422-2657

Innovation Management Consulting, Inc.
209 Dewitt Rd.
Syracuse, NY 13214
Phone: (315)445-8989
Fax: (315)471-2153

M. Clifford Agress
891 Fulton St.
Valley Stream, NY 11580
Phone: (516)825-8955
Fax: (516)825-8955

Destiny Kinal Marketing Consultancy
105 Chemung St.
Waverly, NY 14892
Phone: (607)565-8317
Fax: (607)565-4083

Information Systems Planning
3 Melrose Ln.
West Nyack, NY 10994
Phone: (914)358-6546

Management Insight
96 Arlington Rd.
Williamsville, NY 14221
Phone: (716)631-3319
Fax: (716)631-0203

G.L. Michael, Management Consultants
335 Evans St., Ste. A
Williamsville, NY 14221
Phone: (716)634-5091

NORTH CAROLINA

Chester M. Malanowski
105 Turquoise Creek Dr.
Cary, NC 27513
Phone: (919)460-6600

Ronald A. Norelli & Company
112 S. Tryon St., Ste. 1010
Charlotte, NC 28284
Phone: (704)376-5484
Fax: (704)376-5485

OHIO

Transportation Technology Services
208 Harmon Rd.
Aurora, OH 44202
Phone: (216)562-3596

Delta Planning, Inc.
PO Box 22618
Beachwood, OH 44122
Phone: (216)831-2521
Fax: (216)831-7616

Empro Systems, Inc.
4777 Red Bank Expy., Ste. 1
Cincinnati, OH 45227
Phone: (513)271-2042
Fax: (513)271-2042

Financial Psychology Corporation
6 E. 4th St., Ste. 1204
Cincinnati, OH 45202
Phone: (513)723-0058
Fax: (513)723-0119

Strategic Research Center
1 Corporate Exchange
25825 Science Park Dr.
Cleveland, OH 44122
Phone: (216)831-2410
Fax: (216)464-2308

Cory Dillon Associates
111 Schreyer Pl. E
Columbus, OH 43214
Phone: (614)262-8211

Marketing Advisory Group
2670 Brandon Rd.
Columbus, OH 43221
Phone: (614)481-0033

Ransom & Associates - COMPETITIVEdge Group
106 E. Pacemont Rd.
Columbus, OH 43202
Phone: (614)267-7100

Herman Associates Inc.
PO Box 5351
Fairlawn, OH 44333
Phone: (216)836-5656
Fax: (216)836-3311
Toll Free: 800-227-3566

Young & Associates
PO Box 711
Kent, OH 44240
Phone: (216)678-0524
Fax: (216)678-6219
Toll Free: 800-525-9775

Robert A. Westman & Associates
359 Quarry Ln.
Warren, OH 44483
Phone: (216)856-4149
Fax: (216)856-2564

OKLAHOMA

Innovative Resources Inc.
4900 Richmond Sq., Ste. 100
Oklahoma City, OK 73118
Phone: (405)840-0033
Fax: (405)843-8359

Community & Governmental Consultants, Inc.
Box 1121
Stillwater, OK 74076
Phone: (405)743-3048
Fax: (405)624-9816

OREGON

INTERCON
The International Converting Institute
5200 Badger Rd.
Crooked River Ranch, OR 97760
Phone: (503)548-1447
Fax: (563)548-1618

Talbott ARM
HC 64, Box 120
Lakeview, OR 97630
Phone: (503)947-3482
Fax: (503)947-3482

Management Technology Associates, Ltd.
1618 SW 1st Ave., Ste. 315
Portland, OR 97201
Phone: (503)224-5220

Nudelman & Associates
6443 SW Beaverton Hwy.
Portland, OR 97221
Phone: (503)292-2604
Fax: (503)292-5850

Aldrich, Kilbride & Tatone
1011 Commercial St. NE
Salem, OR 97301
Phone: (503)585-7774
Fax: (503)364-8405
Toll Free: 800-927-7577

PENNSYLVANIA

Problem Solvers for Industry
345 Park Ave.
Box 193
Chalfont, PA 18914
Phone: (215)822-9695

Elayne Howard & Associates, Inc.
3501 Masons Mill Rd., Ste. 501
Huntingdon Valley, PA 19006
Phone: (215)657-9550

GRA, Incorporated
115 West Ave., Ste. 201
Jenkintown, PA 19046
Phone: (215)884-7500
Fax: (215)884-1385

Mifflin County Industrial Development Corporation
Mifflin County Industrial Plaza
One Belle Ave.
Lewistown, PA 17044
Phone: (717)242-0393
Fax: (717)242-1842

Advantage Associates, Inc.
434 Avon Dr.
Pittsburgh, PA 15228
Phone: (412)343-1558
Fax: (412)362-1684

Regis J. Sheehan & Associates
291 Foxcroft Rd.
Pittsburgh, PA 15220
Phone: (412)279-1207

Egbert M. Kipp
745 Thomas St.
State College, PA 16803
Phone: (814)231-0197

Moeller Associates
RD 3, Box 177
Towanda, PA 18848
Phone: (717)265-6523

James W. Davidson Co., Inc.
23 Forest View Rd.
Wallingford, PA 19086
Phone: (610)566-1462

RHODE ISLAND

William L. Keefe
140 Iroquois Rd.
Cumberland, RI 02864
Phone: (401)333-1503

SOUTH CAROLINA

Aquafood Business Associates
PO Box 16190
Charleston, SC 29412
Phone: (803)795-9506
Fax: (803)795-9477

Minus Stage
Box 4436
Rock Hill, SC 29731
Phone: (803)328-0705
Fax: (803)329-9948

TENNESSEE

Daniel Petchers & Associates
8820 Fernwood CV
Germantown, TN 38138
Phone: (901)383-1749
Phone: (901)755-9896

Dean Winn
1114 Forest Harbor, Ste. 300
Hendersonville, TN 37075
Phone: (615)264-1743
Fax: (615)824-7601
Toll Free: 800-737-8382

RCFA Physician Managers Inc.
9724 Kingston Pike
Knoxville, TN 37922
Phone: (615)531-0176

Growth Consultants of America
3917 Trimble Rd.
PO Box 158382
Nashville, TN 37215
Phone: (615)383-0550
Fax: (615)269-8940
Toll Free: 800-230-0550

TEXAS

Erisa Adminstrative Services Inc.
12325 Haymeadow Dr., Bldg. 4
Austin, TX 78750
Phone: (512)250-9020
Fax: (512)250-9487

R. Miller Hicks & Company
1011 W. 11th St.
Austin, TX 78703
Phone: (512)477-7000

M.A. Moses & Associates
1801 Heatherglen Ln.
Austin, TX 78758
Phone: (512)837-2417

Rellstab Associates
7709 Long Point Dr.
Austin, TX 78731
Phone: (512)345-1684
Fax: (512)345-2622

Market Development Services, Inc.
5350 Montrose Dr.
Dallas, TX 75209
Phone: (214)352-7247
Fax: (214)357-1835

Peter Schaar
3515 Haynie Ave.
Dallas, TX 75205
Phone: (214)528-7162
Fax: (214)528-7162

Jaime & Associates International
Bureau of Accountants and Consultants
1731 Montana Ave.
El Paso, TX 79902
Phone: (915)532-7188

The Dowdle Poe Co.
4610 Westin Dr.
Fulshear, TX 77441
Phone: (713)346-2560
Fax: (713)346-2558

Arnott & Associates, Inc.
PO Box 923
Grapevine, TX 76099
Phone: (817)430-1258
Fax: (817)491-4818

PROTEC
4607 Linden Pl.
Pearland, TX 77584
Phone: (713)997-9872
Fax: (713)997-9895

Industrial Distribution Consultants, Inc.
PO Box 2530
Port Aransas, TX 78373
Phone: (512)749-7123
Fax: (512)749-7123

Business Strategy Development Consultants
PO Box 690365
San Antonio, TX 78269
Phone: (210)696-8000
Fax: (210)696-8000
Toll Free: 800-927-BSDC

Tom Welch Financial
PO Box 791555148
San Antonio, TX 78279
Phone: (210)737-7022
Fax: (210)737-7022

UTAH

Millet Consulting Group
575 E. 4500 S, Ste. B-230
Salt Lake City, UT 84107
Phone: (801)265-8724
Fax: (801)261-2529

CAPCON, Ltd.
8746 S. Rustler Rd.
Sandy, UT 84093
Phone: (801)943-6339

VIRGINIA

Elliott B. Jaffa
2530-B S. Walter Reed Dr.
Arlington, VA 22206
Phone: (703)931-0040

Koach Enterprises - USA
5529 N. 18th St.
Arlington, VA 22205
Phone: (703)241-8361
Fax: (703)241-8623

RGT Management Group, Inc.
1611 S. Walter Reed Dr., Ste. 102
Arlington, VA 22204
Phone: (703)553-0774
Toll Free: 800-368-9098

Transportation Management Systems, Inc.
11317 Beach Mill Rd.
Great Falls, VA 22066
Phone: (703)444-0995
Fax: (703)444-6089

Barringer, Huff & Stuart
310 Fifth St.
Lynchburg, VA 24504
Phone: (804)528-2356
Fax: (804)528-2357

Performance Support Systems
601 Thimble Shoals Blvd., Ste. 207
Newport News, VA 23606
Phone: (804)873-3700
Fax: (804)873-3288

Charles Scott Pugh
4101 Pittaway Dr.
Richmond, VA 23235
Phone: (804)560-0979

John C. Randall and Associates, Inc.
PO Box 15127
Richmond, VA 23227
Phone: (804)746-4450
Fax: (804)747-7426

The Dynex Group
5345 Fairfield Blvd.
Virginia Beach, VA 23464
Phone: (804)497-5561
Fax: (804)497-0986

Arthur L. Pepperman, II, Consultant
241 McLaws Cir., Ste. 101
Williamsburg, VA 23185
Phone: (804)253-1495
Fax: (804)253-1295

WASHINGTON

B.A.S.I.C. Consultants, Inc.
10020 A Main St., Ste. 352
Bellevue, WA 98004
Phone: (206)454-0341
Fax: (206)649-8809

Perry L. Smith Consulting
800 Bellevue Way NE, Ste. 400
Bellevue, WA 98004
Phone: (206)462-2072
Fax: (206)462-5638

Management Consultants, Inc.
1322 44th Ave. SW
Seattle, WA 98116
Phone: (206)935-3388

Northwest Trade Adjustment Assistance Center
900 4th Ave., Ste. 2430
Seattle, WA 98164
Phone: (206)622-2730
Fax: (206)622-1105

Spectrum West
4711 NE 50th
Seattle, WA 98105
Phone: (206)524-5958
Fax: (206)524-7826

Business Planning Consultants
S. 3510 Ridgeview Dr.
Spokane, WA 99206
Phone: (509)928-0332
Fax: (509)921-0842

WEST VIRGINIA

MarkeTech Communications
PO Box 35
Montrose, WV 26283
Phone: (304)637-0805

WISCONSIN

White & Associates
5349 Somerset Ln. S
Greenfield, WI 53221
Phone: (414)281-7373
Fax: (414)282-3245

SMALL BUSINESS ADMINISTRATION
REGIONAL OFFICES

This section contains a listing of Small Business Administration offices arranged numerically by region. Service areas are provided. Contact these for a referral to the nearest field office.

Region 1

U.S. Small Business Administration
155 Federal St., 9th Fl.
Boston Massachusetts 02110
Phone: (617)451-2030
Fax: (617)565-8681
Serves: Connecticut, Maine, Massachusetts, New Hampshire, Rhode Island, and Vermont

Region 2

U.S. Small Business Administration
26 Federal Plz., Rm. 3100
New York New York 10278
Phone: (212)264-1450
Serves: New Jersey, New York, Puerto Rico, and the Virgin Islands

Region 3

U.S. Small Business Administration
475 Allendale Rd., Ste. 201
King of Prussia Pennsylvania 19406
Phone: (215)962-3700
Fax: (215)962-3743
Serves: Delaware, the District of Columbia, Maryland, Pennsylvania, Virginia, and West Virginia

Region 4

U.S. Small Business Administration
1735 Peachtree St. NE
Atlanta Georgia 30367-8102
Phone: (404)347-4999
Fax: (404)347-2355
Serves: Alabama, Florida, Georgia, Kentucky, Mississippi, North Carolina, South Carolina, and Tennessee

Region 5

U.S. Small Business Administration
300 Riverside Plz., Ste. 1975 S
Chicago Illinois 60606-6611
Phone: (312)353-5000
Fax: (312)353-3426
Serves: Illinois, Michigan, Minnesota, Ohio, and Wisconsin

Region 6

U.S. Small Business Administration
8625 King George Dr., Bldg. C
Dallas Texas 75235-3391
Phone: (214)767-7643
Fax: (214767-7870
Serves: Arkansas, Louisiana, New Mexico, Oklahoma, and Texas

Region 7

U.S. Small Business Administration
911 Walnut St., 13th Fl.
Kansas City Missouri 64106
Phone: (816)426-3316
Fax: (816)426-5559
Serves: Iowa, Kansas, Missouri, and Nebraska

Region 8

U.S. Small Business Administration
633 17th St., 7th Fl.
Denver Colorado 80202
Phone: (303)294-7186
Fax: (303)294-7153
Serves: Colrado, Montana, North Dakota, South Dakota, Utah, and Wyoming

Region 9

U.S. Small Business Administration
71 Stevenson St., 20th Fl.
San Fancisco California 94105
Phone: (415)744-6402
Serves: American Samoa, Arizona, California, Guam, Hawaii, Nevada, and the Trust Territory of the Pacific Islands

Region 10

U.S. Small Business Administration
2601 4th Ave., Ste. 440
Seattle Washington 98121
Phone: (206)553-5676
Serves: Alaska, Idaho,
Oregon, and Washington

SMALL BUSINESS DEVELOPMENT CENTERS

This section contains a listing of all Small Business Development Centers organized alphabetically by state or country name, then by city, then by agency name.

Alabama

Auburn University
Small Business Development Center
108 College of Business
Auburn Alabama 36849
Phone: (205)844-4220
Fax: (205)844-4268
Contact: Harry Burdy

University of Alabama at Birmingham
Small Business Development Center
1601 11th Ave. S
Birmingham Alabama 35294
Phone: (205)934-6760
Fax: (205)934-0538
Contact: Vernon Nabors

University of North Alabama
Small Business Development Center
Box 5248, Keller Hall
Florence Alabama 35632
Phone: (205)760-4629
Fax: (205)760-4813
Contact: Kerry Gaflin

Alabama A&M University
University of Alabama (Huntsville)
North East Alabama
Regional Small Business Development Center
225 Church St. NW
PO Box 168

Huntsville Alabama 35804
Phone: (205)535-2061
Fax: (205)535-2050
Contact: Jeff Thompson

Jacksonville State University
Small Business Development Center
700 Pelham Rd. N
114 Merrill Hall
Jacksonville Alabama 36265
Phone: (205)782-5271
Fax: (205)782-5124
Contact: Pat W. Shaddix

Livingston University
Small Business Development Center
Sta. 35
Livingston Alabama 35470
Phone: (205)652-9661
Contact: Charlie Cook

University of South Alabama
Small Business Development Center
College of Business
Mobile Alabama 36688
Phone: (205)460-6004
Fax: (205)460-6246
Contact: Cheryl Coleman

Alabama State University
Small Business Development Center
915 S. Jackson St.
Montgomery Alabama 36195
Phone: (205)269-1102
Fax: (205)265-9144
Contact: Kenneth Walker

Troy State University
Small Business Development Center
102 Bibb Graves
Troy Alabama 36082
Phone: (205)670-3771
Fax: (205)670-3636
Contact: Janet W. Kervin

Alabama International Trade Center
University of Alabama
Small Business Development Center
PO Box 870396

Martha Parham W.
Tuscaloosa Alabama 35487
Phone: (205)348-7621
Fax: (205)348-6974

University of Alabama
Small Business Development Center
Bighood Hall, Rm. 250
PO Box 870397
Tuscaloosa Alabama 35487
Phone: (205)348-7011
Fax: (205)348-9644
Contact: Paavo Hanninen

Alaska

Alaska Business Development Center
3335 Artic Blvd., Ste. 203
Anchorage Alaska 99503
Phone: (907)562-0335
Fax: (907)562-6988

University of Alaska (Fairbanks)
Small Business Development Center
510 2nd Ave., Ste. 101
Fairbanks Alaska 99701
Phone: (907)456-1701
Toll Free: 800-478-1701
Fax: (907)456-1873
Contact: Theresa Proenza

University of Alaska (Juneau)
Small Business Development Center
400 Willoughby, Ste. 211
Juneau Alaska 99801
Phone: (907)463-3789
Toll Free: 800-478-6655
Fax: (907)463-5670

University of Alaska (Matanuska-Susitna)
Small Business Development Center
1801 Parks Hwy., Ste. C-18
Wasilla Alaska 99654
Phone: (907)373-7232
Fax: (907)373-2560
Contact: Marian Romano

Arizona

Central Arizona College
Small Business Development Center
8470 N. Overfield Rd.
Coolidge Arizona 85228
Phone: (520)426-4444
Fax: (520)426-4234

Central Arizona College
Small Business Development Center
8470 N. Overfield Rd.
Coolidge Arizona 85228
Phone: (520)426-4444
Fax: (520)426-4234

Coconina County Community College
Small Business Development Center
3000 N. 4th St., Ste. 25
Flagstaff Arizona 86004
Phone: (602)526-5072
Fax: (602)526-8693
Contact: Mary Ann Stanton

Northland Pioneer College
Small Business Development Center
PO Box 610
Holbrook Arizona 86025
Phone: (602)537-2976
Fax: (602)524-2227
Contact: Joel Eittreim

Mohave Community College
Small Business Development Center
1971 Jagerson Ave.
Kingman Arizona 86401
Phone: (602)757-0894
Fax: (602)757-0836
Contact: Jenee Miles

Gateway Community College
Small Business Development Center
108 N. 40th St.
Phoenix Arizona 85034
Contact: Kathy Evans

Rio Salado Community College
Small Business Development Center
301 Roosevelt St., Ste. B
Phoenix Arizona 85003
Phone: (602)238-9603
Fax: (602)340-1627
Contact: Marti McCorkindale

Yavapai College
Small Business Development Center
117 E. Burley St., Ste. 206
Prescott Arizona 86301
Phone: (602)778-3088
Fax: (602)778-3109
Contact: Richard Senopole

Eastern Arizona Community College
Small Business Development Center
1111 Thatcher Blvd.
Sanford Arizona 85546
Phone: (520)687-1904

Cochise College
Small Business Development Center
901 N. Colombo, Rm. 411
Sierra Vista Arizona 85635
Phone: (602)459-9778
Fax: (602)459-9212
Contact: Debbie Elver

Eastern Arizona College
Small Business Development Center
622 College Ave.
Thatcher Arizona 85552
Phone: (602)428-8590
Fax: (602)428-8462
Contact: Greg Ross

Pima Community College
Small Business Development Center
4903 E. Broadway Blvd., No. 101
Tucson Arizona 85709
Phone: (602)748-4906
Fax: (602)748-4585
Contact: Linda Andrews

Arizona Western College
Small Business Development Center
281 W. 24th St.

Century Plz., No. 152
Yuma Arizona 85364
Phone: (602)341-1650
Fax: (602)726-2636
Contact: Hank Pinto

Arkansas

Henderson State University
Small Business Development Center
1100 Henderson St.
Arkadelphia Arkansas 71999
Phone: (501)230-5000
Fax: (501)230-5144

University of Central Arkansas
Small Business Development Center
College of Business Administration
Burdick Business Admin. Bldg., Rm. 212
201 Donaghey Ave.
Conway Arkansas 72035
Phone: (501)450-3190
Fax: (501)450-5302

Small Business Development Center
BADM 1172
University of Arkansas at Fayetteville
College of Business-BA 117
Fayetteville Arkansas 72701
Phone: (501)575-5148
Fax: (501)575-4013

University of Arkansas at Little Rock
Regional Office (Fort Smith)
Small Business Development Center
1109 S. 16th St.
PO Box 2067
Fort Smith Arkansas 72902
Phone: (501)785-1376
Fax: (501)785-1964

University of Arkansas at Little Rock
Regional Office (Harrison)
Small Business Development Center
1818 Hwy. 62-65-412 N
PO Box 190
Harrison Arkansas 72601
Phone: (501)741-8009
Fax: (501)741-1905

California

University of Arkansas at Little Rock
Regional Office (Hot Springs)
Small Business Development Center
835 Central Ave., Box 402D
Hot Springs Arkansas 71901
Phone: (501)624-5448

University of Arkansas at Little Rock
Regional Office (Magnolia)
Small Business Development Center
600 Bessie
PO Box 767
Magnolia Arkansas 71753
Phone: (501)234-4030
Fax: (501)234-0135

University of Arkansas at Little Rock
Regional Office (Pine Bluff)
Small Business Development Center
The Enterprise Center III
400 Main, Ste. 117
Pine Bluff Arkansas 71601
Phone: (501)536-0654
Contact: Mike Brewer

Harding University
Small Business Development Center
Mabee School of Business
Blakeny and Center Sts.
Searcy Arkansas 72149
Phone: (501)279-4000
Fax: (501)279-4078

Arkansas State University
Small Business Development Center
PO Drawer 2650
State University Arkansas 72467
Phone: (501)972-3517
Fax: (501)972-3868

University of Arkansas at Little Rock
Regional Office (Stuttgart)
Small Business Development Center
301 S. Grand, Ste. 101
Stuttgart Arkansas 72160
Phone: (501)673-8707
Fax: (501)673-8707

Central Coast
Small Business Development Center
6500 Soquel Dr.
Aptos California 95003
Phone: (408)479-6136
Contact: Elza Minor

Sierra College
Small Business Development Center
560 Wall St., Ste. J
Auburn California 95603
Phone: (916)885-5488
Fax: (916)823-4142
Contact: Mary Wollesen

Weill Institute
Small Business Development Center
1330 22nd St., Ste. B
Bakersfield California 93301
Phone: (805)395-4148
Contact: Jeffrey Johnson

Butte College Tri-Counties
Small Business Development Center
260 Cohasset Rd., Ste. A
Chico California 95926
Phone: (916)895-9017
Fax: (916)895-9094

Southwestern College
Small Business Development
and International Trade Center
900 Otay Lakes Rd., Bldg. 1600
Chula Vista California 91910
Phone: (619)421-2156
Contact: Mary Wylie

Satellite Lake County
Small Business Development Center
PO Box 4550
15322 Lakeshore Dr.
Hilltop Prof Ctr., Ste. 205
Clearlake California 95422
Phone: (707)995-3440
Contact: Dana Parker

North Coast
Small Business Development Center
779 9th St.
Crescent City California 95531
Phone: (707)464-2168
Contact: Fran Clark

North Coast Satellite Center
408 7th St., Ste. "E"
Eureka California 95501
Phone: (707)445-9720
Contact: Duff Heuttner

Central California
Small Business Development Center
1999 Tuolumne St., Ste. 650
Fresno California 93721
Phone: (209)278-4946
Fax: (209)278-6964
Contact: Dennis Winans

Gavilan College
Small Business Development Center
7436 Monterey St.
Gilroy California 95020
Phone: (408)847-0373
Contact: Peter Graff

Accelerate Technology Assistance
Small Business Development Center
University of California, Irvine
Graduate School of Management, No. 230
Irvine California 92717
Phone: (714)856-8366
Fax: (714)856-8469
Contact: Tiffany Haugen

Greater San Diego Chamber of Commerce
Small Business Development Center
4275 Executive Sq., Ste. 920
La Jolla California 92037
Phone: (619)232-0124
Contact: Lisa Hasler

Export Small Business Development Center
of Southern California
110 E. 9th, Ste. A669
Los Angeles California 90079
Phone: (213)892-1111

Fax: (213)892-8232
Contact: Gladys Moreau

Merced Satellite Center
1632 N St.
Merced California 95340
Phone: (209)385-7312
Fax: (209)383-4959

Valley Sierra
Small Business Development Center
1012 11th St., Ste. 300
Modesto California 95354
Phone: (209)521-6177
Contact: Kelly Bearden

Napa Valley College
Small Business Development Center
1556 First St., Ste. 103
Napa California 94559
Phone: (707)253-3210
Contact: Michael Kauffman

East Bay Small Business Development Center
2201 Broadway, Ste. 701
Oakland California 94612
Phone: (510)893-4114
Contact: Selma Taylor

Export Satellite Center
300 Esplanade Dr., Ste. 1010
Oxnard California 93030
Phone: (805)981-4633
Contact: Heather Wicka

East Los Angeles County
Small Business Development Center
363 S. Park Ave., Ste. 100
Pomona California 91766
Phone: (909)629-2247
Contact: Toni Valdez

Inland Empire Small Business Development Center
2002 Iowa Ave., Ste. 110
Riverside California 92507
Phone: (714)781-2345
Fax: (714)781-2353
Contact: Terri Corrazini Ooms

Greater Sacramento Area
Small Business Development Center
1787 Tribute Rd., Ste. A
Sacramento California 95815
Phone: (916)263-6580
Fax: (916)263-6571

Silicon Valley/San Mateo County
Small Business Development Center
111 N. Market St., No. 150
San Jose California 95113
Phone: (408)298-7694
Fax: (408)971-0680

Orange County Small Business Development Center
901 E. Santa Ana Blvd., Ste. 101
Santa Ana California 92701
Phone: (714)647-1172
Fax: (714)835-9008
Contact: Gregory Kishel

Redwood Empire Small Business Development Center
520 Mendosino Ave., Ste. 210
Santa Rosa California 95403
Phone: (707)527-4435
Contact: Charles Robins

San Joaquin Delta College
Small Business Development Center
814 N. Hunter St.
Stockton California 95202
Phone: (209)474-5089
Contact: Gillian Murphy

Solano County
Small Business Development Center
320 Campus Ln.
Suisan City California 94585
Phone: (707)864-3382
Contact: Edward Schlenker

Southwest Los Angeles County
Small Business Development Center
21221 Western Ave., Ste. 110
Torrance California 90501
Phone: (310)782-3861
Fax: (310)782-8607
Contact: Bart Hoffman

Northern Los Angeles
Small Business Development Center
14540 Victory Blvd., Ste. 206
Van Nuys California 91411
Phone: (818)373-7092
Fax: (818)373-7740
Contact: Lance Stevenson

Colorado

Adams State College
Small Business Development Center
Business Bldg., No. 105
Alamosa Colorado 81102
Phone: (719)589-7372
Contact: Peggy Micklich

Aurora Small Business Management Program
16000 E. Centretech Pky., Ste. A201
Aurora Colorado 80011
Phone: (303)360-4745

Community College of Aurora
Small Business Development Center
9905 E. Colfax
Aurora Colorado 80010
Contact: Randy Johnson

Front Range Community College (Boulder)
Small Business Development Center
Boulder Chamber of Commerce
2440 Pearl St.
Boulder Colorado 80302

Pueblo Community College (Canon City)
Small Business Development Center
402 Valley Rd.
Canon City Colorado 81212
Phone: (719)275-5335
Fax: (719)275-4400
Contact: Elwin Boody

Pikes Peak Community College
Small Business Development Center
Colorado Springs Chamber of Commerce
PO Drawer B
Colorado Springs Colorado 80901
Phone: (719)635-1551
Contact: Harrry Martinez

Colorado Northwestern Community College
Small Business Development Center
50 Spruce Dr.
Craig Colorado 81625
Phone: (303)824-7078
Fax: (303)824-3527
Contact: Ken Farmer

Delta Small Business Development Center
Delta Montrose Vocational School
1765 US Hwy. 50
Delta Colorado 81416
Phone: (303)874-8772
Contact: Steve Schrock

Colorado Association of Commerce and Industry (CACI)
Manager of Government Affairs
1776 Lincoln, Ste. 1200
Denver Colorado 80203
Phone: (303)831-7411
Fax: (303)860-1439

Community College of Denver
Small Business Development Center
Greater Denver Chamber of Commerce
1445 Market St.
Denver Colorado 80202
Phone: (303)620-8076
Fax: (303)534-3200
Contact: Carolyn Love

Fort Lewis College
Small Business Development Center
295 A Girard
Durango Colorado 81301
Phone: (303)247-9634
Fax: (303)247-9513
Contact: Bard Heroy

Front Range Community College (Fort Collins)
Small Business Development Center
1609 Oakridge Dr.
PO Box 270490
Fort Collins Colorado 80527
Phone: (303)226-0881
Fax: (303)825-6819

Morgan Community College (Fort Morgan)
Small Business Development Center
300 Main St.
Fort Morgan Colorado 80701
Phone: (303)867-4424
Fax: (303)867-3352
Contact: Lori Slinn

Colorado Mountain College (Glenwood Springs)
Small Business Development Center
215 9th St.
Glenwood Springs Colorado 81601
Contact: Russell Disberger

Mesa State College
Small Business Development Center
304 W. Main St.
Grand Junction Colorado 81505
Phone: (303)248-7314
Fax: (303)241-0771
Contact: Joe Bell

Greeley/Weld Chamber of Commerce
Small Business Development Center
Aims Community College
1407 8th Ave.
Greeley Colorado 80631
Phone: (303)352-3661
Fax: (303)352-3572
Contact: David Sanchez

Reed Rocks Community College
Small Business Development Center
13300 W. 6th Ave.
Lakewood Colorado 80401
Phone: (303)987-0710
Contact: Jayne Reiter

Lamar Community College
Small Business Development Center
2400 S. Main
Lamar Colorado 81052
Phone: (719)336-8141
Fax: (719)336-2448
Contact: Elwood Gillis

Small Business Development Center
Arapahoe Community College
South Metro Chamber of Commerce

7901 S. Park Plz., Ste. 110
Littleton Colorado 80120
Phone: (303)795-0142
Contact: Selma Kristel

Pueblo Community College
Small Business Development Center
900 W. Orman Ave.
Pueblo Colorado 81004
Phone: (719)549-3224
Contact: Rita Friberg

Morgan Community College (Stratton)
Small Business Development Center
PO Box 28
Stratton Colorado 80836
Phone: (719)348-5546
Fax: (719)348-5887
Contact: Ronnie Carr

Trinidad State Junior College
Small Business Development Center
136 W. Main St.
Davis Bldg.
Trinidad Colorado 81082
Phone: (719)846-5645
Fax: (719)846-5667
Contact: Dennis O'Connor

Colorado Mountain College (Vail)
Small Business Development Center
1310 Westhaven Dr.
Vail Colorado 81657
Phone: (303)476-4040
Fax: (303)479-9212

Front Range Community College (Westminster)
Small Business and International Development Center
3645 W. 112th Ave.
Westminster Colorado 80030
Phone: (303)460-1032
Fax: (303)466-1623
Contact: Michael Lenzini

Connecticut

Bridgeport Regional Business Council
Small Business Development Center
10 Middle St., 14th Fl.

Bridgeport Connecticut 06604
Phone: (203)335-3800
Contact: Juan Scott

The Greater Danbury Chamber of Commerce
Small Business Development Center
72 West St.
Danbury Connecticut 06810
Phone: (203)743-5565
Fax: (203)794-1439

Quinebaug Valley Community College
Small Business Development Center
742 Upper Maple St.
Danielson Connecticut 06239
Phone: (203)774-1130
Contact: Roger Doty

East Hartford Chamber of Commerce
Small Business Development Center
763 Burnside Ave.
East Hartford Connecticut 06108
Phone: (203)289-0239
Fax: (203)289-0230

North Central Connecticut Chamber of Commerce
Small Business Development Center
111 Hazard Ave.
Enfield Connecticut 06082
Phone: (203)763-2396
Fax: (203)749-1822

Glastonbury Chamber of Commerce
Small Business Development Center
2400 Main St.
Glastonbury Connecticut 06033
Phone: (203)659-3587
Fax: (203)659-0102

University of Connecticut (Groton)
Small Business Development Center
Administration Bldg., Rm. 300
1084 Shennecossett Rd.
Groton Connecticut 06340
Phone: (203)449-1188
Contact: William Lockwood

Hartford Enterprise Zone
Small Business Development Center
10 Prospect St.
Hartford Connecticut 06103
Phone: (203)543-8635
Fax: (203)722-6402

Greater New Haven Chamber of Commerce
Small Business Development Center
195 Church St.
New Haven Connecticut 06506
Phone: (203)773-0782
Contact: Neal Wehr

Chamber of Commerce of Southeastern Connecticut
Small Business Development Center
105 Hutington St.
New London Connecticut 06320
Phone: (203)443-8332
Fax: (203)444-1529

Cooperative Extension
University of Connecticut
Small Business Development Center
562 New London Turnpike
Norwich Connecticut 06360
Phone: (203)887-1608
Fax: (203)886-1164

Old Saybrook Chamber of Commerce
Small Business Development Center
PO Box 625
Old Saybrook Connecticut 06475
Phone: (203)388-3266
Fax: (203)388-3266

Southwestern Area Commerce
and Industry Association (SACIA)
Small Business Development Center
1 Landmark Sq., Ste. 230
Stamford Connecticut 06901
Phone: (203)359-3220
Contact: George Ahl

Torrington Chamber of Commerce
Small Business Development Center
PO Box 59
Torrington Connecticut 06790
Phone: (203)482-6586
Fax: (203)489-8851

Greater Waterbury Chamber of Commerce
Small Business Development Center
83 Bank St.
Waterbury Connecticut 06702
Phone: (203)757-0701
Fax: (203)756-3507

University of Connecticut (Greater Hartford Campus)
Small Business Development Center
1800 Asylum Ave.
West Hartford Connecticut 06117
Phone: (203)241-4986
Contact: Richard Rogers

Eastern Connecticut State University
Small Business Development Center
83 Windham St.
Willimantic Connecticut 06226
Phone: (203)456-5349
Contact: Roger Doty

Delaware

Delaware State University
School of Business and Economics
Small Business Development Center
Price Hall
1200 DuPont Hwy.
Dover Delaware 19901
Phone: (302)678-1555
Fax: (302)739-2333

Delaware Technical and Community College
Small Business Development Center
PO Box 610
Georgetown Delaware 19947
Phone: (302)856-1555
Fax: (302)856-5779

District of Columbia

Gallaudet University
Small Business Development Center
800 Florida Ave., NE
Washington District of Columbia 20002
Phone: (202)651-5312
Fax: (202)651-5516

George Washington University
National Law Center
Small Business Clinic
720 20th St. NW
Washington District of Columbia 20052
Phone: (202)994-6260
Contact: Susan Jones

Florida

Florida Atlantic University
Office of International Trade
PO Box 3091
Boca Raton Florida 33431
Phone: (407)367-2271
Fax: (407)367-2272

Florida Atlantic University (Boca Raton)
Small Business Development Center
777 Glades Rd.
Boca Raton Florida 33431
Phone: (407)362-5620
Fax: (407)362-5623

Florida Atlantic University (West Palm Beach)
Small Business Development Center
777 Glaze Rd.
Boca Raton Florida 33371
Phone: (407)362-5620

Casselberry
Seminole Community College
Small Business Development Center
4590 S. Highway 17-92
Casselberry Florida 32707
Phone: (407)834-4404
Fax: (407)339-1224

Brevard Community College (Cocoa)
Small Business Development Center
1519 Clearlake Rd.
Cocoa Florida 32922
Phone: (407)632-1111
Fax: (407)634-3725

Dania Small Business Development Center
46 SW 1st Ave.
Dania Florida 33004
Phone: (305)987-0100

Stetson University
Small Business Development Center
Campus Box 8417
Deland Florida 32720
Phone: (904)822-7326
Fax: (904)822-7430

Florida Atlantic University Commercial Campus
Small Business Development Center
1515 W. Commercial Blvd., Rm. 11
Fort Lauderdale Florida 33309
Phone: (305)771-6520
Contact: John Hudson

Edison Community College
Small Business Development Center
8099 College Pky. SW
Fort Myers Florida 33919
Phone: (813)489-9200
Fax: (813)489-9051

University of South Florida (Fort Myers)
Small Business Development Center
8111 College Pkwy.
Fort Myers Florida 33919
Phone: (813)432-5500
Fax: (813)432-5599

Indian River Community College
Small Business Development Center
3209 Virginia Ave.
Fort Pierce Florida 34981
Phone: (407)462-4756

Fort Walton Beach
University of West Florida
Small Business Development Center
1700 Martin Luther King, Jr. Blvd., Rm. 250
Fort Walton Beach Florida 32547
Phone: (904)863-6543
Fax: (904)863-6564

Small Business Development Center (Fort Walton Beach)
414 Mary Esther Cutoff
Fort Walton Beach Florida 32548
Phone: (904)244-1036

University of North Florida
Small Business Development Center
PO Box 2518
Gainesville Florida 32602
Phone: (904)377-5621
Fax: (904)377-0288

University of North Florida
Small Business Development Center
College of Business
4567 St. John's Bluff Rd. S
Bldg. 11, Rm. 2163
Jacksonville Florida 32224
Phone: (904)646-2476
Fax: (904)646-2476

Florida Keys Community College
Small Business Development Center
5901 W. College Rd.
Key West Florida 33040
Phone: (305)296-9081

Lake City
Lake City Community College
Small Business Development Center
226 N. Marlon St.
Lake City Florida 32055
Phone: (904)646-2476
Fax: (904)646-2567

Lynn Haven
Gulf Coast Community College
Small Business Development Center
2500 Minnesota Ave.
Lynn Haven Florida 32444
Phone: (904)271-1108
Fax: (904)271-1109

Brevard Community College (Melbourne)
Small Business Development Center
3865 N. Wickham Rd.
Melbourne Florida 32935
Phone: (407)632-1111
Fax: (407)232-1111

Florida International University (North Miami Campus)
Small Business Development Center
Academic Bldg. No. 1, Rm. 350
Miami Florida 33180
Phone: (305)940-5790

Florida International University (Tamiami Campus)
Small Business Development Center
PC 39
Miami Florida 33199
Phone: (305)348-2272
Fax: (305)348-2965

Miami Dade Community College
Small Business Development Center
627 SW 27th Ave.
Miami Florida 33150
Phone: (305)237-3800

Ocala Small Business Development Center
110 E. Silver Springs Blvd.
Ocala Florida 34475
Phone: (904)629-8051
Fax: (904)629-7651

University of Central Florida
Small Business Development Center
College of Business Administration, 309
PO Box 161530
Orlando Florida 32816
Phone: (407)823-5554
Fax: (407)823-3073

Valencia Community College
Small Business Development Center
PO Box 3208
Orlando Florida 32802
Phone: (407)299-5000

Palm Beach Community College
Small Business Development Center
North Campus
3160 PGA Blvd.
Palm Beach Gardens Florida 33410
Phone: (407)624-7222

Palm Beach Gardens
Florida Atlantic University
Small Business Development Center
Northrop Center
3931 RCA Blvd., Ste. 3106
Palm Beach Gardens Florida 33410
Phone: (407)625-9196
Fax: (407)625-9895

Florida State University (Panama City)
Small Business Development Center
Barron Bldg.
4750 Collegiate Dr.
Panama City Florida 32405
Phone: (904)872-4655

Florida Small Business Development Network
University of West Florida
19 W. Garden St., Ste. 300
Pensacola Florida 32501
Phone: (904)444-2060
Fax: (904)444-2070
Contact: Jerry Cartwright

Procurement Technical Assistance Program
Small Business Development Center
11000 University Pky., Bldg. 8
Pensacola Florida 32514
Phone: (904)474-2919
Fax: (904)474-2126

St. Petersburg Community College
Small Business Development Center
3200 34th St. S
St. Petersburg Florida 33711
Phone: (813)341-4414

University of South Florida (St. Petersburg)
Small Business Development Center
128 5th Ave. S
St. Petersburg Florida 33701
Phone: (813)893-9529

Small Business Development Center (Sarasota)
5700 N. Tamiami Trl.
Bldg. PME, Rm. 117
Sarasota Florida 34243
Phone: (813)359-4292

Florida Agricultural and Mechanical University
Small Business Development Center
1157 Tennessee St.
Tallahassee Florida 32301
Phone: (904)599-3407
Fax: (904)561-2049

Florida State University (Downtown Office)
Small Business Development Center

1605 Eastwood Office Plz., Ste. 1
Tallahassee Florida 32308
Phone: (904)644-6524

SBDC Training Center
Skipper Palms Shopping Center
1111 Westshore Blvd., Annex B
Tampa Florida 33607
Phone: (813)974-4371

Tampa
University of South Florida
Small Business Development Center
1111 North Westshore Blvd., Ste. 201B
Tampa Florida 33607
Phone: (813)554-2341
Fax: (813)554-2356

University of South Florida (Tampa)
Small Business Development Center
College of Business Adminstration
1111 N. Westshore Blvd., Ste. 201-B
Tampa Florida 33607
Phone: (813)974-4274
Toll Free: 800-733-7232
Fax: (813)554-2356

Georgia

Darton College
Southwest Georgia District
Small Business Development Center
230 S. Jackson St., Ste. 333
Business & Technology Ctr.
Albany Georgia 31701
Phone: (912)430-6740
Contact: Sue Ford

Georgia State University
Small Business Development Center
Box 874
University Plz.
Atlanta Georgia 30303
Phone: (404)651-3550
Contact: Lee Quarterman

Morris Brown College
Small Business Development Center
643 Martin Luther King, Jr., Dr. NW
Atlanta Georgia 30314
Phone: (404)220-0233

Augusta College
Small Business Development Center
1061 Katherine St.
Augusta Georgia 30910
Phone: (706)737-1790

University of Georgia (Brunswick)
Small Business Development Center
1107 Fountain Lake Dr.
Brunswick Georgia 31520
Phone: (912)264-7343

Columbus College
Small Business Development Center
928 45th St.
North Bdlg., Rm. 523
Columbus Georgia 31904
Phone: (706)649-7433

DeKalb Small Business Development Center
DeKalb Chamber of Commerce
750 Commerce Dr., Ste. 201
Decatur Georgia 30030
Phone: (404)378-8000

Gainesville Small Business Development Center
455 Jesse Jewell Pky., Ste. 302
Gainesville Georgia 30501
Phone: (404)531-5681

Gwinnet Technical Institute
Small Business Development Center
1250 Atkinson Rd.
PO Box 1505
Lawrenceville Georgia 30246
Phone: (404)339-2287

Central Georgia District
Small Business Development Center
PO Box 13212
Macon Georgia 31208
Phone: (912)751-6592
Contact: David Mills

Kennesaw State College
Small Business Development Center
PO Box 444
Marietta Georgia 30061
Phone: (404)423-6450
Contact: Carlotta Roberts

Clayton State College
Small Business Development Center
PO Box 285
Morrow Georgia 30260
Phone: (404)961-3440

Floyd Junior College
Small Business Development Center
PO Box 1864
Rome Georgia 30162
Phone: (706)295-6326

Southeast Georgia District
Small Business Development Center
450 Mall Blvd., Ste. H
Savannah Georgia 31406
Phone: (912)356-2755
Contact: Harry O'Brien

University of Georgia (Statesboro)
Small Business Development Center
325 S. Main St.
Statesboro Georgia 30458
Phone: (912)681-5194

Valdosta Small Business Development Center
Baytree W. Professional Offices, Ste. 9
1205 Baytree Rd.
Valdosta Georgia 31601
Phone: (912)245-3738

Warner Robins Small Business Development Center
151 Osigian Blvd.
Warner Robins Georgia 31088
Phone: (912)953-9356
Fax: (912)953-9376

Hawaii

Manoa Innovation Center
Small Business Development Center
2800 Woodlawn Dr., Ste. 238
Honolulu Hawaii 96822
Phone: (808)539-3800
Fax: (808)539-3799

Maui Community College
Small Business Development Center
Maui Research and Technology Center
590 Lipoa Pky.
Kihei Hawaii 96753
Phone: (808)875-2402
Fax: (808)875-2452

Kauai Community College
Small Business Development Center
8-1901 Kaumualii Hwy.
Lihue Hawaii 96766
Phone: (808)246-1748
Fax: (808)245-5102
Contact: Randy Gingras

Idaho

Boise State University
Small Business Development Center
1910 University Dr.
Boise Idaho 83725
Phone: (208)385-3875
Contact: James Hogge

Panhandle Area Council (Coeur d'Alene)
Small Business Development Center
11100 Airport Dr.
Hayden Idaho 83835
Phone: (208)772-0587
Fax: (208)772-6196

Idaho State University (Idaho Falls)
Small Business Development Center
2300 N. Yellowstone
Idaho Falls Idaho 83401
Phone: (208)523-1087
Toll Free: 800-658-3829
Contact: Mary E. Capps

Lewis-Clark State College
Small Business Development Center
8th Ave. & 6th St.
Lewiston Idaho 83501
Phone: (208)799-2465
Contact: Helen LeDoeuf

Idaho State University (Pocatello)
Small Business Development Center
1651 Alvin Ricken Dr.
Pocatello Idaho 83201
Phone: (208)232-4921
Toll Free: 800-232-4921
Contact: Paul Cox

North Idaho College
Small Business Development Center
525 W. Clearwater Loop
Post Falls Idaho 83854
Phone: (208)769-3285
Fax: (208)769-3223

Panhandle Area Council (Sandpoint)
Small Business Development Center
804 Airport Way
Sandpoint Idaho 83864
Phone: (208)263-4073
Fax: (208)263-4609

College of Southern Idaho
Small Business Development Center
PO Box 1238
Twin Falls Idaho 83303
Phone: (208)733-9554
Fax: (208)733-9316
Contact: Cindy Bond

Illinois

Aledo Chamber of Commerce
Small Business Development Center
PO Box 261
Aledo Illinois 61231
Phone: (309)582-5373

Waubonsee Community College (Aurora Campus)
Small Business Development Center
5 E. Galena Blvd.
Aurora Illinois 60506
Phone: (708)892-3334
Contact: Mike O'Kelley

Spoon River College
Small Business Development Center
23235 N. County 22
Canton Illinois 61520
Phone: (309)647-4645
Fax: (309)647-6498

Southern Illinois University at Carbondale
Small Business Development Center
College of Business Administration
Carbondale Illinois 62901
Phone: (618)536-2424
Contact: Dennis Cody

John A. Logan College
Small Business Development Center
RR 2
Carterville Illinois 62918
Phone: (618)985-6506
Fax: (618)985-2248
Contact: Richard Fyke

Kaskaskia College
Small Business Development Center
Shattuc Rd.
Centralia Illinois 62801
Phone: (618)532-2049
Fax: (618)532-4983
Contact: Richard McCullum

Parkland College
Small Business Development Center
2400 W. Bradley Ave.
Champaign Illinois 61821
Phone: (217)351-2556
Fax: (217)351-2581

Back of the Yards Neighborhood Council
Small Business Development Center
1751 W. 47th St.
Chicago Illinois 60609
Phone: (312)523-4419

Fax: (312)254-3525
Contact: Paul Landniak

Chicago Association of Neighborhood
Development Organization
Small Business Development Center
343 S. Dearborn St., Ste. 910
Chicago Illinois 60604
Phone: (312)939-7171
Fax: (312)939-7236

Chicago Small Business Development Center
DCCA James R. Thompson Center
100 W. Randolph, Ste. 3-400
Chicago Illinois 60601
Phone: (312)814-6111
Fax: (312)814-1749
Contact: Carson Gallagher

Chicago State University
Small Business Development Center
9501 S. King Dr.
Chicago Illinois 60628
Phone: (312)995-2000

Cosmopolitan Chamber of Commerce
Small Business Development Center
1326 S. Michigan Ave.
Chicago Illinois 60605
Phone: (312)786-0212
Fax: (312)786-9079

Daley College
Small Business Development Center
7500 S. Pulaski Rd., Bldg. 200
Chicago Illinois 60652
Phone: (312)735-3000
Fax: (312)838-7524

Eighteenth Street Development Corp.
Small Business Development Center
1839 S. Carpenter
Chicago Illinois 60608
Phone: (312)733-2287
Fax: (312)733-7315
Contact: Maria Munoz

Greater North Pulaski Development Corp.
Small Business Development Center

4054 W. North Ave.
Chicago Illinois 60639
Phone: (312)384-2262
Contact: Paul Peterson

Greater Southwest Development Corporation
Small Business Development Center
2601 W. 63rd St.
Chicago Illinois 60629
Phone: (312)436-4448
Fax: (312)471-8206

Greater Westside Development Corporation
Small Business Development Center
3555 W. Roosevelt Rd.
Chicago Illinois 60624
Phone: (312)762-2440

Industrial Council of Northwest Chicago
Small Business Development Center
2023 W. Carroll
Chicago Illinois 60612
Phone: (312)421-3941
Contact: Alex Viorst

Latin American Chamber of Commerce
Small Business Development Center
2539 N. Kedzie, Ste. 11
Chicago Illinois 60647
Phone: (312)252-5211
Fax: (312)252-7065
Contact: Martin Sandoval

Little Village Chamber of Commerce
Small Business Development Center
3610 W. 26th St., 2nd Fl.
Chicago Illinois 60623
Phone: (312)521-5387
Fax: (312)521-5252

The Neighborhood Institute
Small Business Development Center
2255 E. 75th St.
Chicago Illinois 60649
Phone: (312)933-2021
Fax: (312)933-2039

North River Commission
Small Business Development Center

4745 N. Kedzie
Chicago Illinois 60625
Phone: (312)478-0202

Olive-Harvey Community College
Small Business Development Center
Heritage Pullman Bank
1000 E. 111th St., 7th Fl.
Chicago Illinois 60628
Phone: (312)291-6296
Fax: (312)660-4847
Contact: Jerry Chambers

Southeast Chicago Development Commission
Small Business Development Center
9204 S. Commercial. Rm. 415
Chicago Illinois 60617
Phone: (312)731-8755
Fax: (312)731-8618

Truman College-Economic Development
Small Business Development Center
1145 W. Wilson
Chicago Illinois 60640

University Village Association
Small Business Development Center
925 S. Loomis St.
Chicago Illinois 60607
Phone: (312)243-4045
Fax: (312)243-4684

Women's Business Development Center
Small Business Development Center
8 S. Michigan, Ste. 400
Chicago Illinois 60603
Phone: (312)853-3477
Fax: (312)853-0145
Contact: Paul Carlin

McHenry County College
Small Business Development Center
8900 U.S. Hwy. 14
Crystal Lake Illinois 60012
Phone: (815)455-6098
Fax: (815)455-3999
Contact: Don Glaze

Danville Area Community College
Small Business Development Center
28 W. North St.
Danville Illinois 61832
Phone: (217)442-7232
Fax: (217)442-6228
Contact: Ed Adrain

Richland Community College
Small Business Development Center
1 College Pk.
Decatur Illinois 62521
Phone: (217)875-7200
Fax: (217)875-6965

Northern Illinois University
Small Business Development Center
Department of Management
305 E. Locust
Dekalb Illinois 60115
Phone: (815)753-1403
Contact: Joanne Rouse

Sauk Valley Community College
Small Business Development Center
173 Illinois Rte. 2
Dixon Illinois 61021
Phone: (815)288-5605
Fax: (815)288-5958
Contact: Tom Gospodarczyk

Black Hawk College
Small Business Development Center
301 42nd Ave.
East Moline Illinois 61244
Phone: (309)762-3661
Contact: Donna Scalf

East St. Louis Small Business Development Center
DCCA, State Office Bldg.
10 Collinsville
East St. Louis Illinois 62201
Phone: (618)583-2272
Fax: (618)588-2274
Contact: Karen Pinkston

Southern Illinois University at Edwardsville
Small Business Development Center
Center for Advanced Manufacturing and Production

Campus Box 1107
Edwardsville Illinois 62026
Phone: (618)692-2452
Contact: Jim Mager

Elgin Community College
Small Business Development Center
1700 Spartan Dr., Office B-15
Elgin Illinois 60123
Phone: (708)697-1000
Contact: Craig Fowler

Evanston Business and Technology Center
Small Business Development Center
1840 Oak Ave.
Evanston Illinois 60201
Phone: (708)866-1841
Fax: (708)866-1841

Highland Community College
Small Business Development Center
206 S. Galena
Freeport Illinois 61032
Phone: (815)232-1366
Fax: (815)235-1366
Contact: Chuck Mufich

Geneseo Chamber of Commerce
Small Business Development Center
200 N. State St.
Geneseo Illinois 61254
Phone: (309)944-2686

College of DuPage
Small Business Development Center
22nd Street & Lambert Rd.
Glen Ellyn Illinois 60137
Phone: (708)858-2800
Contact: David Gray

College of Lake County
Small Business Development Center
19351 W. Washington St.
Grayslake Illinois 60030
Phone: (708)223-3614
Contact: Arthur Cobb, Jr.

Southeastern Illinois College
Small Business Development Center
325 E. Poplar, Ste. A
Harrisburg Illinois 62946
Phone: (618)252-8528
Fax: (618)252-0210
Contact: Becky Williams

Rend Lake College
Small Business Development Center
Rte. 1
Ina Illinois 62846
Phone: (618)437-5321
Fax: (618)437-5321
Contact: Lisa Payne

Joliet Junior College
Small Business Development Center
Renaissance Center, Rm. 319
214 N. Ottawa St.
Joliet Illinois 60431
Phone: (815)727-6544
Fax: (815)722-1895
Contact: Denise Mikulski

Kankakee Community College
Small Business Development Center
4 Dearborn Sq.
Kankakee Illinois 60901
Phone: (815)933-0376
Fax: (815)933-0380
Contact: JoAnn Seggebruck

Western Illinois University
Small Business Development Center
216 Seal Hall
Macomb Illinois 61455
Phone: (309)298-1128
Contact: Dan Voorhis

Lake Land College
Small Business Development Center
5001 Lakeland Blvd.
South Route No. 45
Mattoon Illinois 61938
Phone: (217)234-5253
Contact: Daniel Sulsberger

Maple City Business and Technology Center
Small Business Development Center
620 S. Main St.
Monmouth Illinois 61462
Phone: (309)734-4664
Fax: (309)734-8579
Contact: Carol Cook

Heartland Community College
Small Business Development Center
1226 Towanda Plz.
Normal Illinois 61761
Phone: (217)875-7200
Fax: (217)875-6965
Contact: Maureen Ruski

Illinois Valley Community College
Small Business Development Center
Rte. 1, Bldg. 11
Oglesby Illinois 61348
Phone: (815)223-1740
Fax: (815)224-3033
Contact: Boyd Palmer

Illinois Eastern Community College
Small Business Development Center
401 E. Main St.
Olney Illinois 62450
Phone: (618)395-3011
Fax: (618)392-2773
Contact: John Spitz

William Raney-Harper College
Small Business Development Center
1200 W. Algonquin Rd.
Palatine Illinois 60067
Phone: (708)397-3000
Fax: (708)925-6043

Moraine Valley College
Small Business Development Center
10900 S. 88th Ave.
Palos Hills Illinois 60465
Phone: (708)974-5468
Fax: (708)974-0078
Contact: Hilary Gereg

Bradley University
Small Business Development Center
1501 Bradley Ave.
141 N. Jobst Hall, 1st Fl.
Peoria Illinois 61625
Phone: (309)677-3075
Contact: Roger Luman

Illinois Central College
Small Business Development Center
124 SW Adams St., Ste. 300
Peoria Illinois 61602
Phone: (309)676-7500
Fax: (309)676-7534
Contact: Susan Gorman

Quincy Procurement Assistance Center
Small Business Development Center
301 Oak St.
Quincy Illinois 62301
Phone: (217)228-5511

Triton College
Small Business Development Center
2000 5th Ave.
River Grove Illinois 60171
Phone: (708)456-0300
Fax: (708)456-0049
Contact: Meredith Jaszczek

Rock Valley College
Small Business Development Center
1220 Rock St., Ste. 180
Rockford Illinois 61102
Phone: (815)968-4087
Contact: Beverly Kingsley

South Suburban College
Small Business Development Center
15800 S. State St.
South Holland Illinois 60473
Phone: (708)596-2000
Toll Free: 800-248-4772
Fax: (708)596-1125

Small Business Development Center
Lincoln Land Community College
200 W. Washington
Springfield Illinois 62701

Phone: (217)524-3060
Contact: Freida Schreck

Shawnee Community College
Small Business Development Center
Shawnee College Rd.
Ullin Illinois 62992
Phone: (618)634-9618
Fax: (618)634-9028
Contact: Donald Denny

Governors State University
Small Business Development Center
University Park Illinois 60466
Phone: (708)534-5000
Contact: Christine Cochrane

Indiana

Bloomington Area
Small Business Development Center
116 W. 6th St., No. 100
Bloomington Indiana 47404
Phone: (812)339-8937

Columbus Area
Small Business Development Center
4920 N. Warren Dr.
Columbus Indiana 47203
Phone: (812)372-6480
Toll Free: 800-282-7232
Fax: (812)372-0228

Southwestern Indiana
Small Business Development Center
100 NW 2nd St., Ste. 200
Evansville Indiana 47708
Phone: (812)425-7232
Fax: (812)421-5883

Northeast Indiana
Small Business Development Center
1830 Wayne Trace
Fort Wayne Indiana 46803
Phone: (219)426-0040
Fax: (219)424-0024

Northlake
Small Business Development Center
487 Broadway, Ste. 103
Gary Indiana 46402
Phone: (219)882-2000

Indianapolis Regional
Small Business Development Center
342 N. Senate Ave.
Indianapolis Indiana 46204
Phone: (317)261-3030
Fax: (317)261-3053

Southern Indiana
Small Business Development Center
PO Box 843
Jeffersonville Indiana 47130
Phone: (812)288-6451
Toll Free: 800-742-6763
Fax: (812)284-8314

Kokomo-Howard County
Small Business Development Center
106 N. Washington
Kokomo Indiana 46901
Phone: (317)457-5301
Fax: (317)452-4564

Greater Lafayette Area
Small Business Development Center
PO Box 311
Lafayette Indiana 47902
Phone: (317)742-2394
Fax: (317)742-6276

LaPorte
Small Business Development Center
414 Lincolnway
LaPorte Indiana 46350
Phone: (219)326-7232
Fax: (219)324-7349

Southeastern Indiana
Small Business Development Center
301 E. Main St.
Madison Indiana 47250
Phone: (812)265-3127
Fax: (812)265-2923

Northwest Indiana
Small Business Development Center
8002 Utah St.
Merrillville Indiana 46410
Phone: (219)756-7232

East Central Indiana
Small Business Development Center
401 S. High St.
PO Box 842
Muncie Indiana 47308
Phone: (317)284-8144
Fax: (317)741-5489

Northwest Indiana
Small Business Development Center
6100 Southport Rd.
Portage Indiana 46368
Phone: (219)762-1696
Toll Free: 800-693-6786
Fax: (219)763-2653

Richmond-Wayne County
Small Business Development Center
33 S. 7th St.
Richmond Indiana 47374
Phone: (317)962-2887
Fax: (317)966-0882

South Bend Area
Small Business Development Center
300 N. Michigan
South Bend Indiana 46601
Phone: (219)282-4350
Fax: (219)236-1056

Terre Haute Area
Small Business Development Center
Indiana State University
School of Business, Rm. 510
Terre Haute Indiana 47809
Phone: (812)237-7676
Toll Free: 800-227-7232
Fax: (812)237-7675

Iowa

Iowa State University
Small Business Development Center
ISU Branch Office
137 Lynn Ave.
Ames Iowa 50014
Phone: (515)292-6355
Toll Free: 800-373-7232
Fax: (515)292-0020
Contact: Steve Carter

DMACC Small Business Development Center
Circle West Incubator
PO Box 204
Audubon Iowa 50025
Phone: (712)563-2623
Fax: (712)563-2301
Contact: Lori Harmening-Webb

University of Northern Iowa
Small Business Development Center
Business Bldg., Ste. 5
Cedar Falls Iowa 50614
Phone: (319)273-2696
Fax: (319)273-6830
Contact: Lyle Bowlin

Iowa Western Community College
Small Business Development Center
2700 College Rd., Box 4C
Council Bluffs Iowa 51502
Phone: (712)325-3260
Fax: (712)325-0189
Contact: Rhonda Helms

Southwestern Community College
Small Business Development Center
1501 W. Townline Rd.
Creston Iowa 50801
Phone: (515)782-4161
Fax: (515)782-3312
Contact: Paul Havick

Eastern Iowa Community College District
Eastern Iowa Small Business Development Center
304 W. 2nd St.
Davenport Iowa 52801
Phone: (319)322-4499

Fax: (319)322-8241
Contact: Jon Ryan

Drake University
Small Business Development Center
Drake Business Center
Des Moines Iowa 50311
Phone: (515)271-2655
Fax: (515)271-4540
Contact: Benjamin Swartz

Northeast Iowa Small Business Development Center
Dubuque Area Chamber of Commerce
770 Town Clock Plz.
Dubuque Iowa 52001
Phone: (319)588-3350
Fax: (319)557-1591
Contact: Charles Tonn

University of Iowa
Small Business Development Center
108 Papajohn Business Administration Bldg., Ste. S160
Iowa City Iowa 52242
Phone: (319)335-4057
Toll Free: 800-253-7232
Fax: (319)335-1956
Contact: Paul Heath

Kirkwood Community College
Small Business Development Center
2901 10th Ave.
Marion Iowa 52302
Phone: (319)377-8256
Fax: (319)377-5667
Contact: Carol Thompson

North Iowa Area Community College
Small Business Development Center
500 College Dr.
Mason City Iowa 50401
Phone: (515)421-4342
Fax: (515)423-0931
Contact: Richard Petersen

Indian Hills Community College
Small Business Development Center
525 Grandview Ave.
Ottumwa Iowa 52501
Phone: (515)683-5127

Fax: (515)683-5263
Contact: Bryan Ziegler

Western Iowa Tech Community College
Small Business Development Center
5001 E. Gordon Dr.
Box 265
Sioux City Iowa 51102
Phone: (712)274-6418
Toll Free: 800-352-4649
Fax: (712)276-0502
Contact: Dennis Bogenrief

Iowa Lakes Community College (Spencer)
Small Business Development Center
Gateway North Shopping Center
Hwy. 71 N
Spencer Iowa 51301
Phone: (712)262-4213
Fax: (712)262-4047
Contact: John Beneke

Southeastern Community College
Small Business Development Center
Drawer F
West Burlington Iowa 52655
Phone: (319)752-2731
Toll Free: 800-828-7322
Fax: (319)752-4957
Contact: Deb Daniel

Kansas

Cowley County Community College
Small Business Development Center
125 S. 2nd
PO Box 1147
Arkansas City Kansas 67005
Phone: (316)442-0430
Toll Free: 800-593-2222
Fax: (316)441-5350

Butler County Community College
Small Business Development Center
600 Walnut
Augusta Kansas 67010
Phone: (316)775-1124
Fax: (316)775-1370

Colby Community College
Small Business Development Center
1255 S. Range
Colby Kansas 67701
Phone: (913)462-3984
Fax: (913)462-4600

Dodge City Community College
Small Business Development Center
2501 N. 14th Ave.
Dodge City Kansas 67801
Phone: (316)225-1321
Toll Free: 800-742-9519
Fax: (316)225-0918

Great Plains Development, Inc.
Small Business Development Center
Box 1116
Dodge City Kansas 67801
Phone: (316)227-6406
Fax: (316)225-6051

Emporia State University
Small Business Development Center
207 Cremer Hall
Emporia Kansas 66801
Phone: (316)343-5308
Fax: (316)341-5418

Barton County Community College
Small Business Development Center
Rte. 3, Box 1362
Great Bend Kansas 67530
Phone: (316)792-2701
Fax: (316)792-1356

Fort Hays State University
Small Business Development Center
1301 Pine St.
Hays Kansas 67601
Phone: (913)628-5340
Fax: (913)628-1471

Pioneer Country Development, Inc.
Small Business Development Center
Box 248
Hill City Kansas 67642
Phone: (913)674-3488
Fax: (913)674-3496

Hutchinson Community College
Small Business Development Center
815 N. Walnut, Rm. 225
Hutchinson Kansas 67501
Phone: (316)665-4950
Toll Free: 800-289-3501
Fax: (316)665-8354

Kansas City (Kansas) Community College
Small Business Development Center
7250 State Ave.
Kansas City Kansas 66112
Phone: (913)334-1100
Fax: (913)596-9609

University of Kansas
Small Business Development Center
734 Vermont St., Ste. 104
Lawrence Kansas 66044
Phone: (913)843-8844
Fax: (913)865-4400

Seward County Community College
Small Business Development Center
PO Box 1137
Liberal Kansas 67905
Phone: (316)624-1951
Toll Free: 800-373-9951
Fax: (316)629-2725

Kansas State University (Manhattan)
Small Business Development Center
College of Business Administration
2323 Anderson Ave., Ste. 100
Manhattan Kansas 66502
Phone: (913)532-5529
Fax: (913)532-5827

Decatur County Economic Development
Small Business Development Center
132 S. Penn
Oberlin Kansas 67749
Phone: (913)475-3441

Johnson County Community College
Small Business Development Center
CEC Bldg., Rm. 223
Overland Park Kansas 66210
Phone: (913)469-3878
Fax: (913)469-4415

Pittsburg State University
Small Business Development Center
Shirk Hall
Pittsburg Kansas 66762
Phone: (316)235-4920
Fax: (316)232-6440

Pratt Community College
Small Business Development Center
348 N.E. Sr-61
Pratt Kansas 67124
Phone: (316)672-5641
Toll Free: 800-794-3091
Fax: (316)672-5288

Kansas Institute of Technology
Small Business Development Center
131 Crompton Rd.
Salina Kansas 67401
Phone: (913)825-0275

Kansas State University (Salina)
Small Business Development Center
2409 Scanlan Ave.
Salina Kansas 67402
Phone: (913)826-2622

Washburn University of Topeka
Small Business Development Center
School of Business
101 Henderson Learning Center
Topeka Kansas 66621

Kentucky

Ashland Small Business Development Center
Morehead State University College of Business
PO Box 830
207 15th St.
Ashland Kentucky 41105
Phone: (606)329-8011
Contact: Kimberly A. Jenkins

Western Kentucky University
Bowling Green Small Business Development Center
245 Grise Hall
Bowling Green Kentucky 42101
Phone: (502)745-2901
Contact: Rick Horn

Southeast Community College
Southeast Small Business Development Center
Chrisman Hall, Rm. 113
Cumberland Kentucky 40823
Phone: (606)589-4514
Contact: Cortez Davis

Elizabethtown Small Business Development Center
238 W. Dixie Ave.
Elizabethtown Kentucky 42701
Phone: (502)765-6737
Contact: Denver Woodring

Northern Kentucky University
Small Business Development Center
BEP Center, Rm. 463
Highland Heights Kentucky 41099
Phone: (606)572-6524
Contact: Sutton Landry

Hopkinsville Small Business Development Center
Murray State University
300 Hammond Dr.
Hopkinsville Kentucky 42240
Phone: (502)886-8666
Contact: Mike Cartner

Lexington Area Small Business Development Center
University of Kentucky
227 Business and Economics Bldg.
Lexington Kentucky 40506
Phone: (606)257-7666
Contact: William Morley

Bellarmine College
Small Business Development Center
School of Business
2001 Newburg Rd.
Louisville Kentucky 40205
Phone: (502)452-8282
Contact: Thomas G. Daley

University of Louisville
Small Business Development Centers
Center for Entrepreneurship and Technology
Burhans Hall, Shelby Campus
Louisville Kentucky 40292
Phone: (502)852-7854
Contact: Lou Dickie

Morehead State University
Small Business Development Center
207 Downing Hall
Morehead Kentucky 40351
Phone: (606)783-2895
Contact: Wilson Grier, Consultant

Murray State University
West Kentucky Small Business Development Center
College of Business and Public Affairs
Business Bldg., Rm 253
Murray Kentucky 42071
Phone: (502)762-2856
Contact: Rosemary Miller

Owensboro Small Business Development Center
Murray State University
3860 U.S. Hwy. 60 W
Owensboro Kentucky 42301
Phone: (502)926-8085
Contact: Mickey Johnson

Pikeville Small Business Development Center
Moorehead State University
Rte. 7
110 Village St.
Pikeville Kentucky 41501
Phone: (606)432-5848
Contact: Mike Morley

Eastern Kentucky University
South Central Small Business Development Center
107 W. Mt. Vernon St.
Somerset Kentucky 42501
Phone: (606)678-5520
Contact: Donald R. Snyder

Louisiana

Capital Small Business Development Center
Southern University
9613 Interline Ave.
Baton Rouge Louisiana 70809
Phone: (504)922-0998
Contact: Greg Spann

Southeastern Louisiana University
Small Business Development Center
College of Business Administration
Box 522, University Sta.
Hammond Louisiana 70402
Phone: (504)549-3831
Contact: William Joubert

University of Southwestern Louisiana
Acadiana Small Business Development Center
Box 43732
College of Business Administration
Lafayette Louisiana 70504
Phone: (318)265-5344
Contact: Dan Lavergne

McNeese State University
Small Business Development Center
College of Business Administration
Lake Charles Louisiana 70609
Phone: (318)475-5529
Contact: Paul Arnold

Northeast Louisiana University
Small Business Development Center
College of Business Administration, Rm. 2-57
Monroe Louisiana 71209
Phone: (318)342-1224
Contact: Lesa Lawrence

Northwestern State University
Small Business Development Center
College of Business Administration
Natchitoches Louisiana 71497
Phone: (318)357-5611
Contact: Mary Lynn Wilkerson

Loyola University
Small Business Development Center
College of Business Administration
Box 134
New Orleans Louisiana 70118
Phone: (504)865-3474
Contact: Ronald Schroeder

Southern University--New Orleans
Small Business Development Center
College of Business Administration
New Orleans Louisiana 70126

Phone: (504)286-5308
Contact: Jon Johnson

University of New Orleans
Small Business Development Center
College of Business Administration, Rm. 368Tm=
Lakefront Campus
New Orleans Louisiana 70148
Phone: (504)286-6978
Contact: Ivan Miestchovich

Louisiana Tech University
Small Business Development Center
College of Business Administration
Box 10318, Tech Sta.
Ruston Louisiana 71272
Phone: (318)257-3537
Contact: Mike Matthews

Louisiana State University at Shreveport
Small Business Development Center
College of Business Administration
1 University Pl.
Shreveport Louisiana 71115
Phone: (318)797-5144
Contact: James O. Hicks

Nicholls State University
Small Business Development Center
College of Business Administration
PO Box 2015
Thibodaux Louisiana 70310
Phone: (504)448-4242
Contact: Weston Hall

Maine

Androscoggin Valley Council of Governments (AVCOG)
Small Business Development Center
125 Manley Rd.
Auburn Maine 04210
Fax: (207)783-5211

Eastern Maine Development Corp.
Small Business Development Center
PO Box 2579
Bangor Maine 04401
Phone: (207)942-6389
Toll Free: 800-339-6389

Fax: (207)942-3548
Contact: Ron Loyd

Northern Maine Regional Planning Commission
Small Business Development Center
PO Box 779
Caribou Maine 04736
Fax: (207)493-3108

University of Maine at Machias
Small Business Development Center
Math & Science Bldg.
9 O'Brien Ave.
Machias Maine 04654
Phone: (207)255-3313
Fax: (207)255-4864

Southern Maine Regional Planning Commission
Small Business Development Center
255 Main St.
PO Box Q
Sanford Maine 04073
Phone: (207)324-0316

North Kennebec Regional Planning Commission
Small Business Development Center
7 Benton Ave.
Winslow Maine 04901
Phone: (207)873-0711
Fax: (207)873-5723

Coastal Enterprises, Inc. (Wiscasset)
Small Business Development Center
Water St.
PO Box 268
Wiscasset Maine 04578
Phone: (207)882-7552
Fax: (207)882-7552

Maryland

Western Region
Advance Technical Center
Small Business Development Center
3 Commerce Dr.
Cumberland Maryland 21502
Toll Free: 800-457-7232
Fax: (301)777-7504

Western Region
Small Business Development Center
3 Commerce Dr.
Cumberland Maryland 21502
Phone: (301)724-6716
Toll Free: 800-457-7233

National Business League
of Southern Maryland, Inc.
Small Business Development Center
9200 Basil Ct., Ste. 210
Landover Maryland 20785
Phone: (301)772-3683
Fax: (301)772-0730

Suburban Washington Region
Small Business Development Center
9201 Basil Ct., Rm. 115
Landover Maryland 20785
Phone: (301)925-5032
Contact: Tom McLamore

Montgomery College (Rockville)
Small Business Development Center
Continuing Education
51 Mannakee St.
Rockville Maryland 20850
Phone: (301)251-7940
Fax: (301)251-7937

Salisbury State University
Eastern Shore Region
Small Business Development Center
1101 Camden Ave.
Salisbury Maryland 21801
Phone: (410)543-6000
Fax: (410)548-3313

Southern Region
Small Business Development Center
235 Smallwood Village Center
Waldorf Maryland 20602
Phone: (800)762-7232
Toll Free: 800-762-SBDC
Fax: (301)645-9082

Eastern Region - Upper Shore
c/o Chesapeake College
Small Business Development Center
PO Box 8
Wye Mills Maryland 21679
Phone: (410)827-5286
Fax: (410)827-5286

Massachusetts

Boston College
Metropolitan Boston
Small Business Development Center
Regional Office
96 College Rd., Rahner House
Chestnut Hill Massachusetts 02167
Phone: (617)552-4091
Contact: John McKiernan

Southeastern Massachusetts
Small Business Development Center
Regional Office
University of Massachusetts/Dartmouth
200 Pocasset St.
PO Box 2785
Fall River Massachusetts 02722
Phone: (508)673-9783
Contact: Clyde Mitchell

Salem State College
North Shore Massachusetts
Small Business Development Center
Regional Office
197 Essex St.
Salem Massachusetts 01970
Phone: (508)741-6639
Contact: Frederick Young

University of Massachusetts/Amherst
Western Massachusetts
Small Business Development Center
Regional Office
101 State St., Ste. 424
Springfield Massachusetts 01103
Phone: (413)737-6712
Contact: Dianne Fuller Doherty

Clark University
Central Massachusetts

Small Business Development Center
Regional Office
950 Main St.
Dana Commons
Worcester Massachusetts 01610
Phone: (508)793-7615
Contact: Lawrence Marsh

Michigan

Ottawa County Economic Development Office, Inc.
Small Business Development Center
6676 Lake Michigan Dr.
Allendale Michigan 49401
Phone: (616)892-4120
Fax: (616)895-6670

Michigan Energy and Resource
Research Association (MERRA)
Specialty Small Business Development Center
PO Box 130500
Ann Arbor Michigan 48113
Phone: (313)930-0034
Fax: (313)930-0145

Huron County Economic Development Corp.
Small Business Development Center
Huron County Bldg., Rm. 303
Bad Axe Michigan 48413
Phone: (517)269-6431
Fax: (517)269-7221

Kellogg Community College
Small Business Development Center
450 North Ave.
Battle Creek Michigan 49017
Phone: (616)965-3931
Toll Free: 800-955-4KCC
Fax: (616)962-4290

Lake Michigan College Corporation and
Community Development
Small Business Development Center
2755 E. Napier
Benton Harbor Michigan 49022
Phone: (616)927-3571
Fax: (616)927-4491

Ferris State University
Small Business Development Center
Alumni 226
901 S. State St.
Big Rapids Michigan 49307
Phone: (616)592-3553
Fax: (616)592-3539

Wexford-Missaukee
Small Business Development Center
222 Lake St.
Cadillac Michigan 49601
Phone: (616)775-9776
Fax: (616)775-1440

Tuscola County Economic Development Corp.
Small Business Development Center
194 N. State St.
Caro Michigan 48723
Phone: (517)673-2849
Fax: (517)673-2517

Detroit Economic Growth Corp.
150 W. Jefferson, Ste. 1500
Detroit Michigan 48226
Phone: (313)963-2940
Fax: (313)963-8839

Michigan Small Business Development Center (Detroit)
2727 2nd Ave., Rm. 107
Detroit Michigan 48201
Contact: Ron Hall

University of Detroit Mercy
NILAC Small Business Development Center
PO Box 19900
Detroit Michigan 48219
Phone: (313)993-1115
Fax: (313)993-1052

Michigan State University
International Business Development Center
7 Eppley Center
East Lansing Michigan 48824
Phone: (517)353-4336
Toll Free: 800-852-5727
Fax: (517)432-1009

First Step, Inc.
Small Business Development Center
2415 14th Ave. S
Escanaba Michigan 49829
Phone: (906)786-9234
Fax: (906)786-4442

Genesee Economic Area Revitalization, Inc.
Small Business Development Center
412 S. Saginaw St.
Flint Michigan 48502
Phone: (313)238-7803
Toll Free: 800-488-7803
Fax: (313)238-7866

Grand Rapids Area Chamber of Commerce
Small Business Development Center
The Walers Bldg.
111 Pearl St.
Grand Rapids Michigan 49503
Phone: (616)771-0300
Fax: (616)771-0318

Grand Rapids Chamber of Commerce
Small Business Development Center
111 Pearl, NW
Grand Rapids Michigan 49503
Phone: (616)771-0300
Fax: (616)771-0318

Oceana County Economic Development Corp.
PO Box 168
Hart Michigan 49420
Phone: (616)873-7141
Fax: (616)873-4177

Comerica Small Business Development Center
Commerica SB Nevel Ctr.
14048 Woodward
Highland Park Michigan 48203
Phone: (313)222-2956

Hillsdale County IDC
2 N. Howell St.
Hillsdale Michigan 49242
Phone: (517)437-3200
Fax: (517)437-3735

Michigan Technological University
Small Business Development Center
Bureau of Industrial Development
1400 Townsend Dr.
Houghton Michigan 49931
Phone: (906)487-3170
Fax: (906)487-2463

Western U.P. Planning and Development Region
326 Sheldon Ave.
PO Box 365
Houghton Michigan 49931
Phone: (906)482-7205
Fax: (906)482-9032

Livingston County Small Business Development Center
207 M Michigan Ave.
PO Box 138
Howell Michigan 48843
Phone: (517)546-4020
Fax: (517)546-4115

Greater Gratiot Development, Inc.
Small Business Center
136 Main
Ithaca Michigan 48847
Phone: (517)875-2083
Fax: (517)875-2990

Jackson Business Development Center
414 N. Jackson St.
Jackson Michigan 49201
Phone: (517)787-0442
Fax: (517)787-3960

Kalamazoo College
Small Business Development Center
Stryker Center for Management Studies
1327 Academy St.
Kalamazoo Michigan 49007
Phone: (616)337-7354
Fax: (616)337-7352

Lansing Community College
Small Business Development Center
PO Box 40010
Lansing Michigan 48901
Phone: (517)483-1921
Fax: (517)483-1675

Lapeer Development Corp.
Small Business Development Center
449 McCormick Dr.
Lapeer Michigan 48446
Phone: (810)667-0080
Fax: (810)667-3541

Thumb Area Community Growth Alliance
Small Business Development Center
3270 Wilson St.
Marlette Michigan 48453
Phone: (517)635-3561
Fax: (517)635-2230

Northern Economic Initiative Corp.
Small Business Development Center
1009 W. Ridge St.
Marquette Michigan 49855
Phone: (906)228-5571
Fax: (906)228-5572

Monroe County Community College
Monroe Small Business Center
1555 S. Raisinville Rd.
Monroe Michigan 48161
Phone: (313)242-7300
Toll Free: 800-462-5114
Fax: (313)242-9711

Macomb County Business Assistance Network
Small Business Development Center
115 S. Groesbeck Hwy.
Mount Clemens Michigan 48043
Phone: (810)469-5118
Fax: (810)469-6787

Central Michigan University
Small Business Development Center
256 Applied Business Studies Complex
Mount Pleasant Michigan 48859
Phone: (517)774-3270
Fax: (517)774-2372

Muskegon Economic Growth Alliance
Small Business Development Center
349 W. Webster Ave., Ste. 104
PO Box 1087
Muskegon Michigan 49443
Phone: (616)722-3751

Toll Free: 800-235-3866
Fax: (616)728-7251

Oakland County Economic Development Group
Executive Office Bldg.
1200 N. Telegraph Rd., Dept. 412
Pontiac Michigan 48341
Phone: (810)858-0732
Fax: (810)858-1080

St. Clair County Community
Small Business Development Center
323 Erie St.
PO Box 5015
Port Huron Michigan 48061
Phone: (313)984-3881
Toll Free: 800-553-2427
Fax: (313)984-2852

Saginaw Future, Inc.
Small Business Development Center
301 E. Genesee, 3rd Fl.
Saginaw Michigan 48607
Phone: (517)754-8222
Fax: (517)754-1715

West Shore Community College
Small Business Development Center
Business and Industrial Development Institute
3000 N. Stiles Rd.
Scottville Michigan 49454
Phone: (616)845-6211
Fax: (616)845-0207

Montcalm Community College
Small Business Development Center
2800 College Dr. SW
Sidney Michigan 48885
Phone: (517)328-2111
Fax: (517)328-2950

Downriver Small Business Development Center
15100 Northline Rd.
Southgate Michigan 48195
Phone: (313)281-3418

Sterling Heights Area Chamber of Commerce
Small Business Development Center
12900 Hall, Ste. 110

Sterling Heights Michigan 48313
Phone: (810)731-5400
Fax: (810)731-3521

Greater Northwest Regional
Small Business Development Center
PO Box 506
Traverse City Michigan 49685
Phone: (616)929-5000
Fax: (616)929-5012

Northwestern Michigan College
Small Business Development Center
Center for Business and Industry
1701 E. Front St.
Traverse City Michigan 49684
Phone: (616)922-1105
Fax: (616)922-1722

Traverse Bay Economic Development Corp.
Small Business Development Center
202 E. Grandview Pky.
PO Box 387
Traverse City Michigan 49685
Phone: (616)946-1596
Fax: (616)946-2565

Traverse City Area Chamber of Commerce
Small Business Development Center
202 E. Grandview Pky.
PO Box 387
Traverse City Michigan 49685
Phone: (616)947-5075
Fax: (616)946-2565

Michigan International Business
Development Metro Extension Center
1300 W Long Lake Rd.
Troy Michigan 48098
Phone: (810)952-5800
Fax: (810)952-1875

Saginaw Valley State University
Small Business Development Center
Business and Industrial Development Institute
7400 Bay Rd.
University Center Michigan 48710
Phone: (517)790-4000
Toll Free: 800-968-9500
Fax: (517)790-1314

Warren Chamber of Commerce
Small Business Development Center
30500 Van Dyke, Ste. 118
Warren Michigan 48093
Phone: (810)751-3939
Fax: (810)751-3995

Ypsilanti Area Chamber of Commerce
Small Business Development Center
301 W. Michigan Ave., Ste. 101
Ypsilanti Michigan 48197
Phone: (313)482-4920
Fax: (313)483-0400

Minnesota

Bemidji State University
Small Business Development Center
1500 Birchmont Dr. NE
Bemidji Minnesota 56601
Phone: (218)755-2000

Normandale Community College
Small Business Development Center
9700 France Ave. S
Bloomington Minnesota 55431
Phone: (612)832-6560
Fax: (612)832-6352

Brainerd Technical College
Small Business Development Center
300 Quince St.
Brainerd Minnesota 56401
Phone: (218)828-5302
Toll Free: 800-247-2574
Fax: (218)828-5340

Southwestern Technical College (Canby Campus)
Small Business Development Center
1011 1st St. W
Canby Minnesota 56220
Phone: (507)223-7252
Toll Free: 800-658-2535
Fax: (507)223-5291

University of Minnesota at Duluth
Small Business Development Center
10 University Dr., 150 SBE
Duluth Minnesota 55812

Phone: (218)726-7298
Fax: (218)726-6337

East Grand Forks Technical Institute
Small Business Development Center
PO Box 111
Highway 220 N
East Grand Forks Minnesota 56721
Phone: (218)773-3441
Toll Free: 800-451-3441
Fax: (218)773-4502

Normandale Community College
Small Business Development Center
4900 Viking Dr.
Edina Minnesota 55435
Phone: (612)832-6221
Fax: (612)823-6352

Faribault City Hall
Small Business Development Center
208 NW 1st Ave.
Faribault Minnesota 55021
Phone: (507)334-2222
Fax: (507)334-0124

Itasca Development Corp.
Grand Rapids Small Business Development Center
19 NE 3rd St.
Grand Rapids Minnesota 55744
Phone: (218)326-9411
Fax: (218)327-2242

Itasca Development Corporation
Small Business Development Center
19 NE 3rd St.
Grand Rapids Minnesota 55744
Phone: (218)327-2241
Fax: (218)327-2242

Hibbing Community College
Small Business Development Center
1515 E. 25th St.
Hibbing Minnesota 55746
Phone: (218)262-6700
Toll Free: 800-224-4422
Fax: (218)262-6717

Rainy River Community College
Small Business Development Center
Hwys. 11 & 71
International Falls Minnesota 56649
Phone: (218)285-2255
Fax: (218)285-2239

Southwestern Technical College (Jackson Campus)
Small Business Development Center
401 West St.
Jackson Minnesota 56143
Phone: (507)847-3320
Toll Free: 800-658-2522
Fax: (507)847-5383

Southwest State University
Small Business Development Center
Science and Technical Resource Center
Marshall Minnesota 56258
Phone: (507)537-7386
Toll Free: 800-642-0684
Fax: (507)537-6094

Minnesota Project Outreach Corp.
Small Business Development Center
The Mill Pl., Ste. 400
111 3rd Ave. S
Minneapolis Minnesota 55401
Phone: (612)672-3490
Toll Free: 800-325-3073
Fax: (612)339-5214

University of St. Thomas
Small Business Development Center
1000 LaSalle Ave., Ste. 100
Minneapolis Minnesota 55403
Phone: (612)962-4500
Fax: (612)962-4410

Moorhead State University
Small Business Development Center
PO Box 303, MSU
Moorhead Minnesota 56563
Phone: (218)236-2289
Fax: (218)236-2280

Pine Technical College
Small Business Development Center
1000 4th St.

Pine City Minnesota 55063
Phone: (612)629-7340
Fax: (612)629-7603

Southwestern Technical College (Pipestone Campus)
Small Business Development Center
Box 250
Pipestone Minnesota 56164
Phone: (507)825-5471
Toll Free: 800-658-2330
Fax: (507)825-4656

Hennepin Technical College
Small Business Development Center
1820 N. Xenium Lane
Plymouth Minnesota 55441
Phone: (612)550-7218
Fax: (612)550-7272

Red Wing Technical Institute
Small Business Development Center
2000 W. Main St., Ste. 324
Red Wing Minnesota 55066
Phone: (612)388-4079

Rochester Community College
Small Business Development Center
Hwy. 14 E
851 30th Ave SE
Rochester Minnesota 55904
Phone: (507)285-7536
Fax: (507)280-5502

Dakota County Technical College
Small Business Development Center
1300 E. 145th St.
Rosemount Minnesota 55068
Phone: (612)423-8262
Fax: (612)322-5156

St. Cloud State University
Small Business Development Center
4191 2nd St. S.
St. Cloud Minnesota 56301
Phone: (612)255-4842
Fax: (612)255-4957

University of St. Thomas
Small Business Development Center
23 Empire Dr.
St. Paul Minnesota 55103
Phone: (612)962-4500

Thief River Falls Technical Institute
Small Business Development Center
1301 Hwy. 1 E
Thief River Falls Minnesota 56701
Phone: (218)681-5424
Toll Free: 800-222-2884
Fax: (218)681-5519

Mesabi Community College
Small Business Development Center
820-N 9th Ave., Alcott Plaza, Ste. 140
Virginia Minnesota 55792
Phone: (218)741-4251
Fax: (218)741-4249

Wadena Technical College
Small Business Development Center
PO Box 566
Wadena Minnesota 56482
Phone: (218)631-3530
Fax: (218)631-9207

North/East Metro Technical College
Small Business Development Center
3300 Century Ave. N
White Bear Lake Minnesota 55110
Phone: (612)779-5764

Winona State University
Small Business Development Center
Somsen Hall, Rm. 111
PO Box 5838
Winona Minnesota 55987
Phone: (507)457-5088

Mississippi

Northeast Mississippi Community College
Small Business Development Center
Holiday Hall, Ste. 303
Booneville Mississippi 38829
Phone: (601)728-7751
Fax: (601)720-7464

Delta State University
Small Business Development Center
PO Box 3235
Cleveland Mississippi 38733
Phone: (601)846-4236
Fax: (601)846-4235

East Central Community College
Small Business Development Center
PO Box 129
Decatur Mississippi 39327
Phone: (601)635-2111
Fax: (601)635-4031

Jones County Junior College
Small Business Development Center
900 Court St.
Ellisville Mississippi 39437
Phone: (601)477-4165
Fax: (601)477-4166

Gulf Coast Community College
Small Business Development Center
Jackson County Campus
PO Box 100
Gautier Mississippi 39553
Phone: (601)497-9595
Fax: (601)497-9604

Mississippi Delta Community College
Small Business Development Center
1656 E. Union St.
PO Box 5607
Greenville Mississippi 38702
Phone: (601)378-8183
Fax: (601)378-5349

Mississippi Contract Procurement Center
Small Business Development Center
3015 12th St.
PO Box 610
Gulfport Mississippi 39502
Fax: (601)864-2969

Pearl River Community College
Small Business Development Center
Rte. 9, Box 1325
Hattiesburg Mississippi 39401
Phone: (601)544-0030
Fax: (601)544-0032

Jackson State University
Small Business Development Center
Jackson Enterprise Center, Ste. A-1
931 Hwy. 80 W
Box 43
Jackson Mississippi 39204
Phone: (601)968-2795
Fax: (601)968-2796

Millsaps College
Small Business Development Center
Dr. David Culpepper
Jackson Mississippi 39210
Phone: (601)974-1000
Fax: (601)974-1260

University of Southern Mississippi
Small Business Development Center
USM Gulf Park Campus
Beach Park Place
Long Beach Mississippi 39560
Phone: (601)865-4578
Fax: (601)865-4581
Contact: Lucy Betcher

Alcorn State University
Small Business Development Center
1000 ASU Dr.
PO Box 90
Lorman Mississippi 39096
Phone: (601)877-6684
Fax: (601)877-6256

Meridian Community College
Small Business Development Center
910 Hwy. 19 N
Meridian Mississippi 39307
Phone: (601)482-7445
Fax: (601)482-5803

Mississippi State University
Small Business Development Center
PO Drawer 5288
Mississippi State Mississippi 39762
Phone: (601)325-8684
Fax: (601)325-4016

Copiah-Lincoln Community College
Small Business Development Center

Natchez Campus
Natchez Mississippi 39120
Phone: (601)445-5254
Fax: (601)445-5254

Hinds Community College
Small Business Development Center
& International Trade Center
PO Box 1170
Raymond Mississippi 39154
Phone: (601)857-3537
Toll Free: 800-725-7232
Fax: (601)857-3535

Holmes Community College
Small Business Development Center
412 W. Ridgeland Ave.
Ridgeland Mississippi 39157
Phone: (601)853-0827
Fax: (601)853-0844

Northwest Mississippi Community College
Small Business Development Center
8700 Northwest Dr.
South Haven Mississippi 38671
Phone: (601)342-1570

Southwest Mississippi Community College
Small Business Development Center
College Dr.
Summit Mississippi 39666
Phone: (601)276-3890
Fax: (601)276-3867

Itawamba Community College
Small Business Development Center
653 Eason Blvd.
Tupelo Mississippi 38801
Phone: (601)680-8515
Fax: (601)680-8423

Missouri

Southeast Missouri State University
Small Business Development Center
222 N. Pacific
Cape Girardeau Missouri 63701
Phone: (314)290-5965
Fax: (314)290-5651
Contact: Frank "Buz" Sutherland

University of Missouri--Columbia
Small Business Development Center
1800 University Pl.
Columbia Missouri 65211
Phone: (314)882-7096
Fax: (314)882-6156
Contact: Frank Siebert

Missouri Southern State College
Small Business Development Center
3950 Newman Rd.
107 Matthews Hall
Joplin Missouri 64801
Phone: (417)625-9313
Fax: (417)625-9782
Contact: Jim Krudwig

Rockhurst College
Small Business Development Center
1100 Rockhurst Rd.
VanAckeren Hall, Rm. 205
Kansas City Missouri 64110
Phone: (816)926-4572
Fax: (816)926-4646
Contact: Judith Burgen

Small Business Development Center
2470 E. Linwood Blvd., Ste. 400
Kansas City Missouri 64109
Phone: (816)926-4572

Northeast Missouri State University
Small Business Development Center
207 E. Patterson
Kirksville Missouri 63501
Phone: (816)785-4307
Fax: (816)785-4357
Contact: Glen Giboney

Northwest Missouri State University
Small Business Development Center
423-N. Market
Maryville Missouri 64468
Phone: (816)562-1701
Fax: (816)582-3071

Mineral Area College
Small Business Development Center
PO Box 1000

Park Hill Missouri 63601
Phone: (314)431-4593
Fax: (314)431-6807

Three Rivers Community College
Small Business Development Center
Business Incubator Bldg.
3019 Fair St.
Poplar Bluff Missouri 63901
Phone: (314)686-3499
Fax: (314)686-5467
Contact: John Bonifield

Center for Technology Transfer
and Economic Development
University of Missouri--Rolla
Nagogami Ter., Bldg. 1, Rm. 104
Rolla Missouri 65401
Contact: Don Myers

University of Missouri--Rolla
Small Business Development Center
Engineering Management Bldg., Rm. 223
Rolla Missouri 65401
Phone: (314)341-4561
Fax: (314)341-6567
Contact: Bob Laney

Missouri Western State College
Small Business Development Center
3003 Fredrick Ave.
St. Joseph Missouri 64506
Phone: (816)232-4461
Fax: (816)364-4873

St. Louis Community College
Small Business Development Center
Continuing Education
3400 Pershall Rd.
St. Louis Missouri 63135
Phone: (314)595-4219

St. Louis University
Small Business Development Center
3642 Lindell Blvd.
St. Louis Missouri 63108
Phone: (314)534-7232
Fax: (314)534-7023
Contact: Virginia Campbell

Southwest Missouri State University
Small Business Development Center
Center for Business Research
901 S. National
Box 88
Springfield Missouri 65804
Phone: (417)836-5685
Fax: (417)836-6337
Contact: Jane Peterson

Central Missouri State University
Small Business Development Center
Grinstead Bldg., Rm. 75
Warrensburg Missouri 64093
Phone: (816)543-4402
Fax: (816)543-8159
Contact: Cindy Tanck

Central Missouri State University
Center for Technology
Grinstead, No. 75
Warrensburg Missouri 64093
Contact: Bernie Sarbaugh

Montana

Billings Area Business Incubator
Small Business Development Center
2720 3rd Ave. N., Ste. 300
Billings Montana 59101
Phone: (406)256-6875
Fax: (406)256-6877

Gallatin Development Corp.
Rozeman Small Business Development Center
321 E. Main, Ste. 413
Bozeman Montana 59715
Phone: (406)587-3113
Fax: (406)587-9565
Contact: Darrell Berger

Rural Economic Development Incubator (REDI)
Butte Small Business Development Center
305 W. Mercury, Ste. 211
Butte Montana 59701
Phone: (406)782-7333
Fax: (406)782-9675
Contact: Ralph Kloser

Bear Paw Development Corp.
Havre Small Business Development Center
PO Box 1549
Havre Montana 59501
Phone: (406)265-9226
Fax: (406)265-3777
Contact: Randy Hanson

Flathead Valley Community College
Kalispell Small Business Development Center
777 Grandview Dr.
Kalispell Montana 59901
Phone: (406)756-3833
Fax: (406)756-3815
Contact: Dan Manning

Missoula Business Incubator
Missoula Small Business Development Center
127 N. Higgins, 3rd Fl.
Missoula Montana 59802
Phone: (406)728-9234
Fax: (406)721-4584
Contact: Leslie Jeasen

Eastern Plains RC&D
Sidney Small Business Development Center
123 W. Main
Sidney Montana 59270
Phone: (406)482-5024
Fax: (406)482-5306
Contact: Dwayne Heintz

Nebraska

Chadron State College
NBDC-Chadron
Administration Bldg.
Chadron Nebraska 69337
Phone: (308)432-6282
Contact: Cliff Hanson

University of Nebraska at Kearney
NBDC-Kearney
Welch Hall
19th St. and College Dr.
Kearney Nebraska 68849
Phone: (308)234-8344
Contact: Kay Payne

University of Nebraska at Lincoln
NBDC-Lincoln
Cornhusker Bank Bldg., Ste. 302
11th and Cornhusker Hwy.
Lincoln Nebraska 68521
Phone: (402)472-3358
Contact: Larry Cox

Mid-Plains Community College
NBDC-North Platte
416 N. Jeffers, Rm. 26
North Platte Nebraska 69101
Phone: (308)534-5115
Contact: Dean Kurth

Nebraska Small Business Development Center
Omaha Business and Technology Center
2505 N. 24 St., Ste. 101
Omaha Nebraska 68110
Contact: Tom McCabe

University of Nebraska at Omaha
Small Business Development Center
60th & Dodge Sts.
College of Business Administration, Rm. 407
Omaha Nebraska 68182
Phone: (402)554-2521
Fax: (402)554-3747
Contact: Robert Bernier

Peru State College
NBDC-Peru
T.J. Majors Hall, Rm. 248
Peru Nebraska 68421
Phone: (402)872-2274
Contact: David Ruenhall

Western Nebraska Community College
NBDC-Scottsbluff
Nebraska Public Power Bldg.
1721 Broadway, Rm. 408
Scottsbluff Nebraska 69361
Phone: (308)635-7513
Contact: Ingrid Battershell

Wayne State College
NBDC-Wayne
Connell Hall
200 E. 10th St.

Wayne Nebraska 68787
Phone: (402)375-7479
Contact: Loren Kucera

Nevada

Carson City Chamber of Commerce
Small Business Development Center
1900 S. Carson St., Ste. 100
Carson City Nevada 89702
Phone: (702)882-1565
Contact: Larry Osborne

Northern Nevada Community College
Small Business Development Center
901 Elm St.
Elko Nevada 89801
Phone: (702)738-8493
Contact: John Pryor

Incline Village Chamber of Commerce
Small Business Development Center
969 Tahoe Blvd.
Incline Village Nevada 89451
Phone: (702)831-4440

University of Nevada at Las Vegas
Small Business Development Center
Box 456011
Las Vegas Nevada 89154
Phone: (702)895-3362
Contact: Sharolyn Craft

North Las Vegas
Small Business Development Center
19 W. Brooks Ave.
North Las Vegas Nevada 89030
Phone: (702)399-6300

University of Nevada at Reno
Small Business Development Center
College of Business Administration
Mail Stop 032, Rm. 411
Reno Nevada 89557
Phone: (702)784-1679
Contact: Sam Males

Tri-County Development Authority
Small Business Development Center

50 W. 4th St.
PO Box 820
Winnemucca Nevada 89446
Phone: (702)623-5777
Contact: Terri Williams

New Hampshire

New Hampshire Small Business Development Center
Office of Economic Initiatives
Heidelberg-Harris Bldg.
Durham New Hampshire 03824
Contact: Michelle Emig

University of New Hampshire
Small Business Development Center
15 College Rd.
108 McConnell Hall
Durham New Hampshire 03824
Phone: (603)862-2200
Contact: Liz Lamoureaux

Keene State College
Small Business Development Center
Blake House
Keene New Hampshire 03431
Phone: (603)358-2602
Contact: Dick George

Small Business Development Center
PO Box 786
Littleton New Hampshire 03561
Phone: (603)444-1053
Contact: Liz Matott

Small Business Development Center (Manchester, NH)
1001 Elm St.
Manchester New Hampshire 03101
Phone: (603)625-5691
Contact: Bob Ebberson

Nashua Chamber of Commerce
Small Business Development Center
188 Main, Ste. 100
Nashua New Hampshire 03060
Phone: (603)881-8333
Fax: (603)881-7323

New Hampshire Small Business Development Center
c/o Center for Economic Development
188 Main St.
Nashua New Hampshire 03060
Contact: Bob Wilburn

Plymouth State College
Small Business Development Center
Hyde Hall
Plymouth New Hampshire 03264
Phone: (603)535-2523
Contact: Janice Kitchen

New Jersey

Greater Atlantic City Chamber of Commerce
Small Business Development Center
1301 Atlantic Ave.
Atlantic City New Jersey 08401
Contact: William McGinley

Rutgers University Schools of Business
Small Business Development Center
Business and Science Bldg., 2nd Fl.
Camden New Jersey 08102
Phone: (609)757-6221
Contact: Patricia Peacock

Brookdale Community College
Small Business Development Center
Newman Springs Rd.
Lincroft New Jersey 07738
Phone: (908)842-1900
Contact: Bill Nunnally

Rutgers University
Small Business Development Center
Ackerson Hall, 3rd Fl.
180 University Ave.
Newark New Jersey 07102
Contact: Brenda Hopper

Bergen Community College
Small Business Development Center
400 Paramus Rd.
Paramus New Jersey 07652
Phone: (201)447-7841
Fax: (201)447-7495

Mercer County Community College
Small Business Development Center
1200 Old Trenton Rd.
Trenton New Jersey 08690
Phone: (609)586-4800
Contact: Herb Spiegel

Kean College
Small Business Development Center
Morris Ave. and Conant
Union New Jersey 07083
Phone: (908)527-2954
Contact: Mira Kostak

Warren County Community College
Small Business Development Center
Rte. 57 W, RD No. 1, Box 55A
Washington New Jersey 07882
Phone: (908)689-7613
Contact: Jonathan Andrews

New Mexico

New Mexico State University at Alamogordo
Small Business Development Center
1000 Madison
Alamogordo New Mexico 88310
Phone: (505)434-5272
Contact: Dwight Henry

Albuquerque Technical-Vocational Institute
Small Business Development Center
525 Buena Vista SE
Albuquerque New Mexico 87106
Phone: (505)224-4246
Contact: Roslyn Block

New Mexico State University at Carlsbad
Small Business Development Center
PO Box 1090
Carlsbad New Mexico 88220
Phone: (505)887-6562
Contact: Larry Coalson

Clovis Community College
Small Business Development Center
417 Schepps Blvd.
Clovis New Mexico 88101
Phone: (505)769-4136
Contact: Roy Miller

Northern New Mexico Community College
Small Business Development Center
1002 N. Onate St.
Espanola New Mexico 87532
Phone: (505)753-7141
Contact: Darien Cabral

San Juan College
Small Business Development Center
203 W. Main St., Ste. 201
Farmington New Mexico 87401
Phone: (505)326-4321
Contact: Brad Ryan

University of New Mexico at Gallup
Small Business Development Center
PO Box 1395
Gallup New Mexico 87305
Phone: (505)722-2220
Contact: Barbara Stanley

New Mexico State University at Grants
Small Business Development Center
709 E. Roosevelt Ave.
Grants New Mexico 87020
Phone: (505)287-8221
Contact: Clemente Sanchez

New Mexico Junior College
Small Business Development Center
5317 Lovington Hwy.
Hobbs New Mexico 88240
Phone: (505)392-4510
Contact: Don Leach

New Mexico State University--Dona Ana Branch
Small Business Development Center
Dept. 3DA, Box 30001
Las Cruces New Mexico 88003
Contact: Terry Sullivan

Luna Vocational-Technical Institute
Small Business Development Center
PO Drawer K
Las Vegas New Mexico 87701
Phone: (505)454-2595
Contact: Michael Rivera

University of New Mexico at Los Alamos
Small Business Development Center
PO Box 715
Los Alamos New Mexico 87544
Phone: (505)662-0001
Contact: Jim Greenwood

University of New Mexico at Valencia
Small Business Development Center
280 La Entrada
Los Lunas New Mexico 87031
Phone: (505)865-9596
Contact: Andrew Thompson

Eastern New Mexico University at Roswell
Small Business Development Center
PO Box 6000
Roswell New Mexico 88201
Phone: (505)624-7133
Contact: Eugene Simmons

Western New Mexico University
Small Business Development Center
PO Box 2672
Silver City New Mexico 88062
Phone: (505)538-6320
Contact: Linda Kay

Tucumcari Area Vocational School
Small Business Development Center
PO Box 1143
Tucumcari New Mexico 88401
Phone: (505)461-4413
Contact: Richard Spooner

New York

SUNY at Albany
Small Business Development Center
Draper Hall, Rm. 107
135 Western Ave.
Albany New York 12222
Phone: (518)442-5577
Fax: (518)442-5582

Binghamton University
Small Business Development Center
PO Box 6000
Vestal Pky. E

Binghamton New York 13902
Phone: (607)777-4024
Fax: (607)777-4029

State University of New York
Small Business Development Center
74 N. Main St.
Brockport New York 14420
Phone: (716)232-7310
Fax: (716)637-2102

Bronx Community College
Small Business Development Center
McCracken Hall, Rm 14
W. 181st & University Ave.
Bronx New York 10453
Phone: (718)220-6464
Fax: (718)563-3572

Bronx Community College
Small Business Development Center
McCracken Hall
W. 181st St. and University Ave.
Bronx New York 10471
Phone: (718)220-6464
Fax: (718)563-3572

Kingsboro Community College
Small Business Development Center
2001 Oriental Blvd.
Bldg. T4
Brooklyn New York 11235
Phone: (718)368-4619
Fax: (718)368-4629

State University of New York at Buffalo
Small Business Development Center
BA 117
1300 Elmwood Ave.
Buffalo New York 14222
Phone: (716)878-4030
Fax: (716)878-4067

Corning Community College
Small Business Development Center
24-28 Denison Pky. W
Corning New York 14830
Phone: (607)962-9461
Toll Free: 800-358-7171
Fax: (607)936-6642

Mercy College/Westchester Outreach Center
Small Business Development Center
555 Broadway
Dobbs Ferry New York 10522
Phone: (914)674-7485
Fax: (914)693-4996

State University of New York at Farmingdale
Small Business Development Center
Campus Commons Bldg.
2350 Route 110
Farmingdale New York 11735
Phone: (516)420-2765
Fax: (516)293-5343

State University of New York Geneseo
Small Business Development Center
1 College Circle
Geneseo New York 14454
Phone: (716)245-5429
Fax: (716)245-5430

York College/City University of New York
Small Business Development Center
94-50 159th St.
Science Bldg. Rm. 107
Jamaica New York 11451
Phone: (718)262-2880
Fax: (718)262-2881

Jamestown Community College
Small Business Development Center
PO Box 20
Jamestown New York 14702
Phone: (716)665-5754
Toll Free: 800-522-7232
Fax: (716)665-6733

Small Business Development Center
1 Development Ct.
Kingston New York 12401
Phone: (914)339-1322
Fax: (914)339-1631

Pace University
Small Business Development Center
1 Pace Plz.
New York New York 10038
Phone: (212)346-1899
Fax: (212)346-1613

Pace University/Harlem Outreach Center
Small Business Development Center
163 W. 125th St., Rm. 1307
New York New York 10027
Phone: (212)865-4299
Fax: (212)346-1613

Onondaga Community College/Oswego Outreach Center
Small Business Development Center
44 W. Bridge St.
PO Box 4067
Oswego New York 13126
Phone: (315)343-1545
Fax: (315)343-1546

Clinton Community College
Small Business Development Center
136 Clinton Pointe Dr.
Alpert House
Plattsburgh New York 12901
Phone: (518)562-4260
Fax: (518)563-9759

State University of New York
Small Business Development Center
74 Main St.
Rockport New York 14420
Phone: (716)232-7310
Fax: (716)637-2102

Niagara County Community College
Small Business Development Center
3111 Saunders Settlement Rd.
Sanborn New York 14132
Phone: (716)693-1910
Fax: (716)731-3395

Long Island University at Southhampton
Small Business Development Center
Abneay Peak, Montauk Highway
Southampton New York 11968
Phone: (516)287-0059

State University at Stony Brook
Small Business Development Center
Harriman Hall, Rm. 109
Stony Brook New York 11794
Phone: (516)632-9070
Fax: (516)632-7176

Polytechnic University/Westchester Outreach Center
Small Business Development Center
10 College Rd.
Suffern New York 10901
Phone: (914)356-0370
Fax: (914)356-0381

Rockland Community College
Small Business Development Center
145 College Rd.
Suffern New York 10901
Phone: (914)356-0370
Fax: (914)356-0381

Onondaga Community College
Small Business Development Center
4969 Excell Bldg.
Rte. 173
Syracuse New York 13215
Phone: (315)492-3029
Fax: (315)492-3764

State University Institute of Technology
Small Business Development Center
PO Box 3050
Utica New York 13504
Phone: (315)792-7546
Fax: (315)792-7554

Jefferson Community College
Small Business Development Center
Coffeer St.
Watertown New York 13601
Phone: (315)782-9262
Fax: (315)782-6901

North Carolina

Small Business and Technology Development Center
(Northwestern Region)
Appalachian State University
Walker College of Business
Boone North Carolina 28608
Phone: (704)262-2492
Fax: (704)262-2027

University of North Carolina at Chapel Hill
Central Carolina Regional
Small Business Development Center

608 Airport Rd., Ste. B
Chapel Hill North Carolina 27514
Phone: (919)962-0389
Fax: (919)962-3291

University of North Carolina at Charlotte
Small Business and Technology Development Center
(Southern Piedmont Region)
8701 Mallard Creek Rd.
Charlotte North Carolina 28262
Phone: (704)548-1090
Fax: (704)548-9050

Western Carolina University
Small Business and Technology
Development Center (Western Region)
Center for Improving Mountain Living
Bird Bldg.
Cullowhee North Carolina 28723
Phone: (704)227-7494
Fax: (704)227-7422

Elizabeth City State University
Small Business and Technology
Development Center (Northeastern Region)
Campus Box 874
Elizabeth City North Carolina 27909
Phone: (919)335-3247

Fayetteville State University
Cape Fear Small Business and
Technology Development Center
PO Box 1334
Fayetteville North Carolina 28302
Phone: (910)486-1727
Fax: (910)486-1949

North Carolina A&T State University
Northern Piedmont Small Business and
Technology Development Center
(Eastern Region)
C. H. Moore Agricultural Research Center
Greensboro North Carolina 27411
Phone: (910)334-7005

East Carolina University
Small Business and Technology
Development Center (Eastern Region)
Willis Bldg.
300 East 1st St.
Greenville North Carolina 27858
Phone: (919)328-6157

Pembroke State University
Office of Economic Development and SBTDC
Small Business Development Center
Pembroke North Carolina 28372
Phone: (910)521-6603
Fax: (910)521-6550

University of North Carolina at Wilmington
Small Business and Technology Development Center
(Southeast Region)
601 S. College Rd.
Cameron Hall, Rm. 131
Wilmington North Carolina 28403
Phone: (910)395-3744

Winston-Salem State University
Northern Piedmont Small Business and Technology Center
PO Box 13025
Winston-Salem North Carolina 27110
Phone: (910)750-2030

North Dakota

Bismarck Regional Small Business Development Center
400 E. Broadway, Ste. 416
Bismarck North Dakota 58501
Phone: (701)223-8583
Contact: Jan M. Peterson

Devils Lake Outreach Center
Small Business Development Center
417 5th St.
Devils Lake North Dakota 58301
Toll Free: 800-445-7232

Dickinson Regional Center
Small Business Development Center
314 3rd Ave. W
Drawer L
Dickinson North Dakota 58602
Phone: (701)227-2096
Contact: Bryan Vendsel

Fargo Regional Small Business Development Center
417 Main Ave., Ste. 402
Fargo North Dakota 58103
Phone: (701)237-0986
Fax: (701)235-6706
Contact: Jon Girinager

Procurement Assistance Center
Small Business Development Center
417 Main Ave.
Fargo North Dakota 58103
Phone: (701)237-9678
Toll Free: 800-698-5726
Fax: (701)235-6706

Grafton Outreach Center
Small Business Development Center
PO Box 633
Grafton North Dakota 58237
Toll Free: 800-445-7232

Grand Forks Regional Small Business Development Center
1407 24th Ave. S, Ste. 201
The Hemmp Center
Grand Forks North Dakota 58201
Phone: (701)772-8502
Contact: Gordon Snyder

North Dakota Small Business Development Center
210 10th St. SE
Jamestown North Dakota 58401
Phone: (701)252-9243
Fax: (701)252-4837

Minot Outreach Center
Small Business Development Center
4215 E. Burdick Expressway
Minot North Dakota 58701
Phone: (701)839-6641

Minot Regional Center
Small Business Development Center
1020 20th Ave. SW
PO Box 940
Minot North Dakota 58702
Phone: (701)852-8861
Contact: George Youngerman

Williston Outreach Center
Tri-County Economic Development Association
Small Business Development Center
PO Box 2047
Williston North Dakota 58801
Toll Free: 800-445-7232

Ohio

Akron Regional Development Board
Small Business Development Center
1 Cascade Plz., 8th Fl.
Akron Ohio 43308
Phone: (216)379-3170
Fax: (216)379-3164

Women's Entrepreneurial Growth Organization (WEGO)
Small Business Development Center
58 W. Center St.
PO Box 544
Akron Ohio 44309
Phone: (216)535-9346
Fax: (216)535-4523

Northwest State Community College
Small Business Development Center
22-600 ST RT 34
Archbold Ohio 43502
Phone: (419)267-5511
Fax: (419)267-3688

Ohio University Innovation Center
Small Business Development Center
Technical & Enterprise Bldg.
20 East Circle Dr., Ste. 153
Athens Ohio 45701
Phone: (614)593-1797
Fax: (614)593-1795

Ohio Hi-Point JVC
Small Business Development Center
112 E. Court St.
Bellefontaine Ohio 43311
Phone: (513)592-3585
Fax: (513)592-3683

West Central Small Business Development Center
Ohio-Point Office
2280 State Rte. 540

Bellefontaine Ohio 43311
Phone: (513)599-3010
Fax: (513)599-2318

Mideast Small Business Development Center
Cambridge Office
1131 Steubenville Ave.
Cambridge Ohio 43725
Phone: (614)439-2822
Fax: (614)439-2822

Greater Stark Development Board
Stark County Small Business Development Center
116 Cleveland Ave. NW, Ste. 600
Canton Ohio 44702
Phone: (216)453-5900
Fax: (216)453-1793

Wright State University--Lake Campus
Small Business Development Center
7600 State Rte. 703
Celina Ohio 45822
Phone: (419)586-2365
Fax: (419)586-0358

Small Business Development Center
University of Cincinnati
IAMS Research Pk., MC189
1111 Edison Ave.
Cincinnati Ohio 45216
Phone: (513)948-2082
Fax: (513)948-2007
Contact: Gloria Parker

Greater Cleveland Growth Association
Small Business Development Center
200 Tower City Center
50 Public Sq.
Cleveland Ohio 44113
Phone: (216)621-3300
Toll Free: 800-562-7121
Fax: (216)621-6013

Columbus Area Chamber of Commerce
Small Business Development Center
Central Ohio Government Marketing Assistance Program
77 S. High St.
PO Box 1001
Columbus Ohio 43266
Phone: (614)221-1321
Fax: (614)469-8250
Contact: Holly Schick

Coshocton County Chamber of Commerce
Small Business Development Center
124 Chestnut St.
Coshocton Ohio 43812
Phone: (614)622-5411
Fax: (614)622-9902
Contact: Blanch Tyree

Dayton Area Chamber of Commerce
Small Business Development Center
Chamber Plz.
5th & Main Sts.
Dayton Ohio 45402
Phone: (513)226-8230
Fax: (513)226-8254

Northwest Technical College
Small Business Development Center
1935 E. 2nd St., Ste. D
Defiance Ohio 43512
Phone: (419)784-3777

Terra Community College
Small Business Development Center
1220 Cedar St.
Fremont Ohio 43420
Phone: (419)332-1002
Fax: (419)334-2300

Enterprise Center
Small Business Development Center
129 E. Main St.
PO Box 756
Hillsboro Ohio 45133
Phone: (513)393-9599
Fax: (513)393-8159

Ashtabula County Economic Development Council, Inc.
Small Business Development Center
36 W. Walnut St.
Jefferson Ohio 44047
Phone: (216)576-9134
Fax: (216)576-5003

Lima Technical College
Small Business Development Center
545 W. Market St., Ste. 305
Lima Ohio 45801
Phone: (419)229-5320
Fax: (419)229-5424

Mid-Ohio Small Business Development Center
246 E. 4th St., 4th Fl.
PO Box 1208
Mansfield Ohio 44901
Phone: (419)525-1614
Toll Free: 800-366-7232
Fax: (419)522-6811

Miami University
Small Business Development Center
311 Upham Hall
Oxford Ohio 45056
Phone: (513)529-4841
Fax: (513)529-1469

Upper Valley Joint Vocational School
Small Business Development Center
8811 Career Dr.
N. Country Rd., 25A
Piqua Ohio 45356
Phone: (513)778-8419
Toll Free: 800-589-6963
Fax: (513)778-9237

Department of Development of the CIC of Belmont County
Small Business Development Center
100 E. Main St.
St. Clairsville Ohio 43950
Phone: (614)695-9678
Fax: (614)695-1536
Contact: Mike Campbell

Sandusky City Schools
Small Business Development Center
407 Decatur St.

Sandusky Ohio 44870
Phone: (419)626-6940
Toll Free: 800-548-6507
Fax: (419)626-9176

Lawrence County Chamber of Commerce
Small Business Development Center
U.S. Rte. 52 & Solida Rd.
PO Box 488
South Point Ohio 45680
Phone: (614)894-3838
Fax: (614)894-3836

Springfield Small Business Development Center
300 E. Auburn Ave.
Springfield Ohio 45505
Phone: (513)322-7821
Fax: (513)322-7874
Contact: Jack Harris

Greater Steubenville Chamber of Commerce
Small Business Development Center of Jefferson County
630 Market St.
PO Box 278
Steubenville Ohio 43952
Phone: (614)282-6226
Fax: (614)282-6285

Toledo Small Business Development Center
300 Madison Ave., Ste. 200
Toledo Ohio 43604
Phone: (419)243-8191
Fax: (419)241-8302

Youngstown State University
Cushwa Center for Entrepeneurship
410 Wick Ave.
Youngstown Ohio 44555
Phone: (216)742-3495
Fax: (216)742-3784

Zanesville Area Chamber of Commerce
Small Business Development Center
205 N. 5th St.
Zanesville Ohio 43701
Phone: (614)452-4868
Toll Free: 800-743-2303
Fax: (614)454-2963

Oklahoma

East Central University
Small Business Development Center
1036 E. 10th St.
Ada Oklahoma 74820
Phone: (405)436-3190
Fax: (405)436-3190

Northwestern Oklahoma State University
Small Business Development Center
Alva Oklahoma 73717
Phone: (405)327-8608
Fax: (405)327-0560

University of Central Oklahoma
Small Business Development Center
100 N. University Blvd.
Edmond Oklahoma 73034
Phone: (405)232-1968

Phillips University
Small Business Development Center
100 S. University Ave.
Enid Oklahoma 73701
Phone: (405)242-7989
Fax: (405)237-1607

Langston University Center
Small Business Development Center
PO Box 667
Langston Oklahoma 73050
Phone: (405)466-3256
Toll Free: 800-501-3435
Fax: (405)466-2909

Lawton Satellite
Small Business Development Center
American National Bank Bldg.
601 SW "D" Ave., Ste. 209
Lawton Oklahoma 73501
Phone: (405)248-4946
Toll Free: 800-522-6154

Northeastern State University
Small Business Development Center
2151 I St. NE
Miami Oklahoma 74354
Phone: (918)540-0575
Fax: (918)540-0575

Rose State College
Small Business Development Center
6420 SE 15th
Midwest Oklahoma 73110
Phone: (405)733-7348
Fax: (405)733-7495

Oklahoma Department of Commerce
Small Business Development Center
PO Box 26980
Oklahoma City Oklahoma 73126
Phone: (405)843-9770
Toll Free: 800-TRY-OKLA
Fax: (405)841-5199

Carl Albert College
Small Business Development Center
1507 S. McKenna
Poteau Oklahoma 74953
Phone: (918)647-4019
Fax: (918)647-1218

Northeastern Oklahoma State University
Small Business Development Center
Oklahoma Small Business Development Center
Tahlequah Oklahoma 74464
Phone: (918)458-0802
Fax: (918)458-2105

Tulsa Satellite
Small Business Development Center
State Office Bldg.
440 S. Houston, Ste. 507
Tulsa Oklahoma 74127
Phone: (918)581-2502
Fax: (918)581-2745

Southwestern Oklahoma State University
Small Business Development Center
100 Campus Dr.
Weatherford Oklahoma 73096
Phone: (405)774-1040
Fax: (405)774-7091

Oregon

Linn-Benton Community College
Small Business Development Center
6500 Pacific Blvd. SW
Albany Oregon 97321
Phone: (503)967-6112
Contact: Dennis Sargent

Southern Oregon State College/Ashland
Small Business Development Center
Regional Services Institute
Ashland Oregon 97520
Phone: (503)482-5838

Central Oregon Community College
Small Business Development Center
2600 NW College Way
Bend Oregon 97701
Phone: (503)383-7290
Contact: Bob Newhart

Southwestern Oregon Community College
Small Business Development Center
340 Central
Coos Bay Oregon 97420
Phone: (503)269-0123
Contact: Jon Richards

Columbia Gorge Community College
Small Business Development Center
212 Washington
The Dalles Oregon 97058
Phone: (503)296-1173
Contact: Bob Cole

Lane Community College
Small Business Development Center
1059 Willamette St.
Eugene Oregon 97401
Phone: (503)726-2255
Contact: Jane Scheidecker

Rogue Community College
Small Business Development Center
214 SW Fourth St.
Grants Pass Oregon 97526
Phone: (503)471-3515
Contact: Lee Merritt

Mount Hood Community College
Small Business Development Center
323 NE Roberts St.
Gresham Oregon 97030
Phone: (503)667-7658
Contact: Don King

Oregon Institute of Technology
Small Business Development Center
3201 Campus Dr. South, Hall 314
Klamath Falls Oregon 97601
Phone: (503)885-1760
Contact: Janie Albert

Eastern Oregon State College
Small Business Development Center
Regional Services Institute
1410 L Ave.
LaGrande Oregon 97850
Toll Free: 800-452-8639
Contact: Joni Gibbens

Oregon Coast Community College
Small Business Development Center
4157 NW Hwy. 101, Ste. 123
PO Box 419
Lincoln City Oregon 97367
Phone: (503)994-4166
Contact: Mike Lainoff

Southern Oregon State College/Medford
Small Business Development Center
Regional Service Institute
229 N. Bartlett
Medford Oregon 97501
Phone: (503)772-3478
Contact: Liz Shelby

Clackamas Community College
Small Business Development Center
7616 SE Harmony Rd.
Milwaukie Oregon 97222
Phone: (503)656-4447
Contact: Jan Stennick

Treasure Valley Community College
Small Business Development Center
88 SW 3rd Ave.
Ontario Oregon 97914

Phone: (503)889-2617
Contact: Kathy Simko

Blue Mountain Community College
Small Business Development Center
37 SE Dorion
Pendleton Oregon 97801
Phone: (503)276-6233
Contact: Grath Davis

Portland Community College
Small Business Development Center
123 NW 2nd Ave., Ste. 321
Portland Oregon 97209
Phone: (503)273-2828
Contact: Robert Keyser

Portland Community College
Small Business International Trade Program
121 SW Salmon St., Ste. 210
Portland Oregon 97204
Phone: (503)274-7482
Contact: Ton Niland

Umpqua Community College
Small Business Development Center
744 SE Rose
Roseburg Oregon 97470
Phone: (503)672-2535
Contact: Terry Swagerty

Chemeketa Community College
Small Business Development Center
365 Ferry St. SE
Salem Oregon 97301
Phone: (503)399-5181
Contact: Bobbie Clyde

Clatsop Community College
Small Business Development Center
1761 N. Holladay Dr.
Seaside Oregon 97138
Phone: (503)738-3347
Contact: Kennetyh McCune

Tillamook Bay Community College
Small Business Development Center
401 B Main St.
Tillamook Oregon 97141
Phone: (503)842-2551
Contact: Mike Harris

Pennsylvania

Lehigh University
Small Business Development Center
621 Taylor St.
Bethlehem Pennsylvania 18015
Phone: (610)758-3980
Fax: (610)758-5205

Clarion University of Pennsylvania
Small Business Development Center
Dana Still Bldg., Rm. 102
Clarion Pennsylvania 16214
Phone: (814)226-2060
Fax: (814)226-2636

Gannon University
Small Business Development Center
Carlisle Bldg., 3rd Fl.
Erie Pennsylvania 16541
Phone: (814)871-7714

West Chester University
Small Business Development Center
906 Springdale Dr.
Exton Pennsylvania 19341
Phone: (610)363-5175
Fax: (610)594-9864

Kutztown University
Small Business Development Center
2986 2nd St.
Harrisburg Pennsylvania 17110
Phone: (717)233-3120

Indiana University of Pennsylvania
Robert Shaw Center
Small Business Development Center
650 S. 13th St.
Indiana Pennsylvania 15705
Phone: (412)357-7915
Fax: (412)357-4514

St. Vincent College
Small Business Development Center
Alfred Hall, 4th Fl.
Latrobe Pennsylvania 15650
Phone: (412)537-4572
Fax: (412)537-0919

Bucknell University
Small Business Development Center
126 Dana Engineering Bldg.
Lewisburg Pennsylvania 17837
Phone: (717)524-1249
Fax: (717)524-1758

St. Francis College
Small Business Development Center
Business Resource Center
Loretto Pennsylvania 15940
Phone: (814)472-3200
Fax: (814)472-3202

LaSalle University
Small Business Development Center
20th & Olney Ave.
Philadelphia Pennsylvania 19141
Phone: (215)951-1416
Fax: (215)951-1488

Temple University
Small Business Development Center
Rm. 6, Speakman Hall, 006-00
Philadelphia Pennsylvania 19122
Phone: (215)204-7282
Fax: (215)204-4554

Dequesne University
Small Business Development Center
Rockwell Hall, Rm. 10, Concourse
600 Forbes Ave.
Pittsburgh Pennsylvania 15282
Phone: (412)434-6233

University of Pittsburgh
Small Business Development Center
The Joseph M. Katz Graduate School of Business
208 Bellefield
315 S. Bellefield Ave.
Pittsburgh Pennsylvania 15260
Phone: (412)648-1544
Fax: (412)648-1638

University of Scranton
Small Business Development Center
St. Thomas Hall, Rm. 588
Scranton Pennsylvania 18510
Phone: (717)941-7588
Toll Free: 800-829-7232
Fax: (717)941-4053

Wilkes University
Small Business Development Center
Hollenback Hall
192 S. Franklin St.
Wilkes-Barre Pennsylvania 18766
Phone: (717)824-4651
Toll Free: 800-572-4444
Contact: Kostas Mallios

Puerto Rico

Interamerican University
Small Business Development Center
Casa Llompart
PO Box 1293
Hato Rey Puerto Rico 00917
Phone: (809)765-2335

University of Puerto Rico at Humacao
Small Business Development Center
Antonio Lopez St.
Casa Roig Annex
Box 10226, CUH Sta.
Humacao Puerto Rico 00661
Phone: (809)850-2500

University of Puerto Rico at Ponce
Small Business Development Center
PO Box 7186
Ponce Puerto Rico 00732
Phone: (809)841-2641
Contact: Elma Santigo

University of Puerto Rico at Rio Piedras
Small Business Development Center
PO Box 21417, UPR Sta.
Rio Piedras Puerto Rico 00931
Phone: (809)763-5933

Rhode Island

University of Rhode Island
Small Business Development Center
24 Woodward Hall
Kingston Rhode Island 02881
Phone: (401)792-2451
Fax: (401)792-4017

Aquidneck Island Small Business Development Center
26 Jacome Way
Middletown Rhode Island 02840
Phone: (401)849-6900
Fax: (401)849-0815
Contact: Sam Carr

Bryant College
Small Business Development Center
7 Jackson Walkway
Providence Rhode Island 02903
Phone: (401)831-1330
Fax: (401)454-2819
Contact: Erwin Robinson

Community College of Rhode Island (Providence Campus)
Small Business Development Center
1 Hilton St.
Providence Rhode Island 02905
Phone: (401)455-6042

Bryant College
Export Assistance Center
Small Business Development Center
1150 Douglas Pike
Smithfield Rhode Island 02917
Phone: (401)232-6111
Fax: (401)232-6416

Rhode Island Small Business Development Center
State Administrative Office
Bryant College
1150 Douglas Pke.
Smithfield Rhode Island 02917
Contact: Douglas Jobling

Community College of Rhode Island (Warwick)
Small Business Development Center
400 East Ave.
Warwick Rhode Island 02886
Phone: (401)825-1000

South Carolina

Aiken/North Augusta Small Business Development Center
171 University Pky., Ste. 100
Aiken South Carolina 29801
Phone: (803)648-6851
Contact: Jackie Moore

University of South Carolina at Beaufort
Small Business Development Center
800 Carteret St.
Beaufort South Carolina 29902
Fax: (803)521-4143
Contact: Martin Goodman

USC Beaufort
Small Business Development Center
801 Cartenet
Beaufort South Carolina 29902
Phone: (803)521-4143
Fax: (803)521-4142

University of South Carolina
Small Business Development Center
PO Box 20339
Charleston South Carolina 29413
Phone: (803)727-2020

Clemson University
Small Business Development Center
College of Commerce and Industry
425 Sirrine Hall
Box 341392
Clemson South Carolina 29634
Phone: (803)656-3227
Contact: Russ Madray

USC Regional Small Business Development Center
University of South Carolina
College of Business Administration
Columbia South Carolina 29201
Phone: (803)777-4907
Fax: (803)777-4403
Contact: Dean Kress

Coastal Carolina College
Small Business Development Center
School of Business Administration
Conway South Carolina 29526
Fax: (803)347-2177
Contact: Tim Lowery

Florence-Darlington Technical College
Small Business Development Center
PO Box 100548
Florence South Carolina 29501
Phone: (803)661-8324
Contact: David Raines

Greenville Chamber of Commerce
Small Business Development Center
24 Cleveland St.
Greenville South Carolina 29601
Phone: (803)271-4259

Upper Savannah Council of Government
Small Business Development Center Exchange Building
PO Box 1366
222 Phoenix St., Ste. 200
Greenwood South Carolina 29648
Phone: (803)941-8050
Contact: George Long

University of South Carolina at Hilton Head
Small Business Development Center
Kiawah Bldg., Ste. 300
10 Office Park Rd.
Hilton Head Island South Carolina 29928
Phone: (803)785-3995
Fax: (803)777-0333
Contact: Jim DeMartin

Aiken/North Augusta Small Business Development Center
Triangle Plz.
215-B Edgefield Rd.
North Augusta South Carolina 29841
Phone: (803)442-3670
Fax: (803)641-3445

South Carolina State University
Small Business Development Center
School of Business Administration
PO Box 7176
Orangeburg South Carolina 29117

Phone: (803)536-8445
Contact: John Gradson

Winthrop University
Wintrop Regional Small Business Development Center
School of Business Administration
119 Thurman Bldg.
Rock Hill South Carolina 29733
Phone: (803)323-2283
Contact: Nate Barber

Spartanburg Chamber of Commerce
Small Business Development Center
PO Box 1636
Spartanburg South Carolina 29304
Phone: (803)594-5080
Contact: Robert Grooms

South Dakota

Aberdeen Small Business Development Center
226 Citizens Bldg.
Aberdeen South Dakota 57401
Phone: (605)622-2252
Fax: (605)622-2667
Contact: Ron Kolbech

Pierre Small Business Development Center
105 S. Euclid, Ste. C
Pierre South Dakota 57501
Phone: (605)773-5941
Fax: (605)773-5942
Contact: Wade Druin

Rapid City Small Business Development Center
444 N. Mount Rushmore Rd., Rm. 208
Rapid City South Dakota 57701
Phone: (605)394-5311
Fax: (605)343-1916
Contact: Matthew Johnson

Sioux Falls Chamber of Commerce
Small Business Development Center
200 N. Phillips, Rm. 302
Sioux Falls South Dakota 57102
Phone: (605)367-5757
Fax: (605)367-5755

Sioux Falls Small Business Development Center
200 N. Phillips, Ste. L103
Sioux Falls South Dakota 57102
Phone: (605)330-6011
Fax: (605)330-6010
Contact: Nancy Straw

Tennessee

Chattanooga State Technical Community College
Small Business Development Center
4501 Amnicola Hwy.
Chattanooga Tennessee 37406
Phone: (615)697-2432
Fax: (615)634-3070

Southeast Tennessee Development District
Small Business Development Center
PO Box 4757
Chattanooga Tennessee 37405
Phone: (615)266-5781
Fax: (615)267-7705

Austin Peay State University
Small Business Development Center
College of Business
Clarksville Tennessee 37044
Phone: (615)648-7674
Fax: (615)648-5985

Cleveland State Community College
Small Business Development Center
Adkisson Dr.
PO Box 3570
Cleveland Tennessee 37320
Phone: (615)478-6247
Toll Free: 800-604-2722
Fax: (615)478-6251

Dyersburg State Community College
Small Business Development Center
1510 Lake Rd.
Dyersburg Tennessee 38024
Phone: (901)286-3201
Fax: (901)286-3271

Jackson State Community College
Small Business Development Center
2046 N. Parkway St.
Jackson Tennessee 38301
Phone: (901)424-5389
Fax: (901)425-2647

East Tennessee State University
Small Business Development Center
College of Business
PO Box 70698
Johnson City Tennessee 37614
Phone: (615)929-5630
Fax: (615)461-7080

Pellissippi State Technical Community College
Small Business Development Center
301 East Church Ave.
Knoxville Tennessee 37915
Phone: (615)525-0277

Memphis State University
Small Business Development Center
Bldg. 1, S. Campus
Memphis Tennessee 38152
Phone: (901)527-1041
Contact: Kenneth J. Burns

Walters State Community College
Tennessee Small Business Development Center
500 S. Davy Crockett Pky.
Morristown Tennessee 37813
Phone: (615)585-2675
Fax: (615)585-2679

Middle Tennessee State University
Small Business Development Center
School of Business
PO Box 487
Murfreesboro Tennessee 37132
Phone: (615)898-2745
Fax: (615)898-2681

Tennessee State University
Small Business Development Center
College of Business
330 10th Ave. No, G2
Nashville Tennessee 37203
Phone: (615)963-7179
Fax: (615)963-7160

Texas

Abilene Christian University
Small Business Development Center
School of Business
648 East Highway 80
Abilene Texas 79601
Phone: (915)670-0300
Fax: (915)670-0311

Alvin Community College
Small Business Development Center
3110 Mustang Rd.
Alvin Texas 77511
Phone: (713)388-4686
Fax: (713)388-4903
Contact: Gina Mattei

West Texas State University
Small Business Development Center
T. Boone Pickens School of Business
1800 S. Washington, Ste. 209
Amarillo Texas 79102
Phone: (806)372-5151
Fax: (806)372-5261

Trinity Valley Community College
Small Business Development Center
500 S. Prairieville
Athens Texas 75751
Phone: (903)675-7403
Fax: (903)675-5199

Austin Small Business Development Center
2211 S. IH 35, Ste. 103
Austin Texas 78741
Phone: (512)326-2256
Fax: (512)447-9825
Contact: Larry Lucero

Lee College
Small Business Development Center
PO Box 818
Rundell Hall
Baytown Texas 77522
Phone: (713)425-6309
Fax: (713)425-6307
Contact: Kenneth Voytek

John Gray Institute/Lamar University
Small Business Development Center
855 Florida Ave.
Beaumont Texas 77705
Phone: (409)880-2367
Fax: (409)880-2201
Contact: Roy Huckaby

Bonham Satellite
Chamber of Commerce
Small Business Development Center
1201 E. 9th St.
Bonham Texas 75418
Phone: (903)583-7565
Fax: (903)583-6706

Bonham Small Business Development Center
Sam Rayburn Library
Bonham Texas 75418

Blinn College
Small Business Development Center
902 College Ave.
Brenham Texas 77833
Phone: (409)830-4137
Fax: (409)830-4116
Contact: Phillis Nelson

Brazos Valley
Small Business Development Center
4001 E. 29th St., Ste. 175
Bryan Texas 77802
Phone: (409)260-5222
Fax: (409)260-5208

Bryan/College Station Chamber of Commerce
Small Business Development Center
PO Box 3695
Bryan Texas 77805
Phone: (409)823-3034
Fax: (409)822-4818
Contact: Sam Harwell

American National Bank--Corpus Christi
Small Business Development Center
PO Box 6469
Corpus Christi Texas 78466
Contact: R.J. Sandoval

Corpus Christi Chamber of Commerce
Small Business Development Center
1201 N. Shoreline
Corpus Christi Texas 78403
Phone: (512)888-6161
Fax: (512)888-5627
Contact: Phil Vasquez

Corsicana Small Business Development Center
120 N. 12th St.
Corsicana Texas 75110
Phone: (903)874-0658
Toll Free: 800-320-7232
Fax: (903)874-4187

Bill J. Priest Institute for Economic Development
North Texas-Dallas Small Business Development Center
1402 Corinth St.
Dallas Texas 75215
Phone: (214)565-5826
Fax: (214)565-5857
Contact: Elizabeth Klimback

Texas Center for Government Contracting
Small Business Development Center
1402 Corinth
Dallas Texas 75215
Phone: (214)565-5842
Fax: (214)565-5857

Grayson County College
Small Business Development Center
6101 Grayson Dr.
Denison Texas 75020
Phone: (903)786-3551
Toll Free: 800-316-7232
Fax: (903)463-5284

Denton Small Business Development Center
PO Box P
Denton Texas 76202
Phone: (817)380-1849
Fax: (817)382-0040

Best Southwest
Small Business Development Center
214 S, Main, Ste. 101D
Duncanville Texas 75116
Phone: (214)709-5878
Toll Free: 800-317-7232
Fax: (214)709-6089

DeSoto Small Business Development Center
2145 Main, Ste. 101-D
Duncanville Texas 75116
Phone: (214)709-5878
Toll Free: 800-717-7232

University of Texas--Pan American
Small Business Development Center
1201 W. University Dr.
Center for Entrepreneurship & Economic Development
Edinburg Texas 78539
Phone: (512)381-3361
Fax: (512)381-2322
Contact: Irene Sanchez-Casas

El Paso Community College
Small Business Development Center
103 Montana Ave., Ste. 202
El Paso Texas 79902
Phone: (915)534-3410
Fax: (915)534-3420
Contact: Rogue Segura

Tarrant County Junior College
Small Business Development Center
Mary Owen Center
1500 Houston St.
Fort Worth Texas 76102
Phone: (817)336-7851
Fax: (817)560-6929

Cooke County Community College
Small Business Development Center
1525 W. California
Gainesville Texas 76240
Phone: (817)668-4220

Galveston College
Small Business Development Center
4015 Avenue Q
Galveston Texas 77550

Phone: (409)740-7380
Fax: (409)740-7381
Contact: Joe Harper

Hillsboro Small Business Development Center
SOS Bldg.
PO Box 619
Hillsboro Texas 76645
Phone: (817)582-2555
Fax: (817)582-7591

Houston International Trade Center
Small Business Development Center
1100 Louisiana, Ste. 500
Houston Texas 77002
Phone: (713)752-8404
Contact: Louis Saldarriaga

Houston Small Business Development Center
2700 W. W. Thorne Dr., Ste. A-127
Houston Texas 77073
Phone: (713)443-5477
Fax: (713)443-5402

North Harris Montgomery CC District
Small Business Development Center
250 N. Sam Houston Pky.
Houston Texas 77060
Phone: (713)591-9320
Fax: (713)359-1612
Contact: Ray Laughter

Texas Information Procurement Service
Small Business Development Center
1100 Louisiana, Ste. 500
Houston Texas 77002
Contact: Jack Ruoff

Texas International Trade Center
Small Business Development Center
1100 Louisiana, Ste. 500
Houston Texas 77002
Contact: Luis Saldarriaga

Texas Product Development Center
Small Business Development Center
1100 Louisiana, Ste. 500
Houston Texas 77002
Phone: (713)752-8400

Fax: (713)752-8484
Contact: Susan Macy

University of Houston
Small Business Development Center
1100 Louisiana, Ste. 500
Houston Texas 77002
Phone: (713)752-8444
Fax: (713)752-8484
Contact: Elizabeth Gatewood

Sam Houston State University
Small Business Development Center
College of Business Administration
PO Box 2056
Huntsville Texas 77341
Phone: (409)294-3737
Fax: (409)294-3612
Contact: Bob Barragan

Kingsville Chamber of Commerce
Small Business Development Center
635 E. King
Kingsville Texas 78363
Phone: (512)595-5088
Fax: (512)592-0866
Contact: Gilbert Soliz

Brazosport College
Small Business Development Center
500 College Dr.
Lake Jackson Texas 77566
Phone: (409)265-7208
Fax: (409)265-2944
Contact: Patricia Leyendecker

Laredo Development Foundation
Small Business Development Center
Division of Business Administration
616 Leal St.
Laredo Texas 78041
Phone: (512)722-0563
Fax: (210)722-6247
Contact: David Pulg

Kilgore
Small Business Development Center
110 Triple Creek Dr., Ste. 70
Longview Texas 75601

Phone: (903)757-5857
Toll Free: 800-338-7232
Fax: (903)753-7920

Kilgore College
Small Business Development Center
300 S. High
Longview Texas 75601
Phone: (903)753-2642
Fax: (903)236-7600

Northwest Texas
Small Business Development Center
2579 S. Loop 289, Ste. 114
Lubbock Texas 79423
Phone: (806)745-1637
Fax: (806)745-6207
Contact: Craig Bean

Northwest Texas Region
Small Business Development Center
2579 S. Loop 289, Ste. 114
Lubbock Texas 79423
Phone: (806)745-3973
Fax: (806)745-6717

Angelina College
Small Business Development Center
PO Box 1768
Lufkin Texas 75902
Contact: Chuck Stemple

Midlothian Satellite
Small Business Development Center
330 N. 8th St., Ste. 203
Midlothian Texas 76065
Phone: (214)775-8500

Northeast Texas Community College
Small Business Development Center
PO Box 1307
Mount Pleasant Texas 75456
Phone: (903)572-1911
Toll Free: 800-357-7232
Fax: (903)572-0598

University of Texas--Permian Basin
Small Business Development Center
College of Management
4901 E. University
Odessa Texas 79762
Phone: (915)552-2000
Fax: (915)552-2433

Paris Junior College
Small Business Development Center
Small Business Development Center
2400 Clarksville St.
Paris Texas 75460
Phone: (903)784-1802
Fax: (903)784-1801

Collin
Small Business Development Center
4800 Preston Park Blvd., Box 15
Plano Texas 75093
Phone: (214)985-3770
Fax: (214)985-3775

Collin County Community College
Small Business Development Center
Piano Market Sq.
2000 E. Spring Creek Pky., No. 109
Plano Texas 75074
Phone: (214)881-0506
Phone: (214)985-3775

Angelo State University
Small Business Development Center
2601 West Ave. N
Campus Box 10910
San Angelo Texas 76909
Phone: (915)942-2098
Fax: (915)942-2038
Contact: Harlan Bruha

South Texas Border Small Business Development Center
University of Texas, San Antonio
1222 N. Main St., Ste. 450
San Antonio Texas 78212
Contact: Robert McKinley

University of Texas at San Antonio
South Texas Border Small Business Development Center
1222 N. Main St., Ste. 450

San Antonio Texas 78212
Phone: (512)224-0791
Fax: (512)222-9834
Contact: Robert McKinley

The University of Texas at San Antonio
Regional Office/Technology Center
Small Business Development Center
UTSA Downtown
1222 N. Main Ave., Ste. 450
San Antonio Texas 78212
Phone: (210)558-2460
Phone: (210)558-2450
Phone: (210)558-2458

UTSA International
Small Business Development Center
801 S. Bowie St.
San Antonio Texas 78205
Phone: (210)227-2997
Fax: (210)222-9834
Contact: Sara Jackson

Houston Community College System
Small Business Development Center
13600 Murphy Rd.
Stafford Texas 77477
Phone: (713)499-4870
Fax: (713)499-8194
Contact: John Fishero

Tarleton State University
Small Business Development Center
School of Business Administration
Box T-0650
Stephenville Texas 76402
Phone: (817)968-9330
Fax: (817)968-9329

College of the Mainland
Small Business Development Center
8419 Emmett F. Lowry Expy.
Texas City Texas 77591
Phone: (409)938-7578
Fax: (409)935-5186
Contact: Ed Socha

Tyler Junior College
Small Business Development Center
1530 South SW Loop 323, Ste. 100
Tyler Texas 75701
Phone: (903)510-2975
Fax: (903)510-2978

Middle Rio Grande Development Council
Small Business Development Center
209 N. Getty St.
Uvalde Texas 78801
Phone: (512)278-2527
Fax: (512)278-2929
Contact: Brenda Blackwood

University of Houston--Victoria
Small Business Development Center
700 Main Center, Ste. 102
Victoria Texas 77901
Phone: (512)575-8944
Fax: (512)575-8852
Contact: Carde Parks

McLennan Community College
Small Business Development Center
4601 N. 19th, Ste. A-15
Waco Texas 76708
Phone: (817)750-3600
Fax: (817)756-3620

Wharton County Junior College
Small Business Development Center
Administration Bldg., Rm. 102
911 Boling Hwy.
Wharton Texas 77488
Phone: (409)532-0604
Fax: (409)532-2201
Contact: Lynn Polson

Midwestern State University
Small Business Development Center
Division of Business Administration
3400 Taft Blvd.
Wichita Falls Texas 76308
Phone: (817)689-4373
Fax: (817)689-4374

Utah

Southern Utah University
Small Business Development Center
351 W. Center
Cedar City Utah 84720
Phone: (801)586-5400
Fax: (801)586-5493
Contact: Greg Powell

Snow College
Small Business Development Center
345 West 1st North
Ephraim Utah 84627
Phone: (801)283-6890
Fax: (801)283-6913
Contact: Lynn Schiffman

Utah State University
Small Business Development Center
E. Campus Bldg., Rm. 24
Logan Utah 84322
Phone: (801)750-2277
Fax: (801)750-3317
Contact: Franklin C. Prante

Weber State University
Small Business Development Center
College of Business and Economics
Ogden Utah 84408
Phone: (801)626-7232
Fax: (801)626-7423
Contact: Bruce Davis

Utah Valley State College
Utah Small Business Development Center
800 West 1200 South
Orem Utah 84058
Contact: Michael Finnerty

College of Eastern Utah
Small Business Development Center
451 East 400 North
Price Utah 84501
Phone: (801)637-1995
Fax: (801)637-4102
Contact: Gary Ward

Brigham Young University
Small Business Development Center
Graduate School of Management
790 Tanner Bldg.
Provo Utah 84602
Phone: (801)378-4636

Utah Basin Applied Technology Center
Utah Small Business Development Center
1100 E. Lagoon, 124-5
Roosevelt Utah 84066
Phone: (801)722-4654
Contact: Scott Bigler

Dixie College
Small Business Development Center
225 South 700 East
St. George Utah 84770
Phone: (801)673-4811
Fax: (801)673-8552
Contact: Eric Pedersen

Vermont

Northwestern Vermont
Small Business Development Center
Greater Burlington Industrial Corp
PO Box 786
Burlington Vermont 05402
Phone: (802)862-5726
Fax: (802)860-1899
Contact: William A. Farr

Vermont Technical College
Small Business Development Center
PO Box 422
Randolph Vermont 05060
Phone: (802)728-9101
Fax: (802)728-3026
Contact: Donald L. Kelpinski

Southwestern Vermont
Small Business Development Center
Rutland Industrial Development Corp.
PO Box 39
Rutland Vermont 05701
Phone: (802)773-9147
Fax: (802)773-2772
Contact: James B. Stewart

Northeastern Vermont Small Business Development Center
PO Box 640
St. Johnsbury Vermont 05819
Phone: (802)748-1014
Fax: (802)748-1223
Contact: Joseph P. Wayne

Southeastern Vermont Small Business Development Center
Springfield Development Corp.
PO Box 58
Springfield Vermont 05156
Phone: (802)885-2071
Fax: (802)885-3027
Contact: Norbert B. Johnston

Virgin Islands

University of the Virgin Islands (Charlotte Amalie)
Small Business Development Center
8000 Nicky Center, Ste. 202
Charlotte Amalie Virgin Islands 00802
Contact: Chester Williams

University of the Virgin Islands
Small Business Development Center
Sunshine Mall
Sion Farm, Ste. 104
Federicksted Virgin Islands 00840
Phone: (809)778-8270
Fax: (809)778-7629

Fredriksted Small Business Revolving Loan Fund
Small Business Development Agency
Box 6400
St. Thomas Virgin Islands 00804
Phone: (809)774-8784
Fax: (809)774-4390

Virgin Islands
Small Business Development Agency
Box 6400
St. Thomas Virgin Islands 00804
Phone: (809)774-8784
Fax: (809)774-4390

Virginia

Arlington Small Business Development Center
George Mason University, Arlington Campus
3401 N. Fairfax Dr.
Arlington Virginia 22201
Phone: (703)993-8128
Fax: (703)993-8130
Contact: Paul Hall

Mount Empire Community College
Southwest Small Business Development Center
Drawer 700, Rte. 23, S.
Big Stone Gap Virginia 24219
Phone: (703)523-6529
Contact: Tim Blankenbeder

Western Virginia SBDC Consortium
New River Valley
Small Business Development Center
Virginia Tech
Blacksburg Virginia 24061
Phone: (703)231-4004
Fax: (703)552-0047
Contact: David Shanks

Western Virginia SBDC Consortium
VPI & SU
Economic Development Assistance Center
404 Clay St.
Blacksburg Virginia 24061
Contact: Michael Hensley

Central Virginia
Small Business Development Center
918 Emmet St., Ste. 200
Charlottesville Virginia 22903
Phone: (804)295-8198
Contact: Charles Kulp

Northern Virginia
Small Business Development Center
George Mason University
4260 Chain Bridge Rd., Ste. B-1
Fairfax Virginia 22030
Phone: (703)993-2131
Fax: (703)993-2126
Contact: Michael Kehoe

Longwood College (Farmville)
Small Business Development Center
515 Main St.
Farmville Virginia 23901
Phone: (804)395-2086
Fax: (804)395-2539
Contact: Gerald L. Hughes

Rappahannock Region
Small Business Development Center
1301 College Ave.
Seacobeck Hall
Fredericksburg Virginia 22401
Phone: (703)899-4076
Fax: (703)899-4373
Contact: Jeffrey R. Sneddon

Small Business Development Center
of Hampton Roads, Inc. (Hampton)
Thomas Nelson Community College
PO Box 9407
Hampton Virginia 23670
Phone: (804)825-2957
Fax: (804)825-2960

James Madison University
Small Business Development Center
JMU College of Business
Zane Showker Hall, Rm. 523
Harrisonburg Virginia 22807
Phone: (703)568-3227
Contact: Karen Wigginton

Lynchburg Regional
Small Business Development Center
147 Mill Ridge Rd.
Lynchburg Virginia 24502
Phone: (804)582-6170
Contact: Barry Lyons

Dr. William E. S. Flory
Small Business Development Center
10311 Sudley Manor Dr.
Manassas Virginia 22110
Phone: (703)335-2500
Contact: Laura Decker

Small Business Development Center
of Hampton Roads, Inc. (Norfolk)
420 Bank St.
PO Box 327
Norfolk Virginia 23501
Phone: (804)622-6414
Fax: (804)622-5563
Contact: William J. Holloran, Jr.

New River Valley
Small Business Development Center
New River Valley Planning
District Commission Office
1612 Wadsworth St.
PO Box 3726
Radford Virginia 24143
Phone: (703)731-9546
Fax: (703)831-6093

Southwest Virginia Community College
Southwest Small Business Development Center
PO Box SVCC
Richlands Virginia 24641
Phone: (703)964-7345
Fax: (703)964-9307
Contact: R. Victor Brungart

Capital Area
Small Business Development Center
403 E. Grace St.
Richmond Virginia 23219
Phone: (804)648-7838
Fax: (804)648-7849
Contact: Taylor Cousins

Virginia Small Business Development Center
1021 E. Cary St., 11th Fl.
Richmond Virginia 23219

Blue Ridge Small Business Development Center
Western Virginia SBDC Consortium
310 1st St., SW Mezzanine
Roanoke Virginia 24011
Phone: (703)983-0717
Contact: John Jennings

Longwood
Small Business Development Center
South Boston Branch

515 Broad St.
PO Box 1116
South Boston Virginia 24592
Phone: (804)575-0044
Contact: Carroll Thackston

Loudoun County
Small Business Development Center
21515 Ridge Top Cir., Ste. 220
Sterling Virginia 20166
Phone: (703)430-7222
Fax: (703)430-9562

Warsaw Small Business Development Center
106 W. Richmond Rd.
PO Box 490
Warsaw Virginia 22572
Phone: (804)333-0286
Fax: (804)333-0187

Wytheville Small Business Development Center
Wytheville Community College
1000 E. Main St.
Wytheville Virginia 24382
Phone: (703)228-6751
Fax: (703)228-2542
Contact: Rob Edwards

Washington

Grays Harbor College
Small Business Development Center
1602 Edward P. Smith Dr.
Aberdeen Washington 98520
Phone: (206)538-4021

Bellevue Community College
Small Business Development Center
3000 Landerholm Circle
Bellevue Washington 98009
Phone: (206)641-2265

Bellevue Small Business Development Center
Bellevue Community College
3000 Landerholm Circle SE
Bellevue Washington 98007
Phone: (206)643-2888
Contact: Bill Huenefeld

Western Washington University
Small Business Development Center
415 Parks Hall
Bellingham Washington 98225
Phone: (206)650-3899
Contact: Lynn Trzynka

Whatcom Community College
Small Business Development Center
237 W. Kellogg Rd.
Bellingham Washington 98226
Phone: (206)676-2170

Centralia Community College
Small Business Development Center
600 W. Locust St.
Centralia Washington 98531
Phone: (206)736-9391
Contact: Don Hayes

Washington Small Business Development Center
347 W. 2nd, Ste. A
Colville Washington 99114
Phone: (509)684-4571
Fax: (509)684-4788

Columbia Basin College--TRIDEC
Small Business Development Center
901 N. Colorado
Kennewick Washington 99336
Phone: (509)735-6222
Contact: Glynn Lamberson

Edmonds Community College
Small Business Development Center
20000 68th Ave. W
Lynnwood Washington 98036
Phone: (206)640-1500
Contact: Jack Wicks

Edmonds Community College
Small Business Development Center
2000 68th Ave., W
Lynwood Washington 98036
Phone: (206)640-1500
Fax: (206)640-1532

Big Bend Community College
Small Business Development Center

7662 Chanute St., Bldg. 1500
Moses Lake Washington 98837
Phone: (509)762-6289
Contact: Ed Baroch

Skagit Valley College
Small Business Development Center
2405 College Way
Mount Vernon Washington 98273
Phone: (206)428-1282
Contact: Peter Stroosma

Okanogan County Council for
Economic Development (OCCED)
Small Business Development Center
Box 741
Okanogan Washington 98840
Phone: (509)826-5107
Fax: (509)826-1812

DTED, Business Assistance Center
Small Business Development Center
PO Box 42516
Olympia Washington 98504
Phone: (206)586-4854

Washington State University (Olympia)
Small Business Development Center
721 Columbia St. SW
Olympia Washington 98501
Phone: (206)753-5616
Contact: Douglas Hammel

Wenatchee Valley College
Small Business Development Center
PO Box 741
Omak Washington 98841
Phone: (509)826-5107
Fax: (509)826-1812

Port Angeles
Small Business Development Center
PO Box 1085
Port Angeles Washington 98362
Phone: (206)457-7793
Fax: (206)452-9618

Washington State University (Pullman)
Small Business Development Center
Kruegle Hall, Ste. 135
Pullman Washington 99164
Phone: (509)335-1576
Contact: Lyle M. Anderson

Duwamish Industrial Education Center
Small Business Development Center
6770 E. Marginal Way S
Seattle Washington 98108
Phone: (206)764-5375
Contact: Ruth Ann Halford

International Trade Institute
North Seattle Community College
Small Business Development Center
9600 College Way N
Seattle Washington 98103
Phone: (206)527-3733
Contact: Ann Tamura

South Seattle Community College
Community College District 6
Small Business Development Center
6000 16th Ave. SW
Seattle Washington 98108
Phone: (206)764-5375
Fax: (206)764-5838

Washington Management Advisory Services
Small Business Development Center
2401 4th Ave., 3rd Fl.
Seattle Washington 98121
Contact: Conrad Rosing

Washington Small Business Development Center (Seattle)
180 Nickerson, Ste. 207
Seattle Washington 98109
Phone: (206)464-5450
Fax: (206)464-6357
Contact: Bill Jacobs

Washington State University (Spokane)
Small Business Development Center
W. 601 1st St.
Spokane Washington 99204
Phone: (509)456-2781
Contact: Terry Chambers

Pierce College
Small Business Development Center
9401 Farwest Dr. SW
Tacoma Washington 98498
Phone: (206)964-6500
Fax: (206)964-6746

Washington Small Business Development Center (Tacoma)
950 Pacific Ave., Ste. 300
PO Box 1933
Tacoma Washington 98401
Phone: (206)272-7232
Contact: Neil Delisanti

Columbia River Economic Development Council
Small Business Development Center
100 E. Columbia Way
Vancouver Washington 98660
Phone: (206)737-2021
Fax: (206)696-6431
Contact: Dennis Hanslits

Wenatchee Small Business Development Center
Grand Central Bldg.
25 N. Wenatchee Ave.
Wenatchee Washington 98801
Phone: (509)662-8016
Contact: Charles DeJong

Yakima Valley College
Small Business Development Center
PO Box 1647
Yakima Washington 98907
Phone: (509)575-2284
Contact: Corey Hansen

West Virginia

West Virginia Small Development Center
1115 Virginia St. E.
E. Capitol Complex
Charleston West Virginia 25301
Phone: (304)348-2960
Contact: Hazel Kroesser

Fairmont State College
Small Business Development Center
Locust Ave.
Fairmont West Virginia 26554
Phone: (304)367-4125
Fax: (304)366-4870

Marshall University
Small Business Development Center
1050 4th Ave.
Huntington West Virginia 25755
Phone: (304)696-3093
Contact: Edna McClain

West Virginia Institute of Technology
Small Business Development Center
Engineering Bldg., Rm. 102
Montgomery West Virginia 25136
Phone: (304)442-5501
Fax: (304)442-3307

West Virginia University
Small Business Development Center
PO Box 6025
Morgantown West Virginia 26506
Phone: (304)293-5839
Fax: (304)293-5652

West Virginia University, Parkersburg
Small Business Development Center
Rte. 5, Box 167-A
Parkersburg West Virginia 26101
Phone: (304)424-8277

Shepherd College
Small Business Development Center
120 N. Princess St.
Shepherdstown West Virginia 25443
Phone: (304)876-5261
Toll Free: 800-344-5231
Fax: (304)876-3101

West Virginia Northern Community College
Small Business Development Center
1701 Market St.
College Sq.
Wheeling West Virginia 26003
Phone: (304)233-5900
Fax: (304)232-8187

Wisconsin

University of Wisconsin--Eau Claire
Small Business Development Center
Schneider Hall, Rm. 113
Eau Claire Wisconsin 54702
Phone: (715)836-5811

University of Wisconsin--Green Bay
Small Business Development Center
460 Wood Hall
Green Bay Wisconsin 54301
Phone: (414)465-2089
Contact: Jim Holly

University of Wisconsin--Parkside
Small Business Development Center
T284, 900 Wood Rd. Box 2000
Kenosha Wisconsin 53141
Phone: (414)595-2189
Contact: Patricia Deutsch

University of Wisconsin--La Crosse
Small Business Development Center
323 N. Hall
La Crosse Wisconsin 54601
Phone: (608)785-8782
Contact: George Weyer

University of Wisconsin--Madison
Small Business Development Center
975 University Ave.
Madison Wisconsin 53706
Phone: (608)263-7680
Contact: Joan Gillman

University of Wisconsin--Milwaukee
Small Business Development Center
929 N. 6th St.
Milwaukee Wisconsin 53203
Phone: (414)227-3240
Contact: Patrick Milne

University of Wisconsin--Oshkosh
Small Business Development Center
Clow Faculty Bldg., Rm. 157
Oshkosh Wisconsin 54901
Phone: (414)424-1453
Contact: John Mozingo

University of Wisconsin--Stevens Point
Small Business Development Center
Lower Level Main Bldg.
Stevens Point Wisconsin 54481
Phone: (715)346-2004
Contact: Mark Stover

University of Wisconsin--Superior
Small Business Development Center
29 Sundquist Hall
Superior Wisconsin 54880
Phone: (715)394-8351
Contact: Loren Erickson

University of Wisconsin--Whitewater
Small Business Development Center
Carlson Bldg., No. 2000
Whitewater Wisconsin 53190
Phone: (414)472-3217
Contact: Carla Lenk

Wyoming

Casper
Small Business Development Center
111 W. 2nd St., Ste. 502
Casper Wyoming 82601
Phone: (307)234-6683
Fax: (307)577-7014

Laramie County Enterprise Center
1400 E. College Dr.
Cheyenne Wyoming 82007
Phone: (307)778-1222
Fax: (307)637-4883

Eastern Wyoming Community College
Small Business Development Center
Douglas Branch
203 S. 6th St.
Douglas Wyoming 82633
Phone: (307)358-5622
Fax: (307)358-5625

Northern Wyoming Community College District
Business and Industry Center
1001 Plaza, Ste. 110
Gillette Wyoming 82716
Phone: (307)686-0297
Fax: (307)682-7927

State Office
Wyoming Small Business Development Center
PO Box 3275
Laramie Wyoming 82071
Phone: (307)766-2363
Contact: Dave Mosley

Northwest Community College
Small Business Development Center
146 S. Bent, No. 103
Powell Wyoming 82435
Phone: (307)686-0254
Toll Free: 800-442-2946

Rock Springs
Small Business Development Center
731C St., No. 321
PO Box 1168
Rock Springs Wyoming 82902
Phone: (307)352-6894
Toll Free: 800-348-5205
Fax: (800)348-5205

Glossary

Glossary of Small Business Terms

ACE
See Active Corps of Executives

Accounts payable
See Trade credit

Active Corps of Executives (ACE)
(See also Service Corps of Retired Executives)
A group of volunteers for a management assistance program of the U.S. Small Business Administration; volunteers provide one-on-one counseling and teach workshops and seminars for small firms.

Adaptation
The process whereby an invention is modified to meet the needs of users.

Adaptive engineering
The process whereby an invention is modified to meet the manufacturing and commercial requirements of a targeted market.

Adverse selection
The tendency for higher-risk individuals to purchase health care and more comprehensive plans, resulting in increased costs.

Agency costs
Costs incurred to insure that the lender or investor maintains control over assets while allowing the borrower or entrepreneur to use them. Monitoring and information costs are the two major types of agency costs.

Antitrust immunity
(See also Collective ratemaking)
Exemption from prosecution under antitrust laws. In the transportation industry, firms with antitrust immunity are permitted—under certain conditions—to set schedules and sometimes prices for the public benefit.

Applied research
Scientific study targeted for use in a product or process.

Asians
A minority category used by the U.S. Bureau of the Census to represent a diverse group that includes Aleuts, Eskimos, American Indians, Asian Indians, Chinese, Japanese, Koreans, Vietnamese, Filipinos, Hawaiians, and other Pacific Islanders.

Assets
Anything of value owned by a company.

Average cost
Total production costs divided by the quantity produced.

Balance Sheet
A financial statement listing the total assets and liabilities of a company at a given time.

Bankruptcy
The condition in which a business cannot meet its debt obligations and petitions a federal district court either for reorganization of its debts or for liquidation of its assets.

Basic research
Theoretical scientific exploration not targeted to application.

Basket clause
A provision specifying the amount of public pension funds that may be placed in investments not included on a state's legal list (see separate citation).

BDC
See Business development corporation

BIDCO
See Business and industrial development company

Birth
See Business birth

Blue chip security
A low-risk, low-yield security representing an interest in a very stable company.

Blue sky laws

A general term that denotes various states' laws regulating securities.

Bond

(See also General obligation bond; Taxable bonds; Treasury bonds)

A written instrument executed by a bidder or contractor (the principal) and a second party (the surety or sureties) to assure fulfillment of the principal's obligations to a third party (the obligee or government) identified in the bond. If the principal's obligations are not met, the bond assures payment to the extent stipulated of any loss sustained by the obligee.

Bonding requirements

Terms contained in a bond (see separate citation).

Brand name

The part of a brand, trademark, or service mark that can be spoken. It can be a word, letter, or group of words or letters.

Bridge financing

A short-term loan made in expectation of intermediate-term or long-term financing. Can be used when a company plans to go public in the near future.

Broker

One who matches resources available for innovation with those who need them.

Business and industrial development company (BIDCO)

A private, for-profit financing corporation chartered by the state to provide both equity and long-term debt capital to small business owners (see separate citations for equity and debt capital).

Business birth

The formation of a new establishment or enterprise. The appearance of a new establishment or enterprise in the Small Business Data Base (see separate citation).

Business contractions

The number of establishments that have decreased in employment during a specified time.

Business death

The voluntary or involuntary closure of a firm or establishment. The disappearance of an establishment or enterprise from the Small Business Data Base (see separate citation).

Business development corporation (BDC)

A business financing agency, usually composed of the financial institutions in an area or state, organized to assist in financing businesses unable to obtain assistance through normal channels; the risk is spread among various members of the business development corporation, and interest rates may vary somewhat from those charged by member institutions. A venture capital firm in which shares of ownership are publicly held and to which the Investment Act of 1940 applies.

Business dissolution

For enumeration purposes, the absence of a business that was present in the prior time period from any current record.

Business entry

See Business birth

Business exit

See Business death

Business expansions

The number of establishments that added employees during a specified time.

Business failure

Closure of a business causing a loss to at least one creditor.

Business format franchising

(See also Franchising)

The purchase of the name, trademark, and an ongoing business plan of the parent corporation or franchisor by the franchisee.

Business license

A legal authorization in document form issued by municipal and state governments and required for business operations.

Business name

(See also Business license; Trademark)

Enterprises must register their business names with local governments usually on a "doing business as" (DBA) form. (This name is sometimes referred to as a "fictional name.") The procedure is part of the business licensing process and prevents any other business from using that same name for a similar business in the same locality.

Business norms
See Financial ratios

Business permit
See Business license

Business plan
A document that spells out a company's expected course of action for a specified period, usually including a detailed listing and analysis of risks and uncertainties. For the small business, it should examine the proposed products, the market, the industry, the management policies, the marketing policies, production needs, and financial needs. Frequently, it is used as a prospectus for potential investors and lenders.

Business proposal
See Business plan.

Business service firm
An establishment primarily engaged in rendering services to other business organizations on a fee or contract basis.

Business start
For enumeration purposes, a business with a name or similar designation that did not exist in the prior time period.

Cafeteria plan
See Flexible benefit plan

Capacity
Level of a firm's, industry's, or nation's output corresponding to full practical utilization of available resources.

Capital
Assets less liabilities, representing the ownership interest in a business. A stock of accumulated goods, especially at a specified time and in contrast to income received during a specified time period. Accumulated goods devoted to production. Accumulated possessions calculated to bring income.

Capital intensity
(See also Debt capital; Equity midrisk venture capital; Informal capital; Internal capital; Owner's capital; Second-hand capital; Seed capital; Venture capital)
The relative importance of capital in the production process, usually expressed as the ratio of capital to labor but also sometimes as the ratio of capital to output.

Caribbean Basin Initiative
An interdisciplinary program to support commerce among the businesses in the nations of the Caribbean Basin and the United States. Agencies involved include the Agency for International Development, the U.S. Small Business Administration, the International Trade Administration of the U.S. Department of Commerce, and private sector groups.

Catastrophic care
Medical and other services for acute and long-term illnesses that cost more than insurance coverage limits or that cost the amount most families may be expected to pay with their own resources.

CDC
See Certified development corporation

Certified development corporation (CDC)
A local area or statewide corporation or authority (for profit or nonprofit) that packages U.S. Small Business Administration (SBA), bank, state, and/or private money into financial assistance for existing business capital improvements. The SBA holds the second lien on its maximum share of 40 percent involvement. Each state has at least one certified development corporation. This program is called the SBA 503 Program.

Certified lenders
Banks that participate in the SBA guaranteed loan program (see separate citation). Such banks must have a good track record with the U.S. Small Business Administration (SBA) and must agree to certain conditions set forth by the agency. In return, the SBA agrees to process any guaranteed loan application within three business days.

Champion
An advocate for the development of an innovation.

Closely held corporation
A corporation in which the shares are held by a few persons, usually officers, employees, or others close to the management; these shares are rarely offered to the public.

Code of Federal Regulations
Codification of general and permanent rules of the federal government published in the Federal Register.

Code sharing
See Computer code sharing

GLOSSARY

Coinsurance

(See also Cost sharing)

Upon meeting the deductible payment, health insurance participants may be required to make additional health care cost-sharing payments. Coinsurance is a payment of a fixed percentage of the cost of each service; copayment is usually a fixed amount to be paid with each service.

Collateral

Securities, evidence of deposit, or other property pledged by a borrower to secure repayment of a loan.

Collective ratemaking

(See also Antitrust immunity)

The establishment of uniform charges for services by a group of businesses in the same industry.

Commercial insurance plan

See Underwriting

Commercialization

The final stage of the innovation process, including production and distribution.

Common stock

The most frequently used instrument for purchasing ownership in private or public companies. Common stock generally carries the right to vote on certain corporate actions and may pay dividends, although it rarely does in venture investments. In liquidation, common stockholders are the last to share in the proceeds from the sale of a corporation's assets; bondholders and preferred shareholders have priority. Common stock is often used in first-round start-up financing.

Community development corporation

A corporation established to develop economic programs for a community and, in most cases, to provide financial support for such development.

Computer code sharing

An arrangement whereby flights of a regional airline are identified by the two-letter code of a major carrier in the computer reservation system to help direct passengers to new regional carriers.

Consortium

A coalition of organizations such as banks and corporations for ventures requiring large capital resources.

Consumer price index

A measure of the fluctuation in prices between two points in time.

Continuation coverage

Health coverage offered for a specified period of time to employees who leave their jobs and to their widows, divorced spouses, or dependents.

Contractions

See Business contractions

Convertible preferred stock

A class of stock that pays a reasonable dividend and is convertible into common stock (see separate citation). Generally the convertible feature may only be exercised after being held for a stated period of time. This arrangement is usually considered second-round financing when a company needs equity to maintain its cash flow.

Convertible securities

A feature of certain bonds, debentures, or preferred stocks that allows them to be exchanged by the owner for another class of securities at a future date and in accordance with any other terms of the issue.

Copayment

See Coinsurance

Copyright

A legal form of protection available to creators and authors to safeguard their works from unlawful use or claim of ownership by others. Copyrights may be acquired for works of art, sculpture, music, and published or unpublished manuscripts. All copyrights should be registered at the Copyright Office of the Library of Congress.

Corporate financial ratios

(See also Industry financial ratios)

A relationship between key figures found in a company's financial statement. The relationship is in the form of a numeric value, and is used to evaluate risk and company performance. Also known as Financial averages, Operating ratios, and Business ratios.

Corporation

A legal entity, chartered by a state or the federal government, recognized as a separate entity having its own rights, privileges, and liabilities distinct from those of its members.

Cost containment

Actions taken by employers and insurers to curtail rising healthcare costs; for example, increasing employee cost sharing (see separate citation), requiring second opinions, or preadmission screening.

Cost sharing

The requirement that health care consumers contribute to their own medical care costs through deductibles and coinsurance (see separate citations). Cost sharing does not include the amounts paid in premiums. It is used to control utilization of services; for example, requiring a fixed amount to be paid with each health care service.

Cottage industry

(See also Home-based business)
Businesses based in the home in which the family units are the labor force and family-owned equipment is used to process the goods.

Credit Rating

A letter or number calculated by an organization (such as Dun & Bradstreet) to represent the ability and disposition of a business to meet its financial obligations.

Cyclical peak

The upper turning point in a business cycle.

Cyclical trough

The lower turning point in a business cycle.

DBA

See Business name

Death

See Business death

Debenture

A certificate given as acknowledgment of a debt (see separate citation) secured by the general credit of the issuing corporation. A bond, usually without security, issued by a corporation and sometimes convertible to common stock.

Debt

(See also Long-term debt; Mid-term debt; Securitized debt; Short-term debt)
Something owed by one person to another. Financing in which a company receives capital that must be repaid; no ownership is transferred.

Debt capital

Business financing that normally requires periodic interest payments and repayment of the principal within a specified time.

Debt financing

See Debt capital

Debt securities

Loans such as bonds and notes that provide a specified rate of return for a specified period of time.

Deductible

A set amount that an individual must pay before any benefits are received.

Demand shock absorbers

A term used to describe the role that some small firms play by expanding their output levels to accommodate a transient surge in demand.

Demonstration

Showing that a product or process has been modified sufficiently to meet the needs of users.

Deregulation

The lifting of government restrictions; for example, the lifting of government restrictions on the entry of new businesses, the expansion of services, and the setting of prices in particular industries.

Disaster loans

Various types of physical and economic assistance available to individuals and businesses through the U.S. Small Business Administration (SBA). This is the only SBA loan program available for residential purposes.

Diseconomies of scale

The condition in which the costs of production increase faster than the volume of production.

Dissolution

See Business dissolution

Distribution

Delivering a product or process to the user.

GLOSSARY

Doing business as (DBA)
See Business name

Economic efficiency
The use of productive resources to the fullest practical extent in the provision of the set of goods and services that is most preferred by purchasers in the economy.

Economically disadvantaged
See Socially and economically disadvantaged

Economies of scale
See Scale economies

8(a) Program
A program authorized by the Small Business Act that directs federal contracts to small businesses owned and operated by socially and economically disadvantaged individuals.

Employee leasing
A contract by which employers arrange to have their workers hired by a leasing company and then leased back to them for a management fee. The leasing company typically assumes the administrative burden of payroll and provides a benefit package to the workers.

Employee tenure
The length of time an employee works for a particular employer.

Employer identification number
The business equivalent of a social security number. Assigned by the U.S. Internal Revenue Service.

Enterprise
An aggregation of all establishments owned by a parent company. An enterprise may consist of a single, independent establishment or include subsidiaries and other branches under the same ownership and control.

Entrepreneur
A person who takes the risk of organizing and operating a new business venture.

Entry
See Business entry

Equity
(See also Common Stock; Equity midrisk venture capital)

The ownership interest. Financing in which partial or total ownership of a company is surrendered in exchange for capital. An investor's financial return comes from dividend payments and from growth in the net worth of the business.

Equity capital
See Equity; Equity midrisk venture capital

Equity financing
See Equity; Equity midrisk venture capital

Equity midrisk venture capital
An unsecured investment in a company. Usually a purchase of ownership interest in a company that occurs in the later stages of a company's development.

Equity partnership
A limited partnership arrangement for providing start-up and seed capital to businesses.

Equity securities
See Equity

Equity-type
Debt financing subordinated to conventional debt.

Establishment
A single-location business unit that may be independent (a single-establishment enterprise) or owned by a parent enterprise.

Establishment and Enterprise Microdata File
See U.S. Establishment and Enterprise Microdata File

Establishment birth
See Business birth

Establishment Longitudinal Microdata File
See U.S. Establishment Longitudinal Microdata File

Evaluation
Determining the potential success of translating an invention into a product or process.

Experience rating
See Underwriting

Exit
See Business exit

Export license

A general or specific license granted by the U.S. Department of Commerce required of anyone wishing to export goods. Some restricted articles need approval from the U.S. Departments of State, Defense, or Energy.

Failure

See Business failure

Fair share agreement

(See also Franchising)
An agreement reached between a franchisor and a minority business organization to extend business ownership to minorities by either reducing the amount of capital required or by setting aside certain marketing areas for minority business owners.

Feasibility study

A study to determine the likelihood that a proposed product or development will fulfill the objectives of a particular investor.

Fictional name

See Business name

Fiduciary

An individual or group that hold assets in trust for a beneficiary.

Financial analysis

The techniques used to determine money needs in a business. Techniques include ratio analysis, calculation of return on investment, guides for measuring profitability, and break-even analysis to determine ultimate success.

Financial intermediary

A financial institution that acts as the intermediary between borrowers and lenders. Banks, savings and loan associations, finance companies, and venture capital companies are major financial intermediaries in the United States.

Financial ratios

See Corporate financial ratios; Industry financial ratios

Financing

See First-stage financing; Second-stage financing; Third-stage financing

First-stage financing

(See also Second-stage financing; Third-stage financing)
Financing provided to companies that have expended their initial capital, and require funds to start full-scale manufacturing and sales. Also known as First-round financing.

503 Program

See Certified development corporation

Flexible benefit plan

A plan that offers a choice among cash and/or qualified benefits such as group term life insurance, accident and health insurance, group legal services, dependent care assistance, and vacations.

FOB

See Free on board

Format franchising

See Business format franchising; Franchising

Franchising

A form of licensing by which the owner—the franchisor—distributes or markets a product, method, or service through affiliated dealers called franchisees. The product, method, or service being marketed is identified by a brand name, and the franchisor maintains control over the marketing methods employed. The franchisee is often given exclusive access to a defined geographic area.

Free on board (FOB)

A pricing term indicating that the quoted price includes the cost of loading goods into transport vessels at a specified place.

Frictional unemployment

See Unemployment

Full-time workers

Generally, those who work a regular schedule of more than 35 hours per week.

Garment registration number

A number that must appear on every garment sold in the United States to indicate the manufacturer of the garment, which may not be the same as the label under which the garment is sold. The U.S. Federal Trade Commission assigns garment registration numbers.

Gatekeeper

A key contact point for entry into a network.

GDP

See Gross domestic product

General obligation bond

A municipal bond secured by the taxing power of the munici-pality. The Tax Reform Act of 1986 limits the purposes for which such bonds may be issued and establishes volume limits on the extent of their issuance.

GNP

See Gross national product

Goods sector

All businesses producing tangible goods, including agricul-ture, mining, construction, and manufacturing businesses.

GPO

See Gross product originating

Gross domestic product (GDP)

The part of the nation's gross national product (see separate citation) generated by private business using resources from within the country.

Gross national product (GNP)

The most comprehensive single measure of aggregate eco-nomic output. Represents the market value of the total output of goods and services produced by a nation's economy.

Gross product originating (GPO)

A measure of business output estimated from the income or production side using employee compensation, profit income, net interest, capital consumption, and indirect business taxes.

HAL

See Handicapped assistance loan program

Handicapped assistance loan program (HAL)

Low-interest direct loan program through the U.S. Small Business Administration (SBA) for handicapped persons. The SBA requires that these persons demonstrate that their disability is such that it is impossible for them to secure employment, thus making it necessary to go into their own business to make a living.

Health maintenance organization (HMO)

An organization of physicians and other health care profes-sionals who provide a wide range of services to subscribers and their dependents on a prepaid basis

Health provider

An individual or institution that gives medical care. Under Medicare, an institutional provider is a hospital, skilled nursing facility, home health agency, or provider of certain physical therapy services.

Hispanic

A person of Cuban, Mexican, Puerto Rican, Latin American (Central or South American), European Spanish, or other Spanish-speaking origin or ancestry.

HMO

See Health maintenance organization

Home-based business

(See also Cottage industry)

A business with an operating address that is also a residential address (usually the residential address of the proprietor).

Hub-and-spoke system

A system in which flights of an airline from many different cities (the spokes) converge at a single airport (the hub). After allowing passengers sufficient time to make connections, planes then depart for different cities.

Idea

An original concept for a new product or process.

Income

Money or its equivalent, earned or accrued, resulting from the sale of goods and services.

Income statement

A financial statement that lists the profits and losses of a company at a given time.

Incorporation

The filing of a certificate of incorporation with a state's secretary of state, thereby limiting the business owner's liability.

Incubator

A facility designed to encourage entrepreneurship and mini-mize obstacles to new business formation and growth, particularly for high-technology firms, by housing a number of fledgling enterprises that share an array of services, such as meeting areas, secretarial services, accounting, research library, on-site financial and management counseling, and word processing facilities.

Independent contractor

An individual considered self-employed (see separate citation) and responsible for paying Social Security taxes and income taxes on earnings.

Indirect health coverage

Health insurance obtained through another individual's health care plan; for example, a spouse's employer-sponsored plan.

Industrial development authority

The financial arm of a state or other political subdivision established for the purpose of financing economic development in an area, usually through loans to nonprofit organizations, which in turn provide facilities for manufacturing and other industrial operations.

Industry financial ratios

(See also Corporate financial ratios)

Corporate financial ratios averaged for a specified industry. These are used for comparison purposes and reveal industry trends and identify differences between the performance of a specific company and the performance of its industry. Also known as Industrial averages, Industry ratios, Financial averages, and Business or Industrial norms.

Inflation

Increases in volume of currency and credit, generally resulting in a sharp and continuing rise in price levels.

Informal capital

Financing from informal, unorganized sources; includes informal debt capital such as trade credit or loans from friends and relatives and informal equity capital from informal investors.

Initial public offering (IPO)

A corporation's first offering of stock to the public.

Innovation

The introduction of a new idea into the marketplace in the form of a new product or service or an improvement in organization or process.

Internal capital

Debt or equity financing obtained from the owner or through retained business earnings.

Intrapreneurship

The state of employing entrepreneurial principles to nonentrepreneurial situations.

Invention

The tangible form of a technological idea, which could include a laboratory prototype, drawings, formulas, etc.

IPO

See Initial public offering

Job tenure

A period of time during which an individual is continuously employed in the same job.

Joint marketing agreements

Agreements between regional and major airlines, often involving the coordination of flight schedules, fares, and baggage transfer. These agreements help regional carriers operate at lower cost.

Joint venture

Venture in which two or more people combine efforts in a particular business enterprise, usually a single transaction or a limited activity, and agree to share the profits and losses jointly or in proportion to their contributions.

Labor force

Civilians considered eligible for employment who are also willing and able to work.

Labor force participation rate

The civilian labor force as a percentage of the civilian population.

Labor intensity

(See also Capital intensity)

The relative importance of labor in the production process, usually measured as the capital-labor ratio; i.e., the ratio of units of capital (typically, dollars of tangible assets) to the number of employees. The higher the capital-labor ratio exhibited by a firm or industry, the lower the capital intensity of that firm or industry is said to be.

Labor surplus area

An area in which there exists a high unemployment rate. In

procurement (see separate citation), extra points are given to firms in counties that are designated a labor surplus area; this information is requested on procurement bid sheets.

Laboratory prototype

See Prototype

Large business-dominated industry

Industry in which a minimum of 60 percent of employment or sales is in firms with more than 500 workers.

LBO

See Leveraged buy-out

Legal list

A list of securities selected by a state in which certain institutions and fiduciaries (such as pension funds, insurance companies, and banks) may invest. Securities not on the list are not eligible for investment. Legal lists typically restrict investments to high quality securities meeting certain specifications. Generally, investment is limited to U.S. securities and investment-grade blue chip securities (see separate citation).

Leveraged buy-out (LBO)

The purchase of a business or a division of a corporation through a highly leveraged financing package.

License

(See also Business license)

A legal agreement granting to another the right to use a technological innovation.

Limited partnerships

See Venture capital limited partnerships

Liquidity

The ability to convert a security into cash promptly. Loans.

Loans

See Disaster loans; SBA direct loans; SBA guaranteed loans; SBA special lending institution categories

Local development corporation

An organization, usually made up of local citizens of a community, designed to improve the economy of the area by inducing business and industry to locate and expand there. A local development corporation establishes a capability to finance local growth.

Long-haul rates

Rates charged by a transporter in which the distance travelled is more than 800 miles.

Long-term debt

An obligation that matures in a period that exceeds five years.

Low-grade bond

A corporate bond that is rated below investment grade by the major rating agencies (Standard and Poor's, Moody's).

Macro-efficiency

(See also Economic efficiency)

Efficiency as it pertains to the operation of markets and market systems.

Management and technical assistance

A term used by many programs to mean business (as opposed to technological) assistance.

Management Assistance Programs

See SBA Management Assistance Programs

Mandated benefits

Specific treatments, providers, or individuals required by law to be included in commercial health plans.

Market evaluation

The use of market information to determine the sales potential of a specific product or process.

Market failure

The situation in which the workings of a competitive market do not produce the best results from the point of view of the entire society.

Market information

Data of any type that can be used for market evaluation, which could include demographic data, technology forecasting, regulatory changes, etc.

Market research

A systematic collection, analysis, and reporting of data about the market and its preferences, opinions, trends, and plans; used for corporate decision-making.

Master Establishment List (MEL)

A list of firms in the United States developed by the U.S. Small Business Administration; firms can be selected by industry, region, state, standard metropolitan statistical area (see separate citation), county, and zip code.

Maturity

(See also Term)

The date upon which the principal or stated value of a bond or other indebtedness becomes due and payable.

Medicaid (Title XIX)

A federally aided, state-operated and administered program that provides medical benefits for certain low-income persons in need of health and medical care who are eligible for one of the governments's welfare cash payment programs, including the aged, the blind, the disabled, and members of families with dependent children where one parent is absent, incapacitated, or unemployed.

Medicare (Title XVIII)

A nationwide health insurance program for disabled and aged persons. Health insurance is available to insured persons without regard to income. Monies from payroll taxes cover hospital insurance and monies from general revenues and beneficiary premiums pay for supplementary medical insurance.

MEL

See Master Establishment List

Metropolitan statistical area (MSA)

A means used by the government to define large population centers that may transverse different governmental jurisdictions. For example, the Washington, D.C., MSA includes the District of Columbia and contiguous parts of Maryland and Virginia because all of these geopolitical areas comprise one population and economic operating unit.

Mezzanine financing

See Third-stage financing

MESBIC

See Minority enterprise small business investment corporation

MET

See Multiple employer trust

Micro-efficiency

(See also Economic efficiency)

Efficiency as it pertains to the operation of individual firms.

Microdata

Information on the characteristics of an individual business firm.

Mid-term debt

An obligation that matures within one to five years.

Midrisk venture capital

See Equity midrisk venture capital

Minimum premium plan

A combination approach to funding an insurance plan aimed primarily at premium tax savings. The employer self-funds a fixed percentage of estimated monthly claims and the insurance company insures the excess.

Minority Business Development Agency

Contracts with private firms throughout the nation to sponsor Minority Business Development Centers to provide minority firms with advice and technical assistance on a fee basis.

Minority enterprise small business investment corporation (MESBIC)

A federally funded private venture capital firm licensed by the U.S. Small Business Administration to provide capital to minority-owned businesses (see separate citation).

Minority-owned business

Businesses owned by those who are socially or economically disadvantaged (see separate citation).

Mom and Pop business

A small store or enterprise having limited capital, principally employing family members.

Moonlighter

A wage-and-salary worker with a side business.

MSA

See Metropolitan statistical area

Multi-employer plan

A health plan to which more than one employer is required to contribute and that may be maintained through a collective bargaining agreement and required to meet standards prescribed by the U.S. Department of Labor.

Multiple employer trust (MET)
A self-funded benefit plan generally geared toward small employers sharing a common interest.

National income
Aggregate earnings of labor and property arising from the production of goods and services in a nation's economy.

Net assets
See Net worth

Net income
The amount remaining from earnings and profits after all expenses and costs have been met or deducted. Also known as Net earnings.

Net worth
(See also Capital)
The difference between a company's total assets and its total liabilities.

Network
A chain of interconnected individuals or organizations sharing information and/or services.

Nonbank bank
A bank that either accepts deposits or makes loans, but not both. Used to create many new branch banks.

Noncompetitive awards
A method of contracting whereby the federal government negotiates with only one contractor to supply a product or service.

Nonprofit
An organization that has no shareholders, does not distribute profits, and is without federal and state tax liabilities.

Norms
See Financial ratios

Optimal firm size
The business size at which the production cost per unit of output (average cost) is, in the long run, at its minimum.

Owner's capital
Debt or equity funds provided by the owner(s) of a business; sources of owner's capital are personal savings, sales of assets, or loans from financial institutions.

P & L
See Profit and loss statement

Part-time workers
Normally, those who work less than 35 hours per week. The Tax Reform Act indicated that part-time workers who work less than 17.5 hours per week may be excluded from health plans for purposes of complying with federal nondiscrimination rules.

Part-year workers
Employees who work less than 50 weeks per year.

Partnership
Two or more parties who enter into a legal relationship to conduct business for profit. Defined by the U.S. Internal Revenue Code as joint ventures, syndicates, groups, pools, and other associations of two or more persons organized for profit that are not specifically classified in the IRS code as corporations or proprietorships.

Patent
A grant made by the government to an inventor, assuring the sole right to make, use, and sell an invention for a period of 17 years.

PC
See Professional corporation

Peak
See Cyclical peak

Pension
A series of payments made monthly, semiannually, annually, or at other specified intervals during the lifetime of the pensioner. The term is sometimes used to denote the portion of the retirement allowance financed by the employer's contributions.

Pension fund
A fund established to provide for the payment of pension benefits; the collective contributions made by all of the parties to the pension plan.

Permit
See Business license

Plan
See Business plan

Pooling
An arrangement for employers to achieve efficiencies and lower health costs by joining together to purchase group health insurance or self-insurance.

PPO
See Preferred provider organization

Preferred lenders program
See SBA special lending institution categories

Preferred provider organization (PPO)
A contractual arrangement with a health care services organization that agrees to discount rates in return for faster payment and/or a patient base.

Premiums
The amount of money paid to an insurer for health insurance under a policy. The premium is generally paid periodically (e.g., monthly), and often is split between the employer and the employee. Unlike deductibles and coinsurance or copayments (see separate citations), premiums are paid for coverage whether or not benefits are actually used.

Prime-age workers
Employees 25 to 54 years of age.

Prime contract
A contract awarded directly by the U.S. Federal Government.

Private company
See Closely held corporation

Private placement
A method of raising capital by offering for sale an investment or business to a small group of investors (generally avoiding registration with the Securities and Exchange Commission or state securities registration agencies). Also known as Private financing or Private offering.

Procurement
(See also 8(a) Program; Small business set asides)
A contract from an agency of the federal government for goods orservices from a small business.

Product development
The stage of the innovation process where research is translated into a product or process through evaluation, adaptation, and demonstration.

Product franchising
An arrangement for a franchisee to use the name and to produce the product line of the franchisor or parent corporation.

Production
The manufacture of a product.

Production prototype
See Prototype

Professional corporation (PC)
Organized by members of a profession such as medicine, dentistry, or law for the purpose of conducting their professional activities as a corporation. Liability of a member or shareholder is limited in the same manner as in a business corporation.

Profit and loss statement (P & L)
The summary of the incomes (total revenues) and costs of a company's operation during a specific period of time. Also known as income and expense statement.

Proposal
See Business plan

Proprietorship
The most common legal form of business ownership; about 85 percent of all small businesses are proprietorships. The liability of the owner is unlimited in this form of ownership.

Prospective payment system
A cost-containment measure included in the Social Security Amendments of 1983 whereby Medicare payments to hospitals are based on established prices, rather than on cost reimbursement.

Prototype
A model that demonstrates the validity of the concept of an invention (laboratory prototype); a model that meets the needs of the manufacturing process and the user (production prototype).

Prudent investor rule or standard
A legal doctrine that requires fiduciaries to make investments using the prudence, diligence, and intelligence that would be used by a prudent person in making similar investments. Because fiduciaries make investments on behalf of third-party beneficiaries, the standard results in very conservative in-

vestments. Until recently, most state regulations required the fiduciary to apply this standard to each investment. Newer, more progressive regulations permit fiduciaries to apply this standard to the portfolio taken as a whole, thereby allowing a fiduciary to balance a portfolio with higher-yield, higher-risk investments. In states with more progressive regulations, practically every type of security is eligible for inclusion in the portfolio of investments made by a fiduciary, provided that the portfolio investments, in their totality, are those of a prudent person.

Public equity markets

Organized markets for trading in equity shares such as common stocks, preferred stocks, and warrants. Includes markets for both regularly traded and nonregularly traded securities.

Public offering

General solicitation for participation in an investment opportunity. Interstate public offerings are supervised by the U.S. Securities and Exchange Commission.

Rate of return

(See also Yield)

The yield obtained on a security or other investment based on its purchase price or its current market price. The total rate of return is current income plus or minus capital appreciation or depreciation.

Realignment

See Resource realignment

Recession

Contraction of economic activity occurring between the peak and trough (see separate citations) of a business cycle.

Regulated market

A market in which the government controls the forces of supply and demand, such as who may enter and what price may be charged.

Regulation D

A vehicle by which small businesses make small offerings and private placements of securities with limited disclosure requirements. It was designed to ease the burdens imposed on small businesses utilizing this method of capital formation.

Regulatory Flexibility Act

An act requiring federal agencies to evaluate the impact of their regulations on small businesses before the regulations are issued and to consider less burdensome alternatives.

Research

The initial stage of the innovation process, which includes idea generation and invention.

Research and development financing

A tax-advantaged partnership set up to finance product development for start-ups as well as more mature companies.

Resource mobility

The ease with which labor and capital move from firm to firm or from industry to industry.

Resource realignment

The adjustment of productive resources to interindustry changes in demand.

Resources

The sources of support or help in the innovation process, including sources of financing, technical evaluation, market evaluation, management and business assistance, etc.

Retained business earnings

Business profits that are retained by the business rather than being distributed to the shareholders as dividends.

Risk capital

See Venture capital

S corporations

See Sub chapter S corporations

SBA

See Small Business Administration

SBA direct loans

Loans made directly by the U.S. Small Business Administration (SBA); monies come from funds appropriated specifically for this purpose. In general, SBA direct loans carry interest rates slightly lower than those in the private financial markets and are available only to applicants unable to secure private financing or an SBA guaranteed loan.

SBA 503 Program

See Certified development corporation

SBA guaranteed loans

Loans made by lending institutions in which the U.S. Small

Business Administration (SBA) will pay a prior agreed-upon percentage of the outstanding principal in the event the borrower of the loan defaults. The terms of the loan and the interest rate are negotiated between the borrower and the lending institution, within set parameters.

SBA loans

See Disaster loans; SBA direct loans; SBA guaranteed loans; SBA special lending institution categories

SBA Management Assistance Programs

(See also Active Corps of Executives; Service Corps of Retired Executives; Small business institutes program)
Classes, workshops, counseling, and publications offered by the U.S. Small Business Administration (SBA).

SBA special lending institution categories

U.S. Small Business Administration (SBA) loan program in which the SBA promises certified banks a 72-hour turnaround period in giving its approval for a loan, and in which preferred lenders in a pilot program are allowed to write SBA loans without seeking prior SBA approval.

SBDB

See Small Business Data Base

SBDC

See Small business development centers

SBI

See Small business institutes program

SBIC

See Small business investment corporation

SBIR Program

See Small Business Innovation Development Act of 1982

Scale economies

The decline of the production cost per unit of output (average cost) as the volume of output increases.

Scale efficiency

The reduction in unit cost available to a firm when producing at a higher output volume.

SCORE

See Service Corps of Retired Executives

Second-stage financing

(See also First-stage financing; Third-stage financing)
The working capital for the initial expansion of a company that is producing and shipping and has growing accounts receivable and inventories. Also known as Second-round financing.

Secondary market

A market established for the purchase and sale of outstanding securities following their initial distribution.

Secondary worker

Any worker in a family other than the person who is the primary source of income for the family.

Secondhand capital

Previously used and subsequently resold capital equipment (e.g., buildings and machinery).

Securitized debt

A marketing technique that converts long-term loans to marketable securities.

Seed capital

Venture financing provided in the early stages of the innovation process, usually during product development.

Self-employed person

One who works for a profit or fees in his or her own business, profession, or trade, or who operates a farm.

Self-funding

A health benefit plan in which a firm uses its own funds to pay claims, rather than transferring the financial risks of paying claims to an outside insurer in exchange for premium payments.

Service Corps of Retired Executives (SCORE)

(See also Active Corps of Executives)
Volunteers for the SBA Management Assistance Program who provide one-on-one counseling and teach workshops and seminars for small firms.

Service firm

See Business service firm

Service sector

Broadly defined, all U.S. industries that produce intangibles, including the five major industry divisions of transportation, communications, and utilities; wholesale trade; retail trade;

finance, insurance, and real estate; and services.

Set asides

See Small business set asides

Short-haul service

A type of transportation service in which the transporter supplies service between cities where the maximum distance is no more than 200 miles.

Short-term debt

An obligation that matures in one year.

SIC codes

See Standard Industrial Classification codes

Single-establishment enterprise

See Establishment

Small business

An enterprise that is independently owned and operated, is not dominant in its field, and employs fewer than 500 people. For SBA purposes, the U.S. Small Business Administration (SBA) considers various other factors (such as gross annual sales) in determining size of a business.

Small Business Administration (SBA)

An independent agency of the federal government which provides assistance in loans, management, and advocating interests before other federal agencies.

Small Business Data Base

(See also U.S. Establishment and Enterprise Microdata File; U.S. Establishment Longitudinal Microdata File)
A collection of microdata (see separate citation) files on individual firms developed and maintained by the U.S. Small Business Administration.

Small business development centers (SBDC)

Centers that provide support services to small businesses, such as individual counseling, SBA advice, seminars and conferences, and other learning center activities. Most services are free of charge, or available at minimal cost.

Small business development corporation

See Certified development corporation

Small business-dominated industry

Industry in which a minimum of 60 percent of employment or

sales is in firms with fewer than 500 employees.

Small Business Innovation Development Act of 1982

Federal statute requiring federal agencies with large extramural research and development budgets to allocate a certain percentage of these funds to small research and development firms. The program, called the Small Business Innovation Research (SBIR) Program, is designed to stimulate technological innovation and make greater use of small businesses in meeting national innovation needs.

Small business institutes (SBI) program

Cooperative arrangements made by U.S. Small Business Administration district offices and local colleges and universities to provide small business firms with graduate students to counsel them without charge.

Small business investment corporation (SBIC)

A privately owned company licensed and funded through the U.S. Small Business Administration and private sector sources to provide equity or debt capital to small businesses.

Small business set asides

Procurement (see separate citation) opportunities required by law to be on all contracts under $10,000 or a certain percentage of an agency's total procurement expenditure.

Smaller firms

For U.S. Department of Commerce purposes, those firms not included in the Fortune 1000.

SMSA

See Metropolitan statistical area

Socially and economically disadvantaged

Individuals who have been subjected to racial or ethnic prejudice or cultural bias because of their identity as a member of a group, without regard to their qualities as individuals, and whose abilities to compete are impaired because of diminished opportunities to obtain capital and credit.

Sole proprietorship

An unincorporated, one-owner business, farm, or professional practice.

Special lending institution categories

See SBA special lending institution categories

Standard Industrial Classification (SIC) codes

Four-digit codes established by the U.S. Federal Government to categorize businesses by type of economic activity; the first two digits correspond to major groups such as construction and manufacturing, while the last two digits correspond to subgroups such as home construction or highway construction.

Standard metropolitan statistical area (SMSA)

See Metropolitan statistical area

Start

See Business start

Start-up financing

Financing provided to companies either completing product development and initial marketing or already in business for one year or less, but that have not sold their product commercially.

Stock

(See also Common stock; Convertible preferred stock)
A certificate of equity ownership in a business.

Stop-loss coverage

Insurance for a self-insured plan that reimburses the company for any losses it might incur in its health claims beyond a specified amount.

Structural unemployment

See Unemployment

Sub chapter S corporations

Corporations that are considered noncorporate for tax purposes but legally remain corporations.

Subcontract

A contract between a prime contractor and a subcontractor, or between subcontractors, to furnish supplies or services for performance of a prime contract or a subcontract.

Surety bonds

Bonds providing reimbursement to an individual, company, or the government if a firm fails to complete a contract. The U.S. Small Business Administration guarantees surety bonds in a program much like the SBA guaranteed loan program (see separate citation).

Swing loan

See Bridge financing

Target market

The clients or customers sought for a business' product or service.

Tax number

(See also Employer identification number)
A number assigned to a business by a state revenue department that enables the business to buy goods wholesale without paying sales tax.

Taxable bonds

An interest-bearing certificate of public or private indebtedness. Bonds are issued by public agencies to finance economic development.

Technical assistance

See Management and technical assistance

Technical evaluation

The assessment of technological feasibility.

Technology

The method in which a firm combines and utilizes labor and capital resources to produce goods or services; the application of science for commercial or industrial purposes.

Technology transfer

The movement of information about a technology or intellectual property from one party to another for use.

Tenure

See Employee tenure

Term

(See also Maturity)
The length of time for which a loan is made.

Terms of a note

The conditions or limits of a note; includes the interest rate per annum, the due date, and transferability and convertibility features, if any.

Third-party administrator

An outside company responsible for handling claims and performing administrative tasks associated with health insurance plan maintenance.

Third-stage financing
(See also First-stage financing; Second-stage financing)
Financing provided for the major expansion of a company whose sales volume is increasing and that is breaking even or profitable. These funds are used for further plant expansion, marketing, working capital, or development of an improved product. Also known as Third-round or Mezzanine financing.

Time deposit
A bank deposit that cannot be withdrawn before a specified future time.

Trade credit
Credit extended by suppliers of raw materials or finished products. In an accounting statement, trade credit is referred to as "accounts payable."

Trade name
The name under which a company conducts business, or by which its business, goods, or services are identified. It may or may not be registered as a trademark.

Trademark
A graphic symbol, device, or slogan that identifies a business. A business has property rights to its trademark from the inception of its use; however, it is still prudent to register all trademarks with the Trademark Office of the U.S. Department of Commerce.

Translation
See Product development

Treasury bills
Investment tender issued by the Federal Reserve Bank in amounts of $10,000 that mature in 91 to 182 days.

Treasury bonds
Long-term notes with maturity dates of not less than seven and not more than twenty-five years.

Treasury notes
Short-term notes maturing in less than seven years.

Trough
See Cyclical trough

UL
See Underwriters Laboratories

Underwriters Laboratories (UL)
One of several private firms that tests products and processes to determine their safety. Although various firms can provide this kind of testing service, many local and insurance codes specify UL certification.

Underwriting
A process by which an insurer determines whether or not and on what basis it will accept an application for insurance. In an experience-rated plan, premiums are based on a firm's or group's past claims; factors other than prior claims are used for community-rated or manually rated plans.

Unfunded accrued liability
The excess of total liabilities, both present and prospective, over present and prospective assets.

Unemployment
The joblessness of individuals who are willing to work, who are legally and physically able to work, and who are seeking work. Unemployment may represent the temporary joblessness of a worker between jobs (frictional unemployment) or the joblessness of a worker whose skills are not suitable for jobs available in the labor market (structural unemployment).

Uniform product code (UPC)
A computer-readable label comprised of ten digits and stripes that encodes what a product is and how much it costs. The first five digits are assigned by the Uniform Produce Code Council, and the last five digits, by the individual manufacturer.

Unit cost
See Average cost

UPC symbol
See Uniform product code

U.S. Establishment and Enterprise Microdata (USEEM) File
A cross-sectional database containing information on employment, sales, and location for individual enterprises and establishments with employees that have a Dun & Bradstreet credit rating.

U.S. Establishment Longitudinal Microdata (USELM) File
A database containing longitudinally linked sample microdata on establishments drawn from the U.S. Establishment and

Enterprise Microdata file (see separate citation).

U.S. Small Business Administration 503 Program
See Certified development corporation

USEEM
See U.S. Establishment and Enterprise Microdata File

USELM
See U.S. Establishment Longitudinal Microdata File

VCN
See Venture capital network

Venture capital
(See also Equity; Equity midrisk venture capital)
Money used to support new or unusual business ventures that exhibit above-average growth rates, significant potential for market expansion, and are in need of additional financing to sustain growth or further research and development; equity or equity-type financing traditionally provided at the commercialization stage, increasingly available prior to commercialization.

Venture capital company
A company organized to provide seed capital to a business in its formation stage, or in its first or second stage of expansion. Funding is obtained through public or private pension funds, commercial banks and bank holding companies, small business investment corporations licensed by the U.S. Small Business Administration, private venture capital firms, insurance companies, investment management companies, bank trust departments, industrial companies seeking to diversify their investment, and investment bankers acting as intermediaries for other investors or directly investing on their own behalf.

Venture capital limited partnerships
Designed for business development, these partnerships are an institutional mechanism for providing capital for young, technology-oriented businesses. The investors' money is pooled and invested in money market assets until venture investments have been selected. The general partners are experienced investment managers who select and invest the equity and debt securities of firms with high growth potential and the ability to go public in the near future.

Venture capital network (VCN)
A computer database that matches investors with entrepreneurs.

Withholding
Federal, state, social security, and unemployment taxes withheld by the employer from employees' wages; employers are liable for these taxes and the corporate umbrella and bankruptcy will not exonerate an employer from paying back payroll withholding. Employers should escrow these funds in a separate account and disperse them quarterly to withholding authorities.

Working capital
Refers to a firm's short-term investment of current assets, including cash, short-term securities, accounts receivable, and inventories.

Yield
(See also Rate of return)
The rate of income returned on an investment, expressed as a percentage. Income yield is obtained by dividing the current dollar income by the current market price of the security. Net yield or yield to maturity is the current income yield minus any premium above par or plus any discount from par in purchase price, with the adjustment spread over the period from the date of purchase to the date of maturity.

GLOSSARY

Bibliography

Bibliography

Abramovitch, Ingrid. "Myth of the Gunslinger" in *Success*, (Vol. 41, No. 2, March 1994, pp. 34-40)

Abrams, Rhonda M. "Business Plan Stumbling Blocks" in *Working Woman*, (October 1994, pp. 45-48)

-----. "The Six Secrets of Strategic Growth" in *Working Woman*, (March 1995, pp. 50-51, 78)

Abramson-Shoemaker, Marcy. "Visions of Success" in *Small Business Opportunities*, (Vol. 6, No. 6, November 1994, pp. 54, 56)

Ackerly, Leone. "9 Steps To Franchise Success" in *Small Business Opportunities*, (Vol. 7, No. 1, January 1995, pp. 72, 90)

Adams, Robert L. *Ten Second Business Forms*. Holbrook, MA: Bob Adams, Inc., 1990.

"After the Covers: What are They Up To Now?" in *Chain Store Age Executive*, (Vol. 70, No. 7, July 1994, pp. 19-33)

Alderman, Lesley. "Selling Your Business" in *Money: Money Guide Supplement*, (1994, pp. 91)

Aldrich, Howard E. and Marlene C. Fiol. "Fools Rush In? The Institutional Context of Industry Creation" in *Academy of Management Review*, (Vol. 19, No. 4, October 1994)

Alexander, T.M., Sr. *Beyond the Timberline: The Trials & Triumphs of a Black Entrepreneur*. Edgewood, MD: M.E. Duncan Company, Inc., 1992.

Allison, Lynn. "Franchise Fundamentals" in *New Business Opportunities*, (November 1990, pp. 36-42)

Anderson, Joan Wester. "Working Around the Family" in *Income Opportunities*, (October 1993, pp. 60-61, 90)

Andreasen, Alan R. *Cheap but Good Market Research*. Homewood, IL: Business One Irwin, 1991.

Applegate, Jane. "Company for Sale" in *Working Woman*, (Vol. 17, No. 6, June 1992, pp. 38-40)

-----. "Essential Books for Start-ups" in *Working Woman*, (February 1995, pp. 54)

Arden, Lynie. "Home-Based Franchises" in *Income Opportunities*, (Mid-March 1990, pp. 51-52)

Aronoff, Craig E. and John L. Ward. "Golden Goose Mathematics" in *Nation's Business*, (Vol. 83, No. 1, January 1995, pp. 54-55)

Babicky, Jacqueline L. and Larry Field and Norman C. Pricher. "Focus on: Small Business" in *Journal of Accountancy*, (Vol. 177, No. 5, May 1994, pp. 41)

Babner, Jeffrey A. "MLM: Opportunities Abound" in *Entrepreneur: Buyer's Guide to Franchise and Business Opportunities*, (Vol. 22, No. 11, 1995, pp. 28-35)

"Back To School" in *Entrepreneur*, (Vol. 22, No. 13, December 1994, pp. 38)

Baechler, Mary. "Death of a Marriage" in *Inc.*, (Vol. 16, No. 4, April 1994, pp. 74-78)

Bahls, Jane Easter. "Ad It Up" in *Entrepreneur*, (Vol. 22, No. 13, December 1994, pp. 47)

-----. "Terms of Agreement" in *Entrepreneur*, (Vol. 22, No. 9, September 1994, pp. 72-75)

Baird, Michael L. *Engineering Your Start-Up: A Guide for the High-Tech Entrepreneur*. Belmont, CA: Professional Publications, Inc., 1992.

Bandele, Gabriel. *Do for Self: One Hundred of the Best Businesses for Africans in the 21st Century*. Washington, DC: Bandele Publications, 1992.

Banfe, Charles. *Entrepreneur: From Zero to Hero*. New York, NY: Van Nostrand Reinhold, 1991.

Bangs, David H., Jr. *Cash Flow Control Guide: Methods to Understand & Control Small Business's Number One Problem.* Dover, NH: Upstart Publishing Company, Inc., 1989.

-----. *Managing by the Numbers: Financial Essentials for the Growing Business.* Dover, NH: Upstart Publishing Company, Inc., 1992.

-----. *The Market Planning Guide: Gaining & Maintaining the Competitive Edge.* Dover, NH: Upstart Publishing Company, Inc., 1989.

-----. *The Personnel Planning Guide: Successful Management of Your Most Important Asset.* Dover, NH: Upstart Publishing Company, Inc., 1989.

-----. *The Start Up Guide: A One-Year Plan for Entrepreneurs.* Dover, NH: Upstart Publishing Company, Inc., 1989.

Barefoot, Jo Ann S. "Next Up, Scrutiny of Small-Business Lending" in *ABA Banking Journal,* (Vol. 87, No. 2, February 1995, pp. 34-40)

Barkemeyer, Erica. *Eighty-Plus Great Ideas for Making Money at Home: A Guide for the First-Time Entrepreneur.* New York, NY: Walker & Co., 1992.

-----. *Eighty-Plus Great Ideas for Making Money: A Guide for the First-Time Entrepreneur.* New York, NY: Ivy Books, 1993.

Barlow, Stephanie. "Breaking the Bank" in *Entrepreneur,* (May 1993, pp. 78, 80-82)

-----. "Competing with the Giants" in *Sporting Goods Business,* (Vol. 27, No. 2, February 1994, pp. 78-81)

Barreto, Humberto. *The Entrepreneur in Micro-Economic Theory: Disappearance & Explanation.* New York, NY: Routledge, Chapman & Hall, Inc., 1990.

Basye, Jennifer. *How to Become a Successful Weekend Entrepreneur: Secrets of Making an Extra 100 Dollars or More Each Week Using Your Spare Time.* Roseville, CA: Prima Publishing, 1993.

Batchelor, Andrew J., Jr. *Business Planning for the Entrepreneur.* Sausalito, CA: Tangent Publishing, 1990.

Baucus, David A. and Melissa S. Baucus and Sherrie E. Human. "Choosing a Franchise" in *Journal of Small Business Management,* Vol. 31, No. 2, April 1993, pp. 91-104)

Beale, Dorr D. *Dorr Entrepreneur.* New York, NY: Carlton Press, Inc., 1992.

Bell, J. Perry. *Doing Business with Integrity: One Man's Story.* De Forest, WI: Bell Press.

Bell, Judy K. *Disaster Survival Planning: A Practical Guide for Businesses: Everything You Need to Know to Develop, Implement, & Test Your Own Recovery Plans.* Port Hueneme, CA: Disaster Survival Planning, Inc., 1991.

Benson, Benjamin. *Your Family Business.* Homewood, IL: Business One Irwin, 1991.

Berard, Diane. "Family Circus" in *CA Magazine,* (Vol. 127, No. 1, January/February 1994, pp. 38-42)

Berle, Gustav. *The Green Entrepreneur: Business Opportunities That Can Save the Earth & Make You Money.* Blue Ridge

-----. "Treasure Hunt" in *Business Start-ups,* (October 1994, pp. 80-84)

"Better Together: Perspectives" in *Franchising World,* (Vol. 27, No. 1, January/February 1995, pp. 12-23)

Biddulph, David L. "An Untapped Market: The Home-Based Business" in *Direct Marketing,* (April 1991, pp. 37-38)

"Big Ideas for Your Small Business" in *Changing Times,* (November 1989, pp. 57-60)

Bovard, James. "The IRS Wages War on the Self-Employed" in *Insight,* (Vol. 10, No. 4, January 24, 1994, pp. 6)

Bowles, Erksine. "Quick Change' in *Entrepreneur,* (Vol. 22, No. 9, September 1994, pp. 208)

Bradford, Marcia. "Effective Relief?" in *Entrepreneur,* (Vol. 23, No. 2, February 1995, pp. 150, 152)

-----. "A New Chapter" in *Entrepreneur,* (Vol. 22, No. 9, September 1994, pp. 204-207)

Brainer, David. "A New Way to Get Funding for Your Business" in *Successful Opportunities*, (April 1990, pp. 36-38)

Branch, Shelly. "B. E. Franchise 50 Report: Tapping into Low-Cost Franchising" in*Black Enterprise*, (Vol. 23, No. 2, September 1992, pp. 66-72)

"Brochures Should Be Written with Specific Reader in Mind" in *Denver Business Journal*, (Vol. 46, No. 1, September 16, 1994, pp. 23)

Brogdon, Anthony. *Being an Entrepreneur in Alabama.* Detroit, MI: Multi Business Concepts, 1991.

-----.*Being an Entrepreneur in California.* Detroit, MI: Multi Business Concepts, 1991.

-----.*Being an Entrepreneur in Colorado.* Detroit, MI: Multi Business Concepts, 1991.

-----. *Being an Entrepreneur in Florida.* Detroit, MI: Multi Business Concepts, 1991.

-----. *Being an Entrepreneur in Georgia.* Detroit, MI: Multi Business Concepts, 1989.

-----. *Being an Entrepreneur in Illinois.* Detroit, MI: Multi Business Concepts, 1991.

-----.*Being an Entrepreneur in Louisiana.* Detroit, MI: Multi Business Concepts, 1991.

-----.*Being an Entrepreneur in Maryland.* Detroit, MI: Multi Business Concepts, 1991.

-----.*Being an Entrepreneur in Michigan.* Detroit, MI: Multi Business Concepts, 1991.

-----.*Being an Entrepreneur in Minnesota.* Detroit, MI: Multi Business Concepts, 1991.

-----.*Being an Entrepreneur in New Jersey.* Detroit, MI: Multi Business Concepts, 1991.

-----.*Being an Entrepreneur in New York.* Detroit, MI: Multi Business Concepts, 1991.

-----. *Being an Entrepreneur in Ohio.* Detroit, MI: Multi Business Concepts, 1991.

-----. *Being an Entrepreneur in Pennsylvania.* Detroit, MI: Multi Business Concepts, 1991.

-----. *Being an Entrepreneur in Texas.* Detroit, MI: Multi Business Concepts, 1991.

-----.*Being an Entrepreneur in Washington, DC.* Detroit, MI: Multi Business Concepts, 1991.

-----. *Twenty-Three Principles to Being a Successful Entrepreneur: The Block Buster.* Detroit, MI: Multi Business Concepts, 1989.

Brokaw, Leslie. "How To Start an Inc. 500 Company" in *Inc. 500*, (Vol. 16, No. 11, 1994, pp. 51-52, 54, 57-58, 60, 63-65)

Brokaw, Leslie and David Whitford. "Then and Now" in*Inc.*, (Vol. 16, No. 9, September 1994, pp. 69-70, 75-77)

Brooksbank, Roger. "The Anatomy of Marketing Positioning Strategy" in*Marketing Intelligence & Planning*, (Vol. 12, No. 4, 1994, pp. 10-14)

Broome, Jr., J. Tol. "A Loan at Last?" in *Nation's Business*, (Vol. 82, No. 8, August 1994, pp. 40-43)

-----. "How to Write a Business Plan" in *Nation's Business*, (Vol. 81, No. 2, February 1993, pp. 29-30)

Brown, Ann. "A Sweet Deal" in*Black Enterprise*, (Vol. 25, No. 2, September 1994, pp. 30-32)

Brown, Carolyn M. and Cassandra Hayes. "Leveling the Field" in *Black Enterprise*, (Vol. 25, No. 1, August 1994, pp. 33)

Brown, Caryne. "Business Busters" in*Black Enterprise*, (Vol. 23, No. 4, November 1992, pp. 75-85)

-----. "Checks & Balances" in*Income Opportunities*, (Vol. 30, No. 2, February 1995, pp. 130-136)

Brown, John O. *The Small Business Guide to the Malcolm Baldrige National Quality Award: Proven Strategies for Building Quality into Your Organization.* Homewood, IL: Business One Irwin, 1995.

Brown, Michael. "The Changing Face of Leadership" in *Nation's Business*, (Vol. 83, No. 1, January 1995, pp. 41-42)

BIBLIOGRAPHY

Budman, Matthew. "Apprentices Begin Apprenticing in the U.S." in*Across the Board*, (Vol. 31, No. 1, January 1994, pp. 36-37)

Building Wealth. Dover, NH: Upstart Publishing Company, Inc., 1992.

Bursten, Steven C. *The Bootstrap Entrepreneur*. Nashville, TN: Thomas Nelson Inc., 1993.

Business of Your Own Staff. *So You're Thinking about Starting a Business: A Comprehensive Business Start up Manual*. Nashville, TN: Business of Your Own, 1988.

-----. *Starting a Business to Sell Your Artwork*. Nashville, TN: Business of Your Own, 1988.

-----. *Starting a Business to Sell Your Craft Items*. Nashville, TN: Business of Your Own, 1988.

-----. *Starting a Clothing Boutique*. Nashville, TN: Business of Your Own, 1988.

-----. *Starting a Day Care Center*. Nashville, TN: Business of Your Own, 1988.

------. *Starting a Franchise*. Nashville, TN: Business of Your Own, 1988.

-----. *Starting a Gift Shop*. Nashville, TN: Business of Your Own, 1988.

-----. *Starting a Home Based Business*. Nashville, TN: Business of Your Own, 1988.

-----. *Starting a Mail Order Business*. Nashville, TN: Business of Your Own, 1988.

-----. *Starting a Secretarial Service*. Nashville, TN: Business of Your Own, 1988.

-----. *Starting an Antique Shop*. Nashville, TN: Business of Your Own, 1988.

Business Planning Guide. Dover, NH: Upstart Publishing Company, Inc., 1992.

Buskirk, Richard H. *Program for Writing Winning Business Plans*. Denver, CO: Creative Management Unlimited, Inc.

Byron, Peg. "Quick Fix" in*Income Opportunities*, (Vol. 30, No. 3, March 1995, pp. 88, 90)

Caffey, Andrew A. "A Closer Look" in*Entrepreneur: Buyer's Guide To Franchise and Business Opportunities*, (Vol. 22, No. 11, 1995, pp. 20, 22, 24-27)

Caimano, Sal. "Crawl...Walk...Run! The Right Way to Test a Telemarketing Campaign" in*Target Marketing*, (Vol. 17, No. 5, May 1994, pp. 28-29)

Callan, Katherine. "Capture the Future" in *Success*, (Vol. 40, No. 10, December 1993, pp. 63-70)

Callan, Katherine and Michael Warshaw. "The 25 Best Business Schools for Entrepreneurs: The Whiz Kids" in *Success*, (Vol. 41, No. 7, September 1994, pp. 38-42)

Calvin, Robert J. "The Price Is Right" in *Small Business Reports*, (Vol. 19, No. 6, June 1994, pp. 9-13)

"Can This Business Be Franchised" in*Success*, (Vol. 41, No. 5, June 1994, pp. 73-75)

Case, John. "Buy Now—Avoid the Rush" in *Inc. Magazine*, (February 1991, pp. 36-45)

"Cashing In On Coupons" in *Small Business Opportunities*, (Vol. 6, No. 5, September 1994, pp. 26-28, 90)

Casson, Mark. *The Entrepreneur: An Economic Theory*. Brookfield, VT: Ashgate Publishing Co., 1992.

Clayton, Sue. "Under Cover" in *Business Start-Ups*, (Vol. 7, No. 3, March 1995, pp. 58-62)

Clift, Vicki. "On-Line Marketing: Hot Opportunity or a Trendy Novelty" in *Marketing News*, (Vol. 28, No. 22, October 24, 1994, pp. 13, 43)

-----. "Problem-solving Approach Works Best for Small Professional Firms" in*Marketing News*, (Vol. 28, No. 6, March 14, 1994, pp. 15)

Cohen, William A. *The Entrepreneur & Small Business Marketing Problem Solver*. New York, NY: John Wiley & Sons, Inc., 1991.

-----. *The Entrepreneur & Small Business Problem Solver.* New York, NY: John Wiley & Sons, 1990.

Common Sense Editors. Creating Customers. Dover, NH: Upstart Publishing Company, Inc., 1992.

"Competing With Category Killers" in *Chain Store Age Executive*, (Vol. 70, No. 5, May 1994, pp. S31)

"Contesting Unemployment Claims" in *Small Business Reports*, (Vol. 19, No. 7, July 1994, pp. 37)

Cooper, Bob. "Key Factors in Selecting the Best Location for Your Company" in *Telemarketing Magazine*, (Vol. 12, No. 8, February 1994, pp. 44-45)

Cosgriff, John and Leonard Sliwoski. "Turning to the Government" in *Practical Accountant*, (Vol. 27, No. 6, June 1994, pp. 37-44)

"Could You Succeed in Small Business" in *Business Horizons*, (September/October 1989, pp. 65-69)

Covello, Joseph A. *The Complete Book of Business Plans: Simple Steps to Writing a Powerful Business Plan.* Naperville, IL: Sourcebooks, Inc., 1992.

Cromie, Stan. "Entrepreneurship: The Role of the Individual in Small Business Development" in *IBAR*, (Vol. 15, 1994, pp. 62-75)

Crowner, Robert P. *Developing a Strategic Business Plan with Cases: An Entrepreneur's Advantage.* Homewood, IL: Richard D. Irwin, Inc., 1990.

Cullinane, John J. *Entrepreneur's Survival Guide: One Hundred One Tips for Managing in Good Times & Bad.* Homewood, IL: Business One Irwin, 1992.

Cushman, Robert F., ed. *Business Opportunities in the United States: The Complete Reference Guide to Practices & Procedures.* Homewood, IL: Business One Irwin, 1992.

Dailey, Gene. *Secrets of a Successful Entrepreneur: How to Start & Succeed at Running Your Own Business.* Pleasanton, CA: K & A Publications, 1993.

Danco, Leon. "Fighting Families Can Lose War Against Competition" in *Crain's Small Business*, (Vol. 3, No. 1, January 1995)

Davis, Eileen. "How to Control Workers' Comp" in *Small Business Reports*, (Vol. 17, No. 8, August 1992, pp. 29-39)

Davis, Karen Zehring. "Suddenly, Last Summer" in *Entrepreneur*, (Vol. 22, No. 13, December 1994, pp. 14)

Davidson, Jeffrey P. *Marketing for the Home-Based Business.* Holbrook, MA: Bob Adams, Inc., 1990.

Dawson, George M. *Borrowing for Your Business: Winning the Battle for the Banker's Yes.* Dover, NH: Upstart Publishing Company, Inc., 1991.

Dears, Donn D. *The Entrepreneur as CEO: Building a Business.* Plano, TX: WDD Corporation Publishing Divison, 1991.

-----. *The New Entrepreneur: How to Get Started in Business.* Plano, TX: WDD Corporation Publishing Division, 1992.

Delaney, Joan. "Cutting Down on Absenteeism" in *Black Enterprise*, (Vol. 25, No. 8, March 1995, pp. 39)

-----. "Entrepreneurial Problem Solver; Finding a Financial Mentor" in *Executive Female*, (Vol. 17, No. 4, July-August 1994, pp. 28)

-----. "A Strategy For Growth" in *Black Enterprise*, (Vol. 25, No. 4, November 1994)

DeMott, John S. "Out on a Limb and on Their Own" in *Nation's Business*, (Vol. 82, No. 3, March 1994, pp. 33-34)

Denalli, Jacqueline Lynn. "Patent Primer" in *Business Start-Ups*, (Vol. 6, No. 9, September 1994, pp. 22, 24-25)

Denton, Keith D. and Peter Richardson. "Globally Competitive: It's a Matter of the Right Attitude" in *Business Forum*, (Vol. 17, No. 2, Spring 1992, pp. 22-25)

Dible, Donald M. *Up Your Own Organization: A Handbook for Today's Entrepreneur.* New York, NY: Simon & Schuster Trade.

"A Directory of Export Services The Trade Information Center: One-Stop Shop" in *Business America*, (Vol. 113, No. 9, 1992, pp. 8-13)

"Do You Need a Designer Logo?" in *Income Opportunities*, (Vol. 30, No. 2, February 1995, pp. 76)

"Does Size Matter?" in *Economist*, (Vol. 331, No. 7867, June 11, 1994, pp. 66)

Dodge, Robert H. and John E. Robbins. "An Empirical Investigation of the Organizational Life Cycle Model for Small Business Development and Survival" in *Journal of Small Business*.

Doscher, Robert S. "How to Create New Products" in *Target Marketing*, (Vol. 17, No. 1, January 1994, pp. 40-42)

Doyle, Patricia A. *Sit & Grow Rich: Petsitting & Housesitting for Profit.* Dover, NH: Upstart Publishing Company, Inc., 1993.

Duffy, Maureen Nevin. "Buying Knowledge" in *Income Opportunities*, (Vol. 29, No. 9, September 1994, pp. 70-74)

-----. "Lost in (Ad) Space" in *Income Opportunities*, (Vol. 29, No. 11, November 1994, pp. 118)

Duncan, Harley T., and Verenda C. Smith. "State Efforts: Small Business" in *National Public Accountant*, (Vol. 37, No. 2, February 1992, pp. 38-41)

Dwyer, Don. Target Success: *How You Can Become a Successful Entrepreneur -- Regardless of Your Background.* Holbrook, MA: Bob Adams, Inc., 1993.

Dwyer, Steve. "Requiem for a Small Jobber" in *National Petroleum News*, (Vol. 86, No. 8, July 1994, pp. 16)

"Easy As Pie: Slicing into Stores with a Clear-cut Marketing Plan" in *Houston Business Journal*, (Vol. 23, No. 37, January 31, 1994)

Eckert, Lee A. *Small Business: An Entrepreneur's Plan.* Fort Worth, TX: Dryden Press, 1993.

Edmond, Alfred. "The B. E. Franchise Start-Up Guide" in *Black Enterprise*, (September 1990, pp. 73-75)

Edwards, Pamela and Peter Turnbull. "Finance for Small and Medium-Sized Enterprises: Information and the Income Gearing Challenge" in *International Journal of Bank Marketing*.

Eechambadi, Naras V. "Does Advertising Work?" in *McKinsey Quarterly*, (No. 3, 1994, pp. 117-129)

Endoso, Joyce. "New Study Predicts Unsurpassed Growth in Franchising" in *Franchising World*, (April 1990, pp. 20-25)

Englander, Debra Wishik. "Investing Dollars and Sense in a Friend's Business" in *Black Enterprise*, (Vol. 24, No. 9, April 1994, pp. 46)

Entrepreneur Magazine Staff. *Complete Guide to Owning a Home Based Business.* New York, NY: Bantam Books, Inc., 1990.

-----. *One Hundred & Eleven Businesses You Can Start for Under $10,000.* New York, NY: Bantam Books, Inc., 1991.

-----. *One Hundred & Sixty-Eight More Businesses Anyone Can Start & Make a Lot of Money.* New York, NY: Bantam Books, Inc., 1991.

-----. *One Hundred Eighty-Four Businesses Anyone Can Start.* New York, NY: Bantam Books, Inc., 1990.

Erhrman, Kenneth A. "Finding a Lawyer for Your Business" in *Nation's Business*, (Vol. 82, No. 4, April 1994, pp. 34-35)

Estess, Patricia Schiff. "Comeback Kids" in *Entrepreneur*, (Vol. 23, No. 2, February 1995, pp. 77-79)

-----. "Family Value" in *Entrepreneur*, (Vol. 22, No. 13, December 1994, pp. 58)

Evans, Arlene. "What's in a Logo?" in *Small Business Opportunities*, (Vol. 7, No. 3, May 1995, pp. 12, 82)

Evanson, Davis R. "A Fair To Remember" in *Entrepreneur*, (Vol. 23, No. 2, February 1995, pp. 38-39)

Falbe, Cecilia M. and Thomas C. Dandridge. "Franchising as a Strategic Partnership" in *International Small Business Journal*, (Vol. 10, No. 3, April-June 1992, pp. 40-52)

Feinglass, Arthur. "Marketing Magic" in *Small Business Opportunities*, (Vol. 6, No. 5, September 1994, pp. 44, 90)

Ferenc, Jeff. "Keys to Success? For Starters, Here Are 15" in *Contractor*, (Vol. 41, No. 11, November 1994, pp. 12)

Ferrell, O.C. *Business: A Changing World*. Homewood, IL: Richard D. Irwin, Inc., 1992.

Finley, Allen C. and Robert W. Pricer. "Raising Money From Your Bank" in *In Business*, (April 1990, pp. 21-23)

Fisher, Jerry. "Say No More" in *Entrepreneur*, (Vol. 23, No. 2, February 1995, pp. 142, 144)

Fisk, Irwin W. "Attention, Franchise Shoppers" in *Entrepreneur*, (January 1991, pp. 94-99)

Foegen, George J. *Business Plan Guidebook with Financial Spreadsheets*. Fort Worth, TX: Dryden Press, 1990.

Forbes, Christine. "The Homebased Psyche" in *Entrepreneur*, (March 1990, pp. 76-81)

"Franchise Finds" in *Small Business Opportunities*, (Vol. 7, No. 1, January 1995, pp. 88)

Frank, Mixson. "Profits After 5" in *New Business Opportunities*, (April 1990, pp. 40-42)

Fraser, Jill Andresky. "Audit Tip Sheet" in *Inc.*, (Vol. 16, No. 4, April 1994, pp. 118)

-----. "A Costly Start-Ups Wise Moves" in *Inc.*, (Vol. 16, No. 9, September 1994, pp. 125)

Freedman, David M. "Do You Have a Plan?" in *In Business*, (April 1990, pp. 12-14)

Freeman, Gregory. "St. Louis: Bringing Minorities into the Mainstream" in *Black Enterprise*, (Vol. 24, No. 10, May 1994, pp. 64)

Frohbieter-Mueller, Jo. "Is the Price Right?" in *Income Opportunities*, (Vol. 29, No. 9, September 1994, pp. 102-104)

-----. "Shattering the Myth" in *Income Opportunities*, (Vol. 29, No. 7, July 1994, pp. 34)

Fromberg, Jeff. "The Money Is Out There . . . How To Get It" in *Agency Sales Magazine*, (Vol. 24, No. 2, February 1994, pp. 15-17)

Gajeway, Charles H. "Building a Better Business Plan" in *Home Office-Computing*, (February 1990, p. 30)

Gangemi, Robina A. "Agency To Client: Do It Yourself" in *Inc.*, (Vol. 16, No. 12, November 1994, pp. 125)

Garrett, Echo Montgomery. "Franchises That Capitalize On Solving Our Problems" in *Inc.*, (Vol. 16, No. 9, September 1994, pp. 106-109)

-----. "Interview With The Franchisee" in *Inc.*, (Vol. 16, No. 12, November 1994, pp. 148-152, 154)

-----. "Up and Comers: How Can You Tell a Good Deal?" in *Inc.*, (Vol. 16, No. 9, September 1994, pp. 100-103, 105)

-----. "Who Makes the Perfect Franchisee?" in *Inc.*, (Vol. 16, No. 12, November 1994, pp. 142-144, 146-147)

Gaskill, LuAnn Ricketts and Howard E. Van Auken and Ronald A. Manning. "A Factor Analytic Study of the Perceived Causes of Small Business Failure" in *Journal of Small Business Management*, (Vol. 31, No. 4)

Gelder, Alice A. *World Business Desk Reference: How to Do Business with 192 Countries by Phone, Fax, & Mail*. Homewood, IL: Business One Irwin, 1994.

"Gift Certificates—The People's Choice" in *Incentive*, (Vol. 169, No. 2, February 1995, pp. SS3-SS26)

Gilbert, Dale L. *Complete Guide to Starting a Used Bookstore*. Dover, NH: Upstart Publishing Company, Inc., 1991.

Gite, Lloyd. "Worth sinking your teeth into" in *Black Enterprise*, (Vol. 25, No. 8, March 1995, pp. 40)

Glink, Ilyce R. "Where To Look for Money Now" in *Working Woman*, (Vol. 19, No. 10, October 1994, pp. 56-62)

"Going for Broke" in *Inc. Magazine*, (September 1990, pp. 34-44)

Goldberg, Cheryl J. "Tax Driver" in *Entrepreneur*, (Vol. 22, No. 13, December 1994, pp. 22)

Gomes, Glenn M. and James F. Morgan. "Meeting the Wrongful Discharge Challenge: Legislative Options for Small Business" in *Journal of Small Business Management*, (Vol. 30, No. 4)

Gottschalk, Jack. *Promoting Your Professional Services.* Homewood, IL: Business One Irwin, 1991.

Greco, Susan. "The Complete New-Business Survival Guide" in *Inc.*, (Vol. 14, No. 7, July 1992, pp. 48-66)

-----. "Pay Bonuses for Profits" in *Inc.*, (Vol. 17, No. 2, February 1995, pp. 107)

Grensing-Pophal, Lin. "Tentative Targets" in *Income Opportunities*, (Vol. 30, No. 3, March 1995, pp. 96, 100-101)

Griffin, Cynthia E. "Basic Training" in *Business Start-Ups*, (Vol. 7, No. 3, March 1995, pp. 12)

-----. "Financial Forecast" in *Entrepreneur*, (Vol. 22, No. 13, December 1994, pp. 97-100)

-----. "Low-Interest Loans For Small Companies" in *Entrepreneur*, (Vol. 22, No. 13, December 1994, pp. 18)

-----. "Pairing Up" in *Entrepreneur*, (Vol. 22, No. 9, September 1994, pp. 60-62)

-----. "Site Seeing" in *Business Start-ups*, (October 1994, pp. 54-58)

Growth Company Starter Kit: "How to" for: Business Plans, Financing, Operations. Coopers & Lybrand.

Gundry, Lisa K. and Charles W. Prather and Jill R. Kickul. "Building the Creative Organization" in *Organizational Dynamics*, (Vol. 22, No. 4, Spring 1994, pp. 22-37)

Haake, Timothy M. "Is Regulatory Relief on the Horizon?" in *Do-It-Yourself Retailing*, (Vol. 166, No. 5, May 1994, pp. 210)

Haber, Jeffry R. "Nonprofit Competition With Small Business: A Roadmap Leading to Answers" in *Nonprofit World*, (Vol. 12, No. 3, May/June 1994, pp. 14-18)

Hall, Betty. "Yes, You Can Create Your Own Job" in *Public Relations Journal*, (Vol. 50, No. 6, June/July 1994, pp. 18-20)

Hall, Phil. "Make Listeners Your Customers" in *Nation's Business*, (Vol. 82, No. 6, June 1994, pp. 53R)

Hanke, Ed. "Marketing: A Little Something Extra" in *Credit Union Management*, (Vol. 17, No. 2, February 1994, pp. 33-35)

Harper, Stephen C. *The McGraw-Hill Guide to Starting Your Own Business: A Step-by-Step Blueprint for the First-Time Entrepreneur.* New York, NY: McGraw-Hill, Inc., 1991.

Harris, Marlys J. "Run Your Company Smarter" in *Money*, (Vol. 23, No. 11, November 1994, pp. 136-140)

Helm, Kathy K. *Becoming an Entrepreneur in Your Own Setting.* Chicago, IL: American Dietetic Association, 1990.

"Helping Small- and Medium-Sized Businesses" in *Business America*, (Vol. 115, No. 9, September 1994, pp. 40-51)

Henricks, Mark. "Brain Power" in *Entrepreneur*, (Vol. 23, No. 2, February 1995, pp. 54-55)

-----. "Head Start" in *Business Start-Ups*, (Vol. 6, No. 8, September 1994, pp. 78, 80, 82)

-----. "A New Chapter" in *Entrepreneur*, (April 1991, pp. 163-169)

-----. "Tax Driver" in *Entrepreneur*, (Vol. 22, No. 13, December 1994, pp. 32)

Henze, Geraldine. *Winning Career Moves: A Guide to Improving Your Work Life.* Homewood, IL: Business One Irwin, 1992.

Herbig, Paul and James E. Golden and Steven Dunphy. "The Relationship of Structure to Entrepreneurial and Innovative Success" in *Marketing Intelligence & Planning*, (Vol. 12, No. 9, 1994)

Heyart, Dorothy and Gail Popyk. "Money Guide" in *Crain's Small Business*, (Vol. 3, No. 1, January 1995, pp. 4-6)

Hiccks, Tyler G. "Ten Easy-to-Start Home Businesses" in *Income Opportunities*, (December 1993, pp. 51-56, 91, 93-95, 97)

Hierl, Thomas. "Look at Every Option - And Beyond" in *Nation's Business*, (Vol. 79, No. 7, July 1991, pp. 9)

Hill, Earlene J. "Trade Secrets" in *Entrepreneur*, (January 1992, pp. 287-294)

Hill, et al., Shannon. "Franchise and Business Opportunities Listings" in *Entrepreneur: Buyer's Guide to Franchise and Business Opportunities*, (Vol. 22, No. 11)

Hise, Phaedra. "The Deal Maker" in *Inc.*, (Vol. 15, No. 13, December 1993, pp. 129-130)

-----. "The Last Hurdle" in *Inc.*, (Vol. 16, No. 1, January 1994, pp. 50)

-----. "Patently Unsafe: Inventors Beware" in *Inc.*, (Vol. 16, No. 12, November 1994, pp. 36)

Hisrich, Robert D. *Entrepreneurship*. Homewood, IL: Richard D. Irwin, Inc., 1989.

-----. *On Your Own*. Homewood, IL: Business One Irwin, 1991.

-----. *The Woman Entrepreneur: Starting, Financing, & Managing a Successful Business*. New York, NY: Free Press, 1990.

Hite, Peggy A. and Toby Stock and Bryan C. Cloyd. "Reasons for Preparer Usage by Small Business Owners: How Compliant Are They?" in *National Public Accountant*, (Vol. 37, No. 2, February)

Hodgetts, Richard. *Effective Small Business Management*. Fort Worth, TX: Dryden Press, 1992.

Hoffman, Gary. "Striking the Faustian Bargain" in *Corporate Detroit*, (Vol. 12, No. 11, November 1994, pp. 38-39)

Hogsett III, Randall M. and William J. Radig. "Employee Crime: The Cost and Some Control Measures" in *Review of Business*, (Vol. 16, No. 2, Winter 1994, pp. 9-14)

Hoke, Pete. "The Lure of Mail Order" in *Direct Marketing*, (Vol. 57, No. 6, March 1994, pp. 42-44)

Holland, Sandra. "Select a Business Site" in *Income Opportunities*, (October 1991, pp. 64, 74)

Holtz, Herman. *Complete Work-at-Home Companion: Everything You Need to Know to Prosper as a Home-Based Entrepreneur or Employee*. Roseville, CA: Prima Publishing, 1993.

"Home-based Business Opportunity" in *Business Start-Ups*, (Vol. 6, No. 9, September 1994, pp. 33)

"Hot Areas for Small Business" in *Black Enterprise*, (Vol. 24, No. 4, November 1993, pp. 54)

"The Hottest Industries for New Business Opportunities" in *Black Enterprise*, (Vol. 25, No. 8, March 1995)

"How to Fight Your Franchisor and Win" in *Money: Money Guide Supplement*, (1994, pp. 28-32)

Huber, Janean. "About Face" in *Entrepreneur*, (Vol. 23, No. 2, February 1995, pp. 166)

-----. "Code of Honor?" in *Entrepreneur*, (Vol. 22, No. 9, September 1994, pp. 216-218)

-----. "Combat Zone" in *Entrepreneur*, (Vol. 22, No. 9, September 1994, pp. 100)

-----. "Home Front: Best Bets for 1994" in *Business Start-Ups*, (December 1993, pp. 10, 12-13)

-----. "Home Runs" in *Entrepreneur*, (Vol. 22, No. 13, December 1994, pp. 63)

-----. "The Quiet Revolution" in *Entrepreneur*, (September 1993, pp. 77-81)

-----. "The Road Ahead" in *Entrepreneur: Buyer's Guide To Franchise and Business Opportunities*, (Vol. 22, No. 11, 1995, pp. 6-8, 10-13)

-----. "What's Next?" in *Entrepreneur*, (Vol. 22, No. 9, September 1994, pp. 144-151)

Huffman, Frances. "Eleven Businesses You Can Run From Home" in *Homebased Business*, (Winter 1990, pp. 29-32)

-----. "Ten Best Businesses to Run Part Time" in *New Business Opportunities*, (April 1990, pp. 45-50)

Jacobs, Joseph J. *Anatomy of an Entrepreneur: Family, Culture, & Ethics*. San Francisco, CA: ICS Press, 1991.

Jackson, Alan W. "It's All In The Plan" in *Small Business Reports*, (Vol. 19, No. 6, June 1994, pp. 38-43)

Jailer, Mildred. "Home Business Start-Up Basics" in *Income Opportunities*, (Mid-September 1990, pp. 54-56)

Johnson, Gene H., Rudolph S. Lindbeck, and Winston N. McVea, Jr. "Traps To Avoid When Purchasing a Business" in *Journal of Financial Planning*, (Vol. 7, No. 1, January 1994, pp. 38-41)

Jondahl, Terri. "The Marketing Game" in *Texas Banking*, (Vol. 83, No. 2, February 1994, pp. 3, 12)

Kao, John. *The Entrepreneur*. Englewood Cliffs, CA: Prentice Hall, 1990.

Kassebaum, Robert. "Factors To Consider" in *Small Business Opportunities*, (Vol. 7, No. 3, May 1995, pp. 20, 74)

Kaufman, Lorraine R. "Call Guides: Tools of the Trade" in *Target Marketing*, (Vol. 17, No. 4, April 1994, pp. 20-22)

Kellmayer, John. "Tax Credits" in *Small Business Opportunities*, (Vol. 7, No. 3, May 1995, pp. 10)

Kennedy, Nancy. "The Business of Education" in *Income Opportunities*, (Vol. 29, No. 9, September 1994, pp. 58-62)

-----. "Should You Franchise Your Business?" in *Income Opportunities*, (Vol. 30, No. 2, February 1995, pp. 42-43, 44, 46, 48, 50, 52)

Kennedy, Shawn. "Saying Goodbye to Corporate America" in *Black Enterprise*, (Vol. 22, No. 11, June 1992, pp. 312-318)

King, Ruth Anne. "Ten Steps to Creating Your Business Plan" in *Income Opportunities*, (December/January 1991, pp. 55-56)

Kirkpatrick, Randall. "Creating the Video Classroom" in *Income Opportunities*, (Vol. 29, No. 9, September 1994, pp. 76-80)

Klein, Fred. *Handbook on Building a Profitable Business: An Expert's Step-by-Step Presentation on How to Make Money in Business*. Seattle, WA: Entrepreneurial Workshops Publications, 1990.

Knight, Brian, & the Associates of Country Business Inc. Staff. *Buy the Right Business -- At the Right Price*. Dover, NH: Upstart Publishing Company, Inc.

Knight, Russell M. "Criteria Used by Venture Capitalists: A Cross Cultural Analysis" in *International Small Business Journal*, (Vol. 13, No. 1, October/December)

Kotite, Erika. "Franchise Outlook" in *Entrepreneur: Buyer's Guide to Franchise and Business Opportunities*, (Vol. 22, No. 11, 1995, pp. 42-48)

-----. "Is Franchising For You?" in *Entrepreneur: Buyer's Guide To Franchise and Business Opportunities*, (Vol. 22, No. 11, 1995, pp. 14, 16-18)

-----. "Keeping Tabs" in *Entrepreneur*, (Vol. 22, No. 13, December 1994, pp. 43)

-----. "Store Wars" in *Entrepreneur*, (July 1992, pp. 158-162)

Kraft, Ronald D. *Strategic Planning for the Entrepreneur*. La Mesa, CA: Center Publications, 1991.

Kressel, Henry and Bruce Guile. "The Wrong Question" in *Inc.*, (Vol. 17, No. 3, March 1995, pp. 27)

Kriegman-Chin, Michele. "Entrepreneurial Skills 101" in *Income Opportunities*, (Vol. 29, No. 9, September 1994, pp. 64-68)

Kuehl, Charles. *Small Business: Planning & Management*. Fort Worth, TX: Dryden Press, 1990.

Lane, Amy. "Many Sides Push Reform of Single Business Tax" in *Crain's Small Business*, (Vol. 3, No. 1, January 1995, pp. 9)

Leavenworth, Geoffrey. "Big Savings for Small Companies" in *Business & Health*, (Vol. 13, No. 1, January 1995, pp. 38-42)

Legette, Cynthia. "Key Strategies for Smart Marketing to African Americans" in *Public Relations Journal*, (Vol. 50, No. 7, Aug/Sep 1994, pp. 38-39)

Levine, Jeffrey P. *Doing Business in Chicago*. Homewood, IL: Business One Irwin, 1990.

Levine, Sumner N., ed. *The Business One Irwin Business & Investment Almanac, 1992*. Homewood, IL: Business One Irwin, 1991.

Levy, Richard C. "How to Market Your Invention" in*Income Opportunities*, (March 1991, pp. 65, 66, 70, 96-112, 119)

-----. "The Million Dollar Idea: How to Sell and Protect Your Brainchild" in*Income Opportunities*, (March 1990, pp. 59-63)

Lewis, Herschell Gordon. "Little Words Mean a Lot" in *Catalog Age*, (Vol. 10, No. 10, October 1993, pp. 88-91)

Lisoskie, Pete. *Networking Your Way to Profits: How to Create a Customer Network That Keeps Them Coming Back.* Newbury Park, CA: Business Toolbox, 1992.

Lorenz-Fife, Iris. "Resource Guide: Small-Business Help From the Government" in*Entrepreneur*, (April 1990, pp. 218-223)

-----. "SBA Lends a Hand" in *New Business Opportunities*, (April 1990, pp. 10-15)

Lownes, Millicent G. *Entrepreneurially Yours: A Compilation of Articles about Starting and Managing a Small Business.* Nashville, TN: Business of Your Own, 1990.

-----. *The Purple Rose Within: A Woman's Basic Guide for Developing a Business Plan.* Business of Your Own, 1989.

Ludden, LaVerne.*Mind Your Own Business: Getting Started as an Entrepreneu*r. Indianapolis, IN: JIST Works, Inc., 1993.

Lunt, Penny. "Does Telemarketing Have to be Annoying?" in *ABA Banking Journal*, (Vol. 86, No. 6, June 1994, pp. 59-62)

-----. "What Truly Deters Check Fraud?" in*Banking Journal*, (Vol. 87, No. 2, February 1995, pp. 74-78)

Lynn, Jacqueline. "Franchise Advantage" in *Entrepreneur*, (Vol. 23, No. 2, February 1995, pp. 132, 134-137)

-----. "Required Reading" in*Business Start-Ups*, (Vol. 7, No. 3, March 1995, pp. 30)

Mack, Gracian. "The Art of Financial Mapping" in *Black Enterprise*, (October 1994, pp. 83-84, 86, 89-90)

-----. "Fueling the Growth of Black Companies" in *Black Enterprise*, (Vol. 25, No. 4, November 1994, pp. 158-159, 162, 164)

-----. "Keeping Track of Your Cashflow" in*Black Enterprise*, (October 1994, pp. 93-94, 96)

Mackay, Harvey. "Five Little Words" in*Successful Meetings*, (Vol. 43, No. 2, February 1994, pp. 28)

Malaborsa, Sylvie. "All About Network Marketing" in*Income Opportunities*, (September 1992, pp. 53-55, 65-66)

Malburg, Christopher R. *Business Plans to Manage Day to Day Operations: Real-Life Results for Small Business Owners & Operators.* New York, NY: John Wiley & Sons, Inc., 1993.

Mangelsdorf, Martha E. "Growing with the Flow" in*Inc.*, (Vol. 16, No. 11, 1994, pp. 88-90)

-----. "Growth in a Developing Market" in*Inc. 500*, (Vol. 16, No. 11, 1994, pp. 92, 94, 96, 98-99)

-----. "The Hottest Entrepreneurs in America" in*Inc.*, (Vol. 14, No. 13, December 1992, pp. 88-103)

-----. "Start-up Funding: Consider the Sources" in*Inc.*, (Vol. 6, No. 8, August 1994, pp. 32)

Mamis, Robert A. "Me & My Banker" in*Inc.*, (Vol. 17, No. 3, March 1995, pp. 43-45, 48)

-----. "The Secrets of Bootstrapping" in *Inc.*, (Vol. 13, No. 9, September 1991, pp. 52-70)

Marullo, Gloria Gibbs. "In Your Best Interest" in *Business Start-Ups*, (Vol. 7, No. 3, March 1995, pp. 24-27)

-----. "Price Pointers" in *Business Start-Ups*, (Vol. 6, No. 9, September 1994, pp. 102, 104-105)

Matthews, John.*The Beginning Entrepreneur.* Lincolnwood, IL: NTC Publishing Group, 1993.

Matura, Richard J. "Fighting Fraud" in*Income Opportunities*, (Vol. 29, No. 11, November 1994, pp. 114, 116)

Matusky, Gregory. "The Real Money in Franchising" in*Inc.*, (Vol. 16, No. 9, September 1994, pp. 110-114)

Maurer, Michael. "Real Money Starts Here" in*Crain's Detroit Business*, (Vol. 10, No. 41, October 10-16, 1994, pp. 1, 26)

May, Bruce E. "Adequacy, Availability & Quality of Legal Services for Small Businesses: A South Dakota Study" in *South Dakota Business Review*, (Vol. 53)

Maynard, Roberta. "Are You Ready to Go Public?" in *Nation's Business*, (Vol. 83, No. 1, January 1995, pp. 30-32)

-----. "Branching Out" in *Nation's Business*, (Vol. 82, No. 11, November 1994, pp. 53)

McCune, Jenny C. "Job One: Find Money" in *Success Magazine*, (Vol. 41, No. 10, December 1994, pp. 23-33)

-----. "The Open Corporation" in *Small Business Reports*, (Vol. 19, No. 7, July 1994, pp. 31)

McDermott, Kevin. "The Hard Facts About Franchising" in *D & B Reports*, (Vol. 42, No. 5, September/October 1993, pp. 36-38)

McKee, Bradford. "Ties That Bind Large and Small" in *Nation's Business*, (Vol. 80, No. 2, February 1992, pp. 24-26)

McKee, Daryl. "Targeted Industry Marketing: Strategy and Techniques" in *Economic Development Review*, (Vol. 12, No. 2, Spring 1994, pp. 4-12)

McKee, Thomas B. "Finding and Helping the Mom-and-Pops" in *Chain Store Age Executive*, (Vol. 70, No. 10, October 1994, pp. 104)

McKenzie, R.A. *Successful Business Plans for Architects.* New York, NY: McGraw-Hill, Inc., 1992.

McLaughlin, Kevin. "A Welcome Addition" in *Entrepreneur*, (January 1990, p. 211)

Meeks, Fleming and Nancy Rotenier. "Am I Going to Mind Sweeping the Floors?" in *Forbes*, (Vol. 152, No. 11, November 8, 1994, pp. 142-148)

Megginson, William L. *Small Business Management: An Entrepreneur's Guide to Success.* Homewood, IL: Richard D. Irwin, Inc., 1993.

Mello, John P. "Have Calculator, Will Franchise" in *CFO: The Magazine for Senior Financial Executives*, (Vol. 10, No. 11, November 1994, pp. 21)

Mendosa, Rick. "A Match Made In Fiber Optics" in *Hispanic Business*, (Vol. 16, No. 9, September 1994, pp. 24, 26)

Merrill, Ronald E. and Henry D. Sedgewick. "To Thine Own Self Be True" in *Inc.*, (Volume 16, No. 8, August 1994, pp. 50-56)

Miller, Holly A. "Instant Success: Buy an Existing Business" in *Income Opportunities*, (December/January 1991, p. 66)

Miller, Jack V. *Fat Hogs & Dead Dogs: How to Use Ideas, Inventions & Patents to Win the War for Your Markets & Profits.* Pasadena, CA: Design Technology Corporation, 1990.

Mitchell, Lee. *A Moving Stairway: From Home-Making to Business-Making in Eight Dynamic Steps.* Dunbridge, OH: Selective Marketing Corporation, 1991.

Mooney, Sean. *Insuring Your Business: What You Need to Know to Get the Best Insurance Coverage for Your Business.* New York, NY: Insurance Information Institute, 1993.

Montgomery, Robin. "Home Alone" in *Small Business Opportunities*, (Vol. 6, No. 5, September 1994, pp. 50)

Moran, Peter J. "Telemarketing Saves the Day" in *Association Management*, (Vol. 46, No. 5, May 1994, pp. 152)

More, Carol. "Planning for Projects" in *Income Opportunities*, (Vol. 29, No. 7, July 1994, pp. 44)

Morrisey, Michael A., Gail A. Jensen, and Robert J. Morlock. "Small Employers and the Health Insurance Market" in *Health Affairs*, (Vol. 13, No. 5, Winter 1994, pp. 149-161)

Moskowitz, Robert K. *The Small Business Computer Book: A Guide in Plain English.* Dover, NH: Upstart Publishing Company, Inc., 1993.

Mosley, Jr., Thomas E. "Marketing Your Invention" in *Income Opportunities*, (March 1993, pp. 56-57, 76, 78, 80, 82)

Mount, Jeffrey. "Why Take Sides?" in *Inc.*, (Vol. 17, No. 3, March 1995, pp. 29)

Mulcahy, Colleen. "Insurers Tap Into Small Employer 401(k) Market" in *National Underwriter*, (Vol. 99, No. 2, January 9, 1995, pp. 2)

Murphy, Anne. "Hot Spots" in *Inc. 500*, (Vol. 16, No. 11, 1994, pp. 37-40, 42, 44, 46)

Murphy, Cindy. "Keeping Small Businesses Healthy" in *Franchising World*, (Vol. 27, No. 1, January/February 1995, pp. 56-57)

Murphy, H. Lee. "The Future is...Wow" in *Crain's Small Business*, (February 1995, pp. 1, 21)

Nadler, Paul S. "SBA Loans: Tales from the Front" in *Commercial Lending Review*, (Vol. 9, No. 4, Fall 1994, pp. 83-86)

Napier, Nan. "Change is Big Even for a Little Guy" in *Business Quarterly*, (Vol. 59, No. 2, Winter 1994, pp. 21-27)

National Nurses in Business Association. *How I Became a Nurse Entrepreneur: Tales from Fifty Nurses in Business.* Petaluma, CA: National Nurses in Business Association, 1991.

National Plan Service, Inc. Staff, Ed. *America's Best Project Plans.* Elmhurst, IL: National Plan Service, Inc., 1990.

Nelton, Sharon. "Beating Back The Competition" in *Nation's Business*, (Vol. 82, No. 9, September 1994, pp. 18-20)

-----. "A Flexible Style of Management" in *Nation's Business*, (Vol. 82, No. 12, December 1993, pp. 24-31)

Nitschke, Martha. *How to Start Your Own One Hundred Thousand Dollar Nursing Agency: With As Little As One Week's Salary.* Wilmington, NC: Entrepress, 1991.

O'Connell, Vanessa. "The Six Best Ways to Raise Cash" in *Money: Money Guide Supplement*, (1994, pp. 34-39)

O'Dell, William F. "Effective Business Decision Making" in *Small Business Reports*, (Vol. 17, No. 3, March 1992, pp. 68-71)

O'Donnell, Michael. *Writing Business Plans That Get Results: A Step-by-Step Guide.* Chicago, IL: Contemporary Books, Inc., 1991.

Oliver, Joseph R. "Self-employment Tax: Maximizing Benefits, Minimizing Costs" in *National Public Accountant*, (Vol. 40, No. 2, February 1995, pp. 28-32)

"On Small Business Benefits, Conventional Thinking is Wrong" in *Business & Health*, (Vol. 12, No. 7, July 1994, pp. 10)

"One Hundred One Home Business Money Makers" in *Income Opportunities*, (Mid-March 1993, pp. 35-38, 50, 52, 54, 56, 58, 60-65)

Orlando, Louis A. "Mistakes That Three Out of Four Businesses Make" in *National Public Accountant*, (Vol. 40, No. 1, January 1995, pp. 12)

Osteryoung, Jerome and Richard L. Constand and Donald Nast. "Financial Ratios in Large Public and Small Private Firms" in *Journal of Small Business Management*, (Vol. 30, No. 3, July 1992)

Padgett, Tania. "Venturing into Business" in *Black Enterprise*, (Vol. 25, No. 9, April 1995, pp. 38)

Page, Abbie C. "An Investor's View" in *In Business*, (January/February 1990, pp. 32-33)

Pagett, Tania. "Venturing Into Business" in *Black Enterprise*, (Vol. 25, No. 9, April 1995, pp. 38)

Parkin, Bond L. *The Florida Entrepreneur.* Sarasota, FL: Pineapple Press, Inc., 1993.

Pearson, Bill. "Competing in the '90s" in *Stores*, (Vol. 76, No. 5, May 1994, pp. 79-80)

-----. "An Independent Point of View" in *Stores*, (Vol. 76, No. 3, March 1994, pp. 57-58)

-----. "Price Advertising - The Winner by Default" in *Stores*, (Vol. 77, No. 1, January 1995, pp. 173-174)

Perkins, Ron. *How to Find Your Treasure in a Gift Basket.* Costa Mesa, CA: Home Income Publishing, 1991.

Perry, Nancy J. "Borrowing Against Collateral You May Not Know You Have" in *Money*, (Vol. 23, No. 11, November 1994, pp. 114-116)

Perry, Robert L. "Affordable Fast Food" in *Income Opportunities*, (Vol. 29, No. 8, August 1994, pp. 22, 24, 26, 28, 30-31)

-----. "Beyond the Basics" in*Income Opportunities*, (Vol. 29, No. 7, July 1994, pp. 24, 26)

-----. "Catch the High-Tech Wave" in *Income Opportunities*, (Vol. 29, No. 7, July 1994, pp. 16, 18, 20, 22)

-----. "Caveat Emptor" in*Income Opportunities*, (Vol. 30, No. 3, March 1995, pp. 76-78, 80)

-----. "Cease & Desist" in*Income Opportunities*, (Vol. 29, No. 9, September 1994, pp. 48-56)

-----. "Exclusive Franchise Report: Cease & Desist" in*Income Opportunities*, (Vol. 30, No. 2, February 1995, pp. 64-72)

-----. "False Promises" in*Income Opportunities*, (Vol. 29, No. 11, November 1994, pp. 36-40)

-----. "Mobile Merchandising" in*Income Opportunities*, (Vol. 30, No. 3, pp. 52, 54, 56, 58)

-----. "Money from Home" in*Income Opportunities*, (Vol. 29, No. 11, November 1994, pp. 28-34)

-----. "New & Noteworthy" in*Income Opportunities*, (Vol. 29, No. 9, September 1994, pp. 40-46)

-----. "The Platinum Zoo: This Year's Best Franchises" in *Income Opportunities*, (Vol. 30, No. 2, February 1995, pp. 20-21)

Perwin, Jean S. "Tricks of the Trademark" in*Entrepreneurial Woman*, (October 1991, pp. 12, 14-15)

Phillips, Debra. "Northern Exposure" in*Entrepreneur*, (Vol. 23, No. 2, February 1995, pp. 80, 82)

Pinson, Linda.*The Home-Based Entrepreneur: The Complete Guide to Working at Home*. Dover, NH: Upstart Publishing Company, Inc., 1993.

-----. *Keeping the Books: Basic Recordkeeping & Accounting for the Small Business*. Dover, NH: Upstart Publishing Company, Inc., 1993.

-----.*The Woman Entrepreneur*. Tustin, CA: Out of Your Mind & Into the Marketplace, 1992.

Posner, Bruce G. "How to Finance Anything" in *Inc. Magazine*, (February 1993, pp. 54, 56-58, 62, 64, 66, 68)

"Power Of The People?" in *Entrepreneur*, (Vol. 22, No. 13, December 1994, pp. 16)

Pratt, Shannon. *Valuing Small Businesses & Professional Practices*. Homewood, IL: Business One Irwin, 1993.

Price, Courtney. "The Pros & Cons of Buying a Business" in *Black Enterprise*, (Vol. 25, No. 4, November 1994, pp. 143-153)

Propst, C. L. and H. N. Hoppes. "Need R & D Funds? Check with the Government" in*Research & Development*, (Vol. 28, June 1986, pp. 68)

Radloff, Laura. "Trading Up" in*Entrepreneur*, (Vol. 23, No. 2, February 1995, pp. 170-171)

Rainsford, Peter. "The Small Business Institute: Hands-On Learning" in *Cornell Hotel & Restaurant Administration Quarterly*, (Vol. 33, No. 4, August 1992)

Randle, Wilma. "When Employees Lie, Steal, or Cheat" in *Working Woman*, (January 1995)

Raphael, Beth. "Restructure for Profitability" in *Bank Management*, (Vol. 70, No. 6, November/December 1994, pp. 78-82)

Raphel, Murray. "Reviving the Dying Store" in *Direct Marketing*, (Vol. 56, No. 7, November 1993, pp. 20-21)

-----. "What Do Customers Want?" in*Direct Marketing*, (Vol. 57, No. 2, June 1994, pp. 22-23)

-----. "Who Speaks for the Small Retailer?" in*Direct Marketing*, (Vol. 57, No. 7, November 1994, pp. 30-32)

Ratliff, Susan. *How to Be a Weekend Entrepreneur: Making Money at Craft Fairs, Trade Shows & Swap Meets*. Phoenix, AZ: Marketing Methods Press, 1991.

Remesch, Kim. "Breaking the Bank" in *Entrepreneurial Woman*, (November 1990, pp. 60-63)

Rensi, Ed. "Franchising: American Business in High Gear" in *Franchising World*, (Vol. 27, No. 1, January/February 1995, pp. 7-10)

"Resources on Franchising" in *Nation's Business*, (Vol. 81, No. 4, April 1993, pp. 54-55)

Restaurant Planning Guide. Dover, NH: Upstart Publishing Company, Inc., 1992.

Reynolds, Paul. "The Truth About Start-ups" in *Inc.*, (Vol. 17, No. 2, February 1995, pp. 23-24)

Reynolds, Rhonda. "Government Trade Loans" in *Black Enterprise*, (Vol. 25, No. 7, February 1995, pp. 42)

-----. "Setting Up at Home" in *Black Enterprise*, (Vol. 24, No. 12, July 1994, pp. 36-38)

Rickard, Leah. "Focus Groups Go to College" in *Crain's Detroit Business*, (Vol. 10, No. 47, November 21-27, 1994, pp. 11)

Rifkin, Glenn. *The Ultimate Entrepreneur: The Story of Ken Olsen & Digital Equipment Corporation*. Roseville, CA: Prima Publishing, 1990.

Riggs, D. Frederick. "Find Financing" in *Income Opportunities*, (December/January 1991, p. 57)

Rogers, et al., Cheryl "Get Rich in '95" in *Small Business Opportunities*, (Vol. 7, No. 1, January 1995, pp. 20, 22, 24, 26, 28, 30, 32, 34, 36, 38-40, 42-45)

Roha, Ronaleen R. "Your Home Business: A Winning Game Plan" in *Changing Times*, (February 1991, pp. 63-65)

Rose, Ronit Addis. "Get Cash Now!" in *Success*, (Vol. 38, No. 10, December 1991, pp. 26-32)

-----. "Money Now" in *Success*, (December 1990, pp. 29-36)

Rosenfeld, Stuart A. "Danish Modern 1994: Designing Networks in North America" in *CMA Magazine*, (Vol. 68, No. 3, April 1994, pp. 24-26)

Rosenthal, Edmond M. "Reversal of Fortune" in *Income Opportunities*, (Vol. 30, No. 2, February 1995, pp. 54-55, 58-62)

Roush, Matt. "Head Above the Water" in *Crain's Detroit Business*, (Vol. 10, No. 51, December 19-25, 1994, pp. 1, 14)

-----. "When Up Means Down" in *Crain's Detroit Business*, (Vol. 11, No. 4, January 23-29, 1995, pp. 38-39)

Rowland, Mary. "Keeping It In the Family" in *Nation's Business*, (Vol. 83, No. 1, January 1995, pp. 63-64)

-----. "Mistakes Your Growing Company Needs To Avoid" in *Money Money Guide Supplement*, (1994, pp. 76-81)

Ruby, Gale Cohen. "Basic Training" in *Entrepreneur*, (Vol. 22, No. 13, December 1994, pp. 129-134)

Ryan, J.D. *Small Business: An Entrepreneur's Plan*. Fort Worth, TX: Dryden Press, 1990.

Schell, Jim. *The Brass Tacks Entrepreneur*. New York, NY: Henry Holt & Company, 1993.

Schutt, David and Yong Lim, Eds. *Pratt's Guide to Venture Capital Sources*. New York, NY: Venture Economics Inc., 1992.

Scott, Matthew S., Rhonda Reynolds and Cassandra Hayes. "Twenty-five Years of Blacks in Financing" in *Black Enterprise*, (Vol. 25, No. 3, October 1994, pp. 146-149)

Seglin, Jeffrey L. "How Can You Survive the Regulators?" in *Inc.*, (Vol. 16, No. 9, September 1994, pp. 62-64)

Sherlock, Marie. "Ads For Your Biz" in *Small Business Opportunities*, (Vol. 6, No. 5, September 1994, pp. 10)

Sherman, Richard W. "The Shared Foreign Sales Corporation: A Tax Saving Opportunity for Small Business" in *National Public Accountant*, (Vol. 39, No. 12)

Singletary, Michelle L. and Kevin D. Thompson. "So, You Want to Buy a Business?" in *Black Enterprise*, (April 1991, pp. 47-56)

Sitterly, Connie. *The Female Entrepreneur*. Menlo Park, CA: Crisp Publications, Inc., 1993.

"Slaying the Giant -- Without Cash" in *Nation's Business*, (Vol. 82, No. 9, September 1994, pp. 21)

Small, Linda Lee. "Surviving the Superstore Steamroll" in *Working Woman*, (Vol. 19, No. 7, July 1994, pp. 62-64)

BIBLIOGRAPHY

Solomon, Stephen D. "Staking a Claim on the Internet" in *Inc.*, (Vol. 16, No. 3, 1994, pp. 87-92)

Soslow, Robin and Daniel J. McConville and Ben Warner and Patrice D. Raia. "Top 10 Cities for International Companies" in *World Trade*, (Vol. 5, No. 8, October 1992, pp. 32-44)

Sotkin, Joan. *Starting Your Own Business: An Easy-to-Follow Guide for the New Entrepreneur.* Laguna Hills, CA: Build Your Business, Inc., 1993.

Sperry, Paul S. *Complete Guide to Selling Your Business.* Dover, NH: Upstart Publishing Company, Inc., 1992.

Sprouse, Mary L. "Timely Ways to Cut Your Taxes" in *Money Guide Supplement*, (1994, pp. 68-70)

"Starting on a Shoestring" in *New Business Opportunities*, (March 1990, pp. 26-28)

Steinberg, Carol. "Grow Or Die" in *Success*, (Vol. 41, No. 6, July/August 1994, pp. 65-67)

Stevens, Chris. *The Entrepreneur's Guide to Developing a Basic Business Plan.* Northbrook, IL: S.K. Brown Publishing, 1991.

Stevens, Mark. "Listing Your Company on a Stock Exchange" in *D & B Reports*, (Vol. 40, No. 2, March/April 1992, pp. 62-63)

Stevenson, Howard H. *New Business Ventures & the Entrepreneur.* Homewood, IL: Richard D. Irwin, Inc., 1994.

Stewart, Robert L. "Developing a Simple Agency Marketing Plan" in *Rough Notes*, (Vol. 138, No. 2, February 1995, pp. 14-16)

Stodder, Gayle Sato. "And Stay Out!" in *Entrepreneur*, (Vol. 22, No. 9, September 1994, pp. 54)

-----. "Damage Control" in *Entrepreneur*, (Vol. 22, No. 13, December 1994, pp. 40)

-----. "Gone Fishing" in *Entrepreneur*, (Vol. 23, No. 2, February 1995, pp. 60-61)

-----. "License To Win" in *Entrepreneur*, (Vol. 23, No. 2, February 1995, pp. 158, 160-161)

Stone, Heather E. "Alphabet Soup" in *Inc.*, (Vol. 16, No. 12, November 1994, pp. 31-32)

Strozier, Geraldine M. "It's Not So Elementary, Watson" in *Entrepreneur*, (January 1990, pp. 69-73)

Sublette, Guen. "Home Grown" in *Business Start-Ups*, (Vol. 7, No. 3, March 1995, pp. 36-47)

Sulkis, Karen. "Back to Business" in *Business Start-ups*, (October 1994, pp. 8)

-----. "O Pioneers!" in *Entrepreneur*, (Vol. 22, No. 9, September 1994, pp. 138-143)

Swain, Liz. "Retailers Share Strategies for Competing with Superstore Giants" in *Pet Product News*, (Vol. 48, No. 3, March 1994, pp. 23)

Szabo, Joan C. "Borrowing Money from Loved Ones" in *Nation's Business*, (Vol. 82, No. 11, November 1994, pp. 40)

Taka, Iwao and Wanda D. Foglia. "Ethical Aspects of Japanese Leadership Style" in *Journal of Business Ethics*, (Vol. 13, No. 2, February 1994, pp. 135-148)

Taylor, Charlotte. "On Hold" in *Entrepreneur*, (Vol. 22, No. 9, September 1994, pp. 76-78)

-----. "Pizza De Resistance" in *Entrepreneur*, (Vol. 22, No. 13, December 1994, pp. 50)

Taylor, Ted. M. *Secrets to a Successful Greenhouse Business.* Melbourne, FL: Green Earth Publishing Company, 1991.

Tehrani, Nadji. "How Telemarketing Saved a Small Company from Bankruptcy" in *Telemarketing*, (Vol. 13, No. 7, January 1995, pp. 3-4)

Thackray, John. "Hatching Uncle Sam's Entrepreneurs" in *Management Today*, (November 1993, pp. 54-56)

Thomas, Dan. "What To Do With A Lousy Business" in *Management Review*, (Vol. 83, No. 6, June 1994, pp. 40-43)

Three Keys to Obtaining Venture Capital. Coopers & Lybrand.

"Tips on People Management" in *D&B Reports*, (Vol. 43, No. 2, March/April 1994, pp. 60)

"The Top 10 Home-Based Businesses to Start Now!" in *Small Business Opportunities*, (March 1994, pp. 22-24, 26, 28, 30, 32, 34, 36-39)

Turell, Robert L. "Medical Self-Defense" in *Small Business Reports*, (Vol. 17, No. 6, June 1992, pp. 60-64)

Turner, Alison. "Global Got Ahead with Help From the SBA" in *South Florida Business Journal*, (Vol. 14, No. 36, April 29, 1994, pp. 17A)

Ubois, Jeff. "Setting Up Shop (in SOHO)" in *Working Woman*, (October 1994, pp. 65-69)

Urquhart III, James R. "IRS May Reclassify Independent Contractors" in *San Diego Business Journal*, (Vol. 15, No. 6, February 7, 1994, pp. 6A)

Van Fleet, Mark. "The U.S. Chamber of Commerce: The Voice of Business" in *Business America*, (Vol. 113, No. 23, November 16, 1992, pp. 18-20)

"Video Ventures" in *Small Business Opportunities*, (Vol. 6, No. 5, September 1994, pp. 68)

"Volumes of Bank Bashing" in *Detroit Free Press Business Monday*, (February 20, 1995, Section F)

Wagner, Stephen. "Twenty-Five Best Home-Based Businesses to Start Right Now" in *Income Opportunities*, (Mid-March 1990, pp. 47-50)

Wallace, Elizabeth. "Bank On It!" in *Entrepreneur*, (May 1993, pp. 85-88)

Warshaw, Robin. "Start a Home Business With $500—Or Less" in *Woman's Day*, (October 2, 1990, pp. 34-38)

Washer, Louise. "The Fast Trackers" in *Working Woman*, (March 1995, pp. 44-48, 86)

-----. "Home Alone: Small Business Strategies" in *Working Woman*, (Vol. 18, No. 3, March 1993, pp. 45-50)

-----. "Is Bigger Better?" in *Working Woman*, (March 1995, pp. 39-40, 42, 90)

-----. "Marketing 101: Finding Your First Customer" in *Working Woman*, (Vol. 17, No. 10, October 1992, pp. 53-54)

Watts, Christina F. "Home Is Where the Business Is" in *Black Enterprise*, (Vol. 25, No. 4, November 1994, pp. 128-138)

-----. "SCORE Points to Success" in *Black Enterprise*, (Vol. 25, No. 6, January 1995, pp. 38)

Weinstein, Bob. "Price Pointers" in *Entrepreneur*, (Vol. 23, No. 2, February 1995, pp. 48, 50-)

-----. "True Stories" in *Entrepreneur*, (July 1992, pp. 169-173)

Weylman, C. Richard. "Much Maligned, the Telephone Still Has Its Place" in *National Underwriter*, (Vol. 99, No. 6, February 6, 1995, pp. 14)

"What an Idea!" in *Family Circle*, (October 1989, pp. 34-38)

White, Sally Button. "Marketing Strategies That Get Results" in *Money: Money Guide Supplement*, (1994, pp. 20-22)

Whittemore, Meg. "Four Paths to Franchising" in *Nation's Business*, (October 1989, pp. 75-85)

-----. "Franchising Beats the Recession" in *Nation's Business*, (Vol. 80, No. 3, March 1992, pp. 55-64)

-----. "Less a Parent, More a Partner" in *Nation's Business*, (Vol. 82, No. 3, March 1994, pp. 49-57)

-----. "New Directions in Franchising" in *Nation's Business*, (Vol. 83, No. 1, January 1995, pp. 45-52)

-----. "The Second Generation" in *Nation's Business*, (Vol. 82, No. 6, June 1994, pp. 57-64)

-----. "Shopping Malls Attract Small Firms" in *Nation's Business*, (Vol. 80, No. 12, December 1992, pp. 53-56)

Wiesendanger, Betsy. "Home is Where the Customer Is" in *Sales & Marketing Management*, (Vol. 144, No. 9, August 1992, pp. 54)

Winninger, Thomas J. "Your Secret Weapon" in *Success*, (Vol. 42, No. 1, February 1995, pp. 48A-48H)

Zagury, Carolyn S. *Nurse Entrepreneur: Building the Bridge of Opportunity*. Long Branch, NJ: Vista Publishing, Inc., 1993.

Zate, Maria. "No Place Like Home" in *Hispanic Business*, (Vol. 16, No. 9, September 1994, pp. 50, 52)

Ziegler, Mel. *The Republic of Tea: Letters to a Young Entrepreneur.* New York, NY: Doubleday, 1992.

Zoghlin, Gil. *From Executive to Entrepreneur: Making the Transition.* New York, NY: AMACOM, 1991.

Zuckerman, Laurie B. *On Your Own: A Woman's Guide to Building a Business.* Dover, NH: Upstart Publishing Company, Inc., 1990.